EARLY
JUDAISM

EARLY JUDAISM

The Exile to the Time of Jesus

FREDERICK J. MURPHY

Hendrickson Publishers, Inc.
P.O. Box 3473
Peabody, Massachusetts 01961-3473

Early Judaism, from the Exile to the Time of Jesus is a completely revised version of *The Religious World of Jesus: An Introduction to Second Temple Palestinian Judaism,* published in 1991 by Abingdon Press.

Printed in the United States of America

First printing—April 2002

Library of Congress Cataloging-in-Publication Data

Murphy, Frederick James.
    Early Judaism: the exile to the time of Jesus / Frederick J. Murphy.
    p. cm.
    Includes bibliographical references and indexes.
    Rewriting of the author's The religious world of Jesus.
    ISBN 1-56563-087-4 (alk. paper)
    1. Jews—History—To 70 A.D. 2. Judaism—History—To 70 A.D. 3.
Bible. O.T.—Criticism, interpretation, etc. 4. Jesus
Christ—Jewishness. I. Murphy, Frederick James. Religious world of
Jesus. II. Title.
    DS121 .M97 2002
    296'.09'014—dc21
                                                        2001006926

COPYRIGHT
ACKNOWLEDGMENTS
AND CREDITS

Dedication

For my parents, Hazel L. and James F. Murphy,
Of blessed memory,
"Remember that it was of your parents you were born;
How can you repay what they have given to you?"
(Sirach 7:28)

And for Lieutenant Thomas E. Spencer
Worcester Fire Department
Of blessed memory,
A true hero, and a true friend

TABLE OF CONTENTS

PREFACE

In 1991, I published *The Religious World of Jesus: An Introduction to Second Temple Palestinian Judaism* (Nashville: Abingdon). I wrote that book because, although I had for years taught a course on Second Temple Judaism, I had not found a suitable text for the course. The present text is *The Religious World* rewritten.

The Jewish origins of Christianity have long fascinated me. From my first acquaintance with the Hebrew Bible, I have found that everything I learned about ancient Israel and Judaism contributed immensely to my understanding of Jesus and earliest Christianity. Of course, I was not the first to discover this. But I soon also discovered that a new movement in the study of the New Testament and Christian origins was attempting to set the record straight concerning the nature of ancient Judaism, Jesus' Jewishness, and the relationships of different forms of ancient Christianity and Judaism. Earlier Christian scholars who studied Judaism as a "background" for Christianity had often denigrated Judaism. Older scholarship often presented it as the religion that had been surpassed by Christianity. Jesus, the Jewish messiah, had come, and the Jews had missed it. Now, Gentile Christianity was the true Israel, the embodiment of Jeremiah's prediction of a "new covenant," heir to the promises enunciated in what was now termed the Old Testament. This strand of Christian theology is called supersessionism because Christianity is thought to supersede Judaism.

As I studied the Hebrew Bible and Jewish texts written in the later Second Temple period, I discovered that this new movement was well justified. I learned things that most of us in this field now consider rather obvious but that are far from evident to many others who are not professional biblical scholars. Late Second Temple Judaism was not the empty shell I thought it was after reading the New Testament and Christian theologians. Instead, it was an immensely rich and inspiring mix of all sorts of things that ultimately traced themselves back to Sinai. I found that ancient Judaism was not a monolith, enslaved to a legalistic and ritualistic worldview that blinded it to the important things in life. Rather, it was the source of much that was good in Christianity, and it was home to countless Jews who survived difficult conditions by remaining loyal to their God. Ancient Judaism was varied and vibrant. I also came to think of earliest Christianity as another form of Judaism, one that eventually went its own way.

Finally and perhaps most important, I discovered that Jesus was a Jew. This was my most revolutionary discovery, although that may seem odd, since virtually no one in their right mind would deny that Jesus was a Jew. But to affirm the Jewishness of Jesus has meant many things to many people. A classic strain in Christian theology and scholarship has been that Jesus, though a Jew, was unique among Jews. Only he truly understood Israel's God, and only he knew God's will. Finding it impossible to reach any but a few Jews, Jesus founded a movement that was in effect a different religion, open to Gentiles. The entire Christ event showed Israel in a poor light. Some Christians protested that they had a very high view of Judaism, but that they just did not have a high regard for most of Jesus' Jewish contemporaries. But I now am convinced that Jesus always saw himself as a Jew within the covenant and obedient to Torah. This insight has made me and many others rethink a whole range of issues—the person and work of Jesus, the nature of ancient Judaism and Christianity and their relationship, messiahship, the character of priestly religion and the temple, the meaning of what scholars used to think of as ancient "Jewish nationalism," the emergence of rabbinic Judaism, and so on.

I first became interested in Judaism because I am a Christian. As I investigated the roots of Christianity, I found them to be Jewish. But it became evident that to look at Judaism only through the eyes of Christianity was to distort it. I slowly learned that it is impossible to appreciate Christianity's Jewish roots properly without "forgetting" about Christianity for a while. That is, one must approach Judaism in its own right and in its own terms. Otherwise we will not understand Jesus' own religion, and we will also misunderstand the earliest Christians.

Learning something new is always a matter of comparison. We can remain abysmally ignorant of ourselves when we do not compare, when we operate from within closed systems that to us are self-evident, when we do not open ourselves up to other ways of thinking and living, at least by trying to understand them. It is difficult to carry out healthy and illuminating comparisons when we are unwilling to change our minds somewhat on how we see each thing being compared. Comparisons between Christianity, Judaism, and other religions will bear fruit when each term of the comparison is seen in new ways. But we must always remember not to compare apples with oranges, as Krister Stendahl, one of my graduate-school professors, often says. Too often the highest ideals of Christianity are compared to the real-life, on-the-ground reality of Judaism. Such comparisons are rigged and serve Christian propaganda, not understanding.

This process of learning and, in many cases, unlearning has been for me one of the most meaningful and enjoyable aspects of being a biblical scholar. It has taught me much about Judaism, Christianity, and God. It has brought me into contact with a myriad of scholars who have taught me both in person and through their books and articles and to whom I am deeply grateful. The purpose of this textbook is to pass this experience on to others. It is the product of seventeen years of teaching at the College of the Holy Cross and of my earlier studies as a graduate student at Harvard. Year after year I observe how this way of looking at things deepens my students' understanding.

This book tries to balance the effort to appreciate Judaism for its own sake, on the one hand, and the desire to shed light on Jesus and the early Christians, on the other. This balance serves students well. My students at Holy Cross have been especially inspiring to me as young adults who are intelligent, committed, and remarkably open to new ways of seeing familiar things. More than anything else, it is their continued positive feedback and encouragement that makes me eager to continue teaching in this field. What means most to me is that the rewriting of this textbook will enable me to offer it once again to my students. I can only hope that it also is of use to teachers and students elsewhere.

I am grateful for the opportunity Hendrickson Publishers has given me to improve my original work and make it available once more. Biblical scholars know how rapidly Hendrickson has grown in recent years in offerings that benefit us all. I am especially thankful to Hendrickson's former editorial director, Patrick Alexander. For years he encouraged my labors, and it gave me great satisfaction finally to be able to work together with him on this project. He helped me to rethink how to present this material. His insightful (and often witty) suggestions made this a much better book and will help me in my future projects. I am also deeply appreciative of the professional and generous way in which John Kutsko, Associate Editorial Director of Hendrickson, took on this project and shepherded it to its completion. He has been a pleasure to work with.

Holy Cross continues to support me in numerous ways. The administration and staff do all that they can to encourage scholarship, with the support and understanding of the trustees, who realize how important for the quality of the college it is to balance teaching and scholarship. The Department of Religious Studies is still one of the best places anywhere to work. We share much in common but also are different in many ways, and this chemistry helps to form a professional, supportive, and creative environment for us all. Joel Villa and Ken Scott have been unfailingly helpful and patient as they have helped me often on computer matters. Dr. Jim Hogan, Director of Library Services at Holy Cross, and his excellent staff have been exemplary in their constant and cheerful support of my scholarship and teaching. A special thanks to my good friend Father Jim Mazzone for the delightful exegetical lunches. Thanks also to Ray Delisle for his constant friendship and support, personally and professionally. I wish most of all to thank my family, Leslie, Rebecca, and Jeremy. They are my solid foundation, and without them I would have nothing on which to build.

I dedicate this revised book to three people. First of all, I dedicate it to my mother, just as I dedicated the original version to her. Life did not deal her an easy hand, and I will never forget her example. I now add my father to the dedication. He died in June of 1997. They were good people, and I miss them both.

Finally, in the preface to *The Religious World of Jesus,* I thanked Tom Spencer "for the music." Tom was a dear friend of mine and my family for many years (though not enough). He was a firefighter, a model family man, an accomplished athlete, and—not least—an opera devotee. He taught me to love opera, and we often enjoyed it together (when he wasn't trouncing me at tennis). On December 3, 1999, Tom and five other Worcester firefighters died in a tragic fire. Firefighters entered a burning abandoned storehouse to rescue homeless people who they thought might be there, and then others went in to rescue their brothers. Six did not come out. Tom was among them.

Tom would have smiled at this dedication, and then made some wisecrack to make us all laugh—I guarantee it. I miss his humor and his friendship. He was one of the finest people I have ever known. He lives on in his courageous wife, Kathy, and in his three talented and extraordinary children, Patrick, Casey, and Dan.

ABBREVIATIONS

Hebrew Bible/Old Testament

Gen	Genesis
Exod	Exodus
Lev	Leviticus
Num	Numbers
Deut	Deuteronomy
Josh	Joshua
Judg	Judges
1–2 Sam	1–2 Samuel
1–2 Kgs	1–2 Kings
1–2 Chr	1–2 Chronicles
Neh	Nehemiah
Ps/Pss	Psalms
Prov	Proverbs
Isa	Isaiah
Jer	Jeremiah
Ezek	Ezekiel
Dan	Daniel
Hos	Hosea
Nah	Nahum
Hab	Habakkuk
Hag	Haggai
Zech	Zechariah
Mal	Malachi

New Testament

Matt	Matthew
Rom	Romans
1–2 Cor	1–2 Corinthians
Gal	Galatians

| Phil | Philippians |
| Rev | Revelation |

Apocrypha and Septuagint

Bar	Baruch
1–2 Esd	1–2 Esdras
1–2 Macc	1–2 Maccabees
Sir/Ecclus	Sirach/Ecclesiasticus
Tob	Tobit
Wis	Wisdom of Solomon

Old Testament Pseudepigrapha

Apoc. Ab.	*Apocalypse of Abraham*
2 Bar.	*2 Baruch (Syriac Apocalypse)*
1 En.	*1 Enoch (Ethiopic Apocalypse)*
Jub.	*Jubilees*
T. Levi	*Testament of Levi*
T. Mos.	*Testament of Moses*

Dead Sea Scrolls and Related Texts

1QH	*Thanksgiving Hymns*
1QpHab	*Commentary on Habakkuk*
1QM and 4QM	*War Rule*
1QS	*Community Rule*
1QSa	*Messianic Rule*
4Q171	*Commentary on Psalms*
4QpNah	(4Q169) *Commentary on Nahum*
4QFlor	(4Q174) *Midrash on the Last Days*
4QTest	(4Q175) *Messianic Anthology* or *Testimonia*
4QMessAp	(4Q521) *Messianic Apocalypse*
CD	*Damascus Document*

Philo

| *Embassy* | *On the Embassy to Gaius* |
| *Moses* 1, 2 | *On the Life of Moses* 1, 2 |

Josephus

Ag. Ap.	*Against Apion*
Ant.	*Jewish Antiquities*
J. W.	*Jewish War*

Life   *The Life*

Mishnah, Talmud, and Related Literature

m.   Mishnah
Meg.   *Megillah*

Technical Abbreviations

AB   Anchor Bible
ABD   *Anchor Bible Dictionary.* Edited by D. N. Freedman. 6 vols. New York: Doubleday, 1992
AI   *The Apocalyptic Imagination: An Introduction to Jewish Apocalyptic Literature.* J. J. Collins. 2d ed. Grand Rapids: Eerdmans, 1998
AMWNE   *Apocalypticism in the Mediterranean World and the Near East.* Proceedings of the International Colloquium on Apocalypticism, Uppsala, August 12–17, 1979. Edited by D. Hellholm. Tübingen: Mohr (Siebeck), 1983
ANRW   *Aufstieg und Niedergang der römischen Welt: Geschichte und Kultur Roms im Spiegel des neueren Forschung.* Edited by W. Haase and H. Temporini. Berlin: de Gruyter, 1972–
APOT   *The Apocrypha and Pseudepigrapha of the Old Testament.* Edited by R. H. Charles. 2 vols. Oxford: Clarendon, 1913
BA   *Biblical Archaeologist*
BASOR   *Bulletin of the American Schools of Oriental Research*
B.C.E.   before the Common Era
BJRL   *Bulletin of the John Rylands University Library of Manchester*
BTB   *Biblical Theology Bulletin*
CBQ   *Catholic Biblical Quarterly*
CBQMS   Catholic Biblical Quarterly Monograph Series
CDSSE   *The Complete Dead Sea Scrolls in English.* Translated and edited by G. Vermes. New York: Penguin, 1997
C.E.   Common Era
CRINT   Compendia rerum iudaicarum ad Novum Testamentum
CurBS   *Currents in Research: Biblical Studies*
E   The Elohist source of the Pentateuch
EJMI   *Early Judaism and Its Modern Interpreters.* Edited by R. A. Kraft and G. W. E. Nickelsburg. Atlanta: Scholars Press, 1986
HBD   *Harper's Bible Dictionary*
HeyJ   *Heythrop Journal*
HR   *History of Religions*
HSM   Harvard Semitic Monographs
HTR   *Harvard Theological Review*
HUCA   *Hebrew Union College Annual*

IDB	*The Interpreter's Dictionary of the Bible.* Edited by G. A. Buttrick. 4 vols. Nashville: Abingdon, 1962
IDBSup	*Interpreter's Dictionary of the Bible: Supplementary Volume.* Edited by K. Crim. Nashville: Abingdon, 1976
IFAJ	*Ideal Figures in Ancient Judaism.* Edited by G. W. E. Nickelsburg and J. J. Collins. Chico, Calif.: Scholars Press, 1980
J	The Yahwist source of the Pentateuch
JBL	*Journal of Biblical Literature*
JJS	*Journal of Jewish Studies*
JSJ	*Journal for the Study of Judaism in the Persian, Hellenistic, and Roman Periods*
JTS	*Journal of Theological Studies*
NIB	*The New Interpreter's Bible*
NJBC	*The New Jerome Biblical Commentary.* Edited by R. E. Brown, J. A. Fitzmyer, and R. E. Murphy. Englewood Cliffs, N.J.: Prentice-Hall, 1990
NRSV	New Revised Standard Version [translation of the Bible]
NTS	*New Testament Studies*
OTP	*Old Testament Pseudepigrapha.* Edited by J. H. Charlesworth. 2 vols. Garden City: Doubleday, 1983–1985
OTT	*Old Testament Theology.* G. von Rad. London: SCM, 1965
P	The Priestly source of the Pentateuch
RB	*Revue biblique*
RelSRev	*Religious Studies Review*
RevQ	*Revue de Qumran*
SBLDS	Society of Biblical Literature Dissertation Series
SBT	Studies in Biblical Theology
SNTSMS	Society for New Testament Studies Monograph Series
SSV	*Scriptures, Sects, and Visions: A Profile of Judaism from Ezra to the Jewish Revolts.* M. E. Stone. Philadelphia: Fortress, 1980
VT	*Vetus Testamentum*

INTRODUCTION

I came to the study of ancient Judaism from a Christian background, and I presently teach in a Roman Catholic college. I am fully committed to understanding ancient Judaism for its own sake and in its own terms, but at the same time I examine it for what it can say about Jesus and the earliest Christians. I have tried, however, to minimize the extent to which Christian interests distort our study of ancient Judaism. Otherwise we will not understand ancient Judaism and so will not attain our goal of allowing it to shed light on specifically Christian concerns.

GOING BEYOND THE CANON

Most students interested in studying ancient Israel, Jesus Christ, Christian origins, or Scripture will choose a course named something like "Introduction to the Old Testament" or "Introduction to the New Testament." This would be a logical choice because those courses examine foundational documents of Christianity and Judaism. *Foundational* means that the Hebrew Bible and the New Testament are foundations for the two religions. ("Hebrew Bible" is a more neutral term because "Old Testament," better translated "Old Covenant," assumes that there is a "New Covenant" and so puts us already in the context of Christian theology. Our aim, however, is to study ancient Judaism on its own terms.) Texts contained in the New Testament and Hebrew Bible belong to the *canon*. This word comes from the Greek word *kanōn*, meaning a reed of fixed length used for measuring. The canon of Judaism or Christianity is that body of writings accepted as authoritative and normative. Belief and practice are measured and judged by these writings. By choosing to include some writings in the canon and exclude others from it, each religion has defined its contours. The normativity of the included texts is expressed through the notion that they are *inspired*—that is, that God is responsible for them in some way. There is a range of ways in which inspiration can be defined, from the idea that the writers were inspired much as poets are, to the literalistic conviction that God dictated every word and letter. Belief in inspiration does not necessarily deny a substantial human role in the production of Scripture.

This book does not confine itself to the canon, because our interest is in the historical circumstances in which its constitutive books were written, including cultural and social aspects of that world. We wish to consider everything that counts as evidence for what people did, thought, and felt in the ancient world, as well as for what their cultural, social, political, and economic institutions were like. Fortunately, there is a large body of extracanonical Jewish literature from the first century C.E. and preceding centuries to aid us in our study.

The original impetus for this book came from an interest in teaching about the world in which Jesus Christ lived, first-century Jewish Galilee and Judea. But that world cannot be fully appreciated by plunging directly into it. Singling out the first century without examining the events and persons leading up to it would build certain distortions into the study, especially if what is desired is a sympathetic understanding of the groups and people who made up first-century Jewish society in the land of Israel. The Second Temple period (520 B.C.E. to 70 C.E.) has a clear beginning and end, and its character, although it develops over time, is somewhat consistent. The building of the second temple was a new beginning in Israel's history, society, and religion. In crucial ways, Israel was very different at the beginning of the Second Temple period from what it was just before that. Likewise, the destruction of the second temple by the Romans in 70 C.E. marked a radical change in Israel. The change went beyond the loss of a physical temple. It had profound implications for every aspect of Jewish life and society.

Chapter 1 at one end, and chapters 10 and 11, at the other, supply a frame within which Second Temple Judaism can be viewed. Chapter 1 lays the groundwork for the rest of the book by discussing Israel before the Second Temple period. It introduces persons, groups, events, and issues in preexilic and exilic Israel that are key to understanding Second Temple Judaism. Chapter 10, after discussing the war against the Romans and the fall of Jerusalem, indicates the direction Judaism took in subsequent years, and then analyzes two Jewish texts written after the war. Chapter 11 looks at several Christian interpretations of Jesus written after the destruction of Jerusalem.

THE STUDY OF HISTORY

For some, it may seem strange to examine biblical books from a historical point of view. But since the ancient texts were produced in a social and historical context quite different from that of modern readers, part of the task of interpretation must be to try to appreciate how the writings made meaning in their own contexts. *Historical criticism* is a mode of analysis that aims to discover through historical methods—the critical examination of textual and material evidence—what the authors themselves meant and how their texts would have been interpreted by their original audiences. The study takes place in dialogue with what is known of the ancient world in which the documents were produced. There are potential problems with the method: (a) it at times assumes that one can get back to the bare, uninterpreted "facts" of a situation; (b) it sometimes identifies truth with the original meaning of the text, so that historical knowledge is privileged almost to the exclusion of other ways of making sense of the text; (c) it may not critically examine its own presuppositions—philosophical, social, and political. These problems must be addressed by all who engage in historical criticism. It would be a mistake, however, simply to reject the quest for historical knowledge. To explain why this is so, a few observations are appropriate.

We prize history highly, even when we know little about it. It is a powerful statement today to say that something did or did not happen. With respect to Jesus Christ, Christians often think that the picture that they have of Jesus is identical to the historical Jesus, the Palestinian Jew of two thousand years ago. They feel secure in their interpretation of Jesus because it corresponds with their reading of the Gospels, which to them are pure history. Further, it is often assumed that first-century Palestinian Jewish society is accurately portrayed in the Gospels. To neglect historical study is to leave such assumptions unchallenged.

Failing to ask historical questions would also make it impossible to have even tentative answers to what brought us to where we are. The nature of society and religion today is a result of decisions made, thoughts developed, and institutions constructed in the past. If we ignore these decisions, thoughts, and institutions, we neglect an essential key to understanding the present.

For both Christians and Jews, there are theological reasons for taking history seriously. Each tradition teaches that God is encountered in history, in the real-life interactions of people in their everyday world. Whether the subject be ancient Israel, grappling with world empires, or Jesus Christ in conflict with priestly and Roman authorities, both traditions seek not to escape from history but to understand it. The rereading and rewriting of sacred stories and history, evident in the Bible itself, attests to a basic drive in each of these religions to find meaning in past events.

The writing of history is no easy matter. For the period under consideration here, the sources are not so plentiful and varied as we would wish. Further, our presuppositions color the way we read what evidence there is. An example would be the debate about miracles among Christian scholars over the past few centuries. Those who believe that God operates through miracles think that the miracles narrated in the Bible actually happened. Rationalistic critics explain them away as products of a nonscientific worldview, as psychosomatic phenomena, or as explicable events of nature. Historical research will not resolve the difficulty. There are basic differences of worldview that result in varying readings of the same evidence.

To write history is not simply to chronicle events. Even if historians could agree on a set of events as actually having happened, we would have only a chronicle, a list of events. Historical analysis does not just list facts but tries to connect them, analyze them, discover their causes and effects, and investigate their meaning within their historical, economic, political, cultural, and social contexts. But how we bring discrete facts into a coherent whole is not simply a matter of scientific investigation. Our explanation of events will be determined by our belief about what causes what, what people and societies are like, and how the universe works.

An everyday example of talking about the past shows how problematic is the view that description of the past can be unfettered by personal opinion or bias. Suppose thirty students take the same course and meet a year later to discuss what happened. They are all eyewitnesses, but their experiences of the class can differ substantially. Was the professor organized or chaotic, clear or confusing, interesting or boring? Was the workload easy, hard, or moderate? Were the exams fair or unfair? Were the professor's comments on the paper helpful or not? It is the rare class that will not elicit the full range of possible comments. A student's experience of a class will depend on what the student's interests are, what sort of background she or he has, how much work the student does, and who the student is, as well as on what actually transpires in the classroom. Hopefully, all students will be able to agree on some basic facts about the course a year later—course title, required books, professor's name, although even here memory may lapse—but as soon as the conversation shifts to more significant questions, such as how good or fair or insightful the course was, there is plenty of room for disagreement.

If eyewitnesses give different descriptions of a common experience a short time after it occurs, there is still more room for disagreement when it comes to events in the distant past. If you have studied American history, you know who George Washington is. You know when he was born, when he died, where he lived, what offices he held, and so on. But do you know what he had for breakfast before an important battle? Probably not. Historians do not find his breakfast significant. But if you think that diet determines behavior, Washington's eating habits are crucial. This is an extreme example, but conflicts become quite real, for example, when a conservative capitalist historian compares analyses with a Marxist. The way we look at the world, the way we think things work, will affect what we choose to tell and how we tell it.

There is no such thing as uninterpreted history. History is interpretation. Interpretation implies a worldview, conceptual frameworks, a philosophical stance on the part of the interpreter, whether acknowledged or not. When one writes history for an audience with which one shares a broad base of common assumptions, the assumptions appear self-evident and do not seem to need examination. In a pluralistic society, such history becomes problematic. In the history of a religion, the matter becomes more acute, since one's attitude toward religion colors what questions are asked and how they are answered. If one thinks that religion is primarily a psychological phenomenon, then psychology will explain it; if it is a political phenomenon, political analysis will explain it.

History as interpretation comes into play on two levels in this book. One level is that of modern scholarship. The same evidence can be interpreted in varying ways by different scholars. Sometimes disagreement is due to scarcity or ambiguity of evidence. At other times, different conclusions come from different assumptions, convictions, and even temperaments. On another level, the primary sources offer interpretations of their own world or of a world that is in the past for them. Part of the task of the historian is to analyze the viewpoints of the sources so that their worldviews and biases can be taken into account when they are used to write history.

THE APPROACH OF THIS BOOK

This book draws on various methodologies. The historical method furnishes a basic framework in which all questions are asked. Because this book deals with texts, it also uses literary criticism, attending to the literary genre of the works studied and seeking to appreciate them as literature. Literary study has a historical dimension because biblical and related texts employ genres, languages, and thought patterns from the ancient world. Because of the importance of social context, this book asks questions proper to anthropology and sociology, disciplines particularly appropriate for the study of groups. Anthropology, in particular, holds much promise for the study of ancient Israel and Christianity because it is accustomed to studying foreign cultures. Because the social sciences raise issues of societal structure, symbol systems, culture, the relationships of politics, economics, kinship, and religion, and so on, they can help flesh out historical studies so as to provide a richer and more accurate picture of the ancient world. The study of language is relevant, since the texts studied here were originally written primarily in

Hebrew, Aramaic, and Greek and survive in an even greater variety of languages. English translations are already interpretations of the texts, since it is impossible to translate a text without interpreting it.

This book covers an immense stretch of Israel's history. Choices must be made about what to treat in detail, what to summarize, which issues to raise, and so on. The choices make for a particular reading of the period that should be challenged and supplemented by other readings. But we must begin somewhere. Our aim is to make accessible some of the best recent research on Second Temple Judaism. Our reconstruction will be fairly mainstream, noting along the way issues that are being debated.

PRIMARY SOURCES

Primary sources are those dating from the period being studied. It is crucial to read the primary sources listed at the beginning of each chapter and mentioned in the body of the chapter. This book aims to foster familiarity with the primary evidence, which mainly consists of textual sources. Extensive portions of primary sources are reproduced to ensure that the reader will examine them and not be content with generalizations arising from their analysis. But even reading such passages is not sufficient. The documents discussed should be seen as wholes. The primary texts should be read in their entirety to achieve familiarity with them, to place the passages discussed into a fuller context, and even to challenge readings argued in this book, by attending to alternative passages or by reading the same ones in a different light. Where the primary texts are too lengthy to be read in their entirety, I rely on teachers to assign reasonable amounts of reading tailored to their own approaches.

Because of the importance of primary documents, much of this book consists of description and analysis of these documents. When possible, the history emerges through analysis of documents. Such an approach results in greater familiarity with the sources and supplies a firsthand view of how to treat sources critically, taking into account their genre, worldview, and biases. It also gives full weight to the sources as *part* of the history being studied. For example, the Gospels say something about the historical Jesus, but they also are historically important for what they say about the early Christians who wrote them.

STEREOTYPES OF JUDAISM

When we limit our study to the canon of the Hebrew Bible or the New Testament, certain viewpoints and prejudices are reinforced that are supported by the principles of selection that led to the formation of the canon in the first place. That is especially true with respect to the New Testament. The New Testament's treatment of Judaism is, on the whole, biased. As long as New Testament texts are the only ones studied in detail, it is very difficult to break down negative stereotypes of Jews and Judaism that are contained in the texts and that continue to influence Christian perception. Analyzing the apostle Paul or the Gospel of Mark can reinforce stereotypes unless our study simultaneously maintains a running commentary demonstrating that what they say is a one-sided view of Judaism. Even so, when the ongoing principle of organization is a Christian book, Judaism will be distorted somewhat.

A course on Second Temple Judaism, rather than simply on the canonical texts, has the luxury of presenting a fairer and more balanced portrait of Jewish society and of groups such as priests, Sadducees, Pharisees, Roman procurators, city crowds, Jewish rebels, and so on. Students are then better prepared to read New Testament texts because of their broader and deeper appreciation of first-century Judaism. This cannot be accomplished as well by means of background information presented along the way in the study of the New Testament or by short chapters at the beginnings of New Testament introductions. And students will more likely take the Jewishness of Jesus and the earliest Christians seriously; they will recognize countless ways in which an understanding of Second Temple Judaism helps them comprehend what Jesus does and says and perhaps even how he thinks. One can see Jesus *within* Judaism, which is crucial for appreciating him as a historical figure.

In general, this book does not criticize stereotypes of Judaism systematically or directly. Rather, it tries to present fairly and in a historical framework the Judaism of Jesus' day. A sympathetic understanding of another group, even if it does not lead to acceptance of its worldview, makes it more difficult to operate on the basis of stereotypes. One cannot see all Jews as legalists if one reads their texts and observes their actions. One cannot listen with equanimity to the Gospel of John saying that the Jews cried out, "We have no king but Caesar," when one knows that a few years later many Jews would sacrifice their lives opposing Roman injustice. One will be far less apt to set Jesus over against Judaism, or blindly blame the Jews for the death of Jesus or for rejecting him as Messiah, if one learns to see Jesus as *part* of Second Temple Judaism.

An important goal of this book is to challenge a view that sees Judaism as monolithic. Therefore, it stresses and illustrates the variety of ways of being Jewish in the Second Temple period. One might even say that its subject is the Judaisms of the Second Temple era.

SELECT BIBLIOGRAPHY

Gager, John G. *The Origins of Anti-Semitism: Attitudes toward Judaism in Pagan and Christian Antiquity.* New York: Oxford University Press, 1983.

Iggers, Georg G. *Historiography in the Twentieth Century: From Scientific Objectivity to the Postmodern Challenge.* Hanover, N.H.: Wesleyan University Press, 1997.

Ruether, Rosemary. *Faith and Fratricide: The Theological Roots of Anti-Semitism.* New York: Seabury, 1974.

Saldarini, Anthony J. "Judaism and the New Testament." Pages 27–53 in *The New Testament and Its Modern Interpreters.* Edited by Eldon J. Epp and George MacRae. Atlanta: Scholars Press, 1989.

Stone, Michael E.. "The Sources and Our View of Reality" and "Hidden Streams in Judaism: Essene Scrolls and Pseudepigrapha." *SSV,* 49–70.

CHAPTER 1

ISRAEL BEFORE THE SECOND TEMPLE PERIOD

PRIMARY READINGS: Genesis ✦ Exodus ✦ Leviticus ✦ Numbers ✦ Deuteronomy

We are about to take a fascinating journey through a key time in Israel's history. Jerusalem's second temple was built from 520 to 515 B.C.E. and lasted until the Romans destroyed it in 70 C.E., six hundred years later. In our travels, we shall meet a wide cast of characters—priests, prophets, kings, emperors, scribes, messiahs, and many others. And we shall learn about the origins of rabbinic Judaism and Christianity. These two great world religions of our day are really siblings, children of the same parent—Second Temple Judaism. An appreciation of Second Temple Judaism in all its variety and richness is needed to understand either religion in depth.

We cannot, however, jump directly into the Second Temple period. By then, Israel already had a long history, developed institutions, complex legal, historical, and theological traditions, and a diversified social structure. This chapter gives an overview of these elements.

THE STORY OF ISRAEL

The first books of the Hebrew Bible tell the stories that shaped Israel's self-understanding. Whether or not the events in these stories happened precisely as described is not our present concern. Jews of the Second Temple period did not do the sort of critical historical work that characterizes the modern age. They took their sacred stories as accurate representations of their history and of God's dealings with them. So we must be familiar with these stories.

THE TIME BEFORE ABRAHAM

Genesis 1–11 covers the period from the creation to the time of Abraham. It takes up myths common to many cultures in the ancient Near East—

the flood, for example—and adapts them to its own purposes. One theme in Genesis is that before Abraham humanity repeatedly failed to obey God. A second theme is that God always grants humanity another chance. A third is that God's plans for the world often encounter obstacles, not the least of which is human intransigence, but God overcomes all obstacles.

According to the Bible, the God of Israel is creator of the entire world. The making of the first humans, Adam and Eve, is the crowning work of creation. God places the humans in the garden of Eden and forbids them to eat from the tree of the knowledge of good and evil (Gen 3). Tricked by the serpent, they eat the forbidden fruit, thinking they will thereby attain equality with God. (Note that the serpent is not called Satan in Genesis. This identification comes much later in history.) God expels them from the garden so that they will not eat of the tree of life and live forever. This is called the *fall*. God curses the ground so that cultivation will be difficult. God curses the snake; it will be most hated of all creatures. God tells Eve that her childbirth will be painful and that she must be subject to her husband. Adam learns that he must eventually die. So Genesis claims that God intended a harmonious creation, with humans at its apex, but that humans ruined this plan through disobedience. Humanity's ills, even death itself, are due to human disobedience, and things are completely different after the fall than they were before.

B.C.E. and C.E.

The abbreviations A.D. and B.C. stand for *Anno Domini* (Latin for "in the year of our Lord") and "before Christ," respectively. They assume a Christian point of view, dating all history in terms of Jesus Christ, but we wish to examine Judaism in its own right. Scholars commonly use the abbreviations C.E. and B.C.E., meaning "Common Era" and "before the Common Era." The Common Era is the time in history shared by Jews and Christians.

Evil now grows until God resolves to destroy humanity with a flood (Gen 6:7). Only Noah is righteous, so God saves him and his family. At God's command, Noah builds a large boat, an ark, and fills it with his family and with every kind of animal. After the flood kills every animal and human on earth except those in the ark, the waters abate and the ark's passengers emerge to begin God's creation anew. God promises Noah that he will never again destroy the world by water, and creates the rainbow as a reminder of this promise, called a "covenant" (Gen 9:13–17).

In Noah, humans get a second chance, but they are soon up to their old tricks. In Gen 11, they decide to build a tower reaching into heaven, thus challenging God. It is called the tower of Babel. Babel is the Hebrew word for

Babylon, and the tower is said to be built in the land of Shinar, which also indicates the land of Babylon. The tower incident recalls Adam and Eve's desire to be equal to God. Before the tower episode, all humans have spoken a single language. But God now causes them to speak many languages, making cooperation on the tower impossible. This myth explains the origins of the various human languages and the different nations.

THE MOTHERS AND FATHERS OF ISRAEL (CA. 1800–1600 B.C.E.)

Genesis 12–50 tells of Israel's patriarchs (Abraham, Isaac, Jacob, and Jacob's twelve sons) and matriarchs (Sarah, Rebekah, Rachel, and Leah). A theme connecting the stories is that fulfillment of the promises to Abraham encounters multiple obstacles that God must overcome. A common expression of this theme is that women who transmit the promise are barren— Sarah (Gen 11:30), Rebekah (25:21), Rachel (29:31; 30:1–2), and perhaps Leah (29:31, 35; 30:9)—but God cures their barrenness.

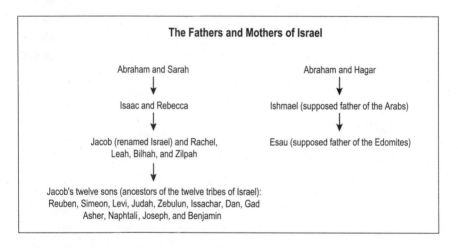

Against the background of humanity's failure to live up to God's demands, God says to Abraham,

> Go from your country and your kindred and your father's house to the land that I will show you. I will make of you a great nation, and I will bless you, and make your name great, so that you will be a blessing. I will bless those who bless you, and the one who curses you I will curse; and in you all the families of the earth shall be blessed. (Gen 12:1–3)

God's promise to Abraham is threefold: (a) land; (b) numerous progeny that will become a great nation; (c) God's blessing on Abraham and, through him, on all nations. The relationship between God and Abraham is called a covenant in Gen 15 and 17. Genesis 17 designates circumcision (the cutting off of the male foreskin) as the sign of the covenant between God and Abraham's descendants. Abraham leaves his Mesopotamian home and journeys to Canaan (the biblical name for Israel during this age). Abraham, his son Isaac, Isaac's son Jacob, and Jacob's offspring live there as "sojourners," that is, as resident aliens.

Palestine

"Palestine" is a name often applied in biblical scholarship to the lands on the eastern coast of the Mediterranean Sea that are the setting for much of the biblical narrative. The name derives from "Philistines," which designates traditional enemies of Israel living on the Mediterranean coast west and southwest of Jerusalem. The Greek historian Herodotus (fifth century, B.C.E.) records the first use of "Palestine" for a broader region. The Bible calls the land "Canaan" before it is taken over by the Israelites. Afterwards, it is known as the land of Israel. After the Babylonian exile, the Persian empire calls much of the area the Province Beyond the River (the Euphrates River), but when Jewish exiles return and rebuild Jerusalem, the area around the city is called "Judah." In Roman times, "Judea" means the area around Jerusalem, but it could also designate a broader area; for example, the kingdom of Herod the Great. After the Jews revolted in 132–135 C.E. and were defeated, the Roman emperor Hadrian ceased using the term *Provincia Judea* in favor of *Provincia Syria Palaestina,* or just *Palaestina.* During the first half of the twentieth century, Britain administered the area and called it Palestine. In 1947, the nation of Israel was founded. Today, Israel shares the area with the Palestinians, who live in Israel, in adjacent lands under Israel's control, and in neighboring Arab lands.

In Gen 32:24–28, Jacob spends a night wrestling with an angel; in the end, he exacts a blessing from the angel, who changes Jacob's name to Israel because, as the angel says, "you have striven with God and with humans, and have prevailed" (32:28). The angel interprets "Israel" to mean "he who strives with God." Jacob's descendants collectively receive this new name. They are called *bene Yisrael,* literally, "sons of Israel" or "children of Israel." They are a single extended family.

Genesis 37, 39–50 tells of Joseph, eleventh of Jacob's twelve sons, much favored by his father, who gives Joseph a multicolored coat. His jealous brothers sell him into slavery, and he ends up in Egypt. Because of false accusations, Joseph finds himself in prison there. He accurately interprets the dreams of some fellow prisoners and so gains Pharaoh's attention. By interpreting Pharaoh's dreams, he helps Egypt avoid the consequences of a terrible seven-year famine. Consequently, he assumes high office in Egypt. Famine

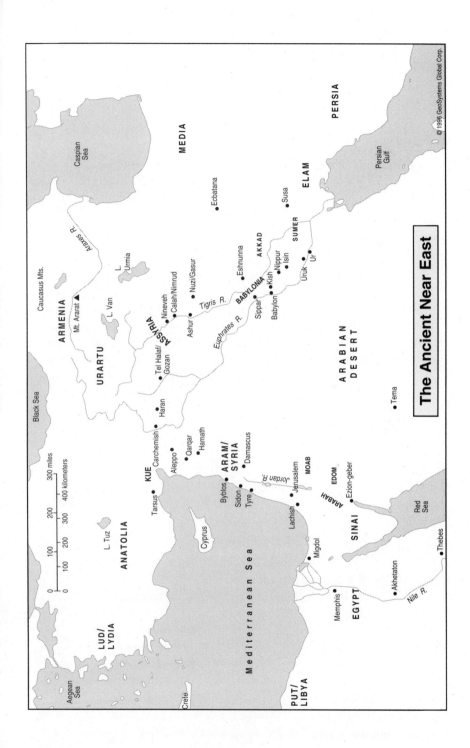

The Ancient Near East

later afflicts Canaan, forcing Jacob's sons to travel to Egypt for food. The brothers encounter Joseph and they reconcile, and then Jacob and his sons settle in Egypt. This sets the stage for the exodus.

EXODUS FROM EGYPT (CA. 1280 B.C.E.)

Hundreds of years pass, and Jacob's twelve sons become twelve large tribes. A pharaoh who is disturbed and threatened by Israel's growth ascends the throne. He decrees death for Israel's male babies and reduces Israel to slavery. Now Moses is born. Fearing he will be killed, his mother hides the baby for three months and then sets him adrift on the Nile in a basket. Pharaoh's daughter discovers the basket and raises Moses as her own. The name Moses is probably Egyptian in origin, perhaps meaning "is born," as in Egyptian names such as that of the famous king, Thutmose. When Moses reaches adulthood, he kills an Egyptian who is mistreating an Israelite (Exod 2:11–12). Moses is apparently aware of his Israelite connection. He then flees to the desert of the Sinai Peninsula and settles down with a tribe called the Midianites. He marries the daughter of a Midianite priest (2:15–22). While Moses is herding his father-in-law's flock at Mount Sinai, God appears to him in a bush that, although burning, miraculously is not consumed (3:1–4). God commissions Moses to go to Pharaoh to demand the Israelites' release.

Despite Moses' entreaties, Pharaoh refuses to release Israel, so God sends ten plagues upon Egypt, one after another. Since the first nine fail to convince Pharaoh, God sends a tenth—the killing of the firstborn of the Egyptians and their animals. God tells the Israelites to kill lambs and smear the blood on their doorposts. When the angel of death kills the Egyptian firstborn, the houses with blood are passed over, an event later commemorated at Passover. This plague convinces Pharaoh to let the people go. As Israel departs Egypt, Pharaoh changes his mind and pursues them. The Israelites are pinned between the Egyptian army and the Sea of Reeds *(Yam Suf)*. ("Reed Sea" is the correct translation of this Hebrew phrase. The idea that Moses led the people through the Red Sea has no foundation in the Hebrew text, but later Jewish and Christian tradition interpreted it as the Red Sea, and Hollywood graphically depicted the crossing of the Red Sea in the movie "The Ten Commandments.") God rescues them by splitting the sea and allowing them to pass through. The Egyptians are overwhelmed and drowned by the returning waters when they attempt to follow.

The Israelites now travel through the desert to God's mountain, led by a pillar of cloud during the day and a pillar of fire at night. The pillars symbolize God's guiding and protective presence. God satisfies the people's needs in the desert despite their frequent complaints. When they are hungry, he feeds them with manna (miraculous food) and with quails (Exod 16; Num 11). When they are thirsty, he brings a spring of water out of a rock for them (Exod 17; Num 20:2–13). However, God also punishes them from time to time for their lack of trust and their disobedience. In several instances, the people escape God's ultimate wrath only through Moses' intercession (e.g., Exod 32:7–14; Num 14:13–24).

MOUNT SINAI

The people arrive at Sinai (Exod 19:1) and stay eleven months. The Sinai material, most of it laws, occupies the rest of the book of Exodus, all of Leviticus, and just under ten chapters of Numbers. The sheer bulk of material indicates the importance of Sinai. God says to Moses,

> Thus you shall say to the house of Jacob, and tell the Israelites: You have seen what I did to the Egyptians, and how I bore you on eagles' wings and brought you to myself. Now therefore, if you obey my voice and keep my covenant, you shall be my treasured possession out of all the peoples. Indeed, the whole earth is mine, but you shall be for me a priestly kingdom and a holy nation. (Exod 19:3–6)

God makes a covenant with all Israel, reminding them of what he has already done for them. If they obey God's laws, they will be God's own possession and will continue to receive divine help.

The Sinai theophany (i.e., an appearance of God) dramatically portrays God's holiness, might, and majesty. The divine presence is marked by smoke and fire and the quaking of the mountain (Exod 19:18). Caution in approaching God acknowledges God's otherness and might, and no one but approved intermediaries may even touch the mountain (19:10–13, 23–25). The people and priests must purify themselves before encountering God (19:10–15, 22). Moses ascends the mountain alone and spends forty days and nights there receiving God's law, which begins with the Decalogue, the Ten Commandments (20:2–17; see also Deut 5:6–21).

Exodus 24 narrates a covenant ceremony. Animals are sacrificed, and Moses takes the blood and throws half against an altar he has built. "Then he took the book of the covenant, and read it in the hearing of the people; and they said, 'All that the LORD has spoken we will do, and we will be obedient' " (24:7). Moses then throws the remaining blood on the people and says, "See the blood of the covenant that the LORD has made with you in accordance with all these words" (24:8). Whatever the precise meaning of this ritual, it establishes a close connection between God and the people, even a "blood" relation, and it commits the people to obey God's Torah (the Hebrew word for God's law; see below).

God tells the Israelites to construct an ark, a box containing the stone tablets on which the covenantal commands are written. The ark symbolizes God's throne or footstool, the divine presence in the community. The ark has two cherubim (angelic figures) who spread their wings over the ark in a protective gesture. God also tells Israel how to build the sanctuary, a tent where God appears to Moses. The ark and the sanctuary accompany the Israelites when they leave Sinai and set out across the desert (Num 10). God selects the tribe of Levi to serve in the sanctuary. Members of this tribe carry the sacred objects (ark, tent, etc.). Aaron, brother of Moses and member of the tribe of Levi, becomes the first priest, and his descendants are named as legitimate priests to offer the prescribed sacrifices. Other members of the tribe are referred to as Levites, and they are often portrayed as lower clergy who aid the sons of Aaron in their cultic tasks.

Leviticus 8 describes the ordination of Aaron and his sons. Important to the ceremony is their anointment with oil by Moses. Anointing, the pouring of oil on their heads, symbolizes their being set aside for a special task. The Hebrew word for "anointed one" is *mashiah,* and in the Greek the word is translated *christos,* from which "Christ" comes. As we shall see, kings were also anointed, as were some others.

ENTRANCE INTO THE LAND (CA. 1250–1200 B.C.E.)

In Num 13–14 the people refuse God's order to enter Canaan because they fear its inhabitants. God angrily condemns the people to wander in the desert for forty years, the length of a generation. (The number forty becomes a standard length in the Bible—Moses is on Mount Sinai for forty days and nights, Israel must wander in the desert for forty years, many kings rule for about forty years, and so on.) Israel may not enter the promised land until the rebellious generation dies. In Deut 34, when Moses himself is about to die, he passes on his authority to Joshua, who will lead the people into the promised land. Deuteronomy highlights Moses' uniqueness: "Never since has there arisen a prophet in Israel like Moses, whom the LORD knew face to face" (34:10).

Israel conquers Canaan in three major campaigns. The book of Joshua ends with Joshua's farewell speech, in which he enjoins exclusive worship of God (Josh 23), and a covenant ceremony, in which the people pledge service to God alone (Josh 24). Joshua's speech reminds the people of what God has done for them. He warns that if they fail to obey God, they will lose the land. The Israelites are to avoid contact with the Canaanites, especially through marriage, because this would bring temptations to idolatry.

THE JUDGES (CA. 120–1020 B.C.E.)

When Israel first settles in the promised land, its leaders are called judges. The institution of judgeship lasts until the rise of the monarchy (ca. 1020 B.C.E.). Despite their title, the judges do not function primarily as judicial personnel. They are charismatic (spirit-filled) leaders raised up by God to respond to particular crises, usually military. Under their leadership, all or some of the tribes act in concert. Judges do not pass on their authority to their posterity. Given the patriarchal nature of ancient Israel, it is remarkable that one of the important judges is a woman, Deborah (Judg 4–5).

THE MONARCHY (CA. 1020–587 B.C.E.)

The first book of Samuel recounts the miraculous birth of Samuel, who is judge, prophet, and priest. He is a transitional figure, presiding over Israel's passage from a loose confederation of tribes to a monarchy. During Samuel's lifetime, Israel confronts the Philistines, new arrivals who settle on the coast, build strong cities, and threaten Israel's highland territory. Ultimately, only intertribal unity under a monarchy allows Israel to end the Philistine threat. As Samuel nears the end of his life, the Israelites approach him, demanding a king. God instructs him to anoint Saul king (ca. 1020 B.C.E.). Saul is of the tribe of Benjamin, settled just to the north of the territory of the southern tribe of Judah. Because Saul later disobeys God, God does not let him found a dynasty. God chooses David as Israel's new king, and to that end, Samuel anoints David in 1 Sam 16. But Saul continues to reign for a time.

David originally belongs to Saul's entourage, but they part company when Saul becomes jealous over David's military victories. David flees Saul and becomes head of a group of bandits (1 Sam 22). After Saul's death in battle (ca. 1000 B.C.E.), David becomes king of Judah, and he rules the south for seven years before he manages to incorporate the northern tribes into his kingdom (2 Sam 5:1–5). David finally overcomes resistance to his rule in the north, a resistance led by Saul's family and supporters. Eventually he establishes a united kingdom and then conquers the Philistines. He also takes the Jebusite city of Jerusalem, located between the tribes of Judah and Benjamin, and makes it his capital, bringing to it the ark to symbolize God's protection of himself, Jerusalem, and the monarchy.

In 2 Sam 7, David wants to build a temple for God, but through the prophet Nathan, God tells David that Solomon, David's son and successor, will build the temple. The later years of David's reign are troubled by struggles between his sons, and the Bible supplies a theological interpretation for this turmoil: David seduced Bathsheba, wife of Uriah the Hittite, one of his soldiers,

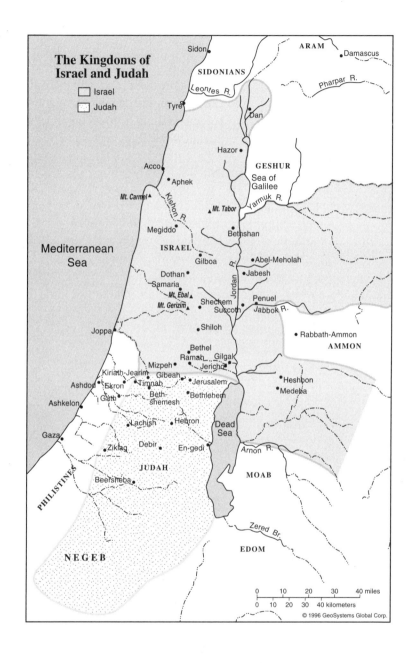

The Kingdoms of
Israel and Judah

☐ Israel
▨ Judah

then had Uriah killed and married Bathsheba. Nathan announces God's condemnation of this transgression and predicts troubles within David's family.

Bathsheba later gives birth to Solomon, and the books of 1 and 2 Kings tell Israel's story from his reign (ca. 961–922 B.C.E.) to the Babylonian exile in the sixth century B.C.E. They begin with Solomon's ambitious building programs, especially the building of the temple. Solomon alienates the northern tribes by placing heavy demands on them, and at his death they successfully revolt under Jeroboam and form an independent kingdom (922 B.C.E.). The Bible attributes this to Solomon's sin in introducing foreign religious influences by marrying many foreign wives. From now on there are two kingdoms that worship Yahweh—the northern kingdom, called Israel, and the southern one, called Judah. Hence, there is ambiguity about the name Israel, because it can mean either the northern kingdom or all who worship Yahweh, north and south. Jeroboam builds two shrines as national and royal sanctuaries, Bethel in the south and Dan in the north.

Nathan's importance in the David story illustrates the key role prophets play in bringing God's word to the kings and their subjects. Another such prophet, Elijah, of the ninth century B.C.E., spends most of his career proclaiming God's anger to the northern king Ahab (ruled 869–850 B.C.E.) and his foreign wife, Jezebel, who worships the god Baal and promotes Baal worship in Israel.

In 722 B.C.E., the kingdom of Israel falls to the expanding Assyrian Empire. The Assyrians deport the prominent citizens and resettle the northern kingdom with foreigners. In the south, Hezekiah takes the throne (ruled ca. 715–687 B.C.E.). He reforms Judah by abolishing places of worship outside Jerusalem, thus bringing the cult under closer control by the king and Jerusalem's priests. The move facilitates enforcement of Hezekiah's program of purifying the cult of foreign influences. Hezekiah's reform is part of a broader policy of resisting foreign domination.

Hezekiah's son, Manasseh (ruled 687–642 B.C.E.), undoes the reforms of his father and rebuilds cultic places outside Jerusalem (2 Kgs 21:1–18). Josiah (ruled 640–609 B.C.E.) reverts to the political and religious policies of Hezekiah.

THE END OF THE KINGDOM OF JUDAH

Babylonia takes over Judah in 605 B.C.E. Judah does not rest easy under the Babylonian yoke. The Babylonian king, Nebuchadnezzar, exiles prominent citizens in 597 B.C.E. to pacify the area, but there is peace for only a decade. When Judah is again rebellious, the Babylonians come again in force. In 587 B.C.E., Jerusalem falls and its king is deported to Babylonia. The following verses describe what then transpires:

> He [Nebuchadnezzar's general] burned the house of the LORD, the king's house, and all the houses of Jerusalem; every great house he burned down. All the army of the Chaldeans [another name for Babylonians] who were with the captain of the guard broke down the walls around Jerusalem. Nebuzaradan the captain of the guard carried into exile the rest of the people who were left in the city and the deserters who had defected to the king of Babylon—all the rest of the population. But the captain of the guard left some of the poorest people of the land to be vinedressers and tillers of the soil. (2 Kgs 25:9–12)

Another deportation takes place five years later, in 582 B.C.E. The events of 597, 587, and 582 deprive Judah of leaders, craftsmen, smiths, soldiers, and courtiers. Judah enters the third decade of the sixth century with its capital destroyed, its upper classes and skilled workmen exiled, its leadership decimated, and its population depleted.

THE EXILE

The exile brings to Israel not just material devastation but a challenge to its entire worldview. It seems to many that Babylonia's gods are far stronger than the Lord of Israel. God no longer even possesses an earthly temple. God's land is desolate, and God's people are dispersed. The monarchy is no more. It is the end of an era and one of the greatest watersheds in Israel's history. The time of the first temple is at an end. Unfortunately, the Bible does not go on to furnish a history of the exile, as it does of the preexilic era. We do, however, have three prophetic voices from this period that shed some light on it.

Jeremiah prophesies from 627 to 582 B.C.E. He preaches a message of social justice similar to that found in the book of Deuteronomy, a message deeply rooted in Israel's covenantal traditions. Jeremiah supports King Josiah's reforms. He is bitterly disappointed in the failure of Josiah's successors to live up to these ideals. In a famous "temple sermon," Jeremiah excoriates those who come to the temple seeking God (Jer 7). He tells them that the temple will not protect them, nor will God live among them, unless they follow God's will with respect to social justice and other matters, especially idolatry:

> Thus says the LORD of hosts, the God of Israel: Amend your ways and your doings, and let me dwell with you in this place. Do not trust in these deceptive words: "This is the temple of the LORD, the temple of the LORD, the temple of the LORD." For if you truly amend your ways and your doings, if you truly act justly one with another, if you do not oppress the alien, the orphan, and the widow, or shed innocent blood in this place, and if you do not go after other gods to your own hurt, then I will dwell with you in this place, in the land that I gave of old to your ancestors forever and ever. . . . Has this house, which is called by my name, become a den of robbers in your sight? (7:3–7, 11)

Jeremiah 26 retells the story of Jeremiah's temple sermon. There many think he should die for his words against the temple. He escapes, perhaps because he has some friends in high places. Uriah, another prophet of the time who preaches the same message, is not so lucky—he is executed (26:20–24).

In oracles (words of God, delivered by a prophet) from between the first two deportations (597 and 587 B.C.E.), Jeremiah voices disapproval of the Israelite community left in Judah and commends the exiles in Babylonia as those in whom Israel's future rests (24:5–7). He predicts that their exile will last seventy years, and he tells them to settle into Babylonia peacefully in the meantime (Jer 29). Jeremiah predicts that God will make a "new covenant" with Israel, in which God's Torah will be written on their hearts (31:31–34).

Ezekiel also prophesies during the early stages of the exile (593–571 B.C.E.). His prophetic commissioning happens during an awe-inspiring vision of God on a heavenly chariot and with an angelic entourage (Ezek 1–3)—a vision that caught the imagination of later writers, particularly those who wrote apocalypses. Ezekiel is a priest, and he uses priestly concepts and language liberally. He attributes Israel's exile to its openness to foreign religious influences, which have polluted Jerusalem and God's temple. God departs from the temple in Ezek 9–11, allowing it to be destroyed. In chapters 40–48, Ezekiel prophesies a restoration of Jerusalem and its temple. Ezekiel 43 pictures God returning to the temple in a blaze of glory. In chapter 44, Ezekiel insists that only Zadokite priests—those descended from Solomon's high priest Zadok—should serve at the altar. There was in fact no such restriction in the Second Temple period, but Zadokites were prominent.

A third prophetic voice from the exilic period is that of Second Isaiah (the prophet behind Isa 40–55). When a Persian general, Cyrus the Great, arises and conquers the Babylonian Empire, Second Isaiah sees this as God's action on behalf of Israel. He correctly expects Cyrus to allow Israel to return home and rebuild. Second Isaiah even says that Cyrus is the messiah because he does God's work (44:24–45:7). He envisages universal salvation, not just salvation for Israel, and expects that when God rescues Israel from exile, the nations will take notice and realize that Israel's God is the true God, the only God, the God who created everything. This relates to another theme that permeates Second Isaiah—monotheism. Second Isaiah's monotheism is univocal and strong. It sounds a note that will be heard throughout the Second Temple period and beyond—there is but one God, the creator, and God is the God of Israel.

SELECTED TOPICS

SOURCES OF THE HEBREW BIBLE

The Bible contains many different books, themselves constructed from a variety of earlier sources. Those sources are long gone, but through careful, close reading, their basic tendencies emerge. Each source had its own viewpoint. So, given the variety of books in the Bible and the different sources they used, we find many voices in the Bible representing many viewpoints.

Genesis, Exodus, Leviticus, and Numbers represent a combination of three major sources, called J, E, and P. "J" stands for the Yahwist, a source especially fond of the proper name Yahweh for Israel's God. ("J" comes from the German spelling, *Jahwist;* German scholars first identified the source.) J seems to have originated in the south, that is, in Judah. "E" stands for the Elohist, so named because it calls God *Elohim* (Hebrew for "god" or "gods") until it reaches the time of Moses. E probably originated among the northern tribes. "P" refers to the Priestly source. Priests were the final editors of the Pentateuch. It is not certain whether these priestly editors ever constructed a connected, independent narrative apart from J and E. Through redaction (incorporation into a larger epic, rearrangement, rewriting) of Israel's traditions (material, both narrative and legal, handed down through the ages), P tried to make sense of the disaster of 587 B.C.E.

Deuteronomy 12–26 is an exposition of God's law with a number of characteristics, among them: a conception of Israel's relationship to God as one of a covenant with mutual obligations, critical acceptance of the monarchy, concern for social justice, resistance to foreign religious influences, centralization of the cult, and belief that obedience to God brings success and disobedience brings misfortune. This exposition was embellished in several stages. With the exile, chapters were added to the beginning and end of Deuteronomy to adapt it to the new circumstances. The Deuteronomistic History (Deuteronomy through 2 Kings) applies the viewpoint of Deut 12–26 to the period from Moses to the exile. Israelites are evaluated according to their conformity to the Deuteronomistic interpretation of Mosaic traditions. Faithfulness to the covenant brings blessing, and violation brings curses.

Hezekiah and Josiah were two kings who tried to reform Judah's religion according to the principles of Deut 12–26. Manasseh tried to undo the reforms of his father, Hezekiah. The Deuteronomistic History blames the exile on Manasseh (2 Kgs 21:11–15; 23:26–27; 24:3–4). There is an intriguing story about Josiah's reform in 2 Kgs 22. While repairing the temple, the priests find "the book of the law" that was lost or neglected.

The prophetess Huldah assures Josiah that it is indeed God's word, and on the basis of this book, Josiah pursues reforms. Scholars see the book as some form of the original core of Deuteronomy. This is the first instance known in Israel of a normative book—that is, this book makes a conscious claim to exclusive authority. This writing was a significant step in the formation of the written Bible.

Prophets play a major role in Deuteronomistic History, where they act as God's spokespersons. God often predicts events through them, and the narrative demonstrates that the predictions are always true. Prophets are central players in the action as well. In Deut 34:10, it is said that Moses was the greatest of Israel's prophets (see 18:15–22; 34:10–12; Num 12:6–8). Samuel is considered a prophet in 1 Sam 9:6–9. Prophets challenge royal abuses.

Covenant

A *covenant* is a formal agreement between two parties. Covenants can be between equals or between superiors and inferiors. The covenant at Sinai is conditional, and it is like a suzerainty covenant. A suzerain is an emperor who rules over kings to whom he allows a degree of autonomy. The basic pattern of a suzerainty treaty has five elements:

(1) an identification of the suzerain (God, in the Israelite covenant);

(2) a historical preamble in which the suzerain's acts on behalf of the vassal are listed (e.g., Israel's liberation from Egypt);

(3) stipulations of the treaty that must be kept by the vassal (all of God's commands to Israel);

(4) a list of witnesses;

(5) blessings and curses.

The Torah exhibits features of the covenant pattern. In Exod 20:2, God says, "I am the LORD your God," where "LORD" represents God's proper name, Yahweh (see below). This corresponds to the first element of the pattern, where the suzerain identifies himself. The verse continues, "who brought you out of the land of Egypt, out of the land of slavery." This is the historical preamble, where the suzerain says what he has done for the vassal. (The covenant form may be responsible for the frequency in the Bible of similar phrases. Israel often used the covenant model to describe its relation to God.) The body of law that follows constitutes the covenant stipulations. Witnesses appear in Deuteronomy: heaven and earth witness to the covenant (Deut 30:19). Positive and negative results of obeying or disobeying the stipulations are clear throughout the Torah, and they are made explicit as blessings and curses of the covenant in Deut 27–28.

Two Hebrew words frequently associated with God characterize his role in the covenant—*hesed* and *emet*. *Hesed* is what God does for Israel. It is translated "steadfast love" or "loving kindness." It is what Israel gets from God in the covenant. The other word *emet,* means "faithfulness": God will do what God promises. So within the covenant, Israel can count on God for blessings and benefits, and it can be sure that God will be faithful and trustworthy: "All the paths of the LORD are steadfast love and faithfulness, for those who keep his covenant and his decrees" (Ps 25:10). In another typical covenant formulation, God says to Israel, "I will take you as my people, and I will be your God" (Exod 6:7).

TORAH

The Hebrew word *torah* is usually translated "law," but it really has a broader meaning. Before the exile and probably for some time afterward, *torah* meant "instruction" by God on some cultic or legal matter, usually through a priest. Deuteronomy represents a narrowing of the term *torah* when it refers to itself as the definitive *book* of law. Even the king is subject to this book: "He [the king] shall have a copy of this law *[torah]* written for him in the presence of the levitical priests" (17:18). Deuteronomy is meant to be definitive: "You must diligently observe everything that I command you; do not add to it or take anything from it" (12:32).

Torah

The Hebrew *torah* originally meant "instruction" on legal and religious matters. In the postexilic period, Torah came to mean especially the first five books of the Bible, with its centerpiece in the covenant at Sinai. When other books were brought together with the first five books to form a sacred collection, the later books were considered commentary on the Torah. In rabbinic literature, the idea of Oral Torah emerges, designating authoritative traditions that were originally oral, legal and nonlegal. In its broadest sense, Torah can designate all of Jewish life as marked by the community's relationship with the God of Sinai.

In the Hebrew Bible, *torah* most often refers to the commands given to Moses on Sinai. When the Pentateuch came together in the postexilic period, Deuteronomy became part of the larger collection, and the five-scroll collection became known as "the Torah." Although the Pentateuch contains much legal material, it is not merely a collection of laws. It tells the story of creation, of the patriarchs and matriarchs, of Israel's election, of the exodus and desert wanderings, and so on. It recounts the relationship between God and Israel and is paradigmatic for all time.

THE GOD(S) OF THE FATHERS

Exodus 3 tells of Moses meeting God in the burning bush on Mount Sinai. God tells Moses to go to Egypt and tell Pharaoh to let the Israelites leave their slavery in Egypt. Then the following interchange takes place:

> But Moses said to God, "If I come to the Israelites and say to them, 'The God of your ancestors has sent me to you,' and they ask me, 'What is his name?' what shall I say to them?" God said to Moses, "I AM WHO I AM." He said further, "Thus you shall say to the Israelites, 'I AM has sent me to you.' " God also said to Moses, "Thus you shall say to the Israelites, 'The LORD, the God of your ancestors, the God of Abraham, the God of Isaac, and the God of Jacob, has sent me to you': This is my name forever, and this my title for all generations. Go and assemble the elders of Israel, and say to them, 'The LORD, the God of your ancestors, the God of Abraham, of Isaac, and of Jacob, has appeared to me, saying: I have given heed to you and to what has been done to you in Egypt.' " (3:13–16)

(The NRSV translation uses "LORD" in small capital letters to render the proper name of Israel's God, Yahweh. Beginning in the last centuries B.C.E. and continuing into the present time, Jews have had such respect for the name of God that they pronounce it only under special circumstances. When they encounter the sacred name in the Hebrew text, they substitute *Adonai,* literally meaning "Lord." The NRSV respects this usage.)

This passage has undergone development, as indicated by the three beginnings to God's response ("God said," "He said further," "God also said"), and by its repetitiveness. The passage has been reworked because the mysterious name Yahweh needed explanation, but even the explanation is unclear. What is most striking about this passage is that it implies that Israel will not know whom Moses means when he says, "The God of your ancestors has sent me to you." The God who interacts with the patriarchs does so under different names, such as El Shaddai and El Elyon (e.g., Gen 14:20; 17:1; 35:11). This suggests that each patriarch had his own clan god and that only after the patriarchal period was each clan god seen as a manifestation of the one God, Yahweh. According to this later recognition, originally independent stories of patriarchs were rewritten to form a connected narrative of one God in continuous interaction with the patriarchs, now seen as a single family in successive generations. In other words, Israel's understanding of itself and of God developed over time.

A passage from Exodus supports this suggestion: "God . . . said to [Moses]: 'I am the LORD. I appeared to Abraham, Isaac, and Jacob as God Almighty [Hebrew: *El Shaddai*], but by my name 'The LORD' [Yahweh] I did not make myself known to them" (Exod 6:2–3). This is P's explanation of the fact that only at the time of Moses did Israel come to know Yahweh. In contrast to P, J claims that Yahweh was already recognized and worshiped in the time of Enosh, grandson of Adam (Gen 4:26), and implies that the patriarchs knew Yahweh by name (see Gen 12:1). P relays the more accurate account of what happened, since it is improbable that P would invent the idea that the patriarchs did not know God by name. Israel's idea of God developed over time and in response to its experiences. As a community worshiping Yahweh, its history really began at Sinai. As it redefined itself, it read its own history differently. As its self-understanding grew and changed, it rewrote its own story to reflect the changes. The process of rewriting traditions is typical of the Bible and continues into the postbiblical period and into Christianity.

Israel was noteworthy in the ancient world in that, unlike other peoples, it was monotheistic—that is, it believed in only one God. At least this was the case in the postexilic period. Numerous texts from the preexilic period suggest that at that earlier time Israel had not always been strictly monotheistic. Rather, it subscribed to monolatry, the worship of one God, although it acknowledged the existence of others. Indeed, the continuing battle of the prophets and others against polytheism and even against idolatry within Israel demonstrates that many Israelites were open to other religions throughout the preexilic period. The first of the Ten Commandments says, "You shall have no other gods before me" (Exod 20:3). The language here suggests the presence of other gods whom Israel might prefer to Yahweh. The text develops the idea of avoiding idols: "You shall not make for yourself an idol, whether in the form of anything that is in heaven above, or that is on the earth beneath, or that is in the water under the earth. You shall not bow down to them or worship them; for I the LORD your God am a jealous God" (20:4–5). This prohibition of making an image of any human, animal, or heavenly being became a hallmark of Israel's religion. It was applied also to making images of Israel's God, so that those outside Israel sometimes marveled that Israel's religion forbade images, or, in technical terms, was *aniconic*.

HOLY WAR

Most wars were to some degree religious in the ancient world. People consulted and depended on gods to help them against their enemies. Israel was no exception. God was conceptualized as a mighty warrior who would fight for the people (Deut 20). The song celebrating Israel's escape from Egypt (Exod 15) proclaims a divine military victory over the Egyptians: "The LORD is a warrior" (15:3). Since God is in the midst of the people as they fight, soldiers must be ritually pure, as if for participation in the cult (Josh 3:5; Num 5:3; see "Priestly Religion," below, for an explanation of ritual purity). Because God wins the victory, to God belong the spoils of war (Hebrew: *herem*). No one else may touch them except under God's explicit instructions. If they do, they incur the Lord's anger (Josh 7). God often demands that the spoils be destroyed.

MONARCHY

We have already heard the story of Israel's first kings—Saul, David, and Solomon. When David became king, Jerusalem had not yet been conquered by the Israelite tribes. The city lay on the central mountain range near the border between the northern and southern tribes. A shrewd politician, David saw the advantage in choosing for his capital a city that lay between the two major tribal divisions (north and south) and did not belong to either of them. His choice was analogous to the choice of Washington, D.C., as capital of the United States, which lies between the northern and southern states and is not located within any state. David conquered Jerusalem, made it his capital, and moved the ark of the covenant there.

David successfully subdued the Philistine threat and extended Israelite hegemony over most of the coast and highlands and into the territory across the Jordan (Ammon, Moab, and Edom) and northward to the Euphrates River. He now ruled people not part of the original tribal confederacy. Troops continued to be raised through tribal processes, and revenue was raised not by taxes on the tribes but through tribute imposed on the areas he conquered. Thus, David's kingship did not destroy all tribal institutions and ideals, but the institution of monarchy was bound to bring radical changes in Israel over time. Monarchy was inherently hierarchical. David exemplified the danger of royal abuse when he used his power to seduce Bathsheba and eliminate her husband (2 Sam 11).

Solomon transformed Israel into a typical ancient Near Eastern monarchy. He engaged in large building programs both inside Jerusalem and throughout his kingdom. The temple was one of his most enduring buildings, and his palace was even more impressive than the temple. Solomon built fortifications throughout his kingdom and raised a standing army with a strong chariot contingent. He established an elaborate and expensive court. For such expenditures he needed substantial revenues. Since the basis of the economy was agriculture, he had to expropriate peasant "surpluses." As his expenses grew, so did his taxes, supplemented by tolls from those who passed through his kingdom and by profits from trade. Solomon also required labor for his projects. To manage his empire and to exploit its resources, he drew up twelve administrative districts. Significantly, the boundaries of the twelve districts did not match those of the twelve tribes. The districts not only helped him administer the empire but also hastened the breakdown of old tribal divisions and weakened old institutions and social structures that embodied different, more egalitarian values based on tribal autonomy.

Israel was located on a corridor of land between Egypt and the other great world powers. Much of Israel's history must be read in this context. When Israel's more powerful neighbors were in decline, its strategic location worked in its favor. David and Solomon could maintain a strong kingdom during the tenth century B.C.E. because the states that traditionally exercised hegemony over the area (Egypt, Assyria, Babylonia) were in decline. At other times Israel was besieged by foreign nations because of its strategic significance. Assyrians, Egyptians, Babylonians, Persians, Greeks, and Romans succeeded each other in ruling the small strip of land.

Given the originally loose organization of the tribes and the fact that the Davidic dynasty belonged to the southern tribe of Judah, it is not surprising that resistance to the new order arose in the north. Jeroboam revolted and founded his own kingdom. Although the northern kingdom emerged in reaction to Solomon's harsh demands, its kings soon followed his example by establishing an empire that aspired to a role in international politics and had a court, standing army, temples, and forced labor. King Omri of the northern kingdom built Samaria as his capital. Foreign alliances led to an increase there in foreign religious and social practices.

Four and a half centuries of monarchy changed Israel forever. Norman Gottwald finds four "enduring structural effects" of the Israelite monarchy (pp. 323–25). The first was political centralization. Both the northern and southern kingdoms now each had a state with powers of taxation and conscription, a monopoly on force, standing armies, and a large bureaucracy. The second effect was social stratification with its attendant inequities. The third was that the possession of land shifted from families and clans and tribes to the hands of a rich upper class. Finally, the state was now fully involved in international trade, diplomacy, and war, which was expensive. Since the major source of wealth was agriculture, the peasants bore the brunt of the new expenses.

An attempt to limit the abuses of kingship can be seen in Deut 17:16–20:

He [the king] must not acquire many horses for himself, or return the people to Egypt in order to acquire more horses, since the LORD has said to you, "You must never return that way again." And he must not acquire many wives for himself, or else his heart will turn away; also silver and gold he must not acquire in great quantity for himself. When he has taken the throne of his kingdom, he shall have a copy of this law written for him in the presence of the levitical priests. It shall remain with him and he shall read in it all the days of his life, so that he may learn to fear the LORD his God, diligently observing all the words of this law and these statutes, neither exalting himself above other members of the community nor turning aside from the commandment, either to the right or to the left, so that he and his descendants may reign long over his kingdom in Israel.

The king is subject to many restrictions. He must be an Israelite and not a foreigner (17:15). The king is not to be exalt "himself above other members of the community," nor is he to amass riches, take multiple wives, become too strong militarily, or pursue foreign alliances. All this is summed up in the idea that the king is subject to God's law, now contained in a specific book (notice the language, "this law *[torah]*" and "these statutes"). If he obeys God's law, in which social justice figures prominently, God will permit him to continue his rule.

Royal propaganda found in the Bible depicts the king's function as enforcing proper worship of Yahweh and adherence to the divine ideal of justice for all Israelites. Psalm 72 supplies an example. Among its petitions for prosperity, success, and victory for the king, the psalm prays that the king might dispense God's justice, particularly with respect to the needy:

> Give the king your justice, O God,
>   and your righteousness to a king's son.
> May he judge your people with righteousness,
>   and your poor with justice. . . .
> May he defend the cause of the poor of the people,
>   give deliverance to the needy,
>   and crush the oppressor. . . .
> For he delivers the needy when they call,
>   the poor and those who have no helper.
> He has pity on the weak and the needy,
>   and saves the lives of the needy.
> From oppression and violence he redeems their life;
>   and precious is their blood in his sight. (Ps 72:1–2, 4, 12–14)

A key passage encapsulating the Davidic royal ideal, which in the Second Temple period becomes the basis of messianic hope, is 2 Sam 7. David offers to build God a house (a temple), and the prophet Nathan responds by using the word "house" in the sense of a dynasty. David will not build God a house; God will build David a house. God will have a special relation to the king, who rules on earth for God. This special relationship is expressed in terms of sonship:

> Moreover the LORD declares to you that the LORD will make you a house. When your days are fulfilled and you lie down with your ancestors, I will raise up your offspring after you, who shall come forth from your body, and I will establish his kingdom. He shall build a house for my name, and I will establish the throne of his kingdom forever. I will be a father to him, and he shall be a son to me. When he commits iniquity, I will punish him with a rod such as mortals use, with blows inflicted by human beings. But I will not take my steadfast love from him, as I took it from Saul, whom I put away from before you. Your house and your kingdom shall be made sure forever before me; your throne shall be established forever. (2 Sam 7:11–16)

Psalm 2 was probably recited in the temple at the coronation of a new Israelite king. The ideal time for subject peoples to revolt against an overlord was at a change of command owing to the death of the emperor. This is the situation behind the psalm—Israel's vassals see their chance for independence. Before they can accomplish their aim, God anoints the new king and puts him on Mount Zion:

> The kings of the earth set themselves,
>   and the rulers take counsel together,
>   against the LORD and his anointed [messiah], saying,
> "Let us burst their bonds asunder,
>   and cast their cords from us."
> He who sits in the heavens laughs;
>   the LORD has them in derision.
> Then he will speak to them in his wrath,
>   and terrify them in his fury, saying,
> "I have set my king on Zion, my holy hill." (Ps 2:2–6)

The new king recites the next words of the psalm:

> I will tell of the decree of the LORD:
> He said to me, "You are my son;
>   today I have begotten you.
> Ask of me, and I will make the nations your heritage,
>   and the ends of the earth your possession.
> You shall break them with a rod of iron,
>   and dash them in pieces like a potter's vessel." (Ps 2:7–9)

"You are my son, today I have begotten you" is an adoption formula. In some other Near Eastern nations, the king was considered literally a son of the god. Israel does not see the king as divine but nonetheless speaks of him as son of God.

Gottwald summarizes the characteristics ideally expected of the Davidic kings and relates them to later messianic hopes:

> In one way or other the Judahite kings were judged to be (1) in a distinctive filial relation to Yahweh; (2) intermediaries between Yahweh and his people; (3) exemplars of piety and obedience to Yahweh; and (4) executors of Yahweh's justice domestically and among the nations. From these roots sprang the later "messianism" associated with the Davidic dynasty. (p. 336)

PROPHECY

Prophecy in ancient Israel was a varied phenomenon. It was prevalent primarily during the time of the monarchy but existed before that time and continued into the Second Temple period. Some prophets worked for the royal or cultic establishment, and others were outside it. For some, prophesying was a full-time job, but others were also priests or shepherds or had some other occupation. Some had disciples and others did not. Some wrote their words down, others had their words written down by their followers, and the words of yet others were never recorded at all. Some were considered true prophets, and others false. The common denominator among all of the prophets is that each claimed to speak for God. They were intermediaries between God and people. Characteristic of the prophets is the messenger formula that introduces many of their proclamations: "Thus says the LORD."

The prophets were acutely aware that the people had obligations in their relationship with God and that they frequently failed to live up to these obligations. They often criticized the people, the king, or whoever violated the covenant. Oracles of judgment threatened transgressors with punishment. Oracles of salvation promised God's blessings on those who had obeyed God, or on the people as a whole after the punishment. The prophets spoke to their own times. Understanding the prophets entails appreciating their historical circumstances and the particular problems they addressed.

The most famous prophets are those whose words were collected in books. The written words of the prophets were transmitted and applied to new situations, supplemented with later oracles, rewritten, edited, and arranged in larger works. This complex process is evident in the book of Isaiah. Isaiah 1–39 contains oracles from a prophet living in Jerusalem in the eighth century B.C.E. Isaiah 40–55 is the work of a prophet living in the Babylonian exile sometime around 538 B.C.E. Isaiah 56–66 consists of oracles uttered during the early postexilic period. All sixty-six chapters are collected under the name of Isaiah. Even this description oversimplifies the book of Isaiah, for within the sections scholars have discerned later additions. The assumption of the ancient editors of the prophetic words is that since the prophets speak the word of God, this word is valid for all generations and should be preserved and reapplied to new circumstances.

The prophets were fully engaged in Israel's life—economic, political, and religious. The prophet Samuel presided over Israel's transition from tribal federation to monarchy by anointing the first two kings, Saul and David. King Ahab drew sharp attack from the prophets Elijah and Elisha, and Elisha anointed Jehu to overthrow Ahab's line and create a new dynasty in the north. The prophets did not distinguish between politics, economics, culture, and religion: Amos condemned the social injustices of the northern kingdom, Hosea censured Israel's devotion to the Canaanite god Baal, Isaiah of Jerusalem warned kings Ahaz and Hezekiah against foreign alliances, Jeremiah condemned Judah for failing to institute religious and social reform.

There was much room for disagreement among prophets. A claim to speak for God was no guarantee that one did so. One prophet might attack the message of another, and society might reject a given prophet as a lunatic or a schemer. Famous clashes between prophets include Jeremiah's confrontation with Hananiah in Jer 28 and Micaiah ben [son of] Imlah's disagreement with four hundred prophets in 1 Kgs 22.

THE WISDOM TRADITION

The word "wisdom" was prominent in the ancient world and could mean different things. In Israel's wisdom movement, wisdom resulted from applying human reason to lived experience. It consisted of prescriptions for life and how it should be lived. The clan passed down the accumulated wisdom of countless generations. This was folk wisdom. Certain members of a clan or a tribe attained a reputation for greater wisdom than others.

Wisdom

Wisdom, a term in the Hebrew Bible (OT) standing for many things ranging from the technical skill of the artisan (Exod 36:8) to the art of government (1 Kgs 3:12, 28). It also designates simple cleverness (2 Sam 14:2), especially the practical skill of coping with life (Prov 1:5; 11; 14), and the pursuit of a lifestyle of proper ethical conduct (Prov 2:9–11 and throughout). Wisdom is also seen as belonging properly to God (Job 28), associated with creation (Prov 8:22–31), and even identified with the Torah or Law (Ecclus 24:23). (Murphy, "Wisdom," 1135)

Israel's wisdom entered a new stage with the advent of monarchy. The bureaucracy created by Solomon's kingdom required professional scribes who could read and write. Not many people were literate in the ancient world. Scribes were educated men who served as record keepers, advisors, diplomats, teachers, tutors to the ruling class, and in other capacities. Kingdoms needed a battery of scribes to keep records, read correspondence, write decrees, read and write laws, and more. Scribes became an integral part of Israelite government and society. Among the scribes were the intellectuals of ancient Israel, called "the wise" or "the sages." An adjective sometimes applied to the activity and literary products of the wise is *sapiential,* which comes from the Latin *sapientia,* meaning "wisdom." Since literacy was, for the most part, confined to royal circles and urban elites, the sages belonged to these classes. Since contact with other kingdoms and empires was common in the Solomonic court, sages were open to outside influences. In the ancient Near East, there was an international wisdom tradition that shared literary genres, themes, ways of teaching, and so on.

The Bible portrays Solomon as an extremely wise man. His reputation arises from his role in creating and developing a royal scribal establishment. Three canonical or deuterocanonical (i.e., accepted as canonical by Catholics but not by Jews or Protestants) works—Proverbs, Qoheleth (also called Ecclesiastes), and Wisdom—are ascribed to Solomon, but few scholars would maintain that he is their real author. In the portrayal of Solomon in 1 Kgs 3, we learn something about Israelite wisdom. Solomon's wisdom is, first of all, that of a ruler: he rules wisely. He is also a wise judge. First Kings 4:32–33 contains further instances of Solomon's alleged wisdom: "He composed three thousand proverbs, and his songs numbered a thousand and five. He would speak of trees, from the cedar that is in the Lebanon to the hyssop that grows in the wall; he would speak of animals, and birds, and reptiles, and fish." The proverb is the form most characteristic of wisdom. Proverbs—short sayings containing general reflections on life—are the product of human reason acting on everyday experience to discern the way things work. "A stitch in time saves nine," "You can't win 'em all," and "The early bird gets the worm" are all proverbs. They carry the conviction of common sense, which attests to their origin in the cumulative experience of a group, not just an individual. Although today we sometimes think of proverbs as simplistic, there is an element of truth to every proverb, and this accounts for its survival and repetition. Even today the quotation of a proverb brings the weight of commonly accepted truth to the conversation.

Ancient sages were interested in the way everything worked—nature, family, the court, politics, and so on. Solomon's knowledge of trees, animals, and fish shows his wisdom, for the wisdom tradition conceived of the universe as an organic whole, and it prized knowledge in all spheres of experience. Segmentation of knowledge is a modern development. For ancient Israel, knowledge about nature was knowledge that affected humans. Proverbs aimed at discovering the sense behind things. To learn how the world worked was also to learn how one should fit into it, how one should act. The ultimate aim of the wisdom tradition was practical and successful living.

The wisdom tradition assumed that there was a discoverable order in the universe. Primary evidence for the way things worked was not so much a sacred text or even Israel's sacred covenantal traditions as the human experience in the world. As the Second Temple period progressed, however, wisdom became more explicitly interested in Israel's sacred traditions. Eventually wisdom became identified with Torah (e.g., in Sir 24), so that Torah was the perfect expression of that order in the universe that was also accessible, to some degree, through human experience. This implied universalistic claims for Torah. Later the rabbis would claim that God consulted Torah when creating the world. Wisdom, which is feminine in both Hebrew *(hokmah)* and Greek *(sophia),* became personified as a woman who enjoyed a close relationship with God and even played a role in creation (e.g., Prov 8, Sir 24, Bar 3, Wis 7). Perhaps the development of personified wisdom fulfilled a deep human need to see the feminine in God. Other religions had female deities.

The books from the wisdom tradition are Proverbs, Job, Ecclesiastes (otherwise known as Qoheleth, Hebrew for "Preacher"), and two deuterocanonical works—Sirach (also known as the Wisdom of Jesus ben Sirach, or Ecclesiasticus) and the Wisdom of Solomon. Wisdom influence is also present in other canonical works (especially in Psalms), deuterocanonical texts (such as Baruch), and in Israelite and Jewish material outside the canon. The books of Job and Ecclesiastes deserve special attention here. Both date to the Second Temple period. Job looks critically at the alleged connection between behavior and worldly rewards and punishments. It challenges the notion that only the wicked suffer. Ecclesiastes challenges a simplistic "wisdom" that has life completely figured out. The book stresses human limitations and sees life as inherently impenetrable. It is famous for characterizing all of life under the sun as "vanity." These two books fascinate modern readers because they reject facile answers to the mysteries and contradictions of life.

PRIESTLY RELIGION

Priestly religion means Jewish religion insofar as it focused upon the temple, its personnel (the priests and their attendants), and its activities.

Priestly religion was a system whose parts cohered and functioned as a whole. The system had an implied worldview, expressed by rituals and institutions. It was thus a *symbolic* system. This system's influence extended well beyond the confines of the temple because it was replicated in the political, economic, social, and cultural realities of ancient Israel. So the priestly system sheds light not just on supernatural entities or on Israel's religion but on Israelite society as a whole. Indeed, Israel's priestly religion gave its society coherence and meaning.

Our own religious beliefs and practices are often self-evident to us, and we usually do not examine them critically or "objectively." Other religions seem strange to us, since we do not share their cultural or religious assumptions. One way to understand other religions sympathetically is to see them as analogous to ones more familiar or to analyze them as particular instances of the common human effort to make sense of life—an endeavor pursued even outside explicitly religious contexts. To facilitate such comparisons, we will investigate some meaning-producing activities.

CATEGORIES, BOUNDARIES, FEELINGS, AND RITUALS

The human world is not just physical; it also has intellectual and emotional content. Humans need to make sense of the world. Essential to this process of making meaning is determining where things and people belong. To decide where things belong is to classify them, to put them into categories. Categories imply distinctions, and distinctions mean drawing boundaries or lines. Boundaries are drawn between one place and another, between one time and another, between one person or group and another. To be aware of boundaries is to know where you are, what belongs to you, what belongs to your group, and what does not. The clearer the boundaries, the clearer the categories.

Categories are invested with feelings. People learn to feel one way about one category and another way about another. They also learn how categories are arrayed with respect to one another. The sum of such classifications forms a symbolic system, a "map" of reality for those who accept it. Through socialization, both deliberate and unplanned, the symbolic system or universe is passed down to successive generations as "simply the way things are" (see Berger; Berger and Luckman). If the system is coherent, then it is replicated throughout society, and the replication reinforces the system. The system is often thought to be God-given.

People and things often cross from one category into another. In many such crossings, some sort of ritual, presided over by a professional, is often required to acknowledge and legitimate the boundary crossing. There are also rituals that put something or someone back in the proper place when dislocation occurs. Of course, there are persons, things, and experiences that simply do not fit the system.

PLACE.   Boundaries between places can be physical, such as rivers or oceans. They can also be purely conventional, such as national boundaries. A U.S. citizen who steps over the Canadian border is only a few feet farther north. Nonetheless, that person is now in a different country, with different traditions, leaders, laws, and institutions. Boundaries that exist primarily in human minds are nonetheless real. The crossing of a national boundary, if done legally, is often accompanied by a ritual presided over by an official of the political system—the offering of the passport, the inspection of papers and baggage, and a stamping of the passport to indicate official approval of entrance.

TIME.   As with physical categories, some temporal catagories are provided by nature. The seasons, day and night, and phases of the moon create natural temporal categories. But natural categories are inadequate for complex human needs. For example, consider "company time" and "my own time." People resent working for the company on their own time, and the company often forbids doing something personal on company time. Similarly, people feel differently about Saturdays than they do about Mondays.

Rituals mark the passing from one time to another. This is evident in the stages of a person's life. Baptism or circumcision marks the entrance into a religious community. A ritual called the birthday party marks the passage from one year to the next. Confirmation or a Bar or Bat Mitzvah ceremony signals the passing from childhood to young adulthood. Graduation from college often marks the beginning of full adulthood.

THINGS.   Identical things can belong to quite different categories. Most people feel differently about what belongs to themselves than about what belongs to others. Two identical pairs of jeans can evoke quite different feelings. To take possession of a pair of jeans from a pile belonging to the store, one goes through a ritual called buying, which includes taking the jeans to a salesperson, giving this person some paper or metal called money, and getting a piece of paper documenting the ritual, called a receipt. This process does not change the jeans physically. They are the same after the procedure as before. But they are different in one's eyes and in the eyes of society.

PEOPLE.   Boundaries between countries are boundaries between both places and people. A U.S. citizen is different from a Canadian citizen. The words "us" and "them" indicate the distinction. To change from one group to another, one must undergo a ritual or series of rituals, such as naturalization. Belonging to one religion is different from belonging to another. Passing from one religion to another requires a ritual to mark the passage. Social boundaries are crossed at marriage, graduation, entering a profession, buying a house, or having a first child. Each crossing is marked by a ritual.

VALUES AND FEELINGS.   Societal and individual values are inscribed in the boundaries people draw and the feelings associated with these boundaries. Because cultures differ, their stake in certain kinds of lines may be different. In the United States, private property is a prominent cultural value. Lines drawn around property are important and frequently find physical expression in fences or hedges. Ignoring such markers can arouse animosity.

Because individualism is such a strong value in American culture, boundaries defining the individual are well marked. Body odors that blur bodily boundaries by letting one's body impinge on another's space are suppressed. Likewise, many do not like to be touched by anyone not within a certain range of close friends and family, or perhaps not even by them.

Everyday life supplies examples of strong feelings aroused when categories are mixed. A child protests if different categories of food even touch each other on his or her plate or if someone else drinks from his or her glass. Even if one is convinced that dog food is the most nutritious food available, one is still repulsed by the idea of eating it because "dog food is for dogs." A germ-conscious culture rationalizes this, claiming that such feelings arise from a desire to avoid what is unhealthy. But this ignores the fact that many such "rules" have no scientific basis, and also misses the symbolic system implied by such rules.

A society's categories can change over time. Civil rights laws enacted in the United States in the second half of the twentieth century are a dramatic example. Previously the categories of black and white had been kept separate by laws, but boundaries between black and white then became unlawful. This aroused intense discomfort among some people. When boundaries change, anxiety rises because one's world is passing out of existence.

CATEGORIES OF PRIESTLY RELIGION.   The following table shows some of the people, places, times, and things considered sacred in priestly religion:

Places	Temple, Mount Zion, Jerusalem, land of Israel
Persons	High priest, priests, Levites, Israelite men, Israelite women (in descending order of holiness)
Times	Sabbath, feasts (especially Passover, Weeks, Tabernacles, Day of Atonement)
Things	Things that belong to the temple, the parts of sacrifices belonging to God, spoils of holy war

PRIESTLY TERMS: CLEAN, PURE, AND HOLY

CLEANNESS.   "Clean" and "unclean" are terms central to priestly religion. To understand these terms, it is useful to think of how we use the term "dirt." Dirt is matter out of place (see Douglas). When we see a freshly tilled garden, we do not say, "What a dirty place!" Although there is soil everywhere in the garden, it belongs there, so it is not "dirt." But after working in the garden all day, we do not sprawl out on the best couch. We are "dirty," meaning that soil is on us, where it does not belong. Soil has become dirt. And we should wash and change clothes before sitting on the couch, since otherwise garden dirt will be transferred to the couch, where it does not belong. If dirt gets into the home, we get rid of it. This is a process of purification, of removing dirt. The fact that soil can be thought of as dirt, as matter out of place, implies that things have their place, and this implies a system, which in turn implies categories that in turn imply lines and relationships between categories. Thus clean/dirty (unclean) and pure/impure are appropriate metaphors for speaking of systems and violations of those systems.

HOLINESS AND PURITY.   Today holiness is often identified with morality. This is misleading when applied to ancient priestly religion. There holiness designates what belongs to God and so does not belong to humanity or to the profane realm. God is by definition holy, so anything that belongs to God is also holy (another word for "holy" is "sacred"). There are degrees of holiness: the closer one comes to God, the holier one must be. The word "sanctuary" denotes the place where God is to be found and is derived from the Latin word *sanctus,* which means "holy."

Purity is related to holiness. For a person to be pure (or clean) means to be free of anything offensive to God and therefore to be able to approach God as closely as one's position in society allows. To become pure when one is not, one undergoes a ritual effecting the passage from impurity to purity. This is often conceptualized as "washing." Similarly, objects need to be purified to be in God's presence, and those which are holy should not be defiled.

Rules about who can and who cannot approach God in the sanctuary are thought to have been given by God. They protect God's holiness. They protect the people as well, for to approach God in an inappropriate manner is dangerous. God is powerful and may react strongly to the approach of an impure person. Purity rules institutionalize categories and make the boundaries clearer. To cross such boundaries without proper rituals or without being in the proper state is to be out of place in the system and to invite disaster. An example is found in the story of David bringing the ark to Jerusalem:

> When they came to the threshing floor of Nacon, Uzzah reached out his hand to the ark of God and took hold of it, for the oxen shook it. The anger of the LORD was kindled against Uzzah; and God struck him there because he reached out his hand to the ark; and he died there beside the ark of God. (2 Sam 6:6–7)

Uzzah was only trying to keep the ark from falling. But he was not authorized to touch the ark, and he paid the price for his presumption.

Basic Definitions

Holy: Closely associated with God.
Sacred: Synonymous with "holy."
Profane: "Everyday," not belonging in a special way to God's sphere.
Dirt: That which is out of place in the system.
Abomination: That which is so abhorrent to God that it has no place in the system.
Clean: Free of what is displeasing to God.
Unclean: Not conforming with God's purity rules and therefore unable to come into God's presence.
Pure: Synonymous with "clean."
Impure: Synonymous with "unclean."
Purity rules: Rules set up to define and guard the proper boundaries between the pure and the impure.

THE TEMPLE: ISRAEL'S SACRED PLACE

THE TEMPLE BUILDING. The temple's architecture symbolized God's presence and made possible the interchange between God and humans; at the same time, it maintained firm boundaries between the sacred and the natural worlds. The temple consisted of three rooms in a row. It was oriented on an east-west axis, with the entrance to the temple on the east. The innermost room was the *debir*, translated the "inner room," the "holy of holies," or the "most holy place." In Solomon's temple, the ark of the covenant, symbol of God's presence, was in the holy of holies. The room was a perfect cube, twenty cubits to a side (one royal cubit equals 20.9 inches), with no windows or lamps. The cherubim over the ark were large carvings of strange and frightening winged creatures, there to protect the ark and so to protect God. Access to the holy of holies was strictly limited.

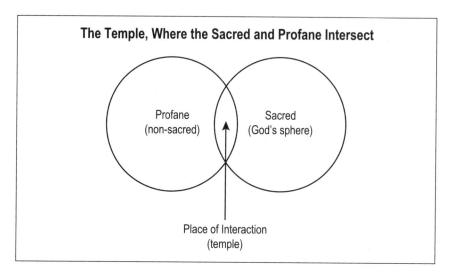

Only the high priest could enter, and only once a year, on the Day of Atonement.

The middle room of the temple was the largest. It was forty cubits long, twenty wide, and thirty high. It was called the *hekal*, meaning "great house" or "palace," also translated "holy place," and it was the site of most of the activity inside the temple. This room contained the small altar on which incense was offered, ten golden lampstands arranged five on a side, and a golden table for the "bread of the presence" (bread continually offered to God). Priests had daily access to this room. The holy place was more accessible than the holy of holies and less accessible than the parts of the temple where nonpriests could go. It represented a high state of holiness but was less holy than the inner sanctuary.

The third room, through which one entered the holy place, was the porch—in Hebrew, *ulam.* It was only ten cubits deep, twenty cubits wide, and thirty cubits high. This was the antechamber to the holy place, corresponding to the entry of a dwelling.

Steps led down from the vestibule's entrance to the area in front of the temple. As one looked down the steps, there was a large altar for burnt offerings to the left (north) with a ramp leading up to it, and on the right (south) was a large "sea of bronze," presumably for ritual washings. The area immediately surrounding the temple was enclosed by a wall. Only the priests had access to this enclosed courtyard.

TEMPLE AND DYNASTY.   David used the ark, symbol of God's covenant relationship with the people, to unite the Israelite tribes. God's presence in Jerusalem signified divine approval of the Davidic dynasty. It also made Jerusalem a holy city, focus of God's protective presence. Solomon's first priority as king was to build a temple for God. Dynasties of the ancient Near East proved their legitimacy by demonstrating the gods' support for their rule. There was no better way to demonstrate this approval than a god's willingness to live beside the king. Therefore, the founding of dynasties was accompanied by the building of temples, royal sanctuaries. Solomon built the temple on Zion, a hill in Jerusalem. The name Zion can denote the temple, the hill on which it was built, or Jerusalem as a whole, which owes its significance to God's presence.

TEMPLE AS THE PRESENCE OF GOD. At the completion of Solomon's temple, a fourteen-day feast was held. It began with the bringing of the ark to the temple.

> Then the priests brought the ark of the covenant of the LORD to its place, in the inner sanctuary of the house, in the most holy place, underneath the wings of the cherubim. . . . And when the priests came out of the holy place, a cloud filled the house of the LORD, so that the priests could not stand to minister because of the cloud; for the glory of the LORD filled the house of the LORD. (1 Kgs 8:6, 10–11)

The priests bring the ark to the holiest part of the temple. God's presence is too much for humans to endure, so the priests cannot remain in the temple while the cloud is there. The Israelites knew that God could not be limited or restricted to one place, but the divine presence among them had to be tangible and reliable. Two verbal devices for conveying this tension appear in 1 Kgs 8. God's "glory" is present in the temple, and the divine "name" dwells there (8:16). Both phrases are circumlocutions for God, expressing that God is present but cannot be contained. *Glory* is a word characteristic of the Priestly source, and "name" is a favorite circumlocution for God's presence in the Deuteronomistic sources.

The dynamics of holiness are visible in the theophany at Sinai.

> The LORD said to Moses: "Go to the people and consecrate them today and tomorrow. Have them wash their clothes and prepare for the third day, because on the third day the LORD will come down upon Mount Sinai in the sight of all the people. You shall set limits for the people all around, saying, 'Be careful not to go up the mountain or to touch the edge of it. Any who touch the mountain shall be put to death.' . . . Even the priests who approach the LORD must consecrate themselves or the LORD will break out against them." (Exod 19:10–12, 22)

In this passage, the verb "consecrate" *(qiddesh)* means "to make holy," and it is accomplished by washing. Even washing only enables people of the proper category, priests, to approach God closely, and even priests must undergo a consecration, or purification, before they can approach.

God was the source of life, fertility, prosperity, and strength. God's presence in the temple was necessary for these things to be realized, and the presence of the temple on Mount Zion and in Jerusalem made them a holy mountain and a holy city. This basic presupposition is evident in the book of Psalms, the hymnbook of the temple. People who participated in the cult would hear the words of the psalms and learn from them. Psalm 48, for example, was probably written for pilgrims to Jerusalem:

> Great is the LORD and greatly to be praised
>   in the city of our God.
> His holy mountain, beautiful in elevation,
>   is the joy of all the earth,
> Mount Zion, in the far north,
>   the city of the great King.
> Within its citadels God
>   has shown himself a sure defense.
> Then the kings assembled,
>   they came on together.
> As soon as they saw it, they were astounded;
>   they were in panic, they took to flight;
> trembling took hold of them there,
>   pains as of a woman in labor,
> as when an east wind shatterst
>   the ships of Tarshish.
> As we have heard, so have we seen
>   in the city of the LORD of hosts,
> in the city of our God,
>   which God establishes forever.
> We ponder your steadfast love, O God,
>   in the midst of your temple.
> Your name, O God, like your praise,
>   reaches to the ends of the earth.
> Your right hand is filled with victory.
>   Let Mount Zion be glad,
> let the towns of Judah rejoice
>   because of your judgments.
> Walk about Zion, go all around it,
>   count its towers,

consider well its ramparts;
    go through its citadels,
that you may tell the next generation
    that this is God,
our God forever and ever.
    He will be our guide forever.

This psalm lauds God's strength. Because of the divine presence, Mount Zion is invincible, and foreign kings tremble at the very sight of it. To see Jerusalem's fortifications is to behold God's strength. The "city of our God" will last "forever." The psalmist tells the pilgrims to tour the city, looking at its ramparts and citadels so that they might tell their posterity, "This is God." God's "steadfast love" here is *hesed,* what God has graciously done for the people. The people recall these gracious deeds in the temple, for God is available there and can be thanked. Zion is beautiful and lofty, and all the world delights in it. It is the place where God speaks, delivering divine judgments. We shall refer to this complex of beliefs about Zion as "Zion ideology." We do not use ideology here in a pejorative sense but to indicate that these ideas could have important practical effects on Israel's society.

Photograph of a model of the Jerusalem temple in the late Second Temple period.
Herod the great rebuilt the temple and it's environs on a grand scale.
The model is located in Jerusalem.

TEMPLE PERSONNEL: ISRAEL'S SACRED PERSONS

PRIESTS AND LEVITES.   Israel's priesthood was hereditary. God chose the tribe of Levi to serve in the sanctuary. Within this tribe, God chose Aaron and his descendants to be the higher clergy, who carried out the sacrifices and entered the temple to minister to God. Other members of the priestly tribe, the Levites, formed a lower clergy. They had different functions at different times. They frequently appear as servants and gatekeepers in the temple. In the postexilic period, they had a prominent role in worship as singers and were teachers of Torah.

A story in Num 16 suggests that the establishment of a professional priesthood did not come without a struggle. Korah, a Levite, leads a rebellion against Moses and Aaron in the desert. Protesting against their authority, Korah's followers say, "You have gone too far! All the congregation are holy, every one of them, and the LORD is among them. So why then do you exalt yourselves above the assembly of the LORD?" (Num 16:3). Holiness was an attribute of all the people, because according to the covenant they were all God's people. In Exod 19:6, God says, "You shall be for me a priestly kingdom and a holy nation." The challenge, then, was to legitimate a special class who were holier than the people and so could approach God more closely. Moses' answer to Korah includes the following:

> "The man whom the LORD chooses shall be the holy one. You Levites have gone too far!" Then Moses said to Korah, "Hear now, you Levites! Is it too little for you that the God of Israel has separated you from the congregation of Israel, to allow you to approach him in order to perform the duties of the Lord's tabernacle, and to stand before the congregation and serve them? He has allowed you to approach him, and all your brother Levites with you; yet you seek the priesthood as well!" (Num 16:7–10)

"To approach him" is a cultic term meaning to approach God in the sanctuary. Different divisions of the clergy were allowed different degrees of closeness to God. God decided who could approach. Aaron is called "the holy one" because he could come closest to God. The Levites were also allowed to approach God closely, though less so, and this meant that they were "separated . . . from the congregation of Israel" and stood "before the congregation and serve[d] them." But there was a divinely ordained hierarchy within the clergy. To challenge this hierarchy was to challenge God. Degrees of holiness of parts of the temple were replicated in degrees of holiness of segments of the community.

ORDINATION.   The ordination ceremony for Aaron and his sons, narrated in Lev 8–9, highlights many features of the priesthood. First, the priest was washed, a symbol for washing away impurities and for separation from the profane world (8:6). Next he was dressed in priestly robes (8:7–9). To take off and put on clothing of special significance is a familiar act both in religious contexts and outside them. Here the clothing signifies the priest's special role as mediator between God and people. The priest was anointed with oil as a sign of his special designation by God (8:10–12). Finally, Aaron and his sons had sacrifices placed in their hands so that they could fulfill their priestly duty of offering them to God.

LAW.   As cultic mediators between Israel and God, priests spoke for God. Moses says of them, "They teach Jacob your ordinances, and Israel your law" (Deut 33:10). It was up to priests to decide who and what was pure. God says to Aaron, "You are to distinguish between the holy and the common, and between the unclean and the clean; and you are to teach the people of Israel all the statutes that the LORD has spoken to them through Moses" (Lev 10:10–11). Israel depended on access to God in the cult for its well-being, and the priests controlled this access.

CULT AND SOCIETY.   One's position with respect to the cult corresponded to one's position in society. This is an example of replication. In descending order of degree of access to the cult were the high priest, the other priests, Levites, and laypersons. Women could not be priests or Levites, nor did they participate in temple activities as much as men. Gentiles were denied access to the cult and so were outside the covenant community. Between Gentiles and pure Israelites were various classes of persons, some of whom never had access to the cult, such as eunuchs (Deut 23:1; probably because they were not "whole" or were unable to pass on their covenantal status through procreation) or children born out of wedlock (Deut 23:2; because their lineage and so their covenantal status was questionable). Temporary hindrances to participation in the cult included leprosy (not what is known as leprosy today, but any serious and obvious skin disorder), nocturnal emissions by males, and contact with a corpse. These examples show that purity was not only a matter of morality. For temporary impurities, purifications were prescribed.

The temple, especially as enhanced by Herod the Great around the turn of the era, symbolized the structure of society because it included a court for men of Israel, located outside that of the priests, and another for women of Israel, placed outside that of the men. It also had a court for Gentiles, which was still further from the temple. Thus degrees of access to the cult by priests,

Jewish men, Jewish women, and Gentiles were symbolized in the architecture of the temple precincts, as illustrated by the following figure of the outside world:

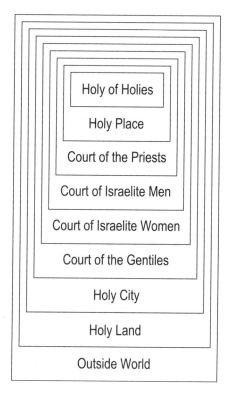

ECONOMIC SUPPORT.   Each tribe was to inherit a specific part of the land of Israel, but Levi received no land. Instead the priests and Levites lived off the cult. Rules for sacrifice gave to the priests much of the animal sacrificed or grain offered. Tithing was the practice of giving a tenth of agricultural products to the priests. Besides the proceeds from tithes and sacrifices, the priests received the firstfruits of the land and the herds. (Even firstborn human children should theoretically have been offered to God, but they were ransomed by animal sacrifices.) The land and Israel belonged to God, and therefore their produce did, too. Offering the firstfruits to God freed the rest for Israel's use. Giving offerings to the priests was giving them to God because the priests belonged to God. In addition to priestly dues, Jews had to pay a temple tax during the Second Temple period. Besides money belonging directly to the temple, it held private deposits for safekeeping. Thus the temple functioned as a bank. The considerable riches within its walls attracted the attention of various foreign rulers, who tried and sometimes succeeded in gaining access to them.

SACRIFICES: MAKING THINGS SACRED

SACRIFICE AS GIFT.   The word "sacrifice" comes from the Latin *facere*, "to make," and *sacer*, "holy" or "sacred." To sacrifice something was to make it holy, to give it to God. It was to transfer it from the realm of the profane into the realm of the sacred. A ritual was necessary to make the transfer, and this ritual was the sacrifice that God prescribed. Animal sacrifice meant killing the animal, pouring its blood out at the foot of the altar (thereby giving its life to God), and burning all or part of the animal on the altar.

CLEAN ANIMALS, ACCEPTABLE OFFERINGS.   One could offer to God only what was acceptable. What was acceptable to the Israelites corresponded to what was acceptable to God. Israel, like most peoples, saw its own likes and dislikes, taboos and categories, as self-evident and God-given, and so societal features were replicated in the cult. Further, in sacrifice the people gave something of its own to God, so Israel's offerings came only from its domestic animals. Purity rules that governed what Israel could eat were replicated in rules that said what was permissible to sacrifice to God. The animals offered had to be unblemished.

Much ink has been spilled over Israel's taboos concerning animals. The most famous taboo is pork. But pigs get no special attention in Israel's literature until the second century B.C.E., and then only because pigs were the sacrificial animals of those with whom the Jews were in conflict (see ch. 3, below, concerning the persecution by King Antiochus IV, in which Jews were forced to eat pork). Before that, pigs were just one instance, among many, of forbidden animals.

One popular explanation of such taboos focuses on hygiene, suggesting that purity rules excluded animals that were risky to eat because of disease. But this could explain only a very small percentage of cases. A glance at Lev 11 shows that the hygiene theory cannot fully explain Israel's categorization of animals. Another theory is that of historical survivals. It sees the purity laws as quaint survivals from an earlier and more primitive time in Israel's past. Assumed by the theory is an evolution of Israelite religion toward a more spiritual and ethical religion embodied in the prophets. There are several problems with such a theory. First, it does not explain the specifics of the purity rules. Second, it has a narrow concept of religion, seeing "real" religion as spiritual and playing down its material and social expressions. Third, the theory forces an evolutionary scheme on Israel's religion. Fourth, although the prophets attacked the idea of sacrifice without accompanying ethical behavior, they did not attack the cult or sacrifice as an institution, as if the very idea of a cult was displeasing to God. We must never forget that dietary rules are enshrined in Torah as demands made by God.

The best explanation of the biblical purity rules concerning animals comes from anthropologist Mary Douglas. She sees purity rules as a symbolic system. Purity rules exist to define categories of things, people, and times, to draw firm boundaries between these categories, and to relate the categories in an integrated system. Leviticus 11 organizes the animal world, dividing it into three major divisions: air, water, and land. It sees as clean (edible by Israel) animals that belong clearly to one category or another. Proper land animals are whatever "has divided hoofs and is cleft-footed and chews the cud." Proper water animals are those with fins and scales. Proper air animals do not eat blood or other dead animals, can fly, and hop on two legs (so insects, e.g., are not pure). Animals that "swarm" on the land do not fit the categories. Swarming is a type of movement that should belong to sea animals—schools of fish, for example. Some things seem "right" to the Israelites and others do not. Something that does not fit existing categories is repulsive and is called an "abomination." In our own day, part of the reason for unease with bats may be that "mice" are not supposed to fly. The replusiveness of snakes may be partially due to the fact that they have no feet or legs and crawl on their belly, unlike other land animals.

SACRIFICE AS FOOD.   If sacrifice meant giving something to God and if this something was usually food, did Israel think that God needed to be fed? The conception of sacrifice as food lies behind Lev 3:11: "Then the priest shall turn these into smoke on the altar as a food offering by fire to the LORD." Such a conception was probably the origin of the frequent term "sweet-smelling" as applied to sacrifices. Nonetheless, the Hebrew Bible seldom speaks of sacrifices as food. Protest against a more literal understanding of sacrifice as food appears in Ps 50:12–13: "If I were hungry, I would not tell you; for the world and all that is in it is mine. Do I eat the flesh of bulls, or drink the blood of goats?" The psalm may be criticizing a popular understanding of sacrifice. Similarly there is little or no evidence for seeing the sacrificial feasts as attempts at mystical union with God or as endeavors to assimilate the life force of the animal. The basic idea of much of Israelite sacrifice seems to have been that of a gift in thanksgiving for a favor or in hopes of getting God's favor.

BLOOD.   A holocaust—an offering entirely burned on the altar—was relatively rare. Usually only parts of the animal were burned. Some of the rest (all of the rest, if it was a sin offering) was eaten by the priests as their portion, and some (if it was a peace offering) was eaten by those who brought the sacrifice. God always received the blood, which was poured out at the foot of the altar. The life of the animal was in the blood, and life belonged only to God. Humans were strictly forbidden to consume the blood.

If anyone of the house of Israel or of the aliens who reside among them eats any blood, I will set my face against that person who eats blood, and will cut that person off from the people. For the life of the flesh is in the blood; and I have given it to you for making atonement for your lives on the altar; for, as life, it is the blood that makes atonement. (Lev 17:10–11)

ATONEMENT. The word "atonement" comes from the English phrase "at one," in the sense of being at one with someone. When a person was separated from God for any reason, it was necessary to have some mechanism by which to regain the status of being at one with God. The word translated "atone" or "expiate" in most texts is the Hebrew word *kipper*. The root meaning of this word is "to cover over," and when used in the context of sacrifices, it seems to mean "to wipe off," "to purge," "to purify." Its object was not usually a person but a thing—the sanctuary, for example. This is clear in the case of the *hatta'th,* usually translated "sin offering." It was not a gift to appease an angry God but a means of purging (cleansing) the sanctuary. A better translation for *hatta'th* would be "purification offering."

The basic idea was that sin defiled the sanctuary. The sanctuary was like a magnet that attracted the "dirt" caused by the sins of the people. The degree of a sin's seriousness determined the extent to which the defilement penetrated the sanctuary. The sanctuary could be purged of lesser sins by "washing off" the outer altar with the blood of the sin offering. Once a year the high priest entered the holy of holies to cleanse it of the defilement caused by sins, on the Day of Atonement, *Yom Kippur.* It was necessary to purge God's dwelling from the defilement caused by the sin of the people because eventually the accumulation of defilement would make it impossible for God to remain there.

It would be wrong to think that Israel had a mechanistic system whereby one's inner disposition did not matter for forgiveness of sin. This is belied by the numerous expressions of sorrow for, and confession of, sin throughout the Hebrew Bible, expressions found in the sacrificial laws themselves (Lev 5:5; 16:21). Furthermore, the sins to be atoned for were both ethical and ritual. Today we may see a big difference between the ethical and the ritual, but for ancient Israel, God decreed both categories of commandments. A more adequate approach for us is to see the sacrificial system as a symbolic system. It assumed that the presence of the divine is a necessary but not a guaranteed circumstance. Human acts that were improper in the presence of God were thought of as producing a kind of dirt that must be washed away. Sacrificial activity accomplished this in ways dictated by God, and so it was successful if done correctly and with the right intention.

The ritual for the Day of Atonement (Lev 16) illustrates the process of cleansing on that day. The ark of the covenant was in the holy of holies. On top of it was a cover, the holiest part of the ark. It was called the "mercy seat" (in Hebrew, *kapporeth,* from the same root as *kipper*). It was this part of the ark that had to be cleansed. According to Lev 16, the high priest used a bull's blood to make atonement for himself. He then used the blood of a goat to make atonement for the people. The guilt of the people was symbolically placed upon another goat, the scapegoat, and it was driven into the desert.

ISRAEL'S SACRED TIMES

SABBATH.   Every seventh day was a Sabbath, on which no work could be done and special sacrifices were offered. Israel thus obeyed God's command, "Remember the sabbath day, and keep it holy" (Exod 20:8), by setting aside a portion of every week for God.

DAY OF ATONEMENT.   The Day of Atonement occurred once a year, in the fall. Of the sacred times, fasting was prescribed for this day alone because it was (and is) a time of sorrow for sins. As noted above, on this day the high priest entered the holy of holies and purified the mercy seat on top of the ark.

PILGRIMAGE FEASTS.   There were three pilgrimage feasts, feasts on which Jewish men were supposed to make their way to Jerusalem. They were Passover–Unleavened Bread, Weeks, and Booths. Each feast was agricultural. When the Israelites turned from a nomadic to a farming lifestyle, they adopted the agricultural feasts of the land and made them into reminders of Israel's history.

PASSOVER–UNLEAVENED BREAD.   Passover–Unleavened Bread combined two feasts. Unleavened Bread was a spring agricultural feast celebrating the barley harvest and lasting seven days. It was customary to make unleavened barley loaves. A sheaf of the firstfruits of barley was brought to the temple and offered to God. At some point, Unleavened Bread was combined with Passover. Today Passover refers to the entire eight-day festival.

The origin and history of Passover is complex. The Hebrew name, *pesach,* may be from the Hebrew verb *p-s-ch,* "to limp." This may be explained by a limping dance performed early in the history of the rite. The Israelite feast was probably originally a spring lambing festival, meant to ward off evil spirits at the beginning of a new nomadic year. The Bible takes the word to mean "passing over."

During the Second Temple period, the ritual for Passover–Unleavened Bread consisted of two parts. The first involved the temple and the priesthood. The second was domestic. If possible, one traveled to Jerusalem and procured a room and a lamb with which to celebrate Passover. At 3 P.M. on the eve of Passover (the Jewish day goes from sunset to sunset), the lambs were slaughtered in the temple by the Levites, and the blood and certain portions were given to God. The rest was returned to the offerer. In the second part of the ritual, the lamb was brought back to the room to be roasted and eaten.

Exodus 12–13 is the longest biblical description of Passover. It associates the rites of both Passover and Unleavened Bread with the exodus of the Israelites from Egypt. Unleavened bread is explained by the fact that the Israelites had to bake loaves without leaven because of the haste with which they fled Egypt. The blood ritual is a memorial of the fact that when the angel of death killed the firstborn of the Egyptians, he passed over the Israelite dwellings that had blood smeared on the doorposts.

WEEKS.   The feast of Weeks (also known by the names Feast of Harvest, of Pentecost, of Firstfruits, and of Assembly) marked the wheat harvest. It was held fifty days after the feast of Unleavened Bread. Because of the fifty days, it was known among Greek-speaking Jews as Pentecost (from the Greek *pentēkostos,* meaning "fiftieth").

BOOTHS.   Booths (also called Tabernacles, Sukkoth, Ingathering) was a seven-day feast to mark the autumn harvest of olives and fruits. It was marked by water libations—probably to ensure adequate rainfall during the winter rainy season—nightly dancing in the temple precincts under the light of menorahs, processions with the lulab (palm branches to which were attached twigs of myrtle, willow, and a citron), and the building of booths in which to live. The booths may go back to the custom of guarding olive trees during harvesting by living among them in makeshift shelters. Leviticus's historicizing rationale for the booths is, "So that your generations may know that I made the people of Israel live in booths when I brought them out of the land of Egypt" (Lev 23:43).

ANCIENT JEWISH SOCIETY

Recent study applies sociological and anthropological questions to ancient Israel. Here are some concepts and approaches assumed in the following chapters.

SOCIETY

Society is used broadly here to denote the full communal life of a given group, characterized by the ways in which its cultural system works through regularized patterns of interaction between members of the group and with outsiders. *Culture* refers to an array of interconnected symbols, values, historical information, customs, and institutions shared by a group of people. Culture holds a society and a people together and is passed on and adapted from generation to generation. Culture allows a group to survive over time and to adapt to changes in environment and technology. Hanson and Oakman relate culture to society as follows: "The cultural system 'envelops' the social system, and the social system makes values, norms, statuses, and roles of the cultural system operational" (p. 195). Politics, kinship, religion, and economics are closely related and cannot be easily separated in ancient cultures.

Kinship means family relationships, although such relationships may not mean quite the same thing to the ancients as they do to us today. *Politics* means the set of mechanisms and interactions, formal and informal, by which power is distributed and exercised. *Economics* means the arrangements determining the production, distribution, and consumption of goods and services. *Religion* indicates a complex consisting of a belief-system and a set of practices enabling humans to understand and interact with the sacred. Within the broad category of religion, ideology indicates the system of beliefs and theories that underpins a particular sociopolitical outlook.

Hanson and Oakman define a social domain as "an institutional system or constellation of social institutions" (p. 196). If we think in terms of four basic social domains—kinship, politics, economics, and religion—we can see that these domains are arranged differently in modern society than they were in ancient society. In modern America, for example, economics tends to be foundational, deeply affecting the other three domains. This was not true in ancient society. Indeed, there does not seem to be any concept of an independent economy there. Rather, the things that we associate with the economy—production, consumption, exchange—were "embedded" in the two explicit domains, kinship and politics, as was religion. The table "Social System," adapted from Hanson and Oakman (p. 15), expresses in graphic form this societal structure.

KINSHIP

Kinship designates aspects of society dealing with family. This social domain is the most fundamental for ancient Israel. *Family* does not mean simply the nuclear family but is a broader term, encompassing what might be called the extended family. Ancient Israel thought of itself as descended from a single ancestor, Abraham, and it considered that its twelve tribes descended from the twelve sons of Jacob, who was renamed Israel. Therefore, Israel called itself *bene Yisrael,* the "children (literally: sons) of Israel," often translated "Israelites." In Israel's kinship system, the male was dominant. Descent was reckoned through the male and so was patrilineal, and the society was patrilocal, meaning that the married couple would live with or near the husband's relatives, not the wife's. Marriage was endogamous—one looked to one's own group for a spouse. Still, frequently in the preexilic period and in the early postexilic period, an Israelite man was permitted to seek a wife outside Israel provided that the woman joined Israel. Reforms, such as the Deuteronomic reform and the later reforms of Ezra and Nehemiah, often targeted such unions as a danger to Israel and a mark of disloyalty to God, who had decreed Israel's cultural and religious laws.

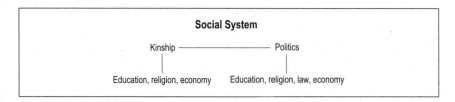

Because of Israel's emphasis on kinship, genealogies (lists of one's ancestors) were important. Genealogies constitute a kind of human geography or map by which an individual and a group can situate themselves in relation to each other and to everyone else. Israel thought of itself as a special kinship group within the human family. Certain groups in Israel placed great importance on genealogies, since these documented their place in society and attested to family honor. Such groups included the priests and the members of royal families, whose status was based on heredity.

POLITICS

Politics was also a fundamental social domain in the ancient world. Politics deals with the public exercise of power and authority. Politics in ancient Israel had little to do with representative democracy, human rights, and so on, and its political life cannot be judged by these modern concepts. More fundamental to public life in Israel and elsewhere in the ancient world is the patron-client system. Societies constructed according to this model are built vertically. Patrons are higher in society than their clients, and therefore they are able to supply them with basic necessities, such as employment, food, honor and status, land, legal assistance, and influence. In return, the client gives the patron public honor, political support, information, and so on. In modern Western societies, patronage is seen as corrupt and inimical to a society built on merit, but ancient societies were structured differently. And although patronage is not a value in our society, it still plays a role. Note, for example, the proverb "It's not what you know; it's whom you know."

During the monarchical period, Israel comprised at first one and then two autonomous or semiautonomous kingdoms. Much of Israel's story concerns how these kingdoms navigated the politics of the ancient Near East. For most of the Second Temple period, Israel had no monarchy and was part of large empires. For a brief period from the second to the first centuries B.C.E., it attained independence under the priestly family of the Hasmoneans.

RELIGION

In ancient Jewish society, religion was not an entity independent of other aspects of society. Rather, it was a set of symbols, beliefs, practices, and social structures thought to be of divine origin, embedded in politics and kinship. Ancient Jews knew nothing of separation between church and state. God's will, expressed in divine oracles mediated by prophets and priests, touched every aspect of Israelite and Jewish life. ("Israelite" refers to the preexilic period and "Jewish" to the postexilic period. For an explanation, see ch. 2.) Israel's sacred law dealt not only with ritual and morality but also with civil and criminal law. It governed political structures, military preparations, and the prosecution of warfare. Political institutions were expressions God's will. In all this, Israel was not much different from cultures contemporary with it.

> Religious belief and practice were part of the family, ethnic and territorial groups into which people were born. People did not choose their religion, nor did most social units or groups have members with different religions. Religion was integral to everything else and inseparable from it. People might worship new gods in addition to the old ones and engage in additional cultic practices, but they remained what they were culturally and socially. Radical conversion to another religion and rejection of one's inherited beliefs and behavior meant (and still mean today in such societies) separation and alienation from family and hereditary social group. Thus, involvement with religion is in itself political and social involvement in the broad sense of those terms. (Saldarini, 5)

ECONOMICS

Throughout the Second Temple period, Israel was an agrarian society. During most of this period, it belonged to large empires that were also primarily agrarian. Peasants working the land accounted for around 90 percent of the population. Given certain technological implements, especially the plow, the peasants could produce more than they consumed. But ancient agrarian societies were not free-market economies. The peasants' surplus was usually taken by rich landowners, priests, and central governments. Taxes were a substantial burden. Peasants usually lived at little better than subsistence levels, and their surplus went to support the aristocracy and the military.

SOCIAL CLASSES

Social structure in agrarian empires was hierarchical, and there was little social mobility. Belonging to a social class usually entailed having a certain level of material wealth, but it was not always true that this guaranteed membership in a certain class. The following is a definition of *social class* that does justice to the complexity of the phenomenon in ancient societies. A class is

> a large body of persons who occupy a position in a social hierarchy by reason of their manifesting similarity of valued objective criteria. These latter include kinship affiliation, power and authority, achievements, possessions, and personal attributes. Achievements involve a person's occupational and educational attainments; possessions refer to material evidences of wealth; moral attributes include one's religious and ethical beliefs and actions; and personal attributes involve speech, dress and personal mannerisms. (Sjoberg, 109, quoted in Saldarini, 25)

This definition of social class shows that many variables went into defining a class. Therefore, there was some overlap between groups and classes.

Ancient Jewish society was highly stratified. The nine-class schema in the table "Classes in Ancient Society" fits ancient Jewish society fairly well (Saldarini, 39–45, following Lenski, 214–96). The classes fall into two main categories, upper and lower. There was no real middle class. Groups that would be considered middle class in a modern setting so depended on the ruling class in ancient society that they did not constitute a middle class in the usual meaning of the term. We call them retainers.

Classes in Ancient Society (following Lenski)	
Upper Classes	**Lower Classes**
Ruler	Peasants
Ruling class	Artisans
Retainers	Unclean
Merchants	Expendable
Priests	

The ruler was in a class by himself because of his power and wealth. The ruling class comprised 2 percent or less of the population. Because it controlled society, it was usually wealthy. In ancient societies, wealth usually flowed from social position; the converse is true in modern Western societies.

The retainers served the needs of the ruling class. They may have composed about 5 percent of the population, and they performed military, bureaucratic, scribal, educational, financial, and religious functions. Some retainers were close to the ruling class, and others were lower on the social scale. There was some overlap between the ruling class and the retainer class; for example, the foremost scribes were members of the ruling class. The merchant class, the fourth class, probably overlapped the upper and lower classes.

Priests formed the fifth class, and again some overlap existed between the priestly class and the ruling class. At times the high priest, along with other prominent priests and rich landowners, ruled Judah. At other times priests were subordinate to other authorities, such as the Herodian rulers of the first century B.C.E. and the first century C.E. Because of their relation to the central institutions of Israel—temple and Torah—priests retained some independent influence and power even when subject to other authorities. Priesthood was hereditary, but not everyone of priestly lineage belonged to the central families of the upper classes. There were poor priests who lived as artisans or peasants, just as there were priests among the retainer classes, such as scribes.

There were four lower classes. The peasants formed the bulk of the population because of the agrarian nature of ancient Jewish society. The artisan class was probably 3 to 7 percent of the population. Like the peasants, they probably earned just about enough to survive, although it is possible that some, if their skills were rare enough, received higher wages. The other two lower classes were the unclean and the expendable. The unclean performed tasks distasteful to the rest of the population, such as mining and tanning. The expendable class, estimated to be about 5 to 10 percent of the population in ancient societies, consisted primarily of peasants driven off their land through economic pressures. Some of them banded together and lived by raiding villages and caravans.

THE ANCIENT CITY

Ancient cities were not like modern cities; they existed to serve the needs of the ruling class. The cities were where the ruling class lived, along with their retainers. Activities related to the control of society—political, economic, religious, educational, and military functions—took place in the cities. Most city residents did not actively work the land, and, conversely, most peasants did not live in the major cities. Members of the lower classes who lived in the cities served the upper classes, for the most part. The temple in Jerusalem, for example, required craftsmen and workers for its rebuilding under Herod and for its maintenance.

DYADIC PERSONALITY

Individualism is an integral aspect of the cultural systems of modern Western societies. Today compound words with the prefix "self-" proliferate. One must strive for self-fulfillment, self-determination, self-satisfaction, self-motivation, for a healthy self-image, for being a self-starter. One must stand on one's own two feet. Dependency is considered negative. Inhabitants of the ancient world thought far more in terms of groups. Being a good and loyal member of a group was a more important value to them than to us. This way of being has been called *dyadic personality*. It means that a person defines himself or herself primarily in relation to one or more groups.

HONOR AND SHAME

Basic to Israel's social values were honor and shame. Honor and shame operate in all societies, and even citizens of modern Western democracies can still understand their force, especially when one is praised or disgraced in a particularly public way. But in ancient societies, where most human interaction was face-to-face, where the majority of the population was quite limited in social and geographical mobility, and where physical goods and social status were in short supply, honor and shame figured prominently. Marriages were contracted to maintain or increase the honor of the family, women were closely guarded as those most capable of bringing shame on the family, clients helped their patrons to maintain honor and prestige, rulers depended on various strategies to sustain and increase their honor so as to strengthen their rule, and so on. One's honor had to be acknowledged by others. The degree of one's honor corresponded with one's place in society.

PATRIARCHY

Studying the Bible from a feminist point of view has brought to the fore the role of gender in ancient Israel. *Gender* goes beyond simple biological differences between males and females and highlights the social construction of roles assigned to women and men.

Feminist criticism cannot be summarized in a short space, but two features deserve special mention. First, it describes and critiques the patriarchal nature of the societies and texts it studies. *Patriarchy* organizes society along hierarchical lines that subordinate women to men. The word comes from the Greek words *patēr,* meaning "father," and *archē,* meaning "sovereignty" or "dominion." Literally, it indicates a situation in which the father is the leader, and all are subject to him. By analogy, the term applies to most of the ancient world and, indeed, to most societies throughout history. Feminist study seeks to unmask such structures of domination and thus to liberate women and others who have been subordinated and marginalized.

A second major feature of feminist biblical criticism has been to reclaim the role of women in Israel's history. Women contributed to Israel in essential but usually gender-determined ways, such as bearing children, keeping the home, supporting their husbands, and so on. Some feminist criticism highlights the overlooked importance of such roles. Further, scholarship looks closely at women who contributed in more unusual ways to Israel's history. Deborah the judge, for example, rescued Israel from its enemies (Judg 4–5). The prophetess Huldah evaluated and declared legitimate the book found in the temple during the reign of Josiah (2 Kgs 22). Other women exercised power in society in more traditional ways, such as influencing their husbands, using sexual attraction to accomplish goals, and so on.

CONCLUSION

This chapter provides a basis and a framework for the rest of this book. Israel of the Second Temple period was heir to stories, symbols, concepts, customs, and institutions that originated and were developed during the preexilic period. To some degree, the following study investigates how Israel changed and how it remained the same as it traveled through history.

SELECT BIBLIOGRAPHY

Alt, Albrecht. "The God(s) of the Fathers." Pages 1–77 in *Essays on Old Testament History and Religion*. Garden City, N.Y.: Doubleday, 1968.

Anderson, Bernhard. *Understanding the Old Testament*. 4th ed. Englewood Cliffs, N.J.: Prentice-Hall, 1986.

Baltzer, Klaus. *The Covenant Formulary in Old Testament, Jewish, and Early Christian Writings*. Philadelphia: Fortress, 1971.

Batto, Bernard. *Slaying the Dragon: Mythmaking in the Biblical Tradition*. Louisville: Westminster/John Knox, 1992.

Berger, Peter L. *The Sacred Canopy: Elements of a Sociological Theory of Religion*. New York: Doubleday, 1967.

Berger, Peter L., and Thomas Luckman. *The Social Construction of Reality: A Treatise in the Sociology of Knowledge*. New York: Doubleday, 1966.

Bright, John. *A History of Israel*. 3d ed. Philadelphia: Westminster, 1981.

Clements, R.E. *God and Temple.* Philadelphia: Fortress, 1965.

Cody, Aelred. *A History of Old Testament Priesthood.* Rome: Pontifical Biblical Institute, 1969.

Crenshaw, James L. *Old Testament Wisdom: An Introduction.* Atlanta: John Knox, 1981.

Douglas, Mary. *Purity and Danger: An Analysis of the Concepts of Pollution and Taboo.* London: Routledge & Kegan Paul, 1966.

Durkheim, Emile. *The Elementary Forms of Religious Life.* New York: Macmillan, 1915.

Edersheim, Alfred. *The Temple: Its Ministry and Services.* Updated ed. Peabody, Mass.: Hendrickson, 1994.

Finley, Moses. *The Ancient Economy.* 2nd ed. Berkeley: University of California, 1985.

Gammie, John G. *Holiness in Israel.* Minneapolis: Fortress, 1989.

Geertz, Clifford. *The Interpretation of Cultures: Selected Essays.* New York: Basic Books, 1973.

Gottwald, Norman K. *The Hebrew Bible: A Socio-Literary Introduction.* Philadelphia: Fortress, 1985.

Grabbe, Lester L. *Judaism from Cyrus to Hadrian.* 2 vols. Minneapolis: Fortress, 1992.

Hanson, K. C., and Douglas Oakman. *Palestine in the Time of Jesus: Social Structures and Social Conflicts.* Minneapolis: Fortress, 1998.

Hayes, John H., and J. Maxwell Miller. *Israelite and Judaean History.* Philadelphia: Westminster, 1977.

Hiebert, Theodore. "Warrior, Divine." *ABD* 6:876–80.

Hillers, D. R. *Covenant: The History of a Biblical Idea.* Baltimore: Johns Hopkins University Press, 1969.

Knight, Douglas A., and Gene M. Tucker, eds. *The Hebrew Bible and Its Modern Interpreters.* Chico, Calif.: Scholars Press, 1985.

Laffey, Alice. *An Introduction to the Old Testament: A Feminist Perspective.* Philadelphia: Fortress, 1988.

Leach, Edmund. *Culture and Communication: The Logic by Which Symbols Are Connected.* Cambridge: Cambridge University Press, 1976.

Lemche, Niels Peter. *Ancient Israel: A New History of Israelite Society.* Sheffield: JSOT, 1988.

Lenski, Gerhard E. *Power and Privilege: A Theory of Social Stratification.* New York: McGraw, 1966.

Levenson, Jon D. *Sinai and Zion: An Entry into the Jewish Bible.* Minneapolis: Winston, 1985.

Malina, Bruce. *Christian Origins and Cultural Anthropology: Practical Models for Biblical Interpretation.* Atlanta: John Knox, 1986.

————. *The New Testament World: Insights from Cultural Anthropology.* Atlanta: John Knox, 1981.

Matthews, Victor H. *Manners and Customs in the Bible.* Rev. ed. Peabody, Mass.: Hendrickson, 1991.

Matthews, Victor H., and Don C. Benjamin. *Social World of Ancient Israel 1250–587 BCE.* Peabody, Mass: Hendrickson, 1993.

Matthews, Victor H., and James C. Moyer. *The Old Testament: Text and Context.* Peabody, Mass.: Hendrickson, 1997.

Meyers, Carol L. "Temple, Jerusalem." *ABD* 6:350–69.

Milgrom, Jacob. "Atonement in the OT." *IDBSup* 78–82.

————. *Studies in Cultic Theology and Terminology.* Leiden: Brill, 1983.

Murphy, Roland E. "Wisdom." *HBD* 1135–36.

————. *Wisdom Literature.* Grand Rapids: Eerdmans, 1981.

Neusner, Jacob. *The Idea of Purity in Ancient Judaism.* Leiden: Brill, 1973.

————. *Torah: From Scroll to Symbol in Formative Judaism.* Philadelphia: Fortress, 1985.

Niditch, Susan. *War in the Hebrew Bible: A Study in the Ethics of Violence.* New York: Oxford, 1993.

Noth, Martin. *The History of Israel.* Rev. ed. New York: Harper & Brothers, 1960.

Patai, Raphael. *Man and Temple in Ancient Jewish Myth and Ritual.* New York: Ktav, 1967.

Rad, Gerhard von. *Wisdom in Israel.* Nashville: Abingdon, 1972.

Rylaarsdam, J. C. "Passover and Feast of Unleavened Bread." *IDB* 3:663–68.

Saldarini, Anthony J. *Pharisees, Scribes, and Sadducees in Palestinian Society: A Sociological Approach.* Wilmington: Michael Glazier, 1988.

Schüssler Fiorenza, Elizabeth. "Feminist Hermeneutics." *ABD* 2:783–91.

Sjoberg, Gideon. *The Preindustrial City: Past and Present.* New York: Free Press, 1960.

Smith, Jonathan Z. *To Take Place: Toward Theory in Ritual.* Chicago: University of Chicago Press, 1987.

Sweeney, Marvin A. "Tithe." *HDB* 1078–79.

Turner, Victor. *The Ritual Process: Structure and Anti-structure.* Chicago: Aldine, 1969.

Vaux, Roland de. *Ancient Israel: Its Life and Institutions.* New York: McGraw-Hill, 1965.

Wilson, Robert R. *Prophecy and Society in Ancient Israel.* Philadelphia: Fortress, 1980.

CHAPTER 2

THE RESTORATION

PRIMARY READINGS: Haggai ◆ Zechariah 1–8 ◆ Isaiah 56–66 ◆ Malachi ◆ Ezra ◆ Nehemiah

The Deuteronomistic History ends with Israel far from home in a foreign land. Israel's bitter experiences threw its view of the world into question. Was Israel's God really the creator God? Had God abandoned Israel? What would now become of the many promises God had made to Israel? Was the covenant irreparably broken? The Babylonian exile changed everything for Israel. It was a shattering event. But Israel did not forsake its identity. Rather, it set about making sense of what had happened by looking to the traditions, customs, and institutions that it still had at its disposal. When the chance came for Israel to return to its land and rebuild, many were ready. They returned to the land to lay the foundations of a new society on the ruins of the old. We call this the *restoration*.

The present chapter begins ou discussion of the Second Temple period proper. Here we cover the time from the rebuilding of the temple (520–515 B.C.E.) to the eve of the conquest of Judah by Alexander the Great in 332 B.C.E. The Bible supplies a narrative for the preexilic period, but, as we have seen, it leaves most of the events of the exile to our imagination. As we enter the postexilic period, we get a bit more help in reconstructing Israel's history. The main sources for the period are the books of Ezra and Nehemiah. Four prophetic books provide eyewitness reflections—Haggai, Zechariah 1–8, Isaiah 56–66, and Malachi.

THE RETURN TO JUDAH

Important segments of Judah's population were exiled to Babylon in 587 B.C.E. In 539 the Persian king Cyrus conquered the Babylonians and permitted the exiles to return to their homeland. His plan for ruling his vast empire was to establish local governments loyal to himself. Judah was especially important because of its strategic location between Persia and Egypt.

There were several major returns of Jewish exiles over the next century and a half, sometimes led by Jews who had become prominent in the Persian government. The first was led by a Jewish court official named Sheshbazzar in 538 (Ezra 1:5–11; 5:13–16). The book of Ezra says that Cyrus gave Sheshbazzar the temple's sacred vessels to bring back to Jerusalem and that he laid the foundations of a new temple. How much he accomplished is unclear, but when the temple construction was resumed in 520, not much progress had been made. The return in 538 was either of limited scope or it was not very successful.

Main Dates (B.C.E.)	
539	Cyrus the Persian conquers the Babylonians
538	Decree of Cyrus allowing the Jews to return to Judah—first return of the exiles
520	Next return of exiles; rebuilding of the temple resumed
515	Temple finished
445	Nehemiah comes to Judah as governor
Possible dates: 458, 428, or 398	Ezra comes to Judah with written Torah

In 520, Zerubbabel and Joshua set off for Judah with a large group of exiles. The Persians appointed Zerubbabel governor of the province and named Joshua high priest. Ezra 3–6 describes the rebuilding of the temple under their leadership (520–515), although some material dealing with later events disrupts these chapters (see 4:7–23). Not all inhabitants of the area were happy with the rebuilding. When Nebuchadnezzar destroyed Jerusalem, some of Israel's neighbors took advantage of the situation and expanded into Judah's territory, and so they did not welcome the exiles back. Further, the Samaritans seem to have opposed the rebuilding, as did powerful people to the east of the Jordan. Each expected the reestablishment of Jerusalem to disturb the balance of power in the region. Even Israelite peasants who had never gone into exile may not have been anxious to submit to the authority of return exiles, most of whom had been born in Babylonia.

The conflict between the returning exiles and the Yahweh worshipers in Judah who had not been deported was more than simply a power struggle. It also concerned concepts of what it meant to be Israel. The exiles had spent much time reflecting on and reworking their traditions, developing a form of Judaism that responded to their new situation. This meant new interpretations of the Mosaic law. One cannot assume at this period that all Yahweh worshipers would subscribe to and interpret identically one monolithic Mosaic law. Those left in the land might oppose the customs, laws, and attitudes brought back and imposed on them by the returning exiles.

Terminology: "Jews" and "Israelites"

The most common designation for Israel in the Hebrew Bible is "Children of Israel." Use of the term "Israel" is confusing when applied to the time of the divided monarchy, for it can mean either the northern kingdom alone or both kingdoms taken together. Once the northern kingdom went out of existence in the eighth century B.C.E., the kingdom of Judah still called itself Israel. In the Second Temple period, the area that formerly constituted the kingdom of Judah was called Judah or later Judea. It is from these names that we get the term "Jew." There is still room for debate precisely when the Greek *Ioudaios* (literally, "Judean") is to be translated "Jew" and when it means "Judean," that is, one from Judea.

Some inhabitants of the land wanted to join in the rebuilding of the temple:

> When the adversaries of Judah and Benjamin heard that the returned exiles were building a temple to the LORD, the God of Israel, they approached Zerubbabel and the heads of families and said to them, "Let us build with you, for we worship your God as you do, and we have been sacrificing to him ever since the days of King Esar-haddon of Assyria who brought us here." But Zerubbabel, Jeshua [another form of the name Joshua], and the rest of the heads of families in Israel said to them, "You shall have no part with us in building a house to our God; but we alone will build to the LORD, the God of Israel, as King Cyrus of Persia has commanded us." (Ezra 4:1–3)

According to this passage, the returning exiles encountered a group that traced its origins to the colonization of the northern kingdom by the Assyrians. These were the Samaritans. The returning exiles did not recognize them as legitimate Yahweh worshipers and declined their involvement in rebuilding the temple. Indeed, the Samaritans might have had mixed motives in offering their help. The Persians had been ruling the area through a local Samaritan governor, who undoubtedly wanted to assert his hegemony over the developing Judahite community. The Samaritans, rejected by the returned exiles, tried to stop the building by warning the Persian emperor (now Darius I; ruled 522–486 B.C.E.) that the Jews resettled in Jerusalem would rebel against him, but Darius overruled the protesters.

The builders finished their work, and Israel celebrated the dedication of the temple and resumed worship in the temple "as it is written in the book of Moses" (Ezra 6:18). The restored cult is seen as a fulfillment of Mosaic law.

The following passage describes the first Passover in the land celebrated by the returned exiles:

> On the fourteenth day of the first month the returned exiles kept the passover. For both the priests and the Levites had purified themselves; all of them were clean. So they killed the passover lamb for all the returned exiles, for their fellow priests, and for themselves. It was eaten by the people of Israel who had returned from exile, and also by all who had joined them and separated themselves from the pollutions of the nations of the land to worship the LORD, the God of Israel. (6:19–21)

Noteworthy is the repetition of the phrase "returned exiles." They are the ones who celebrate Passover. Others may join them only if they "separate" themselves from the "pollutions of the nations of the land," which implies adopting the view of Torah held by the returned exiles. Separation from people of different views and practices included rejection of anything that diluted the pure monotheism now held by the exilic community, a monotheism that was to characterize Second Temple Judaism as a whole. But separation also meant avoiding anything else deemed inconsistent with Mosaic Torah as interpreted by the exiles.

The separation of the returned exiles and those who joined them emphasized communal boundaries. These boundaries were expressed in terms of ritual purity—who could and who could not legitimately celebrate the Passover. Defining the community properly was a matter of survival. Sociologically speaking, not to maintain clear boundaries would result in assimilation into a larger culture where self-identity would be lost; religiously speaking, God demanded pure worship and would punish anyone who defiled it.

HAGGAI

A large group returned to Judah under Zerubbabel, but many Jews remained in Babylonia. Jeremiah had encouraged them to settle in and do well there, and this they had done (Jer 29). In contrast, Jerusalem lay in ruins, and the land was either untended or cultivated by those hostile to the exiles. Besides, most Jews in Babylonia had never seen Judah. For many, therefore, going to Judah was not an attractive prospect.

Arriving in Judah, many of the returnees felt there were needs more urgent than rebuilding the temple. They needed to construct houses, tend fields, and defend themselves. The prophets Haggai and Zechariah, however, urged the new community to begin rebuilding the temple right away (Ezra

5:1–2). The book of Haggai preserves four oracles, precisely dated. The first (Hag 1:1–15), from 520 B.C.E., addresses Zerubbabel and Joshua:

> Thus says the LORD of hosts: These people say the time has not yet come to re-build the LORD's house. Then the word of the LORD came by the prophet Haggai, saying: Is it a time for you yourselves to live in your paneled houses, while this house lies in ruins? Now therefore thus says the LORD of hosts: Consider how you have fared. You have sown much, and harvested little; you eat, but you never have enough; you drink, but you never have your fill; you clothe yourselves, but no one is warm; and you that earn wages earn wages to put them into a bag with holes. (1:2–6)

The returned exiles think that they are too busy with survival to build the temple. Harvests are not good, and there is a shortage of food, drink, clothing, and housing. But the oracle connects the sad state of the people with their neglect of the temple:

> You have looked for much, and, lo, it came to little; and when you brought it home, I blew it away. Why? says the LORD of hosts. Because my house lies in ruins, while all of you hurry off to your own houses. Therefore the heavens above you have withheld the dew, and the earth has withheld its produce. And I have called for a drought on the land and the hills, on the grain, the new wine, the oil, on what the soil produces, on human beings and animals, and on all their labors. (1:9–11)

Haggai has a priestly view of religion and the temple and condemns the "practical" opinion that attending to physical needs is more crucial than maintaining the cult. A truly practical view of the world, however, holds that God controls rain and crops. Unless the people please God, God inflicts famine and drought. Building the temple and instituting proper worship are the only way to insure the well-being of the settlers. A narrative section (1:12–15) indicates that Zerubbabel, Joshua, and the people heed the word of God and begin to build. Accordingly, God assures them that he is with them (1:13).

Nearly two months after the first oracle, another one is given (2:1–9). The people have been working on God's house but are discouraged by its un-inspiring architecture. God tells them to take heart, for this house will eventually be even greater than Solomon's temple: "Once again, in a little while, I will shake the heavens and the earth and the sea and the dry land; and I will shake all the nations, so that the treasure of all nations shall come, and I will fill this house with splendor, says the LORD of hosts" (2:6–7). The prophet expects all the nations to pay tribute to God in Jerusalem. From this small beginning, God will bring earthshaking results. These grand expectations recall

Second Isaiah, who predicts that God's actions on behalf of Israel will convince the entire world that Israel's God is the true and only God.

Haggai's third oracle (2:10–19) comes two months after the second. God invites the people to contrast how they fared before beginning the temple with how they now fare. Harvests have improved, and God says that it is because the people are now paying attention to the temple.

God sends Haggai a fourth oracle on the same day as the third:

> Speak to Zerubbabel, governor of Judah, saying, I am about to shake the heavens and the earth, and to overthrow the throne of kingdoms; I am about to destroy the strength of the kingdoms of the nations, and overthrow the chariots and their riders; and the horses and their riders shall fall, every one by the sword of a comrade. On that day, says the LORD of hosts, I will take you, O Zerubbabel my servant, son of Shealtiel, says the LORD, and make you like a signet ring; for I have chosen you, says the LORD of hosts. (2:21–23)

God is the heavenly warrior battling the nations. The very title "Lord of hosts" means "leader of armies," for "hosts" (multitudes) was used in this sense. God will attack and overthrow the foreign nations. The language echoes Exod 15, which describes the crossing of the Reed Sea in terms of holy war: "Horse and rider he has thrown into the sea. . . . Pharaoh's chariots and his army he cast into the sea" (Exod 15:1, 4). The oracle expects God to fight for Israel as at the exodus.

God has "chosen" Zerubbabel, descendant of David, to be the divine "signet ring." A signet ring bears the king's official seal, with which the king's ministers signed decrees. For God to make Zerubbabel like a signet ring means that Zerubbabel represents God on earth. Zerubbabel's rule will replace the rule of those whom God is about to defeat. The political implications of this are clear. From the Persian point of view, the suggestion is seditious. We do not know of a revolt under Zerubbabel, but Darius I did not rise to power without a struggle. It was common in the ancient world for subject nations to make a bid for independence when their overlords were experiencing a difficult transfer of power, and Haggai may have wanted Israel to do this. For Haggai, the new temple raised hopes for a complete restoration, including an independent state.

ZECHARIAH 1–8

The first eight chapters of the book of Zechariah originated in the early postexilic period. Chapters 9–14 were added later, so we do not treat them here. Zechariah addresses the same situation as does Haggai. He repeatedly presents a picture of an ideal, restored Jerusalem, protected by God: "For I will be a wall of fire all around it, says the LORD, and I will be the glory within it" (2:5). His expectation that all Jewish exiles will return to Judah becomes a stock feature in other postexilic hopes for a glorious future.

Like Haggai and Second Isaiah, Zechariah 1–8 portrays the restoration of Zion as affecting the whole world. Israel's foreign oppressors acted as instruments of God, but they overstepped their bounds and punished Israel too harshly. Therefore, God will punish them (1:15).

> See now, I am going to raise my hand against them, and they [the Gentiles] shall become plunder for their own slaves [Israel]. Then you will know that the LORD of hosts has sent me. Sing and rejoice, O daughter Zion! For lo, I will come and dwell in your midst, says the LORD. Many nations shall join themselves to the LORD on that day, and shall be my people; and I will dwell in your midst. And you shall know that the LORD of hosts has sent me to you. The LORD will inherit Judah as his portion in the holy land, and will again choose Jerusalem. (2:9–12)

When God fully restores Jerusalem, all nations will recognize it as the capital of the only true God. The entire population of the earth will become God's people. This is the sort of universalism displayed by Second Isaiah as well.

Zechariah contains many visions. The prophet frequently receives a vision, asks what it means, and receives an interpretation. This pattern becomes a feature of later apocalypses (see ch. 4, below). Zechariah's fourth vision begins, "Then he showed me the high priest Joshua standing before the angel of the LORD, and Satan standing at his right hand to accuse him" (3:1). The term "high priest" is not used before the exile. Although a chief priest existed in the preexilic period, the use of this new title corresponds to the increased influence and power of the head priest in the postexilic period, due to the absence of a monarch.

Zechariah 3 portrays heaven as a courtroom where Satan accuses Joshua. This is Satan's first appearance in the pages of the Hebrew Bible. The Hebrew text says "the satan" *(hasatan),* meaning "the accuser." Satan is the prosecuting attorney in God's court. He plays a similar role in Job 1–2. At this early stage of tradition, Satan is not God's enemy but a heavenly figure, probably an angel. We noted in chapter 1, above, that Gen 3 does not identify the serpent in the garden of Eden as Satan. This association took place later, when the figure of Satan developed into a leader of demons (see ch. 4, below).

When Satan accuses Joshua in Zech 3, God objects: "And the LORD said to Satan, 'The LORD rebuke you, O Satan! The LORD who has chosen Jerusalem rebuke you! Is not this man a brand plucked from the fire?' " (3:2). God does not deny that Joshua deserves criticism. Indeed, his dirty clothes signify that he (or the people, since he represents them) is impure. But God compares the high priest to a survivor of a fire: Joshua and the Judahite community have been rescued from the exile and are all that remains of God's people. Given the extraordinary circumstances, it makes no sense to hold Joshua accountable for his unworthiness. Accordingly, God commands that Joshua be stripped of his dirty clothes and dressed in pure, clean, priestly vestments. This makes him fit to be God's high priest. The symbolic action of taking off and putting on clothes parallels the same action in Lev 8, where Aaron and his sons are ordained as priests. The difference is that in Lev 8 Aaron and his sons put off profane clothes to put on sacred vestments. They move from being laymen to being priests, from being ordinary members of Israel to being mediators between God and people. Joshua, on the other hand, puts off sacred vestments that had been defiled by Israel's sin and puts on clean vestments. This is not the initiation of the priesthood but its renewal. It signifies a new, divinely sanctioned start for the already established priesthood.

Joshua now receives a promise expressed in terms of priestly ideology: "Thus says the LORD of hosts: If you will walk in my ways and keep my requirements, then you shall rule my house and have charge of my courts, and I will give you the right of access among those who are standing here" (3:7). "Here" means the heavenly court. If Joshua follows God's Law, he will have charge of the temple and its precincts and will have access to God in heaven. There is a close association between the precincts of the Jerusalem temple and heaven itself because, in accord with priestly religion, the temple is where God is present and accessible.

Zechariah 3 ends with another divine promise: "I am going to bring my servant the Branch" (3:8b). "Branch" is a title that occurs elsewhere (Isa 4:2; 11:1; Jer 23:5; 33:15). In Isa 11:1, it appears in a prophecy of salvation in which Isaiah promises that a Davidic king will fulfill God's will and bring righteousness to the land. Peace will reign on earth, and Jerusalem will be the center of a world restored to the idyllic state that God always intended. The two occurrences of "Branch" in Jeremiah also refer to the perfect Davidic king. The most plausible referent for "Branch" in Zech 3:8 is a Davidic king. The center of this hope may have been Zerubbabel, probably a descendant of David. Zechariah 3 may imply the same kind of hope as did Hag 2:20–23, for a Jewish state with a Davidic descendant at its head. In 3:8–10, the rule of the Branch is associated with God's removal of guilt from the land and with fertility for the land.

Chapter 4 contains a vision whose point is that, through God's strength, Zerubbabel is to build the second temple. The vision is of a golden lampstand with seven lamps, recalling the seven-branched lampstand in Solomon's temple (Exod 25:31–40). Two olive trees flank the lampstand, supplying it with oil. Zechariah asks, " 'What are these two olive trees on the right and the left of the lampstand?' And a second time [he] said to him, 'What are these two branches of the olive trees, which pour out the oil through the two golden pipes?' " (Zech 4:11–12). An angel explains, "These are the two anointed ones [messiahs] who stand by the Lord of the whole earth" (4:14). Anointing is done with oil, so olive trees, the sources for olive oil, are appropriate symbols for the messiahs. Zechariah sees two anointed ones supplying the lamp with oil, thus keeping the cult in operation. The vision graphically portrays the dual nature of leadership in the postexilic community. Aaron was anointed at Sinai to minister to God in his sanctuary (Lev 8:12), and Saul and David were anointed kings over Israel (1 Sam 10:1; 16:12–13). Zechariah's vision brings the two kinds of leaders (priestly and royal) together and balances them. This is a theologizing of the politicoreligious structure of the restored community, established under Persian authority. Zerubbabel the governor and Joshua the high priest constitute this dual leadership in Zechariah's time.

In the eighth vision, Zechariah receives instructions from God.

> Collect silver and gold from the exiles—from Heldai, Tobijah, and Jedaiah—who have arrived from Babylon; and go the same day to the house of Josiah son of Zephaniah. Take the silver and gold and make a crown, and set it on the head of the high priest Joshua son of Jehozadak; say to him: Thus says the LORD of hosts: Here is a man whose name is Branch: for he shall branch out in his place, and he shall build the temple of the LORD. It is he that shall build the temple of the LORD; he shall bear royal honor, and shall sit upon his throne and rule. There shall be a priest by his throne, with peaceful understanding between the two of them. (Zech 6:10–13)

This passage is confusing. As it reads, Joshua, the high priest, is to be crowned, be called Branch, build the temple, bear royal honor, sit on a throne, and have a priest by his side. All of these accomplishments would be more suitable for a king. But Joshua cannot be both king and priest because priests come from the tribe of Levi while kings should be descended from David, of the tribe of Judah. Further, Zech 3 records that Zerubbabel builds the temple, but here Joshua does so. In addition, the royal figure in Zech 6 has a priest by his throne, implying that the royal figure is not himself a priest.

These considerations make it plausible that the passage originally referred to Zerubbabel and that at some point the passage was altered to refer to Joshua. Both the prophecy about the signet ring in Hag 2:23 and that about the Branch in Zech 3:8 may reflect a time when Judah attempted to win independence by taking advantage of the unrest in the Persian Empire, early in the reign of Darius I. In this interpretation, the attempt failed, and the oracle originally referring to Zerubbabel was emended to refer to Joshua. Such reapplication of prophetic predictions happens often. In its present form, the oracle in Zech 6 combines priestly and royal elements; the high priest has become civil ruler also. The suggestion that the oracle originally referred to Zerubbabel is conjectural, but in any case the combination of royal and priestly elements in the figure of Joshua in Zech 6 reflects a period when leadership roles in Judah were changing and the high priesthood was gaining power. Several centuries later, Israel achieved a brief period of independence, and its rulers were from a priestly family that also took on the title of king (see ch. 3, below).

THIRD ISAIAH (ISA 56–66)

Second Isaiah (Isa 40–55) was written during the exile. Its oracles presume a situation of exile, but one in which liberation is near. The oracles collected in Third Isaiah (Isa 56–66) show that the situation has changed. Now the prophet (or prophets) is in Judah. In fact, the oracles reflect several different situations and perhaps different prophets in postexilic Judah. They follow the tradition of Second Isaiah in their language, imagery, and hopes. They expect the kind of restoration Second Isaiah envisaged and reflect disappointment that such a restoration has not occurred. Dating the oracles precisely is not possible, but a plausible relative dating can be established. The group that produced the oracles returned to Judah either in 538 or 520 B.C.E. At first they were optimistic about the fulfillment of Second Isaiah's predictions, but then optimism soured. The group lost power and influence in the restored community, and they decided that the priests in power and the people as a whole were not fulfilling the covenant.

Oracles proclaiming the glorious restoration of Zion appear in Isa 60–62 as well as 57:14–21, 63:1, 65:17–25, and 66:10–14. In the manner of Second Isaiah, chapters 60–62 begin with the prophet addressing Zion itself (cf. Isa 40). All nations will be in darkness, but God will shine on Zion. Therefore, the nations who once oppressed Jerusalem will come to its light and praise God, bringing treasures to offer God in Jerusalem. The gates of Jerusalem will be left open because of the endless stream of Gentiles bringing gifts (60:11; cf. Hag 2:7):

> The descendants of those who oppressed you
>> shall come bending low to you,
> and all who despised you
>> shall bow down at your feet;

they shall call you the City of the LORD,
    the Zion of the Holy One of Israel.
Whereas you have been forsaken and hated,
    with no one passing through,
I will make you majestic forever,
    a joy from age to age.
You shall suck the milk of nations,
    you shall suck the breasts of kings;
and you shall know that I, the LORD, am your Savior
    and your Redeemer, the Mighty One of Jacob. (60:14–16)

God is savior because he brings rescue from exile. God is also called Israel's redeemer here. A redeemer "buys back" someone from slavery.

    Isaiah 61 pictures a glorious restoration. The prophet says,

The spirit of the Lord GOD is upon me,
    because the LORD has anointed me;
he has sent me to bring good news to the oppressed,
    to bind up the brokenhearted,
to proclaim liberty to the captives,
    and release to the prisoners;
to proclaim the year of the LORD's favor,
    and the day of vengeance of our God;
    to comfort all who mourn;
to provide for those who mourn in Zion—
    to give them a garland instead of ashes,
the oil of gladness instead of mourning,
    the mantle of praise instead of a faint spirit.
They will be called oaks of righteousness,
    the planting of the LORD, to display his glory.
They shall build up the ancient ruins,
    they shall raise up the former devastations;
they shall repair the ruined cities,
    the devastations of many generations. (Isa 61:1–4)

In the Hebrew Bible, the spirit of God is not an entity separate from God; it is a way of speaking about God's activity. By asserting that he has the spirit of God, the prophet claims to be God's agent, as he does also by asserting that God has anointed him, that is, made him a messiah. It is more common to find anointing associated with a king or a priest, but here the prophet is figuratively anointed (anointed with the spirit) to perform a specific task. Third Isaiah proclaims good news to those who are unhappy in Zion: Jerusalem will be restored and the renewed community will be "planted" there. The ancient ruins will be rebuilt.

Isaiah 61:6 contains a new element: "But you shall be called priests of the LORD, you shall be named ministers of our God." Third Isaiah addresses not just priests, however, but all Israel. The priesthood has been extended to the entire people because they are all holy to the Lord, living in Jerusalem and serving God there (cf. Exod 19:6, and Korah's objection in Num 16 to a professional priesthood). All Israel have become priests to the nations, for humanity now recognizes Israel's special, mediating status in God's eyes.

Third Isaiah has a universalistic vision of God's restored cult. This reflects the universalism of Second Isaiah. All Gentiles who keep God's covenant, especially the Sabbath, can join God's people (cf. Zech. 2:9–12, above):

> And the foreigners who join themselves to the LORD,
>   to minister to him, to love the name of the LORD,
>   and to be his servants,
> all who keep the sabbath, and do not profane it,
>   and hold fast my covenant—
> these I will bring to my holy mountain,
>   and make them joyful in my house of prayer;
> their burnt offerings and their sacrifices
>   will be accepted on my altar;
> for my house shall be called a house of prayer
>   for all peoples. (Isa 56:6–7)

This "democratized" vision of the restored community, where all Israel are priests and all nations are within the covenant, may have contributed to the clash between the group behind Third Isaiah and the priests installed by the Persians. The books of Ezra and Nehemiah envisage a more closed and exclusivistic community than does Third Isaiah.

Chapter 62 assumes that Jerusalem has not yet been rebuilt, but the prophet has not lost hope. He vows to continue petitioning God for salvation: "For Zion's sake I will not keep silent, and for Jerusalem's sake I will not rest, until her vindication shines out like the dawn, and her salvation like a burning torch. . . . Upon your walls, O Jerusalem, I have posted sentinels; all day and all night they shall never be silent. You who remind the LORD, take no rest, and give him no rest until he establishes Jerusalem and makes it renowned throughout the earth" (62:1, 6–7). The central section of Third Isaiah ends on a note of expectation that Jerusalem will be restored and salvation will come to the people (62:11–12).

Another oracle from this early, optimistic period recalls Second Isaiah's claim (43:18–19) that what God now does surpasses anything God has done before: "For I am about to create new heavens and a new earth; the former things shall not be remembered or come to mind. But be glad and rejoice forever in what I am creating; for I am about to create Jerusalem as a joy, and its people as a delight" (65:17–18).

Other oracles reveal that Third Isaiah's hopes did not materialize. A central complaint seems to be that the group supported by the Persian crown was exclusivistic with respect to cult, power, and social status. The visionaries themselves are excluded. They protest, "For you are our father, though Abraham does not know us and Israel does not acknowledge us; you, O LORD, are our father; our Redeemer from of old is your name" (63:16). The beginnings of the restoration were promising, but the results were disappointing: "Your holy people took possession for a little while; but now our adversaries have trampled down your sanctuary" (63:18).

For Third Isaiah, the line between those whom God accepts and those God does not accept is found within Israel itself. The prophet uses the word "servant" to designate the faithful within Israel, as distinguished from the rest of Israel. Servant is a common word in Second Isaiah, sometimes signifying the prophet and at other times referring to all of Israel. Here it applies only to part of Israel. Third Isaiah implies that even the name Israel must be changed so as to underline the failure of the majority of the old community and the foundation of a new community:

> Therefore thus says the Lord GOD:
> My servants shall eat,
>   but you shall be hungry;
> my servants shall drink,
>   but you shall be thirsty;
> my servants shall rejoice,
>   but you shall be put to shame;
> my servants shall sing for gladness of heart,
>   but you shall cry out for pain of heart,
>   and shall wail for anguish of spirit.
> You shall leave your name to my chosen to use as a curse,
>   and the Lord GOD will put you to death;
> but to his servants he will give a different name. (65:13–15)

Isaiah 58 addresses those who, like Haggai, expected that once the cult was back in operation, all would be well for Israel. God says,

> Yet day after day they seek me
>   and delight to know my ways,
> as if they were a nation that practiced righteousness
>   and did not forsake the ordinance of their God;
> they ask of me righteous judgments,
>   they delight to draw near to God.

"Why do we fast, but you do not see?
    Why humble ourselves, but you do not notice?"
Look, you serve your own interest on your fast day,
    and oppress all your workers.
Look, you fast only to quarrel and to fight
    and to strike with a wicked fist.
Such fasting as you do today
    will not make your voice heard on high.
Is such the fast that I choose,
    a day to humble oneself?
Is it to bow down the head like a bulrush,
    and to lie in sackcloth and ashes?
Will you call this a fast,
    a day acceptable to the LORD?
Is not this the fast that I choose:
    to loose the bonds of injustice,
    to undo the thongs of the yoke,
to let the oppressed go free,
    and to break every yoke?
Is it not to share your bread with the hungry,
    and bring the homeless poor into your house;
when you see the naked, to cover them,
    and not to hide yourself from your own kin? (58:2–7)

The phrase "delight to draw near to God" refers to the cult. "To draw near" is to approach God in the temple. Similarly, to "ask righteous judgments" of God is probably to go to the sanctuary to get proper *torah*, instruction, from the priests. Third Isaiah proclaims that the cult is useless without social justice. To serve God in the temple while ignoring the needs of one's fellow humans is futile. In contrast to Haggai, Third Isaiah does not say that God demands cultic service in return for blessing. Rather, caring for the poor, the hungry, the oppressed, and the homeless wins God's favor. Jerusalem will not be rebuilt until God is satisfied with Israel's record of social justice (58:12). This accords with the view of Jeremiah earlier, especially as expressed in his temple sermon (Jer 7, 26).

MALACHI (CA. 500–450 B.C.E.)

Malachi prophesied after the temple was rebuilt and the cult was functioning. He opposed intermarriage. He directs his prophecies primarily against the priests, whom he regards as lax in practice and teaching:

For the lips of a priest should guard knowledge, and people should seek instruction *[torah]* from his mouth, for he is the messenger of the LORD of hosts. But you have turned aside from the way; you have caused many to stumble by your instruction; you have corrupted the covenant of Levi, says the LORD of hosts, and so I make you despised and abased before all the people, inasmuch as you have not kept my ways but have shown partiality in your instruction. (Mal 2:7–9)

Malachi expresses his indictment in the context of his perception that all the world recognizes Israel's God as the true God: "For from the rising of the sun to its setting my name is great among the nations, and in every place incense is offered to my name, and a pure offering; for my name is great among the nations, says the LORD of hosts" (1:11); "For I am a great King, says the LORD of hosts, and my name is reverenced among the nations" (1:14).

Key Figures in the Restoration

Joshua: First high priest of the restoration.

Zerubbabel: Jewish governor of Judah, subject to the Persians, while Joshua was high priest. Some may have based messianic hopes on him.

Haggai: A prophet who insisted that the rebuilding of the temple be the main priority of the restored community in Judah.

Zechariah: A prophet, contemporary with Haggai, who also encouraged the rebuilding of the temple. He had visions of the renewal of the priesthood and of the restoration of Jerusalem in glory.

Malachi: Prophet of the restoration; his precise dating is uncertain. He criticized the priesthood.

Third Isaiah: Probably a number of prophets who saw themselves as in the tradition of Second Isaiah. For them, the restoration fell short of the expectations of Second Isaiah, and so they criticized Israel's ruling establishment, the cult in particular.

Nehemiah: Jewish cupbearer to the Persian king. Commissioned as governor of Judah, he rebuilt Jerusalem's walls, instituted land reform, and reformed the cult, providing for its support. He opposed mixed marriages and insisted on strict observance of the Sabbath.

Ezra: A Jew of the Babylonian exile who was sent by the Persian king to reform Israel according to the written Torah. He opposed mixed marriages.

Malachi is especially upset over improper sacrifices (blemished animals), marriages with Gentiles, divorce, and tithes. A more general list of shortcomings of Israel includes social justice:

Then I will draw near you for judgment; I will be swift to bear witness against the sorcerers, against the adulterers, against those who swear falsely, against those who oppress the hired workers in their wages, the widow and the orphan, against those who thrust aside the alien, and do not fear me, says the LORD of hosts. (3:5)

Malachi predicts the coming of God for judgment. Before judgment, God sends a forerunner.

> See, I am sending my messenger *[mal'aki]* to prepare the way before me, and the Lord whom you seek will suddenly come to his temple. The messenger of the covenant in whom you delight—indeed, he is coming, says the LORD of hosts. But who can endure the day of his coming, and who can stand when he appears? For he is like a refiner's fire and like fullers' soap; he will sit as a refiner and purifier of silver, and he will purify the descendants of Levi and refine them like gold and silver, until they present offerings to the LORD in righteousness. Then the offering of Judah and Jerusalem will be pleasing to the LORD as in the days of old and as in former years. (3:1–4)

The temple service is interpreted as "seeking" God, but Malachi says that when the one who is sought suddenly comes to the temple, what happens will shock the worshipers. God will purify the cult and priesthood as with fire.

Malachi 4:5 identifies the coming messenger with Elijah: "Lo, I will send you the prophet Elijah before the great and terrible day of the LORD comes. He will turn the hearts of parents to their children and the hearts of children to their parents, so that I will not come and strike the land with a curse." Elijah was the ninth-century prophet who reportedly did not die but was taken into heaven in a fiery chariot (2 Kgs 2:11–12). The legend that Elijah was assumed in a fiery chariot gave rise to speculation about his return. According to Mal 4, Elijah will return to reform Israel before the judgment. In the first century C.E., the Gospels claim that some thought that Jesus was the returned Elijah. For Matthew and Mark, John the Baptist was the returned Elijah, who prepared the way for Jesus.

Malachi, like Third Isaiah, questions neither the priestly system nor the validity of the covenant. Indeed, each of them assumes the validity of both covenant and cult. But Malachi indicts the Jewish community for failing to live up to God's demands. Both Malachi and Third Isaiah criticize the establishment, for different reasons. Both expect God to punish the people for their transgressions, but neither expects that to be the end of the story. As in the past, God will preserve a refined Israel.

DATING EZRA AND NEHEMIAH

Ezra and Nehemiah, Jews of the Babylonian exilic community, returned to Judah at different times with royal authority to perform certain tasks. The books of Ezra and Nehemiah put Ezra first in the narrative and say that Ezra came in the seventh year of King Artaxerxes of Persia (458 B.C.E.), while

Nehemiah came in the twentieth year of his rule (445 B.C.E.). But scholars question this schema. The writer claims that Ezra came to promulgate a written law, but he does not promulgate that law until Nehemiah's arrival thirteen years later (Neh 8). Further, although Ezra and Nehemiah are both agents of the Persian crown and are in Jerusalem together according to the narrative, they have little to do with each other even though their tasks are related; their connection in the text is superficial. There are two fairly independent blocks of material in Ezra-Nehemiah, one dealing with Ezra and the other with Nehemiah.

In all likelihood, Nehemiah was first, for the following reasons. Nehemiah lists the exiles who had returned to Judah previously but does not mention the return under Ezra. He comes to a Jerusalem without walls and almost deserted, but when Ezra arrives, the city is rebuilt and has walls. Nehemiah holds office in Judah while Eliashib is high priest whereas Ezra may be contemporary with Eliashib's grandson Jehohanan. We can reconcile this reconstruction with the text of Ezra by identifying the Artaxerxes under whom Ezra returned with Artaxerxes II (ruled 404–358 B.C.E.). Then Ezra would have arrived in Judah ca. 398 B.C.E. Even so, placing Ezra before Nehemiah, as does the writer of Ezra-Nehemiah, would not affect most of what is said below.

THE MISSION OF NEHEMIAH

The book of Nehemiah claims to incorporate Nehemiah's memoirs (Neh 1–7; 11:1–2; 12:31–43; 13:4–31). The memoirs may be authentic. Nehemiah was a Jew prominent in the court of the Persian emperor Artaxerxes I (ruled ca. 465–424 B.C.E.). He was Artaxerxes' cupbearer, a position of trust. According to the book of Nehemiah, he hears in 445 B.C.E. that the Jewish community in Judah is doing badly and that Jerusalem is in a poor, unfortified state, and so he requests permission to go to Judah to rebuild Jerusalem's walls. The king sends him there with letters to the other governors of the area, telling them not to hinder his work.

When the rulers of Samaria and of Ammon (across the Jordan) hear of Nehemiah's mission, they are displeased. A strong and defensible Judah is bad news for them. Upon arrival in Jerusalem, Nehemiah inspects the walls by night for fear of resistance (2:11–16). When restoration begins, he stations a guard around the working parties, and the workers themselves bear arms (4:15–20). The work is completed despite harassment. Because Jerusalem is an unpleasant place to live, lots are cast (a process similar to throwing dice) to choose 10 percent of Judah's population to live there (11:1–2).

Broken walls are not Nehemiah's only problem. He finds a society living contrary to Mosaic law. The first issue is land. The people complain:

> For there were those who said, "With our sons and our daughters, we are many; we must get grain, so that we may eat and stay alive." There were also those who said, "We are having to pledge our fields, our vineyards, and our houses in order to get grain during the famine." And there were those who said, "We are having to borrow money on our fields and vineyards to pay the king's tax. Now our flesh is the same as that of our kindred; our children are the same as their children; and yet we are forcing our sons and daughters to be slaves, and some of our daughters have been ravished; we are powerless, and our fields and vineyards now belong to others." (5:2–5)

Jewish peasants are squeezed between famine and taxes. The unscrupulous rich take advantage of conditions to mire the peasants in debt, seize their fields, and even enslave them.

Nehemiah responds swiftly:

> I was very angry when I heard their outcry and these complaints. After thinking it over, I brought charges against the nobles and the officials; I said to them, "You are all taking interest from your own people." And I called a great assembly to deal with them, and said to them, "As far as we were able, we have bought back our Jewish kindred who had been sold to other nations; but now you are selling your own kin, who must then be bought back by us!" (5:6–8)

Nehemiah's insistence on social justice echoes ancient covenantal law. Deuteronomy is driven by the principle that Israelites are brothers and sisters and are to treat one another as such. One Israelite does not charge another interest, an Israelite never refuses help to the poor, and an Israelite does not retaliate if loans are not repaid because the debtor cannot do so. Nehemiah sees the opposite attitude on the part of the rich and says, "The thing that you are doing is not good. Should you not walk in the fear of our God, to prevent the taunts of the nations our enemies?" (5:9). The nobles relent and return the land they have seized and the interest they have charged. Nehemiah sets an example by foregoing his food allowance as governor "because of the heavy burden of labor on the people" (5:18).

Nehemiah 8–10 describes a covenant ceremony that supposedly took place when Nehemiah and Ezra were in Jerusalem together. It is more likely, however, that Neh 8–9 belongs to the Ezra story and Neh 10 belongs to that of Nehemiah. (We will treat chs. 8–9 later, in connection with Ezra's mission.)

In Neh 10, the people make a number of promises. First, they promise to refuse to marry anyone outside the covenant people (10:30). Family structure, marriage strategy, and ideology usually correspond in any society. Jewish defensive marriage strategy corresponded with attempts to create strong self-identity and well-defined borders. Such a concern lies behind the inclusion of long lists of those who returned from the exile (Ezra 2:1–70; Neh 7:6–73), those who helped to build the temple (Neh 3), those who signed the covenant (10:1–27), and those living in Jerusalem under Nehemiah (11:3–26). These lists help define who stands where with regard to the community. The list in Neh 7 begins by emphasizing the continuity of the Judahite community with the returned exiles: "Then my God put it into my mind to assemble the nobles and the officials and the people to be enrolled by genealogy. And I found the book of the genealogy of those who were the first to come back" (7:5). Several generations after the initial return, Nehemiah considers those who originally came back as the foundation of the community.

Second, the people promise to observe the Sabbath (10:31). Sabbath observance was vital during the exile because it distinguished Israel from the people around them. Since they no longer had their sacred space, the Jerusalem temple, and since their sacred festivals could not be celebrated properly in the absence of the temple, a greater weight fell on the sacred time, the Sabbath, which could still be celebrated, even away from the land of Israel. For the same reason, it is possible that circumcision became more important, since it also was a "portable" symbol of Israel's identity as God's people.

Other promises by the people concerned maintaining the cult (10:32–39). They pledge financial support in the amount of one-third of a shekel (the contribution later became obligatory and was increased to half a shekel). They agree to supply the temple with wood for sacrifices, to bring offerings of firstfruits, and to pay tithes to the Levites. The leaders live in Jerusalem, and the people decide that a tenth of the rest of the people should live there, too. They choose who should live in Jerusalem by casting lots, a typically biblical way of making such a decision that assumes God will make the lots fall a certain way so that the result will accord with God's will. Then the Law is read publicly (13:1), and "when the people heard the law, they separated from Israel all those of foreign descent" (13:3).

Nehemiah governed for twelve years, then returned to the Persian court. After an interval, he came back to Judah. The rest of the book of Nehemiah concerns his return to Judah. Now he must deal with a certain Tobiah from the land of Ammon across the Jordan. Tobiah's name indicates that he is Jewish and a worshiper of Yahweh. (The ending "-iah" at the end of a name is short for Yahweh, and the Hebrew for "good" is *tob*. Thus "Tobiah" means "Yahweh is good.") Tobiah had opposed Nehemiah on his first mission, using his alliances and marriage connections to the upper class in Judah against Nehemiah (6:17–19). Tobiah's business interests may have been jeopardized by Nehemiah's land reform and financial policies.

During Nehemiah's second stay in Judah, he discovers that Eliashib the priest has given Tobiah a room in the temple previously reserved for cultic materials. Eliashib did so because "he was related to Tobiah" (13:4). A room in the well-fortified temple serves as a place for the safekeeping of Tobiah's property. Nehemiah ejects Tobiah from the temple for having desecrated the sacred precincts. He orders the defiled rooms cleansed and the cultic materials previously stored there returned (13:4–9).

Nehemiah also finds that the people's promise to support the Levites through tithes has not been honored. The Levites have been forced to abandon their posts in the temple to work in the fields. Nehemiah reverses this situation, restoring the Levites to their proper functions. He then discovers that the Sabbath is not being observed, for trade is carried out on every Sabbath. Nehemiah forbids this practice, and when traders persist in coming to the city on the Sabbath, he commands that the city gates be closed. This ends the violation (13:10–22).

Finally, Nehemiah learns that his earlier prohibition of mixed marriages has not been observed. He finds Jewish children speaking the languages of the surrounding peoples and unable to speak the language of Judah (13:23–24).

> And I contended with them and cursed them and beat some of them and pulled out their hair; and I made them take an oath in the name of God, saying, "You shall not give your daughters to their sons, or take their daughters for your sons or for yourselves. Did not King Solomon of Israel sin on account of such women? Among the many nations there was no king like him, and he was beloved by his God, and God made him king over all Israel; nevertheless, foreign women made even him to sin. Shall we then listen to you and do all this great evil and act treacherously against our God by marrying foreign women?" (13:25–27)

Nehemiah is especially disturbed when he discovers that the high priest's son has married into the family of Sanballat, governor of Samaria:

> And one of the sons of Jehoiada, son of the high priest Eliashib, was the son-in-law of Sanballat the Horonite; I chased him away from me. Remember them, O my God, because they have defiled the priesthood, the covenant of the priests and the Levites. (13:28–29)

By marrying a foreign woman, a Samaritan, the priest brings her into intimate contact with God's temple. Such a mixing of things that do not belong together defiles the temple.

*Detail from a bas-relief of Persian archers in ceremonial dress. Darius I of Persia
(ruled 522–486 B.C.E.) commissioned this work for his royal palace in Susa.*

Acts of Nehemiah

Rebuilds the walls of Jerusalem (Neh 2:11–4:23)
Repopulates Jerusalem (11:1–2)
Institutes land reform (ch. 5)
Reforms support for the cult (10:32–39; 13:10–14):
  Temple tax; wood offering; firstfruits; offering of firstborn; tithes to support the Levites
Organizes temple tasks (12:44–47)
Ejects Tobiah from the temple and purifies it (13:4–9)
Strictly enforces Sabbath regulations against business (10:31; 13:15–22)
Prohibits intermarriage with Gentiles (10:30; 13:23–29)

EZRA'S MISSION (DATE UNCERTAIN: 458, 428, OR 398 B.C.E.)

Ezra makes his appearance in Ezra 7. Ezra 7–10 and Neh 8–9 contain his story. Since his lineage goes back to "Aaron the chief priest" through Zadok, he has impeccable priestly credentials. In addition, "he was a scribe skilled in the law of Moses that the LORD the God of Israel had given; and the king granted him all that he asked, for the hand of the LORD his God was upon him" (Ezra 7:6). In this passage, being a scribe means more than merely being able to read and write. It also means being knowledgeable regarding the content and application of the Torah of Moses. Further, Ezra is sent by the Persian king. He is therefore a priest, a scribe, and an agent of the Persian crown.

Ezra comes to Judah with a group of exiles—lay persons, priests, and Levites (Ezra 7:7–9). The text says that God favors him, since he is dedicated to Torah: "For the gracious hand of his God was upon him. For Ezra had set his heart to study the law of the LORD, and to do it, and to teach the statutes and ordinances in Israel" (7:9–10). The king of Persia sends him to Judah with royal contributions to the temple and with the news that the temple and its staff will be tax-exempt. The king's commission (7:12–26) reads in part,

> For you are sent by the king and his seven counselors to make inquiries about Judah and Jerusalem according to the law of the LORD your God, which is in your hand. . . . And you, Ezra, according to the God-given wisdom you possess, appoint magistrates and judges who may judge all the people in the province Beyond the River who know the laws of your God; and you shall teach those who do not know them. All who will not obey the law of your God and the law of the king, let judgment be strictly executed on them, whether for death or for banishment or for confiscation of their goods or for imprisonment. (7:14, 25–26)

All Judah is to be ruled by the law of God in Ezra's hand, the law book brought back from Babylonia. It is crucial to note that Ezra comes back from the Jewish community in Babylonia, and that he brings the Torah from there in written form—it is something that he can hold in his hand. The Torah is to be the law of Judah and has the power of the Persian government behind it. The very fact that Ezra must bring the written Torah from Babylonia, that the people hear it as something new to some extent, and that Persian power is needed to enforce it shows that this Torah has undergone change. Even its nature as a written, normative document or collection of documents appears to be something new. This is a step toward the canonization of sacred writings. A normative, written Torah means that those who can read can interpret it; this, in turn, means that Israel can depend less on the priestly establishment to interpret God's will. Now Torah interpretation begins to play a strategic role in much of the interaction of Second Temple Jewish groups.

Ezra probably brought some form of what we now know as the first five books of the Bible. Undoubtedly, Ezra's Torah had deep roots in Israel's past, but it represented the end result of a process of compilation, editing, and interpretation by the Babylonian Jewish community. Most significantly, it was now written. It is very common in the history of religions to see reforms or innovations that claim to be a simple reinstitution of what was there from the beginning. Ezra is to teach the law to the inhabitants of Judah, to appoint judges who understand and can apply that law, and to punish harshly those who do not accept it. In the process, he is also to enforce the king's law. He is an agent of the Persian crown and derives his power from that source.

Israel had lived for four and a half centuries under the rule of independent or at least semi-independent Israelite monarchs. A royal ideology had developed in which the kings were the guarantors of the Mosaic law and covenant, and in return they were assured, at least in the case of the Davidic dynasty, that their rule would last forever. Now, ironically, a crown of a different sort guaranteed the Mosaic law. Judah had to obey the Law as interpreted by the exilic community, and the Persians insured obedience. Restored Judah thus differed in two critical ways from the Judah of the preexilic period. First, there was no native monarchy. Second, Judah was now governed by a law that to some degree was fixed in writing and backed by a foreign power.

A major step in Nehemiah's reform was to abolish mixed marriages so that the returned community could remain pure. Ezra found that the reforms had still not taken root:

> The officials approached me and said, "The people of Israel, the priests, and the Levites have not separated themselves from the peoples of the lands with their abominations, from the Canaanites, the Hittites, the Perizzites, the

Jebusites, the Ammonites, the Moabites, the Egyptians, and the Amorites. For they have taken some of their daughters as wives for themselves and for their sons. Thus the holy seed has mixed itself with the peoples of the lands, and in this faithlessness the officials and leaders have led the way." When I heard this, I tore my garment and my mantle, and pulled hair from my head and beard, and sat appalled. (Ezra 9:1–3)

The priestly viewpoint of the writer (and perhaps of Ezra himself) is apparent here. Israel is a holy race that must be kept "separated" from other nations and not "mix" with them.

Ezra's next step shows his power of enforcement:

They made a proclamation throughout Judah and Jerusalem to all the returned exiles that they should assemble at Jerusalem, and that if any did not come within three days, by order of the officials and the elders all their property should be forfeited, and they themselves banned from the congregation of the exiles. (10:7–8)

For the book of Ezra, the returned exiles are the true Israel. When they arrive in Jerusalem, all Jews are ordered to divorce their non-Jewish wives. There follow lists of those who do so. A substantial number of priests, Levites, and laypersons are in these lists.

Nehemiah 8–9 narrates the covenant ceremony by which the people of Judah pledged to obey the Law that Ezra brought to them. The process takes many days. Here is a condensed version of the first day:

All the people gathered together into the square before the Water Gate. They told the scribe Ezra to bring the book of the law of Moses, which the LORD had given to Israel. Accordingly, the priest Ezra brought the law before the assembly, both men and women and all who could hear with understanding. This was on the first day of the seventh month. He read from it facing the square before the Water Gate from early morning until midday, in the presence of the men and the women and those who could understand; and the ears of all the people were attentive to the book of the law. The scribe Ezra stood on a wooden platform that had been made for the purpose. . . . And Ezra opened the book in the sight of all the people, for he was standing above all the people; and when he opened it, all the people stood up. . . . The Levites helped the people to understand the law, while the people remained in their places. So they read from the book, from the law of God, with interpretation. They gave the sense, so that the people understood the reading. (Neh 8:1–4a, 5, 7b–8)

The entire community is allegedly present to hear and understand the Law. Ezra's qualifications as scribe and priest are stressed. The Law is in the form of a book. Ezra stands above the crowd in full view of all. They can see clearly that he is reading, so they know that the words are not his own but come directly from the book. The people stand out of respect for God's word. One can sense here the power the book will have in the community, that it will become a source of religious authority rivaling even the priesthood and the temple establishment.

The role of the Levites in this passage is not entirely clear. Although Ezra reads the Law, so do they. But whereas Ezra simply reads the Law, the Levites help the people understand it. How they do this is disputed. In particular, questions surround the Hebrew translated "they gave the sense." Some scholars understand it to mean that the Levites translate the Law from Hebrew into Aramaic. The main language of the Jews in Judah and Babylonia during the Second Temple period became Aramaic, the official language of the Persian empire. An alternative view is that the Levites interpret the Law for the people. The Law's application is not obvious, and the people might need teachers to explain its demands.

On the second day, Ezra and the people come together to study the Law. They find prescriptions for the celebration of the Feast of Booths (Neh 8:13–18). The commandments for the feast seem new to the people, and since it is the time for Booths, they set about celebrating it properly. The text makes a surprising statement: "For from the days of Jeshua [Joshua] the son of Nun to that day the people of Israel had not done so" (8:17). What this means historically is a matter for discussion. It is unlikely that Israel had not celebrated the feast at all since Joshua's day. It may mean that Israel had not done so as a single assembly, or perhaps that they had not done so in the way prescribed by Ezra's Torah. In any case, the writer plainly considers Ezra's version of the Law to be something new. Despite its newness, Ezra's Law claims to derive from Moses himself.

Ezra epitomizes the transition between the preexilic and postexilic periods: he was a priest, a direct descendant of Aaron; he was a scribe, which meant he was skilled in God's Torah; and he was an agent of the Persian government. In the preexilic period, there was no fixed law book until toward the end of the monarchy, under Josiah (2 Kgs 22). Israelite kings reigned over Israel, and the priests gave legal instructions *(torah)*. In the postexilic period, the Israelite monarchy had been replaced in some of its functions by a combination of native priestly rule and Persian rule; the Law was becoming a book with a status potentially independent of the temple establishment; and any scribe could, in theory, pick up the law book and read and interpret it in a way unfavorable to the priests in power. At the very time that the internal power of the temple was increased because of the absence of the Israelite monarchy, another power center, based on interpretation of Torah, was created.

The new situation helped pave the way for such later movements as the Pharisees and the Jesus movement, which depended on the written Torah for their self-understanding and ability to appeal to others. At the same time, Israel had to learn to live under foreign rule. The written Torah, promulgated by authority of the Persian crown, became a flexible instrument that simultaneously gave Israel its abiding identity and provided it with the means to adapt to new circumstances.

Some scholars challenge the picture of Ezra contained in Ezra-Nehemiah, with good reason. Later traditions tend to glorify those whom they consider significant. The idea that Ezra was granted sweeping powers to reform Jewish society in Judah seems unrealistic to many. His portrait may be a way to enshrine ideals dear to the writers of these books. But this does not mean that the information about Ezra contained in Ezra-Nehemiah is not useful for reconstructing postexilic Judahite history. Scholars generally agree that the Torah and the Deuteronomistic History were compiled in the Babylonian Diaspora and were brought back to Judah by Jews under the auspices of the Persian Empire. The written Torah they brought back had roots in preexilic Israel, but the Babylonian Jewish community brought it into existence as such. The precise role that Ezra played in all this is debated, but given the traditions Israel preserved about him, it may have been substantial.

Main Elements of Ezra's Activity, according to Ezra-Nehemiah

Brings the written Torah to Judah
Establishes a judiciary to enforce Torah and the Persian king's law
Abolishes mixed marriages and prohibits intermarriage

WRITTEN TORAH AND CANON

Ezra's introduction of the written Torah to Judah was a major step in the formation of the Bible, so we take this opportunity to reflect further on its development. Today we take for granted the existence of a written Bible. This collection of authoritative books is called the canon, from the Greek word *kanōn,* meaning "reed" or "measuring rod." In some sense, the Jewish and Christian religions can be "measured" by means of their respective Scriptures. The Catholic Bible differs from that of Jews and Protestants in that it contains seven more books, collectively called the Apocrypha (meaning "hidden away," or not to be used for public reading) or the deuterocanonical books (meaning a "second" ["deutero-"] group of canonical texts). Catholic Bibles integrate the deuterocanonical books into the Old Testament, while Protestant and ecumenical Bibles put them in a separate collection.

The Christian Old Testament is roughly equivalent to the Jewish Scriptures, although the order of books is different. The Christian Old Testament begins with the five books of Moses (also called the Pentateuch—Genesis, Exodus, Leviticus, Numbers, and Deuteronomy), then has the Deuteronomistic History (Deuteronomy through 2 Kings—from a literary and thematic point of view, Deuteronomy belongs to the Deuteronomistic History but it was also included in the Pentateuch), then Chronicles and Ezra-Nehemiah, followed by Esther, Job, Psalms, Proverbs, Ecclesiastes, and the Song of Songs; significantly, the prophets come at the end. The last book of the Old Testament, Malachi, ends with a prediction that the prophet Elijah will return before God's day of judgment in order to warn people and reform society. The gospels of Matthew and Mark, the first two books of the New Testament, suppose that John the Baptist was Elijah returned, and that Elijah, in the person of John, came to prepare Jesus' way (not God's way, as in Malachi). Therefore, the very order of books in the Christian Old Testament contains a message: it signifies that the entire history of Israel points to the coming of Jesus Christ. The Elijah/John the Baptist identification makes one testament flow smoothly into the other.

The Jewish Bible is most frequently called Tanak or Mikra. "Mikra" means simply "writing" or "scripture." "Tanak" is an acronym formed of the words *torah, nebi'im,* and *ketubim. Torah* refers to the first five books of the Bible, the so-called books of Moses. It is the most sacred part of the Jewish canon, and the rest of the Bible and indeed the rest of Jewish literature can be seen as commentary on Torah. *Nebi'im* means "Prophets," here broadly conceived to include not just those whom Christians consider to be prophets but also what we know as the historical books (called the former prophets—Joshua, Judges, 1–2 Samuel, 1–2 Kings). The justification for this categorization is that since the historical books are inspired, they are written by prophets. Finally, *ketubim* means "Writings"; this section contains the rest of the canonical books. The Jewish Scriptures end with the books of Ezra-Nehemiah and Chronicles (considered part of the Writings). This order points to the importance of the building of the temple and the celebration of a divinely ordained cult in Jerusalem. First and Second Chronicles rewrites the Deuteronomistic History, and a main principle of the rewriting is to see the point of Israel's history, and of the reigns of David and Solomon in particular, as the foundation of the Jerusalem cult. We have seen in this chapter how Ezra-Nehemiah carries this concern forward.

Tracing the exact steps in the formation of the Bible is not easy. Indeed, a clear selection of the canonical texts in both Judaism and Christianity happened only after the Second Temple period. It should also be kept in mind that codices, that is, books, were developed only in the first centuries C.E.; thus, when we speak of collections before this, we literally mean collections of discrete scrolls. Still, we can discern some signposts marking the development of what were to become canonical collections.

The story recounting that a written Torah was given to Moses on Sinai contains important theological points for both Judaism and Christianity. Although few critical scholars would take this story literally, it recognizes that the Torah of later ages was, in some sense, continuous with Israel's laws, practices, beliefs, and stories from the preexilic period. The finding of a book of Torah in the temple during the reign of King Josiah, at the end of the seventh century B.C.E., was remembered by later generations as the basis of Josiah's religious reforms (2 Kgs 22). Most scholars consider it to have been the core of the book of Deuteronomy. When the elite of Judahite society went into exile in Babylonia in the first half of the sixth century B.C.E., they took with them this early form of Deuteronomy and updated it to take account of the exile. Also during the exile, a group of priestly editors, using the sources J and E (described in ch. 1, above) and adding their own material, wrote down what are now the first four books of the Bible. Combined with Deuteronomy, they make up the Torah, also known as the Pentateuch. Many think that it was some form of the Pentateuch that Ezra brought back to Judah.

Literary production in the Babylonian Jewish community was not limited to the Pentateuch. Deuteronomy itself, the fifth book of the Pentateuch, was brought up to date by the addition of chapters to its beginning and end, and a history of Israel up to the time of the exile was written on the basis of Deuteronomistic ideas. We call this the Deuteronomistic History. Along with the writings of the prophets themselves, these constitute the second major division of Jewish scripture, the Prophets. All other books fall into the category of Writings. Most think that some time before the second century B.C.E., the categories of the Torah and the Prophets were fairly well set but that the category of the Writings remained fluid until around the end of the first century C.E. The prologue to the book of Sirach knows of a tripartite division of the sacred books, but the third division seems vague. It speaks of "the Law and the Prophets and the others that followed them," "the Law and the Prophets and the other books of our ancestors," and "the Law itself, the Prophecies, and the rest of the books." These words were written in the second half of the second century B.C.E. The categories of the Law and the Prophets are common in the New Testament (Matt 5:17; 7:12; 22:40; Luke 16:16; John 13:15; 24:14; Rom 3:21). Luke also speaks of Moses and the Prophets (16:29, 31), which indicates the same division.

The Dead Sea Scrolls (see ch. 5, below) were preserved by a Jewish sect that existed from the middle of the second century B.C.E. until 68 C.E. The scrolls provide evidence for the sacred status of most books now in the Bible, but they also demonstrate that other works were sacred to the sect. Certainly the Torah and the Prophets were privileged collections, given the way they are treated in sectarian documents, but the sect did not seem to have a clear and exclusive list that would correspond to our Bible.

The development of a written Scripture was crucial to events in Second Temple Judaism and beyond. Whenever Jews or Christians use their Bibles, they owe a debt to the Second Temple Jews responsible for its existence.

CONCLUSION

This chapter examines the reestablishment of Israel in Judah after the Babylonian exile. Loss of temple and land caused shifts of emphasis in the religion of the exilic community. Circumcision and Sabbath observance increased in significance. The exilic community collected and rewrote sacred narratives and legal rulings and forged them into a new written form that became the written Torah.

When Cyrus, the Persian emperor, allowed the exilic community to return to Jerusalem and rebuild the city and the temple, the monarchy was not reestablished. The returned exiles initially established a dual leadership consisting of Zerubbabel, perhaps a Davidic descendant, and Joshua, the high priest. Soon the high priest emerged as sole leader.

Not all were content with the restored community. Those behind Third Isaiah felt excluded from power and clashed with the priestly establishment. Malachi criticized the priesthood for its practices and teachings. Nehemiah met opposition both inside the Judahite community and outside it. Ezra came to Judah as a reformer. The Torah, whose final redaction was a priestly one, reinforced priestly hegemony in the restored community, but the very fact of a written Torah was to make possible other centers of authority in Israel that were based not on hereditary priesthood but on knowledge and interpretation of Torah. So Torah served both to unify the community and to make disagreements possible within it.

SELECT BIBLIOGRAPHY

Ackroyd, Peter R. *Exile and Restoration: A Study of Hebrew Thought of the Sixth Century B.C.* Philadelphia: Westminster, 1986.

———. *1 and 2 Chronicles, Ezra, Nehemiah.* London: SCM, 1973.

———. *Israel under Babylon and Persia.* Oxford: Oxford University Press, 1970.

Ackroyd, Peter R., and C. F. Evans, eds. *The Cambridge History of the Bible: From the Beginnings to Jerome.* New York: Cambridge University Press, 1970.

Anderson, Bernhard. Chapter 15 in *Understanding the Old Testament.* 4th ed. Englewood Cliffs, N.J.: Prentice-Hall, 1986.

Bickermann, Elias. *From Ezra to the Last of the Maccabees: Foundations of Post-biblical Judaism.* New York: Schocken, 1962.

Blenkinsopp, Joseph. *Ezra-Nehemiah: A Commentary.* Philadelphia: Westminster, 1989.

———. "Interpretation and the Tendency to Sectarianism: An Aspect of Second Temple History." Pages 1–26 in *Aspects of Judaism in the Graeco-Roman Period.* Vol. 2 of *Jewish and Christian Self-Definition.* Edited by E. P. Sanders, A. I. Baumgarten, and Alan Mendelson. Philadelphia: Fortress, 1981.

Bright, John. *A History of Israel.* 3d ed. Philadelphia: Westminster, 1981.

Fishbane, Michael. *Biblical Interpretation in Ancient Israel.* New York: Oxford University Press, 1985.

Friedman, Richard Elliott. "Torah (Pentateuch)." *ABD* 6:605–22.

Gottwald, Norman K. Chapters 9, 10, and 12 in *The Hebrew Bible: A Socio-literary Introduction.* Philadelphia: Fortress, 1985.

Hanson, Paul. *The Dawn of Apocalyptic: The Historical and Sociological Roots of Jewish Apocalyptic Eschatology.* Rev. ed. Philadelphia: Fortress, 1979.

Leiman, Sid. *The Canonization of Hebrew Scripture: The Talmudic and Midrashic Evidence.* Hamden, Conn.: Archon Books, 1976.

Peterson, David L. *Haggai and Zechariah 1–8.* Philadelphia: Westminster, 1984.

Sanders, James A. "Canon." *ABD* 1:837–52.

———. *From Sacred Story to Sacred Text.* Philadelphia: Fortress, 1987.

Smith, Morton. *Palestinian Parties and Politics That Shaped the Old Testament.* New York: Columbia, 1971.

Stone, Michael. "Exile, Restoration, and the Bible." *SSV* 19–25.

CHAPTER 3

HELLENISM, JUDAISM, AND THE MACCABEES

PRIMARY READINGS: 1 and 2 Maccabees • Sirach

HISTORICAL OVERVIEW

ALEXANDER CONQUERS THE WORLD

Alexander the Great was the sort of person to inspire legends. Born son of the king of Macedonia, a land to the north of Greece, he was tutored in his youth by the famous Greek philosopher Aristotle. The language and culture of its southern neighbors influenced Alexander's homeland, and Aristotle taught Alexander that Greek culture was superior to any other. The word "barbarian" comes from a Greek word denoting anyone who did not speak Greek.

The Greeks had always been accomplished soldiers, and they often hired themselves out to foreigners as mercenaries. But the Greeks spent as much time fighting one another as they did fighting foreigners. The basic political unit of Greece was the city-state; Athens and Sparta were the most famous. Although the city-states sometimes banded together to fight, the political structure, combined with mountainous terrain between many of the cities, tended to keep them fragmented. Alexander's father, King Philip V of Macedonia, dreamed that if he could somehow unite the Greek city-states under his leadership, they would be invincible. This awesome Greek power could then turn against its traditional enemy to the east, the Persian Empire. Philip saw the Persian Empire as ripe for the plucking.

Philip did not live to see his dream come true, for he was assassinated in 336 B.C.E. But his son Alexander, a mere twenty years old, took up his father's cause with a vengeance. He brutally subdued the Greek mainland and then turned east. The Greeks had old scores to settle with the Persians. Persia had repeatedly tried to conquer them but failed because of Greek military prowess combined with natural barriers—sea and mountains. But the Persians did snatch Greek colonies in western Asia Minor (also called Anatolia; now Asian Turkey). The Persians were unprepared for Alexander's onslaught. Their emperor, Darius III, faced Alexander in three major battles but lost each time. Darius finally died at the hands of his own men in 330, with Alexander hot on his heels. Alexander took the Persian capital of Persepolis and burned it. This settled another old score—the burning of the Acropolis in Athens by the Persians in 480.

Within ten years, Alexander conquered an area now home to the modern nations of Turkey, Syria, Lebanon, Israel, Jordan, Egypt, Iraq, Iran, Afghanistan, and Pakistan. It was an astonishing achievement. He was anxious to press on into India, but his soldiers refused and forced him to turn back in 326. Their ambition did not match his. They were far from home and tired of war. He had no choice but to yield and died shortly afterward, in 323.

The sheer size of the area Alexander seized testifies to his energy, military brilliance, and visionary ambition. He inaugurated a new period in the history of the eastern Mediterranean and the Near East: the Hellenistic era stretches from the time of Alexander's conquests to the Roman takeover of Judea in 63 B.C.E. (Henceforth in this book, the area around Jerusalem is called Judea, the name by which the Romans called it.) The word "Hellenistic" comes from the Greek word for Greece, *Hellas*. During the Hellenistic period, Greek culture, political forms, and language spread widely throughout the eastern Mediterranean and the Near East.

Main Dates (B.C.E.)

333	Alexander's first important victory over the Persians
Third century	Ptolemaic control of Judah
200	The Seleucid Antiochus III takes Judah from the Ptolemies
175	Antiochus IV ascends the Seleucid throne and the Hellenistic reform begins in Jerusalem
167	Antiochus IV begins his persecution of the Jews; the Maccabean revolt begins
164	Death of Antiochus IV; the Maccabees retake Jerusalem and the temple and rededicate it, instituting the feast of Hanukkah
161	Death of Judah Maccabee
152	Jonathan, brother of Judah Maccabee, becomes high priest
150	Approximate date for the founding of the Qumran community
142	Jonathan killed; his brother Simon succeeds him as high priest
63	The Romans take possession of the Jewish kingdom

The Jewish homeland lay on a narrow strip of arable land wedged between the Mediterranean Sea to the west and deserts to the east. It formed a natural bridge between Egypt and the traditional powers to the north and east, such as Persia. Alexander coveted Egypt, so he had to secure Judea. It is questionable whether he even knew exactly who the Jews were, but they stood in his path, a dangerous place to be. As the great tide of Alexander's forces swept over the eastern Mediterranean, the Jews were caught up in its turmoil. They did not resist Alexander militarily. Some perhaps even saw his arrival as an opportunity to escape Persian control. But their incorporation into Alexander's growing empire was to change their world forever. Alexander's conquest of Judea initiated a socially stormy and intellectually fertile period in Israel's history that compares in importance to the earlier events of the exile and the restoration.

ALEXANDER'S SUCCESSORS

When Alexander died, he left the new empire in the hands of his generals, often called the "successors" (Greek: *diadochoi*). Each general took responsibility for a different part of the empire, and these soon became independent kingdoms squabbling with each other for the largest share of the imperial pie. After about two decades of bitter and destructive warfare, the kingdoms reached an uneasy equilibrium. The two most important kingdoms for our interests were the Ptolemaic in Egypt and the Seleucid in Syria and Mesopotamia.

But the world was not to be carved up so easily, particularly the part that was home to the Jews. Both the Seleucids and the Ptolemies claimed Judea. Although an agreement in 301 gave it to the Seleucids, the Ptolemies already occupied it and refused to give it up. The two dynasties fought war after war in the third century B.C.E., but Judea remained in the hands of the Ptolemies until 200 B.C.E., when Antiochus III finally brought it under Seleucid rule. The shift from Ptolemaic to Seleucid rule was to have disastrous consequences for the Jews.

In 175 B.C.E., the Seleucid Antiochus IV Epiphanes came to the throne. He made the fatal decision in 167 to force Greek culture on Judea and to outlaw the Jewish religion. Jews had lived under foreign domination for centuries, but this was too much. To outlaw Torah was to destroy Israel's identity as a people and to deprive them of their relationship with their God. The Jews revolted, led by a priestly family who became known as the Maccabees. In the following decades, the Jews gradually won first religious freedom, then political independence, and finally an empire. But the fledgling Jewish empire was no match for the next conquerors. In 63 B.C.E., the Romans conquered Jerusalem and brought Jewish independence to an end.

Two Empires Compared

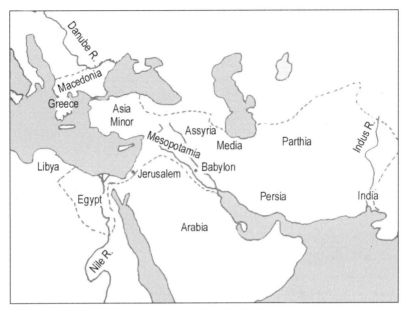

The Empire of Alexander the Great

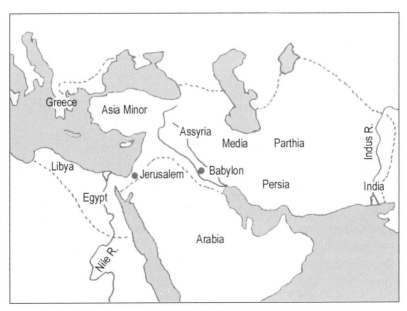

The Persian Empire

HELLENISM

THE GREEK CITY

Greek culture was based on the polis, the city-state. Even before Alexander, the Greeks had established colonies in western Asia Minor and elsewhere and had modeled cities there on Greek city-states. Ideally, the Greek city, wherever located, was autonomous, but when part of an empire, its independence was often limited. The city was ruled by its citizens, that is, prominent land-owning males. From time to time, the citizenry would assemble in a meeting called the *ekklēsia* (a term later adopted by Christians and translated "church"). It was impractical for a large body to operate the Greek city on a daily basis, so this function was entrusted to a city council.

Today anyone visiting a new city expects to find certain things characteristic of almost any city—a city center of some sort, a city hall, a courthouse, perhaps an entertainment district or at least some movie theaters, malls, hotels, bus stations, often an airport, and so on. Since most cities have many of the same features, people can go from city to city without facing great inconvenience. Greek cities were also similar to one another in many ways. Their institutions embodied and nurtured Greek tradition and culture. One institution was the marketplace, the agora. It was a large open square, often surrounded by porticoes, porches with open sides and a roof held up by rows of columns. Most people went to the agora at least occasionally. Perhaps the best modern analogy is the mall. Because of the opportunity it offered to reach many people, the Hellenistic agora served as a marketplace not just for goods but also for ideas. Philosophers could get a hearing there, as could religious missionaries.

Theaters and gymnasia were important fixtures of the Greek city. In the theater, plays immortalized Greek mythology, and society was both praised and satirized. The gymnasium was far more than a place for sports, although sports were important and helped to actualize the Greek idea of a sound mind in a strong body. It also served social functions—for example, as a meeting place for political clubs and as a kind of high school for Greek boys, where they learned the classics and received military training. The gymnasium was key to preserving, transmitting, and spreading Greek culture, and training new generations of citizens. The Greek city also contained temples to its gods. Worship of the city's deities was a civic duty, since the well-being of the city depended on the favor of the gods. Civic and religious life were closely related, so shrines were found in gymnasia, theaters, and elsewhere.

To spread Hellenism, Alexander and his successors built new cities, restructured and chartered old ones on the Greek model, and organized clusters of towns as a city. Not known for their modesty, they often named the cities after themselves. Alexander named many cities after himself including the most enduring and influential city that he founded, Alexandria in Egypt, which survives even today. The Ptolemies made it a showplace of Hellenistic culture and education. During the Hellenistic period it was the world's most important intellectual center, and during the early Roman period, Alexandria, Rome, and Antioch were the three most important cities of the empire.

Hellenism

The Hellenistic period was initiated by the conquests of Alexander the Great and ended with the Roman conquest of the eastern Mediterranean. *Hellenism* refers to the spread of the Greek language and Greek cultural and political forms throughout the eastern Mediterranean and the Near East during that time. This resulted in an interaction between Greek and local cultures that formed a new cultural reality, neither simply Greek nor local.

SYNCRETISM—A MIX OF CULTURES

A useful analogy for understanding Hellenism and its resultant mixture of cultures is British colonial control of India. Colonial control affected India deeply, and English became an important language for the country. But India did not become England by any stretch of the imagination. Similarly, the regions under Hellenistic political control changed considerably, but they did not simply become Greece.

The trickle of interaction between Greece and lands under Persian rule before Alexander became a flood after his conquests. Although Alexander believed in the superiority of Greek culture, he was somewhat open to other cultures. Indeed, Greeks for a long time had been fascinated with the cultures they discovered through their traders and mercenaries. There was also philosophical justification for being open to other cultures. The Stoics, an important philosophical school, held up the ideal of the cosmopolis (from the Greek *kosmos,* meaning "world," and *polis,* meaning "city"). They thought of the whole world as a single city and of all people as inhabitants of this city. But in practice this ideal was based on the conviction of the superiority of Greek culture and Greek institutions. To unify the world, Alexander had to make it Greek. This made the Hellenistic empires potentially more dangerous to local cultures than any previous empire, something the Jews were soon to learn.

But cultural influence did not run in just one direction. Greek culture was inevitably influenced by the foreign cultures onto which it was grafted. Alexander himself encouraged the interaction between different cultures. He actively promoted contact between his soldiers and the conquered peoples. He himself married a foreign princess, and he encouraged his troops to wed foreign women. Persians became leaders in his army, bodyguards, and members of his court. He even roused the resentment of some of his subordinates by taking on the trappings of the Persian emperor. After Alexander's time, local areas sometimes accepted, sometimes resisted Greek influence. When the local peoples accepted Greek ways, these were always mixed with local influences. Thus Hellenism looked different in Egypt than in Judea, different in Judea than in Asia Minor.

Scholars call mixing of cultures syncretism. *Syncretism* means the interaction between cultures and ideas to create a new entity. For example, present-day Jewish and Christian notions of God combine Israelite and Greek elements. A God intimately involved with a specific group of people whose history constitutes "salvation history" is biblical. An unchanging and impassive God, the unmoved mover, comes from Greek philosophers. Such mixing of Greek and biblical notions characterized Judaism in the Hellenistic period.

Greek culture was most influential in cities, but there were degrees of influence even here. Hellenism was less apparent among the lower than the upper classes, and there might be different attitudes toward Hellenism within the upper classes themselves. Hellenization was strongest where trade and other sorts of interaction were greatest, and was less apparent in isolated mountain towns in Asia Minor or parts of the highlands of Judea. So a poor peasant in the Palestinian countryside might speak little or no Greek and would certainly not have read Plato or Aristotle or been trained in a gymnasium. The upper classes of Jerusalem, on the other hand, might well know Greek and adopt Greek ways.

To speak to one another, humans need a common language. Once this is in place, mutual influence on every level can occur. And once a single language becomes dominant, it is in the interest of everyone who wishes to be part of the larger world to learn it. The official language in the vast area now ruled by Macedonians and Greeks was Greek, so native peoples had a powerful incentive to learn it. An added motivation was the possibility of advancing socially through education. Of course, not everyone born in the Hellenistic world could advance economically, politically, and socially. Ancient society was marked by stability and hierarchy, and social mobility was fairly rare as compared with the modern world. Still, avenues to higher levels of society were wider and more traveled in the Hellenistic period than previously. Since the Hellenistic empires shared strong cultural similarities, particularly in the major cities, culture was to some degree international. "Greek" no longer necessarily referred to nationality but to culture. A "Greek" was now one who spoke Greek and was immersed in Hellenistic culture. Geographical and social mobility for such Greeks was easier because of the large number of places where Greek was spoken and Greek culture understood.

ALIENATION

We are familiar with the concept of culture shock. It can occur when a person moves from one culture into another or when one's familiar culture is besieged by new and challenging ideas, values, and institutions. It can be felt by the newly arrived immigrant, by the American who moves from a small town to a large city, or by those who see the land of their birth undergoing demographic changes. Although some embrace such changes, others are threatened by them. A negative reaction can, even today, express itself in religious terms. It certainly did in the Hellenistic world.

Peoples previously ruled by their own kings or by a Persian government with no interest in cultural hegemony now found themselves confronted by an active and vigorous cultural imperialism. Greek-style cities were springing up all over the eastern Mediterranean and the Near East. Greek was heard everywhere. One's religion and worldview now had to reckon with a great variety of other religions and worldviews. Many reacted to the emerging international culture with apprehension and even hostility. But even those opposed to Hellenism often found themselves influenced by it over time.

As life became more complex and as politics were determined by enormous empires often at war with each other, it seemed that control of individual and national life no longer rested with local powers. Economic pressure increased as native populations financed the Hellenistic wars through taxes. Wars periodically disrupted economic activity. Fate, elevated to the status of a goddess in Greece and Rome, became important as a force in people's lives. Astrology was popular because, if you could not control your fate, you might as well know what it is. Local cultures that had religious worldviews in which their gods supported native leaders experienced a degree of what has been called *cognitive dissonance*—that is, a disconnect between their beliefs and the actual state of the world. For example, Jews might ask why they no longer had a king, since God promised David that one of his descendants would always be on the throne of Israel (2 Sam 7:16). To deal with such issues, some religions developed elaborate systems and mythologies in which superhuman evil forces were at work in historical events. Hope was generated through apocalyptic or messianic expectations. Philosophy and religion changed to meet the new challenges and furnished ways for people to survive the overturning of their worlds.

The Parthenon, located on the Acropolis in Athens, built in the fifth century B.C.E. The Parthenon was the temple of the goddess Athena and was a major symbol of Greek culture.

HELLENISTIC PHILOSOPHY

There were schools in the ancient world devoted to the teachings of each of the great philosophers—Plato (Platonism), Aristotle (Aristotelianism or Peripateticism), Zeno (Stoicism), and Diogenes (Cynicism)—and in the spirit of the Hellenistic age, they influenced one another. The schools contributed to Hellenistic culture, especially since they were engaged not just in metaphysical speculation but in discussions of the good life and how to live, what might be called ethics. Their concepts influenced religious groups as well, and we can trace Stoic and Platonic influence among hellenized Jews and then among Christians. A brief sketch of Platonic and Stoic thought will therefore prove fruitful.

Plato (427–347 B.C.E.) and the school of thought that originated with him, Platonism, considered the human person as divided into body and soul, the soul being trapped in the body as in a prison. The goal was to escape the body. This was possible, to some extent, even in this life by looking beyond the world of appearance and change and meditating on what is good, true, and beautiful. At death, the soul was released from the body and ascended to pure ideal realms above. Plato also spoke of the existence of spiritual beings called demons. At a minimum, Plato contributed to Hellenistic conceptions of the dualistic nature of the universe (divided into the material, changing world accessible to sense perceptions, and the ideal, unchanging world accessible to the intellect), the body-soul dichotomy, mystical meditation, and the belief in spirits.

Stoicism contributed the idea of the cosmopolis, the "global village" so to speak, where all people are brothers and sisters. This ideal was imperfectly fulfilled in Hellenistic culture itself. Stoics conceived of the universe analogous to a human person, with body and soul, but they thought of the soul as material of a finer sort than the body. What others might call God they called the world soul or Logos (Greek for "word," "mind," "reason"). The rational element of the universe ordered and held everything together. Thus, the Stoics were pantheists, believing in the unity and divinity of the universe. They saw conventional religion as an allegorical expression of the relation of humanity to the one Logos, and so they favored religious practices and mythologies but interpreted them allegorically. Each human mind was a particular instance of the world soul coming to consciousness, and when a human died, his or her soul would return to the world soul. Since all humans were related in this way, they were all equal, all brothers and sisters, and so should love one another. For the Stoics, happiness consisted of conforming with one's nature. They felt that one should not make one's happiness depend upon what one could not have, and so they aimed at not desiring what they could not have.

HELLENISTIC RELIGION

Luther Martin looks at Hellenistic religions from the point of view of three "strategies of existence." The first is piety. "Piety, then, designates the traditional system of conventional practices concerning the home and family and, by extension, those practices which surround and are part of being at home in one's world under the rule of a family of gods" (p. 11). This strategy supports the social system. It is public and accessible to all. Such would be a fair characterization of the religion of Ezra and Nehemiah, for example, or the civic religion of the Greek cities. The second strategy is mystery. For those engaged in this strategy, the order of the world was not apparent, and one needed to establish a special relationship with some god or goddess for protection. The third strategy is gnosis. In this view, one needed special, esoteric knowledge in order to be saved from a world that was evil. This knowledge could come through special revelations or through enlightened teachers. A given religion, such as Judaism, could have various expressions that fit into each of these strategies. An important issue for religions in the Hellenistic era is how they changed and how they remained the same. Judaism of the Hellenistic era was not identical with any of its past expressions. It was slowly changed by the Hellenistic world. Still, it had much in common with those past expressions.

Many Hellenistic religions thrived both in their lands of origin and in foreign lands. The Jews had important communities in Babylonia, Egypt, Asia Minor, Greece, and even Rome. They were a substantial community in Alexandria. Jews living outside the homeland are collectively called the *Diaspora*. A common characteristic of religions in their land of origin was resistance to Hellenism through nationalistic or messianic movements (see Eddy). Native cultures emphasized their ancient pasts, sometimes reviving old forms, languages, texts, and practices in an effort to maintain their identities in the face of Hellenism. Apocalypticism (see ch. 4, below) arose during this period at least partially in response to the new circumstances created by Hellenism. This is not to say, however, that resistance was the only possible response to Hellenism. As we shall see, even in the Jewish homeland there were many Jews who welcomed Hellenism, and even the resisters were influenced by it. In the expressions of these religions outside the homeland, hellenization was sometimes more deeply embedded than in the homeland. Ancient religions translated their traditions into Greek and interpreted them for Hellenistic audiences. Reinterpretation of sacred texts used allegorical methods to build bridges between the texts and Hellenistic ideas and modes of thought.

For many religions of the ancient world before the Hellenistic period, humanity's task was to fit into the cosmic order. They were dominated by what Martin calls "piety." In the Hellenistic period, however, traditional ways of looking at the world were shaken, and the order of the universe was no longer so apparent to many, so "mystery" and "gnosis" became more important. Many experienced the world as threatening. Religions of individual salvation became more popular, and people looked to gods and goddesses for liberation from the evil world. Divinities sometimes seemed remote and had to be reached by mystical means. Voluntary religious associations for the worship of a specific deity became popular. Members paid dues, followed rules of behavior, and submitted to some authority. These associations created a sense of security in an unsure world and often met for meals to enhance a sense of community.

One special type of religious association was called a *mystery*. Mysteries were supposed to be kept secret, so information about them is limited. They focused on the individual. Each mystery originated in a specific locale but was not restricted to it. Through an initiation ceremony, a person gained close association with a god or goddess. Access to the divine was thus guaranteed, as well as divine protection in this life and the next.

The Hellenistic world was not, for the most part, monotheistic. True, Stoics could allegorically interpret the variety of divinities as expressions of the one Logos, and some philosophers challenged polytheism. And identifications were made between different divinities, so that Syrian deities could be seen as manifestations of Greek ones, for example. Nonetheless, most people believed that there were many divine beings and that it was a wise idea to stay on the good side of as many as might affect one's well-being. It is therefore not surprising that Jewish insistence on worship of Yahweh alone was perceived at times as strange and perhaps even antisocial. Service to the gods was a civic duty, and in the Diaspora, Jewish refusal to participate in worship of city gods could be interpreted as hostile to the political order. Jews were not always seen in this way, but such an interpretation could surface when there were other reasons for conflict between Jews and non-Jews.

Diaspora Judaism

It was once conventional to make an absolute distinction between Diaspora and Palestinian Judaism. Supposedly, Diaspora Jews were completely hellenized, while Palestinian Jews were resistant to hellenization. But this view has been disproved by recent study, which shows that Palestinian Jews were indeed exposed to Hellenism and were changed by it, as evidenced in their writings, inscriptions, institutions, and so on. Still, there were differences between Palestinian Jewish communities and those in the Diaspora. A few words about Diaspora Judaism will provide some background for our discussion of Palestinian Jews.

In the Diaspora, Jews were in the minority. In Judea, they were the majority. In the Diaspora, Jews spoke Greek as their native tongue. In Judea, the language was primarily Aramaic, or perhaps in some cases Hebrew, though some Greek also was spoken. Even peasants and artisans may have had enough Greek to carry on trade and basic interaction with Greek speakers. Contrasts between Diaspora and homeland suggest that although Jews in both locations were hellenized, hellenization was more widespread and deeper in the Diaspora than in Judea, with exceptions. The bulk of Jewish literature presenting Judaism in Hellenistic literary forms and philosophical concepts comes from the Diaspora.

We have already mentioned a sizeable and important Jewish community in Alexandria. One of its members was the famous Philo of Alexandria, who lived from the end of the first century B.C.E. to the middle of the first century C.E. He left behind an extensive body of writings, in which he uses philosophy to interpret Scripture. We also have fragments of retellings of biblical stories in Greek dramatic and epic forms (see *OTP*; Collins; Barclay). But the intellectual, artistic, and cultural interaction between Judaism and its Hellenistic environment was not limited to the Diaspora. Major sources for the first century C.E. are the writings of a priest from Jerusalem named Josephus, who saw himself as an intermediary between his fellow Jews and the wider Hellenistic world.

A crucial accomplishment of Diaspora Jews was the translation of their sacred writings from Hebrew and Aramaic into Greek. Jewish legend preserved in Philo, Josephus, and a text called the *Letter of Aristeas* says that Ptolemy II Philadelphus (ruled 282–246 B.C.E.) wished to make the library of Alexandria the greatest in the world, and so he planned to include the Jewish Scriptures in it. One version says that Ptolemy brought seventy-two Torah scholars from Judea to translate the Hebrew Bible into Greek. They finished their task in precisely seventy-two days. The Greek version of the Bible that they completed is called the Septuagint, from the Latin word for "seventy." Philo adds that the translators, working separately, miraculously agreed on every word of the translation. He takes this to indicate the divine origin of the translation; the point is that the Greek version was as inspired as the original Hebrew. This was important for Diaspora Jews whose native language was Greek. It gave them direct access to the sacred word.

Despite the miraculous elements of the legends about the Septuagint, most scholars accept that such Greek translations began to be produced in the third century B.C.E. in the Diaspora, probably Egypt. The original translation perhaps covered only the first five books of the Bible. Other books were translated over the next couple of centuries.

JEWS IN THE HOMELAND IN THE HELLENISTIC PERIOD

THE SOURCES

Specific events often assume a larger profile in the minds of the "little guys" of history than they do in the estimation of the elites. Alexander's conquest of Judea was cataclysmic for Judea's inhabitants, but for Alexander it was only one relatively small step in his subjection of the East. Our sources for this period derive not from accounts of Alexander's exploits but from the Jews themselves, mainly 1 and 2 Maccabees. Fortunately, they are in the form of histories, and so they are generous with their supply of names, dates, and events (perhaps too generous, since they sometimes make for rather dense reading). The two works agree on many facts, and both were written by loyal Jews. But they also differ in important ways.

Two other literary sources originated in second-century B.C.E. Judea—
Daniel and the *Animal Apocalypse,* both apocalypses written around 165
B.C.E. (the next chapter will discuss these works). The first-century C.E. Jewish historian Josephus discusses the period, but since most of what he says derives from 1 and 2 Maccabees, he does not provide much independent
information. As we shall see in chapter 5, other Jewish writings from the second century, particularly some of those written or used by the community
behind the Dead Sea scrolls, also help to illumine this period.

ISRAEL UNDER GREEK RULE

During the third century B.C.E., Judea was part of the Ptolemaic Empire. The Ptolemies inherited the centralized system of ancient Egypt, in
which everything belonged to the pharaoh and everything was controlled
from the capital. The Ptolemies adopted this system and made bureaucratic
control even tighter than that of the pharaohs. Taxation was heavy.

The Seleucid king Antiochus III finally managed to wrest Judea from
the Ptolemies in 200 B.C.E. He was called "the Great" because he regained
much of the territory his predecessors had lost over the years. The shift to
Seleucid rule was to have earthshaking consequences for the Jews. But the rising power of Rome was to tarnish Antiochus's successes. The Romans defeated Antiochus III in western Asia Minor in 190 B.C.E. and ordered the
Seleucids out of Asia Minor.

When Antiochus III captured Jerusalem, he granted its inhabitants the
right to live according to their ancestral laws, embodied in the Torah. His
grant continued what had been the case under the Ptolemies as well—the
Jews were allowed to live by Torah insofar as this did not interfere with foreign policy or taxation. In 175 B.C.E., a new king arose, Antiochus IV
Epiphanes. "Epiphanes" is a title meaning "God manifest." At this time, a
Jewish party favoring hellenization was influential in Jerusalem. It consisted
of some priests and members of the upper class. Tensions started to build between hellenizers and more conservative inhabitants of Jerusalem and Judea,
and Antiochus IV figured he could resolve the conflict by outlawing Judaism.
This led to open revolt, led by Mattathias and his five sons, who were priests.
Mattathias died early in the revolt, and his son Judah assumed command.
Judah was called "Maccabee," meaning "hammer," probably because of his
military successes. During the next decades the Maccabees, the name by
which all the brothers are known, won first religious and then political independence from the Seleucids and established an independent Jewish kingdom. The Maccabees, once established as the rulers of Judea, were called the
Hasmoneans after one of their ancestors.

Important Terms

Diaspora: Jews living outside the land of Israel
Hasmoneans: Dynastic name of the Maccabean family when it assumed power
Hellenistic reform: An attempt by Jewish priests in Jerusalem to adapt to Hellenism and to make Jerusalem a Hellenistic city
Maccabees: Five brothers of a priestly family who revolted against the Seleucids
Ptolemies: Hellenistic dynasty ruling from Alexandria in Egypt
Seleucids: Hellenistic dynasty ruling from Antioch in Syria

THE VERSION OF EVENTS IN 2 MACCABEES

God defends his temple. Those who would attack it do so at their peril unless for some reason God lets them do so. This is a basic theme in 2 Maccabees. God defends the temple both through supernatural means and through the Maccabees.

Second Maccabees tells us of events from the high priesthood of Onias III, which began around 190 B.C.E., up to the Jews' defeat of the Syrian general Nicanor in 161 B.C.E. It condenses a five-volume work by Jason of Cyrene (in north Africa), a Jew of the Diaspora (note his Greek name). Both the original work and the condensation were written in Greek. Jason wrote toward the end of the second century, and so the condensation belongs somewhere in the first century B.C.E. Second Maccabees interprets history theologically. The author tells of supernatural events such as the appearance of angels who fight God's enemies. The book is more detailed and probably more accurate than 1 Maccabees regarding the events leading to the Jewish revolt against Antiochus IV.

SOCIAL CONFLICT AND TEMPLE IDEOLOGY

Second Maccabees 3:1 paints a picture of the idyllic harmony that existed before the troubles under Antiochus: "The holy city was inhabited in unbroken peace and the laws were strictly observed because of the piety of the high priest Onias and his hatred of wickedness." Here is the ideal. The high priest is devoted to the Torah, and the result is peace. Then comes trouble: "But a man named Simon, of the tribe of Benjamin, who had been made captain of the temple, had a disagreement with the high priest about the administration of the city market" (3:4). We are not sure what the precise duties of a captain of the temple were, but the Greek word implies some sort of oversight of the temple's activities. Simon's disagreement with Onias III is about financial matters.

Because Simon does not prevail, he sets about stirring up trouble for
Onias. He goes to the Seleucids and reveals that there is a lot of money in the
temple. The temple was, among other things, a financial institution. Because
of the wealth that flowed to it from tithes, contributions, and the temple tax,
it had substantial funds of its own. It also served as a secure bank for the
upper class. The Seleucids were in chronic need of money, and they periodically raided temple funds throughout the empire. Simon hopes his report
will ingratiate him to the Seleucids. The king sends his representative
Heliodorus to seize the money. When he arrives, the place is in an uproar.
Onias pleads with Heliodorus not to confiscate the funds: "He [Onias] said
that it was utterly impossible that wrong should be done to those people who
had trusted in the holiness of the place and in the sanctity and inviolability of
the temple that is honored throughout the whole world" (3:12).

When Heliodorus comes to the temple to take its money, angels appear,
who beat him to within an inch of his life. The point is clear: "They recognized clearly the sovereign power of God" (3:28). The city is overjoyed, but
Onias is too prudent to get carried away. He does not want to provoke
Antiochus, and so he offers a sacrifice of atonement for Heliodorus, who is
cured. Then Heliodorus proclaims God's power. It is frequent in such stories
that the enemy, the one who attacked Israel or God or the temple, becomes a
witness to God's power and sovereignty:

> Then Heliodorus offered sacrifice to the Lord and made very great vows to the
> Savior of his life, and having bidden Onias farewell, he marched off with his
> forces to the king. He bore testimony to all concerning the deeds of the su-
> preme God, which he had seen with his own eyes. (3:35–36)

When he returns to the king, the king asks him whom he would suggest
sending on another such mission. Heliodorus's response shows a touch of
irony:

> When the king asked Heliodorus what sort of person would be suitable to send
> on another mission to Jerusalem, he replied, "If you have any enemy or plotter
> against your government, send him there, for you will get him back thoroughly
> flogged, if he survives at all; for there is certainly some power of God about the
> place. For he who has his dwelling in heaven watches over that place himself
> and brings it aid, and he strikes and destroys those who come to do it injury."
> (3:37–39)

THE HELLENISTIC REFORM

In 175 B.C.E., Antiochus IV Epiphanes comes to the throne. This
marks the beginning of a catastrophic time for Judean Jews. According to

2 Maccabees, it starts when Jason, Onias's brother, wants more aggressive hellenization of Judea and usurps his brother's position by making King Antiochus an offer he cannot refuse.

> When Seleucus died and Antiochus, who was called Epiphanes, succeeded to the kingdom, Jason the brother of Onias obtained the high priesthood by corruption, promising the king at an interview three hundred sixty talents of silver, and from another source of revenue eighty talents. In addition to this he promised to pay one hundred fifty more if permission were given to establish by his authority a gymnasium and a body of youth for it, and to enroll the people of Jerusalem as citizens of Antioch. When the king assented and Jason came to office, he at once shifted his compatriots over to the Greek way of life.

> He set aside the existing royal concessions to the Jews, secured through John the father of Eupolemus, who went on the mission to establish friendship and alliance with the Romans; and he destroyed the lawful ways of living and introduced new customs contrary to the law. He took delight in establishing a gymnasium right under the citadel, and he induced the noblest of the young men to wear the Greek hat. There was such an extreme of hellenization and increase in the adoption of foreign ways because of the surpassing wickedness of Jason, who was ungodly and no true high priest, that the priests were no longer intent upon their service at the altar. Despising the sanctuary and neglecting the sacrifices, they hurried to take part in the unlawful proceedings in the wrestling arena after the signal for the discus-throwing, disdaining the honors prized by their ancestors and putting the highest value upon Greek forms of prestige. For this reason heavy disaster overtook them, and those whose ways of living they admired and wished to imitate completely became their enemies and punished them. It is no light thing to show irreverence to the divine laws—a fact that later events will make clear. (4:7–17)

Israel's high priest was to serve for life. Jason's appointment departs from this practice. Jason (his Greek name perhaps indicates his sympathies) ousts his brother by paying Antiochus for the office. In other Hellenistic religions, there were periodic changes of priests. Wealthy persons paid for the honor of being priest for a time. Antiochus does what was normal in other Hellenistic contexts, but it does not fit the Jewish context. He does, however, appoint a Jew, and one who is of a high-priestly family.

Jason and his allies aim to make Jerusalem a Greek city. As in any Greek city, only land-owning male inhabitants will be citizens. The gymnasium trained young men to assume citizenship. Accordingly, Jason applies for permission to establish "a gymnasium and a body of youth for it" (4:9). Jerusalem's establishment as a full-fledged Greek city means that it needs a new name, and since Antiochus is its official founder, the city is named after him.

The new citizens are enrolled as "citizens of Antioch." Jerusalem already has the institution of "elders," which consists of the heads of the leading families. It is probably these men who will become the city council.

The stage is set for the shifting of Jason's countrymen over to the "Greek way of life." "He set aside the existing royal concessions to the Jews." That is, permission given to the Jews by Antiochus III to live by their ancestral laws (Torah) is abrogated so that Jason can modify the Law where necessary to accommodate Hellenistic elements, or as the text has it, to introduce "new customs contrary to the law." Conservatives are bound to take offence.

Jason immediately sets about transforming Jerusalem. To add insult to injury, he locates the gymnasium "right under the citadel," right near the temple itself. Since Greek religious rites would be part of gymnasium activity, we can imagine the horror of many Jews at this new development. Further, young men may compete in the gymnasium naked (the word "gymnasium" comes from the Greek word for "naked," *gymnos*). Nakedness offended Jewish sensibilities. However, 2 Maccabees does not mention nakedness as an issue.

The passage reports that many youth of the upper class wear the "Greek hat." The author's shock at this seems almost silly unless we call to mind the universal importance of such cultural symbols. Dress is important in every society, more so in traditional societies. The appearance of jeans on youth around the world some time ago signified American influence. Wearing a suit and tie to a job interview signals respect. Orthodox Jewish men can often be identified by their black clothing, black hats, beards, and so on. Clothing carries a message. So our author, in taking offense at the Greek hat, is really pointing out something quite significant.

The author is particularly upset that the priests have been caught up in the wave of hellenization. The priests who live and serve at Jerusalem are members of Judea's upper classes. They have the most contact with the larger world and the most to gain from expanded contacts. Young priests accept hellenization happily and join the Greek games in the gymnasium.

The passage ends with what is really the theme of the book: "It is no light thing to show irreverence to the divine laws—a fact that later events will make clear" (4:17). Here the author states his conclusions beforehand. Readers know that anyone who opposes God will pay.

THE MOTIVES OF THE HELLENISTIC REFORMERS

The hellenizers probably did not think that they were abandoning their ancestral way of life. They did not stop worshiping God, nor did they introduce Greek rites into the temple or cease sacrificing. They did change some customs, but Judaism had always adapted to new situations, and the hellenizers may have considered this simply keeping up with the times. In their eyes, the financial and political advantages of hellenization outweighed the consequences of losing a few outmoded customs, as a verse from 1 Maccabees suggests: "In those days certain renegades came out from Israel and misled many, saying, 'Let us go and make a covenant with the Gentiles around us, for since we separated from them many disasters have come upon us' " (1 Macc 1:11). That these people were "lawless" (without Torah) is a judgment that was perhaps not shared by all. We cannot assume that they themselves thought that they were lawless. But as far as 2 Maccabees is concerned, the hellenizers violate Torah. Writing after the events, the author has the benefit of hindsight. He knows civil war, persecution by Antiochus, and war against the Greeks will follow. In 2 Macc 4:16–17, these tragedies are seen as punishment for disobeying Torah.

ANTIOCHUS IV BRUTALIZES JERUSALEM

Three years after Jason becomes high priest, Menelaus, brother of the Simon who was captain of the temple and made trouble for Onias III, outbids Jason for the high priesthood. Ironically, Jason falls victim to his own tactics and withdraws to the safety of Transjordan. Meanwhile, Antiochus IV marches to Egypt, which he always wanted to bring under his control (2 Macc 5:1). When a false rumor circulates that Antiochus has been killed, Jason thinks this is his chance to make a comeback (5:5). He attacks Jerusalem and besieges Menelaus in fortifications near the temple. In Egypt, Antiochus meets that old nemesis of Seleucid ambition, the Romans. His expansion into Egypt is against Roman interests. The Romans demand that Antiochus leave Egypt, and he has to obey. Hearing that Judea is in revolt, Antiochus attacks Jerusalem mercilessly, so that "there was a massacre of young and old, destruction of boys, women, and children, and slaughter of young girls and infants" (5:13). Antiochus invades the temple and steals its treasures (5:15–16). He has killed two birds with one stone: he has subdued Judea and obtained spoils to finance his considerable expenditures.

But why did God not act? After all, when Heliodorus tried to plunder the temple, he almost paid with his life. The text explains why Antiochus got away with it:

> Antiochus was elated in spirit, and did not perceive that the Lord was angered for a little while because of the sins of those who lived in the city, and that this was the reason he was disregarding the holy place. But if it had not happened that they were involved in many sins, this man would have been flogged and turned back from his rash act as soon as he came forward, just as Heliodorus

had been, whom King Seleucus sent to inspect the treasury. But the Lord did not choose the nation for the sake of the holy place, but the place for the sake of the nation. Therefore the place itself shared in the misfortunes that befell the nation and afterward participated in its benefits; and what was forsaken in the wrath of the Almighty was restored again in all its glory when the great Lord became reconciled. (5:17–20)

This explanation is in the Deuteronomistic tradition, which claims that evildoing brings punishment and doing good brings reward. When God is angry at Israel, he allows the temple to suffer. When God is reconciled to Israel, the temple is restored.

Antiochus leaves Judea, but things do not improve. The king leaves behind officials of "barbarous" character who oppress the people. Then he sends another army to Jerusalem to attack the people deceitfully. He establishes a permanent garrison in Jerusalem in a fortification on what was called the "city of David," a hill just to the south of the temple.

Then they fortified the city of David with a great strong wall and strong towers, and it became their citadel [Greek: *akra*]. They stationed there a sinful people, men who were renegades [Greek: *andras paranomous,* which can mean "lawless men" or "men who act contrary to the law"]. These strengthened their position; they stored up arms and food, and collecting the spoils of Jerusalem they stored them there, and became a great menace. (1 Macc 1:33–35)

The foreign troops stationed in Jerusalem are a hateful presence to the Jews. Their demands for food and other supplies are heavy, and they bring with them their own gods and religions, abhorrent to strict observers of Torah. Their presence defiles the sanctuary (1:36–40). The situation is deteriorating, particularly for Jews who interpret the Torah strictly and conservatively. The *akra* is a thorn in Israel's side for the next two decades.

RELIGIOUS PERSECUTION

The next step in this drama is almost unbelievable. Antiochus IV decided to outlaw Judaism completely and to punish brutally anyone who opposed him. Israel had certainly been through terrible times before. It had been conquered and reconquered, and had lost its land, its sacred city, and its temple. It had even been exiled. But never before had it been forbidden to be itself, to practice Torah. Now this inconceivable event took place.

Exactly why Antiochus tried to stamp out Judaism is debated. Some depict him as mentally unstable, others as a champion of hellenization, others as anxious to unite his diverse empire. But we must remember that the hellenization of Jerusalem was initiated by upper-class Jews, not by Antiochus, and that the struggle over hellenization was also a power struggle between upper-class factions. Political unrest in Judea was a problem to Antiochus. He needed a stable and loyal Judea, for the area could too easily slip through his fingers. He knew that part of what the Jews were fighting over was Torah, and may have thought that if he eliminated Torah, this would help pacify Judea. He may even have thought that his Jewish allies, those who wanted hellenization in the first place, would approve. After all, he was only carrying hellenization through to its logical conclusion.

Antiochus's terrible decrees appear in 2 Macc 6:1–11 and 1 Macc 1:41–64. Copies of the Torah are destroyed, possessors of the Torah are put to death, circumcision is forbidden, Jewish sacrifices and rites are prohibited, altars are built to foreign gods, Jews are forced to participate in idolatrous sacrifices, and they are compelled to eat pork, an unclean meat. An altar to Olympian Zeus is set up in the temple, and sacrifices are offered on it. This is truly a horrific day for Israel.

Chapters 6 and 7 of 2 Maccabees tell of martyrs for the cause of Torah. In chapter 6, an old man named Eleazar refuses to eat pork and is savagely tortured and killed. In chapter 7, a mother and her seven sons undergo the same fate in front of Antiochus. The sons make speeches addressed to Antiochus, their persecutor, before they die. They attribute Israel's suffering to its own sins. Nonetheless, they say that if they die loyal to Torah, God will raise them to new life. The idea of resurrection is something we have not encountered so far. There is not much idea of an afterlife in the Hebrew Bible. Sheol, where all humans go after death, is a place of rather shadowy existence. It certainly would not correspond to an afterlife with rewards and punishments—heaven and hell—with which we are familiar from later periods. But now resurrection makes its appearance as part of the Jewish argument against Antiochus. Resurrection appears as a solution to the age-old problem of why the wicked prosper and the righteous suffer. The second son says to Antiochus, "You accursed wretch, you dismiss us from this present life, but the King of the universe will raise us up to an everlasting renewal of life, because we have died for his laws" (7:9). The sons are confident that God will punish Antiochus for his cruelty. Explaining injustice by positing an afterlife where all get their just deserts becomes more prevalent as time goes on, especially in apocalyptic literature (see ch. 4, below).

The seventh son predicts that God will punish Antiochus, and asks God to have mercy on Israel "and through me and my brothers to bring to an end the wrath of the Almighty that has justly fallen on our whole nation" (7:38). He is saying that the brothers' suffering might be instrumental in causing God to be merciful. The efficacy of the sufferings of one or a few for the whole people first appears in the Suffering Servant song of Second Isaiah (Isa

52:13–53:12). Here the context is different, but the idea of vicarious suffering is similar.

The story of the martyrdoms of Eleazar, the mother, and her seven sons was so powerful that it became the subject of another book shortly afterward, 4 Maccabees. This book defends Judaism brilliantly in a Hellenistic context. Philosophers often remarked on the importance of having reason control the passions. Fourth Maccabees shows that the martyrs refused to yield to their passions, such as fear of pain and desire for comfort, and instead followed reason, which the author equates with God's law.

Second Maccabees tells of God's punishment of Antiochus: the king goes to Persia to rob more temples, and there he is struck with a terrible illness. Like Heliodorus when he was beaten by the angels, Antiochus acknowledges the power of God: "It is right to be subject to God; mortals should not think they are equal to God" (2 Macc 9:12; perhaps a reference to his royal title Epiphanes, "God manifest"). To make up for his sins, he vows to free Jerusalem, to make its citizens equal to those of Athens, and so on. But it is too late and he dies. "So the murderer and blasphemer, having endured the more intense suffering, such as he had inflicted on others, came to the end of his life by a most pitiable fate, among the mountains in a strange land" (9:28). The author goes on to tell of the purification and rededication of the temple and of further conflicts between the Jews and Seleucids. The book ends on a note of victory, with Judah Maccabee conquering the Seleucid general Nicanor. "And from that time the city has been in the possession of the Hebrews. So I will here end my story" (15:37).

THE VERSION OF EVENTS IN 1 MACCABEES

The main character of 2 Maccabees is, in a sense, the temple itself. It is perfectly able to defend itself, as Heliodorus and Antiochus could attest, to their chagrin. Thus the book features supernatural events. First Maccabees, on the other hand, focuses more on the Maccabees themselves as great heroes, chosen by God to liberate Jerusalem and then to rule. When people and leaders acclaim the Hasmonean Simon as high priest in 1 Macc 14:27–45, they simply recognize God's will; it is the climax and point of the book. The book serves as a legitimation of Hasmonean rule.

First Maccabees was written around 100 B.C.E. It begins its story with Alexander the Great but within ten verses gets to its real interest, the reign of Antiochus IV of Syria in 175 B.C.E. and its effects on Israel. Most of the book deals with the leadership of four men—three of the Maccabee brothers (Judah, Jonathan, Simon) and Simon's son, John Hyrcanus I. (Although the books of the Maccabees call the first brother mentioned here Judas, they do so because they are written in Greek, where it would be unusual for a man's name to end in -*ah*.) The original language of 1 Maccabees was probably Hebrew, but it survives in Greek and Latin. It is strongly pro-Hasmonean and was written to prove that Hasmonean leadership was divinely ordained and that God chose the Maccabees to liberate Israel from Seleucid oppression. The book does not narrate the supernatural events found in 2 Maccabees, and so it sounds realistic to modern ears.

MATTATHIAS BEGINS THE REVOLT

After telling of Antiochus's persecution, 1 Maccabees introduces the Maccabees in chapter 2. They decide that, given how dangerous things are in Jerusalem, they should withdraw to their hometown of Modein, twenty miles northwest. The family consists of an elderly priest, Mattathias, and his five sons. They are grief-stricken at the desecration of Jerusalem and the Torah. They are dedicated to Torah and will resist the evil plans of Antiochus IV. But they cannot escape the king's decree even in Modein. When royal agents come to Modein to enforce the decree that all Jews offer idolatrous sacrifice, Mattathias refuses. Not only that, he kills another Jew who complies with the demand. Mattathias, his sons, and their sympathizers then flee to the wilderness. Other pious Jews also flee to the wilderness but are trapped by the king's men, who attack them on the Sabbath. They are too pious to break the Sabbath by fighting and so are slaughtered. Hearing of this, Mattathias and his followers suspend Torah's Sabbath regulations to fight the enemy (2:39–41). Breaking Torah might seem a contradiction of their cause, but the Maccabees find they must break the Torah to save the Torah.

> And Mattathias and his friends went around and tore down the altars; they forcibly circumcised all the uncircumcised boys that they found within the borders of Israel. They hunted down the arrogant, and the work prospered in their hands. They rescued the law out of the hands of the Gentiles and kings, and they never let the sinner gain the upper hand. (2:45–48)

Circumcision is a sign of the covenant between God and Israel. It is also a sign that makes the Jews a distinct people. Some adult Jews, seeking accommodation with the hellenized world, remove the marks of circumcision (1:15; see 1 Cor 7:18). Such a step is especially desirable for those who participate naked in the Greek games.

Mattathias delivers a speech as he is about to die. He reminds his audience of Israel's heroes who trusted in God and were rewarded for it. Such reviews of Israel's past to make a specific point are common in Jewish literature (e.g., Dan 9, Ezra 9, Ps 105). One figure is of particular significance for the Hasmoneans: "Phinehas our ancestor, because he was deeply zealous, received the covenant of everlasting priesthood" (2:54). While Moses was still alive, and before Israel had entered the promised land, the priest Phinehas killed an Israelite, Zimri, son of Salu, because he had married a foreigner, contrary to God's command (Num 25:6–15). His action put to an end a plague God had sent to punish them for having sexual relations with foreign women and worshipping their god. As a reward, God said, "I hereby grant him [Phinehas] my covenant of peace. It shall be for him and for his descendants after him a covenant of perpetual priesthood, because he was jealous for his God, and made atonement for the Israelites" (Num 25:12–13). In 1 Macc 2:26, the narrator compares to Phinehas's action Mattathias's killing of the Jew who was to sacrifice to the foreign god: "Thus he [Mattathias] burned with zeal for the law, as Phinehas did against Zimri son of Salu." The basis of the Hasmoneans' claim to high priesthood and later to kingship is zeal for the Law, zeal which extends even to being willing to die or kill for Torah.

JUDAH MACCABEE REDEDICATES THE SANCTUARY

Mattathias's son Judah now assumes the mantle of his late father and carries the resistance to a new level through guerilla warfare. His exploits are depicted as holy war, in which God fights with the righteous and makes victory possible. Eventually Judah enters Jerusalem in 164 B.C.E. and takes control of most of it. He fails, however, to penetrate the *akra,* the Seleucid fortress in the city of David.

Judah's first act in Jerusalem is to purify and rededicate the sanctuary. The temple is what makes Jerusalem the holy city, and it symbolizes God's presence with Israel. Rededication of the temple carries the message that God's power is intact and God remains faithful to Israel.

> He [Judah] chose blameless priests devoted to the law, and they cleansed the sanctuary and removed the defiled stones to an unclean place. They deliberated what to do about the altar of burnt offering, which had been profaned. And they thought it best to tear it down, so that it would not be a lasting shame to them that the Gentiles had defiled it. So they tore down the altar, and stored the stones in a convenient place on the temple hill until a prophet should come to tell what to do with them. Then they took unhewn stones, as the law directs, and built a new altar like the former one. (1 Macc 4:42–47)

The passage features cultic, priestly language. The use of the temple precincts for unholy, foreign rites makes it unfit for the worship of God. Purification is necessary (the purification theme is also stressed in 2 Macc 10). The very stones are contaminated and must be replaced. But stones that were previously dedicated to sacred use must not be simply discarded. At a loss about what to do with the old altar, they decide to wait for God's instructions, which they expect to come through a future prophet. No prophet is available to the Hasmoneans, reflecting a belief that prophecy ceased sometime shortly after the exile. Chapter 9 makes this belief explicit: "So there was great distress in Israel, such as had not been since the time that prophets ceased to appear among them" (9:27). The Jewish historian Josephus expresses the same view two centuries later. But 1 Maccabees expects a renewal of prophecy at some unspecified future date. Later, Christians were to see the outbreaking of the spirit of prophecy as a sign of the end time (see Acts 2).

"Then Judas and his brothers and all the assembly of Israel determined that every year at that season the days of dedication of the altar should be observed with joy and gladness for eight days" (4:59). The Hebrew word for "dedication" is *hanukkah*. The feast instituted by the Maccabees is still celebrated by Jews today. "When the Gentiles all around heard that the altar had been rebuilt and the sanctuary dedicated as it was before, they became very angry, and they determined to destroy the descendants of Jacob who lived among them" (5:1–2). Jews live not only in Judea but also throughout Galilee, Samaria, and Transjordan, in the same cities and areas as Gentiles. When the Seleucid Empire decides to stamp out Judaism, some of the Jews' Gentile neighbors may hope to profit somehow. They may also fear that if the Jews manage to win their independence, the fate of Gentiles in the region will be uncertain.

SELEUCID POWER STRUGGLES AND THE MACCABEES

Around the time of the dedication of the altar, Antiochus IV dies (6:8–16; 164 B.C.E.), and the Seleucids face what is to be a common situation: rival claimants to the Seleucid throne offer the Hasmoneans rewards for helping them. The Jews, in turn, manipulate the warring Seleucids to their own advantage by striking deals with one and then another of them (1 Macc 6–15). When Antiochus IV dies, his nine-year-old son is next in line for the throne. Since the child is too young to rule, Antiochus's general Lysias is the child's regent (i.e., he temporarily rules in his place). He besieges Jerusalem (6:18–54). But when he hears that before his death Antiochus had appointed another man, Philip, as regent and that Philip is trying to seize the government (6:14–15), Lysias has no time to waste on the siege. He quickly settles with Judah by granting religious freedom (6:55–59), but before he leaves, he breaks down Jerusalem's defenses. He then sets out to deal with Philip, whom he defeats.

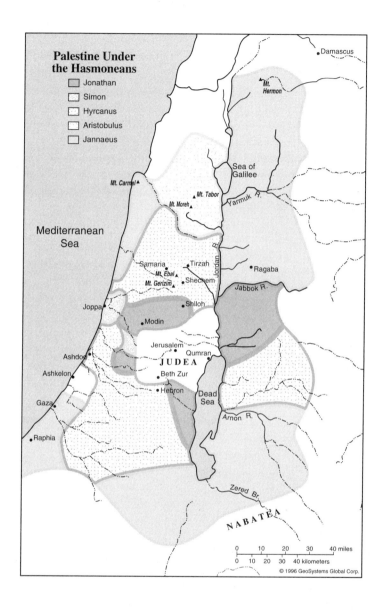

Palestine Under
the Hasmoneans

- Jonathan
- Simon
- Hyrcanus
- Aristobulus
- Jannaeus

Damascus

Mt.
Hermon

Sea of
Galilee

Mt. Carmel

Mt. Tabor

Mt. Moreh

Yarmuk R.

Mediterranean
Sea

Samaria   Tirzah
    Mt. Ebal
Mt. Gerizim   Shechem

Ragaba

Jordan R.

Jabbok R.

Joppa

Shiloh

Modin

Jerusalem
    Qumran
JUDEA
    Beth Zur

Ashdod

Ashkelon

Hebron

Dead
Sea

Gaza

Arnon R.

Raphia

Zered Br.

NABATEA

0   10   20   30   40 miles

0   10   20   30   40 kilometers

© 1996 GeoSystems Global Corp.

A new pretender to the throne, Demetrius I, son of Seleucus IV, kills both Antiochus's young son and Lysias (7:1–4). Demetrius sends Alcimus, a legitimate Jewish priest, to assume the high priesthood. Many Jews, satisfied that religious freedom is restored and a legitimate priest is appointed high priest, consider the war over. But Judah is not so easily satisfied. Legitimate priest or not, Alcimus serves the Seleucids, who have proven themselves untrustworthy. Besides, Judah may now desire, beyond simply religious freedom, independence. In any case, he takes to the wilderness again (7:23–24). He is now taking on not only the Seleucids but also Jews who have made peace with them. Alcimus travels to the king to ask for help against Judah (7:25), who takes the opportunity to recapture Jerusalem, defeating the general, Nicanor, who is sent against him (7:39–50). He then sends an emissary to Rome and negotiates a treaty of friendship with the rising power (8:1–32), although Rome gives the Maccabees no direct help. Judah later meets his end in battle (9:18; 161 B.C.E.).

Another Maccabean brother, Jonathan, now becomes leader (9:28–31). When Demetrius finds himself confronted with yet another royal pretender, Alexander, he turns to Jonathan for help. Jonathan agrees, but then switches his allegiance to Alexander and is rewarded with the high priesthood (10:15–21; 152 B.C.E.). He later loses his life through Seleucid treachery (12:48; 142 B.C.E.).

ACCLAMATION OF THE HASMONEANS

When Jonathan dies, his brother Simon, the last of the Maccabean brothers (John and Eleazar died in battle), comes to power (1 Macc 13). Under Simon the Jews finally take the *akra* (13:49–52; 142 B.C.E.). With the Seleucid garrison in Jerusalem gone, the Jews are more truly independent than before. Later the Jewish leaders and people solemnly declare that Simon is high priest and leader of the nation (140 B.C.E.). This declaration gives the nation's official confirmation to the honors the Maccabees gained by force and diplomacy from the Seleucids. The following are excerpts from the declaration:

> Since wars often occurred in the country, Simon son of Mattathias, a priest of the sons of Joarib, and his brothers, exposed themselves to danger and resisted the enemies of their nation, in order that their sanctuary and the law might be preserved; and they brought great glory to their nation. . . .

> In view of these things King Demetrius confirmed him in the high priesthood, made him one of his Friends, and paid him high honors. For he had heard that the Jews were addressed by the Romans as friends and allies and brothers, and that the Romans had received the envoys of Simon with honor.

> The Jews and their priests have resolved that Simon should be their leader and high priest forever, until a trustworthy prophet should arise, and that he should be governor over them and that he should take charge of the sanctuary and appoint officials over its tasks and over the country and the weapons and the strongholds, and that he should take charge of the sanctuary, and that he should be obeyed by all, and that all contracts in the country should be written in his name, and that he should be clothed in purple and wear gold. (14:29, 38–43)

Though not of the line of Zadok, the Hasmoneans become the established high priestly family. And though not of the line of David, they exercise what amounts to royal power (they wear purple and gold, signs of royalty, and contracts are dated in their names); several decades later they explicitly assume the royal title as well.

HASMONEAN RULE

Simon was assassinated in 134 B.C.E., and his son, John Hyrcanus I, took the throne (ruled 134–104 B.C.E.). Under John, the Jewish state looked more and more like a monarchy, although the title of king was still not used. His son Aristobulus I (ruled 104–103 B.C.E.) was the first to use the title of king. John and his successors expanded the empire through conquest. By the time of Alexander Jannaeus (ruled 103–76 B.C.E.), it reached a size comparable to that of the united kingdom under David and Solomon. Among John's conquests was Samaria, the area situated between Judea to the south and Galilee to the north, former home to the northern kingdom of Israel. In 128 B.C.E., he destroyed the temple the Samaritans built on Mount Gerizim at the beginning of the Hellenistic era. This won him no friends in Samaria and worsened already hostile relations between Jerusalem and Samaria. Another significant conquest was Idumea, south of Judea. There John followed the Hasmonean practice of forcibly circumcising the conquered peoples. Despite this inauspicious beginning, Judaism took root in Idumea (perhaps it already had roots there), and Idumeans began to play an important role in Judean politics. Herod the Great, for example, was an Idumean.

Maccabean Leaders and Hasmonean Rulers (All Dates Are B.C.E.)	
165–161	Judah Maccabee
161–142	Jonathan (first to take title of high priest)
142–134	Simon
134–104	John Hyrcanus I
104–103	Aristobulus I (first to take title of king)
103–76	King Alexander Jannaeus
76–67	Queen Alexandra Salome
76–67	Hyrcanus II (high priest, not king)
67–63	Aristobulus II (high priest, king)
63–40	Hyrcanus II (high priest, not king)

Ironically, as time went by, the Hasmoneans, who began by fighting the hellenizers to defend temple and Torah, became hellenizers themselves. Their Greek names are noteworthy—Hyrcanus, Alexander, Alexandra, Aristobulus, Antigonus. At the same time, those with Greek names also carried Hebrew names—Judah, Jonathan, Simon, John, Jannaeus, and Salome. The Jews were now part of the Hellenistic world, for good or ill. The conquests of Alexander changed Judaism forever.

The Hasmoneans hired Greek mercenaries, and their courts acquired the trappings of a typical Hellenistic court. Parts of the population began to resent their rule. Some opposition may have come from the Hasmoneans' hellenizing tendencies. Other opposition may have been due to simple power struggles. Still more resentment may have resulted from the burdens that a monarchical system imposed. Finally, there may have been those who disapproved of the Hasmonean assumption of royal titles, high priestly honors, or both. A terrible civil war broke out in the reign of Alexander Jannaeus, a brutal leader and an expansionist. Much of the population opposed him and even appealed to the Seleucids for help in 88 B.C.E. But many switched their allegiance back to the Jewish king when they realized that events might result in the reestablishment of Seleucid rule, not a pleasant prospect. Alexander won the war and viciously punished those who rebelled against him.

EXCURSUS: THE HASIDIM

A group called the Hasideans appears in 1 and 2 Maccabees. Their name probably derives from the Hebrew word *hasidim,* meaning "pious ones." It is the same word that lies behind today's designation of some Jews as "Hasidic." Some scholars picture the Hasideans as a coherent group—either scribes or with a scribal contingent—who were respected warriors allied with the Maccabees for a time but who then accepted the Seleucid terms of religious freedom in return for stopping the revolt. According to this view, the group later reacted negatively to the rule of the Hasmoneans and split into two factions, both opposed to Hasmonean rule—the Pharisees and the Essenes. This hypothesis is attractive, especially because it explains the origin of the Pharisees and Essenes, but there is not enough evidence to prove or disprove it.

In 1 Macc 2:42, it is reported that joining the Maccabees in the wilderness was "a company of Hasideans, mighty warriors of Israel, all who offered themselves willingly for the law." The Hasideans appear again in 7:12–14, where they are willing to make peace with Alcimus, the Jewish priest sent by the Seleucids to rule for them. The policy of the Hasideans differs from that of the Maccabees because the latter continue the struggle when Alcimus comes. Perhaps the Hasideans were content with religious freedom, whereas the Maccabees wanted full independence. The Hasideans are associated with scribes.

The final reference to the Hasideans occurs in 2 Macc 14:6. Alcimus says to King Demetrius, "Those of the Jews who are called Hasideans, whose leader is Judas Maccabeus, are keeping up war and stirring up sedition, and will not let the kingdom attain tranquility." If indeed the authors of 1 and 2 Maccabees are using the term to designate a single group, this statement is incompatible with what is known of the Hasideans from 1 Maccabees. There the Hasideans acted contrary to the wishes of Judah Maccabee and made peace with Alcimus (1 Macc 7:13). Judah was not their leader.

What is clear is that under the Maccabees, a coalition was formed between various segments of the population to battle what was perceived as an attack on the divinely ordained Jewish way of life. When the immediate threat was overcome, the coalition dissolved and a number of groups emerged in Jewish society, not all of whom were satisfied with the new state of affairs in the Hasmonean state.

THE BOOK OF SIRACH

Sirach is a fascinating book written in Jerusalem at the beginning of the second century B.C.E. It is the work of a well-to-do scribe and intellectual who was deeply involved in the religion and culture of his day. Exercising the rare skills of reading and writing in a mostly illiterate world, scribes belonged to all strata of society. Our scribe's name was Joshua ben Sira (*ben* being the Hebrew for "son"; the Greek form of his name is Jesus son of Sirach). We shall limit our attention to what Sirach says about scribes and scribal activity in Jerusalem just before the Hellenistic reform.

Sirach paints a portrait of the ideal scribe, whom he considers the wise man. Torah is seen as the height of wisdom, and divine inspiration is the root of all wisdom. But Sirach shows a basic openness to the larger Hellenistic world. A scribe does not neglect foreign wisdom but, rather, is open to knowledge wherever it may be found (Sir 39:4). Sirach thus occupies a middle ground between the Jewish hellenizers, such as Jason the high priest, and the groups who allied against the hellenizing reformers. The very fact that ben Sira writes in his own name (50:27) is unusual in a Jewish context but common in a Hellenistic one.

The book's prologue was written by Sirach's grandson, who brought the book to Egypt and translated it into Greek. The grandson begins:

Many great teachings have been given to us through the Law and the Prophets and the others that followed them, and for these we should praise Israel for instruction and wisdom. Now, those who read the scriptures must not only themselves understand them, but must also as lovers of learning be able through the spoken and written word to help the outsiders. So my grandfather Jesus, who had devoted himself especially to the reading of the Law and the Prophets and the other books of our ancestors, and had acquired considerable proficiency in them, was himself also led to write something pertaining to instruction and wisdom, so that by becoming familiar also with his book those who love learning might make even greater progress in living according to the law.

The prologue claims that true learning lies in the study of God's Torah, although ben Sira's learning also draws on sources outside Scripture, as is common in wisdom works. His vocation is to study and to write and teach about the wisdom that comes from God.

Beginning a long description of the ideal scribe in 38:24–39:11, Sirach writes, "The wisdom of the scribe depends on the opportunity of leisure; only the one who has little business can become wise" (38:24). Other occupations take up too much time for study. Sirach mentions the occupations of farmer, craftsman, blacksmith, and potter, all of whom are consumed with perfecting the skills required for their jobs and with being productive. He acknowledges their integral role in society, but they have no place in the upper echelons of the social structure. In fact, the vast majority of them were illiterate.

> All these rely on their hands,
>   and all are skillful in their own work.
> Without them no city can be inhabited,
>   and wherever they live, they will not go hungry.
> Yet they are not sought out for the council of the people,
>   nor do they attain eminence in the public assembly.
> They do not sit in the judge's seat,
>   nor do they understand the decisions of the courts;
> they cannot expound discipline or judgment,
>   and they are not found among the rulers.
> But they maintain the fabric of the world,
>   and their concern is for the exercise of their trade. (38:31–34)

There follows a contrasting passage on the wise scribe:

> How different is the one who devotes himself
>   to the study of the law of the Most High!
> He seeks out the wisdom of all the ancients,

and is concerned with prophecies;
he preserves the sayings of the famous
   and penetrates the subtleties of parables;
he seeks out the hidden meanings of proverbs
   and is at home with the obscurities of parables.
He serves among the great
   and appears before rulers;
he travels in foreign lands
   and learns what is good and evil in the human lot.
He sets his heart to rise early
   to seek the Lord who made him,
   and to petition the Most High;
he opens his mouth in prayer
   and asks pardon for his sins.
If the great Lord is willing,
   he will be filled with the spirit of understanding;
he will pour forth words of wisdom of his own
   and give thanks to the Lord in prayer.
The Lord will direct his counsel and knowledge,
   as he meditates on his mysteries.
He will show the wisdom of what he has learned,
   and will glory in the law of the Lord's covenant. (38:34–39:8)

This passage illustrates the centrality of religious motivations in scribal activity. The first duty of the scribe is to study "the law of the Most High." The "wisdom of all the ancients" and "prophecies" probably mean Scripture. Inspiration direct from God is central to scribal activity. The scribe rises early to pray, to open his heart to God, and to await inspiration. The true scribe will "glory in the law of the Lord's covenant." The upper-class scribe also preserves and passes on the teachings of notable men, just as the Hellenistic philosophical schools preserve and transmit the teachings of Plato, Aristotle, and Zeno. Parables and proverbs are typical wisdom forms, and meditation on them is a common activity of wisdom teachers.

Scribes are also involved in politics. They are eminent in the public assembly, and the people follow their advice (39:33). They act as judges because they know the Law. They perform their duties among "the great," and they "appear before rulers" (39:4). Scribes are advisors to the ruling class, and some even belong to that class. They are well educated, knowledgeable in international affairs, understanding of the bureaucracy, and learned in history. Ideally, they have traveled "in foreign lands," and they examine foreign wisdom for the fruit it could bear domestically. The ideal of foreign travel and appreciation of foreign wisdom was typical of the Hellenistic age.

Ben Sira is sympathetic to the government headed by the high priest. He ends his book with a lengthy praise of Israel's illustrious ("pious" in the Hebrew and Syriac manuscripts) men. (Compare this with Mattathias's speech in 1 Macc 2, which turns to the heroes of Israel's past for examples of those zealous for the Torah.) The list culminates in an encomium on Simon son of Onias, the high priest. Ben Sira lists Simon's accomplishments, including the repair and fortification of the temple, the digging of a cistern for water, and the reinforcement of Jerusalem's defenses. Then he glories in Simon's cultic role and its significance for Israel:

> How glorious he [Simon] was, surrounded by the people,
>> as he came out of the house of the curtain [the inner sanctuary].
> Like the morning star among the clouds,
>> like the full moon at the festal season;
> like the sun shining on the temple of the Most High,
>> like the rainbow gleaming in splendid clouds. . . .
> When he put on his glorious robe
>> and clothed himself in perfect splendor,
> when he went up to the holy altar,
>> he made the court of the sanctuary glorious. . . .
> Then Simon came down and raised his hands
>> over the whole congregation of Israelites,
> to pronounce the blessing of the Lord with his lips,
>> and to glory in his name;
> and they bowed down in worship a second time,
>> to receive the blessing from the Most High. (50:5–7, 11, 20–21)

Here we see the temple service through the eyes of a participant. We can appreciate the impression made by the worship, especially on pilgrims from afar. The power of the liturgy and the glory of the high priest come across forcefully. The high priest was the conduit for God's blessing and so occupied a crucial role in Israel's life. Political power and religious function coincided.

CONCLUSION

Alexander's conquests changed the world forever. Jews now faced political and cultural imperialism that challenged not only their political institutions but also their religious faith and customs. They reacted in varied ways to the new situation. In the Diaspora, most Jews became part of the Hellenistic world without losing their identity. In Jerusalem, tension developed between Jews who wanted to turn the city into a Greek polis and those who thought that this would violate Torah. When Antiochus thought he could resolve the situation by simply outlawing Judaism, he discovered his mistake the hard way. Within the space of several decades, the Jews had won not only religious freedom but political independence under the leadership of the priestly Hasmoneans. But this independence was to last only until the next conquerors arrived, the Romans.

SELECT BIBLIOGRAPHY

Attridge, Harold. "Jewish Historiography." *EJMI* 311–43.

Barclay, John M. G. *Jews in the Mediterranean Diaspora: From Alexander to Trajan (323 BCE - 117 CE)*. Edinburgh: T&T Clark, 1996.

Bartlett, John R. *1 Maccabees*. Sheffield, England: Sheffield Academic Press, 1998.

———, ed. *Jews in the Hellenistic and Roman Cities*. New York: Routledge, 2002.

Betz, Hans Dieter. "Hellenism." *ABD* 3:127–35.

Bickerman, Elias. *From Ezra to the Last of the Maccabees: Foundations of Post-biblical Judaism*. New York: Schocken, 1962.

———. *The God of the Maccabees: Studies on the Meaning and Origin of the Maccabean Revolt*. Leiden: Brill, 1979.

Coggins, Richard J. *Sirach*. Sheffield, England: Sheffield Academic Press, 1998.

Collins, John J. *Between Athens and Jerusalem: Jewish Identity in the Hellenistic Diaspora*. Grand Rapids, Mich.: Eerdmans, 2000.

———. *Jewish Wisdom in the Hellenistic Age*. Louisville: Westminster John Knox, 1997.

Cumont, Franz. *Astrology and Religion among the Greeks and Romans*. New York: Dover, 1960.

Davies, Philip R. "Hasidim in the Maccabean Period." *JSJ* 28 (1977): 127–40.

DeSilva, David A. *4 Maccabees*. Sheffield, England: Sheffield Academic Press, 1998.

Doran, Robert. *Temple Propaganda: The Purpose and Character of 2 Maccabees*. Washington, D.C.: Catholic Biblical Association of America, 1981.

Eddy, Samuel K. *The King is Dead: Studies in the Near Eastern Resistance to Hellenism, 334–31 B.C.* Lincoln: University of Nebraska Press, 1961.

Farmer, W. R. *Maccabees, Zealots, and Josephus: An Inquiry into Jewish Nationalism in the Greco-Roman Period*. New York: Columbia University Press, 1973.

Feldman, Louis. *Jew and Gentile in the Ancient World: Attitudes and Interactions from Alexander to Justinian.* Princeton: Princeton University Press, 1993.

Goldstein, Jonathan. "Jewish Acceptance and Rejection of Hellenism." Pages 64-87 in *Aspects of Judaism in the Graeco-Roman Period.* Vol 2 of *Jewish and Christian Self-Definition.* Edited by E. P. Sanders, A. I. Baumgarten, and Alan Mendelson. Philadelphia: Fortress, 1981.

———. *I Maccabees: A New Translation with Introduction and Commentary.* AB 41. Garden City, N.Y.: Doubleday, 1976.

———. *II Maccabees: A New Translation with Introduction and Commentary.* AB 41A. Garden City, N.Y.: Doubleday, 1983.

Goodman, Martin, ed. *Jews in a Graeco-Roman World.* Oxford: Clarendon Press, 1998.

Green, Peter. *Alexander to Actium: The Hellenistic Age.* London: Thames & Hudson, 1990.

Gruen, Erich S. *Heritage and Hellenism: The Reinvention of Jewish Tradition.* Berkeley: University of California Press, 1998.

Hadas, Moses. *Hellenistic Culture: Fusion and Diffusion.* New York: Norton, 1972.

Harrington, Daniel J. *The Maccabean Revolt: Anatomy of a Biblical Revolution.* Wilmington: Michael Glazier, 1988.

———. "The Wisdom of the Scribe according to Ben Sira." *IFAJ* 181–88.

Hengel, Martin. *Judaism and Hellenism: Studies in Their Encounter in Palestine during the Early Hellenistic Period.* 2 vols. Philadelphia: Fortress, 1974.

Jones, A. H. M. *The Greek City: From Alexander to Justinian.* Oxford: Clarendon Press, 1940.

Kampen, John. *The Hasideans and the Origin of Pharisaism: A Study on First and Second Maccabees.* Atlanta: Scholars Press, 1988.

Lieberman, Saul. *Greek in Jewish Palestine.* New York: Jewish Theological Seminary, 1942.

———. *Hellenism in Jewish Palestine.* New York: Jewish Theological Seminary, 1950.

Martin, Luther H. *Hellenistic Religions: An Introduction.* Oxford: Oxford University Press, 1987.

Meyers, Eric M., and A. Thomas Kraabel. "Archeology, Iconography, and Nonliterary Remains." *EJMI* 175–210.

Peters, F. E. *The Harvest of Hellenism: A History of the Near East from Alexander the Great to the Triumph of Christianity.* New York: Simon & Schuster, 1970.

Rajak, Tessa. "Hasmonean Dynasty." *ABD* 3:67–76.

Sanders, E. P. "The Covenant as a Soteriological Category and the Nature of Salvation in Palestinian and Hellenistic Judaism." Pages 11–44 in *Jews, Greeks, and Christians: Studies in Honor of W. D. Davies.* Edited by R. Hamerton-Kelly and R. Scroggs. Leiden: Brill, 1976.

Sievers, Joseph. *The Hasmoneans and Their Supporters: From Mattathias to the Death of John Hyrcanus I.* Atlanta: Scholars Press, 1990.

Skehan, P. W., and Alexander DiLella. *The Wisdom of Ben Sira.* AB 39. Garden City, N.Y.: Doubleday, 1987.

Smith, Jonathan Z. "Hellenistic Cults in the Hellenistic Period." *HR* 11 (1971): 236–49.

———. "Hellenistic Religions." Pages 925–27 in vol. 18 of *The Encyclopedia Britannica: Macropedia.* 15th ed. Chicago: University of Chicago Press, 1985.

Stone, Michael. "Hellenism and the Diaspora." *SSV* 87–98.

Tarn, W. W., and G. T. Griffith. *Hellenistic Civilization.* 3d ed. New York: New American Library, 1961.

Tcherikover, Victor. *Hellenistic Civilization and the Jews.* New York: Atheneum, 1977.

CHAPTER 4

APOCALYPTICISM

PRIMARY READINGS: Daniel ◆ *1 Enoch* 1–36; 72–108

In this chapter, we enter a strange world. Journeys to the underworld and to the heavens, appearances of strange, otherworldly beasts, visions that are all but incomprehensible—we find all of these and more in apocalypses. We may be tempted to throw up our hands in frustration at such bizarre literature. But then we would miss an opportunity to grasp a key element of ancient Jewish and Christian thought. A large proportion of Jewish and Christian literature written between the third century B.C.E. and the second century C.E., a five-hundred-year stretch, either is in the form of apocalypses or contains apocalyptic features. Although only two biblical books are apocalypses, Daniel and Revelation, the New Testament is saturated with apocalyptic ideas and imagery, while much Jewish literature in the Hellenistic and Roman periods was heavily influenced by apocalypticism. Jesus and Paul used apocalyptic ideas and images.

Because apocalypticism is dissatisfied with the state of the world and expects God to intervene soon to change things radically, earlier scholarship thought that it was the worldview of fringe groups, groups persecuted by the broader society. Many scholars imagined small "conventicles," communities apart from, and opposed to, the world at large. More recent scholarship has successfully challenged these assumptions, noting that apocalypticism is a scribal phenomenon, requiring, for example, extensive knowledge of traditions and the ability to read and write, traits characteristic of the upper classes, especially the scribal classes, of ancient society. We now realize that dissatisfaction with the world is possible even among the ruling classes, in the face of foreign domination, for instance, where political reality clashes with native traditions. Alternatively, upper-class factions might resent the greater power or authority of other more powerful factions within their own society.

TERMINOLOGY

The terminology used in this chapter may be confusing at first. The most important terms are these: 1) *apocalypse* denotes a literary genre (type); 2) *apocalypticism* is a worldview common to apocalypses; 3) the adjective *apocalyptic* means "typical of apocalypses or apocalypticism." It is still common for the word apocalyptic to be used as a noun, broadly denoting the entire complex of literary genre, worldview, and social movements associated with the apocalyptic worldview.

LITERARY GENRE: APOCALYPSE

Whenever we pick up a piece of literature, our first question is, What sort of literature is it? Our answer will determine how we read the text. We read histories differently than we do novels, newspaper articles differently than poetry, personal letters differently than term papers. We have certain expectations of a written text, and if it does not fit these expectations, we may toss it aside as not making sense.

There is little in the modern reading experience that prepares us for reading apocalypses. In 1979 a team of scholars published the following definition of the genre:

> A genre of revelatory literature with a narrative framework, in which a revelation is mediated by an otherworldly being to a human recipient, disclosing a transcendent reality which is both temporal, insofar as it envisages eschatological salvation, and spatial insofar as it involves another, supernatural world. (*AI* 5)

An apocalypse is first of all a story, a narrative. In the story, a human receives a revelation. The human is called a *seer* ("see-er") because he or she usually sees visions. What is seen is not self-explanatory but needs interpretation by a supernatural being, most often an angel. The temporal aspect of the revelation deals with the future, in which evil is punished and good rewarded. Most apocalypses see this future as short-term—it is coming soon. The revelation is also spatial because there is another space, a supernatural world, in which decisions are made and events happen that determine human history. One can understand what occurs in the human sphere only by knowing what is happening in the supernatural sphere.

Revelations in apocalypses contain information not generally available. It does not matter how much one reads Scripture, exercises sharp intellect, or prays to God. One cannot obtain this information by any means other than direct revelation. This makes it esoteric, that is, accessible only to few. Yet the information is crucial to humans because it concerns the criteria for the final judgment on humans, angels, and demons and because it reveals the course of history and its significance. Because right action depends on right knowledge, wisdom terminology ("wisdom," "the wise," "knowledge," "understanding") abounds in apocalypses. But apocalyptic wisdom is very different from the wisdom of Israel's wisdom tradition. In the latter, human reason applied to everyday life produces knowledge of how the world works and how humans should behave. In contrast, apocalyptic wisdom comes only through direct revelation. Because it is esoteric, the revelation is often called a "mystery" or a "secret." The very means of revelation points to the mysteriousness of the knowledge. The seer goes where others have not gone or sees visions others have not seen. He or she does not understand what is seen. A supernatural being must explain the vision. God is mysterious and remote.

Most apocalypses fall into one of two major types—those with an otherworldly journey and those with a review of history. Broadly speaking, the former type contains speculations about the workings of the universe. This is called *cosmological speculation,* from the Greek word *kosmos,* which denotes an ordered universe. Apocalypses with reviews of history tend to be less interested in the cosmos and more interested in history. Both types assume an intimate connection between the workings of the universe and the events of human history. So, to understand human history, one has to know secrets about the universe.

Almost every apocalypse is pseudonymous (an exception is the book of Revelation in the New Testament). *Pseudonymity* literally means "false name." The person whose name an apocalypse bears is usually not its real author but a prominent figure of the distant past. Pseudonymity makes the apocalypse persuasive, especially given the Hellenistic world's high regard for the past. It is very impressive when a revered hero from centuries past "predicts" the course of history accurately. But most predictions in apocalypses are actually *ex eventu*— that is, they were written after the events they pretend to predict, not before.

Some scholars think that the definition of a genre must specify the genre's function. In other words, we need to answer the question of why something is written. Adela Yarbro Collins explains the function of apocalypses. They are "intended to interpret present, earthly circumstances in light of the supernatural world and of the future, and to influence both the understanding and the behavior of the audience by means of divine authority" (*Early Christian,* 7). That is, apocalypses are really focused on the present. This is somewhat surprising, given the emphasis in apocalypses on past and future. But past and future comment on the present, and it is to address the present that the apocalyptist writes in the first place.

Apocalyptic elements occur in a wide range of Jewish and Christian literature, even in documents that are not apocalypses. The influence of apocalypticism and of the apocalyptic genre cannot be measured merely by a survey of apocalypses. For example, the community whose library was the collection of ancient texts now known as the Dead Sea Scrolls (see next chapter) did not produce apocalypses. Nonetheless it was apocalyptic in its worldview and orientation.

THE APOCALYPTIC WORLDVIEW

The word *eschatology* derives from the Greek word *eschaton,* which means "end" and refers here to the end of the world as presently constituted. Eschatology is the teaching about the eschaton. Scholars differ on how much emphasis to put on eschatology as an element of apocalypticism. Some do not see eschatology as integral to apocalypticism. They see the essence of apocalypticism to be esoteric revelation, and contend that not all apocalypses have an eschatological orientation. Still, all apocalypses contain some sort of eschatology, and for many of them their eschatology is central. We follow what has been the mainstream approach, which is to treat eschatology as important in apocalypticism and central to many apocalypses.

The most important distinguishing characteristic of apocalyptic eschatology is that it involves a transcendence of death. So it answers the age-old dilemma of why the good suffer and the wicked prosper. The answer is that all will get what they deserve but that rewards and punishments will come after death (postmortem).

Apocalypses that stress eschatology often contain the following elements, although not all elements are present in each apocalypse.

Common Features in Apocalypses

(1) urgent expectation of the end of earthly conditions in the immediate future; (2) the end as a cosmic catastrophe; (3) periodization and determinism; (4) activity of angels and demons; (5) new salvation, paradisal in character; (6) manifestation of the kingdom of God; (7) a mediator with royal functions; (8) the catchword "glory"; (9) dualism; (10) a final showdown between good and evil. (*Al* 12, following Koch for the first eight elements, 28–33)

THE END.   The world as presently known will end soon. Something is wrong with the world. The eschaton brings a close to what is bad in the world, and it brings about the reconstitution of things so that everything is as it should be. This can mean different things in different apocalypses—the passing away of the earth and the transfer of the righteous into heaven, the renewal of heaven and earth so that God's original intentions are fulfilled, a temporary messianic kingdom followed by a more radical consummation of history, and so on.

COSMIC CATASTROPHE. The entire universe is involved in the eschaton. Stars fall, the sun and moon stop giving light, and mountains melt, for the cosmos is closely tied to humanity's fate. This conviction is not peculiar to apocalypticism. In the creation stories of Genesis when Adam and Eve disobey God, God punishes both them and the earth (Gen 3:17). Most of this apocalyptic imagery derives from the Hebrew Bible. Consider, for example, the words of the prophet Joel: "The earth quakes before them, the heavens tremble. The sun and the moon are darkened, and the stars withdraw their shining" (Joel 2:10).

PERIODIZATION AND DETERMINISM. Many apocalypses divide history into a number of periods whose progression is foreordained by God and unchangeable. The number is often symbolic—seven, ten, or twelve, for example. The real author of a given apocalypse sees him- or herself as living at the end of the succession of periods, at "the end of times." *Determinism* means that God's plans cannot be changed. Repentance puts one on the right side of God when the end comes, but it will not prevent the end from coming.

ANGELS AND DEMONS. Angels and demons populate apocalypses. Such beings occupy a place in creation somewhere between God and humans. If God needs angelic intermediaries, God must be distant from humans. Evil is personified in supernatural beings—demons, or evil angels—often with a single demon at their head. The most famous leader is Satan. As mentioned earlier, his name in Hebrew, *satan,* means "accuser" or "adversary." Ideas about Satan changed over time. We probably associate him with the serpent in the garden of Eden in Genesis, but Genesis never mentions him. This association came later. (The Hebrew word can also describe a human being as an "adversary" in the Hebrew Bible.) Early traditions about Satan picture him as the prosecuting attorney in the heavenly courtroom (Zech 3; Job 1–2); his job is to accuse humans. By the late Second Temple period, the traditions have so developed that he has become totally evil, opposed to God, and leader of the demons. Various Satan-like figures earn this honor in other traditions—Beelzebul, Mastema, Shemihazah, Azazel, and so on.

NEW SALVATION.   "Salvation" is a noun, and its associated verb is "to save." A good synonym for this is "to rescue." "Rescue" implies that there is some bad situation to be rescued from. Christians often think of salvation as something that happens after death, perhaps rescue from life itself, from sin, or from hell. Before the Hellenistic period, salvation meant rectification of earthly wrongs, such as the overthrow of Israel's enemies and the setting up of an earthly kingdom in Jerusalem. For Second Isaiah (sixth century B.C.E.), for example, salvation means return from the Babylonian exile and rebuilding Jerusalem. But in the Hellenistic period, salvation can be on the other side of death. Apocalyptic salvation always includes transcendence of death, punishment of the wicked and rewarding of the righteous, and the banishment of all that is bad. The effect of this understanding on later Jewish and Christian belief is obvious. The new world anticipated in apocalypticism is paradisal— everything is as it should be. "Paradise" is from a Persian loanword used in the Septuagint to designate the garden of Eden. In the end, creation will be as God meant it to be, as it was in the garden of Eden. The end will be like the beginning.

KINGDOM OF GOD.   "Kingdom of God" means "God's rule." The Hebrew Bible often speaks of God as king (see, e.g., Ps 145). But humanity, supernatural creatures, and creation itself have not acted as if God is king. Evil powers have taken over God's creation. However, God's rule will be restored in the universe at the appropriate time. God's sovereignty is a major concern of apocalypses.

MEDIATOR.   The "mediator with royal functions" can be called a "messiah" *(mashiah)*, a title often applied to Israel's king. Christians took this mediator to be Jesus, who was then called Son of David, Messiah, and Son of God (all terms belonging to kings of the Davidic line). Because Christian scholars have paid special attention to elements of Judaism that were of interest to Christianity, it is often thought that Jewish apocalypticism was always messianic in the strict sense—that is, it involved a messiah. But this distorts the evidence. Messiahs are not always present in Jewish apocalypses.

GLORY.   The word "glory" recalls the terminology of the priestly writer in the Pentateuch, where it indicates the active and powerful presence of God. The word is frequent in apocalyptic literature, which speaks of the seer's access to the divine world, which is glorious, and of the divine becoming powerfully present to the world.

DUALISM. Apocalypticism is dualistic, that is, it divides the cosmos at all levels, natural and supernatural, into two opposing parts—God (or God's angel) against Satan, angels against demons, the righteous against the wicked—in order, ultimately, to explain the human world. The group that uses such language always considers itself to be the righteous, whereas those who oppose it, or, in some cases, *everyone* else, are numbered among the wicked. Apocalypses typically see the righteous as "chosen" by God, as the "elect."

THE FINAL SHOWDOWN. We noted above that there is an issue of sovereignty in apocalypticism. God may have lost control of his creation temporarily, but God will soon come to take it back. But the power of evil is real, and God's enemies are formidable. Apocalypticism believes in the supreme power of God, but God still must use this power to smash God's enemies, and this may take time. So some apocalypses envision a time of struggle between God and his enemies, during which there will be great distress in the world, both human and physical. The word "tribulation" and others like it characterize this time. Sometimes the phrase "messianic woes" is used, meaning that when the messiah comes (if a messiah is expected in the given system), there will be upheaval, trouble, and suffering, even for the righteous. Even where elements of battle are absent, the end time, a time of judgment, can be seen as a time of tribulation.

THE ORIGINS OF JEWISH APOCALYPTICISM

Was apocalypticism Jewish, or was it something that Jews took from the broader Hellenistic world? The question itself oversimplifies. Israel's religion, like most religions, was always in contact with other religions, and it was always being influenced by them; the Bible bears abundant witness to this. As we have seen, interaction between cultures accelerated during the Hellenistic period, and it was then that Jewish apocalypses made their appearance. Cultures in the Hellenistic world mixed native and foreign elements. Apocalypticism did appear outside Judaism during the Hellenistic era (see Eddy), but scholars have discerned Jewish roots for apocalypticism in Israel's wisdom and prophetic traditions. So we turn first to these Jewish traditions.

Like wisdom, apocalypticism sees the structure of the universe as intimately related to human life. Wisdom and apocalypticism share the idea that right understanding is required for right action. But wisdom thinks that understanding is accessible to human reason, while for apocalypticism special revelation is necessary. Interest in cosmology, shared by wisdom and apocalypticism, is not found in prophecy.

Prophecy and apocalypticism agree in being convinced that their messages come through direct revelation. Later prophets, such as Ezekiel and Zechariah, sound rather apocalyptic because they contain mysterious visions that are interpreted. Trips to heaven, common in apocalypses, remind us of the prophet Micaiah ben Imlah's journey to the heavenly council in 1 Kgs 22 and the prophet Isaiah's vision of God's throne (Isa 6). Like prophecy, apocalypticism thinks that God is about to make an appearance on the stage of human history. Both prophecy and apocalypticism expect this appearance to be awesome and spectacular. But prophecy does not expect cosmic transformation, as does apocalypticism, nor does it speak of the transcendence of death. The prophets expect divine punishment or reward to occur in this life. And prophets think that judgment can be averted by repentance. For apocalypticism, however, the end is coming no matter what people do.

Many elements of apocalypses and apocalypticism, therefore, come from Israel's own religious, symbolic, and literary heritage. We see many familiar things in new arrangements. This is hardly surprising; individuals and nations all draw on the past when facing new situations. But the precise constellation of features from Israel's heritage that we find in apocalypses has not been seen before. And there is one truly new element—the transcendence of death.

Among foreign influences, Persian writings of the Hellenistic period share a number of elements with Jewish apocalypses. The periodization of history, dualism, sufferings caused by eschatological battles, resurrection and judgment, the ascent of the soul, and good and evil supernatural forces are present in both bodies of writing. Jewish and Persian apocalyptic writings offer an explanation for, and a solution to, the foreign domination typical of the Hellenistic period (see Eddy). Furthermore, apocalyptic seers are similar to Babylonian wise men (VanderKam; Grayson). But it is perhaps simplistic to trace Jewish apocalypticism to Jewish roots, Persian or Mesopotamian roots, or a combination of the two. Rather, apocalypticism is an expression of one or several aspects of a general Hellenistic *Zeitgeist* (cultural climate).

> Several of the most prominent aspects of the apocalypses involved modifications of biblical tradition that are in accord with widespread ideas of the Hellenistic age: pseudepigraphy, periodization, *ex eventu* prophecy, heavenly journeys, interest in the heavenly world, judgment of the dead. In the earliest Jewish apocalypses these motifs are woven together with considerable originality, and indeed variety, into a composite structure that was distinctively Jewish but was also strikingly new, as over against the earlier biblical tradition. (*AI* 28)

Apocalypticism was therefore both a homegrown product and something that resulted from outside influences, as were many other aspects of Israel's religion.

THE NATURE OF APOCALYPTIC DISCOURSE

Apocalypses are full of strange images and events—fierce beasts combining animal and human traits, fiery and bottomless abysses, marvelous heavenly temples, cosmic struggles, and so on. Apocalyptic language is not simple and straightforward. The strangeness of apocalyptic discourse makes it hard to determine exactly what the images refer to and how they relate to specific historical situations. We modern readers cannot see what apocalypses are talking about, and so we hardly find them relevant to our lives and have trouble seeing how they can help us comprehend ancient Judaism and Christianity.

Apocalyptic images tend to hide what they refer to. Some scholars think that apocalypses are coded messages, meant to pass on information to insiders while concealing the message from others. According to this view, the code must be broken so as to translate apocalyptic images into intelligible language. Unquestionably, there are codes in apocalypses, since apocalypses themselves often supply detailed interpretations for some of their own visions. Scholarly research on each work must include discovering the situation it addresses and, where possible, finding some one-to-one correspondences between elements of the text and entities in the "real world." But this does not mean that the works were meant to hide information from hostile inquirers. Indeed, one wonders how many rulers would really be fooled if they were to stumble across an apocalypse written by a disgruntled subject.

There is a better way to think of apocalyptic language. Apocalypticism uses ancient traditions and mythologies in a symbolically expressive way. The end product is not geared simply to transmit information. Apocalyptic language is like both poetry and mythology. Just as a poem cannot be reduced to simple propositions without losing something essential, so an apocalypse cannot be reduced to the description of an historical situation. Apocalypses also incorporate mythic elements, and apocalyptists are myth producers. Ancient myths, narratives involving supernatural figures, are not simply fantasy but are the narrative expression of deeply held convictions, insights, and feelings about the universe and human experience. Myth is narrative metaphor used to express views and attitudes about realities that can be spoken of only metaphorically.

Apocalypses usually do not quote myths or biblical traditions directly, but they do allude to them. A range of associations, analogies, and resonances is set up, appealing to the most profound levels of thought and feeling. By taking narrative form, apocalypses implicate readers as only stories can. Readers or hearers experience fear, dread, hope, and exultation. Even in a world dominated by sin, they see and feel victory of good over evil, and of their own group over their oppressors. Apocalypses do not just supply new data; they reveal patterns in events, patterns with deep cultural roots, so as to provide a new way of experiencing the world.

Like myths, apocalypses contain basic patterns that can apply to many concrete situations. Fundamental themes such as good against evil, battles between the gods, divine kingship and sovereignty, struggles for order against chaos, renewal of the cosmos, and return to a primeval state are central to many apocalypses. Although each apocalypse was written in a specific situation that it addresses, the vagueness of its references and the primordial nature of its patterns make it both mysterious and applicable to many other analogous situations. The function of such applications is to persuade readers to see the world in a particular way and to interpret the events and persons in one's world as part of a larger drama. It helps one to map one's world, to know who is good and who is bad, and to be assured of one's own ultimate vindication and salvation, or at least to know how to reach that goal.

Among the many apocalypses, two are treated here—*1 Enoch* and the book of Daniel. The former consists of several originally independent apocalypses. The parts that date from the third and second centuries B.C.E. are examined in this chapter. (The *Parables of Enoch* [*1 En.* 37–71] are discussed in ch. 7.) (The translation of *1 Enoch* used here is my own adaptation of Charles's translation, found in *APOT.*)

THE ENOCH LITERATURE: A COMPILATION

First Enoch is a very long, complicated work. Indeed, it is really a collection of documents. Reading it from start to finish is not the best way to approach it, for it results in "overload" and confusion. It is better to read each of its individual documents separately before trying to see the collection as a whole. Scholars divide the book into five originally independent documents. But the story is even more complicated; several of these documents contain originally independent sections. Since the church in Ethiopia preserved *1 Enoch* (also called the *Ethiopic Book of Enoch*), the major manuscript is in Ethiopic. Fragments of the Greek from which the Ethiopic was translated survive, and extensive Aramaic fragments were found at Qumran (see next chapter).

Originally Independent Works Incorporated into *1 Enoch*

Book of the Watchers	*1 En.* 1–36	third century B.C.E.
Similitudes of Enoch	*1 En.* 37–71	first century C.E.
Astronomical Book	*1 En.* 72–82	third century B.C.E.
Book of Dreams	*1 En.* 83–90	second century B.C.E.
Epistle of Enoch	*1 En.* 91–108	second century B.C.E.

Like almost all apocalypses, *1 Enoch* is pseudonymous. We have seen that picking a fictitious author from a long ago time adds credibility to an apocalypse. But why Enoch? Apocalyptic writers chose their seers carefully to maximize the effect. What "credentials" of Enoch's would attract the real authors of the various apocalypses contained in *1 Enoch?*

Enoch lived in the seventh human generation, according to Gen 5. This makes him ancient indeed, and the number seven was thought to be special in the ancient world. (The book of Revelation is structured almost entirely in terms of the number seven.) Genesis 5:24 contains an obscure statement: "Enoch walked with God; then he was no more, because God took him." The ambiguity of this verse sparked speculation among ancient Jews. They interpreted Enoch's walking with God to be his righteousness (walking is an image for behavior in Judaism). The vague statements "he was no more, because God took him," combined with the fact that Enoch is the only human in the genealogy of Gen 5 who is not explicitly said to have died, were taken to mean that Enoch had ascended to heaven while still alive. It was then a short step to the idea that Enoch had traveled to heaven to receive apocalyptic secrets. Thus Enoch was the ideal seer.

THE *BOOK OF THE WATCHERS: 1 ENOCH* 1–36

The *Astronomical Book* (see below) and the *Book of the Watchers* are the two oldest extant apocalypses. They come from the third century B.C.E. The *Book of the Watchers* illustrates the features of an apocalypse so clearly that we shall analyze it at some length here. A "watcher" is an angel who watches in heaven, a sort of heavenly guard. Such angelic watchers also appear in the book of Daniel (4:13, 17, 23). The *Book of the Watchers* is in three parts: an introduction (chs. 1–5), the story of the watchers and of Enoch's heavenly ascent (chs. 6–16), and Enoch's cosmic journeys (chs. 17–36). The book shows signs of having been put together from several originally independent sources.

Chapters 1–5 introduce the *Book of the Watchers*. But since they stand at the beginning of *1 Enoch* as whole, they also introduce the entire compilation. The section begins, "The words of the blessing of Enoch, with which he blessed the elect and righteous, who will be living in the day of tribulation, when all the wicked and godless are to be removed" (1:1). These words echo those in Deuteronomy introducing Moses' final blessing on the Israelite tribes: "This is the blessing with which Moses, the man of God, blessed the Israelites before his death" (Deut 33:1). There is a deliberate parallel set up between Enoch and Moses. The author wants to enhance Enoch's dignity and stature by using language about him that is reminiscent of Moses.

First Enoch 1:1 sets an eschatological tone. Enoch's blessing is for those who live in the "day of tribulation," the time when the final battle between God and his enemies is to take place. On that day, the "wicked and godless are to be removed." This reflects typical apocalyptic dualism—humanity is divided into the wicked and the righteous.

The introduction continues,

> And he took up his parable and said—Enoch, a righteous man, whose eyes were opened by God, saw the vision of the Holy One in the heavens, which the angels showed me, and from them I heard everything, and from them I understood as I saw, but not for this generation, but for a remote one which is to come. (1:2)

Parable is a general term for figurative language. Enoch receives explanations of his visions through angels and comes to understand "everything." The ancient seer learns that the revelation is for a much later time. This supports the literary fiction that Enoch lived in primordial times but speaks of much later times. In reality, the real writer addresses his own situation, which he thinks is the time of "tribulation."

The rest of chapter 1 describes a theophany, an appearance of God:

> The Holy Great One will come forth from his dwelling, and the eternal God will tread upon the earth, on Mount Sinai, and appear from his camp, and appear in the strength of his might from the heaven of heavens. (1:3–4)

God appears as a mighty warrior, recalling holy-war imagery (see Deut 33:2). No one can resist God. Holiness and greatness are attributes of God prominent throughout *1 Enoch*. God is utterly above humans. In *1 En.* 1:3–4, God appears on Sinai. It is appropriate that God should decide to come to earth for the final judgment at the same spot where God came to earth to give Moses the Torah. God's true home is the "heaven of heavens." God's "camp" is military imagery.

Mountains and hills tremble and melt. Destruction falls upon the "ungodly," "but with the righteous he will make peace, and will protect the elect, and mercy shall be upon them" (1:8). The good are "righteous" (obedient to the divine will), and "elect" (God has chosen them). Both terms are common in apocalyptic texts and permeate *1 Enoch*. A heavenly army accompanies God: "And behold! he comes with ten thousand of his holy ones [angels] to execute judgment upon all, and to destroy the ungodly" (*1 En.* 1:9; see Deut 33:2; Dan 7:10). This is divine power at its most awesome.

Chapters 2–5 describe the order of heaven and earth. They are orderly because they obey God's will.

> Observe everything that takes place in the heaven, how they do not change their orbits, and observe the luminaries that are in the heaven, how they all rise and set in order each in its season, and do not transgress against their appointed order. Behold the earth, and give heed to the things that take place on it from first to last, how steadfast they are, how none of the things on earth change, but all of the works of God appear to you. (2:1–2)

Nature's order underscores God's greatness and might. The whole universe follows God's will. In contrast to the modern notion that the universe follows natural laws, Jewish apocalypses conceive of the universe as controlled by supernatural beings. Indeed, the ancients thought of many of the entities in the heavens as personal beings, known by moderns to be natural formations. In this passage, the heavenly luminaries (sun, moon, stars) are capable of obedience or disobedience to God's commands. This view of the universe is laid out more fully in the *Astronomical Book*. But the point of all this concerns humanity. The universe obeys God, but sinners are disobedient (5:3–4). They contrast with the universe.

Judgment is coming. The passage addresses the sinners, "For all of you sinners there shall be no salvation, but on you all shall abide a curse. But for the elect there shall be light and joy and peace, and they shall inherit the earth" (5:6–7). Again, this expresses social dualism—all of humanity is divided into the sinners and the elect. And things are not as they should be. The ones who possess the earth are not the righteous. When God comes, he will change this. Things will be as they should; the righteous will possess the earth. This promise echoes Ps 37:11: "The meek shall inherit the land." This promise is found in other Jewish eschatological scenarios, and it implies an earthly restoration. Jesus refers to this promise in a beatitude: "Blessed are the meek, for they will inherit the earth" (Matt 5:5). As we shall see in the next chapter, the eschatological community of Qumran applied Ps 37:11 to themselves. They saw themselves as the poor who would inherit the land.

Chapters 6–11 are a new section, dealing with the watchers. First we hear of their sins. The watchers' story probably grew out of the following cryptic passage in Genesis:

> When people began to multiply on the face of the ground, and daughters were born to them, the sons of God saw that they were fair; and they took wives for themselves of all that they chose. . . . The Nephilim were on the earth in those days—and also afterward—when the sons of God went in to the daughters of humans, who bore children to them. These were the heroes that were of old, warriors of renown. (Gen 6:1–2, 4)

"Sons of God" means heavenly beings. In the ancient Near Eastern mythology inherited by Israel from its environment, there were many gods and goddesses. In Second Temple Judaism, which was monotheistic, such beings were considered angels. Preexilic Israel, on the other hand, was not necessarily strictly monotheistic. In speaking of "sons of God," Gen 6 may reflect Israel's polytheistic past. The story in Gen 6:1–4 is a fragment of a myth about heavenly beings who were sexually attracted to human women and had intercourse with them. The women then bore children who were greater than humans and less than gods. *First Enoch* 6–11 expands this fragment into a full narrative. The Greeks also had myths in which gods had intercourse with humans; Hercules was the fruit of such a union.

If we read *1 En.* 6–11 carefully, we will notice that there seem to be two distinct stories, told in parallel. The first begins,

> And it came to pass when the children of men had multiplied that in those days were born to them beautiful and comely daughters. And the angels, the children of the heaven, saw and lusted after them, and said to one another: "Come, let us choose wives from among the children of men and beget us children." (6:1–2)

This clearly builds on Gen 6. The leader of the angels in this story is called Semyaza. The angels carry out their plan of taking human wives, and as in Genesis, their offspring are something between humans and gods. These offspring wreak havoc on the earth and attack humans and animals.

Scholars have gained insight into how this narrative may reflect real conditions in Judea of the third century B.C.E. It may be an allegorized account of the successors of Alexander the Great who claimed divinity and who ravaged the earth through their wars (see Nickelsburg, "Apocalyptic"). The armies of Alexander swept into the Jewish homeland, swallowing all in their path. This terrifying invasion must have seemed to many to be supported by cosmic forces. Could these amazing generals be simply human? It would not be surprising if apocalyptic thinkers represented them as beings from another world.

Another interpretation notes the priestly language used to describe the relationship of the angels to the women: "They began to go in to them and to defile themselves with them" (7:1). Such language also shows up in 10:11: "Go, bind Semyaza and his associates who have united themselves with women so as to defile themselves with them in their uncleanness." In this interpretation, the angels symbolize the priests who do not observe proper purity rules (see Suter). This interpretation is supported by God's words in chapter 15. There he tells Enoch, who is interceding for the watchers, to tell the watchers,

> You should intercede for men, and not men for you. Why have you left the high, holy, and eternal heaven, and lain with women, and defiled yourselves with the daughters of men and taken to yourselves wives, and done like the children of earth, and begotten giants as your sons? And though you were holy, spiritual, living the eternal life, you have defiled yourselves with the blood of women, and have begotten children with the blood of flesh. . . . For as for the spiritual ones of the heaven, in heaven is their dwelling. (15:2–4, 7)

This is priestly language of separation. Like belongs with like. Heavenly beings and earthly ones ought not to mix in this way. Such illicit mixing leads to all manner of evil. Similarly, the priests ought to guard their purity so as to remain acceptable to God.

The parallel story in *1 En.* 6–11 sees a different angel, Azazel, as the leader. He shares knowledge with humans that they should not have:

> And Azazel taught men to make swords, and knives, and shields, and breastplates, and made known to them the metals of the earth and the art of working them, and bracelets, and ornaments, and the use of antimony, and the beautifying of the eyelids, and all kinds of costly stones, and all coloring tinctures. And there arose much godlessness, and they committed fornication, and they were led astray, and became corrupt in all their ways. (8:1–2)

As in the Semyaza tradition, human violence is blamed on angels. Knowledge of metalworking is evil because it results in warfare. Knowledge of cosmetics is evil because it results in fornication. There may be an element of disapproval of "modern" culture here; that is, human technological progress has resulted not in improvement but in sin. In fact, it has resulted in too much sex and violence. The parallel to those who today use apocalyptic terms to decry a culture they judge to be offtrack is remarkable. Further, reservations about human knowledge are found throughout the course of history, including our own times. The idea that the gods have secrets humans were not meant to share is expressed in such legends as the Greek myth of Prometheus, punished for stealing fire. The distinction between knowledge attainable by humans on their own and heavenly knowledge not available to them is crucial for apocalypticism. The watchers reveal heavenly knowledge to humans inappropriately and without God's approval. The results are disastrous.

The bringing together of the Semyaza and Azazel traditions says something about how apocalypses were written. Different sources could be combined to employ the strength of multiple traditions. Both traditions claim that what is wrong with the world was caused by angels. This solution to the problem of evil is typically apocalyptic because it explains phenomena in this world by reference to an unseen world of angels and spirits. In the story of Adam and Eve, the presence of evil in the world is the fault of humans. In contrast, in the story of the watchers, it is due to the angels. *First Enoch* 10:8 says it in a nutshell: "To him [Azazel] ascribe all sin." Each of these solutions, however, assumes that the world was created good but was ruined by God's creatures.

In *1 En.* 9, the leaders of the good angels—Michael, Uriel, Raphael, and Gabriel—petition God to respond. God angrily imprisons the bad angels until the Last Judgment. The rebellious angels' offspring kill each other off. There follows an idyllic description of the earth restored to its pristine harmony and resultant fertility and peace (10:16–11:2). Thus the *Book of the Watchers* contains a myth in which angels disturb God's creation, other angels petition God to rectify the situation, and creation is partially restored, in hope of a full restoration in the future.

In chapters 12–16, Enoch makes his grand appearance. He is called "scribe of righteousness"—"scribe" because writing plays an important role in what he does, and "righteousness" because he obeys God. Enoch is commissioned to declare to the sinful watchers their punishment. When he does so, the watchers beg him to compose a petition for forgiveness and to present it to God. Enoch must have a soft heart, for he goes along with their request. He writes the petition but then falls asleep reading it. As he sleeps, he has visions of being carried up to heaven. He sees God's heavenly palace, described in wondrous terms, complete with "fiery cherubim" as guards. The palace is unlike anything on earth—it is hot as fire and cold as ice (14:13).

Enoch now perceives a second house much greater than the first, so that he cannot describe it. He sees God on a throne.

> And I looked and saw a lofty throne: its appearance was as crystal, and its wheels were as the shining sun, and there was the vision of cherubim. And from underneath the throne came streams of flaming fire so that I could not look at it. And the Great Glory sat on it, and his raiment shone more brightly than the sun and was whiter than any snow. None of the angels could enter and

behold his face by reason of the magnificence and glory, and no flesh could behold him. The flaming fire was round about him, and a great fire stood before him, and none around could draw close to him. Ten thousand times ten thousand stood before him, yet he needed no counselor. And the most holy ones who were near him did not leave by night nor depart from him. (14:18–23)

This is certainly a splendid scene. Enoch has come into the very presence of God in heaven. This is one of the many visions of God's throne in Jewish literature (see 1 Kgs 22; Isa 6; Ezek 1; Zech 3; Dan 7; *Apoc. Ab.* 18; *1 En.* 60:2; 90:20; *2 Enoch*; *T. Levi* 3–5; for a Christian example, see Rev 4–5). The throne is pictured as a throne-chariot of the type used by the Canaanite god Baal, which explains the presence of wheels. Ezekiel 1 has a similar picture of God on a throne-chariot. Enoch's vision stresses God's overwhelming might and glory. The Israelites at Mount Sinai were warned not to touch the mountain while God was present, because approaching God so closely was dangerous (Exod 19). In *1 En.* 14, angels and humans cannot come close to God, and they cannot even look directly at the vision. Enoch's visit to heaven gives him tremendous authority because it shows that he receives his information straight from God. The large heavenly entourage befits a heavenly monarch. This scene legitimates all of *1 Enoch*. This legitimating function is evident also in the other throne scenes mentioned.

God sends Enoch back to the watchers to give them a message (ch. 15). Through Enoch, God condemns the watchers for leaving heaven to mix with human women, and says that evil spirits will rise out of the fallen bodies of their offspring, who have killed each other. They will roam the earth, spreading evil and suffering. This explains the presence and activity of evil spirits on earth. God also claims that the only secrets the watchers have managed to divulge to humans are "worthless ones" (16:3). So the author of *1 Enoch* has it both ways—heavenly secrets have been revealed, leading to disaster, but the best secrets are still secret.

Chapters 17–36 recount Enoch's trips through the universe. He visits inaccessible places accompanied by angels who explain to him everything he sees. There is an intense eschatological perspective in these chapters. Enoch observes the fiery abysses prepared for the watchers' punishment, the chambers where dead humans are kept until the great judgment, and the perfect Jerusalem of the future.

In chapters 24–25, Enoch sees a mountain at the ends of the earth where God will descend at the end of time. There is a fragrant tree there.

And as for this fragrant tree, no mortal is permitted to touch it till the great judgment, when He shall take vengeance on all and bring everything to its consummation for ever. It shall then be given to the righteous and holy. Its fruit shall be food to the elect: it shall be transplanted to the holy place, to the temple of the Lord, the Eternal King. Then they shall rejoice with joy and be glad, and into the holy place they shall enter; and its fragrance shall be in their bones, and they shall live a long life on earth, such as your fathers lived. And in their day no sorrow or plague or torment or calamity shall touch them. (25:4–6)

The tree is the tree of life. This is an instance of the apocalyptic principle that the end is like the beginning. In the garden of Eden, Adam and Eve ate of the forbidden tree of knowledge (Gen 3). God threw them out of the garden, fearing that they would also eat of the tree of life and become immortal (Gen 3:22). *First Enoch* 25:4–6 says that this very same tree of life will be available to the elect at the end time. Its fragrance will penetrate their bones and give them "a long life on earth, such as your fathers lived," free of sorrow. The tree of life restores the long life people had aeons ago. The process in Genesis in which human life gets shorter as sin spreads will be reversed. Chapters 28–36 fill out Enoch's cosmic journeys and demonstrate his complete knowledge of the universe.

The author of *1 Enoch* does not address directly and explicitly the problems he faces. This is typical of apocalypses.

Instead, the problem—whatever it was—is transposed to a mythological plane. By telling the story of the Watchers rather than of the Diadochoi or the priesthood, *1 Enoch* 1–36 becomes a paradigm which is not restricted to one historical situation but can be applied whenever an analogous situation arises. (*AI* 51)

This is what Collins calls "apocalyptic multivalence." The story of the watchers is a model that can be applied to a variety of circumstances. The story attributes earthly evil to superhuman agents. It gives hope by asserting the sovereignty of God over these agents and gives assurance of God's eventual judgment on them. The interpretive framework that is created is spatial in that there is a superhuman world determining what happens in this one, and temporal in that a final judgment is coming.

THE *ASTRONOMICAL BOOK: 1 ENOCH* 72–82

The *Astronomical Book* is another version of Enoch's journey through the universe. Here his guide is the angel Uriel (see *1 En.* 9:1; 20:2), who explains what Enoch sees. The book assumes that Enoch has ascended to the heavens. He gets a wonderful tour of the universe and observes the movements of the sun, moon, and stars and the places of the winds. The universe he sees is strictly ordered. And it is not a collection of lifeless objects following universal physical laws. Rather, many angels oversee the movements of the heavenly bodies and the winds. The angels keep the universe running smoothly and according to God's plans. This recalls *1 En.* 2–5, where the order of the cosmos signifies its obedience to God.

The *Astronomical Book's* cosmological interest goes beyond simple curiosity. The author has something more specific in mind, for he is advocating a 364–day calendar. Disputes over the calendar happen in many religions. Christians may be familiar with the differences between Orthodox Christians and Catholics over Christmas and Easter. Agreement on the calendar was important in Judaism. Jewish communities could agree on how to serve God properly in their worship only by agreeing on a common calendar.

Eschatology is featured in chapter 80, where cosmic order breaks down. The sun and moon do not behave as they ought, rain is withheld, crops fail, and the stars stray from their paths. Cosmic disorder is connected to human transgression. Humans do not understand the cosmos properly and end up worshiping the stars (stars were thought to be supernatural beings). It is not clear whether human sin causes cosmic disorder, or humans sin because they are misled by the stars (80:6–7 seems to blame the situation on the stars). But the two are linked. Judgment comes in 80:8: "And evil shall be multiplied upon them, and punishment shall come upon them so as to destroy all."

Chapter 81 seems an addition to the *Astronomical Book* because it does not mention heavenly bodies or calendrical disputes. Enoch discovers that the "deeds of mankind" are written in a heavenly book and that the righteous will be rewarded and the evil punished. The idea that human actions are recorded in heavenly books is common in the ancient Near East and in Jewish and Christian apocalyptic texts. We shall see this notion again. At the judgment, the books will be evidence against the wicked and for the righteous.

THE *APOCALYPSE OF WEEKS: 1 ENOCH* 93:1–10 AND 91:12–17

The *Apocalypse of Weeks* looks like a complete little apocalypse in itself. It probably once existed independently of *1 Enoch*. The entire *Apocalypse of Weeks* is part of the *Epistle of Enoch* (*1 En.* 91–108). In its present location, the sequence of weeks has been disturbed—the first seven weeks occur in *1 En.* 93:1–10, and the last three in 91:12–17—and so we have to rearrange the text a bit to read the apocalypse in sequence. The *Epistle of Enoch* must have been written before 160 B.C.E., since it is mentioned in another work dated to about that time, *Jubilees*. Therefore, the *Apocalypse of Weeks*, too, must predate 160 B.C.E.

At the beginning of the *Apocalypse of Weeks*, Enoch reveals the source of his information: "According to that which appeared to me in the heavenly vision, and which I have known through the word of the holy angels, and have learned from the heavenly tablets" (93:2). Heavenly books foretell the course of history. The *Apocalypse of Weeks* divides history into ten periods called weeks. Within the fiction of the *Apocalypse,* Enoch lives in the first of the periods and foretells the other nine. Periodization of history implies that God controls it. Readers can locate themselves within the periods and so make sense of their own experience. As usual, the author locates himself toward the end of history, in the seventh week, just before the great reversal where the good triumphs.

The seventh week is the period of the Second Temple, although the author does not deem the rebuilding of the temple worth mention. This is striking; it may indicate that he is alienated from the temple establishment of the day. Prophets in the postexilic period raised their voices against the Second Temple priesthood (Third Isaiah and Malachi). Michael Knibb shows that many Jews of the time thought that the exile had not really come to an end because the restoration was not what they had hoped (see Wright).

The seventh week is evil: "And after that in the seventh week shall an apostate generation arise, and many shall be its deeds, and all its deeds shall be apostate" (93:9). An apostate is one who renounces one's religion or is disloyal to God. During this evil period, a group of righteous people arises. "And at its close shall be elected the elect righteous of the eternal plant of righteousness, to receive sevenfold instruction concerning all his creation" (93:10). The group has special knowledge concerning the entire universe. This knowledge sets the elect apart from everyone else. They are "elect," meaning that God chose them, and "righteous," meaning that they are the only ones with a proper relationship to God.

This apocalypse sees history follow a pattern in which evil flourishes and then God separates from the world an elect individual or group. Noah was separated in the second evil period, and Elijah in the sixth. Now the "elect" of the author's own time are separated from the "apostate generation." Since they know they are God's elect, they expect vindication. The rest of the *Apocalypse* confirms this expectation. Again we find a dualistic view that there is a minority of humanity who are God's chosen.

The following table shows the ten weeks of the *Apocalypse of Weeks* and what the author thinks are the major milestones of history.

First week (93:3)	Enoch's birth; good period
Second week (93:4)	Wickedness spreads; Noah saved from flood
Third week (93:5)	Abraham; good period
Fourth week (93:6)	Torah given to Moses; good period
Fifth week (93:7)	Temple built; good period

Sixth week (93:8)	Increasing sinfulness in First Temple period; Elijah; destruction of the first temple
Seventh week (93:9–14)	Apostate generation; emergence of the elect who receive instruction (Second Temple period)
Eighth week (91:12–13)	Sinners delivered to the righteous and punished; new temple built; all humans are righteous
Ninth week (91:14)	Works of the godless vanish; world slated for destruction
Tenth week (91:15–17)	Great judgment; heaven and earth pass away and a new heaven appears; an eternity without sin

Since the real author lives in the seventh week, we look to the weeks that follow to see what he expects in the future. "And after that there shall be another, the eighth week, that of righteousness, and a sword shall be given to it that a righteous judgment may be executed on the oppressors, and sinners shall be delivered into the hands of the righteous" (91:12). The righteous will avenge themselves on their oppressors; this is not a pacifistic book, nor does it leave vengeance entirely to the Lord. "And at its close they shall acquire houses through their righteousness, and a house shall be built for the Great King in glory for evermore" (91:13–14). The righteous will prosper because of their righteousness, the temple will be rebuilt, and the entire human race will look to "the path of righteousness," meaning the will of God as interpreted by the elect group. The ninth and tenth weeks see the punishment of wicked humans and angels, and then an idyllic future untainted by sin. So the writer see a future in which, in his opinion, everything is set straight.

THE *BOOK OF DREAMS: 1 ENOCH* 83–90

The *Book of Dreams* consists of two visions that Enoch describes to his son, Methuselah. Methuselah is known for living longer than anyone else—969 years! (Hence the expression "as old as Methuselah.") In the first vision, Enoch sees catastrophe and is told that his vision concerns "the secrets of all the sin of the earth: it must sink into the abyss and be destroyed with a great destruction" (83:7). Here are the elements of secrecy and cosmic destruction. In chapter 84, Enoch prays that a remnant be spared.

The rest of the book constitutes the second vision; it is an extended allegory that was an independent apocalypse in itself. It is called the *Animal Apocalypse* because in it history is "predicted" with animals representing humans (chs. 85–90). This makes for a rather strange narrative. As is frequent in apocalypses, names of historic figures are not supplied but must be guessed from clues, but in this case most of the clues are quite clear. The climax comes with the rise of the Maccabees, and Judah's death is not mentioned, so the *Animal Apocalypse* must date to sometime around 165 B.C.E. Chapter 86 retells the story of the descent of the angels (represented by stars) to have intercourse with human women (see *Book of the Watchers*). In chapters 87–88, other angels descend to bind the fallen watchers and cast them into the abyss. Throughout the narrative, angels look like humans, while the humans appear as animals. But Noah and Moses are transformed into human figures, suggesting that they become equal to the angels. The righteous frequently attain equality with angels in apocalyptic literature.

Humans who represent what God wanted for humanity seem to be represented by white bulls. Adam is a white bull, as is his son Seth (85:8) and many of Seth's offspring. Noah is a white bull, too (89:1). Only one of Noah's sons (Shem, ancestor of Israel) is a white bull. Humanity seems to deteriorate during the time of the patriarchs. Abraham is a white bull, as is Isaac, but Jacob is a white sheep. Then Israel enters the story; it is represented by sheep. Wild animals (the Philistines) ravage them, and then the Lord anoints Saul, represented by a ram, as king (89:42–44). When Saul mistreats the sheep, God appoints another ram (David) in his stead, who saves them (89:45–49). The northern tribes then go astray, abandoning the temple (89:51); this refers to the division of the kingdom between north (Israel) and south (Judah). Elijah prophesies against the north, is pursued and persecuted, and is brought up to heaven (89:52), as in the Bible.

When the rest of the sheep (Judahites) sin, specified as abandoning the "tower" (the temple) and the "house" (Jerusalem), God forsakes the sheep and destroys tower and house. God then appoints seventy shepherds who rule the sheep during four periods (reminiscent of the four kingdoms of Dan 2 and 7; see "The Book of Daniel," below). It is uncertain who these seventy are. Since they take the form of humans and not animals, they are probably angels; they may be the angelic patrons of the nations. In other words, Israel is ruled by foreigners. The writer sees the entire era from the destruction of Jerusalem by the Babylonians (587 B.C.E.) to his own time (ca. 165 B.C.E.) as one of foreign domination. Nonetheless, all nations fall under angelic authority, and the angels in turn are subject to God. So God's sovereignty is affirmed despite the subjugation of God's people. God orders the seventy shepherds to punish and destroy a precise number of sheep and to protect the rest. In the end, the angels will answer to God. This section ends with the note that the animals burn the tower and the house, and Enoch grieves over the destruction (89:66–67). This, of course, refers to the destruction wrought by the Babylonians in the sixth century B.C.E.

The restoration of Jerusalem and its temple is noted in 89:73, but it is disparaged: "They began again to place a table before the tower, but all the bread on it was polluted and not pure." That is, sacrifices are again offered in the temple, but the restoration is not satisfactory. This disparagement of the second temple matches the attitude found in the *Apocalypse of Weeks,* although there the rebuilding of the temple is not even mentioned. Again we note persistent unhappiness on the part of some with Israel's condition in the Second Temple period. Enoch charges that in this period the sheep become blind and their shepherds abuse their rule. But the picture is not entirely bleak. "Lambs" are born to some of the sheep, and the lambs can "see" (90:6). The sighted lambs are Jews who oppose the Hellenistic reform in Jerusalem. We are now in the real author's situation. There follows a reference to the Maccabean revolt. Judah Maccabee is portrayed as a hero. A sword is given to the sheep (90:19); this apocalypse approves the military means used by the Maccabees. The enemies of the sheep are defeated. Then there is a judgment scene in which God condemns first the watchers, then the seventy angelic patrons of the nations, and then the unfaithful from Israel (90:20–27). The text describes a perfect future in which Jerusalem is rebuilt, "greater and loftier than at first" (90:29). The wild animals who oppressed the sheep are now included in Israel's house but are subject to Israel (90:30). The sheep themselves become "all white," signifying their acceptance by God. Then a white bull is born (90:37; perhaps a messianic figure), and afterwards all become white bulls. Humanity has regained its original state (90:38).

The *Animal Apocalypse* provides a typically apocalyptic solution to the problems of the Hellenistic reform. First, the reform is situated in the sweep of world history, so that readers can see that all history has led up to their own period and that God controls all events. Second, supernatural forces are at work in history and explain it. Third, things will soon be reversed; Israel's oppressors will soon be overthrown by the Maccabees. The result will be a transformed Jerusalem in which true worshipers of God have their rightful place, and Israel's enemies will be punished. Fourth, humanity has fallen from its original position but in the end is restored to its original state. Finally, the *Animal Apocalypse* subscribes to Deuteronomistic theology. Israel's suffering results from its unfaithfulness to the temple. Its subjection to foreigners in the Second Temple period is reconciled with God's ultimate sovereignty and is seen as God's punishment on Israel. But the problems with humanity run deeper than just Israel's sinfulness. The apocalypse presents a rather dim view of humanity, that goes astray, a basic view that could be based on Gen 1–11.

THE *EPISTLE OF ENOCH: 1 ENOCH* 91–108

The most likely date for the *Epistle of Enoch* is the period of hellenization preceding the Maccabean revolt. The *Epistle* specifies that the major sins to be punished are idolatry and social abuses. Wealth leads to self-delusion: "Woe to you, you rich, for you have trusted in your riches, and from your riches you shall depart, because you have not remembered the Most High in the days of your riches" (94:8). The wealth of the rich lures them into thinking that they are self-sufficient, and they forget God. The rich also oppress the righteous: "Woe to you, you mighty, who with might oppress the righteous; for the day of your destruction is coming" (96:8).

The social concerns of the *Epistle of Enoch* emerge in the following verses. "Woe to those who build their houses with sin; for from all their foundations they shall be overthrown, and by the sword they will fall. And those who acquire gold and silver in judgment suddenly shall perish" (94:7). The verse attacks those who live in grand houses bought with ill-gotten gain, and those who take bribes in legal proceedings:

> Woe to you, you sinners, for your riches make you look like the righteous, but your hearts convict you of being sinners, and this fact shall be a testimony against you for a memorial of your evil deeds. Woe to you who devour the finest of the wheat, and drink wine in large bowls, and tread underfoot the lowly with your might. Woe to you who drink water from every fountain, for suddenly you shall be consumed and wither away, because you have forsaken the fountain of life. (96:4–6).

The sinners "look like the righteous." They are well-to-do, prominent in the community, and respected for their wealth and power; their status seems proof of their righteousness. Nonetheless, their actions are unjust. They live well and exploit others. "Drink water from every fountain" may mean that they profit from the labor of others in society, so that they live off of the "lowly." But they do not drink from the fountain that really counts, God's fountain that gives life. The text sees social stratification as the context for sins of the rich against the poor. These accusations sound much like those leveled by earlier prophets against the upper classes of Israelite society (eg. Isa 1–5, Amos 4–6).

The *Epistle* insists on human free will and responsibility for sin: "Sin has not been sent upon the earth, but humans have of themselves created it, and under a great curse shall they fall who commit it" (98:4). The tension between free will and fate was addressed by cultures in the ancient world. Both Jewish and Christian texts wrestle with this issue (e.g., *2 Bar.* 54:15; *4 Ezra* 7:116–18; Rom 9). The *Epistle* rejects the notion that sin is beyond human control.

Those who suffer oppression learn that they will be rewarded and their oppressors punished:

> I swear to you, that in heaven the angels remember you for good before the glory of the Great One; and your names are written before the glory of the Great One. Be hopeful; for previously you were put to shame through ill and affliction; but now you shall shine as the lights of heaven, you shall shine and you shall be seen, and the portals of heaven shall be opened to you. And in your cry, cry for judgment, and it shall appear to you; for all your tribulation shall be visited upon the rulers, and on all who helped those who plundered you. Be hopeful, and cast not away your hope; for you shall have great joy as the angels of heaven. (104:1–4)

Enoch can console the suffering righteous because he has inside information—he knows what is happening in heaven and what is written in the heavenly books. The reward of the righteous includes resurrection and admission to heaven: "You shall become companions of the hosts of heaven [angels]" (104:6).

The idea that there are books in heaven, a common notion in the ancient Near East, fits an apocalyptic worldview in which the unseen world determines the visible world. The books are of various types. Sometimes they are lists of people in God's favor, analogous to lists of citizens in cities (e.g., Exod 32:32–33; Ps 69:28; Isa 4:3). In apocalyptic literature, this becomes a list of those destined for eternal life (Dan 12:1; *1 En.* 47:3; 104:1; 108:7; Rev 3:5). Another notion is that they record actions and so will be used in judgment (e.g., Ps 66:8; Mal 3:16; Neh 13:14; *Jub.* 30:20; *2 Bar.* 24:1). These sorts of books are featured in the two canonical apocalypses (Dan 7:10; Rev 20:12). They may be analogous to the heavenly books Enoch reads in *1 En.* 103:2–3. There is yet another type of heavenly book, one in which earthly events are recorded in advance of their happening (Ps 139:16; Rev 5). This reflects the common idea that God knows everything that is to happen.

A passage at the end of the *Epistle* suggests that the conflict between the author and his opponents was not simply one of social class. It was also scribal conflict, in which there were disagreements over interpretation of Torah:

> Do not be godless in your hearts, and do not lie or alter the words of uprightness, nor consider false the words of the Holy Great One, nor take account of your idols; for all your lying and all your godlessness result not in righteousness but in great sin. And now I know this mystery, that sinners will alter and pervert the words of righteousness in many ways, and will speak wicked words, and lie, and practice great deceits, and write books concerning their words. But when they write down truthfully all my words in their languages, and do not change or subtract anything from my words but write them all down truthfully—all that I first testified concerning them. (104:9–11)

It is not hard to imagine these words addressing upper-class members of Judean society who sought to accommodate themselves to the Hellenistic world and were willing to make changes in ancient customs in order to do so. The *Epistle* refers to books given to the righteous:

> I know another mystery, that books will be given to the righteous and the wise to become a cause of joy and uprightness and much wisdom. And to them shall the books be given, and they shall believe in them and rejoice over them, and then shall all the righteous who have learned from them all the paths of uprightness be recompensed. (104:12–13)

The giving of the books is itself a mystery that is part of the eschatological events. They undoubtedly include the *Epistle of Enoch* itself, perhaps along with other apocalyptic books. If one believes in them, one will have joy and be saved from the disasters to come.

THE BOOK OF DANIEL

Daniel is the only apocalypse in the Hebrew Bible. It was immensely influential in later Jewish and Christian works (see Collins, "Influence"). It was composed during the Maccabean revolt that began in 167 B.C.E., but the stories in chapters 1–6 predate the revolt. So the book falls into two main parts—chapters 1–6 and chapters 7–12. Daniel 1–6 is a third-person narrative where Daniel interprets others' dreams, while Dan 7–12 is a first-person narration concerning Daniel's own dreams and visions—an apocalypse. Chapters 1–6 consist of stories that originally existed independently of the apocalypse, but they are an appropriate prologue to the apocalypse proper.

CHAPTERS 1–6

Enoch was a good choice for an apocalyptic seer. The same is true of Daniel. Daniel is mentioned in Ezek 14:14, 20, where he, along with Job and Noah, are legendary for their righteousness. Daniel 1–6 contains various stories about Daniel, a Jew influential in the royal courts of the kings of Babylonia, Media, and Persia. He is a "wise man" in the technical sense of one who can interpret dreams. Dreams were an important way in which gods communicated with humans in the ancient world.

Is it realistic to think that a Jew could rise high in a foreign court? Daniel is not the only evidence for this. Jews in Babylonia were successful economically, politically, and socially. Those who returned to Judah were supported by the Persian Empire, and when the Greeks took over, many Jews worked well with the new rulers. There was not necessarily antipathy between the Jews and their overlords. But Antiochus's persecution caused many to see Gentile rule as evil, even demonic, and this view finds expression in Dan 7–12. So Gentile rule is seen quite differently in Daniel's two major sections.

In chapter 1, Daniel and three other Jewish youths are recruited for royal service and trained in Chaldean (Babylonian) wisdom. The Chaldeans were known for divination, the art of predicting the future or discovering hidden knowledge through decoding natural events, such as the movements of stars, or through the interpretation of dreams. This art was passed down through successive generations of "wise" ones. Daniel and friends join this professional group of wise men. They are expected to share the life of the court, including eating foods prohibited by Jewish law. Their overseer is reluctant to allow them a different diet because, if they suffer from an ascetic regimen, he will take the blame. The Jewish youths convince him to let them live according to their own customs, and they thrive.

> At the end of the time that the king had set for them to be brought in, the palace master brought them into the presence of Nebuchadnezzar, and the king spoke with them. And among them all, no one was found to compare with Daniel, Hananiah, Mishael, and Azariah; therefore they were stationed in the king's court. In every matter of wisdom and understanding concerning which the king inquired of them, he found them ten times better than all the magicians and enchanters in his whole kingdom. (1:18–20)

Adherence to God's laws brings success. God favors the Jewish youths for their faithfulness and brings them prominence and recognition for their wisdom. Such a story would encourage those forced by Antiochus IV to abandon the Torah or die. Daniel and the others do well not because of their intelligence or hard work but because God gives them wisdom.

The Jews end up being much better at professional wisdom than the Chaldeans themselves. Several of the stories in Dan 1–6 feature events that are contests between Daniel and foreign wise men. This recalls the exodus story, where, in contests before Pharaoh, the powers of Moses and Aaron are found to be greater than those of Egyptian magicians (Exod 7:8–9:12). The superiority of Jewish wisdom and of Israel's God is the more striking when, as happens several times in Dan 1–6, foreigners, even foreign kings, recognize this superiority and render God homage.

In Dan 2, the Babylonian king Nebuchadnezzar has a troubling dream and is desperate to discover its meaning. When he summons his wise men to explain it, he refuses to divulge its contents to them, to see if they have the ability to know the dream without his disclosing it. The wise are unable to tell the king his dream, and so he orders their execution. Daniel requests an audience with the king and then prays. The prayer brings results: "Then the mystery was revealed to Daniel in a vision of the night" (2:19). When he appears before the king, Daniel acknowledges the divine origin of his wisdom in 2:27–28: "No wise men, enchanters, magicians, or astrologers can show to the king the mystery that the king is asking, but there is a God in heaven who reveals mysteries, and he has disclosed to King Nebuchadnezzar what will happen at the end of days."

Daniel tells the king his dream and gives its interpretation (2:31–45). The dream is of a statue with a head of gold, chest and arms of silver, middle and thighs of bronze, legs of iron, and feet of mixed iron and clay. The dream concerns a succession of four kingdoms, declining in quality with time. The first kingdom, represented by gold, is that of Nebuchadnezzar. The second kingdom (the Medes) is silver, the third (the Persians) is bronze, and the last (the Greeks) is a mixture of iron and clay. The four kingdoms are smashed by a rock that is interpreted in 2:44: "And in the days of those kings the God of heaven will set up a kingdom that shall never be destroyed, nor shall this kingdom be left to another people. It shall crush all these kingdoms and bring them to an end, and it shall stand for ever." The four-kingdom schema comes from Hellenistic political prophecy. Daniel "predicts" these kingdoms to Nebuchadnezzar, and so, within the fiction of the book, the fourth kingdom is in the distant future. But in reality, the real author of this episode writes during the fourth kingdom. This is but one of many examples of *ex eventu* prophecy in Daniel. After the last kingdom, God's kingdom will be established. In Daniel, the prophecy means that God will destroy the Seleucid Empire, and an everlasting kingdom—the kingdom of God—will replace it. The content of the king's dream is political—it concerns the rise and fall of kingdoms. But for the apocalyptic author, politics and religion are inseparable, and history is heading inevitably to the time of God's kingdom on earth, replacing and destroying Israel's earthly masters.

This story's view of Daniel's wisdom accords well with his portrayal in chapters 7–12 as the receiver of esoteric wisdom. In both cases, the wisdom involves mysterious dreams that need interpretation.

Chapters 3–6 contain other stories that reinforce the points already made. Chapter 5 tells of Belshazzar's feast, in which cryptic writing appears on the wall during a royal banquet and only Daniel is able to decipher it (hence the familiar phrase "to read the writing on the wall"). Chapter 6 contains the well-known story of Daniel in the lion's den. In this story, the king, the Mede Darius, is trapped into subjecting Daniel to this punishment; he is deeply reluctant to do so and is much relieved when Daniel survives. Indeed, he kills those who plotted to have Daniel killed. This pattern, where plotters almost succeed in having the hero killed but instead are killed themselves, is common in such stories (see Wills). Throughout Dan 1–6, foreign kings admit the sovereignty of Israel's God (2:46–47; 3:28–29; 4:34–35, 37; 6:26–27).

Daniel 1–6 addresses issues faced by Jews subject to foreign rule—the value of Jewish wisdom, customs, and religion as compared with that of foreigners, God's sovereignty in the face of foreign domination, the necessity to observe Torah even when threatened with death, the importance of resisting idolatry, and so on. Each of these issues is sharpened when Antiochus IV tries to stamp out Judaism, a situation reflected in Dan 7–12. The theme in Dan 1–6 of God revealing mysteries of history to Daniel, the chosen wise man, prepares the way for Daniel's role as an apocalyptic seer in chapters 7–12.

CHAPTERS 7–12

At the beginning of chapter 7, Daniel has a dream, awakens, and writes it down. He then recounts his vision: "The four winds of heaven [were] stirring up the great sea, and four great beasts came up out of the sea, different from one another" (7:2–3). The beasts are weird and terrifying, and their very weirdness signifies that they come from another world. They are more frightening than earthly beasts and represent supernatural forces. The interpretation of the vision explains that the beasts stand for oppressive kings and their kingdoms (7:17, 23). Since there are four beasts, this is another instance of the four-kingdom schema encountered in Dan 2. The series climaxes with the fourth beast, representing the Seleucid kingdom. It was "a fourth beast, terrifying and dreadful and exceedingly strong. It had great iron teeth and was devouring, breaking in pieces, and stamping what was left with its feet. It was different from all the beasts that preceded it" (7:7). History leads up to the time in which the author writes, and this time is the culmination of history. Things are at their worst because history has reached its culmination.

In the ancient Near East, the sea often symbolized the forces of chaos. The sea was a god opposed to good order. He rose in rebellion against the god who brought order to the universe. The main god or his ally had to defeat the sea so that an ordered creation, fit for human habitation, could exist (Collins, *Combat Myth;* Batto). The combat myth expressed the idea that order's dominance over chaos was not necessarily permanent and that forces inimical to God were capable of rising again. This explanation was always available to show why things were not as they should be. Particularly at times of crisis, individuals and groups could read historical events in the light of these primordial patterns. The patterns would explain why forces of good were not easily victorious, but they would also give assurance that good would ultimately prevail.

Neo-Assyrian human-headed winged bull from the ninth century B.C.E.
Such strange images may have inspired the sorts of beasts described in Daniel 7
and in the book of Revelation.

In Dan 7, present events are assimilated to these ancient mythic patterns. Events in Judea are seen as a result of a much larger conflict that encompasses history and the cosmos. The scene shifts to heaven:

> As I watched,
>   thrones were set in place,
>   and an Ancient One [literally: Ancient of Days] took his throne,
> his clothing was white as snow,

    and the hair of his head like pure wool;
his throne was fiery flames,
    and its wheels were burning fire.
A stream of fire issued
    and flowed out from his presence.
A thousand thousands served him,
    and ten thousand times ten thousand stood attending him.
The court sat in judgment,
    and the books were opened. (7:9–10)

First Enoch 14 has a throne scene that legitimates the revelations in that book. Daniel has also seen heaven and God. He too can speak with authority. In Daniel's throne scene, he sees God himself sitting on his heavenly throne. He then sees "thrones" set up for members of God's heavenly court. Books are opened containing the deeds of the nations, who are judged on the basis of these books. Judgment in heaven immediately has its effect on earth. Without a transition, the scene shifts abruptly from heaven to earth: "The beast was put to death, and its body destroyed and given over to be burned by fire" (7:11). Decisions taken in heaven determine what happens on earth, and no intermediaries are necessary. God's judgment results in instant defeat for God's foes, both human and supernatural. The very abruptness of the change from heaven to earth reinforces this point.

    After the fourth beast is punished, there follows a scene that greatly influenced later Jewish and Christian apocalyptic literature:

As I watched in the night visions,
I saw one like a human being [literally: like a son of man]
    coming with the clouds of heaven.
And he came to the Ancient One
    and was presented before him.
To him was given dominion
    and glory and kingship,
that all peoples, nations, and languages
    should serve him.
His dominion is an everlasting dominion
    that shall not pass away,
and his kingship is one
    that shall never be destroyed. (7:13–14)

Christians too easily assume that "son of man" here is a title and take it to mean *the* Son of Man, as if we knew just what or who that son of man is. But no text predating Daniel gives a clear indication of what Daniel's author might have meant by the term, aside from the general meaning "human" (e.g., in Ezek 2:1, 3, 6, 8 and throughout Ezekiel). In Dan 7, the appearance of the one who comes on the clouds is *like* that of a human being: "I saw one *like* a son of man" (7:13). Hints in Daniel and in the author's environment, however, help us to make an educated guess about this figure's identity.

Ancient Canaanite mythology, for example, supplies comparable material. El, the Canaanite father of the gods, is called *abu shanima,* probably meaning "father of years." This is similar to the phrase applied to the Jewish God in Dan 7:9, "Ancient of Days." Baal, head god of the Canaanite pantheon when the Israelites settled in Canaan, was El's son. He is traditionally depicted as riding on the clouds; he is a storm god. Baal defeats the god Yam, whose name means "sea," when Yam challenges Baal's power, and Baal thus secures his kingdom. The battle between Baal and Yam is an instance of the combat myth mentioned above; it preserves the order and the sovereignty of the head god. In Dan 7, the figure of one like a son of man riding the clouds into the presence of the Ancient of Days to receive the kingdom after the slaying of the beasts parallels Baal of the Canaanite story. So clearly, Daniel's author is tapping into ancient Near Eastern mythology.

Scholars pose three main suggestions concerning how the son of man is used in Dan 7. One is that he is a messianic figure. But the only references to messiahs in Daniel are in 9:25–26, where they refer to the high priest of the restoration, Joshua, and to the assassinated high priest Onias III. Further, the one like a son of man in Dan 7 is not called "messiah." The first suggestion, therefore, has little to recommend it. The second is that the son of man symbolizes Israel as a whole. This is plausible, but there is a still more compelling suggestion, that the son of man is an angel.

Except for the fact that it is singular, the use of the phrase in 7:13–14 is parallel to that in 10:16, where the angel Gabriel is "in the likeness of the sons of men" (see also 10:5, 18). In 10:5, the angel is simply called a man. Indeed, angels are often depicted as humans. Note that in the *Animal Apocalypse,* contemporary with Daniel, humans are portrayed as animals and angels as humans. Throughout Daniel, angels have the appearance of human beings (8:15; 9:21; 10:5, 16, 18; 12:6, 7). Further, the son of man receives power once exercised by the beasts, which represent kings and kingdoms but also cosmic forces of chaos ancient as the sea. If the one like a son of man is also a superhuman force, capable of being compared to the bestial forces from the sea, then he stands for more than the Jewish community. The most likely solution is that he is an angel. If so, he is probably Michael, Israel's own angel (10:21; 12:1).

The idea that nations are represented by supernatural beings whose fate in heaven determines the fate of their nation on earth comes from Israel's ancient Near Eastern context. It surfaces in Deut 32:8–9: "When the Most High apportioned the nations, when he divided humankind, he fixed the boundaries of the peoples according to the number of the gods; the LORD's own portion was his people, Jacob his allotted share." Earlier, non-Israelite myth saw these "gods" as divinities. Deuteronomy probably considers them heavenly beings less than gods, most likely angels, and indeed the Septuagint translates "gods" as "angels" in Deut 32 (see also Gen 6:2 for the term "sons of God," seen as angels by the *Book of the Watchers*). Each god is assigned a people, and so each nation has an angelic representative. Each nation's history reflects the fate of its angel in the supernatural realm.

Daniel asks an angel to interpret the vision. The angel says, "As for these four great beasts, four kings shall arise out of the earth. But the holy ones of the Most High shall receive the kingdom and possess the kingdom forever— forever and ever" (7:17–18). The interpretation associates the one like a son of man with the "holy ones" (Aramaic: *qaddishin*), since in 7:14 the one like a son of man receives kingship while in 7:18 it is the holy ones who do so. "Holy ones" (Hebrew: *qedoshim*) usually means "angels" in the Hebrew Bible. The same usage occurs in *1 Enoch's* throne scene, where it also refers to angels (14:22–23). "Holy ones" means "angels" in Dan 4:17; 7:21, 22, 25, 27; 8:13, 24. The identification of holy ones with angels sheds light on 7:27: "The kingship and dominion and the greatness of the kingdoms under the whole heaven shall be given to the people of the holy ones of the Most High." The "people of the holy ones" are the people of the angels, the Jews. In other words, the one like a son of man (Michael) and the holy ones receive kingship in the heavenly realm, which corresponds to their people, Israel, receiving kingship in the earthly realm. The same pattern is found in the War Scroll from Qumran (see ch. 5, below). There Israel's angel, Michael, receives dominion among supernatural beings, and Israel reigns on earth (1QM 17:7–8).

The vision continues: "As I looked, this horn made war with the holy ones and was prevailing over them, until the Ancient One came; then judgment was given for the holy ones of the Most High, and the time arrived when the holy ones gained possession of the kingdom" (Dan 7:21–22). The horn is a common representation of strength, particularly royal or military strength. In this vision, the horn is on the fourth beast (the Seleucid Empire) and represents one of its kings, Antiochus IV. He makes war against the angels and even prevails over them, at least for a while. His persecution of Judaism is an attack on heaven itself: "He shall speak words against the Most High, shall wear out the holy ones of the Most High, and shall attempt to change the sacred seasons and the law; and they shall be given into his power for a time, two times, and half a time" (7:25). "Change the sacred seasons" refers to outlawing the divinely appointed feasts and Sabbaths of the Jews. "Change . . . the law" refers to outlawing Torah. Antiochus's persecution will last "a time, two times, and half a time." A "time" is probably a year here, so the persecution is to last three and a half years. This, in fact, was the approximate length of time between the beginning of Antiochus's persecution and the rededication of the temple under Judah Maccabee.

Daniel is concerned with real historical events, just as *1 Enoch* is. Daniel reviews history several times, the same events being narrated in different visions and corresponding interpretations. This is called *recapitulation;* common in apocalypses, it is evident especially in the biblical apocalypses Daniel and Revelation. Recapitulation reinforces basic patterns. For example, in each of Daniel's historical reviews, the rise of oppressive empires leads to a crisis that is resolved by divine intervention. The details vary, but the basic pattern remains the same.

Chapter 8 is a vision and interpretation concerning the history of the world from the Medean and Persian Empires to the death of Antiochus IV. It mentions topics of most interest to the author's contemporaries—the power and extent of the Persian Empire, Alexander's victory over the Persians, the division of Alexander's empire after his death, and Antiochus's rise and persecution of Judaism. The last event gets by far the most attention (8:9–14). The interpretation (8:23–25) emphasizes Antiochus's attack on Judaism. The end of the interpretation promises that Antiochus will be defeated by divine power: "But he shall be broken, and not by human hands" (8:25).

Daniel 9:2 says, "In the first year of his reign, I, Daniel, perceived in the books the number of years that, according to the word of the LORD to the prophet Jeremiah, must be fulfilled for the devastation of Jerusalem, namely, seventy years." This refers to Jeremiah's prediction at the time of the destruction of Jerusalem that the devastation would last seventy years (Jer 25:11–12; 29:10). It leads Daniel to utter a lengthy prayer. The prayer acknowledges that Israel's suffering is due to its own lack of loyalty to the Mosaic covenant, reaffirms God's fidelity to Israel, and petitions for the salvation of Jerusalem and its sanctuary.

After the prayer, an angel tells Daniel that Jeremiah's prediction really refers to "seventy weeks," that is, seventy times seven, or 490 years: "Seventy weeks are decreed for your people and your holy city: to finish the transgression, to put an end to sin, and to atone for iniquity, to bring in everlasting righteousness, to seal both vision and prophet, and to anoint a most holy place" (9:24). This radically reinterprets Jeremiah's words. The anointing of a "most holy place" refers to a full restoration of the temple. If this is not to take place until such a long period after the prophecy of Jeremiah, it implies that the Second Temple was not a full restoration. Jeremiah's prediction was yet to be fulfilled. We noted a similar dissatisfaction with the Second Temple in the *Apocalypse of Weeks* and the *Animal Apocalypse* (see Knibb). The sort of reinterpretation of prophecy found in Dan 9:24 is common in Second Temple Judaism, where ancient prophecies are taken to refer to the interpreter's own time, even if that means departing from the literal meaning of the original prophecy.

The building of the Second Temple appears in 9:25: "Know therefore and understand: from the time that the word went out to restore and rebuild Jerusalem until the time of an anointed prince, there shall be seven weeks; and for sixty-two weeks it shall be built again with streets and a moat, but in a troubled time." The "anointed prince" here is Joshua, the high priest of the restoration. The rebuilding of Jerusalem happens seven weeks (49 years) after its destruction by the Babylonians. The entire Second Temple period, sixty-two weeks of years (434 years), is quickly dismissed as "a troubled time." "After the sixty-two weeks, an anointed one shall be cut off and shall have nothing, and the troops of the prince who is to come shall destroy the city and the sanctuary" (9:26). The "anointed one" is the high priest Onias III, assassinated in 171 B.C.E., and the "prince who is to come" is Antiochus IV. There follows a short account of his actions against the sanctuary. Again, Daniel's interest is in the crisis under Antiochus IV.

Daniel 10 shows that conflicts experienced by the Jews on earth result from battles fought in the supernatural realm. An angel appears to Daniel and speaks of the supernatural battles:

> The prince of the kingdom of Persia opposed me twenty-one days. So Michael, one of the chief princes, came to help me, and I left him there with the prince of the kingdom of Persia, and have come to help you understand what is to happen to your people at the end of days. For there is a further vision for those days. . . .
>
> Now I must return to fight against the prince of Persia, and when I am through with him, the prince of Greece will come. But I am to tell you what is inscribed in the book of truth. There is no one with me who contends against these princes except Michael, your prince. (10:13–14, 20–21)

The princes of kingdoms are the angels in charge of specific nations, and the angels' fate determines the fate of the nations they represent. Within the fiction of the book of Daniel, the Persians presently rule, and Gabriel and Michael (Israel's angel) are fighting Persia's angel. Gabriel and Michael know the future—they will win, and they will then fight Greece's angel. History is determined by God and has only to be played out in heaven and on earth.

Chapter 11 once again traces the course of history from the Persian Empire to the death of Antiochus. The story of Antiochus occupies more than half the chapter. Antiochus pays "heed to those who forsake the holy covenant"

(11:30), meaning that he listens to the hellenizers who want to make Jerusalem a Greek city. There is a contrast between Jews who go along with this apostasy and those who resist: "He shall seduce with intrigue those who violate the covenant; but the people who are loyal to their God shall stand firm and take action" (11:32).

The next verses offer a glimpse of the group behind the book of Daniel:

> The wise among the people shall give understanding to many; for some days, however, they shall fall by sword and flame, and suffer captivity and plunder. When they fall victim, they shall receive a little help, and many shall join them insincerely. Some of the wise shall fall, so that they may be refined, purified, and cleansed, until the time of the end, for there is still an interval until the time appointed. (11:33–35)

The word translated "wise" (Hebrew: *maskilim*) could be rendered "those who make wise," those who teach others. Wisdom here means understanding of the secret plans of God. "Wise" is plural here, and the wise teach others; this may point to a coherent social group that embraces Daniel's views. The book of Daniel itself is one of the ways by which the wise make many understand. Those faithful to Torah will be vindicated, and those who abandon it will see their seducer, Antiochus, suffer the penalty of death at God's hands. In the meantime, some of the wise will fall in the persecution, but this is only a purification.

The reference to a "little help" in Dan 11:34 may mean the Maccabees. The phrase is a bit insulting. Nowhere in Daniel are Jews urged to fight the Seleucids. Daniel wants them to remain faithful to Torah and to wait until God defeats Antiochus. Militant resistance to Seleucid rule and to Antiochus's persecution is of little use, for matters are ultimately decided on another level. This contrasts with the view of the *Animal Apocalypse,* which values the efforts of the Maccabees much more highly.

The "predictions" in chapter 11 end with an authentic prediction about Antiochus's end (11:40–45). But significantly, when the writer ventures into real prediction, he is wrong. He incorrectly predicts that Antiochus will die in Israel. Instead, Antiochus died in Persia in 164 B.C.E. Scholars often date apocalypses by noting when the predictions stop being accurate. The apocalypse was thus written sometime between the last datable event described in its pages and the future about which it is wrong. Daniel, then, was written around 165 B.C.E., since the persecution began in 167 and Antiochus died in 164.

The climactic passage in Daniel is 12:1–3:

> At that time Michael, the great prince, the protector of your people, shall arise. There shall be a time of anguish, such as has never occurred since nations first

came into existence. But at that time your people shall be delivered, everyone who is found written in the book. Many of those who sleep in the dust of the earth shall awake, some to everlasting life, and some to shame and everlasting contempt. Those who are wise shall shine like the brightness of the sky, and those who lead many to righteousness, like the stars forever and ever.

Michael dominates the final scene. As in other apocalyptic scenarios, the final struggle causes great suffering. At Michael's appearance, those who have their names written in the heavenly book are delivered. They are those who have remained faithful to God and Torah. Daniel 12:2 is the only clear affirmation of resurrection in the Hebrew Bible (references in Isa 26:19 and Ezek 37 are figurative). Since this resurrection appearance occurs in the only apocalypse in the Hebrew Bible, belief in resurrection seems to have entered Jewish belief through apocalypticism. But Dan 12 does not envisage general resurrection. Those who are raised are only the very good and the very bad, that is, those who resisted persecution, perhaps to the point of martyrdom, and those who inflicted or aided persecution. The wise get a special reward: they shine like stars for all eternity. Since the stars represent the angels, the wise will join the company of angels. The elect receive the same promise in *1 En.* 104:2 and elsewhere.

In Dan 12:4, the angel says, "But you, Daniel, keep the words secret and the book sealed until the time of the end" (see 12:9). The literary fiction is maintained. The sealing of the books explains how the words of the seer from the sixth century B.C.E. were unknown until four centuries later.

CONCLUSION

Apocalypticism was an important new factor in the worldview of ancient Judaism. It offered a way of showing why Israel's God, the all-powerful, was seemingly helpless in the face of Israel's enemies and their gods. The reason was that the world was not as God had created it. Humans or angels had rebelled against God and disturbed the proper order of creation. As a result, the present world was under the dominion of evil cosmic forces. But they would soon be defeated in a decisive battle with the cosmic forces of good. Apocalyptic seers claimed direct, esoteric revelation from the supernatural world. The revelation was made known to the chosen few who would be saved when the God's wrath finally ravaged the universe. Apocalyptic eschatology features the transcendence of death, a definitive solution to the age-old question about the good suffering and the wicked prospering in this life. Apocalypticism was to furnish key symbols, concepts, and literary forms to late Second Temple Judaism and early Christianity.

SELECT BIBLIOGRAPHY

This chapter depends heavily on the work of John J. Collins, especially *The Apocalyptic Imagination.*

Barr, James. "Jewish Apocalyptic in Recent Scholarly Study." *BJRL* 58 (1975): 9–35.

Batto, Bernard F. *Slaying the Dragon: Mythmaking in the Biblical Tradition.* Louisville: Westminster/John Knox, 1992.

Clifford, Richard J. "History and Myth in Daniel 10–11." *BASOR* 220 (1975): 23–26.

Collins, Adela Yarbro. *The Combat Myth in the Book of Revelation.* Missoula, Mont.: Scholars Press, 1976.

——. *Cosmology and Eschatology in Jewish and Christian Apocalypticism.* Leiden: Brill, 1996.

——. "The Influence of Daniel on the New Testament." Pages 90–112 in *Daniel: A Commentary on the Book of Daniel.* By John J. Collins. Minneapolis: Fortress, 1993.

——. ed. *Early Christian Apocalypticism: Genre and Social Setting.* Semeia 36. Decatur, Ga.: Scholars Press, 1986.

Collins, John J. "Apocalypses and Apocalypticism." *ABD* 1:279–88.

——. "Apocalyptic Eschatology as the Transcendence of Death." *CBQ* 36 (1974): 21–43.

——. *The Apocalyptic Imagination: An Introduction to Jewish Apocalyptic Literature.* 2d ed. Grand Rapids: Eerdmans, 1998.

——. "The Apocalyptic Technique: Setting and Function in the Book of the Watchers." *CBQ* 44 (1982): 91–111.

——. *The Apocalyptic Vision of the Book of Daniel.* HSM 16. Missoula, Mont.: Scholars Press, 1977.

——. "Cosmos and Salvation: Jewish Wisdom and Apocalyptic in the Hellenistic Age." *HR* 17 (1977): 121–42.

——. *Daniel: A Commentary on the Book of Daniel.* Minneapolis: Fortress, 1993.

——. "Jewish Apocalyptic against Its Ancient Near Eastern Environment." *BASOR* 220 (1975): 27–36.

——. *Seers, Sybils, and Sages in Hellenistic-Roman Judaism.* Leiden: Brill, 1997.

——, ed. *Apocalypse: The Morphology of a Genre.* Semeia 14. Missoula, Mont.: Scholars Press, 1979.

Cook, Stephen L. *Prophecy and Apocalypticism: The Postexilic Social Setting.* Minneapolis: Fortress, 1995.

Eddy, Samuel K. *The King Is Dead: Studies in the Near Eastern Resistance to Hellenism.* Lincoln: University of Nebraska Press, 1961.

Grayson, A. K. *Babylonian Historical-Literary Texts.* Toronto: University of Toronto Press, 1975.

Hamerton-Kelly, R. G. "The Temple and the Origins of Jewish Apocalyptic." *VT* 20 (1970): 1–15.

Hanson, Paul D. "Apocalypticism." *IDBSup,* 28–34.

———. *The Dawn of Apocalyptic.* Philadelphia: Fortress, 1975.

Hellholm, David, ed. *Apocalypticism in the Mediterranean World and the Near East.* Proceedings of the International Colloquium on Apocalypticism, Uppsala, August 12–17, 1979. Tübingen: Mohr (Siebeck), 1983.

Himmelfarb, Martha. *Ascent to Heaven in Jewish and Christian Apocalypses.* New York: Oxford University Press, 1993.

———. *Tours of Hell: An Apocalyptic Form in Jewish and Christian Literature.* Philadelphia: Fortress, 1983.

Knibb, Michael. A. "The Exile in the Literature of the Intertestamental Period." *HeyJ* 17 (1976): 253–72.

Koch, K. *The Rediscovery of Apocalyptic.* SBT 2/22. Naperville, Ill.: Allenson, 1972.

Kvanvig, Helge S. *Roots of Apocalyptic: The Mesopotamian Background of the Enoch Figure and of the Son of Man.* Neukirchen-Vluyn, Germany: Neukirchener Verlag, 1988.

Lacocque, Andre. *The Book of Daniel.* Atlanta: John Knox, 1979.

Murphy, Frederick J. "Apocalypses and Apocalypticism: The State of the Question." *CurBS* 2 (1994): 147–79.

———. "The Book of Revelation." *CurBS* 2 (1994): 181–225.

———. *Fallen Is Babylon: The Revelation to John.* Harrisburg: Trinity Press International, 1998.

———. "Introduction to Apocalyptic Literature." *NIB* 7:1–16.

Neusner, Jacob. *A History of the Jews in Babylonia.* 5 vols. Leiden: Brill, 1965–1970.

Nickelsburg, George W. E. "Apocalyptic and Myth in *1 Enoch* 6–11." *JBL* 96 (1977): 383–405.

———. *Resurrection, Immortality, and Eternal Life in Intertestamental Judaism.* Cambridge: Harvard University Press, 1972.

———. "Social Aspects of Palestinian Jewish Apocalypticism." *AMWNE* 639–52.

Olson, Daniel C. "Those Who Have Not Defiled Themselves with Women: Revelation 14:4 and the Book of Enoch." *CBQ* 59 (1997): 492–510.

Plöger, O. *Theocracy and Eschatology.* Richmond: John Knox, 1968.

Rad, Gerhard von. "Daniel and Apocalyptic." *OTT* 2:301–15.

Smith, Jonathan Z. "Wisdom and Apocalyptic." Pages 131–56 in *Religious Syncretism in Antiquity.* Edited by B. Pearson. Missoula, Mont.: Scholars Press, 1975.

Rowland, Christopher. *The Open Heaven: A Study of Apocalyptic in Judaism and Christianity.* New York: Crossroad, 1982.

Russell, D. S. *The Method and Message of Jewish Apocalyptic.* Philadelphia: Westminster, 1964.

Stone, Michael. "New Light on the Third Century" and "Enoch and Apocalyptic Origins." *SSV* 27–47.

Suter, David W. "Fallen Angel, Fallen Priest: The Problem of Family Purity in *1 Enoch* 6–16." *HUCA* 50 (1979): 115–35.

VanderKam, James. *Enoch and the Growth of an Apocalyptic Tradition.* CBQMS 16. Washington, D.C.: Catholic Biblical Association, 1984.

Wainwright, Arthur W. *Mysterious Apocalypse: Interpreting the Book of Revelation.* Nashville: Abingdon, 1993.

Wills, Lawrence M. *The Jew in the Court of the Foreign King: Ancient Jewish Court Legends.* Minneapolis: Fortress, 1990.

Wright, N. T. *The New Testament and the People of God.* Minneapolis: Fortress, 1992.

CHAPTER 5

QUMRAN AND THE DEAD SEA SCROLLS

PRIMARY READINGS: From *CDSSE,* as indicated in section headings

DISCOVERY OF THE SCROLLS

In 1947, a young Bedouin shepherd stumbled upon an amazing deposit of ancient manuscripts. In caves located in steep and rugged cliffs near the northwestern shore of the Dead Sea, Muhammad Ahmed el-Hamed found large earthen jars containing mysterious bundles of cloth and leather. The bundles found their way into the hands of experts and were identified as manuscripts dating from the last two centuries B.C.E. and the first century C.E. The find became known as the Dead Sea Scrolls. Further searches turned up many more manuscripts in neighboring caves. Archaeologists came to recognize that the manuscripts were the library of an ancient Jewish group, and they connected them with the nearby ruins called Qumran. The resultant interest in the scrolls and the ruins has produced enough studies to fill a library. The find has been called the greatest archaeological discovery of the twentieth century.

Controversy swirled around the Dead Sea Scrolls from the moment they came to light, but it increased dramatically in the late 80s and early 90s. We can trace the course of the controversy in numerous publications by the participants, and even in television documentaries (see Vermes in *CDSSE* 1–10 for a brief account). At various times, major news media covered the story. The main issue was access to the scrolls. Since over forty years had passed since their original discovery and since a number of scrolls and fragments had yet to be published, speculation grew about what they contained. News media and individual writers were occasionally attracted to the sensational potential of this issue, suggesting that there was something in the scrolls that would undermine Christianity, for example, and that they were purposely being kept secret for this reason. Several books have claimed that the scrolls describe earliest Christianity and that the founder of the sect was Jesus Christ or John the Baptist. Since many of the scholars who originally had access to the scrolls were Roman Catholic, there was even speculation that the Vatican was involved in a cover-up of potentially damaging information in the texts.

Most serious scholars overwhelmingly rejected these speculations. As the scrolls have been published and analyzed, it has become clear that they contain nothing to justify such extravagant claims. Rather, the main value of the scrolls has been to provide abundant and original evidence of an important sect of Judaism of the mid-to-late Second Temple period. The evidence is invaluable for our understanding of the period and for anyone studying early Judaism or Christianity.

It is true that many of the scrolls were slow to come into the public arena. This was due to a number of factors. First, a large number of scrolls and scroll fragments were entrusted to a very small number of scholars. These scholars did not always devote their full attention to the publication of the scrolls, and delays resulted. Second, since a good deal of reconstruction is necessary, given the deterioration of the scrolls, and since reconstruction itself is a creative scholarly effort, some scholars have been reluctant to release information about the scrolls in their possession until they are satisfied that they have completed their scholarly work. Third, the original scholars who were entrusted with the scrolls tended to pass them on to their own students, in effect excluding others from access to them. Whatever the reasons for the delays, objections to such limited access were well founded. The public and experts in the field had a right to gain access to the scrolls in a timely fashion, and in many cases this did not occur. Only when the scrolls were generally available could an open discussion of their contents take place and differing interpretations of them be based on all the evidence.

The situation changed drastically when scholars and others who did not have the scrolls available to them took steps to gain access. The biggest breakthrough came when the Huntington Library in California, which had photographs of the scrolls, decided to release them to the public in 1991. This action made possible a broader discussion of their content. Of course, this does not mean that all questions were answered. Quite the contrary. But it does mean that possible solutions to many puzzles can now be debated by a larger number of people, all of whom have access to the evidence.

Disagreements about matters large and small are still with us. For this reason, most of what is said in this chapter could be presented differently. But we must begin somewhere, and the important thing is that we become familiar with the scrolls and have some idea of the ways in which they can increase our knowledge of the period we are studying. This chapter follows a fairly mainstream interpretation of the scrolls and their history, with the caution that most of what is said here can be (and has been) subject to disagreement.

Many believe that the scrolls were the library of a group of Essenes. The Essenes were a Jewish sect known from the writings of Josephus, Philo of Alexandria, and Pliny the Elder (a Roman author writing shortly after 70 C.E.). Scholars had long been fascinated by the Essenes, but until the discovery of the Dead Sea Scrolls, they had to be satisfied with the secondhand reports of these three ancient authors. Now the scrolls offer unprecedented insight into the lives and thoughts of this group. Some maintain that the people of the scrolls were not Essenes. True, the scrolls themselves never use the word "Essene." But there are so many similarities between the descriptions of the sect in the scrolls and the characteristics of the Essenes as described by Philo, Josephus, and Pliny that the identification is attractive to a good many scholars (see Vermes in *CDSSE* 47–48; VanderKam, ch. 3). Whether or not the Essene hypothesis is correct, the scrolls continue to be a gold mine of information about Second Temple Palestinian Judaism.

There are three main kinds of scrolls in the collection: (1) manuscripts of the Hebrew Bible; (2) texts written by sect members; (3) noncanonical texts not written by sect members. The Qumran library contains all books of the Hebrew Bible except Esther, though its absence may be a historical accident. Before the discovery of the scrolls, the earliest known manuscripts of the Hebrew Bible dated to the Middle Ages. The discovery has been very helpful to text critics, who try to reconstruct the original text and understand its development and varieties. The manuscripts show that the biblical text was somewhat fluid before it was standardized in the wake of the destruction of Jerusalem in 70 C.E. In other words, there was no one standard text agreed upon by everyone; there were different versions of the sacred texts. Prominent among the noncanonical, nonsectarian documents are fragments from every section of *1 Enoch* except the *Similitudes of Enoch* (*1 En.* 37–71).

This chapter is limited to texts produced by members of the sect, and the treatment is by no means exhaustive. It will look at several of the most important texts and, relying on them, will construct an overall picture of the sect.

There is one important document, the *Temple Scroll* (11QT), whose origin is disputed. It is the longest scroll and consists mostly of detailed regulations for temple and cult. Scholars disagree whether this was written by a member of the Qumran community. Whatever the answer, its presence in Qumran's library attests to the group's interest in temple and cult. The extensive rules in this scroll do not fully correspond to practices in either the First Temple or the Second Temple period. It is perhaps best taken as a somewhat idealistic codification of how the temple will operate in the future, when the sectarians control it.

The following table, taken from VanderKam (p. 30), lists the biblical texts found at Qumran along with the number of copies of each found there. It gives a rough idea of the relative popularity of biblical books at Qumran.

As VanderKam cautions, the actual canon of the Bible was not decided till later, and so a firm distinction between canonical and noncanonical texts can be misleading.

Biblical Scrolls from Qumran

Genesis	15
Exodus	17
Leviticus	13
Numbers	8
Deuteronomy	29
Joshua	2
Judges	3
1–2 Samuel	4
1–2 Kings	3
Isaiah	21
Jeremiah	6
Ezekiel	6
Twelve prophets	8
Psalms	36
Proverbs	2
Job	4
Song of Solomon	4
Ruth	4
Lamentations	4
Ecclesiastes	3
Esther	0
Daniel	8
Ezra	1
Nehemiah	0
1–2 Chronicles	1

HISTORY OF THE COMMUNITY

The scrolls care little about history in the modern sense. While modern history looks for cause and effect on a natural plane, Qumran, like the Bible, looks for the causes of historical events on the supernatural level. And while modern history is cautious about finding a grand narrative that joins many events over a broad period of time, the writers of the scrolls are convinced that their story about God's dealings with Israel in general and themselves in particular is the core and meaning of all history.

Of course, modern scholars must go beyond the sect's views to try to re-construct an accurate history according to critical standards. For decades, scholars have struggled to reconstruct Qumran's history accurately, using ar-chaeological evidence, clues in the texts, and what is known of the period from other sources. One theory concerning Qumran's history, the Maccabean theory (followed here), is the most commonly accepted. (But we must re-member that when it comes to interpreting history, the majority are not al-ways right.)

The archaeologist Roland de Vaux thinks that there were several periods of occupation of the Qumran site. In period Ia, Qumran was settled on a modest scale in the middle of the second century B.C.E. In period Ib, it grew substantially during the reign of John Hyrcanus (134–104 B.C.E.). This pe-riod ended in some sort of catastrophe, perhaps the earthquake of 31 B.C.E. In period II, it was resettled, probably during the reign of Archelaus (4 B.C.E.–6 C.E.), but was destroyed in the Jewish war against the Romans, around 68 C.E. In period III, it was occupied by Roman soldiers.

The main lines of the Maccabean theory are as follows. We have already seen that the Maccabean rebellion against the Seleucids brought together di-verse Jewish groups who then went their separate ways when Hasmonean rule was established. The people who eventually settled at Qumran may have been part of the anti-Seleucid coalition who then had a falling-out with their Hasmonean allies. As the scrolls make a great deal of the supposedly Zadokite credentials of the priests at Qumran, it is possible that the first members of the settlement at Qumran objected when the Hasmoneans, a non-Zadokite family, became high priests, although such an objection is not explicit in the scrolls. At the end of the second century B.C.E., the Hasmoneans also claimed the title of king, reserved, according to some, for Davidic descendants. Members of the sect may have objected to this, and in some of the scrolls there is an expectation of a Davidic messiah, perhaps to re-place the Hasmoneans. But again, the scrolls do not say all this explicitly. Even if the sect at Qumran did not object specifically to the Hasmoneans' as-sumption of the titles of high priest and king, they certainly found much to disagree with them about. The scrolls supply ample evidence for a history of conflict with the priestly establishment in Jerusalem.

Early in the history of the Qumran group, a leader arose called the "Teacher of Righteousness." The Hebrew word translated "teacher," *moreh,* is from the same root as "torah," *torah,* whose basic meaning is "instruction." In some of the scrolls the Teacher opposes the "Wicked Priest," who was at first looked upon favorably by the Teacher's group but then was considered wicked when he became high priest in Jerusalem. Two plausible candidates for identification of the Wicked Priest are Maccabees. The first is Jonathan, appointed high priest by a Seleucid king in 152 B.C.E., and the other is Simon, who became high priest when Jonathan died in 142. The former is more likely. The Teacher's community may have fled Jerusalem when Jonathan became high priest. This would agree with the date assigned to the beginning of the first period of settlement at Qumran, based on archaeological data. Qumran was destroyed by the Romans in 68 C.E., during the revolt begun by the Jews in 66.

Cave four of Qumran. This cave yielded the richest load of ancient manuscripts.

THE NATURE OF THE COMMUNITY

Pliny the Elder says that the Essenes were "a solitary people, the most extraordinary in the world since there are no women (they renounce all sexual desire), they have no money, and they enjoy only the society of the palmtrees" (*Natural History* 5.15.73). He locates them in the vicinity of Qumran. Both Josephus and Philo say that Essenes were celibate and lived in many towns. Josephus adds that there were also married Essenes. The apparent contradictions in these reports—whether they were married or celibate, living in towns or in the wilderness—may not be contradictions so much as descriptions of different sorts of Essenes.

Among the Dead Sea Scrolls are two community rules. Both speak of the nature of the community, its rules, its structure, and so on. The *Community Rule* (1QS; in this customary notation, the number "1" indicates the first cave, "Q" indicates Qumran, and "S" is an abbreviation of the Hebrew word *serek,* meaning "rule," taken as title of the work) pictures a self-contained, celibate community. The *Damascus Document* (CD) assumes that some sect members live in towns, marry, and are in contact with society at large. Despite the differences, the communities reflected in the two scrolls are very similar. Taking both of these documents into account, we can speculate that there were at least two branches of the Essene movement—one, located at Qumran, that was isolated and celibate, the other living in towns, marrying, and in contact with the surrounding society. The picture is doubtlessly more complicated that this. Rather than one, single, uniform group, there may have been a movement, spanning several centuries, that was embodied in different ways at different times and in various places. This seems likely on general principles, and it also fits the variety found within the scrolls.

The community or communities reflected in the scrolls can be characterized under six general rubrics. It was priestly, centered on Torah, sectarian, based on special esoteric revelation, apocalyptic, and highly structured.

PRIESTLY

At the top of Qumran's structure were Zadokite priests. We are therefore not surprised to find typical priestly concerns in the scrolls. Purity was important, for example. Relations between people of different categories were closely regulated. Scholars debate whether members of the sect participated in the sacrifices at Jerusalem. There may have been times in the sect's history when it frequented the temple and times when it did not, and it is also possible that members of the sect differed among themselves, some coming to the temple and others refusing.

But how can a priestly group survive apart from the temple in Jerusalem? The scrolls say that atonement is possible apart from sacrifices. Prayer and Torah observance are declared equivalent to sacrifices in their effect. Such ideas made it possible for the sect to be cut off from Jerusalem without being deprived of the benefits of the sacrificial system. The community conceived of itself as a temple where God was present. One way of expressing this was that the angels were present in the community, since angels are God's attendants. Several allusions to ritual washings and the existence of facilities for such washings at the Qumran ruins suggest that they were important to the sect.

CENTERED ON TORAH

All Jewish groups in some way centered on Torah. The people of Qumran interpreted Torah and prophets in ways that distinguished them from other Jews. Many sectarian interpretations may go back to the Teacher of Righteousness. Qumran claimed that only the Teacher of Righteousness and his community held the key to Torah, because it had been granted to them by God. Since only they knew the correct interpretation of Torah, only they could authentically fulfill it. The Qumran community was the true Israel.

The community thought that it had a "New Covenant" with God. This does not mean a new religion. The Torah of Moses was the basis of the community, as it had always been Israel's foundation. But Israel had not been faithful to the covenant, according to the people of Qumran, and now God had established the sect as the true Israel and had revealed to the Teacher of Righteousness and his followers the true interpretation of Torah. The term "New Covenant" comes from Jer 31:31, "The days are surely coming, says the LORD, when I will make a new covenant with the house of Israel and the house of Judah." The Qumran community saw itself as a fulfillment of this verse, as did the Christian church later (the term translated "Testament" in "New Testament" can better be translated "Covenant," so that the "New Testament" is really the "New Covenant"). Because Qumran covenant did not include all Jews, and because it was based on a new understanding of Torah, Jews needed to undergo a sort of conversion to join the Qumran sect.

A major halakic (legal) dispute between the sect and the Jerusalem establishment concerned the calendar. (*Halakah* is the word for Jewish law. It comes from the word for "to walk" *[halak]*, used to refer to behavior.) Qumran followed a solar calendar, while Jerusalem adhered to a lunar calendar. This was a serious disagreement. It meant that Qumran considered the rest of Judaism in violation of God's will concerning feasts, and conversely, other Jewish groups could accuse Qumran of the same.

SECTARIAN

Sect has a specific meaning in sociology. It denotes a minority group that shares basic symbols and traditions with the dominant society around it but that is also conscious of itself as separate and not in harmony with the dominant religious establishment. Religious sects think of themselves as having the authentic version of the religion while others are purposely evil or in serious error. Sects have clearly defined social boundaries, often reinforced by stringent purity rules. Contact with outsiders is rigidly regulated. Marriage is endogamous—that is, one marries within the sect.

BASED ON SPECIAL ESOTERIC REVELATION

Only members of the community knew God's will. It was disclosed to the Teacher of Righteousness and his successors and was not generally available. The revelation granted to the sect concerned the role of the community as the true Israel, eschatological teaching, interpretation of the Torah, and so on.

APOCALYPTIC

Although there are no full apocalypses among the documents attributed to the Qumran sectaries (members of the sect), there were several apocalypses in their library. Daniel and *1 Enoch* were especially popular. Eight copies of Daniel are attested among the fragments, and eleven manuscripts contain at least part of *1 Enoch*. Qumran shared with apocalypses an interest in angelology and eschatology. Qumran was also apocalyptic in its dualism: the world was in the grips of a cosmic struggle between good and evil; humanity was divided into good and bad. The sectaries looked forward to an imminent eschatological battle in which the powers of good would overcome the powers of evil. Victory was assured because God was all-powerful. God had planned the entire course of history in advance.

The sect's beliefs concerning the afterlife are unclear. There are no unambiguous references to resurrection; some passages seem to imply it. Since the community already lived in the presence of the angels, in a sense resurrection would be anticlimactic. "Everlasting life" is mentioned in the scrolls; it may mean some sort of immortality. Josephus says that the Essenes did not believe in the resurrection of the body but in the immortality of the soul. In any case, the sect was more interested in the defeat of Satan, the overthrow of the unrighteous in Jerusalem, and the restoration of the proper role of the sons of Zadok than in an afterlife.

Qumran expected two messiahs, one priestly and the other royal. These were human, not supernatural beings. They were not said actively to bring in the end time. Their significance rested in the fact that when God would visit the earth, Israel would come to be what it was meant to be. Properly constituted, Israel had at its head a king and a high priest. Both were anointed, and so both were messiahs, just as David and Aaron were both messiahs. The priestly messiah seems to be superior to the royal one.

The community's view of Scripture corresponded to its apocalyptic worldview. Qumran took special interest in prophetic writings and saw them as predicting the sect itself. It also saw other biblical texts not usually considered to be prophetic, such as the book of Psalms, as cryptically predicting events relating to the sect. Exegesis in the scrolls often consisted of showing in detail how biblical texts referred to the sect.

We have seen that esotericism is important to apocalypses. The Teacher of Righteousness received a unique and secret revelation concerning the true interpretation of Torah and the course of the end of the ages. This was then imparted to the faithful who constituted the sect.

Main Characteristics of the Community Reflected in the Scrolls

Priestly	Zadokite priests at the apex of the community; all major decisions made by the priests; concern with purity, atonement, and so on
Centered on Torah	The sect strictly obeyed true Torah as revealed through the Teacher
Sectarian	A minority group considering itself the true Israel; strong social boundaries
Based on special esoteric revelation	Through the Teacher of Righteousness, the sect alone knew God's true revelation concerning Torah, history, eschatology
Apocalyptic	Dualism; esoteric knowledge concerning the unseen world and the future; a strong eschatological orientation; messianism; angelology
Highly structured	Hierarchy based on the priestly nature of the community and the degree of knowledge and observance of Torah

---

HIGHLY STRUCTURED

The community was divided into three main parts—priests (also called the "sons of Zadok"), Levites, and laypeople. The priests were the leaders, responsible for right doctrine and practice. Priests had to be present in any significant gathering. The top officer was called the "Guardian" or the "Master."

He taught the sect how to live in conformity with correct understanding of the Torah, presided over major meetings, and ranked the members on the basis of their adherence to the rule. There would ahve been a need for such a leader once the Teacher of Righteousness had died. The "Council of the Community" was a formal gathering of the members. The *Community Rule* mentions a smaller council of fifteen men, but its place in the structure of the community is uncertain. There was a bursar to attend to the community's finances.

THE *DAMASCUS DOCUMENT* (CD)

This text and the *Community Rule*, to be treated below, are rules of the community. Perhaps more than any of the other texts, these two provide us a window into the sect's life. Each says something about the sect's worldview and contains specific rules that tell us much about community structure and practices.

Geza Vermes dates the *Damascus Document* to around 100 B.C.E. It is unusual among the sectarian scrolls in that it was known before the discoveries near the Dead Sea. Two incomplete medieval copies of the text were discovered in a Cairo synagogue at the end of the nineteenth century. Many fragments of it turned up in three of the Qumran caves. Thus, the document as printed in *CDSSE* is a scholarly reconstruction based on various manuscripts. Vermes has rearranged the document, putting columns XV–XVI before IX because this seems to have been the original order of the text, on the basis of scroll fragments 4Q266 and 270 (in this notation, numbers indicating specific fragments, instead of document titles, come after "Q"). The name of the book comes from references to Damascus within the text. Most scholars do not take these references literally but see them as a symbolic reference to the "exile" from Jerusalem that the sect imposed on itself.

The *Damascus Document* has two major sections—an exhortation and a collection of statutes. It is a good place to begin our study because the exhortation contains a "history" of the world, placing the emergence of the sect within that history as its culmination. A theme is that obedience to God brings blessing and disobedience brings punishment. According to the document, God planned the formation of the sect from all eternity. The following analysis goes through the text in order, and so the reader will benefit most by keeping the text of the *Damascus Document* open in *CDSSE* and referring to it along the way. The same advice applies to the other Dead Sea scrolls we will examine.

SECTION ONE: HISTORY AS EXHORTATION (CD I–VIII)

This section is a sermon, perhaps to be read at an annual covenant renewal ceremony. The sermon frequently uses scriptural language as do most of the other scrolls. This is a community that has immersed itself in the sacred texts we now call the Bible. It begins with a traditional *rib* formula: "Listen now all you who know righteousness, and consider the works of God; for He has a dispute [Hebrew: *rib*] with all flesh and will condemn all those who despise him." The Hebrew word *rib* means something like "lawsuit." The *rib* formula is used in many places throughout the Bible. Its point is that God calls Israel (or all humanity, as here) to a legal reckoning. The relationship between God and Israel has a legal framework through the covenant, where both sides—God and Israel—have obligations. God also has claims on all humanity, and so here God's lawsuit is against "all flesh." These introductory words establish an eschatological tone, since judgment is near.

The preacher reminds the hearers that the temple was destroyed (587 B.C.E.) and many of the people killed because of Israel's sins but God, "remembering the Covenant of the forefathers," let a remnant survive. The idea that God preserves a "remnant" even when he punishes the people is found elsewhere (e.g., Isa 65; Rom 9).

The preacher then relates the story to recent history:

And in the age of wrath, three hundred and ninety years after He had given them into the hand of king Nebuchadnezzar of Babylon, He visited them, and He caused a plant root to spring from Israel and Aaron to inherit His Land and to prosper on the good things of His earth. And they perceived their iniquity and recognized that they were guilty men, yet for twenty years they were like blind men groping for the way. (CD I)

"Wrath" means God's anger at sins. It is a common term in apocalyptic texts, indicating God's anger at sin, working itself out through the eschatological events. The *Damascus Document* alludes to Daniel here, one of the community's favorite books. Daniel also conceives of its own time as the "period of wrath" (Dan 8:19; 11:36). This means that it is a time when the struggle between God and God's enemies is coming to a head. Given the many other references in the scrolls to the Hellenistic crisis and its consequences for Israel, we should take the age of wrath to indicate that time.

Nebuchadnezzar exiled Israel in 587 B.C.E. Three hundred and ninety years after that would be 197 B.C.E., just before the hellenizing reform in Jerusalem. Of course, this figure is undoubtedly symbolic, but even if it is approximately correct, this brings us down to sometime in the second century B.C.E. This would mean that the whole period from 587 to the foundation of the sect was a time of exile. It implies that the Second Temple and its establishment were not a true restoration at all (see Knibb). We have already seen this attitude in the *Animal Apocalypse,* in the *Apocalypse of Weeks,* and in Daniel (see ch. 4, above). So there seems to be a persistent dissatisfaction, on the part of some Jews, with the temple establishment in Jerusalem. For the *Damascus Document,* the true restoration of the covenant community is the sect itself, which emerges four centuries after Nebuchadnezzar's destruction of the temple.

The summary in CD I implies that the group was fairly unorganized and unsure of its goals when it first arose: "For twenty years they were like blind men groping for the way." That could be a period during which they were allied with the Maccabees, first in war and then in the Maccabees' control of Jerusalem. The next stage is crucial for the community: "And God observed their deeds, that they sought Him with a whole heart, and He raised for them a Teacher of Righteousness to guide them in the way of His heart" (CD I). Through the Teacher, God reveals that Israel continues to suffer because it is a "congregation of traitors" that has departed from God's way. The Teacher is opposed by one who "shed over Israel the waters of lies" and was engaged in "abolishing the ways of righteousness." The wicked leader is elsewhere called "the Scoffer" because he scoffs at Torah (see Isa 28:14, 22, 29:20). The Teacher's opponent attacks the Torah itself and thus brings on Israel "the curses of His Covenant" (see Deut 27) and delivers it to "the avenging sword of the Covenant." This reference would be especially appropriate at a covenant renewal ceremony, for part of the covenant formulary was the recital of blessings and curses. The obvious candidate for the wicked leader would be a Hasmonean. The preacher calls the Teacher's enemies "seekers of smooth things," a recurrent phrase in the scrolls, taken from Isaiah (see Isa 30:10). It may mean the Pharisees. In any case, the phrase concerns what the sect considers to be the "easy," "lenient" interpretation of Torah, much less strict than its own. Of course, we are hearing only one side of the story. Neither the Hasmoneans, whose claim to legitimacy rested on their history as defenders of Torah, nor the Pharisees, who had a reputation as experts in Torah and strict observers of it, would have admitted that the criticisms at Qumran had any validity at all.

Torah is not just religious but affects every aspect of life, including politics, so a group challenging the established order is a religious and political threat. Not surprisingly, the Teacher's opponent pursues him. The acts of the Scoffer and his supporters are summed up with contempt: "Their deeds were defilement before Him" (CD II). This is priestly terminology. The behavior of the Teacher's enemies is abominable to God. The Scoffer probably thought that the Teacher was the one threatening the covenant by rebelling against God's representatives in Jerusalem.

The exhortation again addresses the hearers directly, saying, "Hear now, all you who enter the Covenant, and I will unstop your ears concerning the ways of the wicked" (CD II). The "Covenant" is equivalent to the community. Those outside the sect are outside the covenant, even if they are Jewish or worship in the temple. This redefines the covenant.

The preacher begins a narrative whose lesson is that obedience to God brings divine favor and disobedience brings God's anger. It asserts that God foreknew everything:

> \<The sinners> shall have no remnant or survivor. For from the beginning God chose them not; He knew their deeds before ever they were created and He hated their generations, and He hid His face from the Land until they were consumed. For He knew the years of their coming and the length and the exact duration of their times for all ages to come and throughout all eternity. He knew the happenings of their times throughout all the everlasting years. And in all of them He raised for Himself men called by name that a remnant might be left to the Land, and that the face of the earth might be filled with their seed. And He made known His Holy Spirit to them by the hand of His anointed ones, and He proclaimed the truth (to them). But those whom He hated He led astray. (CD II; angled brackets designate my clarifications of the text; parentheses indicate Vermes's clarifications.)

The sinners have already experienced punishment for their sins in the misfortunes that have overtaken Israel, but since they still sin, they will continue to be punished until not a single survivor is left. God even turned his back on the land of Israel so that they might be punished. God knew beforehand everything that was to happen, and provided for the preservation of the covenant by leaving a "remnant." The passage seems to border on predestination, since "from the beginning God chose them \<the sinners> not." Nonetheless, the scrolls in general and this text in particular make it clear that humans do have free choice. This tension between free will and predestination occurs elsewhere in the scrolls.

The remnant spared by God is divinely "called"; it is an elect group. To the elect God makes known the truth through people chosen for the task, called messiahs ("anointed ones"; see also CD VI). It is not certain who these messiahs are, but this shows the flexibility of the term "messiah," since here it is plural and refers to past figures, perhaps prophets. The wicked will be utterly destroyed, but then the earth will be repopulated through "the seed" of the elect. The notions of God's foreknowledge of history and of divine election are both common in apocalypses.

Now the preacher begins a quick review of history. He does this to, as he says, "uncover your eyes that you may see and understand the works of God."

He starts with unspecified "mighty heroes" who stumbled. Then he speaks of the "Heavenly Watchers," whose story we have already read in the *Book of the Watchers* (*1 En.* 1–36). The *Book of the Watchers* was available in the Qumran library. The review of history shows that those (both humans and angels) who obey God prosper while those who "follow after thoughts of the guilty inclination and after eyes of lust" are punished (CD II). The idea that there is a guilty inclination in humanity is also found elsewhere in postbiblical Judaism (see the discussion of *4 Ezra* in ch. 10, below). "Through it <the guilty inclination> their sons perished, and through it their kings were cut off; through it their mighty heroes perished and through it their land was ravaged" (CD III). So humanity almost always seems to go wrong because of this guilty inclination. Besides the heroes and the watchers, the preacher mentions the children of the watchers, humanity before the flood, the children of Noah, the patriarchs Abraham, Isaac, and Jacob (who did not walk in the evil inclination), the Israelites in Egypt, the desert community that was disobedient, and the first members of the covenant (Israel before the sect).

At the end of this dismal history shines the glory of the community of the covenant:

> But with the remnant which held fast to the commandments of God He made His Covenant with Israel for ever, revealing to them the hidden things in which all Israel had gone astray. He unfolded before them His holy Sabbaths and His glorious feasts, the testimonies of His righteousness and the ways of His truth, and the desires of His will which a man must do in order to live. (CD III)

The remnant is the Qumran community. God has revealed to them mistakes and sins that Israel is making that no one else knows. To Qumran has been revealed the correct cultic year with its feasts. Only the community of the covenant truly knows God's will. Prosperity and even survival depend on God, so the divine will is something that one must do "in order to live," and only the community is in a position to do it.

The text goes on to say that the remnant's reward is that God has "built them a sure house in Israel whose like has never existed from former times till now." This refers to the community as temple. The temple is often called a "house" in Israelite and Jewish literature. The community also regains the "glory of Adam"; that is, the sect recaptures the status God originally gave to Adam before he lost it through disobedience. (Note the restoration of humanity in the *Animal Apocalypse* when humans are again represented as white bulls.

The document now speaks of the first members of the community:

> (They were the first men) of holiness whom God forgave, and who justified the righteous and condemned the wicked. And until the age is completed, according

to the number of those years, all who enter after them shall do according to that interpretation of the Law in which the first (men) were instructed. According to the Covenant which God made with the forefathers, forgiving their sins, so shall He forgive their sins also. But when the age is completed, according to the number of those years, there shall be no more joining the house of Judah, but each man shall stand on his watch-tower. (CD IV)

The community sees as God sees, so they know who is truly righteous and who is truly wicked. All who convert to the sect must follow the sect's interpretation of Torah, just as the first members did. Conversion is open to anyone during the present age, but when this age draws to a close, it will be too late. Once the eschatological battle begins and the sides are drawn up, there is no going back. In typical apocalyptic fashion, history consists of a succession of preordained ages.

Before the eschaton, "Belial shall be unleashed against Israel, as He spoke by the hand of Isaiah, son of Amoz, saying, *Terror and the pit and the snare are upon you, O inhabitant of the land*" (CD IV). Here an ancient prophecy (Isa 24:17) is taken to refer directly to the community's own time. This is typical of the way the sect looks at Scripture. Belial is another name for the leader of the demonic armies. Belial dominates the present age and makes war against Israel. "Terror," "pit," and "snare" are then each interpreted as cryptic allusions to sins committed by the Jerusalem priestly establishment. The sins involve "fornication," "riches," and "profanation of the temple." Are these charges literally true, which is always possible, or is exaggeration or even distortion involved? For example, fornication may really mean failure to conform to the marriage laws advocated by the sect. The preacher claims that the sinners in Jerusalem "shall be caught in fornication twice by taking a second wife while the first is alive, whereas the principle of creation is, *Male and female created He them* (Gen. i, 27)" (CD IV). This passage criticizes the marriage practices of those in Jerusalem, among which it may mean divorce when it speaks of having two wives; it criticizes this practice on the basis of Genesis. Jesus does the same thing in Matt 19:3–9. For both the sectarians and Jesus, divorce may be unacceptable because the eschaton is approaching in which, in good eschatological fashion, the original state of the creation is restored. Of course, those who were divorced would have seen nothing wrong with it, and they would have pointed to Torah to support their case.

The legal disputes between the sect and the establishment are summarized as follows: "They defile their holy spirit and open their mouth with a blaspheming tongue against the laws of the Covenant of God saying, 'They are not sure'" (CD V). "Not sure" may mean that the opponents question Qumran's interpretations. But since the sect members see these interpretations as revealed by God, they are outraged that others do not accept them. Their anger is evident in their vehement condemnation of their opponents.

At the end of CD VI is a paragraph dealing with the temple:

> None of those brought into the Covenant shall enter the temple to light His altar in vain. They shall bar the door, forasmuch as God said, *Who among you will bar its door?* And, *You shall not light my altar in vain* (Mal. i, 10). They shall take care to act according to the exact interpretation of the Law during the age of wickedness. They shall separate from the sons of the Pit, and shall keep away from the unclean riches of wickedness acquired by vow or anathema or from the Temple treasure; they shall not rob the poor of His people, to make of widows their prey and of the fatherless their victim (Isa. x, 2). They shall distinguish between clean and unclean, and shall proclaim the difference between holy and profane. They shall keep the Sabbath day according to its exact interpretation, and the feasts and the Day of Fasting according to the finding of the members of the New Covenant in the land of Damascus. They shall set aside the holy things according to the exact teaching concerning them. They shall love each man his brother as himself; they shall succor the poor, the needy, and the stranger. (CD VI)

Because the temple in Jerusalem is defiled, it would be futile to send sacrifices there. God said through Malachi not to "light my altar in vain." What the community should do during the "age of wickedness," the age in which Belial's allies rule Jerusalem, is to obey the Torah strictly, and to do so "according to the finding of the members of the New Covenant." True to the community's priestly nature, decisions about clean and unclean are crucial (see Lev 10:10). Only the members of the sect can accurately distinguish between clean and unclean. The point is reemphasized a few lines down: "They shall keep apart from every uncleanness according to the statutes relating to each one, and no man shall defile his holy spirit since God has set them apart" (CD VII). Holiness means to belong to God, which implies separation from everything that is profane.

Attention to ritual and cultic matters is quite compatible with ethical concerns: "They shall love each man his brother as himself; they shall succour the poor, the needy, and the stranger" (CD VI). Love of one another and social justice are highlighted here, as they are in other priestly writings. It is an unfair generalization to say that priestly concern with rules and ritual necessarily excludes other concerns that we may consider more central to religion. The text elaborates on how sectaries are to relate to each other. They are to be open, not holding grudges. They are to separate from those who do not follow the proper interpretation of Torah. Others are called "sons of the Pit." "The Pit" (Hebrew: *shahat*) is a biblical term found as a synonym for "Sheol" (e.g., Ps 16:10). Originally, Sheol was thought to be a shadowy place where all humans go when they die. As ideas of the afterlife evolved, the Pit was seen as the place for the unrighteous dead. We have seen such places of eternal punishment in the *Book of the Watchers.*

The separation demanded of covenant members works on several levels. Through it, the sect maintains ritual purity, thus guarding God's presence among them. It helps in maintaining strong social boundaries so as to avoid any threat to the community identity from dissenting ideas and practices. It also allows for social control in that the threat of separation from the holy community can keep members in line. That the concept of separation operates in this last way is confirmed by the fact that the punishment transgressors receive is often separation from parts of community life or from the community in general. These tactics may seem unattractive to mainstream modern Americans, who value openness and tolerance. But they make sense to a minority group in a hostile environment. And they may at times be necessary for groups whose very identity is in jeopardy. The same tactics were used by the returning exiles, as we know from the book of Ezra.

The next section of the *Damascus Document* shows that some members lived elsewhere than at Qumran and did marry. This section lays down rules for members "if they live in camps according to the rule of the Land, marrying and begetting children" (CD VII). Those who marry must still obey Torah strictly lest a punishment come upon them whose severity has not been seen since the split of the northern and southern kingdoms (following Isa 7:17). The text then speaks of exile to Damascus. This notion is puzzling. Are we to think that the sect members actually lived in Damascus in Syria? Although a literal reading here has some defenders, most scholars think that the reference to Damascus is symbolic. The reference to Damascus derives from Amos 5:26–27, quoted in CD VII. The *Damascus Document* does not give us an explicit interpretation for Damascus, but since it assigns the other elements of Amos 5:26–27 a symbolic meaning, Damascus doubtless has one, too. Exile to Damascus represents the exile from Jerusalem now suffered by the sect. Then the text cites Num 24:17 as a messianic prophecy: *"A star shall come forth out of Jacob and a sceptre shall rise out of Israel."* This is taken to foretell a messiah who is an interpreter of Torah (the star) and one who is a prince (the scepter). This agrees with the expectation of a priestly and a royal messiah expressed elsewhere in the scrolls.

One is not automatically saved by being in the community. Strict obedience to Torah is necessary. The preacher warns,

> At the time of the former Visitation they were saved, whereas the apostates were given up to the sword; and so it shall be for all the members of His Cove-

nant who do not hold steadfastly to these. They shall be visited for destruction by the hand of Belial. That shall be the day when God will visit. (CD VII–VIII)

The day of judgment is a threat to insincere members of the sect. Transgressors who belong to the community will be given over to Belial for destruction. "The former Visitation" refers to a period of severe punishment of Israel, which the sect escaped. It may well allude to the persecution of Judaism by Antiochus IV, seen as a punishment for the Hellenistic reform. This reading is supported by the next section, which speaks of "the kings of Greece who came to wreak vengeance upon them" (CD VIII).

Later in CD VIII the warning to those not serious about the rules is put in terms that tell us something about how the sect looks at history:

> None of the men who enter the New Covenant in the land of Damascus, and who again betray it and depart from the fountain of living waters, shall be reckoned with the Council of the people or inscribed in its Book from the day of the gathering in of the Teacher of the Community until the coming of the Messiah out of Aaron and Israel.

The "gathering in" of the Teacher is his death. The Teacher's death is apparently in the past. The document anticipates a messianic age. The term "Messiah out of Aaron and Israel" may mean two messiahs. That is, there will be a messiah from Aaron (a priest) and one from Israel (a prince or king). This dual messiahship matches the division—standard in the scrolls—of Israel into a priestly and a lay component.

The *Damascus Document* is more specific about its timetable in the following passage:

> From the day of the gathering in of the Teacher of the Community until the end of all the men of war who deserted to the Liar there shall pass about forty years (Deut. ii, 14). And during that age the wrath of God shall be kindled against Israel; as He said, *There shall be no king, no prince, no judge, no man to rebuke with justice* (Hos. iii, 4). But those who turn from the sin of Jacob, who keep the Covenant of God, shall then speak each man to his fellow, to justify each man his brother, that their step may take the way of God. . . . And every member of the House of Separation who went out of the Holy City and leaned on God at the time when Israel sinned and defiled the Temple, but returned again to the way of the people in small matters, shall be judged according to his spirit in the Council of Holiness. (CD VIII)

There are only forty years between the death of the Teacher and eschatological judgment. The only ones to escape God's wrath are the members of the covenant who have turned their backs on the rest of Israel. Thus an appropriate name for the sect is the "House of Separation." They have fled the "Holy City," Jerusalem, because the temple establishment did not follow the teaching of the Teacher of Righteousness and so was defiling the temple. The "Liar" controls the temple. This passage predicts judgment for members of the sect who deserted to the Liar. Contrasted with these are "all those who hold fast to these precepts, going and coming in accordance with the Law, who heed the voice of the Teacher" (CD VIII).

SECTION TWO: RULES FOR THE COMMUNITY (CD XV–XVI, IX–XIV)

The rest of the *Damascus Document* contains statutes for the community. Laws can make for fairly dull reading, but they are better than other sorts of writing at telling us what daily life was really like. The most important beliefs and values of a society, particularly the sort of traditional society we are studying, take concrete form in laws. The laws of a community are "where the rubber meets the road."

We look at only a portion of the rules here. They begin with regulations to safeguard the sanctity of God's name (Yahweh). The Ten Commandments forbid the use of God's name in vain, that is, swearing falsely using God's name (Exod 20:7; Deut 5:11). In the *Damascus Document*, no one may swear by God's name at all (CD XV). (Jesus makes a similar prohibition in Matt 5:33–37.) But Qumran's rules go still further. Not only is one to avoid the sacred name Yahweh; one may not even use the names Elohim ("God") and Adonai ("Lord"), acceptable substitutes for the sacred name among Jews elsewhere. Swearing by the Torah is also prohibited. The practice of swearing by holy objects such as the temple is attested in Matthew's Gospel, where Jesus forbids swearing by heaven, which is God's throne; earth, which is God's footstool; the temple; or one's own head (Matt 5:33–37). Both the *Damascus Document* and Matthew's Jesus are engaged in what the later rabbis will call building a fence around the Torah. That is, when the Torah commands something, if one institutes a still stricter command, then one will run no risk of violating the more limited, original rule. The stricter rule is a fence. If one does not go past that fence, he or she will not violate the basic Torah command that is inside the fence. Swearing falsely by God's name directly transgresses the second commandment in the Decalogue, "You shall not make wrongful use of the name of the LORD your God" (Exod 20:7). But since the Torah (or heaven, the temple, or one's head) comes from God, one should not swear by that either. Keeping the latter rule helps to safeguard the former.

Entrance into the sect is equivalent to returning to the Torah: "They shall enroll him with the oath of the Covenant which Moses made with Israel, the Covenant to return to the Law of Moses with a whole heart and soul" (CD XV). True knowledge of Torah is granted to the sect alone, so a prospective convert should not be told the statutes until approved by the Guardian.

God is present with the community, which is the true temple. This means God's angels are present, so purity rules must be stringently observed: "No madman, or lunatic shall enter, no simpleton, or fool, no blind man, or maimed, or lame, or deaf man, and no minor, none of these shall enter into the Community, for the Angels of Holiness are [in their midst]" (4Q266; square brackets indicate Vermes's reconstruction of the text). The Hebrew Bible contains similar restrictions on who may enter the temple (e.g., Deut 23:1–6). Those on the fringes of the community cannot be allowed full access to God. Societal structures are replicated in cultic prescriptions. This may seem cruel to modern sensibilities, but we must remember that the sect was bent on keeping the Torah strictly and that the restrictions in Deuteronomy showed what God required if God was to remain present with the community. Attitudes to sickness were different then, too, for it was a prescientific age.

The concern to celebrate feasts according to the solar calendar probably explains the following statement: "As for the exact determination of their times to which Israel turns a blind eye, behold it is strictly defined in the *Book of the Divisions of the Times into their Jubilees and Weeks*" (CD XVI). The book alluded to is *Jubilees,* which was in the Qumran library and so was known to the sect. It advocates a solar calendar.

A section of the statutes deals with relations between members of the community (CD IX). They must not use Gentile law against one another (cf. 1 Cor 6:1–8). There are rules about not bearing grudges and not using the hierarchical structure of the community to belittle others. Reporting of transgressions of Torah is to be done according to a strict procedure that respects and safeguards the one accused. Those who have proven themselves unworthy members of the community cannot be witnesses against other sectarians.

A series of rules safeguards the sanctity of the Sabbath (CD X–XI). The Sabbath became especially important during and after the exile. Sabbath observance became a matter of controversy between Jews and was one of the ways Jewish groups distinguished themselves from one another. This is apparent in the Gospels, where there are Sabbath disputes between Jesus and his opponents. Sabbath rules are quite strict in the *Damascus Document.* Sabbath is decreed to begin not at sunset but slightly before that, so as to "build a fence" around the Sabbath rule and ensure that it is not violated. That is, if one considers Sabbath to begin just before sunset and not at sunset, and if one obeys that stricter rule, then one will not be in danger of violating the less strict rule that is found in Torah, that Sabbath observance begin at sunset. Work in any form is prohibited. A person who falls into water may not be saved on the Sabbath if it involves using a tool such as a ladder or a rope. (See Jesus' question about saving a life on the Sabbath in Mark 3:1–5; Matt 12:9–14; Luke 6:6–11.) No business or anything having to do with money is to be transacted. Cooking is forbidden. On the Sabbath, one must keep one's distance from Gentiles (other rules in this section regulate ordinary interaction with Gentiles). On the Sabbath, one may not help an animal to give birth or help it out of a pit into which it has fallen. On this score, it is interesting to note that Jesus' argument in Matt 12:9–14 assumes that his listeners in the Galilean synagogue would lift a sheep out of a pit, even on the Sabbath. The sectarians are stricter than Jesus' synagogue audience.

Care for Jerusalem's purity appears in the rule prohibiting the sending of sacrifices to Jerusalem by the hand of one who is unclean (CD XI). The same concern emerges in the forbidding of sexual intercourse in the holy city (CD XII). It is not certain whether these rules assume that members of the sect are actually going to Jerusalem to sacrifice, which would contradict CD VI, or are simply "on the books" in anticipation of a time when the sect will control the temple.

The *Damascus Document* also lays down rules for the Guardian's actions. It is clear that the Guardian was a powerful figure in the community. He determined the status of each member within the community, was responsible for teaching them the proper interpretation of Torah, and had to be consulted on business dealings and on divorces.

THE *COMMUNITY RULE* (1QS)

The *Community Rule* is one of the oldest documents of the sect. Like the *Damascus Document,* it gives us an excellent window through which to look at the sect's beliefs and concrete practices. Its present form dates to around 100 B.C.E., but it is composed of earlier documents. It existed in one form or another during most of the sect's life. Its importance is shown by the fact that twelve copies of it are attested. Some fragments of the *Damascus Document* even cite the *Community Rule.*

> It seems to have been intended for the Community's teachers, for its Masters or Guardians, and contains extracts from liturgical ceremonies, an outline of a tractate on the spirits of truth and falsehood, statutes concerned with initiation into the sect and with its common life, organization and discipline, a penal code, and finally a poetic dissertation on the fundamental religious duties of

the Master and his disciples, and on the sacred seasons proper to the Community. *(CDSSE* 97)

LITURGY (1QS I–III).

The first three columns of the *Community Rule* contain part of the liturgy for a covenant renewal ceremony. A reference in column II shows that this liturgy is to be celebrated once a year and that at this time members will be ranked, first according to whether they are priests, Levites, or laypersons and then according to the "perfection of their spirit." This hierarchy ensures that members live according to God's will and constitute "a Community of truth and virtuous humility, of loving-kindness and good intent one towards the other, and (they shall all of them be) sons of the everlasting Company" (1QS II).

Members pledge themselves to do what is good and right before God, "as He commanded by the hand of Moses and all His servants the Prophets" (1QS I). The Guardian is to emphasize the importance of the revealed "appointed times"—times for feasts and for daily prayers. Qumran's dualism is apparent in this liturgy, as it is in the sermon on the two spirits that follows. Humanity is divided into two opposing groups, one belonging to light and the other to darkness, and this is all part of God's design. God has placed each person in one camp or the other. Members must pledge to "love all the sons of light, each according to his lot in God's design, and hate all the sons of darkness, each according to his guilt in God's vengeance." Those who enter the covenant bring to it their "knowledge, powers and possessions." They are fully committed to it with respect to their minds, abilities, and material goods.

"All those who embrace the Community Rule shall enter into the Covenant before God to obey all His commandments so that they may not abandon Him during the dominion of Belial because of fear or terror or affliction." These words assume that the elect are in danger of suffering because of Belial's dominion. Being in the community does not of itself guarantee salvation. One can always backslide. One is always subject to temptation and to the onslaughts of Belial. Although each individual is always in danger and Belial has the upper hand for the time being, eventual victory is assured for the forces of good.

Israel thinks in terms of history, and at key points in its experience it reviews that history. As part of the covenant renewal at Qumran, the priests and Levites first "bless the God of salvation and all His faithfulness [Hebrew: *emet,* a covenantal term]." The people answer, "Amen, Amen." The priests recite God's glorious deeds on behalf of Israel, followed by the Levites listing Israel's sins. Then Israel confesses its sins and praises God for his mercy (1QS

I–II). The Levites curse the "lot of Belial," that is, all those who do not belong to the sect, particularly its enemies within Israel. (In Deut 27:14–26, Levites recite the covenantal curses.) The congregation again responds, "Amen, Amen."

The liturgy does not assume that all entering the covenant do so with pure motives. Priests and Levites together condemn anyone who enters the covenant thinking he can do so in "the stubbornness of his heart," that is, without full assent to Torah. They threaten such people with the covenantal curses. These words echo Deut 29:19–21, where Moses addresses such people and also declares that the covenantal curses will fall on them.

> He shall not be justified by that which his stubborn heart declares lawful, for seeking the ways of light he looks towards darkness. He shall not be reckoned among the perfect; he shall neither be purified by atonement, nor cleansed by purifying waters, nor sanctified by seas and rivers, nor washed clean with any ablution. Unclean, unclean shall he be. For as long as he despises the precepts of God he shall receive no instruction in the Community of His counsel. (1QS III)

The scroll admits that the people it condemns do in fact seek light and do what their heart declares lawful. But this does not excuse the fact that they are in error. Only absolute adherence to the sect's ways brings God's favor. Using the language of priestly religion, the scroll claims that no one who does not give full inner assent to the truth can be purified. Ritual washings are not magic; they are outer signs of an inner conversion. And without the inner conversion, one remains unclean. The liturgical section ends with a statement that ritual washing, combined with an inner determination to obey Torah, effects atonement.

TRACTATE (1QS III–IV)

The *Community Rule* now begins a dissertation on the "nature of all the children of men," apparently meant to be delivered by the Master (1QS III). The scroll itself supplies a table of contents for the presentation: "The kind of spirit which they possess, the signs identifying their works during their lifetime, their visitation for chastisement, and the time of their reward." The section goes on to a general statement that even before creation came into being, God had planned the entire course of it. Then comes a section that states in the clearest possible terms the division of humanity into two parts.

> He has created man to govern the world, and has appointed for him two spirits in which to walk until the time of His visitation: the spirits of truth and injustice. Those born of truth spring from a fountain of light, but those born of in-

justice spring from a source of darkness. All the children of righteousness are ruled by the Prince of Light and walk in the ways of light, but all the children of injustice are ruled by the Angel of Darkness and walk in the ways of darkness.

God is sovereign over all creation, including the Prince of Light and the Angel of Darkness. God created the good and evil spirits and assigned individuals to one or the other. This appears to be a statement of individual predestination, but what follows qualifies this extreme position. The tension between determinism and free will, implied in this position and its qualification, is a tension present in other writings of the period, Jewish and non-Jewish.

The Angel of Darkness not only influences the children of darkness; he also tempts the children of righteousness. This explains how even the righteous can stumble at times. But the Angel of Darkness has power only because God allows it: "But the God of Israel and His Angel of Truth will succour all the sons of light. For it is He who created the spirits of Light and Darkness and founded every action upon them and established every deed [upon] their [ways]." There is no absolute cosmic dualism here, as if there were two equal powers at the apex of creation. Instead, the powers of light and darkness are both subject to the one God.

The next column continues this dualistic strain. In it are catalogs of the deeds of the righteous and of the unrighteous. Notable among the deeds of the righteous are the emphases on "zeal for just laws" and "faithful concealment of the mysteries of truth" (1QS IV). The latter element points to esoteric revelation granted to the sect. The "visitation" of the righteous, their reward at the Lord's visit, is "healing, great peace in a long life, and fruitfulness, together with every everlasting blessing and eternal joy in life without end, a crown of glory and a garment of majesty in unending light." The visitation of the wicked consists of "a multitude of plagues by the hand of all the destroying angels, everlasting damnation by the avenging wrath of the fury of God, eternal torment and endless disgrace together with shameful extinction in the fire of the dark regions."

Now the text takes a remarkable turn. It claims not only that humans are in the camp either of the good or the bad angel but that these spirits struggle in the heart of each individual. Each person has a certain measure of each spirit, and the size of the portion determines the ultimate orientation of the individual. "And the whole reward for their deeds shall be, for everlasting ages, according to whether each man's portion in their two divisions is great or small." This seems to be an attempt to maintain a social dualism while leaving open the possibility of conversion for outsiders and defection for insiders. When the end comes, the evil parts of the righteous will be purged and evil will be destroyed completely.

RULES (1QS V–VI)

The rules section begins with the statement that converts

> separate from the congregation of the men of injustice and shall unite, with respect to the Law and possessions, under the authority of the sons of Zadok, the Priests who keep the Covenant, and of the multitude of the men of the Community who hold fast to the Covenant. Every decision concerning doctrine, property, and justice shall be determined by them. (1QS V)

This passage reaffirms the absolute authority of the Zadokite priests. They have full jurisdiction even over possessions. The text goes on to say that the one entering must take an oath to "return with all his heart and soul to every commandment in the Law of Moses in accordance with all that has been revealed of it to the sons of Zadok, the Priests, Keepers of the Covenant and Seekers of His will." This emphasis on Zadokites recalls that the priests at Qumran considered themselves the true Zadokite priesthood that should be in charge in Jerusalem.

Members cannot associate with those who do not conform to Qumran's rule. Eschatological punishment threatens such people, for "they are not reckoned in His Covenant." They do not seek God's will, so they do not benefit from the purifications of the community, nor can they share in the common meal.

There follow regulations stressing the hierarchy of the community. A new member is ranked "with respect to his understanding and practice of the Law." Every year each member is so ranked. Priests are at the apex of the community, and study of the Law is a priority. Wherever there are ten members, there should be a priest who presides, blessing the firstfruits of bread and wine. Further, "there shall never lack a man among them who shall study the Law continually, day and night, concerning the right conduct of a man with his companion. And the Congregation shall watch in community for a third of every night of the year, to read the Book and to study the Law and to bless together" (1QS VI). All assemblies follow strict rules of order, based on the sect's hierarchy.

Full membership in the community is attained only after a period of probation. The following rules recall Josephus's description of Essene practices. A candidate must be examined by the Guardian "concerning his understanding and his deeds." If found acceptable, he enters a period of instruction in the sect's rules. Then he is examined by the entire congregation. If he passes this test, he lives as a member for a year, but is still excluded from the pure common meal and retains his personal property. If the assembly finds that he has lived the life satisfactorily, then he is admitted to the meal but not to the "Drink of the Congregation." This is a use of food to mark the degree of the candidate's integration into the sect. During the second year, the candidate's property is delivered to the bursar, who keeps it separate from the common property. Then the candidate is again examined. If found worthy, "he shall be inscribed among his brethren in the order of his rank for the Law, and for justice, and for the pure Meal; his property shall be merged and he shall offer his counsel and judgement to the Community" (1QS VI).

PENAL CODE (1QS VI–VII)

Part of the statutes section assigns punishments to specific violations. These statutes concern everyday matters and ensure that the community runs smoothly and that members are at peace with each other and subject to the proper Zadokite authorities.

DUTIES OF MASTER AND DISCIPLES (1QS VIII–XI)

The Torah lays down cultic requirements for atonement, and as a priestly community, the members of the Qumran sect would be especially anxious to fulfill these requirements. Because they felt the temple was defiled, however, they had to separate from it. They were thus deprived of the means for effecting atonement, a crucial and necessary process in priestly religion. Column VIII explains how they solved this dilemma:

> In the Council of the Community there shall be twelve men and three Priests, perfectly versed in all that is revealed of the Law, whose works shall be truth, righteousness, justice, loving-kindness and humility. They shall preserve the faith in the Land with steadfastness and meekness and shall atone for sin by the practice of justice and by suffering the sorrows of affliction. They shall walk with all men according to the standard of truth and the rule of the time.

> When these are in Israel, the Council of the Community shall be established in truth. It shall be an Everlasting Plantation, a House of Holiness for Israel, an Assembly of Supreme Holiness for Aaron. They shall be witnesses to the truth at the Judgement, and shall be the elect of Goodwill who shall atone for the Land and pay to the wicked their reward. It shall be that tried wall, that *precious corner-stone*, whose foundations shall neither rock nor sway in their place (Isa. xxviii, 16). It shall be a Most Holy Dwelling for Aaron, with everlasting knowledge of the Covenant of justice, and shall offer up sweet fragrance. It shall be a House of Perfection and Truth in Israel that they may establish a Covenant according to the everlasting precepts. And they shall be an agreeable offering, atoning for the Land and determining the judgement of wickedness, and there shall be no more iniquity. (1QS VIII)

At the beginning of this passage, a group of fifteen especially knowledgeable in the Law atone for the sins of all. Later in the passage, the community itself functions as a temple. When its members study and observe the Law and when they suffer for their obedience to the will of God, this brings about atonement for the land and insures that God will remain there. Without Qumran, God would leave the land of Israel because it would be completely unclean. The frequent use of the word "house" in this passage is due to the fact that the temple is called a house. The community now becomes the house (temple) where Aaron, the true priests, can dwell. It is a house of holiness because it belongs to God. It "shall offer up a sweet fragrance" because it does what the temple was intended to do through its sacrificial system: send the pleasing odor of sacrifices up to God in heaven.

A later passage reinforces the idea that all sectaries effect atonement:

> They shall atone for guilty rebellion and for sins of unfaithfulness, that they may obtain loving-kindness <Hebrew: *hesed*> for the Land without the flesh of holocausts and the fat of sacrifice. And prayer rightly offered shall be as an acceptable fragrance of righteousness, and perfection of way as a delectable free-will offering. At that time, the men of the Community shall set apart a House of Holiness in order that it may be united to the most holy things and a House of Community for Israel, for those who walk in perfection. The sons of Aaron alone shall command in matters of justice and property, and every rule concerning the men of the Community shall be determined according to their word. (1QS IX)

The passage ends with the declaration that members "shall be ruled by the primitive precepts in which the men of the Community were first instructed until there shall come the Prophet and the Messiahs of Aaron and Israel." When Israel is properly constituted at the end of time, it will have a king and a high priest, both anointed (messiahs). But now a third figure, a prophet, joins these two. In Deut 18:15–19 Moses promises that the Lord will send another prophet like him. The prophet awaited by Qumran is probably the prophet promised by Moses. This is supported by the *Messianic Anthology* or *Testimonia* (4QTest; see below), which collects biblical passages concerning three figures—a prophet (Deut 5:28–29; 18:18–19), a king (Num 24:15–17), and a priest (Deut 33:8–11).

The sectaries believed that the prophet Isaiah had foretold that they would go out into the desert:

> And when these become members of the Community in Israel according to all these rules, they shall separate from the habitation of unjust men and shall go into the wilderness to prepare there the way of Him; as it is written, *Pre-*

pare in the wilderness the way of . . . , make straight in the desert a path for our God (Isa. xl, 3). This (path) is the study of the Law which He commanded by the hand of Moses, that they may do according to all that has been revealed from age to age, and as the Prophets have revealed by His Holy Spirit. (1QS VIII)

In the first century C.E., the early Christians took this same quotation from Isaiah and applied it to John the Baptist. Both the Essenes and the Christians thought that Isaiah spoke of events that concerned them and their group. There follows in columns VIII–IX another section that has the nature of a penal code.

The prose section of the *Community Rule* ends with rules for the Master. The Master must live in perfect accord with God's will and help others in the community to do the same. He must teach the sectaries, and he must judge and rank them. He is to love members of the community and keep separate from "the men of the Pit." He is to reveal God's mysteries to those who have chosen God's way, and conceal them from others.

The scroll ends with a poetic section similar to a psalm. It assumes that the singer is a teacher and echoes several of the themes in the *Thanksgiving Hymns* (1QH). The section begins by declaring that the psalmist will keep all of God's appointed holy days and times for prayer, and it uses sacrificial terminology to describe prayer ("the offering of the lips"). The keeping of God's prescribed order for worship reflects God's order in creation and so demonstrates a concern for order typical of priestly religion. The psalmist then praises God's judgment of his sins and calls God "My Righteousness." Many places in the scrolls, but especially in the psalms, reflect a profound sense of the unworthiness of all humanity. Unworthiness characterizes the sectaries, too, but God has chosen them and made them worthy to stand in the divine presence:

As for me, my justification is with God.
In His hand are the perfection of my way and the uprightness of my heart.
He will wipe out my transgression through His righteousness. (1QS XI)

The psalm goes on to praise God for the essential characteristic of the sect, the possession of God's revelation, which is hidden from all others. The revelation to the sectaries is a gracious act of God. Self-righteousness is inappropriate because one's graced status is not something earned. God's grace allows the psalmist to stand in the midst of the "Holy Ones," the "Sons of Heaven," both terms for angels. The psalmist is rescued from the power of Satan and placed in a new, proper relationship with God.

THE *MESSIANIC RULE* (1QSA)

Vermes dates this document to around the middle of the first century B.C.E. It is a brief text containing rules for the community in the last days, when the messiahs will be present. The scroll illustrates the fact that the present structure and operation of the community accords with an ideal to be fully implemented at the end of time. Although the rule is for the messianic age, the community appears essentially as it does in the *Community Rule* and the *Damascus Document*. It specifies the status of individuals in the community at each stage of life and reaffirms the absolute authority of the sons of Zadok, also called the sons of Aaron. It stresses proper interpretation and observation of Torah and instruction in the "Book of Meditation," perhaps the *Community Rule*. It recalls the angels' presence in the community and the need for strict limits on who may enter it and on how one is to act while belonging to it. Finally, it briefly describes a common meal at which the messiahs of Aaron and of Israel preside. The priestly messiah takes precedence over the royal one. It is significant that the meal resembles the regular common meal of the community. The community even now lives the ideal life desired by God, which will be fully implemented at the end of times.

MIQSAT MA^CASE HA-TORAH (MMT): SOME OBSERVANCES OF THE LAW (4Q394–399)

This text has been at the center of the debate over access to the Dead Sea Scrolls. Many scholars think that it is especially illuminating for the origins of the sect. There were at least six copies of it in the Qumran library. Its editors have suggested that it is a letter from the leader of the sect to the authorities in Jerusalem. The text advocates adherence to the rules it lays out, appeals to its readers to agree, and argues against a third position (perhaps that of the Pharisees). The legal interpretations in this text correspond with other parts of the scrolls and, in a few instances, to what rabbinic literature says were Sadducean positions, as opposed to Pharisaic interpretations.

In its present form, the text begins with a calendar specifying when Sabbaths and major feasts occur. The calendar is a solar one. The text then lists twenty-two instances in which the writer has specific legal rulings on which he disagrees with those to whom he writes. Many today would consider these disagreements rather minor, but they were not minor to members of the sect.

THE *WAR SCROLL* (1QM, 1Q33, 4Q491–497, 4Q471)

The *War Scroll* is a composite work, and remains of multiple copies were found in the Qumran caves. Its earliest sections were probably written when Israel was dealing with the Seleucids in the second century B.C.E., and it was later adapted to the Roman period. The scroll describes the final war between the forces of good and evil, both cosmic and earthly. The main earthly opponents of the righteous are the "Kittim." "Kittim" originally denoted the inhabitants of Citium in Cyprus, was later applied to Israel's Greek overlords, and finally designated the Romans. As in apocalypticism in general, so also in the *War Scroll,* earthly and heavenly, natural and supernatural events correspond.

A comparison between the *War Scroll* and the book of Daniel is instructive. In the book of Daniel, God's judgment determines the fate of Israel's earthly oppressors (Dan 7). A heavenly decree changes political realities on earth. Also, Israel's fate depends on the fate of its heavenly prince, Michael. When Michael conquers the angel of another nation, Israel prevails over that nation on earth. Daniel, however, does not expect Israel to participate in actual warfare. In the *War Scroll,* it is also God who determines the ultimate outcome of the final battle, but the heavenly and earthly levels are more mixed. Spiritual and human forces fight side by side. The righteous do participate in the final battle. This is similar to what appears in the *Animal Apocalypse,* where God accomplishes the victory using the Maccabees, but the Maccabees receive supernatural aid. Like Daniel, however, the *War Scroll* sees Michael's conquest on the cosmic plane as corresponding to Israel's victory on the earthly level.

The first lines of the *War Scroll* state that it is for "the unleashing of the attack of the sons of light against the company of the sons of darkness, the army of Belial." The sect's human enemies are listed, including traditional biblical enemies of Israel such as Edom, Moab, and the Philistines. Also present are the Kittim and the "ungodly of the Covenant." In other words, on one side of the battle is the sect, and on the other everyone else, including "ungodly" Jews.

The battle starts when the "exiled sons of light return from the Desert of the Peoples to camp in the Desert of Jerusalem; and after the battle they shall go up from there (to Jerusalem?)" (1QM I). ("Jerusalem" is supplied by Vermes and is supported by 1QM VII.) Victory is assured because God sides with the righteous. "This shall be a time of salvation for the people of God, an age of dominion for all the members of His company, and of everlasting destruction for all the company of Belial." The battle is waged by human and superhuman forces:

> On the day when the Kittim fall, there shall be battle and terrible carnage be-
> fore the God of Israel, for that shall be the day appointed from ancient times
> for the battle of destruction of the sons of darkness. At that time, the assembly
> of gods and the hosts of men shall battle, causing great carnage; on the day of
> calamity, the sons of light shall battle with the company of darkness amid the
> shouts of a mighty multitude and the clamour of gods and men to (make man-
> ifest) the might of God. And it shall be a time of [great] tribulation for the
> people which God shall redeem; of all its afflictions none shall be as this, from
> its sudden beginning until its end in eternal redemption. (1QM I)

Humans and angels take part in both sides of the battle. The terrific struggle
brings suffering even to the righteous, for this is a real war. The idea that the
righteous will also suffer in the final days is common in apocalyptic thinking.
It recalls the last chapter of Daniel: "At that time Michael, the great prince,
the protector of your people, shall arise. There shall be a time of anguish,
such as has never occurred since nations first came into existence"
(Dan 12:1).

The war unfolds as predetermined by God. This first column says that
the war will take place in seven phases. In three, the righteous will prevail; in
three, the wicked will win; but in the seventh, God will destroy the power of
the wicked forever. This implies a dualism in which good and evil are equally
balanced until God's intervention.

The eschatological war is a holy war in which people and angels fight
alongside one another. As a holy war, its description mixes realistic with unrealistic elements. Prayers, sacrifices, and liturgy are as important as the fighting itself. Military arrangements are determined by purity rules, and no one
who is impure is allowed in the camp. Ritual purity must be constantly maintained in the camps because of the presence of the angels. Purity rules about
who can be in the war camp resemble such rules for the temple as are found
in Deut 23 and elsewhere (see also the strict rules concerning Jerusalem's purity in CD XII, XV–XVI and in other places in the scrolls).

War Scroll 2 anticipates the time when the proper priestly group, those
from Qumran, will again control the temple. It defines parts of the community in terms of their service in the temple:

> They shall rank the chief Priests below the High Priest and his vicar. And the
> twelve chief Priests shall minister at the daily sacrifice before God, whereas the
> twenty-six leaders of the priestly divisions shall minister in their divisions. . . .
> These are the men who shall attend at holocausts and sacrifices to prepare
> sweet-smelling incense for the good pleasure of God, to atone for all His
> congregation, and to satisfy themselves perpetually before Him at the table
> of glory.

The *War Scroll* depicts a time when the specific sacrifices required by Torah would again be offered by pure priests.

In 1QM X–XII, the officers deliver a long speech to strengthen the faithful for war. God is extolled as the almighty creator, and Israel is seen as unique among humans because of its knowledge of God's laws. They are those "who have heard the voice of Majesty and have seen the Angels of Holiness, whose ear has been unstopped, and who have heard profound things" (1QM X). The officers recall David's victories over Israel's enemies. They tell God that the victory is his, not Israel's, and they quote Num 24:17–19, a passage taken to be messianic: *"A star shall come out of Jacob, and a sceptre shall rise out of Israel. He shall smite the temples of Moab and destroy all the children of Sheth. He shall rule out of Jacob and shall cause the survivors of the cities to perish. The enemy shall be his possession and Israel shall accomplish mighty deeds"* (1QM XI).

Israel has learned through a "messiah" (probably the Teacher of Righteousness) that, in the final battle, the hordes of Belial will be defeated because God is on the side of the righteous: "For Thou wilt fight with them from heaven" (1QM XI). God will fight in the final battle as God did in the exodus against Pharaoh, and God's angelic army fights in the battle.

The priests are noncombatants in the final struggle. They sacrifice, pray, and deliver sermons. They are the cultic leaders of the war and must keep themselves separated from the aspects of war that could defile them: "And as the slain men fall, the Priests shall trumpet from afar; they shall not approach the slain lest they be defiled with unclean blood. For they are holy, and they shall not profane the anointing of their priesthood with the blood of nations of vanity" (1QM IX).

The role of the archangel Michael, Israel's prince, is detailed in column XVII:

> This is the day appointed by Him for the defeat and overthrow of the Prince of the kingdom of wickedness, and He will send eternal succour to the company of His redeemed by the might of the princely Angel of the kingdom of Michael. . . . He will raise up the kingdom of Michael in the midst of the gods, and the realm of Israel in the midst of all flesh. Righteousness shall rejoice on high, and all the children of his truth shall jubilate in eternal knowledge.

Michael victorious among the gods (angels) corresponds to Israel exalted among the nations. This is like Dan 7, where Michael (the "one like a son of man"; 7:13) receives dominion in heaven while Israel ("the people of the holy ones of the Most High"; 7:27) receives kingship on earth.

The manuscript of this text from Qumran Cave 1 ends with a hymn to Zion. The result of the great battle will be that Jerusalem, as the center of

God's sovereignty and that of his people, will be the center of the world. All nations will be subject to it.

BIBLICAL INTERPRETATION

Biblical interpretation at Qumran follows the principle that the Bible refers directly to the sect. Prophetic literature was seen as especially rich in allusions to the sect. This is precisely the position of Christians with respect to their own religion: they interpret the Hebrew Bible as if its purpose is to point to Christ and the Christian religion. The Qumran library contains several texts whose literary genre is commentary on Scripture. They cite and comment on a biblical book verse by verse. Each verse is usually followed by the formula "Its interpretation," followed by a decoding of the verse to show its application to the sect. This sort of interpretation is called *pesher*, a Hebrew word meaning "interpretation." The sect does not assume that the author of the biblical text comprehended its full implications. It was the Teacher of Righteousness who was given knowledge of what the deeper meanings of the prophecies were, as is claimed in the commentary on the prophet Habakkuk:

> God told Habakkuk to write down that which would happen to the final generation, but He did not make known to him when time would come to an end. And as for that which He said, *That he who reads may read it speedily:* interpreted this concerns the Teacher of Righteousness, to whom God made known all the mysteries of the words of His servants the Prophets. (1QpHab VII)

THE *COMMENTARY ON HABAKKUK* (1QpHab)

In citations of the commentaries, "p" indicates that the document is a *pesher*, or biblical interpretation, and it is followed by an abbreviation of the biblical book to be explained. The *Commentary on Habakkuk* has been dated, on the basis of paleography, to around 30 B.C.E. It cites Habakkuk verse by verse and explains it in terms of the sect. Although the prophet Habakkuk prophesied sometime between 626 and 587 B.C.E., the Qumran community is not interested in the original context of the prophecies. Their true meaning is not what they meant to Habakkuk but what they mean to the sect. The verse-by-verse decoding of Habakkuk is a method followed by all of the pesharim (plural of "pesher," *pesharim*). It is not simply that the sectaries conceive of themselves as adapting prophecy to the sect's needs. They believe that God foretold specific events in the life of the community, so the pesharim are an important place to look for reconstructing the history of the Qumran community.

The commentary is directed against the priestly establishment in Jerusalem, which opposes the Teacher of Righteousness, as well as against all in Israel who do not believe in the Teacher.

> [Interpreted, this concerns] those who were unfaithful together with the Liar, in that they [did] not [listen to the word received by] the Teacher of Righteousness from the mouth of God. And it concerns the unfaithful of the New [Covenant] in that they have not believed in the Covenant of God [and have profaned] His holy Name. And likewise, this saying is to be interpreted [as concerning those who] will be unfaithful at the end of days. They, the men of violence and the breakers of the Covenant, will not believe when they hear all that [is to happen to] the final generation from the Priest [in whose heart] God set [understanding] that he might interpret all the words of His servants the Prophets, through whom He foretold all that would happen to His people and [His land]. (1QpHab II)

The Teacher encounters opposition not only from the Jerusalem establishment and the majority of Jews but also from some within his own community, those of the new covenant. Evidence for internal conflicts appear also in the scroll of the *Thanksgiving Hymns*. The basic reason for such opposition is that most do not accept that the Teacher, here called "the Priest," is indeed the one who understands the words of the prophets.

Later passages supply more information about the Teacher's opponents:

> *O traitors, why do you stare and stay silent when the wicked swallows up one more righteous than he?* (i,13b). Interpreted <Hebrew: *pishro*, "its interpretation," from *pesher*>, this concerns the House of Absalom and the members of his council who were silent at the time of the chastisement of the Teacher of Righteousness and gave him no help against the Liar who flouted the Law in the midst of their whole [congregation]. (1QpHab V)

The identity of the House of Absalom is not known. Absalom may be the son of David who revolted against his father (2 Sam 15–19), or may be a contemporary of the Teacher of Righteousness, or both. In any case, Hab 1:13b is taken to refer to an incident when the Teacher and one called the Liar had a public confrontation in which the Teacher was abandoned by a group from whom he expected support. The Liar is an important public figure who disagrees with the Teacher on Torah. He may be the same person as the Wicked Priest and the Scoffer (probably a Hasmonean). This event may be one of the occurrences leading to the Teacher's withdrawal from Jerusalem to the desert.

In column VI, Hab 1:14–16 is taken to refer to the Kittim, who "sacrifice to their standards and worship their weapons of war." This describes the Romans well. Josephus says that when the Romans captured the temple in 70 C.E., they set up their standards in the temple court and sacrificed to them (*J. W.* 6.316).

Habakkuk's language is well suited to Qumran's eschatological outlook:

> *If it tarries, wait for it, for it shall surely come and shall not be late* (ii, 3b). Interpreted, this concerns the men of truth who keep the Law, whose hands shall not slacken in the service of truth when the final age is prolonged. For all the ages of God reach their appointed end as He determines for them in the mysteries of his wisdom. (1QpHab VII)

This commentary may have been written when the eschatological battle did not happen as expected. It uses the prophetic word to show that the delay was anticipated in Scripture, and it reaffirms the belief that God's mysterious plans will be actualized without fail.

> *[But the righteous shall live by his faith]* (ii, 4b). Interpreted, this concerns all those who observe the Law in the House of Judah, whom God will deliver from the House of Judgement because of their suffering and because of their faith in the Teacher of Righteousness. (1QpHab VII–VIII)

"All those who observe the Law in the House of Judah" can only mean the members of the sect. This is but one of many references in the scrolls to the suffering undergone by the sectaries. Faith in the Teacher of Righteousness is necessary for deliverance (salvation) here. It is striking that Paul uses the same verse from Habakkuk to show that salvation comes through faith in Jesus Christ (Gal 3:11).

In column VIII, Hab 2:5–8 is interpreted as follows:

> Interpreted, this concerns the Wicked Priest who was called by the name of truth when he first arose. But when he ruled over Israel his heart became proud, and he forsook God and betrayed the precepts for the sake of riches. He robbed and amassed the riches of the men of violence who rebelled against God, and he took the wealth of the peoples, heaping sinful iniquity upon himself. And he lived in the ways of abominations amidst every unclean defilement.

This passage applies to a priest, originally approved by the Teacher's group, who then assumed power and went astray. The Hasmoneans are likely candidates for this description. The Wicked Priest may be the first Hasmonean to assume the title of high priest, Jonathan, who ruled from 152 to 142 as high priest. The pesher considers the Wicked Priest guilty of the kinds of crimes typical of rulers—violence and the amassing of riches. He and his cohorts are spoken of as rebels against God. The last line puts all of this into the language of priestly religion—abomination, uncleanness, defilement.

The condemnation is repeated in the following passage, an interpretation of Hab 2:7–8a:

> Interpreted this concerns the last Priests of Jerusalem, who shall amass money and wealth by plundering the peoples. But in the last days, their riches and their booty shall be delivered into the hands of the army of the Kittim. (1QpHab IX)

John Hyrcanus I (ruled 134–104) and Alexander Jannaeus (ruled 103–76) both conquered substantial portions of territory in Judea and surrounding areas and so reigned over Gentiles. "Plundering the peoples" would fit their reigns. The army of the Kittim is probably the Roman army that took over Judea in 63 B.C.E.

The next section of the commentary speaks of the Wicked Priest's death as a fulfillment of Hab 2:8b:

> Interpreted, this concerns the Wicked Priest whom God delivered into the hands of his enemies because of the iniquity committed against the Teacher of Righteousness and the men of his Council, that he might be humbled by means of a destroying scourge, in bitterness of soul, because he had done wickedly to his elect. (1QpHab IX)

If the Wicked Priest is Jonathan, then the enemies are the Seleucids who killed him by treachery in 142 B.C.E. The Habakkuk commentary considers his death a punishment for the way he treated the Teacher and his followers.

In column XI a confrontation between the Teacher and the Wicked priest is seen as a fulfillment of Hab 2:15:

> Interpreted, this concerns the Wicked Priest who pursued the Teacher of Righteousness to the house of his exile that he might confuse him with his venomous fury. And at the time appointed for rest, for the Day of Atonement, he appeared before him to confuse them, and to cause them to stumble on the Day of Fasting, their Sabbath of repose.

Because Qumran followed a solar calendar and Jerusalem a lunar one, the day on which the Day of Atonement was observed at Qumran did not correspond to its observance by the Jerusalem establishment. The Wicked Priest may have used this discrepancy to confront the Qumran community when it was most vulnerable. The horror with which Qumran viewed this desecration is expressed in the many titles given to the feast—time appointed for rest, Day of Atonement, Day of Fasting, Sabbath of repose. Precisely what happened is unknown, but it certainly made an impression on the sect and illustrates how seriously the priestly establishment took the existence of the Qumran settlement.

A final passage indicating the wickedness of the Jerusalem establishment interprets Hab 2:17. Because the priest tried to harm the "Poor" (here it is a designation of the sectaries), he will be treated as he wished to treat them. The passage continues,

> And as for that which He said, *Because of the blood of the city and the violence done to the land:* interpreted, *the city* is Jerusalem where the Wicked Priest committed abominable deeds and defiled the Temple of God. *The violence done to the land:* these are the cities of Judah where he robbed the Poor of their possessions. (1QHab XII)

The Wicked Priest is in Jerusalem and in charge of the temple and of Judah. His rule defiles the temple. He uses his power to wreak violence against the Poor, the sectaries. He must thus be a Hasmonean priest.

THE *COMMENTARY ON PSALMS* (1Q16, 4Q171, 4Q173)

Most of the text deals with Ps 37. Psalm 37 is a generalized reflection on the injustices of the world and the justice of God. Four points in this short, fragmentary document are of interest here. First, Ps 37:18–19 is taken as referring to "the penitents of the desert who, saved, shall live for a thousand generations and to whom all the glory of Adam shall belong, as also to their seed forever" (4Q171 III). This reference to the glory of Adam reminds us that in apocalyptic thought the end is like the beginning. The glory that Adam lost will be restored to the sect. This idea appears several times in the scrolls. Second, interpreting Ps 37:21–22, the commentary says, "Interpreted, this concerns the congregation of the Poor, who [shall possess] the whole world as an inheritance. They shall possess the High Mountain of Israel [for ever], and shall enjoy [everlasting] delights in his Sanctuary" (4Q171 III). This implies that the sect will control Jerusalem in the end. The third point concerns the Teacher. In this text he is explicitly designated a priest: "Interpreted, this concerns the Priest, the Teacher of [Righteousness whom] God chose to stand before Him, for He established him to build for Himself the congregation of . . . " (4Q171 III). The last point concerns the Wicked Priest, who is said to have tried to put the Teacher of Righteousness to death. The term "poor" is often used in the Bible to refer to innocent victims of injustice (see Pleins). From here it is a short step to apply the term to the "exiled" community that produced the scrolls.

THE *COMMENTARY ON NAHUM* (4QpNAH [4Q169])

This commentary is of special interest because it mentions names of historical figures as it interprets Nah 2:11b. Nahum was originally written between 663 and 612 B.C.E. in reaction to the Assyrian Empire, the empire that destroyed the northern Israelite kingdom in 722 B.C.E. But the pesher takes the prophetic text to refer to Hasmonean times:

> [Interpreted, this concerns Deme]trius king of Greece who sought, on the counsel of those who seek smooth things, to enter Jerusalem. [But God did not permit the city to be delivered] into the hands of the kings of Greece, from the time of Antiochus until the coming of the rulers of the Kittim. But then she shall be trampled under their feet. (4QpNah I)

Antiochus is Antiochus IV Epiphanes (ruled 175–164), and the rulers of the Kittim are the Romans. Demetrius is Demetrius III, a Seleucid who ruled between Antiochus and the coming of the Romans in 63 B.C.E. Jerusalem was plundered by Antiochus but then evaded further capture until the coming of Pompey in 63 B.C.E.

"Interpreted, this concerns the furious young lion [who executes revenge] on those who seek smooth things and hangs men alive, . . . formerly in Israel" (4QpNah I). The "seekers of smooth things" are often thought to be the Pharisees. Many scholars find in the lion a reference to the Hasmonean king, Alexander Jannaeus. The reference accords well with Josephus's story about Jannaeus crucifying eight hundred of his enemies for conspiring with Demetrius III to overthrow him (*Ant.* 13.380–83; *J.W.* 1.96–98). Josephus says elsewhere that the Pharisees were strong opponents of Jannaeus (see ch. 6, below).

MESSIANIC EXEGESIS

The scrolls use the term "messiah" to designate figures of the past, those who conveyed the word of God, probably the prophets (e.g., CD II, V–VI; 1QM XI). But when we speak of a messiah, most often we mean an eschatological leader of Israel, who either brings in the end time or is present when God restores the world and Israel. At Qumran, there are two such eschatological messiahs, one a priest and the other a layman, called the messiahs of

Aaron and Israel (1QS IX; 1QSa II; CD VII). Of these, the priest is dominant.

THE *MESSIANIC ANTHOLOGY* (4QTEST [4Q175])

In addition to the passages already examined, we should look at several texts that contain messianic expectations. The first is the *Messianic Anthology,* or *Testimonia* (a *testimonium* is a collection of texts to prove a point), which collects several biblical texts that speak of three future figures. The first speaks of a future prophet like Moses, the second of a royal messiah, and the last of a future priestly figure. This corresponds with the expectation of a prophet, royal messiah, and priestly messiah such as we saw in 1QS IX above. The text about a prophet is from Deuteronomy:

> *I will raise up for them a Prophet like you from among their brethren. I will put my words into his mouth and he shall tell them all that I command him. And I will require a reckoning of whoever will not listen to the words which the Prophet will speak in my Name.* (Deut. xviii, 18–19)

This same passage is applied to Jesus in Acts 3:17–26. The next biblical passage is from Numbers, which we have already seen interpreted messianically in 1QM XI above:

> *A star shall come out of Jacob and a sceptre shall rise out of Israel; he shall crush the temples of Moab and destroy all the children of Sheth.* (Num xxiv, 15–17)

The priestly figure comes next, through the inclusion of Deut 33:8–11, the blessing of the tribe of Levi. This blessing praises the Levitical priests for their obedience to God, and it gives them the duties of sacrifice and Torah interpretation.

The *testimonium* ends with a quotation of Josh 6:26, which originally forbade the rebuilding of Jericho. It is used here to attack the Jerusalem establishment.

A *MIDRASH ON THE LAST DAYS* (4QFLOR [4Q174])

This text collects and interprets passages from 2 Samuel and the Psalms. It first combines the famous passage from 2 Sam 7, in which God promises to dwell with Israel in Jerusalem, with Exod 15:17–18, in which God is praised for the establishment of the sanctuary. It interprets them as referring to the founding of the community, conceived of as a temple: "He has commanded that a Sanctuary of men be built for Himself, that there they may send up, like the smoke of incense, the works of the Law."

Then the text continues with 2 Sam 7, recalling the promise to David that his son would sit on the throne of Israel and that his son would be God's son and God would be his father. This is interpreted as follows: "He is the Branch of David who shall arise with the Interpreter of the Law [to rule] in Zion [at the end] of time." This is expectation of two messiahs.

Passages from Ps 1, Isaiah, and Ezekiel are then used to condemn the priests in Jerusalem, specifically those sons of Zadok who oppose the sect. Not all sons of Zadok, therefore, belong to the Qumran community.

Finally, the text cites Ps 2, a messianic psalm that speaks of a Gentile uprising "against the Lord and against his Messiah." This is taken to refer to the battle of the last days, between "the elect of Israel"—also referred to as the ones who "shall practice the whole Law . . . of Moses"—and their enemies.

THE *MESSIANIC APOCALYPSE* (4QMESSAP [4Q521])

We noted above that although Qumran was an apocalyptic community, no apocalypses have been found among the writings that can be attributed to the sect itself. Daniel and books of Enoch were popular in the community. It is still debated whether the fragment 4Q521 is an apocalypse although some scholars call it an apocalypse. Interesting for our purposes here is that it speaks of the Messiah, and then it speaks of one who "liberates the captives, restores sight to the blind, straightens the b[ent]." Further, "He will heal the wounded, and revive the dead and bring good news to the poor." Such images recall biblical passages such as Ps 146:7–8 and Isa 61:1. It is not clear whether it is God or the Messiah who performs these miraculous feats. But the connection between the coming of the Messiah and the occurrence of these events is interesting from the point of view of what is said about Jesus in the New Testament.

THE *THANKSGIVING HYMNS* (1QH)

This is a collection of about twenty-five psalms (according to Vermes's counting), echoing the biblical psalms in language, form, and ideas. Qumran's hymns may have been used in the sect's worship. They take the form of individual thanksgivings. Several describe the experience of a teacher betrayed by his own group and persecuted by opponents. According to Vermes's numbering, those are 1, 2, and 7–11. It is possible that those hymns were written by the Teacher of Righteousness, but we cannot know for sure.

The hymns claim that God foreknows everything and that all operates according to his law. They often contrast humanity and God. The psalmist prefaces the following passage by saying that it is not through his own reason but through God's gracious revelation that he understands how things really are:

> These things I know by the wisdom which comes from Thee,
> For Thou hast unstopped my ears to marvellous mysteries.
> And yet I, a shape of clay kneaded in water,
> a ground of shame and a source of pollution,
> a melting-pot of wickedness and an edifice of sin,
> a straying and perverted spirit of no understanding, fearful of
> righteous judgments,
> what can I say that is not foreknown, and what can I utter that is
> not foretold?
> All things are graven before Thee on a written Reminder for
> everlasting ages,
> and for the numbered cycles of the eternal years in all their
> seasons;
> they are not hidden or absent from Thee. (1QH IX)

The psalmist says that God has purified him of his sins and placed him in the company of angels. Because of secret knowledge given him by God, he represents the truth and so is ill-treated by sinners. "But to the elect of righteousness Thou hast made me a banner, and a discerning interpreter of wonderful mysteries" (1QH X). Differing interpretations of Torah are at stake, as is clear from the following: "To the interpreters of error I have been an opponent, [but a man of peace] to all those who see true things." Opponents of the psalmist and his revealed message are considered to be anti-God and partisans of Belial.

Vermes notes that the two main themes of the hymns are knowledge and salvation (*CDSSE* 244). Through knowledge of God's will and submission to it, the psalmist has been saved from the lot of Belial and brought into the company of angels.

> I thank Thee, O Lord,
> for Thou hast redeemed my soul from the Pit,
> and from the Hell of Abaddon
> Thou hast raised me up to everlasting height.
> I walk on limitless level ground,
> and I know there is hope for him
> whom Thou has shaped from dust
> for the everlasting Council.
> Thou hast cleansed a perverse spirit of great sin
> that it may stand with the host of the Holy Ones,
> and that it may enter into community
> with the congregation of the Sons of Heaven. (1QH XI)

"Sons of Heaven" here means angels. We have seen in our study of apocalypticism that the reward of the righteous is often to join the angels. This passage is immediately followed with one that begins, "And yet I, a creature of clay, what am I?"

The "seekers of smooth things" receive much criticism from the psalmist, for they lead Israel astray regarding Torah:

> And they, teachers of lies and seers of falsehood,
>   have schemed against me a devilish scheme,
> to exchange the Law engraved on my heart by Thee
> for the smooth things (which they speak) to Thy people.
> And they withhold from the thirsty the drink of Knowledge,
>   and assuage their thirst with vinegar,
> that they may gaze on their straying,
>   on their folly concerning their feast-days,
>   on their fall into their snares. (1QH XII)

The seekers of smooth things are teachers (probably Pharisees), and their teaching concerns the Torah, particularly the feast days. The psalmist admits that they seek God, but claims that "They seek Thee with a double heart and are not confirmed in Thy truth." The idea that they speak smooth things may be particularly appropriate given Qumran's strict view of the Torah, and the mention of feast days may reflect the calendrical disputes we have already discussed. The structure of the charge, that the opponents neither accept the truth nor allow others to do so, recalls Jesus' criticism of the Pharisees in Matt 23:13: "You lock people out of the kingdom of heaven. For you do not go in yourselves, and when others are going in, you stop them!" Both Jesus' criticism and that of Qumran reflect the sorts of sectarian controversies that characterized late Second Temple Judaism.

The life of the psalmist, perhaps identical in this case with the Teacher of Righteousness, has not been easy. Not only has he faced fierce opposition from others in Israel; members of his own group have not always been faithful to him (see above on the *Commentary on Habakkuk*).

> But I have been [iniquity to] those who contend with me,
> dispute and quarrelling to my friends,
> wrath to the members of my Covenant
> and murmuring and protest to all my companions.
> [All who have ea]ten my bread
>   have lifted their heel against me,
> and all those joined to my Council
>   have mocked me with wicked lips.
> The members of my [Covenant] have rebelled

and have murmured round about me;
they have gone as talebearers
   before the children of mischief
concerning the mystery which Thou hast hidden in me. (1QH XIII)

There is an echo here of Ps 41:9: "Even my bosom friend in whom I trusted, who ate of my bread, has lifted his heel against me." John 13:18 uses the same verse from Psalm 41 to refer to Judas's betrayal of Jesus.

God will not allow Belial to hold sway forever. There will be a great battle, and the unrighteous will fall (1QH XIV). The teacher claims that he is the touchstone by which each one will be judged righteous or unrighteous: "For Thou wilt condemn in Judgement all those who assail me, distinguishing through me between the just and the wicked" (1QH XV).

CONCLUSION

The Qumran community was a sect—a religious group that, to a great degree, shared the dominant religious culture but saw itself as opposed to the religious establishment. The people of Qumran withdrew to the shores of the Dead Sea and waited for the coming of the Lord. They made atonement for the land and prepared the Lord's way through perfect obedience to Torah as interpreted by their founder, the Teacher of Righteousness, and the Zadokite priests who ran the community. Qumran's priestly orientation was expressed in its social structure, which was dominated by the Zadokite priests, and in its theology and ritual, which stressed atonement and cleanness. Its worldview was apocalyptic, expressed in its expectation of an imminent final battle, its belief in esoteric revelation granted to its founder, and in the detailed belief in a supernatural world whose struggles between good and evil were reflected in the earthly realm. The Dead Sea Scrolls have failed to deliver the devastating blow to Christianity that sensation seekers predicted. Instead they have been a gold mine of comparative material for students of Christianity and have contributed greatly to our knowledge of Judaism of the mid-second century B.C.E. to the first century C.E.

SELECT BIBLIOGRAPHY

Beall, Todd. *Josephus' Description of the Essenes Illustrated by the Dead Sea Scrolls.* SNTSMS 58. Cambridge: Cambridge University Press, 1988.

Brown, Raymond. "The Messianism of Qumran." *CBQ* 19 (1957): 53–82.

Callaway, Phillip R. *The History of the Qumran Community: An Investigation.* Sheffield, England: Sheffield Academic Press, 1988.

Charlesworth, James H. "The Origin and Subsequent History of the Authors of the Dead Sea Scrolls: Four Transitional Phases among the Qumran Essenes." *RevQ* 10 (1979–1981): 213–33.

Collins, John J. "Patterns of Eschatology at Qumran." Pages 351–75 in *Traditions in Transformation*. Edited by B. Halpern and J. D. Levenson. Winona Lake, Ind.: Eisenbrauns, 1981.

———. "Qumran." *AI.*

———. *The Scepter and The Star: The Messiahs of the Dead Sea Scrolls and Other Ancient Literature*. New York: Doubleday, 1995.

———. "Was the Dead Sea Sect an Apocalyptic Community?" Pages 25–51 in *Archeology and History in the Dead Sea Scrolls: The New York University Conference in Memory of Yigael Yadin*. Edited by L. H. Schiffman. Sheffield, England: JSOT Press, 1990.

Cross, Frank M. *The Ancient Library of Qumran*. Rev. ed. Grand Rapids: Baker, 1980.

Davies, Philip R. *Qumran*. Cities of the Biblical World. Guildford, England: Lutterworth, 1982.

Fitzmyer, Joseph A. *The Dead Sea Scrolls: Major Publications and Tools for Study*. 2d ed. Missoula, Mont.: Scholars Press, 1977.

Garcia Martinez, Florentino. *The Dead Sea Scrolls Translated: The Qumran Texts in English*. Leiden: Brill, 1994.

Garcia Martinez, Florentino, and Eibert Tigchelaar. *The Dead Sea Scrolls Study Edition*. 2 vols. Grand Rapids: Eerdmans, 1999.

Gärtner, Bertil. *The Temple and the Community in Qumran and the New Testament*. Cambridge: Cambridge University Press, 1965.

Hengel, Martin, James H. Charlesworth, and D. Mendels. "The Polemical Character of 'On Kingship' in the *Temple Scroll:* An Attempt at Dating 11QTemple." *JJS* 37 (1986): 28–38.

Knibb, Michael A. "The Exile in the Literature of the Intertestamental Period." *HeyJ* 17 (1976): 253–72.

Murphy-O'Connor, Jerome. "The Essenes and Their History." *RB* 81 (1974): 215–44.

Pleins, J. David. "Poor, Poverty: Old Testament." *ABD* 5:402–14.

Schiffman, Lawrence. *The Halakhah at Qumran*. Leiden: Brill, 1975.

———. "The New Halakhic Letter (4QMMT) and the Origins of the Dead Sea Sect." *BA* 53 (1990): 64–73.

Smith, Morton. "The Dead Sea Sect in Relation to Ancient Judaism." *NTS* 7 (1960–1961): 347–60.

Ulrich, Eugene, and James Vanderkam, eds. *The Community of the Renewed Covenant: The Notre Dame Symposium on the Dead Sea Scrolls*. Notre Dame, Ind.: University of Notre Dame, 1994.

VanderKam, James C. *The Dead Sea Scrolls Today.* Grand Rapids: Eerdmans, 1994.

Vaux, Roland de. *Archeology and the Dead Sea Scrolls.* London: Oxford University Press, 1973.

Vermes, Geza. *The Complete Dead Sea Scrolls in English.* New York: Penguin, 1997.

Vermes, Geza, and Martin Goodman, eds. *The Essenes according to the Classical Sources.* Sheffield, England: JSOT Press, 1989.

Wilson, Bryan. *Magic and the Millenium: A Sociological Study of Religious Movements of Protest among Tribal and Third-World Peoples.* London: Heinemann, 1973.

———. *Patterns of Sectarianism: Organization and Ideology in Social and Religious Movements.* London: Heinemann, 1967.

CHAPTER 6

SCRIBES, PHARISEES, SADDUCEES, AND SANHEDRIN

PRIMARY READINGS: Matthew ◆ Mark ◆ Luke ◆ John ◆ Readings from Josephus as indicated in the text

Anyone who has ever heard the story of Jesus is familiar with the groups we study in this chapter—scribes, Pharisees, and Sadducees. They seem like "old friends" (or perhaps "old enemies") in the sense that we know them well. But what do we really know about them? How did we get our information? And is this information reliable?

Most Christians know of Second Temple Judaism only through the story of Jesus as told in the gospels of Matthew, Mark, Luke, and John. But the early churches that produced these gospels were bitterly disappointed that Jews as a group had not accepted Jesus as the Messiah. They portrayed this lack of belief as stubborn, sinful, the fruit of willful opposition to God's will, and deceitful. This can hardly be fair. Jesus does not really fit any "job description" of messiah that we have seen or will see in our studies, so it is not surprising that most of his contemporaries did not see him as such. And as the church became less Jewish, in particular when it stopped being subject to Torah, it became even less likely that Jews would convert. Betrayal of God's Torah would be unthinkable.

But, again, the early church was puzzled and pained that the majority of Jews did not see things as it did. Christians used a variety of strategies to respond, prominent among which was the construction of proofs from Scripture. Another of their main strategies was to write the story of Jesus and to portray Jews and their leaders as evil and as opposing Jesus for base motives. Scribes and Pharisees became hypocrites. Priests and elders became deceitful conspirators. The Jewish man or woman in the street became ignorant, gullible, and a tool of bad leaders and demons. If we depend on the Gospels for our picture of Second Temple Judaism, the picture will not be a pretty one.

Suppose for a moment that we are living before the fall of the Soviet Union and the end of the Cold War. In a class on American history, the

professor begins by telling us that the textbook was authored by a noted Soviet historian and this will be our sole source of information. We may decide to keep silent so as not to jeopardize our grade, but would we really be
content? Not likely. We can see instantly that the information we get and
the viewpoints we are exposed to will be biased. This is pretty much what
happens when Christians hear and tell the story of Jesus, thinking that we
have a fair picture of the other characters in the story. But we do not, for the
sources are biased. And the only way we can get a fairer picture is to read
with suspicion, seek other sources, and try not to let our misconceptions
get the better of us.

SCRIBES

THE SCRIBAL PROFESSION

The scribe's occupation was based upon knowledge of reading and writing. Since the literacy rate was low in ancient times, the scribe's function was
crucial. Scribes populated the bureaucracy at every level, from royal court to
peasant village. Village scribes probably had relatively little education and
performed simple functions, such as writing out contracts. At the other end
of the spectrum were scribes who were advisors to the ruler, took care of correspondence, and kept official records of all sorts. Those at the highest level
may even have been members of the ruling class. Most scribes were in the
middle level of the bureaucracy.

Saldarini *(Pharisees)* suggests that the best English word to convey what
the scribe did in ancient societies is "secretary." Secretaries exist at every level
of society and in most organizations. There is a big difference between the
secretary of a third-grade class and the secretary of state. And it would never
occur to us to assume that every secretary at every level in the United States is
a Democrat, or a Republican, or an Independent, or holds the same political
views as every other secretary. It is precisely because "secretary" is such a
broad term, and because it denotes a profession whose duties are analogous,
to some degree, with those of ancient scribes, that Saldarini's suggestion is
enlightening.

Just as secretaries today have no single political or social viewpoint, so in
the ancient world scribes did not have a single point of view. Just as there is
no organization or group that represents all secretaries in the modern world,
so the scribes do not constitute a single, coherent, organized group. In the ancient world, relatively few scribes were at the highest levels of government.
Scribes, like secretaries, attained and kept their position because of their
skills, but they were always subordinate to someone else. They were retainers,

members of a class that existed to serve the governing class. There must have been schools to train scribes. The highest scribes required extensive education, extending well beyond the ability to read and write. As Solomon transformed Israel into a full ancient Near Eastern kingdom, he developed a scribal establishment (see ch. 1, above). This probably accounts for his reputation as a wise man, since the scribes were sometimes thought of as "the wise."

There were scribes within most Jewish groups. Pharisees who interpreted Torah must have been scribes. Essene society, which was centered around Torah and its interpretation, needed scribes, and scholars who study the Dead Sea Scrolls even come to know individual scribes from their handwriting. The priestly establishment required many scribes, and Hasmonean and Herodian rulers employed them. Scribes also wrote and copied apocalypses, including those critical of the Jerusalem establishment.

Scribes

The word *scribe* in Hebrew, Greek, and other languages had a wide range of meaning that changed over time and could denote several social roles. The closest English equivalent is the term "secretary," which refers to roles from that of a typist to a cabinet officer at the highest level of government. In both Semitic and Greek usage, the scribe was commonly a middle-level government official, for example, a "secretary" in charge of the town council (Acts 19:35). (Saldarini, "Scribes," 1012).

JEWISH WRITINGS

In Jewish writings, scribes are often associated with Torah. Scribes were responsible for writing, editing, preserving, and transmitting sacred traditions, and so they were involved in the production of the Bible itself. Likewise, teaching the Law must also have been a scribal activity. One of Israel's most famous scribes was Ezra, who brought the Torah from Persia to Judah around the turn of the fourth century B.C.E. It is significant that Ezra was also a priest, since the teaching of Torah was also a priestly function. Ezra illustrates an overlap between the categories of priest and scribe.

The end of chapter 3, above, used Sir 38–39 as evidence for understanding the role of an upper-class scribe. Sirach notes that the scribe cannot pursue another occupation, since then he would not have time for study. He says that the scribe studies Torah and all ancient wisdom, prophecies, proverbs, and sayings of famous people, that he is close to the ruling class and gives them counsel, that he travels in foreign lands and learns foreign wisdom, and that he seeks inspiration from God.

In rabbinic literature (literature produced by rabbis beginning ca. 200 C.E.), scribes often appear simply as copyists, but they are also legal experts, whose rulings on legal matters are authoritative but do not have the weight of Scripture.

Josephus, the first-century C.E. Jewish historian, confirms the notion that scribes occupied every level of the bureaucracy. They do not appear as a single, organized group in his writings. Josephus does not associate the scribes explicitly with Torah. He speaks of the "scribes of the Temple" as a recognizable group (*Ant.* 11.128; 12.142). In the war against the Romans (66–70 C.E.), the rebels executed many prominent citizens. Among these is a scribe: "After these a priest named Ananias, son of Masbalus, a person of distinction, and Aristeus, the secretary [scribe] of the council [Sanhedrin], a native of Emmaus, and along with them fifteen eminent men from among the people were executed" (*J. W.* 5.532). Aristeus the scribe is included here among the most eminent men of the city and so belongs to the upper classes. This hardly works to his favor here, since he is killed precisely because of his status.

THE NEW TESTAMENT

The New Testament pictures ancient Jewish scribes as a unified group, almost unanimously opposed to Jesus (Mark 12:28–34 is an exception). But it generally lumps together Jewish leadership groups with little regard for their differences. The New Testament does contain some historical information about the scribes, but it must be used critically.

The Gospels concur with other sources in associating scribes with Torah and with government. Saldarini summarizes the roles of scribes in the Gospels:

> The gospels testify most reliably to scribes connected to the government in Jerusalem where their role seems to be as associates of the priests both in judicial proceedings, enforcement of Jewish custom and law and ongoing business in the Sanhedrin. The gospel traditions about scribes may reflect the opposition of many scattered local officials to early Christian communities before and after the war, and perhaps opposition to Jesus also. (*Pharisees,* 268)

PHARISEES

The New Testament gives the Pharisees very bad press. And this has determined how we hear the word "Pharisee" today. If we were to say to someone, "We think you are a real Pharisee," that person would take it an insult. Today "Pharisee" is pretty much synonymous with "hypocrite." With some exceptions, this is how the New Testament presents the Pharisees. Historical research is not equipped to prove or disprove such a judgment, because making a judgment on hypocrisy depends upon getting inside the minds and hearts of persons, particularly hard when we are dealing with those who lived two millennia ago. Nonetheless, it stretches the imagination to think that the thousands of members of a religious group whose difficult and noble goal was to implement God's will in their daily lives were, each and every one of them, hypocrites. That would be remarkable indeed. Historical work on Second Temple Judaism and on the historical Jesus must therefore put such unwarranted and outrageous assumptions aside, in the interests of fairness and historical accuracy.

Many today are also under the impression that the Pharisees were the foremost political power in Galilee and Judea during the time of Jesus. This also is untrue. During the time of Jesus, the Pharisees did not exercise direct political power as a group, and their influence was limited. But as individuals, there were prominent and even powerful Pharisees. Finally, it is very unlikely that the Pharisees brought about the death of Jesus, and indeed a close reading of the New Testament shows that they play little or no role in the events in Jerusalem in the last days of Jesus' life.

Why set the record straight on the Pharisees? It is important for a number of reasons. First, the Pharisees are an important group in late Second Temple Judaism, so if we want to have an accurate picture of that time, we need to correct misapprehensions about them. Second, one of the ways that modern Christian prejudice against Jews in the time of Jesus is expressed is through a negative portrait of the Pharisees; to correct stereotypes, we need to look again at the Pharisees. Third, for those interested in the historical Jesus, an inaccurate picture of the Pharisees will result in a correspondingly inaccurate picture of Jesus. Fourth, the Pharisees had a lot to do with the restructuring of Judaism after the destruction of the temple by the Romans in 70 C.E. This eventually led to rabbinic Judaism, and so Judaism today owes much to the Pharisees.

There are three sources of information on the Pharisees—Josephus, the New Testament, and rabbinic documents. None of the three is objective. Josephus claims to be a Pharisee. The New Testament sees the Pharisees as opponents of Jesus. The rabbis consider the Pharisees as their predecessors. None of the sources is disinterested, so each must be critically assessed.

JOSEPHUS

In several places, Josephus talks about Pharisees, Sadducees, and Essenes together. (For an explanation of who Josephus was see the beginning of chapter 8. The Essenes were discussed in chapter 5, above, and the Sadducees will be examined in "Sadducees," below.) The Essenes differed from the other two groups in that they had less to do with Jerusalem politics and religious life than did the other two groups. The Qumran branch of the movement separated itself entirely from the rest of Israel. It also differed from the Pharisees and the Sadducees in that it left an extensive library, including works by members of the group, whereas no extant work can be confidently traced to either Sadducees or Pharisees.

THE PHARISEES AS PHILOSOPHERS AND INTERPRETERS OF TRADITION. Josephus thinks of himself as an intermediary between the Jewish and non-Jewish worlds. When speaking of Jews and Judaism, he uses terms understandable to Hellenistic audiences. He says that Palestinian Jewish society is divided into three groups—Sadducees, Pharisees, and Essenes. The Greek word he uses here, *hairesis,* is often translated "sect," but that is misleading. *Sect* is a sociological term meaning a religious minority in conscious opposition to the dominant religious establishment. But in the Hellenistic world, this is not what *hairesis* meant. Rather, it denoted a particular option or choice from among prevailing Hellenistic philosophies. The word "school" would be a better translation.

In the following passages, Josephus defines the groups in terms of their positions on philosophical problems understandable to his Hellenistic audience. The passages are taken from two important works of Josephus, the *Jewish War* and the *Jewish Antiquities.*

> The Pharisees, who are considered the most accurate interpreters of the laws, and hold the position of the leading sect, attribute everything to Fate and to God; they hold that to act rightly or otherwise rests, indeed, for the most part with men, but that in each action Fate co-operates. Every soul, they maintain, is imperishable, but the soul of the good alone passes into another body, while the souls of the wicked suffer eternal punishment. (*J. W.* 2.162–163)

> As for the Pharisees, they say that certain events are the work of Fate, but not all; as to other events, it depends upon ourselves whether they shall take place or not. The sect of Essenes, however, declares that Fate is mistress of all things, and that nothing befalls men unless it be in accordance with her decree. But the Sadducees do away with Fate, holding that there is no such thing and that human actions are not achieved in accordance with her decree, but that all things lie within our own power, so that we ourselves are responsible for our well-being, while we suffer misfortune through our own thoughtlessness. (*Ant.* 13.172–173)

> They [Pharisees] follow the guidance of that which their doctrine has selected and transmitted as good, attaching the chief importance to the observance of those commandments which it has seen fit to dictate to them. They show re-

spect and deference to their elders, nor do they rashly presume to contradict their proposals. Though they postulate that everything is brought about by fate, still they do not deprive the human will of the pursuit of what is in man's power, since it was God's good pleasure that there should be a fusion and that the will of man with his virtue and vice should be admitted to the council-chamber of fate. They believe that souls have power to survive death and that there are rewards and punishments under the earth for those who have led lives of virtue or vice: eternal imprisonment is the lot of evil souls, while the good souls receive an easy passage to a new life. Because of these views they are, as a matter of fact, extremely influential among the townsfolk; and all prayers and sacred rites of divine worship are performed according to their exposition. This is the great tribute that the inhabitants of the cities, by practising the highest ideals both in their way of living and in their discourse, have paid to the excellence of the Pharisees. . . .

Whenever [the Sadducees] assume some office, though they submit unwillingly and perforce, yet submit they do to the formulas of the Pharisees, since otherwise the masses would not tolerate them. (*Ant.* 18.12–15, 17)

The theme common to all three passages is that of fate as opposed to free will. This issue has troubled philosophers and theologians from time immemorial, and it is one that remains with us today. American individualism can sometimes assume that everyone is master of his or her own destiny. One gets what one deserves. But paradoxically, we must admit that there is much that is beyond our control. The tension between these two ways of looking at things spills over into politics and public policy, where liberals and conservatives argue over whether criminal behavior is simply the result of people freely deciding to commit crime or whether many factors outside the offender's control lead to the crime. And which is more determinative, one's genes or one's upbringing? The debate has concrete consequences.

Of course, the ancients were not psychologists, or geneticists, or penal-justice theoreticians. But they were sharp observers of human life, and they, too, saw a tension between what was within and what was outside human control. Some thought that fate controlled everything—that is, that things are outside human control. Others thought that humans were entirely in control of their own destiny. But then as now, most probably fell somewhere in between these extremes. Frequently the debate was couched in what we would call religious terms. Hellenistic philosophers debated whether the gods were concerned with human history. Stoics defended the idea of God's providence (oversight of human affairs), and Epicureans denied it. Josephus says in *Life* 12 that the Pharisees are like the Stoics.

Jewish Antiquities 13 assigns to the three Jewish groups different philosophical positions: Essenes say that fate rules all, Sadducees deny fate, and

Pharisees are in between. But these are probably not the expressions Palestinian Jews would use themselves. When Josephus says that the Essenes see fate as "mistress of all things," he may have in mind the apocalyptic determinism of Qumran. The Sadducees, who Josephus says deny fate and believe in free will, are usually seen as resisting messianic hopes and apocalyptic expectations. For them, rewards and punishments are a matter for this life and are due to one's own actions. The Pharisees might hold apocalyptic views and so be seen to believe in fate, and they also defend each individual's freedom to range him- or herself on the side of God or of Satan. Even within apocalypticism, despite its determinism, each individual is free to choose to be on God's side or not. Josephus also mentions the afterlife. He probably has resurrection in mind when he says that the Pharisees believe in an afterlife.

In *J.W.* 2, Josephus credits the Pharisees with being "the most accurate interpreters of the laws." In *Ant.* 18.12, already quoted, he says, "They follow the guidance of that which their doctrine has selected and transmitted as good, attaching the chief importance to the observance of those commandments which it has seen fit to dictate to them." In an earlier chapter, Josephus says, "The Pharisees had passed on to the people certain regulations handed down by former generations and not recorded in the Laws of Moses" (*Ant.* 13.297). At issue is Torah interpretation. The Pharisees developed a large body of tradition that they considered binding, at least for their own group. This tradition eventually developed into the later rabbinic idea of Oral Torah. For the rabbis, Oral Torah was an integral part of the Torah given to Moses on Sinai but was passed down orally through the generations.

THE PHARISEES AS A SOCIAL AND POLITICAL FORCE.   Josephus's attitude toward the Pharisees may have changed over time. We are interested in this not so much for what it tells us about Josephus as for how we should read what he says about the social role of the Pharisees. Josephus writes of the Pharisees in both the *Jewish War* (ca. 75 C.E.) and the *Jewish Antiquities* (ca. 94 C.E.). In the later work, he credits the Pharisees with more political clout than he does in the earlier. A possible reason for the change is that in the 90s the Pharisees, who were an important contingent among those who became the rabbis, were in a position to administer Israel for the Romans and were making a bid to do so. Josephus may have supported them in this bid and rewritten his descriptions of them to make the Romans see them as qualified to rule. If this is correct, then the *War* has a greater claim to historicity where the two sources diverge, at least where the divergence involves increasing the power of the Pharisees in the later source.

In *Ant.* 18.11–17 (see extracts above), Josephus presents the Pharisees as dominant. Their interpretation of Torah prevails. But we have to take this with a grain of salt. As we shall see, the Sadducees were a party of the ruling class. It is hardly likely that they would have allowed the Pharisees to dictate to them. Further, in the years leading up to the Jewish revolt against Rome, the Pharisees play no role Josephus finds worth mentioning, nor do they operate as a group in the account of the revolt in the *War*.

POLITICAL POWER AND INFLUENCE. Suspicions that Josephus alters his picture of the Pharisees are confirmed when we look at his two accounts of their role in the reign of Alexandra Salome (ruled 76–67), wife and successor of Alexander Jannaeus (ruled 103–76). In *J.W.* 1.107–114, the earlier source, Josephus reports that when King Alexander Jannaeus died, he left the kingdom to his wife, Alexandra Salome. She was "the very strictest observer of the national traditions and would deprive of office any offenders against the sacred laws" (*J.W.* 1.108). He goes on:

> Beside Alexandra, and growing as she grew, arose the Pharisees, a body of Jews with the reputation of excelling the rest of their nation in the observances of religion, and as exact exponents of the laws. To them, being herself intensely religious, she listened with too great deference; while they, gradually taking advantage of an ingenuous woman, became at length the real administrators of the state, at liberty to banish and to recall, to loose and to bind, whom they would. In short, the enjoyments of royal authority were theirs; its expenses and burdens fell to Alexandra. She proved, however, to be a wonderful administrator in larger affairs, and, by continual recruiting doubled her army, besides collecting a considerable body of foreign troops; so that she not only strengthened her own nation, but became a formidable foe to foreign potentates. But if she ruled the nation, the Pharisees ruled her.

> Thus they put to death Diogenes, a distinguished man who had been a friend of Alexander, accusing him of having advised the king to crucify his eight hundred victims. They further urged Alexandra to make away with the others who had instigated Alexander to punish those men; and as she from superstitious motives always gave way, they proceeded to kill whomsoever they would. (*J.W.* 1.110–113)

According to this version, during Alexandra's reign the Pharisees are influential but do not hold office. They are advisors. Josephus implies that Alexandra carries out their desires through administrators, even if the Pharisees are the "real" administrators. Josephus's distinction is between real and apparent administrators. The Pharisees are expert in the laws and fulfill them zealously.

In many respects, this is an unflattering portrait. The Pharisees take advantage of a "superstitious" woman who listens to them with "too great deference" and use their influence to wreak vengeance on their enemies. Their vengeance sounds almost indiscriminate. But Josephus does not explain how a woman who is "a wonderful administrator in larger affairs," doubles her army, and earns the respect of neighboring rulers can be deceived by the Pharisees. Here Josephus's bias interferes with his reporting, and his bias seems to be against the Pharisees.

Earlier in the passage, Josephus gives the real reason for Alexandra's support among the people: "Alexander bequeathed the kingdom to his wife Alexandra, being convinced that the Jews would bow to her authority as they would to no other, because by her utter lack of his brutality and by her opposition to his crimes she had won the affections of the populace" (*J. W.* 1.107). Alexandra's support was not due to her relationship with the Pharisees but was a result of her popularity. She was the opposite of her late husband, the hated Alexander Jannaeus. She consulted the Pharisees simply because she followed the laws and knew the Pharisees to be expert in their interpretation.

Some think that the eight hundred crucifixion victims mentioned in this passage were Pharisees and that they are the same as those mentioned in the *Commentary on Nahum* of the Dead Sea Scrolls. If so, it is not surprising that the Pharisees urged Alexandra to punish those who were behind the crucifixions.

The same story is retold in *Ant.* 13.399–418. The essential facts remain the same, but in the *Antiquities,* Alexander gives deathbed advice to his wife to place the Pharisees in power. Alexander says,

> [she] should yield a certain amount of power to the Pharisees, for if they praised her in return for this sign of regard, they would dispose the nation favorably toward her. These men, he assured her, had so much influence with their fellow-Jews that they could injure those whom they hated and help those to whom they were friendly; for they had the complete confidence of the masses when they spoke harshly of any person, even when they did so out of envy; and he himself, he added, had come into conflict with the nation because these men had been badly treated by him. (*Ant.* 13.401–402)

Now Josephus stresses the Pharisees' influence with the people. In fact, Alexandra needs their help in winning over the people. Pharisaic expertise in Torah is not mentioned. Jannaeus even blames all his troubles on his failure to enlist Pharisaic support. Thus, in this later source, Josephus increases the political role of the Pharisees and asserts their popularity. Even here, however, what was probably the real reason for Alexandra's support among the masses surfaces: "As for the queen herself, she was loved by the masses because she was thought to disapprove of the crimes committed by her husband."

The following incident occurred in the time of Herod the Great (ruled 37–4 B.C.E.):

> There was also a group of Jews priding itself on its adherence to ancestral custom and claiming to observe the laws of which the Deity approves, and by these men, called Pharisees, the women (of the court [of Herod]) were ruled. These men were able to help the king greatly because of their foresight, and yet they were obviously intent upon combating and injuring him. At last when the whole Jewish people affirmed by an oath that it would be loyal to Caesar and to the king's government, these men, over six thousand in number, refused to take this oath, and when the king punished them with a fine, Pheroras' wife paid the fine for them. (*Ant.* 17.41–42)

The passage assumes that the Pharisees are not in power during Herod's rule. He merely wants their support. But they oppose him and exercise influence over the women in Herod's court.

The *Jewish War* first mentions the Pharisees in the passage about Alexandra Salome. In *Ant.* 13.288–298, they enter the narrative at an earlier point, during the reign of John Hyrcanus I (ruled 135–104 B.C.E.).

> As for Hyrcanus, the envy of the Jews was aroused against him by his own successes and those of his sons; particularly hostile to him were the Pharisees, who are one of the Jewish schools, as we have related above. And so great is their influence with the masses that even when they speak against a king or high priest, they immediately gain credence. Hyrcanus too was a disciple of theirs, and was greatly loved by them.

As might be expected of this later work, Josephus stresses their influence with the people.

The story goes on to a banquet given by Hyrcanus at which a certain Eleazar tells him he should give up the high priesthood and be content with the kingship. A Sadducee named Jonathan, a close friend of the king, tells him that all the Pharisees support Eleazar and that the king will discover the truth of this claim if he asks them what penalty Eleazar deserves. The Pharisees recommend a relatively light punishment, as is their custom, according to Josephus. Jonathan persuades Hyrcanus to regard this as approval of Eleazar's action. Jonathan "so worked upon him that he brought him to join the Sadducaean party and desert the Pharisees, and to abrogate the regulations which they had established for the people, and punish those who observed them. Out of this, of course, grew the hatred of the masses for him and his sons." The passage concludes, "And so Hyrcanus quieted the outbreak, and lived happily thereafter; and when he died after administering the government excellently for thirty-one years, he left five sons" (*Ant.*

13.293–299). This last bit of information does not fit well with the idea that the people hate him because he no longer follows the Pharisees and that it is impossible to rule without their support. Again, Josephus exaggerates the influence of the Pharisees. Whenever Josephus stresses the Pharisees' great power or influence, it contradicts other aspects of his stories. It is worth noting here that the Sadducees are depicted as the Pharisees' political enemies.

Josephus's *Life* was written after the *Antiquities,* probably around 100 C.E. We would expect, then, that it reflects Josephus's bias, found in the latter work, in favor of the Pharisees, and we are not disappointed. In *Life* 10–12, Josephus claims to have gained personal experience of all three Jewish schools: "So I submitted myself to hard training and laborious exercises and passed through the three courses." Afterward he went to the wilderness and apprenticed himself for three years to a figure named Bannus, who was a figure similar to John the Baptist. All this supposedly happened between his sixteenth and nineteenth years. But this cannot be. Had he spent three years with Bannus, he could not have trained "laboriously" in the three schools. The Essenes alone required a lengthy novitiate, as we know from Josephus's own words and from the Dead Sea Scrolls. So why does Josephus stretch the truth? He wants his audience to consider what he says to be reliable. And since he supposedly knows so much firsthand, his choice of a school becomes important to his readers. He says, "Being now in my nineteenth year I began to govern my life by the rules of the Pharisees, a sect having points of resemblance to that which the Greeks call the Stoic school." Suddenly Josephus asserts that he himself is a Pharisee. We did not learn this from his earlier works. He may be claiming this simply as part of his effort to support the Pharisees' case to the Romans.

Josephus has little to say about Pharisaic involvement on the political scene throughout the first half of the first century C.E. When war with the Romans erupts in 66 C.E., some individual Pharisees make an appearance. When Josephus is appointed general of the revolutionary forces in Galilee, his rival, John of Gischala, sends word to a certain Simon in Jerusalem to try to have Josephus removed:

> This Simon was a native of Jerusalem, of a very illustrious family, and of the sect of the Pharisees, who have the reputation of being unrivalled experts in their country's laws. A man highly gifted with intelligence and judgement, he could by sheer genius retrieve an unfortunate situation in the affairs of state. He was John's old and intimate friend, and, at the time, was at variance with me. On receiving this application he exerted himself to persuade the high-priests Ananus and Jesus, son of Gamalas, and some others of their party to clip my sprouting wings and not suffer me to mount the pinnacle of fame. (*Life* 191–193)

Simon the Pharisee is not a person in power in his own right. His importance rests upon his ability to persuade. His being a Pharisee means only that he is expert in the Torah. He has to persuade those who really hold power, the high priests and "their party."

> Then calling up John's brother he instructed him to send presents to Ananus and his friends, as a likely method of inducing them to change their minds. Indeed Simon eventually achieved his purpose; for, as the result of bribery, Ananus and his party agreed to expel me from Galilee. (*Life* 195–196)

Simon has no power either through legitimate office or through membership in the Pharisees. His task is to convince the high priests and their party. He fails even in this and so resorts to bribery. Thus, although the Pharisees do not have power as a group during the war, individual Pharisees have influence because of their intelligence, knowledge of the Law, wealthy family connections, or friends.

Such a conclusion is supported when a delegation is sent to Galilee to remove Josephus from his command:

> The scheme agreed upon was to send a deputation comprising persons of different classes of society but of equal standing in education. Two of them, Jonathan and Ananias, were from the lower ranks and adherents of the Pharisees; the third, Jozar, also a Pharisee, came of a priestly family; the youngest, Simon, was descended from the high priests. Their instructions were to approach the Galileans and ascertain the reason for their devotion to me. If they attributed it to my being a native of Jerusalem, they were to reply that so were all four of them; if to my expert knowledge of their laws, they should retort that neither were they ignorant of the customs of their fathers; if again, they asserted that their affection was due to my priestly office, they should answer that two of them were likewise priests. (*Life* 196–198)

The Pharisees dominate the delegation in terms of numbers, but Josephus does not say that their being Pharisees will carry weight with the Galileans. The three reasons for the delegates' influence are that they are from Jerusalem, know the laws, and are priests. One of the two priests in the embassy is a Pharisee, but his influence is never said to be due to his being a Pharisee, but only to his knowledge of the Torah or priestly status. Josephus says that the delegation is composed of members from different social classes and that two of the Pharisees were of the "lower ranks." Presumably this means the lower ranks of the upper classes, or perhaps it means that they were retainers, those who served the ruling class proper. One of the priests is a Pharisee, but he seems to rank lower than the priest who is of high priestly descent.

SUMMARY.   Josephus sees the major Pharisaic presence to be in Jerusalem. They were present in the courts of John Hyrcanus, Alexandra Salome, and Herod the Great. The Pharisee Simon, friend of Josephus's rival, John of Gischala, was an influential citizen of Jerusalem. They were rivals of the Sadducees, a party located in Jerusalem.

Josephus represents the Pharisees as politically influential before the time of Herod, but after that time they had much less influence. They were rivals of the Sadducees. After Herod's time, there were Pharisees who were influential because of knowledge of the laws, wealth, family, social connections, or priesthood. But being a Pharisee was not equivalent to holding public office. Nonetheless, the Pharisees were always involved in politics in a wider sense. That is, Torah concerns public life, and to be expert in Torah is to have political opinions and interests of some sort.

Josephus consistently characterizes the Pharisees as knowing the Torah well and having an authoritative body of interpretation. He says that the Pharisees served both John Hyrcanus and Alexandra Salome as experts in Torah. The Pharisees who did so must have been scribes and so belonged to the retainer class. The Pharisees were united by a specific way of interpreting Torah. And they had an interest in, and a program for, society at large. They were a political interest group, "a collectivity which seeks to convert its interests into public law or gain control over social behavior" (Saldarini, *Pharisees*, 312).

THE NEW TESTAMENT

A CRITICAL APPROACH.   Many take for granted the New Testament picture of the Pharisees as narrow-minded legalists, hypocrites, proud men, lovers of money and prestige, who opposed Jesus even to the extent of bringing about his death, simply because he preached a loving religion. Such a distorted view is reflected even in dictionaries. For example, *Merriam-Webster's Collegiate Dictionary* (10th ed.) defines "pharisaical" as "marked by hypocritical censorious self-righteousness." This definition simply reflects actual usage. Such denigration of an important Jewish group comes from taking New Testament descriptions of Jews and Jewish society as historical fact, pure and simple, as if these descriptions were wholly unbiased. Using the New Testament in this way is not only naïve; it is destructive to Judaism, as has been amply demonstrated over the past two thousand years.

We must remember that the Pharisees were very important in the ultimate formation of rabbinic Judaism. Denigration of the Pharisees says something about the Judaism that followed them. If someone approached a Christian today and said that although present-day Christians are fine people, all the apostles were hypocrites, the Christian would likely take offense, and rightly so. How is it different if someone approaches a Jew today and says that he or she has nothing against Jews today but that all of the Pharisees were hypocrites? So preachers, theologians, and scholars who feel free to speak in such a way about the Pharisees because they are simply a "historical group" and not living Jews unwittingly help to perpetuate stereotypes they should be working to undermine.

MATTHEW'S VIEW.   Jesus left no written records. Others reported what he said and did. And those who did the reporting, the authors of the Gospels, produced not histories but documents of faith. This means that we cannot take the Gospels as they stand as simple, unaltered transcripts of what actually happened. There is much good history in the Gospels, and scholars labor mightily to get to it. But the process requires careful, critical study.

Modern biblical scholars realize that the gospel writers had their own viewpoints affecting the way they told the story of Jesus. A large majority of scholars think that Mark wrote first and that Matthew and Luke used Mark as a source. Matthew and Luke also used a source, called Q (for the German *Quelle,* "source"), consisting mostly of sayings of Jesus. The source is no longer extant, so it must be reconstructed by comparing Matthew and Luke. Because of the large amount of material they share, Matthew, Mark, and Luke are called the Synoptics, from the Greek word meaning "to see together." The material in the Gospel of John is, for the most part, independent of that in the first three.

A good deal can be learned about Matthew by observing how he rewrites Mark. Using this method, called "redaction criticism," we see that Matthew harbors special animosity toward the Pharisees. He loves to insert the word "Pharisee" when it is absent from his source. An example is Matt 12:22–36 (cf. Mark 3:19–30). In Mark's version, some scribes come down from Jerusalem when they hear that Jesus is performing exorcisms. They charge, "He has Beelzebul, and by the ruler of the demons he casts out demons" (Mark 3:22). Matthew changes the accusers from scribes to Pharisees. He makes his point still clearer when he repeats the charge in 9:34: "But the Pharisees said, 'By the ruler of the demons he casts out the demons.' "

Another example of Matthew's antipathy toward the Pharisees appears in Matt 15 (cf. Mark 7). Mark's Jesus attacks the Pharisees for their purity rules. Matthew adds verses 12–14:

> Then the disciples approached and said to him, "Do you know that the Pharisees took offense when they heard what you said?" He answered, "Every plant that my heavenly Father has not planted will be uprooted. Let them alone; they are blind guides of the blind. And if one blind person guides another, both will fall into a pit."

Matthew's Jesus denies the Pharisees any divine legitimation. The passage seems to contradict Matt 23:3, where Jesus says that the Pharisees reliably interpret the divine will. The contradiction may indicate that Matthew's community related differently to the Pharisees at various stages of the community's history, or it may mean that Matthew's community respects the authority of the scribes and Pharisees but still hopes that they will recognize Jesus' authority.

Matthew introduces his readers to his view of the Pharisees early. He prefaces Jesus' ministry with an account of John the Baptist, as do the other evangelists. Mark says only that John baptized, preached repentance, and claimed to be the precursor of another, but Matthew and Luke include more of John's teaching. They share verses (which are from Q, not Mark) in which the Baptist accuses his audience of being a "brood of vipers." In Luke 3:7, the accusation is aimed at "the crowds," but in Matt 3:7 it is the "Pharisees and Sadducees" who are so accused. Given Matthew's antipathy toward the Pharisees, it is more likely that he added the words "Pharisees and Sadducees" than that Luke omitted them.

One of Matthew's techniques is to collect traditional sayings of Jesus and put them together into connected "sermons." For example, the Sermon on the Mount occurs only in Matt 5–7. It consists partly of material found scattered throughout the other gospels and partly of material unique to Matthew. Matthew crafts a sermon in Matt 23 as an attack on the "scribes and Pharisees," whom he lumps together as a single group. But scribes were a professional group, whereas Pharisees were not. The majority of scribes were not Pharisees, and it is unlikely that all Pharisees were scribes. This historical inaccuracy immediately makes us wonder whether we ought to take Matt 23 at face value. Did Jesus really deliver this barrage of condemnation aimed at scribes and Pharisees? Furthermore, Jesus' sayings against them here are, in some cases, directed against different groups in Mark and Luke. Luke does accuse the Pharisees of hypocrisy (Luke 11:39–41), excessive attention to legal details to the detriment of justice and love (11:42), and craving public recognition (11:43). But he directs some of the other accusations not at the Pharisees but at lawyers. Again, lawyers and Pharisees were not identical. Lawyers were a professional class; Pharisees were not. For Luke, it is the lawyers, not the Pharisees, who lay on others burdens that they themselves do not lift, who do not enter the kingdom or let others do so, and who murder those whom God sends to them (11:45–52).

Perhaps the strongest attack in Matt 23 is put in priestly terms: "Woe to you, scribes and Pharisees, hypocrites! For you are like whitewashed tombs, which on the outside look beautiful, but inside they are full of bones of the dead and of all kinds of filth. So you also on the outside look righteous to others, but inside you are full of hypocrisy and lawlessness" (23:27–28). In Matt 23 Jesus accuses the scribes and Pharisees of performing religious deeds just to be seen by others, not practicing what they preach, laying on others burdens they themselves are unwilling to bear, refusing to enter the kingdom of God and keeping others out as well, mocking the law of God, attending to legal details and ignoring the demands of faith, justice, and mercy, and being full of extortion and rapacity. The attack is unrelenting.

The chapter reaches a climax in the assertion that the Pharisees murder those whom God sends to them:

> Therefore I send you prophets, sages, and scribes, some of whom you will kill and crucify, and some you will flog in your synagogues and pursue from town to town, so that upon you may come all the righteous blood shed on earth, from the blood of righteous Abel to the blood of Zechariah son of Barachiah, whom you murdered between the sanctuary and the altar. (23:34–35)

The passage reflects the experience of Matthew's community. We cannot simply take this as an accurate measure of Jesus' attitude toward the Pharisees. Matthew has Jesus speak of *future* acts of killing, blaming the scribes and Pharisees in advance for the death of Jesus and all Christian martyrs. Crucifixion is inflicted on more than one, which makes it likely that the reference is both to Jesus' death and to that of later Christians. Scourging and persecution correspond to what Jesus predicts for his followers in Matt 10:17–20. God sends "prophets" and "scribes" to the Jewish leaders; in Matthew these are titles for Christians (10:41; 13:51). Matthew has Jesus say that the blood of all righteous men will fall upon the scribes and Pharisees; "righteous" is a favorite term of Matthew for Christians (10:51; 5:20). Matthew 23 cannot be used uncritically for reconstructing what Jesus thought of the Pharisees, because the material has been reworked by Matthew, and perhaps also by his predecessors in the transmission of the traditions, to address issues in the early church.

The tendency to make the Pharisees look worse is not peculiar to Matthew. Luke also adds several hostile references to them (Luke 5:17, 21; 7:36–50; 11:53; 14:3; 16:14; 18:10–14). The same holds for the Gospel of John, which outdoes even Matthew, Mark, and Luke in portraying the Pharisees as the prime enemies of Jesus. As years passed, Christian hostility to the Pharisees increased. Matthew and Luke (written ca. 85 C.E.) make them look worse than does Mark (ca. 70 C.E.), and John (often dated to the 90s) makes them look worst of all. Why is there such increasing hostility to the Pharisees? A historical answer lies close at hand.

YAVNEH.   During the war between the Jews and the Romans that raged from 66 to 70 C.E. (some Jews resisted several years more at the fortress of Masada), a Pharisee named Johanan ben Zakkai escaped from Jerusalem (in a coffin, the story has it!). The Romans gave him permission to go to the coastal town of Yavneh (also called Jamnia) and to found a school there. After the destruction of Jerusalem in 70 C.E., a group of Pharisees, scribes, and others gathered at Yavneh to restructure Jewish society in the absence of the temple and its establishment. They confirmed the Torah as the center of the life of the Jewish people, and Pharisaic views and principles began to become central. The term "rabbi," previously used as a term of respect for a teacher, took on a more technical sense, meaning an authoritative teacher of Torah. Study of Torah itself became an act of the utmost piety. This emerging, postdestruction Judaism aimed for greater unity than had been the case in Second Temple Judaism.

Older scholarship conceived of this change as a sudden transformation into what we now call rabbinic Judaism, which then rapidly became normative worldwide. Such an overnight transformation is, on the face of it, unlikely, and it is based on an uncritical use of later rabbinic sources, themselves committed to writing beginning only around 200 C.E. This view has now been discredited, largely through the work of Jacob Neusner and his students. Following his lead, scholars now speak of Judaism between the fall of the temple in 70 C.E. and the writing of the Mishnah around 200 C.E. as "formative Judaism" so as to recognize the period of transition (see Neusner, *Formative Judaism*).

Many see the activity at Yavneh as the background against which to read Matthew's Gospel. Matthew sees emerging rabbinic Judaism as the rival of his own group. He portrays Jesus as *the* authoritative Torah teacher (see ch. 11, below). Speaking of the scribes and Pharisees, Jewish interpreters of Torah, Jesus says in Matt 23:6–10,

> They love to have the place of honor at banquets and the best seats in the synagogues, and to be greeted with respect in the marketplaces, and to have people call them rabbi. But you are not to be called rabbi, for you have one teacher, and you are all students. And call no one your father on earth, for you have one Father—the one in heaven. Nor are you to be called instructors, for you have one instructor, the Messiah.

The term "rabbi" did not come into general usage in a technical sense until after the destruction of Jerusalem in 70 C.E. These verses are a Christian attack on the leaders of formative Judaism. They originate after 70 C.E. and pit the authority of Jesus Christ, Messiah, Torah teacher, against that of the Jewish leaders of Matthew's time.

Both the Jewish community at Yavneh and Matthew's community were defining their identities. Each claimed to embody the true interpretation of Torah.

The stage was set for conflict, and it is mainly this conflict that Matthew reflects, more than the conflict between Jesus and the Pharisees. The same can be said of Luke and John. It is especially apparent in John, where the Pharisees assume a degree of power and authority they did not have before 70 C.E.

MARK'S VIEW.   It was once thought that since Mark is older and less polished than Matthew and Luke, he must also be more historically accurate. This theory was disproved at the beginning of the twentieth century. Mark, too, has a theological agenda. Even he does not supply an accurate picture of the Pharisees. He tends to typecast the Pharisees as Jesus' main opponents. For example, one of the stories in Mark 2, when Jesus and his disciples are still in Galilee, begins in the following way: "One sabbath he was going through the grainfields; and as they made their way his disciples began to pluck heads of grain. The Pharisees said to him, 'Look, why are they doing what is not lawful on the Sabbath?' " (Mark 2:23–24). Now Jesus and Pharisees may well have clashed over Sabbath observance. The issue was important in Second Temple Judaism, as evidenced by the Sabbath rules in the Dead Sea Scrolls, for example (CD XI), and there was a fair amount of disagreement among Jews about Sabbath rules. But it is hardly likely that the Pharisees strolled with Jesus on Sabbath walks through Galilean grainfields. Nor is it likely that they were crouched behind the wheat stalks, waiting for a chance to pounce on him. The narrative in Mark 2 was composed to furnish a setting for the sayings of Jesus that follow, sayings that themselves could well be authentic. Once the early Christians assumed that Pharisees were Jesus' primary opponents, they easily gave the Pharisees a conventional narrative role. This also happens in Mark 8:15, 12:13–17, 10:2–10, and elsewhere.

PHARISEES IN THE LIFE OF JESUS.   But things are not so simple. Mark was written before those at Yavneh began to be influential. The Pharisees' importance at Yavneh cannot be blamed entirely for the tendency to blame Pharisees, only for its aggravation. There is no reason to deny the earliest anti-Pharisaic stories some foundation in the life of Jesus. Still, it is a misconception that Jesus spent most of his time opposing the Pharisees.

None of the Synoptic Gospels claims that the Pharisees played an active role in the death of Jesus. The elders, priests, and scribes of Jerusalem were the ones who delivered Jesus to the Romans, and the Romans killed him. John connects the Pharisees more closely to the passion by stating that Judas obtained officers to arrest Jesus from the "chief priests and the Pharisees" (John 18:3), but even John lays ultimate blame for the death of Jesus on the chief priest. In view of the antipathy of the Christian tradition toward the Pharisees, it is striking that they do not figure in the passion and death. If they had played a role, later Christians would surely not have ignored it. And as we shall see when we look at the historical Jesus, he would hardly have been executed for the issues about which he clashed with Pharisees.

Another reason to be suspicious of the dominance of the Pharisees in the Gospels concerns their sphere of influence. Josephus locates the Pharisees in Jerusalem. They go to Galilee as outsiders. This picture confirms the idea that the Pharisees were retainers in the Jerusalem establishment. Galilee was under the rule of Herod Antipas, and historically the Pharisees and Herodians were not friendly. The rabbis preserved traditions indicating that the Pharisees were not influential in Galilee. Yet the Gospels locate the Pharisees primarily in Galilee. It is there that Jesus has most of his confrontations with them. It goes too far to claim that the stories of Jesus' Galilean clashes with the Pharisees lack any basis in fact, since there may have been some Pharisees in Galilee. But it was not their main sphere of influence, and the gospel stories are, in any case, stylized and questionable.

PHARISAIC PRACTICES.   The Pharisees in the New Testament are very dedicated to Torah, its interpretation and application. Their concerns center on Sabbath observance and table fellowship—tithing, ritual purity, and rules about with whom one may eat. They attack Jesus and his followers for working on the Sabbath. When the disciples pluck grain on the Sabbath, the Pharisees criticize them for working on the holy day (Matt 12:1–8; Mark 2:23–28; Luke 6:1–5). Twice in the Synoptics (Mark 3:1–6 and parallels; Luke 13:10–17) and twice in John (5:2–18; 9:1–14; cf. 7:21–24) Jesus clashes with them over whether it is lawful to heal on the Sabbath. According to the Gospels, Pharisees do not permit healing. Rabbinic literature, however, indicates that most Pharisees did permit healing on the Sabbath, at least when the person's life was in danger or when no physical work was required.

Other disputes between Jesus and the Pharisees are over table fellowship, that is, over with whom one might share a meal. Mark 7:1–23 (Matt 15:1–20; see Matt 23:25–26) says that the Pharisees "and all the Jews" (this last is doubtful) have purification procedures for their hands, cups, pots, and bronze vessels before eating. If such rules were followed strictly, the Pharisees would not have been able to eat with those who did not follow the rules. Other eating rules in dispute between Jesus and the Pharisees concern tithing (but Jesus does not disagree with their strict practice; Matt 23:23–24) and fasting (Matt 9:14–17; Mark 2:18–22; Luke 5:33–39). A final issue, raised only in Matt 23:16–22, concerns rules about swearing on sacred things.

The Pharisees in the New Testament have a narrow range of interests. Sabbath observance and eating in the proper state of purity are most important. But this characterization should not be seen as excluding political interest on the part of the Pharisees.

RESURRECTION FROM THE DEAD.   Josephus testifies to Pharisaic belief in an afterlife. This is confirmed by the New Testament. When Paul is on trial before the Jewish Sanhedrin, the narrator says, "The Sadducees say that there is no resurrection, or angel, or spirit; but the Pharisees acknowledge all three" (Acts 23:8).

POSITIVE REFERENCES.   There are a few references to the Pharisees in the New Testament that are positive in tone. In Matt 23:3, Jesus says they are reliable interpreters of Torah. In Luke 13:31, they warn Jesus about Herod. They side with Paul against the Sadducees in Acts 23 on the issue of resurrection. In Acts 15:5, there are Pharisees in the early church. We know about one specific Pharisee who did become a Christian—the apostle Paul (Acts 23:6; Phil 3:5). In Acts 5:33–42, Gamaliel, a Pharisee in the Sanhedrin, advises that body to leave the Christian movement alone lest they interfere with what might be God's work. Gamaliel is a "teacher of the law." This passage also attests to the presence of some Pharisees among the ruling class.

SUMMARY.   As in Josephus, the Pharisees in the New Testament are Torah experts, which makes it likely that at least some of them are scribes, and their interpretation of Torah sets them apart from others. Although they are interested in politics, there is no reliable evidence in the New Testament for assigning them official power. At times they influence those who do hold power, and some Pharisees are found in the upper echelons of Jewish society. The majority of Pharisees probably belonged to the retainer class. Pharisaic interests center on tithing, Sabbath observance, table fellowship, and purity. They probably clashed with Jesus on these issues, but such clashes are exaggerated because of later tensions between the emerging Christian and rabbinic movements.

RABBINIC TRADITIONS

HOLINESS AND PURITY, MEALS AND TITHES.   Rabbinic material relevant to this topic was put into writing from around 200 C.E. to around 600 C.E. These dates raise a problem in using rabbinic sources for historiography. The earliest of the sources appeared over a century after the destruction of Jerusalem by the Romans. Material in the sources was handed down orally before being written down, and the stories and legal traditions were altered in the course of their transmission. Furthermore, the material was generated, preserved, and transmitted to fashion and convey a particular worldview, not for the purpose of recording history. The rabbinic sources must be used with caution.

Perushim or *perishin* is the word in rabbinic literature that lies behind the word "Pharisee." It means "separated ones" or "separatists" and is used for various individuals and groups, some clearly not the Pharisees. Neusner investigates traditions about people who definitely were pre-70 C.E. Pharisees (*Politics,* 18). He finds 371 separate Pharisaic traditions contained in 655 passages (some traditions occur in more than one passage). Of these, 280 traditions in 462 passages concern a Pharisee named Hillel and people associated with him, and the houses of Hillel and Shammai, two Pharisaic schools. This accounts for 75 percent of the total number of traditions about pre-70 C.E. Pharisees. Hillel is obviously a dominant figure for the rabbis, and it is likely that he played a seminal role in the Pharisaic movement. He came to Judea from Babylonia, and his school of Torah interpretation became dominant. Its main rival was the school of Shammai.

"Most of the nearly 700 pericopae pertaining to pre-70 Pharisees concern legal matters, and the largest number of these pertain to, first, agricultural tithes, offerings, and other taboos, and, second, rules of ritual purity— that is, sectarian interests" (Neusner, *Politics,* 83). (A pericope is a short unit of tradition. *Sectarian* means here that which set the Pharisees apart from other Jews.) The Pharisees' seem to have thought that purity rules previously applicable only to temple priests, such as eating meals in a state of purity, could now apply to non-priests, specifically in the context of meals. So the Pharisees saw the table within the home as analogous to the altar in the temple, and they were claiming that in some sense all Jews were priests. The entire people, or at least the portion of the people that followed Pharisaic purity rules, were the dwelling place of God. This made it possible to think of a Judaism without a temple, although the Pharisees were not against the temple. The Pharisaic emphasis on tithing should be seen in the context of table purity. Tithes applied primarily to agricultural products, which comprised the bulk of what was eaten in Israel, so tithing rules affected table fellowship. It is by no means clear, however, that the Pharisees demanded that all Jews follow their practices strictly, or that they considered those who did not to be sinners. The Pharisees were also concerned about Sabbath observance.

Pharisees did not have ritual meals at which they celebrated their community and difference from other groups. They had no analogue to the Christian Eucharist or to the Qumran messianic meal, for example. Sanctification, making things holy, was now a category that applied not just to cultic acts but to every meal in the home. Every meal became a living reminder of God's presence in the midst of the people.

Perushim ("separatists") may have been a negative name conferred by outsiders on the Pharisees but later adopted by them as an appropriate title. Holiness meant being acceptable to God because of separation from anything unpleasing to God, and therefore being able to participate in the cult. This notion of separation is essential to priestly religion. In the course of separating themselves from anything ritually impure, the Pharisees separated themselves from portions of their own society. Pharisaic interpretation of Torah set them apart from other Jews, but they wanted at least some of their interpretations to apply to society at large; they were thus interested in politics. In rabbinic literature, the Pharisees and Sadducees are rivals, as they were in Josephus's story of John Hyrcanus I's banquet. This rivalry concerns ritual purity in rabbinic traditions, but, as stated, purity laws had political consequences.

SUMMARY.   Rabbinic documents depict the Pharisees as a table fellowship group. Rules surrounding their meals were what set them apart from others. This setting apart was for the purpose of being holy, so that they could honor God's presence among them. Such behavior had social, political, and economic consequences and was not merely religious in the modern sense.

The Pharisees

Josephus	Experts in Torah
	Possessed their own traditions concerning Torah
	Believers in an afterlife and in both free will and fate
	Politically influential under several of the Hasmoneans; opponents of Alexander Jannaeus and Herod
	As a group, not an important political force after Herod's reign
	Influential among the people
	Rivals of the Sadducees
New Testament	Experts in Torah
	Possessed their own traditions concerning Torah
	Especially interested in Sabbath observance, tithing, and purity rules concerning table fellowship
	Believers in resurrection, angels, and spirits
	Rivals of the Sadducees
	Opponents of Jesus, although in some passages of Luke they are friendly toward him and in Acts there are Pharisees in the early church
	Allied with the Herodians in opposition to Jesus
	Hypocrites, who do not practice what they preach
Rabbinic literature	Table fellowship group
	Concerned about tithing and purity rules concerning meals
	Adapted temple purity rules to their daily lives
	Concerned about Sabbath observance

REVIEW

We have gone beyond the slanted New Testament evidence. And in so doing, we have seen the New Testament picture supported in some ways and challenged in others.

Because Josephus, the New Testament, and the rabbinic traditions have varied interests, they present different aspects of the Pharisees. Josephus stresses their involvement in politics, the New Testament focuses on their opposition to Jesus, and rabbinic literature preserves material relevant to its own worldview. The Pharisees are first mentioned in the context of the court of the Hasmonean John Hyrcanus I, where they exerted influence for a while and then lost it. They regained it under Alexandra Salome. Given the consistent emphasis on devotion to Torah stressed by all the sources, it is plausible that their original program included a revival of Torah observance in the context of the problems raised by the Hellenistic reform and then in the context of Hasmonean rule. But the Pharisees themselves were influenced by Hellenism. The schools of Hillel and Shammai were, in some ways, similar to Greek philosophical schools. But the Pharisees did want to structure Judaism according to a strict interpretation of Torah. This made the Pharisees a political interest group.

The Pharisees had less influence under Herod the Great, but Herod was unwilling or unable to stamp them out. Even the women of his court were sympathetic to the Pharisees. The Pharisees were not politically powerful in the first century C.E., although they did have influence. A few may have been members of the ruling class. When other groups lost their power bases or had them eroded because of the Roman war, the Pharisees, who were experts in Torah and had been developing a consistent interpretation of it, were ready to help rebuild Judaism according to their own definition.

Purity rules drew boundaries not only between Jews and Gentiles but also between Jews and Jews. The priests had the power to declare clean and unclean (Lev 10:10), which gave them great control in society. But the availability of a written Torah made it possible for others besides priests to interpret purity rules, at least for their own groups. Although primarily laypeople, Pharisees made oral rulings that applied and reinterpreted Torah. Their authority came not from heredity or from being in charge of the temple but from an accurate knowledge of Torah. Whether or not their rulings were followed by anyone outside the group is unclear, but they seem to have been respected for their knowledge and observance of Torah. Through their interpretation of Torah and their application of purity rules to everyday life, the Pharisees were laying the groundwork for the posttemple period, when Torah scholars became dominant in Judaism. Using symbols and institutions that became especially important after the destruction of the first temple, they helped Israel survive the destruction of the second.

Being a Pharisee was not a profession but a particular way of living out being Jewish. The question arises about how the Pharisees made their living. There were some Pharisaic priests, and there were Pharisaic members of the ruling class. They seem to have been the exceptions. Most Pharisees occupied a position in society subordinate to the ruling class but superior to the lower classes (peasants, artisans, and so on).

> Though some Pharisees were part of the governing class, most Pharisees were subordinate officials, bureaucrats, judges and educators. They are best understood as retainers who were literate servants of the governing class and had a program for Jewish society and influence with the people and their patrons. When the opportunity arose, they sought power over society. (Saldarini, *Pharisees,* 284)

The recognition that Pharisees were scribes, judges, teachers, and priests leads to three general observations about groups (*Pharisees,* 280). First, groups are not always mutually exclusive. Individuals can belong to more than one group simultaneously. The Pharisees cut across more than one social class, and more than one profession. Second, groups change over time. The Pharisees under the Hasmoneans may not look exactly like the Pharisees in the first century C.E. In addition, a group may look different in different places. Third, groups can have several aspects or functions. The Pharisees could be both a religious fellowship and a political interest group.

SADDUCEES

Josephus, the New Testament, and rabbinic literature all speak of the Sadducees, but we in fact know little about them. All three sources contrast the Sadducees and the Pharisees. In rabbinic literature, the two groups debate ritual purity and Sabbath observance. The only two solidly established traits of the Sadducees that Josephus and the New Testament agree on are that they were members of the ruling class and they did not believe in resurrection. If the Sadducees were members of the ruling class, they could not have been a sect, since a sect sees itself as different and in opposition to society as a whole and its leaders.

JOSEPHUS

The Sadducees first appear in the same passage—concerning John Hyrcanus I—where the Pharisees first appear (*Ant.* 13.288–298). There both

Pharisees and Sadducees are political interest groups seeking influence with the king. The Pharisees were dominant at first, but then they were ousted in favor of the Sadducees. Both groups retained their interest in politics until the fall of the Second Temple.

Josephus offers four descriptions of the Sadducees. The following passage contrasts them with the Pharisees.

> The Pharisees had passed on to the people certain regulations handed down by former generations and not recorded in the Laws of Moses, for which reason they are rejected by the Sadducaean group, who hold that only those regulations should be considered valid which were written down (in Scripture), and that those which had been handed down by former generations need not be observed. And concerning these matters the two parties came to have controversies and serious differences, the Sadducees having the confidence of the wealthy alone but no following among the populace, while the Pharisees have the support of the masses. (*Ant.* 13.297–298)

The Sadducees did not accept traditional Pharisaic legal rulings. They accepted as authoritative only written traditions, presumably written in Torah. Of course, the Sadducees would have had to apply Torah, but their interpretations may have been less far-reaching and innovative than Pharisaic ones. This conservative tendency would not be surprising if they were associated with the ruling class. Pharisaic rulings applied Torah to everyday life, including parts of Torah previously applied only to priests. Their "democratizing" of the cult might explain Josephus's claim that the masses supported them, although Josephus may exaggerate Pharisaic influence here. Most accept Josephus's assertion that the wealthy supported the Sadducees.

Josephus's other three passages discuss the Pharisees, Sadducees, and Essenes in ways comprehensible to a Hellenistic audience. The model again is that of philosophical schools with set doctrines.

> The Sadducees hold that the soul perishes along with the body. They own no observance of any sort apart from the laws; in fact, they reckon it a virtue to dispute with the teachers of the path of wisdom that they pursue. There are but few men to whom this doctrine has been made known, but these are men of the highest standing. (*Ant.* 18.16–17)

Unlike the Pharisees, the Sadducees did not have a body of authoritative interpretation, and this might explain their readiness to argue, if indeed that is an accurate comment. Josephus's mention of the immortality of the soul might be translated into a Palestinian context as the resurrection of the dead. The Sadducees may have rejected the idea of resurrection because it was not in written Torah.

The Sadducees, the second of the orders, do away with Fate altogether, and remove God beyond, not merely the commission, but the very sight, of evil. They maintain that man has the free choice of good or evil, and that it rests with each man's will whether he follows the one or the other. As for the persistence of the soul after death, penalties in the underworld, and rewards, they will have none of them. The Pharisees are affectionate to one another and cultivate harmonious relations with the community. The Sadducees, on the contrary, are, even among themselves, rather boorish in their behaviour, and in their intercourse with their peers are as rude as to aliens. (*J. W.* 2.164–166).

But the Sadducees do away with Fate, holding that there is no such thing, and that human actions are not achieved in accordance with her decree, but that all things lie within our own power, so that we ourselves are responsible for our well-being, while we suffer misfortune through our own thoughtlessness. (*Ant.* 13.173)

The discussion of Fate should perhaps be read as a dispute about apocalyptic determinism. The Sadducees thus did not subscribe to apocalypticism, perhaps not surprising for members of the ruling class. We should not take our observation too far, however, for apocalypticism is a scribal phenomenon and it does arise among the educated and well-to-do. The ruling elite of a colonized people are perfectly capable of being dissatisfied with the current situation and of expecting God to intervene and change things (see S. Cook).

If the Sadducees were closely associated with the priestly aristocracy, then Josephus's claim that they remove God beyond the very sight of evil would correspond to priestly concerns with ritual purity. Support of the priestly system does not prove that all of the Sadducees were priests, however. It could well be that the party consisted of a coalition of powerful priests and laypersons who were wealthy landowners.

THE NEW TESTAMENT

The New Testament contrasts the Sadducees with the Pharisees when Paul is on trial before the Sanhedrin:

When Paul noticed that some were Sadducees and others were Pharisees, he called out in the council, "Brothers, I am a Pharisee, a son of Pharisees. I am on trial concerning the hope of the resurrection of the dead." When he said this, a dissension began between the Pharisees and the Sadducees, and the assembly was divided. (The Sadducees say that there is no resurrection, or angel, or spirit; but the Pharisees acknowledge all three.) (Acts 23:6–8)

The Torah says little about angels and spirits, but apocalyptic literature is full of them. Josephus hints that the Sadducees refused to believe in resurrection because it was not in Torah. Their reluctance to believe in a universe populated with spirits might have the same basis. Incidentally, this passage shows that its author thought that both the Pharisees and the Sadducees were important in the Sanhedrin, the Jewish council at Jerusalem, to be discussed below.

In Acts 4:1 and 5:17, the Sadducees are associated with, but not identical to, the chief priests and the captain of the temple. This agrees with Josephus's claim that they were supported by the ruling class. The Sadducees appear in the gospels of Mark and Luke only in a controversy over resurrection (Mark 12:18; Luke 20:27). They try to persuade Jesus that belief in resurrection is unreasonable, but Jesus refutes them. Matthew pictures the Sadducees in league with the Pharisees against Jesus (Matt 16:1, 6, 11–12). But an alliance is suspect because only Matthew mentions it, while in Acts, Josephus, and rabbinic literature the Sadducees and Pharisees are rivals.

RABBINIC TRADITIONS

In rabbinic literature, the Sadducees are rivals of the Pharisees, and the two groups argue about purity regulations. Rabbinic traditions are negative toward the Sadducees; this makes sense if the rabbinic movement was dominated by Pharisees.

	The Sadducees
Josephus	Members of the ruling class
	Political influence under John Hyrcanus I
	Rivals of the Pharisees; the masses support the Pharisees, not the Sadducees
	Accept only the written Torah, not the oral interpretations of the Pharisees
	Do not believe in an afterlife
	Believe in free will and not in fate
New Testament	Members of the ruling class, associated with the high priest and with the Jerusalem Sanhedrin
	Rivals of the Pharisees
	Do not believe in the resurrection, angels, or spirits
Rabbinic literature	Rivals of the Pharisees
	Argue with Pharisees over purity regulations

REVIEW

The Sadducees were a segment of the ruling class. They existed at least from the second half of the second century B.C.E. to the destruction of Jerusalem in 70 C.E. They are associated with the chief priests, and Josephus says that Ananus the high priest was a Sadducee (*Ant.* 20.199). They were a political interest group who were often rivals to the Pharisees, but the two groups got along well enough to work together in the Sanhedrin. During Roman rule, they probably shared the view of many in the ruling class that Jews should accept Roman rule and not strive for national independence. The Sadducees were not a sect because they were part of the establishment.

THE SANHEDRIN

For most people familiar with the story of Jesus, the Sanhedrin conjures up images of Jesus standing condemned before a body of hostile Jewish leaders in Jerusalem. Whether or not the Sanhedrin was involved in Jesus' death, it was an important body in the late Second Temple period. The name comes from the Greek *synedrion,* meaning "council." The Sanhedrin was the aristocratic council of Jerusalem. Evidence of this council first shows up in the Greek period. The council is mentioned in a letter of Antiochus III (223–187 B.C.E.) under the title *gerousia,* which is Greek for "council of elders" (*Ant.* 12.138). The *gerousia* is mentioned several times in 1 and 2 Maccabees. There is evidence that the council continued throughout Hasmonean times, but its precise function and status must have depended upon the Hasmoneans to some degree. Herod the Great repressed the Jewish aristocracy, so it is unlikely that the council had independent authority during his rule (37–4 B.C.E.). In the first century, the Romans used the Sanhedrin to help administer Judea.

JOSEPHUS

Josephus uses the term *synedrion* freely, applying it to a variety of groups, all dating to the Roman period. Some were ad hoc gatherings to deal with a problem or situation. Josephus applies *synedrion* to both Jewish and Roman councils, sometimes in the sense of a group of advisors to a ruler. His usage follows that of the Hellenistic world in general, where the word is used for a variety of councils—political, military, economic, and private. Josephus has nothing corresponding to the absolute usage, the Sanhedrin. Saldarini, however, thinks that the evidence from Josephus supports the idea of a permanent city council, corresponding to what is usually meant by the Sanhedrin.

It is very probable that the leading citizens of Jerusalem, priests and nonpriests, had a permanent city council which had power or influence over Judea and the rest of Palestine, depending on political circumstances. Josephus does not give the technical name for this body consistently, nor does he describe its membership or powers, perhaps because they varied greatly over time. Most probably the powerful social leaders at any time were members of it. The functions of this council most probably covered whatever was important to society, including legislative, judicial, temple, and civil matters. (Saldarini, "Sanhedrin," 976).

THE NEW TESTAMENT

New Testament usage of *synedrion* also varies, since it can refer to local courts or councils. But most often it designates a supreme council in Jerusalem. It is in this latter sense that the Sanhedrin appears in the Gospels in connection with the trial of Jesus. The Gospels want to demonstrate that the Jerusalem establishment as a whole opposed Jesus, and they assume that the readers know that the Sanhedrin represents that establishment. Mark 14 tells of a meeting of the Sanhedrin: "They took Jesus to the high priest; and all the chief priests, the elders, and the scribes were assembled. . . . Now the chief priests and the whole council *[synedrion]* were looking for testimony against Jesus to put him to death; but they found none" (Mark 14:53, 55). The passage assumes that the Sanhedrin is an important judicial body in Jerusalem. Throughout the scene, the high priest is in charge. The "chief priests" are the leading priests in Jerusalem, perhaps belonging to the families from which the high priest was usually chosen, along with some other prominent families. The "elders" are the prominent citizens, probably landowners. It is no surprise that there are scribes in the Sanhedrin. The Gospel of John includes Pharisees in the Sanhedrin as it deliberates about Jesus (John 11:45–53).

In Acts 4, the temple captain and some Sadducees happen upon Peter and John preaching about Jesus in the temple. They are brought before the Sanhedrin to be judged: "The next day their rulers, elders, and scribes assembled in Jerusalem, with Annas the high priest, Caiaphas, John, and Alexander, and all who were of the high-priestly family" (Acts 4:5–6; see 4:15). Here the Sanhedrin consists of rulers, elders, scribes, the high priest, and the high priestly family. They judge Peter and John on a matter both religious and political—their preaching of Jesus. In Acts 5:34, Gamaliel, a Pharisee and a teacher of Torah, belongs to the Sanhedrin, and he argues that the fledgling Christian movement ought to be left alone. In Acts 23, both Pharisees and Sadducees are in the Sanhedrin, and Paul pits one against the other by raising the issue of resurrection.

RABBINIC TRADITIONS

The rabbis normally use the Hebrew term *bet din,* "house of judgment," for the Sanhedrin. According to them, there were a variety of sanhedrins. Their function was to judge and to make legal rulings. Rabbinic sources speak of the Sanhedrin as composed of religious scholars. Because Josephus and the New Testament use the term more widely, assigning judicial and political functions to the council, some scholars have posited two Sanhedrins, one political and one religious. Such a division between politics and religion is highly doubtful. The different functions emphasized by different sources probably reflect the divergent interests of the sources or indicate that the terminology used is not fixed and that a variety of councils existed in different places and times.

REVIEW

The evidence for reconstructing the nature of the Sanhedrin is scarce. Josephus uses the term flexibly, the New Testament evidence is affected by its own agenda, and the rabbinic evidence is questionable because of its date and nature. All three sources, however, attest to the existence of a council in Jerusalem that was at times juridical and at times advisory to the high priest. The existence of such a body is likely because the Romans often ruled local areas through aristocratic councils.

CONCLUSION

We have investigated three groups prominent in Israel of the late Second Temple period. The scribes were a professional group found within most Jewish groupings and in most strata of society. The Pharisees and Sadducees were religious and political interest groups with specific stands toward Torah and with specific programs for Jewish society. They are often presented as rivals.

SELECT BIBLIOGRAPHY

Black, Matthew. "Pharisees." *IDB* 3:774–81.
Blenkinsopp, Joseph. "Interpretation and the Tendency to Sectarianism: An Aspect of Second Temple History." Pages 1–26 in vol. 2 of *Jewish and Christian Self-Definition.* Edited by E. P. Sanders. 3 vols. Philadelphia: Fortress, 1980–1982.

Bowker, John. *Jesus and the Pharisees*. Cambridge: Cambridge University Press, 1973.

Carroll, J. T. "Luke's Portrayal of the Pharisees." *CBQ* 50 (1988): 603–21.

Cook, Michael J. *Mark's Treatment of the Jewish Leaders*. Leiden: Brill, 1978.

Cook, Stephen L. *Prophecy and Apocalypticism: The Postexilic Social Setting*. Minneapolis: Fortress, 1995.

Finkelstein, Louis. *The Pharisees: The Sociological Background of Their Faith*. 3d ed. Philadelphia: Jewish Publication Society, 1966.

Gowan, Donald. "The Sadducees" and "The Pharisees." *BBT* 139–55.

Lightstone, Jack. "Sadducees versus Pharisees: The Tannaitic Sources." Pages 206–17 in vol. 3 of *Christianity, Judaism, and Other Greco-Roman Cults: Studies for Morton Smith at Sixty*. 4 vols. Edited by Jacob Neusner. Leiden: Brill, 1975.

Mantel, Hugo. *Studies in the History of the Sanhedrin*. Cambridge: Harvard University Press, 1961.

Neusner, Jacob. *Formative Judaism: Religious, Historical, and Literary Studies, Third Series. Torah, Pharisees, and Rabbis*. Chico, Calif.: Scholars Press, 1983.

———. *From Politics to Piety: The Emergence of Rabbinic Judaism*. 2d ed. New York: Ktav, 1979.

———. *Rabbinic Literature and the New Testament : What We Cannot Show, We Do Not Know*. Valley Forge, Pa.: Trinity Press International, 1994.

———. *The Rabbinic Traditions about the Pharisees before 70*. 3 vols. Leiden: Brill, 1971.

Overman, J. Andrew. *Matthew's Gospel and Formative Judaism: The Social World of the Matthean Community*. Minneapolis: Fortress, 1990.

Parsons, Talcott. *Politics and Social Structure*. New York: Free Press, 1969.

Porton, Gary G. "Diversity in Postbiblical Judaism." *EJMI* 57–80.

Rivkin, Ellis. *The Hidden Revolution: The Pharisees' Search for the Kingdom Within*. Nashville: Abingdon, 1978.

Saldarini, Anthony J. *Pharisees, Scribes, and Sadducees in Palestinian Society: A Sociological Approach*. Wilmington: Michael Glazier, 1988.

———. "Sanhedrin." *ABD* 5:975–80.

Schürer, Emil. "Torah Scholarship" and "Pharisees and Sadducees." Pages 314–414 in vol. 2 of *The History of the Jewish People in the Age of Jesus Christ (175 B.C.–A.D. 135)*. By Emil Schürer. Revised and edited by Geza Vermes, Fargus Millar, and Matthew Black. 3 vols. Edinburgh: T&T Clark, 1973–1987.

Smith, Morton. "Palestinian Judaism in the First Century." Pages 67–81 in *Israel: Its Role in Civilization*. Edited by Moshe Davis. New York: Harper, 1956.

CHAPTER 7

ENTER THE ROMANS

PRIMARY READINGS: *Testament of Moses* (also called *Assumption of Moses*) ◆ *Psalms of Solomon* ◆ *1 Enoch* 37–71 (also called *Similitudes of Enoch*) ◆ selections from Josephus

After the Maccabean revolt, Palestinian Jews ruled themselves for the better part of a century. The Hasmonean family assumed first high-priestly and then royal honors. But Israel's independence ended abruptly when the Romans came to the eastern Mediterranean. This chapter traces Judea's transition from independence to Roman rule. Three documents are examined, the *Psalms of Solomon,* the *Testament of Moses,* and the *Similitudes of Enoch.* Each of them is a voice from the time, telling us how some Jews reacted to the new state of affairs. Finally, there is a short section on the synagogue.

THE HISTORY

FROM ALEXANDER JANNAEUS TO HEROD THE GREAT

The last Hasmonean ruler discussed in chapter 5, above, was Alexander Jannaeus (ruled 103–76 B.C.E.). He was a cruel king whose main interest was in increasing his own power. The Pharisees were his enemies. Much of his reign was marked by warfare, some of it against fellow Jews. His successor was his wife, Alexandra Salome (ruled 76–67 B.C.E.), whom Josephus judged to be a very good ruler, and who was friendly with the Pharisees (see ch. 6, above). As a woman, she could not be high priest. She had two sons, Hyrcanus II and Aristobulus II. According to Josephus, the former was passive, but the latter was ambitious and aggressive. Alexandra appointed Hyrcanus high priest, perhaps because she could control him. Aristobulus was not happy about Hyrcanus's appointment, and after Alexandra's death in 67 B.C.E., he ousted Hyrcanus and ruled until 63 B.C.E.

Just at this moment, the Romans burst upon the scene. The Roman general Pompey was in the eastern Mediterranean, fighting piracy and finishing up a military campaign against Mithradates, king of Armenia. Both Hasmonean brothers, Aristobulus and Hyrcanus, appealed to Pompey for support in their dispute. Other Jews, sick of Hasmonean abuses, asked Pompey to terminate the Hasmonean monarchy altogether. The Romans would probably have brought Judea under their sway one way or another, but the feuding Hasmonean brothers handed Rome the perfect opportunity to hasten it. After some mediation between the brothers, during which Aristobulus once again proved himself less controllable than his brother, Pompey eventually decided to incorporate the area into the empire. He placed Hyrcanus in charge of Judea and subordinated the area to the Roman province of Syria. Appointing Hyrcanus was consonant with the Roman policy of ruling through local elites, and the newly formed Roman province of Syria to the north guarded Roman interests in Judea. In 57 B.C.E., Gabinius, governor of Syria, restricted Hyrcanus's authority to the temple and set up five administrative districts under the control of aristocratic councils.

During the two decades between 49 and 30 B.C.E., Rome was embroiled in internal power struggles. Hyrcanus II and his general Antipater supported Julius Caesar in his wars first against Pompey, then against Ptolemy XIII of Egypt. Caesar won both conflicts. In return for their support, Caesar appointed Hyrcanus ethnarch ("leader of the people") in Jerusalem and made Antipater procurator of Judea (47 B.C.E.). Antipater thus became Caesar's agent in Judea even though he was Idumean. Idumea was the area south of Judea that John Hyrcanus I had conquered and whose inhabitants were forcibly circumcised. Their Judaism was thus rather recent and was suspect in some Judean eyes (see Josephus, *Ant.* 14.403). Julius Caesar granted Antipater Roman citizenship and exempted him from tribute. The Jews were granted freedom of religion, were allowed to rebuild the walls of Jerusalem, and regained some of the lands they had lost in previous years. Antipater's sons administered various parts of the land under Antipater's jurisdiction. The most famous of his sons was Herod, who administered Galilee and made a name for himself by his efficiency in neutralizing resistance forces there.

Julius Caesar was assassinated in 44 B.C.E. In the new power alignment, Antipater and his sons supported Marc Antony. Marc Antony made Herod and his brother Phasael tetrarchs. (In the Greek, a tetrarch was originally the leader of a fourth of a people or territory or one of four rulers. Later the term meant simply a ruler who was less than a king and less than an ethnarch [ruler of a people].) In 43 B.C.E., Antipater was poisoned. It was not long before the upheavals in the Roman Empire tempted the Parthians (rulers of an empire east of the Roman Empire) to invade its eastern reaches. In 40 B.C.E., the Parthians made their move. They captured Jerusalem and installed the Hasmonean Antigonus Mattathias, son of Aristobulus II, as king and high

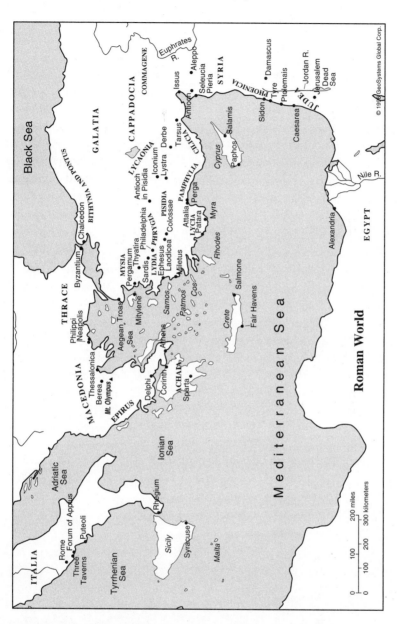

priest. In the same year, the Roman Senate declared Herod king of Judea. He went from Rome to Judea and recaptured Jerusalem in 37 B.C.E. after a three-year struggle. His difficult beginning was followed by a relatively stable rule lasting until 4 B.C.E. Because of his accomplishments, he earned the title "Herod the Great." As with other men called "great," the title does not imply that Herod was morally admirable or that his rule benefited his subjects. It simply recognizes his historical significance.

THE REIGN OF HEROD THE GREAT (37–4 B.C.E.)

Once he secured the kingship, Herod's first priority was to consolidate his power. He had no natural constituency in Judea, since his father was Idumean. Some did not consider him a true Jew. Furthermore, he lacked traditional credentials to be ruler of the Jews. He was not a priest and so could not be high priest. He was not of the Davidic line and so did not have that claim to kingship. Nor did Herod belong to Jerusalem's aristocracy. Herod owed his power to his own cunning and that of his father, Antipater, in supporting the winning sides in Roman power struggles. When Antony met defeat at the hands of Octavian (later to be called Augustus) at Actium in 31 B.C.E. and then committed suicide with Cleopatra in 30 B.C.E., Herod adroitly switched his allegiance to Octavian. Octavian confirmed him in his royal office.

Herod's relations with the Hasmonean family show his difficulties with legitimacy as well as his ruthlessness. To address his legitimacy problem, Herod married into the Hasmonean family. But because he felt threatened by them, he killed many of the Hasmoneans and so vacillated between using the influence of the Hasmonean family and trying to destroy it. His execution of Antigonus Mattathias in 37 B.C.E. may have made him unpopular with some Hasmonean supporters. Then Herod married the Hasmonean princess Mariamne, daughter of Alexander Jannaeus and Alexandra Salome. Although he is said to have loved her, this was also a political marriage; marriages within the ruling class often had political overtones. In 35 B.C.E., Herod wanted to import a high priest from among the priestly families of the Jewish community in Babylonia, probably because he did not think he could trust the Hasmoneans. But he was persuaded to appoint Aristobulus III, the young brother of his wife. Later the same year, Herod arranged for Aristobulus to be drowned at Jericho because he saw him as a threat. He then brought priestly families from the Diaspora to fill the high priesthood.

Herod's reign was full of executions of people whom he suspected, sometimes rightly, of conspiring against him. He seldom seems to have felt secure, and he became known as a cruel and merciless ruler, eager to do away with anyone he saw as a menace. Herod put Mariamne to death in 29 B.C.E. Her two sons by Herod, Alexander and Aristobulus, met the same fate in 7 B.C.E. Josephus provides a glimpse of life under Herod:

> They [the people] resented his [Herod's] carrying out of such arrangements as seemed to them to mean the dissolution of their religion and the disappearance of their customs. And these matters were discussed by all of them, for they were always being provoked and disturbed. Herod, however, gave the most careful attention to this situation, taking away any opportunities they might have (for

agitation) and instructing them to apply themselves at all times to their work. No meeting of citizens was permitted, nor were walking together or being together permitted, and all their movements were observed. Those who were caught were punished severely, and many were taken, either openly or secretly, to the fortress of Hyrcania and there put to death. Both in the city and on the open roads there were men who spied on those who met together. (*Ant.* 15.365–366)

Herod was known as a builder. In the Hellenistic world, building was a medium of propaganda: an ambitious building program signified wealth, power, and stability. Wealth came primarily from peasants' toil, which was the main source of wealth in the ancient world. To some subjects, magnificent buildings were a source of pride. To others, they symbolized the power of a well-entrenched ruler. To still others, they represented economic oppression. Herod's most famous project was the rebuilding of Jerusalem's temple on a scale never before seen, complete with a massive platform surrounded by Hellenistic porticoes. He began the work in 20 B.C.E., and Josephus says that it did not completely cease until 64 C.E., eighty-four years later. The building was substantially finished by the time of Jesus, who taught under its porticoes. For Herod, the temple served the dual purpose of advertising the magnificence of his rule and placating his Jewish subjects.

Herod may have tried to please Jews by his work in Jerusalem, but he used building for other purposes as well. An important motivation was to express his loyalty to Rome. He rebuilt the town of Strato's Tower on the Mediterranean coast and renamed it Caesarea in honor of Caesar. (Caesar was originally the proper name of a Roman family. After the death of Julius Caesar, it became one of the titles of the Roman emperor. The Caesar here is Augustus, formerly Octavian, adopted son of Julius.) Herod also rebuilt Samaria and renamed it Sebaste, from the Greek for the name Augustus. Herod had no qualms about erecting a temple to Augustus in Sebaste and thus showed that Torah had little claim on him, at least in this regard. He also built or rebuilt numerous fortresses to guard his power. Among these was Masada, northwest of the Dead Sea. Atop a high hill surrounded by precipitous cliffs, it was almost impregnable, and its ruins continue to astonish visitors today. In the Jewish-Roman war, a Jewish group held off the Romans there until 73 C.E., three years after Jerusalem had been destroyed and the war effectively won by the Romans.

THE HERODIAN FAMILY

At Herod's death, Rome divided his kingdom among three of his sons, Archelaus, Herod Antipas, and Philip. Archelaus ruled Jerusalem, Judea, and some surrounding territories from 4 B.C.E. to 6 C.E. At first some Judeans hoped that his rule would be less harsh than his father's, but they were sadly disappointed (see Matt 2:22). Ten years later, in 6 C.E., even the Romans admitted that his rule was a failure and banished him to the western Mediterranean. They then instituted direct Roman rule over Judea under a prefect accountable to the Roman governor of Syria.

	Main Dates Concerning the Herodian Family
47 B.C.E.	Antipater, father of Herod, becomes procurator of Judea; Herod assumes control of Galilee
40 B.C.E.	Roman Senate appoints Herod king; Parthians invade Judea and install a Hasmonean as high priest in Jerusalem
37 B.C.E.	Herod takes control of his kingdom
4 B.C.E.	Herod dies and is succeeded by his sons, each of whom rules over a portion of Herod's kingdom: Archelaus over Judea, Herod Antipas over Galilee and Perea, Philip over lands north of Galilee
6 C.E.	Archelaus deposed and banished by the Romans; Romans assume direct administration of Judea
37 C.E.	Former territory of Philip given to Agrippa I, grandson of Herod the Great, as a kingdom
39 C.E.	Herod Antipas deposed and banished by the Romans; his territory and Judea are added to Agrippa's kingdom
44 C.E.	Agrippa I dies
48 C.E.	Agrippa II becomes king of some small territories to the north of Galilee

Herod Antipas (see ch. 8, below) received Galilee and Perea (a territory east of the Jordan) and ruled from 4 B.C.E. to 39 C.E. This was the Herod before whom Jesus appeared just before his crucifixion, according to Luke 23:6–12. Herod Antipas contracted a political marriage with the daughter of King Aretas IV of Nabatea (a land to the east and southeast of the Dead Sea), and then he divorced her to marry his sister-in-law. The Gospels say that John the Baptist was beheaded by Herod Antipas because John protested this second marriage (see Mark 6:17–18 and parallels). Herod Antipas rebuilt Sepphoris in Galilee, which had been destroyed in 4 B.C.E. by the Roman Varus. He also built Tiberias, named for the reigning emperor Tiberius, on the shores of the Sea of Galilee. Sepphoris and Tiberias were the two main cities in Galilee in the first century. The Romans banished Antipas to Gaul in 39 C.E. because Agrippa I accused him of sedition.

Philip took charge of lands north and east of the Sea of Galilee. Though his rule was apparently uneventful, he built a town named Caesarea, often called Caesarea Philippi (see Mark 8:27) to distinguish it from Herod's Caesarea. Philip ruled from 4 B.C.E. until 34 C.E., when the Romans attached his territory to Syria.

Agrippa I was grandson of Herod the Great and son of Aristobulus, one of the two sons of Herod by Mariamne the Hasmonean. He spent time in Rome and was friendly with several influential Romans, as was common in the Herodian family. The Romans made a practice of having family members of their client kings spend time in Rome as a precaution against disloyalty. Among Agrippa's Roman friends was Gaius, nicknamed Caligula, who later ruled as emperor from 37 to 41 C.E. ("Caligula" means "little boots" and was a name from his childhood.) When Caligula became emperor, he awarded to Agrippa the territory that formerly belonged to Philip, and bestowed on him a royal title. In 39, Agrippa became king of Judea and Samaria as well. When Caligula was assassinated in 41, Agrippa played a role in negotiations that led to the choice of Claudius as emperor. At the beginning of Claudius's reign (ruled 41–54), the new emperor was kindly disposed to Agrippa and gave him the rest of what had been Herod the Great's kingdom. Agrippa remained king until his sudden death in 44. (Acts 12 says that he killed the apostle James and arrested Peter. Agrippa's death is considered punishment for blasphemy in Acts 12.) During his short reign, some of Agrippa's acts made his loyalty to Rome suspect, such as convening a meeting of local rulers without Rome's permission. When Agrippa I died, his son, Agrippa II, was only eighteen, and Claudius's advisors warned against giving him his father's kingdom. Instead, Claudius reinstituted direct Roman rule through procurators. Agrippa I was the last Jewish king to rule over Judea.

Agrippa II became king over some small territories north of Galilee in 48 and enjoyed a long rule in spite of the upheavals in Judea and Galilee during his reign. He was the last of Herod's descendants to rule. Although he did not exercise direct power over Judea and Galilee, he had influence there, and he played a minor role in some events in these regions.

PSALMS OF SOLOMON

The *Psalms of Solomon* is a collection of eighteen psalms, none of which are from the biblical Psalter. They date from about the middle of the first century B.C.E. Although the Hebrew originals have been lost, they survive in

Theater at Beth Shean (Scythopolis), a city located between the Jezreel and Jordan valleys in Galilee. Such structures show the influence of Hellenistic and Roman culture in the region.

Greek and Syriac. The psalms express the anger and anguish felt by some Jews at events of the first century B.C.E. They are a reaction to the reign of the Hasmoneans and to the coming of Rome in the person of Pompey. The composers of the psalms cannot be identified as members of any one party in Judaism, although attempts have been made to tie them to the Pharisees. They express a negative evaluation of the Hasmoneans because of Hasmonean social sins, and of Pompey for his defilement of the temple. They look forward to a Davidic messiah who will reform Israel, cast out the Gentiles, and bring the people into conformity with Torah. This section examines only the psalms that directly pertain to the events discussed earlier in this chapter.

Psalm 2 lays ultimate blame for Pompey's attack on Jerusalem at the feet of the city's sinful inhabitants:

> When the sinner grew proud, with a battering-ram he cast down fortified walls,
> And you did not restrain him.
> Alien nations ascended your altar,
>   They trampled it proudly with their sandals;
> Because the sons of Jerusalem had defiled the holy things of the Lord,
>   Had profaned with iniquities the offerings of God. (2:1–3)

The "sinner" is Pompey, who, when he captured Jerusalem, entered the temple and defiled it, an unforgivable sin. But the psalmist believes that God is all-powerful, so if Jerusalem has fallen to foreigners, God must have allowed it. The only reason God would have allowed such an event is that Jerusalem's residents displeased God; the coming of the Romans is really God's punishment on the people. The people's sin is put in terms of defilement of the sanctuary, "the holy things of the Lord." Since the "offerings" are the sacrifices offered by the priests in the temple, the psalm criticizes Jerusalem's priesthood and its ruling class. It praises God for righteous judgment: "God is a righteous judge, and he is no respecter of persons" (2:19), and therefore divine punishment falls on God's own people as well as on Gentile sinners.

But the psalmist then complains that Jerusalem's punishment, though just, has lasted long enough and that those who have carried out the punishment (Pompey and the Romans) are insolent toward God and must be prevented from utterly destroying Israel. God soon responds:

> And I had not long to wait before God showed me the insolent one
>> Slain upon the mountains of Egypt,
> Esteemed of less account than the least, on land and sea;
> His body borne hither and thither on the billows with much insolence,
>> With none to bury him, because he had rejected him with dishonor.
>> (2:30–31)

Pompey died in 48 B.C.E., perishing in Egypt during his war against Julius Caesar. His body indeed went unburied for some time, a mark of great dishonor. The insolent and shameful way Pompey was treated is considered a direct and appropriate punishment for his own insolence in dishonoring Jerusalem. For the psalmist, Pompey was guilty of the sin to which kings were particularly susceptible—refusing to acknowledge God's sovereignty. Other kings about whom we have read in Jewish literature and who refused to accept God's sovereignty were Antiochus IV (2 Macc 9:5–12; Dan 7, 8, 11) and Nebuchadnezzar (Dan 4:19–37). In *1 En.* 62–63, after death there is a judgment in which the kings and mighty of the earth suffer for the same offense. Speaking of Pompey, the psalm says,

> He did not reflect that he was a man,
>> And did not reflect on the latter end;
> He said: I will be lord of land and sea;
>> And he did not recognize that it is God who is great,
>> Mighty in his great strength.
> He is king over the heavens,
>> And judges kings and kingdoms. (2:31–34)

Pompey was called "the Great," but only God is truly great in the estimation of the psalmist.

Psalm 3 mentions resurrection: "But they that fear the Lord shall rise to life eternal, and their life shall be in the light of the Lord, and shall come to an end no more" (3:16).

Psalm 4 castigates some of the psalmist's fellow Jews for only pretending to follow Torah:

> Why do you sit, O profane man, in the council of the pious,
>> Seeing that your heart is far removed from the Lord,
>> Provoking with transgressions the God of Israel?
> Extravagant in speech, extravagant in outward seeming beyond all men,
>> Is he that is severe of speech in condemning sinners in judgment.
> And his hand is first upon him as though he acted in zeal,
>> And yet he is himself guilty in respect of manifold sins and of wantonness.
> (4:1–3)

The very ones who act as judges and claim to uphold Torah are themselves sinners. The psalmist is contemptuous of such hypocrisy. This psalm and the *Psalms of Solomon* in general go into detail about the sins such people commit. They are sexually wanton, they render false judgments in court, and they steal others' property by seemingly legal means. The sinners "utter law guilefully" (4:10). The sins are those of the upper class, those who have the authority to interpret and enforce Torah.

The *Psalms of Solomon* pleads for the destruction of the sinners in Israel, but it also reminds God to remain with the righteous lest they, too, perish:

> Do not make your dwelling far from us, O God;
>> Lest they assail us that hate us without cause.
> For you have rejected them, O God;
>> Do not let their foot trample upon your holy inheritance.
> Chasten us yourself in your good pleasure;
>> But do not give us up to the nations;
> For, if you send pestilence,
>> You yourself give it charge concerning us;
> For you are merciful,
>> And will not be angry to the point of consuming us.
> While your name dwells in our midst, we shall find mercy;
>> And the nations will not prevail against us.
> For you are our shield,
>> And when we call upon you, you listen to us. (7:1–7)

"The nations" are the Gentiles. These are the words of someone who has recently seen Jerusalem captured and defiled by the Romans. The prayer is that God remain with Israel lest it be completely destroyed by the Gentiles.

Psalm 8 bemoans Pompey's defilement of the temple but considers the judgment of God just because it is due to the behavior of Jerusalem's inhabitants:

> God laid bare their sins in the full light of day;
>> All the earth came to know the righteous judgments of God.
> In secret places underground, their iniquities were committed to provoke
>> him to anger;
> They wrought confusion, son with mother and father with daughter;
>> They committed adultery, every man with his neighbor's wife.
> They made covenants with one another with an oath concerning these
>> things;
>> They plundered the sanctuary of God, as though there was no avenger.
> They trampled the altar of the Lord, coming straight from all sorts of
>> uncleanness;
>> And with menstrual blood they defiled the sacrifices, as though these were
>> common flesh.
> They left no sin undone in which they did not surpass the heathen. (8:8–14)

The psalm condemns what it considers sexual sins of those who attend the altar and who thus must be priests. The mention of menstrual blood suggests that the priests are not following Torah as interpreted by the psalmist concerning the time of abstention from intercourse during a woman's menstrual period. The illegitimate crossing of kinship lines in marriage is also listed as a sin of the priests. The charges may be exaggerated, but it is clear that the ruling class was not following the psalmist's marriage rules. The sinners have "plundered the sanctuary." The Jerusalem elite profit illegitimately from temple service.

The psalm goes on to the punishment of the Jewish sinners, which God accomplishes through Pompey:

> God brought him that is from the end of the earth, that smites mightily;
>> He decreed war against Jerusalem and against her land.
> The princes of the land went out to meet him with joy; they said to him:
>> Blessed be your way! Come, enter in with peace.
> They made the rough ways even, before his entering in;
>> They opened the gates to Jerusalem, they crowned its walls.
> As a father enters the house of his sons, so he entered Jerusalem in peace;
>> He established his feet there in great safety.
> He captured her fortresses and the wall of Jerusalem;
>> For God himself led him in safety, while they wandered.
> He destroyed their princes and every one wise in counsel;
>> He poured out the blood of the inhabitants of Jerusalem, like the water of
>> uncleanness.

He led away their sons and daughters, whom they had begotten in
   defilement.
They did according to their uncleanness, even as their fathers had done:
   They defiled Jerusalem and the things that had been hallowed to the name
   of God. (8:16–26)

The one "from the end of the earth, that smites mightily" is Pompey. Rome
seemed like the end of the earth to the Palestinian Jews, and Pompey's prowess in war was legendary. These verses reflect events that we have already
studied. Josephus confirms that the princes of Israel invited Pompey into
their affairs (*Ant.* 14.58–59). Hoping for a favorable decision from Pompey,
Aristobulus at first offered him gifts and turned over fortresses. The gates of
Jerusalem were opened by Jews who hoped that Pompey would arrange the
political situation in their favor. But the Romans' arrival resulted in bloodshed and defilement of the holy city when tension between Aristobulus and
the Romans erupted in violence.

Psalms 17 and 18 express hope for a Davidic messiah. Psalm 17 opens
with the cry that Israel places its hope in God, its savior (17:3). In this case,
salvation consists of liberation from bondage to foreign and domestic oppressors whose activities violate God's law. The group behind the psalms had
somehow to make sense of the fact that, despite their loyalty to the all-powerful God of the universe, they were oppressed and powerless while the wicked
ruled the earth. The solution was to insist still more strongly that God controls all. "The kingdom of our God is for ever over the nations in judgment"
(17:4). Rome might seem all-powerful, but in reality the kingdom of God is
supreme.

The next verses probably refer to the Hasmoneans:

You, O Lord, chose David to be king over Israel,
   And swore to him concerning his seed that never should his kingdom fail
   before you.
But because of our sins, sinners rose up against us;
   They assailed us and thrust us out;
   What you had not promised to them, they took away with violence.
They in no way glorified your honorable name;
   In glory they established a monarchy in place of that which was their
   excellence;
They laid waste the throne of David in tumultuous arrogance. (17:4–6)

Although the Hasmoneans called themselves kings, they could not claim
Davidic lineage. By setting up an illegitimate monarchy, one that promoted
their own glory, they arrogantly ruined David's throne. In reaction to
Hasmonean abuses, the psalm recalls God's promise to David in 2 Sam 7 that

his posterity will always sit upon the throne of Israel. The psalm reminds God of the promise but admits that it was the sinfulness of Israel that led to the absence of a Davidic king.

The psalm looks for a Davidic king who will "shatter unrighteous rulers" and "purge Jerusalem from nations that trample it down to destruction" (17:24–25). Further, he will "thrust out sinners from the inheritance" (17:26), referring to Jewish sinners. The next verses, stating the Davidic messiah's tasks, draw on biblical traditions about the messiah and the ideal Israel.

> And he shall gather together a holy people, whom he shall lead in
>   righteousness,
>   And he shall judge the tribes of the people that has been sanctified by the
>   Lord his God.
> And he shall not suffer unrighteousness to lodge any more in their midst,
>   Nor shall there dwell with them any man that knows wickedness,
>   For he shall know them, that they are all sons of God. (17:28–30)

The king's primary task is to obey Torah and to insure that Israel does the same. "Sons of God" means a community that acts like God's children, completely obedient. The Hebrew Bible speaks of Israel as God's son or sons, as it does also of individual Israelites (see 2 Sam 7:14; Isa 1:2; Hos 11:1; Ps 2:7; Wis 2:13). Particularly instructive as a comparison is Wis 2, where the righteous man is a son of God because of his righteousness. A similar usage is found in Paul, where Christians are the only real children of God because, through incorporation into Jesus Christ, they are the only ones in the proper relation to God and are righteous (Gal 3:26; 4:4–7; Rom 8:12–17; see also John 1:12–13).

The next verses look to the past as the model for the future restoration:

> And he shall divide them according to their tribes upon the land,
>   And neither sojourner nor alien shall sojourn with them any more.
> He shall judge peoples and nations in the wisdom of his righteousness.
>   (17:30–31)

The Davidic era, which is seen as a golden age, will be restored. The twelve tribes will once again live in their allotted areas. As Joshua divided the land among the tribes when Israel first entered the promised land, so the Davidic messiah does here. The theme that the ideal Israel will contain no foreigners emerges, as it did in the critical periods of Josiah's reform (Deuteronomy) and the restoration (Ezra and Nehemiah). Israel will remain pure of foreign influences, but the Davidic king will rule over the whole earth "in the wisdom of his righteousness."

The following verses paint a glorious picture of a restored Jerusalem, seat of God's messiah, home to a purified community:

> And he shall have the heathen nations to serve him under his yoke;
>> And he shall glorify the Lord in a place to be seen of all the earth;
>> And he shall purge Jerusalem, making it holy as of old:
> So that the nations shall come from the ends of the earth to see his glory,
>> Bringing as gifts her sons who had fainted,
>> And to see the glory of the Lord, with which God has glorified it.
> And he shall be a righteous king, taught of God, over them,
> And there shall be no unrighteousness in his days in their midst,
> For all shall be holy and their king the anointed of the Lord.
> For he shall not put his trust in horse and rider and bow,
>> Nor shall he multiply for himself gold and silver for war,
>> Nor shall he gather confidence from a multitude for the day of battle.
> The Lord himself is his king, the hope of him that is mighty through hope
>> in God. (17:32–38)

This messiah's power comes not from military means but from obedience to God. In terms derived from holy war, the psalm declares that battles are won not with cavalry and bows but through devotion to God. The messiah is the opposite of Pompey and of the Hasmoneans, who, rather than recognize God's sovereignty and hope in God, rely on their own power and wealth. Jerusalem's invincibility is assured by its holiness, and the righteousness of its king ensures the righteousness of the people. Other elements of Zion ideology are present here as well. When God intervenes in history, the exiles will return, and all nations will recognize the true God and the divine election of Israel and of Jerusalem. Jerusalem will have been delivered from the "uncleanness of unholy enemies" (17:45).

The Davidic messiah is expected to be "free from sin" (17:41) and "powerful in the holy spirit" (17:42). In the Hebrew Bible, "the spirit" means the presence and activity of God. The psalm sees the messiah as possessing the holy spirit and therefore having understanding, strength, and righteousness (17:42). He will be "shepherd" of God's flock. His words will guide Israel: "His words shall be like the words of the holy ones in the midst of sanctified peoples" (17:49). The "holy ones" are the angels.

Psalm 18 speaks of the people's preparation for this messiah:

> Your chastisement is upon us as upon a first-born, only-begotten son,
>> To turn back the obedient soul from folly wrought in ignorance.
> May God cleanse Israel against the day of mercy and blessing,
>> For the day of choice when he brings back his anointed. (18:4–5)

The suffering of the righteous proves that they are the only son of God, the firstborn. Because God cares for them, they have undergone a purging meant to teach them how to be true sons. When the messiah comes, he will continue the chastening so that the community will remain pure. Israel will live "under the rod of chastening of the Lord's anointed in the fear of his God" (18:8).

Description of the Messiah in the *Psalms of Solomon*

Son of David

King of Israel

Has God as his king

Shepherd of God's flock

Sinless, obedient to Torah

Puts his trust not in wealth or might but in God

Defeats the Gentiles and rules them

Purges Jerusalem, so that exiles return

Brings Israel into conformity with the Torah, making them "sons of God"

Judges the tribes of Israel

Gives each of the twelve tribes its assigned land

The *Psalms of Solomon* allows a glimpse of how some Jews of the first century B.C.E. viewed the reign of the Hasmoneans and the coming of the Romans. They considered themselves God's people, but they thought that the Torah had been betrayed by their priests and princes. They felt justified when the wicked among their fellow Jews suffered at the hands of the Romans, but they lamented the injury done their holy city and temple by Pompey. These Jews looked to their sacred traditions for comfort and found hope in God's promises to David and in the Zion traditions that portrayed a world centered around Jerusalem and its God. They believed that the coming of the Davidic messiah would mean the fulfillment of the divine promises to Israel and the destruction of their oppressors, Jewish and Gentile. They awaited an Israel restored to its glorious state under David.

TESTAMENT OF MOSES

The *Testament of Moses* (sometimes called the *Assumption of Moses* although, in its present form, there is no account of Moses being assumed into heaven) is, as its title indicates, a testament. A testament is the final message of an important figure. Usually the figure is about to die, and he gathers his sons or successor to him for his last words. The *Testament* was originally written during the persecution of Judaism by Antiochus IV in the second century B.C.E., and then it was rewritten to comment on Herod's reign. Chapters 6–7 were inserted into a preexisting document to make it fit the later situation. Rewriting of texts and reapplication of traditions was common in ancient Judaism and Christianity. But the resultant arrangement is confusing. Chapters 6–7 refer to the time of Herod the Great (37–4 B.C.E.), the war of the Roman governor Varus (4 B.C.E.), and the rule of Herod's sons, but the clearest references to Antiochus's persecution in the second century B.C.E. do not occur until chapter 8. We shall see below why the editor did not order the chapters chronologically.

The setting of the *Testament of Moses* comes from the description of Moses' death in Deut 34. Moses is about to die, and he appoints Joshua to succeed him. In the *Testament* he tells Joshua that the world was created for Israel but that this fact had been hidden from the Gentiles so that they would mistreat Israel and unwittingly bring punishment on themselves. Moses instructs Joshua to preserve some books, probably the Pentateuch, "until the day of repentance in the visitation when the Lord will visit them in the consummation of the end of days" (1:18). He then predicts the course of history. Since it is not really Moses making these predictions but writers in the second century B.C.E. and the first century C.E., this is *ex eventu* prophecy, typical of apocalyptic literature. Although the *Testament* is not an apocalypse, it contains apocalyptic elements. The text takes a Deuteronomistic point of view: suffering is punishment for sin, and obedience to Torah brings success. Historical referents within the text are not always certain because the *Testament* follows the common apocalyptic practice of not being explicit. Therefore, all of the identifications we make are interpretations, although in most cases the referents are fairly obvious.

Chapter 2 predicts the entry into the land, the building of the temple, and the breaking away of the ten northern tribes. The north is condemned for breaking away from Jerusalem and for idolatry. The two southern tribes (Judah and Benjamin) are called the "holy tribes." In chapter 3, the destruction of Jerusalem and the Babylonian exile are described. Remarkably, the exile of the southern tribes is blamed on the sins of the northern tribes (3:5).

In chapter 4, an unnamed person, perhaps Daniel, prays to God for the people and is heard (see Dan 9). The Persian emperor Cyrus arises and allows the people to return to Judah and rebuild Jerusalem. The text says, "The two tribes shall continue in their prescribed faith, sad and lamenting because they will not be able to offer sacrifices to the Lord of their fathers" (4:8). Since we know that returning exiles rebuilt the temple and reestablished the cult, this seems to be a denigration of the second temple (see the *Damascus Document*; *1 En.* 89:73; Knibb, "Exile").

Historical Review in the *Testament of Moses*

Chapter 2	Entry into the land
	Periods of judges and kings
	Building of Solomon's temple
	Division of the kingdom into Israel and Judah
	Northern kingdom falls into idolatry
Chapter 3	Nebuchadnezzar's destruction of the temple
	Babylonian exile (blamed on the northern kingdom)
Chapter 4	Daniel prays for Israel
	Cyrus has pity on Israel
	Israel rebuilds Jerusalem but is unable to offer sacrifices
Chapter 5	Division within community concerning the truth
	Israel defiles temple and engages in idolatry
	Israel pollutes the altar with its offerings (Hellenistic reform?)
Chapter 6	Rise of the Hasmoneans, who are both kings and priests
	Hasmoneans do evil in the holy of holies
	Rise of Herod the Great, who rules for thirty-four years
	Herod punishes the Hasmoneans
	Herod's sons appointed to rule
	War of Varus
Chapter 7	Impious men rule who are hedonists and trample on the poor
Chapter 8	The persecution of Judaism, originally referring to Antiochus IV
Chapter 9	Martyrdom of the old man Taxo and his seven sons
Chapter 10	Coming of God's kingdom
	Defeat of Satan
	Apocalyptic signs and cosmic disruptions as God comes forth from his royal throne
	Israel conquers its oppressors, ascends to the heavens, and looks down on the punishment of its enemies

Chapter 5 may describe the time of the Hellenistic reform when it says of the Jews, "They themselves shall be divided as to the truth" (5:2). Because of their sins they will be punished "through the kings who share in their guilt and punish them" (5:1). "Kings" probably refers to the Seleucids, who, in the person of Antiochus IV, were party to the reform but who were God's instrument of punishment during the persecution and subsequent wars. The desecration of Jerusalem and its altar is described in priestly terms:

> They shall turn aside from righteousness and approach iniquity, and they shall defile with pollutions the house of their worship, and they shall go whoring after strange gods. For they shall not follow the truth of God, but some shall pollute the altar with the gifts which they offer to the Lord. They are not priests but slaves, sons of slaves. (5:3–4)

The historical referent of those who "are not priests, but slaves, sons of slaves," who pollute the altar by their very sacrifices, is not clear. It may be a derogatory reference to those who followed Onias III in the priesthood after Jason deposed him. Maybe it is Menelaus, who deposed Jason and whom 2 Maccabees describes as "possessing no qualification for the high priesthood, but having the hot temper of a cruel tyrant and the rage of a savage wild beast" (2 Macc 4:25).

The reference in *T. Mos.* 5:3–4 may be to the Hasmoneans even though the text says they "are not priests," since this statement may be less about their lineage and more about their worthiness to serve at the altar. Chapter 6, however, seems to introduce the Hasmoneans into the text for the first time:

> Then there shall be raised up to them kings bearing rule, and they shall call themselves priests of the Most High God: they shall assuredly work iniquity in the holy of holies. And an insolent king shall succeed them, who will not be of the race of the priests, a man bold and shameless, and he shall judge them as they deserve. And he shall cut off their chief men with the sword, and shall destroy them in secret places, so that no one may know where their bodies are. He shall slay the old and the young, and he shall not spare. Then the fear of him shall be bitter to them in their land. And he shall execute judgments on them as the Egyptians executed upon them, during thirty-four years, and he shall punish them. And he shall beget children, who will succeed him and rule for shorter periods. Into their parts cohorts and a powerful king of the west shall come, who shall conquer them: and he shall take them captive, and burn a part of their temple with fire, and crucify some around their colony.

The Hasmoneans were both kings and priests. According to the author of the *Testament*, their activity insults the temple. Then the text goes on to express in vivid terms the horror of Herod's rule and of the war of Varus that followed it. Herod was not a Hasmonean or even a priest. His harsh treatment of the Hasmoneans and other aristocrats who oppose him is seen as punishment for their sins. The description of Herod's thirty-four-year reign (37–4 B.C.E.) fits what we know of it—it was merciless. The Roman Varus, called "a powerful king of the west" although he was only a provincial governor of Syria, brutally crushed the upheavals following Herod's death.

Chapter 7 denigrates Israel's leaders, presumably the aristocracy of the time after Herod's death and the war of Varus. The chapter accuses these leaders of self-indulgence and of mistreating the poor. Chapter 8 speaks of persecutions that are similar to those that occurred under Antiochus IV. Chapter 9 introduces a Levite named Taxo, who has seven sons. Taxo suggests that the people withdraw to a cave in the wilderness and die there rather than transgress Torah, saying, "If we do this and die, our blood shall be avenged before the Lord" (9:7). Taxo's story is very similar to that of Jews during Antiochus's persecution who preferred slaughter in the wilderness rather than violation of Sabbath (1 Macc 2:29–38).

Chapter 10 is the climax of the book. God comes to retake creation. The text may imply that God comes in response to the death of the martyrs, although their death is not narrated. God's action is described in apocalyptic terms as the reassertion of divine sovereignty over all of creation that had been controlled by Satan. Themes of holy war are recalled as God goes out to battle:

> And then His kingdom shall appear throughout all his creation,
> And then Satan shall be no more,
> And sorrow shall depart with him.
> Then the hands of the angel shall be filled
> Who has been appointed chief,
> And he shall forthwith avenge them on their enemies.
> For the Heavenly One will arise from his royal throne,
> And he will go forth from his holy habitation
> With indignation and wrath on account of his sons.
> And the earth shall tremble: to its confines shall it be shaken:
> And the high mountains shall be made low
> And the hills shall be shaken and fall.
> And the horns of the sun shall be broken and it shall be turned into
>   darkness;
> And the moon shall not give her light, and be turned wholly into blood.
> And the circle of the stars shall be disturbed.
> And the sea shall retire into the abyss,
> And the fountains of waters shall fail,
> and the rivers shall dry up.
> For the Most High shall arise, the Eternal God alone,
> And he will appear to punish the Gentiles,
> And he will destroy all their idols.
> Then you, O Israel, shall be happy,
> And you shall mount upon the necks and wings of the eagle,
> And they shall be ended.
> And God will exalt you,
> And he will cause you to approach the heaven of the stars,
> In the place of their habitation.
> And you shall look from on high and shall see your enemies in Gehenna,

And you shall recognize them and rejoice,
And you shall give thanks and confess your Creator. (10:1–10)

God is angry at the treatment of his "sons," Israel. As God goes forth to battle, the entire cosmos reacts. Sun and moon fail. The stars are disturbed from their places. The earth is devastated. The cosmic scope of the turmoil is typical of apocalyptic scenarios. Such images derive from the Hebrew Bible, for example, Joel:

The earth quakes before them,
    the heavens tremble.
The sun and the moon are darkened,
    and the stars withdraw their shining.
The Lord utters his voice
    at the head of his army;
how vast is his host! (Joel 2:10–11)

The withdrawal of the sea into the abyss, found in *T. Mos.* 10, draws on the ancient Near Eastern symbolism of the sea as that which opposes God, as in Dan 7. All forces opposing God are destroyed.

The author sees all humanity as divided between Jew and Gentile. This is social dualism, typical of the apocalyptic worldview. The Jews are God's sons, attacked by the wicked Gentiles. God's intervention spells defeat of the Gentiles and their descent to hell, whereas Israel ascends to heaven and lives with the stars, considered heavenly beings by the ancient world (in Israel, angels). We have seen several times that being with or like the angels (or stars) is a common reward in these texts. Israel gazes down from its heavenly abode, sees and recognizes its enemies as they are being punished, and takes pleasure in its vindication.

In its present form, the *Testament* ends with Joshua upset that Moses is about to leave. Moses strengthens him with words about God's control of history. In chapter 12, Moses asserts that God has foreseen all of history, as is proven by the "predictions" Moses has just uttered.

The episode of Taxo, the old man with seven sons, in chapter 9 combines elements found in stories that appear in 2 Macc 6 and 7, stories that take place during the time of the persecution of Judaism by Antiochus IV. In 2 Macc 6, an old man named Eleazar refuses to eat pork and so is viciously martyred. In 2 Macc 7, a mother and her seven sons are tortured to death for Torah. The last son killed expresses the hope that their suffering will liberate Israel. He appeals to God "through me and my brothers to bring to an end the wrath of the Almighty that has justly fallen on our whole nation" (2 Macc 7:38). In both the *Testament* and 2 Maccabees, Israel's suffering is acknowledged to be a just punishment for Israel's sins. And in both, the martyrs' deaths bring about the end of Israel's suffering and the punishment of its enemies. In 2 Maccabees, the result is the establishment of the independent Hasmonean kingdom; in the *Testament,* there are cosmic results more typical of apocalypses. Both works expect rewards and punishments after death as well.

If the *Testament of Moses* was originally written to respond to the crisis under Antiochus IV, then both the stories in *T. Mos.* 9 and those in 2 Macc 8 originally addressed the same situation. That a later editor could pick up and adapt the same story to reflect on a later situation is an instance of a common practice in ancient Judaism and Christianity. But this raises the question of why the later editor of the *Testament* placed chapters 6–7, which refer to Herod, Herod's sons, and the war of Varus, *before* chapters 8–9, which seem to refer to the persecution of Judaism by Antiochus IV.

One answer is that chapters 6–7 are simply misplaced, and that they should be placed later, after chapters 8–9. But we must remember that although we have identified persons and events in the text, chapters 2–10 do not contain such specific identifications. There are similarities between the events enumerated in chapter 8 and those that transpired under Antiochus, but the identification is not explicit in the text. But in the present form of the book, it is best not to read chapter 8 as a direct reference to the time of Antiochus, although it was such in the original composition. Rather, the later editor has inserted chapters 6–7 before chapters 8–9 because he saw this description of events under Antiochus as a perfect portrayal of what would happen to bring about the final consummation of Israel's history. That is, he expected that the tragic events under Herod, Varus, and Herod's sons would be followed by a persecution of Judaism analogous to the one under Antiochus. This would then be followed by God's intervention, the glorification of Israel, and the punishment of Israel's enemies. Thus, the very placement of the chapters about the Hasmoneans, Herod, Herod's sons, and Varus is in itself a reinterpretation of the traditions from the time of the crisis under Antiochus IV.

SIMILITUDES OF ENOCH (1 EN. 37–71)

The *Similitudes of Enoch* is an apocalypse. As is common in apocalypses, it does not have clear historical references. But we consider the work here because it probably comes from the period and locale under discussion, provides another example of apocalyptic literature, embodies one reaction to events in Israel under the Romans, and speaks of a savior figure that shows similarities with Christian belief and later Jewish traditions.

Many scholars date the *Similitudes of Enoch* to the first century C.E. although the dating is disputed. The work survives as part of *1 Enoch*. Like the other parts of that collection, it once existed independently. It is the only section of *1 Enoch* whose presence is not attested at Qumran. Its original language was probably Aramaic, but it is preserved in its entirety only in Ethiopic. Its title comes from the fact that it contains three "similitudes" introduced in chapters 38, 45, and 58, framed by an introduction in chapter 37, and has two endings, one in chapter 70 and the other in chapter 71. The word for "similitude," also translated "parable," has a wide range of meaning in ancient Israel, but its basic meaning is any sort of figurative language. Such language operates on the principle of finding similarities between different things. In the context of *1 Enoch*, "similitudes" denotes revelatory discourse, a usage derived from a prophetic milieu.

The *Similitudes* is mainly interested in the fate of the good and the bad, as is usual in apocalypses. The good are "righteous," "elect" ("chosen"), and "holy." They possess secret wisdom that they receive from Enoch. Enoch travels to heaven and sees God and God's agent, also called one with a "countenance like a son of man," the "Righteous One," the "Elect One," and the "Messiah." The heavenly son of man will judge the good and the bad at the end of time. Enoch's trips to heaven and to various parts of the universe provide him with firsthand views of the punishment of the bad and the reward of the good. He brings this knowledge, available only through direct revelation, to the chosen people. Acceptance of this secret knowledge and hope in the son of man will result in salvation.

There is a close relation between the earthly righteous and the heavenly son of man, reflected in their shared titles, "righteous" and "elect" (see Collins, "Heavenly Representative"). The relationship of the son of man to the righteous is like that of the one like a son of man to Israel in Dan 7 and the relationship of the archangel Michael to Israel in Dan 10 and the *War Scroll* from Qumran. He is the people's heavenly patron. The career of the son of man in heaven corresponds to the experience of the righteous on earth. As the son of man remains hidden until his glory is fully revealed at the judgment, so the righteous are not recognized and suffer oppression on earth but will share in the son of man's glory at the end of time, when all is revealed.

Enoch claims, "Till the present day such wisdom has never been given by the Lord of Spirits as I have received" (37:4). "Lord of Spirits" is a frequent title for God in the *Similitudes,* because the *Similitudes* assumes that there is a multitude of spirits, good and bad, operating in the universe and that God is sovereign over them all.

The first parable announces the reward of the good and the punishment of the evil "when the congregation of the righteous shall appear" (38:1). This implies that the righteous are not yet recognized as such. "Those that possess the earth shall no longer be powerful and exalted" at the end of time (38:4; cf. Jesus' beatitude in Matt 5:5: "Blessed are the meek, for they will inherit the earth"; cf. also Ps 37:11; *1 En.* 5:6–7). At that time "shall the kings and mighty perish" (38:4). The enemies of the righteous are thus the kings and mighty of the earth. The judgment will bring the downfall of rulers. This theme appears frequently in apocalyptic literature.

Enoch receives "books of zeal and wrath, and books of disquiet and expulsion" (39:2). Their content coincides with the revelation imparted in the *Similitudes*. Enoch continues,

> And in those days a whirlwind carried me off from the earth,
> And set me down at the end of the heavens.
> And there I saw another vision, the dwelling-places of the holy,
> And the resting-places of the righteous.
> Here my eyes saw their dwellings with His righteous angels,
> And their resting-places with the holy.
> And they petitioned and interceded and prayed for the children of men,
> And righteousness flowed before them as water,
> And mercy like dew upon the earth:
> Thus it is among them for ever and ever.
> And in that place my eyes saw the Elect One of righteousness and faith,
> And I saw his dwelling-place under the wings of the Lord of Spirits.
> And righteousness shall prevail in his days,
> And the righteous and elect shall be without number before him for ever
> and ever. (39:3–7)

Enoch travels to heaven itself, where he views the angels, the righteous who have died, God, and the Elect One resting close to God. The vision is comforting to the righteous still oppressed on earth, because they can see that those who have gone before them, perhaps in martyrdom, are present with the angels and intercede for them. When the days of the Elect One come, righteousness will prevail, and the righteous will live in glory.

God "knows before the world was created what is for ever and what will be from generation to generation" (39:11). Enoch hears "those that sleep not" (probably angels) saying, "Holy, holy, holy is the Lord of Spirits: He fills the world with spirits" (39:12). This echoes the prophet Isaiah's vision in the temple, when he sees God sitting on a throne and the angels singing, "Holy, holy, holy is the LORD of hosts; the whole earth is full of his glory" (Isa 6:3; see Rev 4). The worldview of the *Similitudes* is reflected in the change of "hosts" (meaning God's angelic army) to "Spirits" and by the fact that God fills the earth with spirits instead of divine glory. As is typical of apocalypticism, the universe is full of spirits. God rules them all.

Enoch says that the angel who accompanies him on his tour of heaven shows him "all the hidden things" (40:2). Enoch sees four angels in the presence of God, a feature recalling Ezek 1:4–14 (see Rev 4). The first angel praises God. The second blesses "the Elect One and the elect ones." The third prays and intercedes for those dwelling on earth. The last angel is seen "fending off the satans and forbidding them to come before the Lord of Spirits to accuse them who dwell on earth." This is a bit bizarre for modern sensibilities. After all, does God need protection from his enemies, even in heaven? Apparently so. And who are these "satans"? Modern ears hear "Satan" as a proper name, but in the Hebrew Bible it is a common noun meaning "accuser" or "adversary" (hasatan), as already mentioned. We noted in chapter 2, above, that when applied to a superhuman, angelic figure, "the satan" is the heavenly prosecuting attorney, who stands before God and accuses the high priest of sin (Zech 3; Job 1–2). As the centuries progressed and as Israel began to believe in an unseen world heavily populated with angels and demons, "the satan" became Satan, prince of demons. But in *1 En.* 40, "the satan" has become plural, and God's angelic protector fends off the advances of would-be accusers (satans) of the earthly righteous. In *1 Enoch,* the satans are unwelcome in heaven. In the development of the tradition, the accuser—the satan, once a member of the heavenly host—has been transformed into a multitude of demonic opponents of God.

Chapter 41 portrays nature as obedient to God, having taken an oath to remain faithful to its tasks. This implicitly contrasts nature with the sinners who do not follow God's ways. In the *Book of the Watchers,* this contrast is explicit, as we have seen (*1 En.* 2–5). The next chapter shows that apocalyptic wisdom is accessible only to the elect. The chapter is a hymn about wisdom, personified as a woman:

> Wisdom found no place where she might dwell;
> Then a dwelling-place was assigned to her in the heavens.
> Wisdom went forth to make her dwelling among the children of men,
> And found no dwelling-place:
> Wisdom returned to her place,
> And took her seat among the angels.
> And unrighteousness went forth from her chambers:
> Whom she sought not she found,
> And dwelt with them,
> As rain in a desert
> And dew on a thirsty land. (42:1–3)

Wisdom is now in heaven, not on earth. To obtain wisdom, one must make a trip to heaven; there is no other way. This is characteristic of apocalypticism.

Enoch's trip to heaven makes him the sole source of wisdom for those on earth. To accept his testimony contained in the *Similitudes* is to have wisdom; to reject it is to live in darkness. (Such ideas about wisdom influenced the Gospel of John, where the only way to be in touch with God is through the only one who ever descended from heaven, the Son of Man [e.g., John 1:18; 3:11–15, 31–35].) Not only can wisdom not be found on earth; humanity welcomes her opposite, unrighteousness. The personification of wisdom and her opposite as two women, each of whom tries to woo men, is known from the wisdom tradition (Prov 8–9). Humanity's acceptance of unrighteousness and rejection of wisdom explain the present state of the world.

The hymn to wisdom in *1 En.* 42 contrasts sharply with a hymn from Sirach. There personified wisdom says that she has journeyed through creation and visited every nation. She finds no home in all the earth. Following *1 En.* 42, we would expect her to return to heaven. But God tells her, "Make your dwelling in Jacob, and in Israel receive your inheritance" (Sir 24:8). Wisdom says,

> In the holy tent I ministered before him,
>   and so I was established in Zion.
> Thus in the beloved city he gave me a resting place,
>   and in Jerusalem was my domain.
> I took root in an honored people,
>   in the portion of the Lord, his heritage. . . .
> All this is the book of the covenant of the Most High God,
>   the law that Moses commanded us
>   as an inheritance for the congregations of Jacob.
> It overflows, like the Pishon, with wisdom,
>   and like the Tigris at the time of the first fruits.
> It runs over, like the Euphrates, with understanding,
>   and like the Jordan at harvest time.
> It pours forth instruction like the Nile,
>   like the Gihon at the time of vintage. (Sir 24:10–12, 23–27)

For Sirach, Torah is the source of all wisdom and is available to all. Torah overflows with wisdom and understanding and fills those who accept it. The contrast between Sir 24 and *1 En.* 42 corresponds to the difference between sapiential and apocalyptic wisdom. In sapiential wisdom, wisdom comes from the exercise of human reason on events in the human and natural worlds or, when seen from a more explicitly religious point of view, by the study of Torah. But apocalyptic wisdom comes only through direct revelation and is known only to the elite. Both the wisdom tradition and apocalypticism use the language of wisdom, but they mean something different by it.

Chapter 45 of *1 Enoch* introduces the second parable. Again its subject is judgment. The sinners "denied the name of the Lord of Spirits" (45:2), and they will be denied entrance to heaven and earth. The Elect One judges them:

> On that day my Elect One shall sit on the throne of glory
> And shall try their works,
> And their places of rest shall be innumerable.
> And their souls shall grow strong within them when they see my elect ones,
> And those who have called upon my glorious name:
> Then I will cause my Elect One to dwell among them.
> And I will transform the heaven and make it an eternal blessing and light:
> And I will transform the earth and make it a blessing:
> And I will cause my elect ones to dwell upon it:
> But the sinners and evil-doers shall not set foot on it. (45:3–5)

Here there is a connection between the elect ones on earth, who trust in God's name, and the Elect One in heaven, who will be the judge at the end time. Sinners are excluded from the new heaven and earth, which will be transformed.

Chapter 46 is important for understanding the origins of the figure of the Elect One, the son of man, and for appreciating his function:

> And there I saw One who had a head of days,
> And his head was white like wool,
> And with him was another being whose countenance had the appearance of
>   a man,
> And his face was full of graciousness, like one of the holy angels.
> And I asked the angel who went with me and showed me all the hidden
>   things, concerning that son of man, who he was, and whence he was,
>   and why he went with the Head of Days. And he answered and said to
>   me:
> This is the son of man who has righteousness,
> With whom dwells righteousness,
> And who reveals all the treasures of that which is hidden,
> Because the Lord of Spirits has chosen him,
> And whose lot has pre-eminence before the Lord of Spirits in uprightness for
>   ever. (46:1–3)

This passage depends on Dan 7. The "Head of Days" is God and corresponds to the "Ancient of Days" in Dan 7:9. In *1 Enoch* God's hair is white as wool, and in Daniel God is dressed in white and has hair like pure wool (which probably implies it is also white). God's appearance in both texts signifies extreme age, wisdom, and dignity. Both passages feature one in God's presence who resembles a "son of man." In Dan 7, the one like a son of man is Israel's angelic patron. In the *Similitudes* the son of man is compared to the angels and is the heavenly patron of the elect on earth.

The similarities between *1 En.* 46 and Dan 7 indicate that our seer saw Dan 7 as the key to understanding the oppression of the righteous in his own time. The heavenly representative of the righteous is hidden in God's presence, unknown by the oppressors, and he will come at the end of time to vindicate them. The son of man epitomizes righteousness. He is "chosen" by God and so is "elect." He knows all secret wisdom and is able to disclose that the powerful of the earth will meet a dismal end and the righteous of the earth will be glorified. He combines the attributes of a perfect apocalyptic seer—wisdom, righteousness, and election. We shall see that this leads to a rather startling development in chapter 71. The righteous know this hidden wisdom only because Enoch has revealed it to them.

The rest of the passage identifies the sinners as the powerful:

> And this son of man whom you have seen
> Shall raise up the kings and the mighty from their seats,
> And the strong from their thrones
> And shall loosen the reins of the strong,
> And break the teeth of the sinners.
> And he shall put down the kings from their thrones and kingdoms
> Because they do not extol and praise Him,
> Nor humbly acknowledge whence the kingdom was bestowed upon them.
> And he shall put down the countenance of the strong,
> And shall fill them with shame.
> And darkness shall be their dwelling,
> And worms shall be their bed,
> And they shall have no hope of rising from their beds,
> Because they do not extol the name of the Lord of Spirits.
> And these are they who judge the stars of heaven,
> And raise their hands against the Most High,
> And tread upon the earth and dwell upon it.
> And all their deeds manifest unrighteousness,
> And their power rests upon their riches,
> And their faith is in the gods which they have made with their hands,
> And they deny the name of the Lord of Spirits,
> And they persecute the houses of his congregations,
> And the faithful who hang upon the name of the Lord of Spirits. (46:4–8)

The powerful persecute the community behind the *Similitudes*. Further, they do not acknowledge that their power derives from the Lord of Spirits. Instead, they trust in their own wealth and might and create idols for themselves. Their conduct is an assault on the stars (angels) and God (see Dan 8; 11).

"And in those days shall have ascended the prayer of the righteous, and the blood of the righteous from the earth before the Lord of Spirits" (47:1). Then the holy ones in the heavens will pray "on behalf of the blood of the righteous that has been shed." Members of the community of the righteous have actually shed their blood, and their blood now calls to the Lord for vengeance. Then comes a judgment scene:

> In those days I saw the Head of Days when he seated himself upon the
>   throne of his glory,
> And the books of the living were opened before him:
> And all his host which is in heaven above and his counsellors stood before
>   him,
> And the hearts of the holy were filled with joy;
> Because the number of the righteous had been offered,
> And the prayer of the righteous had been heard,
> And the blood of the righteous been required before the Lord of Spirits.
>   (47:3–4)

The scene recalls the judgment scene of Dan 7. There the Ancient of Days takes his throne in the heavenly court and "the books" are opened. In Daniel the books are heavenly records of human deeds, as they probably are here, too. They will be read at the final judgment, an idea common in the ancient Near East and in apocalypticism. Another common apocalyptic idea in *1 En.* 47 is that a specific number of righteous must be martyred before the eschaton can come. In this passage, the holy ones rejoice because the number has been reached.

The son of man appears again in the next chapter:

> And in that place I saw the fountain of righteousness
> Which was inexhaustible:
> And around it were many fountains of wisdom:
> And all the thirsty drank of them,
> And were filled with wisdom,
> And their dwellings were with the righteous and holy and elect.
> And at that hour that son of man was named
> In the presence of the Lord of Spirits,
> And his name before the Head of Days. (48:1–2)

Enoch is still in heaven. Although wisdom is inaccessible on earth, it is abundant in heaven. Wisdom and righteousness are closely associated because righteousness, being in the proper relationship with God, is possible only to those who really know how things are, the wise. In this scene, the identity of the heavenly son of man is made known, at least in heaven. The next verse says that the son of man was named before the Lord, even before the sun and moon were created. God has planned all in advance, even before creation:

> And for this reason he has been chosen and hidden before him,
> Before the creation of the world and for evermore.
> And the wisdom of the Lord of Spirits has revealed him to the holy and
>   righteous;
> For he has preserved the lot of the righteous,
> Because they have hated and despised this world of unrighteousness,
> And have hated all its works and ways in the name of the Lord of Spirits:
> For in his name they are saved,
> And according to his good pleasure do they have life. (48:6–7)

The community of the righteous on earth is truly alone in the world. They alone know about the son of man and his coming judgment. They have rejected this world and believed in the Lord of Spirits. Only they will be saved.

The next part of the chapter tells of the fate of the sinners:

> In these days downcast in countenance shall the kings of the earth have
>   become,
> And the strong who possess the land because of the works of their hands,
> For on the day of their anguish and affliction they shall not be able to save
>   themselves.
> And I will give them over into the hands of my elect:
> As straw in the fire so shall they burn before the face of the holy:
> As lead in the water shall they sink before the face of the righteous,
> And no trace of them shall any more be found.
> And on the day of their affliction there shall be rest on earth,
> And before them they shall fall and not rise again:
> And there shall be no one to take them with his hands and raise them:
> For they have denied the Lord of Spirits and his Anointed. (48:8–10)

The sinners are the powerful of the earth—kings and large landowners. Their present strength means nothing in the end. They will be handed over to the righteous for punishment. Opponents of the community have denied the name of the Lord and the Lord's Messiah (anointed). The Messiah is the same as the Elect One and the son of man. Chapter 49 is a hymn of praise to the Elect One, with whom reside all wisdom, insight, might, and understanding and to whom it has been given to judge the "secret things."

Chapters 50 and 51 are jubilant accounts of the fate of the righteous. They will be raised from the dead, glorified. They will be saved through the name of the Lord of Spirits, who will have compassion on them. The Elect One will arise and "choose the righteous and holy from among them" (51:2), an act of positive judgment. God says, "And the Elect One shall in those days sit on My throne, and his mouth shall pour forth all the secrets of wisdom and counsel" (51:3); the Elect One possesses divine authority.

Enoch is now carried by a whirlwind to the far west of the universe, where he observes mountains of iron, copper, silver, gold, soft metal, and lead. He learns that the mountains are there to show the power of the Messiah when he comes, for they will melt in his presence. This will demonstrate that at the coming of the Elect One, "none shall be saved, either by gold or by silver, and none be able to escape. And there shall be no iron for war, nor shall one clothe oneself with a breastplate" (52:7–8). Those who are presently powerful will become powerless.

In chapter 53, Enoch views the valley of judgment, where the wicked will be brought. He sees the "angels of punishment abiding there and preparing all the instruments of Satan" (53:3). The wicked are identified as the "kings and the mighty of this earth" (53:5). Enoch learns that when the sinners are destroyed, "the Righteous and Elect One shall cause the house of his congregation to appear" (53:6). In the next chapter, he sees a fiery valley being prepared for the punishment of the evil angels who led humanity astray. The second parable ends with Enoch's vision of the return of Israel's exiles.

Chapter 58 introduces the last parable. It predicts glory, eternal life, and peace for the righteous. The next few chapters show Enoch discovering more secrets of the universe. The theme of eschatological judgment is prominent. God appears as judge on the divine throne in 60:2. Chapters 62 and 63 are an extended judgment scene in which the kings and the mighty are judged by the son of man. The powerful of the earth do not know God, nor do they understand that the community behind the *Similitudes* is the community of the elect, holy, and righteous. Similarly, the son of man is hidden and is revealed only to the elect until the judgment. At the judgment, he will be revealed to all as judge. The ideal situation for the righteous, realized at the end of time, is to be with the son of man forever: "And the Lord of Spirits will abide over them, and with that son of man shall they eat and lie down and rise up for ever and ever" (62:14).

The once powerful sinners beg for the chance to mend their ways and to worship God. They confess, "We have not believed before him nor glorified the name of the Lord of Spirits, nor glorified our Lord, but our hope was in the scepter of our kingdom and in our glory" (63:7). They are denied any opportunity to repent, because it is too late. Their last words are, "Our souls are full of unrighteous gain, but it does not prevent us from descending from the midst thereof into the burden of Sheol" (63:10).

The *Similitudes* has two endings. Chapter 70 is probably the original ending, with chapter 71 added later. Chapter 70 begins,

> And it came to pass after this that his [Enoch's] name during his lifetime was raised aloft to that son of man and to the Lord of Spirits from amongst those who dwell on the earth. And he was raised aloft on the chariots of the spirit and his name vanished among them. (70:1).

This reflects the mysterious end of the biblical Enoch, in which God simply takes him (Gen 5:24). There may also be an allusion to the ascent of Elijah to heaven in a fiery chariot in 2 Kgs 2:11. Enoch's mysterious end, combined with his legendary righteousness, made him an apt patron for the Enoch traditions.

Chapter 71 is a much longer ending that recapitulates Enoch's visions of heaven. Most interesting is an interchange between Enoch and an angel: "And he came to me and greeted me with his voice, and said to me: 'You are the son of man who is born unto righteousness' " (71:14). The identification of Enoch with the son of man is startling. R. H. Charles was so surprised by the identification of Enoch with the son of man that he changed the text from "You are the son of man" to "*This* is the son of man" (*APOT* 237). He thought there must be some mistake in the text. The reader has not been prepared for the complete identification of Enoch with the son of man. It has been suggested that when Christians identified Jesus as the Son of Man on the basis of Dan 7, Jews did the same with Enoch to counter Christian claims. Others find it unlikely that Jews would imitate Christians in this way.

Whatever the reason for the identification of Enoch with the son of man, the *Similitudes* provides some remarkable parallels with Christianity. Although the *Similitudes* does not oppose Torah, it receives almost no attention in the book. Instead, salvation depends on rejection of this world and belief in a hidden world where God controls all. God works through an agent called the son of man, in whom the elect must have faith. The focus is on the son of man, also called the Elect One, the Righteous One, and the Messiah. The Messiah in the *Similitudes* is a supernatural figure, something that has not been seen before in this study but is found in later Jewish works. All of this recalls how early Christianity looks upon Jesus. Jesus is a supernatural person in whom one must have faith to be saved. Further, the titles borne by Enoch's son of man—Messiah, Righteous One, Elect One—are applied to Jesus in Christian traditions.

The importance of the *Similitudes* has often been thought to depend upon whether it was the origin of Christian portrayals of Jesus as Son of Man. The similarities between the *Similitudes* and Christianity, however, do not prove dependence in either direction. At any rate, trying to prove direct influence is too narrow an approach. Collins redirects the discussion to a more fruitful path: "It is apparent that Jewish conceptions of savior figures in this period were variable, but the Similitudes illustrate the kind of speculation that was also at work in the New Testament development of christological titles" (*AI* 193).

The *Similitudes* provides an apocalyptic solution to the problem that its author faces in his own historical circumstances. For him, the rich and powerful are arrogant and oppressive and trust not in God but in their own resources. His solution is to picture a scene of postmortem judgment in which the wealthy and powerful are punished and the righteous rewarded. Also characteristic of apocalypses is that Enoch gains knowledge of God's secrets by his journeys to the heavenly world and to other parts of the universe inaccessible to other human beings. In other words, true wisdom can come only at the initiative of God and through direct revelation.

EXCURSUS: THE SYNAGOGUE

The word "synagogue" comes from the Greek *synagōgē*, meaning "gathering" or "assembly." A synagogue is a gathering for reading and interpretation of Torah, for teaching, and for prayer, and so the word, in the first instance, means a group of people, not a building. The word was eventually applied to a building by extension.

The New Testament, Josephus, Philo, and rabbinic literature all mention synagogues in the first century C.E., but we do not know for sure how and when synagogues first came into being. Since they were so widespread in

Theodotus inscription (see sidebar).

the first century C.E., they must have existed in some form before then. Many have thought the exiled Jews in Babylon must have created something like the synagogue to make up for the loss of the temple and the holy land. As logical as this may be, direct evidence for it is lacking. We do know of Jewish "places of prayer" (Greek: *proseuchai*) in third-century B.C.E. Egypt, and this term also appears in Josephus and the Acts of the Apostles. But the relation of the places of prayer to synagogues is unclear. Archaeology does not help much, since no building predating the first century can clearly claim to be a synagogue. Of course, there may have been synagogues, "gatherings," in private homes or in buildings built for some other purpose. The synagogue most probably predates the first century, but little is known about it.

Josephus stresses the teaching function of the synagogue on the Sabbath:

> He [Moses] appointed the Law to the most excellent and necessary form of instruction, ordaining, not that it should be heard once for all or twice or on several occasions, but that every week men should desert their other occupations and assemble to listen to the Law and to obtain a thorough and accurate knowledge of it. (*Ag. Ap.* 2.175)

Josephus's observations about the importance of weekly reading and interpretation of the Law is supported by Philo (*Moses* 2.216) and by references in the New Testament. Because Torah was central in Jewish life, the institution of the synagogue was crucial. And when the temple was destroyed, Torah and synagogue became still more important.

In 1913, an inscription was discovered on Mount Ophel in Jerusalem (Mount Ophel is a section of the southeast ridge of Jerusalem between the temple mount to the north and the City of David to the south). The inscription is associated with the ruins of a large building. The inscription has been dated to the first century, C.E., although that dating has been disputed (see Kee). It reads as follows.

"Theodotus, son of Vettenus, the priest and *archisynagogos*, son of an *archisynagogos* and grandson of an *archisynagogos,* who built the synagogue for purposes of reciting the Law and studying the commandments, and as a hotel with chambers and water installations to provide for the needs of itinerants from abroad, which his fathers, the elders and Simonides founded." (translation from Meyers, 252)

An *archisynagogos* is a synagogue ruler. This inscription may be evidence that there was a synagogue building in Jerusalem as early as the first century C.E. It confirms Josephus's, Luke's, and Acts's description of synagogue gatherings as occasions to read and teach the Torah. It also illuminates the use of synagogues for purposes of hospitality to traveling Jews.

Jesus' appearance in the synagogue at Nazareth in Luke 4 shows what Luke thought would happen in a synagogue. It begins, "When he came to Nazareth, where he had been brought up, he went to the synagogue on the sabbath day, as was his custom. He stood up to read, and the scroll of the prophet Isaiah was given to him" (Luke 4:16–17). Jesus finds a passage and reads it. Jesus then "rolled up the scroll, gave it back to the attendant, and sat down" (Luke 4:20). The "attendant" is presumably some sort of helper in the synagogue. Jesus then explains the passage. Luke's scene fits what later rabbinic documents say about the synagogue service—it consisted of prayer, readings from the Torah and the Prophets with translation, a sermon, and a blessing (*m. Meg.* 4:3). Translation was necessary because Hebrew was no longer generally spoken by either Palestinian or Diaspora Jews. The number of those able to read the Hebrew text was limited, as was the number of those qualified to expound it.

In Acts, Paul and his companions arrive at Antioch in Asia Minor. "And on the sabbath day they went into the synagogue and sat down. After the reading of the law and the prophets, the rulers of the synagogue sent to them, saying, 'Brethren, if you have any word of exhortation for the people, say it' " (Acts 13:14–15). Here there are readings from the Torah and an explanation of the readings. Apparently the synagogue had "rulers," a somewhat vague term. Perhaps the rulers were the prominent, educated members of the Jewish community.

CONCLUSION

The independent Jewish kingdom of the Hasmoneans was cut short by the arrival of the Romans in the person of Pompey and his army. Rome had long exercised influence in the eastern Mediterranean, and it had gradually reduced the power of the Seleucid Empire. In their own struggles with the Seleucids, the Maccabees had claimed the Romans as allies (1 Macc 8:17–32). In the first century B.C.E., Pompey was in the East to suppress piracy and to make the East safe for Roman interests. When the Hasmoneans asked Rome to intervene in their affairs, Rome responded by taking over. This was the natural extension of a long process.

Herod the Great became king in 40 B.C.E. His rule was oppressive. At his death in 4 B.C.E., his kingdom was divided among his sons Archelaus, Herod Antipas, and Philip. Archelaus's rule lasted only ten years, until the Romans deposed him and instituted direct Roman rule over Judea through procurators.

The three texts examined in this chapter present three reactions to these events. The *Psalms of Solomon* laments Pompey's defilement of the temple and blames the disgrace on the behavior of the Hasmoneans and their supporters among the upper classes of Jerusalem. It yearns for a Davidic messiah who will lead a purified Israel in perfect obedience to God. The *Testament of Moses* has a low opinion of the Hasmoneans and Herod. It anticipates God's coming as warrior in the midst of cosmic disturbances to destroy idolatry and to exalt to the stars those faithful to God. The *Similitudes of Enoch* complains about the abuses of the powerful and accuses them of not recognizing that their power comes from God. It awaits a supernatural figure called the son of man, the Elect One, the Righteous One, and the Messiah, who will judge all people, punishing the powerful and exalting the suffering righteous.

SELECT BIBLIOGRAPHY

Avi–Yonah, Michael, and Zvi Baras, eds. *The Herodian Period.* Vol. 7 of *The World History of the Jewish People.* New Brunswick, N.J.: Rutgers University Press, 1975.

Binder, Donald D. *Into the Temple Courts: The Place of the Synagogues in the Second Temple Period.* Atlanta: Society of Biblical Literature, 1999.

Collins, John J. "The Heavenly Representative: The 'Son of Man' in the *Similitudes of Enoch.*" *IFAJ* 111–33.

―――. "The *Similitudes of Enoch.*" *AI* 177–93.

Garnsey, Peter, and Richard Saller. *The Roman Empire: Economy, Society, and Culture.* Berkeley: University of California Press, 1987.

Goodman, Martin. *The Ruling Class of Judaea: The Origins of the Jewish Revolt against Rome, A.D. 66–70.* Cambridge: Cambridge University Press, 1987.

Grant, Michael. *The Jews in the Roman World.* New York: Scribner's, 1973.

Greenhalgh, P. A. L. *Pompey: The Republican Prince.* Columbia: University of Missouri, 1981.

―――. *Pompey, the Roman Alexander.* Columbia: University of Missouri, 1980.

Kee, Howard Clark, and Lynn H. Cohick, eds. *Evolution of the Synagogue: Problems and Progress.* Harrisburg, Pa.: Trinity Press International, 1999.

Knibb, Michael A. "The Date of the Parables of Enoch: A Critical Review." *NTS* 25 (1978–1979): 345–59.

―――. "The Exile in the Intertestamental Period." *HeyJ* 17 (1976): 253–72.

Leaney, A. R. C. *The Jewish and Christian World, 200 BC to AD 200.* Cambridge: Cambridge University Press, 1984.

Meyers, Eric M. "Synagogue." *ABD* 6:251.

Nickelsburg, George W. E. "The Books of Enoch in Recent Research." *RelSRev* 7 (1981): 210–17.

———. "The Romans and the House of Herod." Pages 195–230 in *Jewish Literature between the Bible and the Mishnah: A Historical and Literary Introduction.* Philadelphia: Fortress, 1981.

———. ed. *Studies on the Testament of Moses.* Cambridge, Mass.: Society of Biblical Literature, 1973.

Saldarini, Anthony J. *Pharisees, Scribes, and Sadducees in Palestinian Society: A Sociological Approach.* Wilmington: Michael Glazier, 1988.

Sandmel, Samuel. *Herod: Portrait of a Tyrant.* Philadelphia: Lippincott, 1967.

Schalit, Abraham. "Herod and His Successors." Pages 36–46 in *Jesus in His Time.* Edited by Hans Jürgen Schultz. Philadelphia: Fortress, 1971.

Seager, Robin. *Pompey: A Political Biography.* Berkeley: University of California, 1979.

Sherwin-White, A. N. *Roman Society and Roman Law in the New Testament.* Oxford: Clarendon Press, 1963.

Smallwood, E. Mary. *The Jews under Roman Rule—from Pompey to Diocletian: A Study in Political Relations.* Leiden: Brill, 1981.

Stern, M. "The Reign of Herod and the Herodian Dynasty." Pages 216–307 in vol. 1 of *The Jewish People in the First Century.* Edited by S. Safrai and M. Stern. 2 vols. CRINT. Assen: Van Gorcum, 1974-1976.

Suter, D. W. *Tradition and Composition in the Parables of Enoch.* SBLDS 47. Missoula, Mont.: Scholars Press, 1979.

———. "Weighed in the Balance: The *Similitudes of Enoch* in Recent Discussion." *RelSRev* 7 (1981): 217–21.

CHAPTER 8

ROMAN RULE

PRIMARY READINGS: Josephus's *Jewish War* and *Jewish Antiquities* 18–20

In 63 B.C.E., Israel's brief period of independence under the Has-moneans came to an abrupt halt. The Roman Empire, which had been slowly creeping eastward for some time, finally swallowed Judea. Over the next 130 years, Jewish-Roman relations had their ups and downs, but they were never easy. They eventually exploded in 66 C.E., when Palestinian Jews entered into full-scale bloody revolt. This chapter traces the story of the Jews in the land of Israel under Roman rule. It covers the time from the death of Herod the Great to the beginning of the Jewish revolt against the Romans. The period is of great importance to Jews, because it immediately precedes the loss of Jerusalem and its temple, events that led to the formation of rab-binic Judaism. It is equally important to Christians because it encompasses the ministry of Jesus and the beginnings of Christianity.

PRELIMINARY TOPICS

JOSEPHUS

Josephus, who lived in Judea and Rome in the first century C.E., is our primary source of information for events in Judea and Galilee in the first cen-tury C.E. Unfortunately, we do not have other sources to check the accuracy of much of what he tells us. Josephus is certainly not unbiased, so we should do our best to understand what his biases are. He was born into Jerusalem's priestly aristocracy in 37 C.E. and died around 100 C.E. He claims Has-monean ancestry through his mother. Josephus was very familiar with the Romans. At age twenty-six, he traveled to Rome to defend fellow priests on an unspecified charge. While there, he won the friendship of Nero's wife, Poppaea. When he returned to Judea, the Jews were about to revolt against Rome. He says that he initially tried to stop the revolt, but, when this proved impossible, he decided to go with the tide, hoping to keep things under control and to take advantage of opportunities to stop the rebellion. His viewpoint probably coincided with that of much of Jerusalem's aristocracy, to which he belonged.

Josephus was commissioned as general of Galilee by the revolutionary government in Jerusalem, which was composed of people of his own class. He had trouble consolidating his control over Galilee—a certain John of Gischala being his major rival—but he was in command of the area when the Romans retook it. Josephus was captured, but he won the favor of the Roman general Vespasian by prophesying that he would become emperor. Ironically, he may have done this by applying to Vespasian a biblical prophecy that referred to a Jewish messiah. When Vespasian did become emperor in 69 C.E., Josephus was freed from his chains and became guide and interpreter for Vespasian's son, Titus, who had assumed his father's command in Judea. After the war finally ended, Josephus went to Rome, where Vespasian's family, the Flavians, became his patrons (hence his Latin name Flavius Josephus). There was even a statue of him erected in Rome.

Josephus wrote four works still extant. In the *Jewish War,* written in the late 70s to explain the war to Diaspora Jews, he plays the role of Roman apologist to his own people. He explains that Roman domination of Israel was God's will, at least for the moment. He blames a few hotheads in Israel for starting the revolution and accuses them of acting contrary to God's will and defiling Jerusalem and the sanctuary with unjustified bloodshed. In the 90s, Josephus wrote the *Jewish Antiquities,* a work retelling Jewish history from creation to the beginning of the Jewish revolt. It overlaps somewhat with the *War,* thus allowing us to compare his different accounts of the same events. The *Antiquities* attempts to make Judaism understandable to a non-Jewish audience. Josephus's *Life* concentrates on justifying his own actions and impugning those of his rivals in Galilee during his command there. Finally, Josephus wrote *Against Apion,* a work defending Judaism against the slurs of an Egyptian named Apion.

THE SAMARITANS

Our familiarity with the term "Samaritan" is due mostly to Jesus' story of the Good Samaritan, in which a Jew is mugged near Jerusalem and left for dead. A priest and a Levite pass him by. But a Samaritan stops and helps. We often take this story simply as an admonition to help our neighbor in need, but this misses the point. There was great animosity between Jews and Samaritans at the time of Jesus, and he is attempting to make the Jews look at Samaritans differently. Since the Samaritans play a role in the story of first-century Jews, we need to look at them more closely.

The Samaritans lived in the region between Judea and Galilee, in and around a city named Samaria, the old capital of the northern kingdom of Israel. In 722 B.C.E., the Assyrians conquered the northern kingdom and exiled many of its people. The following passage is a Judahite, that is, a southern, perspective on what then happened:

> The king of Assyria brought people from Babylon, Cuthah, Avva, Hamath, and Sepharvaim, and placed them in the cities of Samaria in place of the people of Israel; they took possession of Samaria, and settled in its cities. When they first settled there, they did not worship the LORD; therefore the LORD sent lions among them, which killed some of them. So the king of Assyria was told, "The nations that you have carried away and placed in the cities of Samaria do not know the law of the god of the land; therefore he has sent lions among them; they are killing them, because they do not know the law of the god of the land." Then the king of Assyria commanded, "Send there one of the priests whom you carried away from there; let him go and live there, and teach them the law of the god of the land." So one of the priests whom they had carried away from Samaria came and lived in Bethel; he taught them how they should worship the LORD. (2 Kgs 17:24–28)

This passage explains how it could be that the Samaritans had a version of the Torah and claimed to worship the God of Israel but were not really members of Israel. We must remember, however, that this is from a Judahite point of view. The Samaritans saw things quite differently, believing themselves to be the legitimate descendants of the northern kingdom of Israel. Judahite traditions denigrated the Samaritans. The passage from 2 Kings also explains how God allowed the Samaritans to live in the land even though they were not the chosen people. Although the nations that were brought to Samaria worshiped God, they also brought along their own gods, whom they continued to worship. The passage therefore accuses the Samaritans of idolatry, ending with a condemnation: "So these nations worshiped the LORD, but also served their carved images; to this day their children and their children's children continue to do as their ancestors did" (2 Kgs 17:41).

The books of Ezra and Nehemiah are also anti-Samaritan. In Ezra 4, the Samaritans, among others, ask to be allowed to join in the rebuilding of the temple. "Let us build with you, for we worship your God as you do, and we have been sacrificing to him ever since the days of Esar-haddon of Assyria who brought us here" (Ezra 4:2). When the returned exiles spurn the Samaritans' offer, the Samaritans try to subvert the building of the temple. This passage shows Jewish awareness that the Samaritans claimed to worship the same God they did although the Jews did not see the Samaritans as true members of their religion. But we must read such texts with suspicion. Ezra and

Nehemiah reflect the viewpoints of the Babylonian Jewish community or of some segments of the returned exilic community, which was not always in agreement with Judahites who had not gone into exile or had returned at another time. It is by no means clear that relations between Samaritans and Judahites were always negative, at least at this earlier period. This is borne out by the fact that when Nehemiah returned to Judah a second time, he found that the grandson of the high priest had married into the ruling class of Samaria (Neh 13:28).

When Alexander the Great arrived, the Samaritans initially supported but then resisted him. His response was quick and overwhelming: he destroyed the city of Samaria (331 B.C.E.). The ancient city of Shechem became the main city of the area, and the Samaritans built a temple on Mount Gerizim at Shechem. Some time later, when John Hyrcanus I conquered the area, he destroyed the Samaritan temple (128 B.C.E.). This stuck in Samaritan memory. Later, he destroyed Shechem itself (107 B.C.E.).

The Gospel of John is aware of tensions between Jews and Samaritans concerning the proper place to worship. Jesus meets a woman at a well near Mount Gerizim and asks for water. The woman replies, "How is it that you, a Jew, ask a drink of me, a woman of Samaria?" The narrator explains, "Jews do not share things in common with Samaritans" (John 4:9). Later the woman perceives that Jesus is a prophet and says, "Our ancestors worshiped on this mountain, but you say that the place where people must worship is in Jerusalem" (4:20).

Jesus begins his final journey to Jerusalem in the Gospel of Luke as follows:

> He sent messengers ahead of him. On their way they entered a village of the Samaritans to make ready for him; but they did not receive him, because his face was set toward Jerusalem. When his disciples James and John saw it, they said, "Lord, do you want us to command fire to come down from heaven and consume them?" But he turned and rebuked them. Then they went on to another village. (Luke 9:52–56)

The Samaritans were hostile because Jesus was a Jewish pilgrim on his way to Jerusalem. It is likely that many Galilean pilgrims went out of their way to avoid Samaritan territory on their way to Jerusalem. The disciples' offer to call down fire on the Samaritans recalls an incident in the career of the prophet Elijah when he called down fire from heaven. Elijah is known for his opposition to Ahab and Jezebel, king and queen of the northern kingdom of Israel, whose capital was Samaria.

Another incident showing Samaritan hostility to Jerusalem took place under the procurator Coponius (6–8 C.E.):

> When the Festival of Unleavened Bread, which we call Passover, was going on, the priests were accustomed to throw open the gates of the temple after midnight. This time, when the gates were first opened, some Samaritans, who had secretly entered Jerusalem, began to scatter human bones in the porticoes and throughout the temple. (Josephus, *Ant.* 18.29–30)

Human bones were ritually impure and so would defile the temple. The Samaritans' act was clearly hostile to the Jerusalem cult and to the Jews.

The Samaritans were monotheists who considered themselves within the Mosaic covenant. They were conservative in their attitude toward Scripture, for, like the Sadducees, they accepted only a version of the five books of Moses as authoritative and sacred. Some of the differences between the Jewish and the Samaritan Pentateuchs concern specifically Samaritan beliefs, such as the conviction that God's sacred mountain is Gerizim in Samaria and not Zion in Jerusalem. Like the Sadducees, the Samaritans did not accept the idea of resurrection from the dead. Priests were dominant in Samaritanism. Their eschatological expectation included the coming of a prophet like Moses, called the Taheb, "Restorer," a hope based on Deut 18. The same hope of an eschatological prophet like Moses is also visible in the Dead Sea Scrolls (4QTest) and in Peter's description of Jesus in Acts 3.

It is not surprising that the Jews and the Samaritans were enemies. Both claimed to worship the same God, but each denigrated the worship of the other. Religious groups that have much in common can make the bitterest enemies because they fight over of the same symbols. The same dynamic can be observed in Christianity's conflict with Judaism over the centuries. Our study will find other examples of clashes between Jews and Samaritans. The Samaritans still survive as a small community to this day.

PEASANTS AND ARTISANS

First-century peasants and artisans did not write books. For the most part, they were not even literate. Consequently, their side of history is often ignored for lack of evidence. But by combining Josephus's writings with insights about peasant societies generally, we can learn something about activities and attitudes of first-century Jewish peasants.

Peasants lived a restricted life dictated by the need to survive. Material goods were scarce. The family was the basic unit of production and consumption. Local villages and local markets were as far as most peasants traveled in the course of their lives. In Judea and Galilee, pilgrimages to Jerusalem might also have been common, but we cannot assume that the trip was easy or made frequently. In general, peasants were born, grew up, and died in a very small area and with narrow horizons. Their knowledge of the wider world was limited, and they probably came into contact with it primarily through tax collectors and invading armies. Peasants tended to be conservative socially and religiously.

Peasants frequently faced economic pressure. Because agriculture was the basis of most ancient empires, the peasants ultimately paid for wars, royal courts, bureaucracies, and religious establishments. Jewish peasants had to feed their families, help maintain the temple establishment, support the local nobility, and pay taxes to the ruling empire. Famines could be disastrous under such pressures. Hard years led to foreclosures and loss of land to the upper classes (see Neh 5). The Gospels attest to peasants resorting to day labor (Matt 20:1–16) and to tenant farmers working for absentee landlords (Mark 12:1–9).

Artisans were skilled craftsmen, such as potters, stone carvers, and makers of clothing. In modern America, artisans are generally middle class economically. In the ancient world, they were, for the most part, of the lower classes. They probably lived mostly in villages and urban areas. Urban workers may have had more political power than the peasants, since they could mount demonstrations or even riots in the very places where the upper classes lived and so exert direct pressure on the ruling class.

BANDITS

Bandits (Greek: *lēstais*) constituted an important kind of group in the first century. Josephus employs the term in a derogatory way, claiming that Israel's bandits were simple robbers, having only the lowest motives. But he speaks as a Jewish aristocrat, and aristocrats had the most to lose by confrontation with Rome. Research has shown that bandits can be much more than just criminals and has highlighted the social and political sides of banditry. They live in groups and make their living by robbery, at times with the support of the peasantry. Banditry is most likely to occur when the peasants are oppressed and are economically vulnerable and when governments are ineffective. When peasants are pressed by the difficulty of farming, social oppression, taxation, and coercion by the government, sometimes their only option is to abandon their land and live outside the law. This can be prepolitical rebellion—that is, one resisting oppression but not yet having a clear political ideology, agenda, or strategy. Bandits, although they opt out of the political and economic system, may not yet oppose the system itself. Their activity aims at survival and sometimes at righting specific wrongs, not at overthrowing political authorities. If things get bad enough and the bandit groups numerous and large enough, however, widespread banditry can develop into full-scale revolt.

The most famous bandit for English speakers is Robin Hood. In a time of tyrannical and greedy rulers and a powerless peasantry, Robin Hood effected a rough sort of justice. He "stole from the rich and gave to the poor." Through him and his band ("bandits" means members of a band), wealth was redistributed, and the peasants were protected from the violence of the rulers. Of course, this picture is romanticized, but it does tell us about the potential significance of banditry.

Conditions in Israel were ripe for banditry at various points in the first century C.E. The plight of the peasants was described above. Under the Herods, the people paid taxes supporting the Herodian establishment, the temple, and the Roman Empire. The Herodian rulers and then Roman administrators were at times oppressive and ineffective in controlling the population. When a difficult political situation combined with a natural disaster such as a drought, the situation could become explosive. And when religious symbols and systems, which were often all that the people had left to give their lives meaning and to maintain self-respect, were trampled on, the situation could end in violence.

While administering Galilee, Herod the Great captured and executed the most notorious bandit chief in the area, a man named Hezekiah. Hezekiah was no ordinary robber, since his execution was protested by a Galilean contingent that traveled to the Sanhedrin in Jerusalem. Herod's execution of Hezekiah was not just law enforcement but the suppression of resistance to oppression. The support shown for Hezekiah shows that bandits could command the respect and support of other segments of society.

THE "ZEALOTS"

For a long time, scholars thought that there was organized, continuous Jewish resistance to Roman rule throughout the first century and that the goal of the resistance was the ouster of the Romans. Josephus tells of a certain Judah the Galilean who in 6 C.E. founded a "fourth sect" (in addition to Pharisees, Sadducees, and Essenes). The aim of the fourth sect was freedom. It believed that only God could be master of Israel. Foreign domination was unacceptable. The scholarly theory identified this sect with a warlike party, called by Josephus the "Zealots," who were active in Jerusalem in 66–67 (see ch. 10, below). This theory held that the sect of 6 C.E. continued to advocate violence to achieve its aims over the years and that its efforts culminated in revolt against Rome in 66 C.E.

Evidence for the Zealot theory is minimal and ambivalent, and there is much that speaks against it, as we shall see. Over the years, it served Christian interests to portray first-century Jewish society as dominated either by legalistic

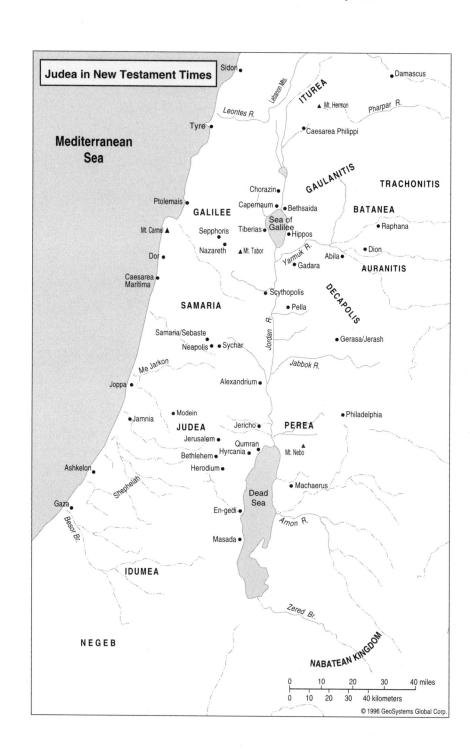

Judea in New Testament Times

Mediterranean Sea

Sidon

Damascus

Lebanon Mts.

ITUREA

▲ Mt. Hermon

Pharpar R.

Leontes R.

Tyre

Caesarea Philippi

GAULANITIS

TRACHONITIS

Chorazin

Capernaum ● Bethsaida

BATANEA

Ptolemais

GALILEE

Sea of Galilee

Raphana

Mt. Carmel ▲

Sepphoris   Tiberias ● Hippos

Nazareth   ▲ Mt. Tabor

Dor

Dion

Yarmuk R.

Abila

Gadara

AURANITIS

Caesarea Maritima

Scythopolis

DECAPOLIS

SAMARIA

Pella

Jordan R.

Samaria/Sebaste

Gerasa/Jerash

Neapolis ● ● Sychar

Me Jarkon

Jabbok R.

Joppa

Alexandrium

Jamnia

● Modein

Philadelphia

JUDEA   Jericho

PEREA

Jerusalem

Qumran

Bethlehem ● Hyrcania   Mt. Nebo ▲

Herodium

Ashkelon

Shephelah

Machaerus

Gaza

Dead Sea

En-gedi

Amon R.

Besor Br.

Masada

IDUMEA

Zered Br.

NEGEB

NABATEAN KINGDOM

| 0 | 10 | 20 | 30 | 40 miles |

| 0 | 10 | 20 | 30 | 40 kilometers |

© 1996 GeoSystems Global Corp.

hypocrites (Pharisees) or violent revolutionaries (Zealots). Jesus was favorably contrasted with each Jewish group. He was pictured as antilegalistic and a pacifist. Chapter 6, above, addressed prejudices against the Pharisees. If it is true that the Zealot theory is also faulty, then the other side of the Christian stereotype of Judaism in the time of Jesus also collapses.

THE SPIRAL OF VIOLENCE

Richard Horsley *(Spiral)* applies to first-century Israel a helpful model of how colonial powers interact with subject peoples. It is called the "spiral of violence." When injustice inflicted on a subject people becomes burdensome enough, they resist it. Initial resistance is often nonviolent and aims simply to remove the injustice. The ruling power may well respond with repression. If so, the subject population can be driven to revolution. The spiral of violence thus has four stages: (a) injustice, (b) resistance, (c) repression, (d) revolt. The stages are not always neatly separated, nor do they always proceed in a simple, linear fashion, but frequently there is a definite progression and intensification of conflict over time. Language used by observers and participants in this spiral encodes value judgments about what is happening. For example, the act of killing someone might be called "terrorism" if done by revolutionaries, but "legitimate use of force" if done by the occupying power. The term "violence" itself usually carries negative connotations and is more likely to be used when describing actions with which one disagrees, whereas "force" might be used to describe the same action if one approves of it. In other words, the very words one uses betray a point of view and are already part of an argument. Keeping these distinctions in mind will help in assessing Josephus's judgments about resisters to Roman rule.

THE HISTORY OF FIRST-CENTURY JEWS IN JUDEA AND GALILEE

THE EAGLE INCIDENT

In 4 B.C.E., Herod the Great fell desperately ill. Many waited eagerly for his death, hoping that it would bring improved conditions. Then the following incident occurred:

> To his other troubles was now added an insurrection of the populace. There were in the capital two doctors with a reputation as profound experts in the laws of their country, who consequently enjoyed the highest esteem of the

whole nation; their names were Judas [the Greek form of the name Judah], son of Sepphoraeus, and Matthias, son of Margalus. Their lectures on the laws were attended by a large youthful audience, and day after day they drew together quite an army of men in their prime. Hearing now that the king was gradually sinking under despondency and disease, these doctors threw out hints to their friends that this was the fitting moment to avenge God's honour and to pull down those structures which had been erected in defiance of their fathers' laws. It was, in fact, unlawful to place in the temple either images or busts or any representation whatsoever of a living creature; notwithstanding this, the king had erected over the great gate a golden eagle. This it was which these doctors now exhorted their disciples to cut down, telling them that, even if the action proved hazardous, it was a noble deed to die for the law of one's country; for the souls of those who came to such an end attained immortality and an eternally abiding sense of felicity; it was only the ignoble, uninitiated in their philosophy, who clung in their ignorance to life and preferred death on a sick-bed to that of a hero.

While they were discoursing in this strain, a rumour spread that the king was dying; the news caused the young men to throw themselves more boldly into the enterprise. At mid-day, accordingly, when numbers of people were perambulating the temple, they let themselves down from the roof by stout cords and began chopping off the golden eagle with hatchets. The king's captain, to whom the matter was immediately reported, hastened to the scene with a considerable force, arrested about forty of the young men and conducted them to the king. Herod first asked them whether they had dared to cut down the golden eagle; they admitted it. "Who ordered you to do so?" he continued. "The law of our fathers." "And why so exultant, when you will shortly be put to death?" "Because, after our death, we shall enjoy greater felicity." (Josephus, *J. W.* 1.648–653)

The young men and their teachers were burned alive.

One of Herod's most notable achievements was the rebuilding of Jerusalem's temple. He perhaps wanted to gain the support of his Jewish subjects by doing so, but he showed disregard for their sensitivities by placing on the temple a golden eagle, symbol of the Roman Empire. The Ten Commandments prohibit such images (Exod 20:4–6; Deut 5:8–10). It is proof of Herod's effectiveness in controlling opposition that no one dared try to remove the eagle until he was thought to be near death and unable to respond.

The decision to remove the eagle was taken by two teachers of Torah renowned for their adherence to Torah. They are not characterized as revolutionaries, in the sense of those who would overthrow the power structure through violent means. They showed no desire to change the political system or to seize power. As far as we know, they only wanted to put an end to a violation of Torah that defiled the temple. They persuaded forty of their students to undertake the task, and no provisions were made for their safety or for armed resistance. Although the students knew that they were endangering their lives, they cut down the eagle in broad daylight, when the temple was full of people. They probably wanted maximum exposure for their deed so as to win popular support.

The scenario of the resisters before Herod follows the pattern of martyrdom trials in Judaism and later in Christianity (e.g., 2 Macc 7). In such trials, the victims are questioned by a ruler who threatens them with punishment or tempts them with favors. They stand firm in their loyalty to God and are then killed mercilessly. The martyrs often make speeches at their trials. A further similarity between the story of the eagle incident and that of the martyrs in 2 Macc 7 is that, in both cases, those on trial express hope for vindication after death.

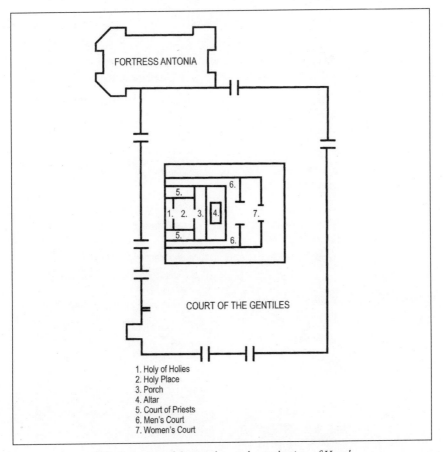

Schematic view of the temple complex at the time of Herod.
The fortress Antonia was used by the Romans to oversee temple activities.

Important Dates (4 B.C.E.–66 C.E.)

4 B.C.E.	Eagle incident Death of Herod the Great Revolts by Hezekiah, Simon, and Athronges War of Varus
6 C.E.	Romans depose Archelaus and rule Judea directly Tax revolt by Judah the Galilean and Saddok the Pharisee
26–36 C.E.	Administration of the prefect Pontius Pilate in Judea Eschatological prophets, including Jesus and John the Baptist
37–41 C.E.	Rule of the Roman emperor Gaius (Caligula)
37–44 C.E.	Agrippa I reigns as king
41–54 C.E.	Rule of the Roman emperor Claudius
44 C.E.	Agrippa I dies, and Judea, Samaria, and Galilee come under the administration of a Roman procurator
44–46 C.E.	Fadus is procurator of Judea He captures and kills Theudas, an eschatological prophet
46–48 C.E.	Tiberius Julius Alexander is procurator, a Jew and nephew of Philo of Alexandria He crucifies two sons of Judah the Galilean
48–52 C.E.	Cumanus is procurator He tramples on Jewish sensitivities and so is removed as procurator Bandits are active
52–60 C.E.	Felix is procurator Bandits, Sicarii, and eschatological prophets (e.g., the "Egyptian") are active Conflicts between priestly factions and classes of priests
54–68 C.E.	Rule of the Roman emperor Nero
60–62 C.E.	Festus is procurator Bandits are active; Festus has some success against them
62–64 C.E.	Albinus is procurator Before he arrives in Judea, the high priest Ananus puts James, the brother of Jesus, to death Albinus accepts bribes from the bandits and levies heavy taxes
64–66 C.E.	Florus is procurator Josephus accuses him of numerous abuses Florus confiscates temple funds

DISTURBANCES IN 4 B.C.E.

As mentioned in chapter 7, above, when Herod died in 4 B.C.E., Augustus Caesar divided the kingdom among Herod's three sons. Herod Antipas received power in Galilee and Perea (across the Jordan), Philip took control of lands to the north of Herod's, and Archelaus took charge of Judea. At first the people of Judea hoped that Archelaus would place a higher value on justice than his father. Archelaus began by listening sympathetically to some of their requests, such as lower taxes and freedom for some of Herod's political prisoners. But then the people dared to ask that the high priest appointed by Herod be deposed so that Archelaus might "choose another man who would serve as high priest more in accordance with the law and ritual purity" (*Ant.* 17.207). Some went further still and demanded punishment for the executioners of those who cut down the eagle. This touched a sensitive area because it would mean punishing Herod's officers and members of the ruling class for suppressing a challenge to Herodian and Roman rule.

Josephus says that the Jews who made the final request did so out of a "desire for innovation" (*Ant.* 17.206). He presumes that his audience will see innovation as negative. In traditional societies, where the weight of custom is heavy and things are perceived as basically static, change itself can appear negative. Such societies contrast markedly with that of the United States, for example, in which change is often seen as progress. But there is another issue here as well. Whether or not something is an innovation depends on one's frame of reference. Josephus sees the request of the protesters as challenging the established order, and so as an innovation. In contrast, the protesters probably saw Herod's aristocracy as an unwanted innovation that led to the violation of Torah.

Soon after Archelaus's coming to power, Passover arrived. During pilgrimage feasts, tremendous crowds of pilgrims poured into Jerusalem, creating a tense situation for authorities. Passover's danger lay not only in the concentration of people but also in the fact that Passover traditions commemorated and celebrated the liberation of Israel from its Egyptian oppressors. Fearing trouble, Archelaus sent armed soldiers to the temple. When some of the people pelted them with stones, Archelaus sent in the cavalry and killed a large number of people. Terrified, many of the people returned home.

Archelaus then sailed for Rome to ask Augustus to grant him the title of king. Other segments of the Herodian family also went to Rome. They would neither oppose Archelaus, Josephus says, because they were his family, nor support him, for they hated him. Later in his narrative, Josephus admits that some of the Herodian family did support Archelaus. They were followed by another Jewish embassy that Josephus defines only by their opposition to Archelaus (*Ant.* 17.299–316). This last group informed Augustus of Herod's tyranny. It is likely, from the nature of their complaints, that they were people of means and prominent in Jewish society. Among other things, they complained that Herod killed members of the nobility and confiscated their estates and that he also showed little regard for the integrity of the Jewish family system, wreaking havoc with marriage rules and rules for sexual conduct. The embassy said that they had initially welcomed Archelaus as leader of the nation, hoping that he would not follow his father's example, but his slaughter of the worshipers proved this to be an empty hope. They petitioned Augustus to annex Judea to the Roman province of Syria, asking only that they be allowed to observe Torah. They said that their conduct would prove that they had no hostile intentions toward Rome.

This Jewish embassy seems to have represented the viewpoint of a sizable portion of the nobility and the retainer class of Judea who had suffered under Herod. They saw no reason they could not live peacefully and submissively under Roman rule, if only they were not oppressed and were allowed to live according to their own customs. In the end, they lost their cause, for Augustus confirmed Archelaus as ethnarch. But their efforts show that Jerusalem's upper classes were not of one mind. Besides the conflict between the Herodians and the Hasmoneans, there were other divisions as well. There were even divisions within the Herodian family itself. This follows the pattern we have seen repeatedly in the Second Temple period.

When Archelaus left for Rome, Israel erupted (*Ant.* 17.250–298). The Roman Sabinus had been left in charge in Judea. Josephus charges that the situation was made volatile by those Jews "very fond of innovation" (*Ant.* 17.251; my translation). Sabinus commanded a military force, and he used it to harass the Jews until they finally rebelled. Josephus accuses Sabinus of acting from greed; in this instance, Josephus blames both Jews and a Roman official for the hostilities. But modern readers can sense a difference in the degree of responsibility. The "innovation" for which Josephus castigates the Jews is really a desire for justice. Further, given Josephus's pro-Roman agenda, his criticism of the Roman official's provocation of the people must be given great weight. It is easy to trace the spiral of injustice, resistance, repression, and revolt in Josephus's narrative. Even Josephus admits that it was only after a length of time and numerous injustices that they resorted to rebellion.

At the feast of Pentecost (Weeks), fifty days after Passover, a large number of pilgrims converged on Jerusalem. Josephus says they came not only to celebrate the feast but also to attack Sabinus. There follows an extensive description of conflicts between Roman soldiers and Jews in which both sides suffered substantial casualties. Battles then erupted throughout Judea between Jews and Gentiles.

Josephus tells the stories of several of these rebels. The first is that of Judah ben Hezekiah, son of Hezekiah the bandit:

> Then there was Judas, the son of the brigand chief Ezekias [the Greek form of the name Hezekiah], who had been a man of great power and had been captured by Herod only with great difficulty. This Judas got together a large number of desperate men at Sepphoris in Galilee and there made an assault on the royal palace, and having seized all the arms that were stored there, he armed every single one of his men and made off with the property that had been seized there. He became an object of terror to all men by plundering those he came across in his desire for great possessions and his ambition for royal rank, a prize that he expected to obtain not through the practice of virtue but through excessive ill-treatment of others. (*Ant.* 17.271–272)

Josephus recalls what a formidable foe Hezekiah had been for Herod in Galilee. Resistance to the ruling class extended to Judah ben Hezekiah. Josephus accuses Judah of wanting power and aspiring to royal rank. Since a Jewish king was an anointed one, a messiah, this meant that Judah had messianic aspirations.

Next comes the story of Simon:

> There was also Simon, a slave of King Herod but a handsome man, who took pre-eminence by size and bodily strength, and was expected to go farther. Elated by the unsettled condition of affairs, he was bold enough to place the diadem on his head, and having got together a body of men, he was himself also proclaimed king by them in their madness, and he rated himself worthy of this beyond anyone else. After burning the royal palace in Jericho, he plundered and carried off the things that had been seized there. He also set fire to many other royal residences in many parts of the country and utterly destroyed them after permitting his fellow-rebels to take as booty whatever had been left in them. . . . Such was the great madness that settled upon the nation because they had no king of their own to restrain the populace by his pre-eminence, and because the foreigners who came among them to suppress the rebellion were themselves a cause of provocation through their arrogance and greed. (*Ant.* 17.273–277)

Simon was active near the Jordan River. He put on a crown and declared himself king, so he, too, had messianic pretensions. As a member of Herod's entourage, he was a servant of the ruling class, and he saw an opportunity to take power. Josephus emphasizes Simon's strength, size, and appearance. At the end of this story, Josephus editorializes that the disturbances resulted from the lack of a king to keep order and from brutal oppression by "foreigners."

Josephus also recounts the history of Athronges:

> Then there was a certain Athronges, a man distinguished neither for the position of his ancestors nor by the excellence of his character, nor for any abundance of means but merely a shepherd completely unknown to everybody although he was remarkable for his great stature and feats of strength. This man had the temerity to aspire to the kingship, thinking that if he obtained it he would enjoy freedom to act more outrageously; as for meeting death, he did not attach much importance to the loss of his life under such circumstances. He also had four brothers, and they too were tall men and confident of being very successful through their feats of strength, and he believed them to be a strong point in his bid for the kingdom. Each of them commanded an armed band, for a large number of people had gathered round them. Though they were commanders, they acted under his orders whenever they went on raids and fought by themselves. Athronges himself put on the diadem and held a council to discuss what things were to be done, but everything depended upon his own decision. This man kept his power for a long time, for he had the title of king and nothing to prevent him from doing as he wished. He and his brothers also applied themselves vigorously to slaughtering the Romans and the king's men, toward both of whom they acted with a similar hatred, toward the latter because of the arrogance that they had shown during the reign of Herod, and toward the Romans because of the injuries that they were held to have inflicted at the present time. (*Ant.* 17.278–281)

Athronges was not from the nobility, nor was he a person of wealth. He was a shepherd. As in the case of Simon, Josephus stresses his size and strength. His area of activity seems to have been Judea. Josephus ascribes low motives to Athronges. Even when Athronges operated in a rather democratic fashion, Josephus insists that he was really reserving all power for himself. As Athronges explicitly claimed kingship, he likewise had messianic claims. He managed to survive for a long time. Although Josephus calls Athronges' motive "wantonness," he admits that he attacked Roman and Herodian troops because of the wrongs they committed.

Josephus ends this section with a generalization about the nature of the disturbances:

> And so Judaea was filled with brigandage. Anyone might make himself king as the head of a band of rebels whom he fell in with, and then would press on to the destruction of the community, causing trouble to few Romans and then only to a small degree but bringing the greatest slaughter upon their own people. (*Ant.* 17.285)

There is no evidence that these bands of rebels had anything to do with each other, so we cannot conclude that this was a single, organized movement.

Since Josephus routinely presents rebellions against Rome as conspiracies of a minority of the Jews with low motives, it is significant that he does not assert that Judah, Simon, and Athronges were in contact with each other or with any other of the "gangs of bandits." He does claim that each of the bandit leaders had royal pretensions which implied the overthrow of Roman and Herodian hegemony. Josephus's generalization here includes the charge that anyone can claim to be king—in Jewish terms, to be a messiah.

Josephus points out that the three rebel leaders did far more damage to their countrymen than to the Romans. The injustices suffered by the lower classes were not inflicted by the Romans alone. In fact, there were probably relatively few Romans in Judea. As elsewhere, the Romans exercised their rule through the local aristocracy, who were oppressive to the common people and to segments of the nobility. It is no accident that the rebels attacked Herodian troops, who were most accessible to the rebels and who represented both the native elites and Roman power. As noted above, the Jewish upper class was not a monolith. The rebels were probably raiding the properties of those who profited from Herod's rule at the expense of other parts of Jewish society—peasants, disenfranchised nobility, disaffected scribes, Pharisees, and so on.

Varus, governor of Syria, came to Galilee and Judea to crush the rebellion. He burned Sepphoris to the ground, enslaving its inhabitants. Other rebellious villages suffered a similar fate. When Varus arrived at Jerusalem, its inhabitants desperately pled their case. They said that they had not favored rebellion but that the crowds of pilgrims for the feast of Weeks were responsible for the trouble. Varus was lenient with those he judged innocent, but he continued mopping-up operations in the countryside. Participants in the revolt were severely punished. Josephus claims that Varus crucified two thousand rebels. Crucifixion was a horrible Roman punishment reserved for political offenders, slaves, and hardened criminals. It not only punished the guilty; it also graphically warned others.

Judah, Simon, and Athronges are each said to aspire to royal rank. We sometimes think that only descendants of David could be kings in Israel. But the Hasmoneans claimed to be kings, and Herod also was called king. Horsley invites us to consider the possibility that there was indeed a popular notion of kingship alive in Judea at this time. This notion did not stress royal lineage but, rather, saw kingship as conferred by God for the good of the people, sometimes to rescue them from their enemies or even from their oppressive rulers. The Bible itself bears witness to how one might think of popular kingship. David and Saul are good examples. The king, in this conception, was not absolute but under God's Law. He was acclaimed by the people. His rule would not result in an oppressively hierarchical society but would preserve the dignity of all Israelites as God's people. This kingship could be revolutionary, overthrowing existing structures. Such kings were often praised for their military prowess or their physical attractiveness. Saul is said to be very tall and handsome (1 Sam 9:2). David is presented as handsome and clever (1 Sam 16:12). Even when Samuel begins to rule unjustly and contrary to God's will, David will not raise his hand against Saul, whom he calls "the LORD's messiah." But after Saul's death, David consolidates his power by ensuring that Saul's family is no threat. Here is an instance of a dynasty being overthrown by a divinely appointed king who later is popularly acclaimed.

Another example of popular kingship is Jeroboam (1 Kgs 12). After the death of David's son Solomon, God raised up Jeroboam to enable the northern tribes to rid themselves of the oppression of the Jerusalem monarchy and to establish the northern kingdom, called Israel. Later, Jehu was instructed by God to lead a successful revolt in the northern kingdom of Israel against King Ahab and his wife, Jezebel, who had incurred God's displeasure because of their idolatry (2 Kgs 9–10).

Popular Kingship: Three Rebels	
Judah (Galilee)	Aspires to royal rank Assaults royal palace and seizes arms Plunders the upper class
Simon (Perea)	Places the crown on his head and is acclaimed king by his followers Handsome, large, of great strength Assaults and plunders the royal palace at Jericho Sets fire to and plunders other royal residences
Athronges (Judea)	Puts the crown on his head and establishes an advisory council A shepherd Of large stature and great strength Has several brothers Attacks the Romans

We can see elements of Israel's notion of traditional popular kingship in Josephus's narrative. Simon's strength and size are mentioned, and he attacks the Herodian establishment. Like David, he is handsome. Athronges, like David, starts as a shepherd and is known for his stature and strong deeds. As with David, his brothers play a role in the narrative (1 Sam 16–17). His rule is somewhat democratic, and he is said to fight Roman and Herodian injustice. Their followers must have seen these heroic figures as God-sent liberators.

Josephus condemns Archelaus's ten-year rule as tyrannical. The prominent men of Judea and Samaria finally appealed to Augustus in 6 C.E., and he agreed that Archelaus should not be ruler. He banished Archelaus to Gaul.

THE TAX REVOLT OF JUDAH THE GALILEAN (6 C.E.)

After removing Archelaus from office, Augustus did not appoint another Herodian over Judea. Instead, he appointed a Roman prefect who was subordinate to the Roman governor of Syria. Roman administrators over territories or provinces could be called prefects, procurators, or governors. Those under the direct control of the emperor or who administered less important provinces were often called prefects or procurators and usually came from the equestrian class (see below), while governors of more important provinces were usually of the Roman senatorial class. We know from a fragmentary inscription discovered in Caesarea, home of Judea's Roman administrator, that Pontius Pilate, administrator from 26 to 36 C.E., was called a prefect.

The prefect had a small body of troops, but he relied on Syria's governor for help should there be large-scale disturbances. He resided in the coastal city of Caesarea, a town of mixed (Jewish and Gentile) population that Herod the Great had rebuilt and renamed in honor of Augustus Caesar. The prefect traveled to Jerusalem for the Jewish festivals because of the potential for trouble, and while there, he occupied the fortress Antonia (named after Marc Antony), overlooking the temple. A permanent garrison of about two hundred men was stationed at Antonia.

The prefect was primarily interested in keeping the peace and in ensuring that taxes were paid, but he had general oversight over all that happened in Judea. He was of the equestrian order of Roman society. Millar and Burton define the order as follows: "Under the emperors the *equites* constituted a second aristocratic order which ranked only below the senatorial order in status. *Equites* in the wider sense provided the officer corps of the Roman army and held a wide range of posts in the civil administration as it developed from its limited beginnings under Augustus" (p. 551). Members of the equestrian order had to be Roman citizens, be of free birth, and enjoy a certain minimum income to qualify for their status. Although the prefect was allowed to make a profit from his tenure, he was answerable to Rome, which expected him to keep the peace. This sometimes prevented gross abuses of the office, since prefects realized that an excess of injustice could stir up the people. Despite this risk, however, they were sometimes insensitive to Jewish concerns, leading to unrest.

As before, the Jewish aristocracy played a major role in the daily running of Judea. The difference was that the Herodians were no longer in charge, and the high priest was the leading Jewish authority under the prefect. The high priest thus gained in power and status under the new arrangement. Similarly, the Sanhedrin was more powerful than under Herod. Herod had established the practice of deposing and appointing high priests as he saw fit. The Romans continued the policy, so the position of the high priest was now dependent on the prefect's decision.

In 6 C.E., Augustus sent Quirinius to Syria to conduct a census for purposes of taxation. Since Judea now fell, to some degree, under the supervision of the province of Syria, Quirinius accompanied Judea's new prefect, Coponius, to deal with matters related to the census. At first the Jews resisted the census, but their high priest, Joazar, son of Boethus, persuaded them not to make trouble. Not all went along with the plan, however. (In addition to the passages discussed here, see *Ant.* 20.102; *J.W.* 2.433; 7.253.)

Although the Jews were at first shocked to hear of the registration of property, they gradually condescended, yielding to the arguments of the high priest Joazar, the son of Boethus, to go no further in opposition. So those who were convinced by him declared, without shilly-shallying, the value of their property. But a certain Judas, a Gaulanite from a city named Gamala [also called Judah the Galilean], who had enlisted the aid of Saddok [the same name as Zadok], a Pharisee, threw himself into the cause of rebellion. They said the assessment carried with it a status amounting to downright slavery, no less, and appealed to the nation to make a bid for independence. They urged that in case of success the Jews would have laid the foundation of prosperity, while if they failed to obtain any such boon, they would win honour and renown for their lofty aim; and that Heaven would be their zealous helper to no lesser end than the furthering of their enterprise until it succeeded—all the more if with high devotion in their hearts they stood firm and did not shrink from the bloodshed that might be necessary. Since the populace, when they heard their appeals, responded gladly, the plot to strike boldly made serious progress; and so these men sowed the seed of every kind of misery, which so afflicted the nation that words are inadequate. When wars are set afoot that are bound to rage beyond control, and when friends are done away with who might have alleviated the suffering, when raids are made by great hordes of brigands [bandits] and men of the highest standing are assassinated, it is supposed to be the common welfare that is upheld, but the truth is that in such cases the motive is private gain. They sowed the seed from which sprang strife between factions and the slaughter of fellow citizens. Some were slain in civil strife, for these men madly had recourse to butchery of each other and of themselves from a longing not to be outdone by their opponents; others were slain by the enemy in war. Then came famine, reserved to exhibit the last degree of shamelessness, followed by the storming and razing of cities until at last the very temple of God was ravaged by the enemy's fire through this revolt. Here is a lesson that an innovation and reform in ancestral traditions weighs heavily in the scale in leading to the destruction of the congregation of the people. In this case certainly, Judas and Saddok started among us an intrusive fourth school of philosophy; and when they had won an abundance of devotees, they filled the body politic with tumult, also planting the seeds of those troubles which subsequently overtook it, all because of the novelty of this hitherto unknown philosophy that I shall now describe. My reason for giving this brief account of it is chiefly that the zeal which Judas and Saddok inspired in the younger element meant the ruin of our cause. (*Ant.* 18.3–10)

As for the fourth of the philosophies, Judas the Galilean set himself up as leader of it. This school agrees in all other respects with the opinions of the Pharisees, except that they have a passion for liberty that is almost unconquerable, since they are convinced that God alone is their leader and master. (*Ant.* 18.23)

The territory of Archelaus was now reduced to a province, and Coponius, a Roman of the equestrian order, was sent out as procurator, entrusted by Augustus with full powers, including the infliction of capital punishment. Under his administration, a Galilean, named Judas, incited his countrymen to revolt, upbraiding them as cowards for consenting to pay tribute to the Romans and tolerating mortal masters, after having God for their lord. This man was a sophist who founded a sect of his own, having nothing in common with the others. (*J. W.* 2.117–118)

We noted earlier in this chapter that scholars once thought that Jewish resistance to Rome in the first century was continuous, organized, and bent on violence. They had in mind a group they called the Zealots, and they thought it was the same group as that founded by Judah the Galilean. But the passages above, the only evidence for Judah's "sect," do not support the theory. In these passages, Josephus states that Judah founded a fourth school of Jewish philosophy in addition to the Pharisees, Essenes, and Sadducees. In *Ant.* 18.9 and 18.25, he blames the school for all subsequent troubles, right up to 66 C.E., when the Jewish revolt erupted. In *Ant.* 18, Josephus claims that the school was "intrusive," caused tumult among the people, and planted the seeds of Israel's future woes. Josephus produces a long list of occurrences in the first century, including civil strife, assassinations, and even famine. All is laid at the doorstep of this new "fourth philosophy."

In the Roman war, a Jewish party called the Zealots is indeed prominent. Some scholars have argued that the Zealots of the war are the same as Judah's group but active several decades later. Because of repression at the beginning of the first century, they supposedly went underground until the 60s, but they were always present, stirring up resistance to Roman rule, assassinating Jewish collaborators, and waiting for a chance to realize their nationalistic program.

ROMAN EMPERORS	OFFICIAL RULERS & PROCURATORS IN PALESTINE			HIGH PRIESTS	BANDITS	MESSIAHS	PROPHETS
Augustus (30 B.C.E.–14 C.E.)	Herod the Great (37–4 B.C.E.)				Hezekiah (ca. 47–38 B.C.E.)		
	Herod Archelaus *Ethnarch of Judea* (4 B.C.E.–6 C.E.)	Herod Philip *Tetrarch of Iturea* (4 B.C.E.–34 C.E.)	Herod Antipas *Tetrarch of Galilee* (4 B.C.E.–39 C.E.)	Joazar son of Boethus (4 B.C.E.)		Judas son of Hezekiah [Ezekias] (ca. 4 B.C.E.)	
				Eleazar son of Boethus (4–? B.C.E.)		Simon (ca. 4 B.C.E.)	
	Coponius (6–9 C.E.)			Jesus son of See (?)		Athronges (ca. 4–2? B.C.E.)	
	Marcus Ambibulus (9–12 C.E.)			Ananus son of Sethi (6–15 C.E.)			
Tiberius (14–37 C.E.)	Annius Rufus (12–15 C.E.)			Ismael son of Phiabi (15–16 C.E.)			
	Valerius Gratus (15–26 C.E.)			Eleazar son of Ananus (16–17 C.E.)			
				Simon son of Camithus (17–18 C.E.)			
	Pontius Pilate (26–36 C.E.)	[Iturea, Batanea Trachonitus and Auranitis attached to Province of Syria (34–41 C.E.)]		Joseph Caiaphas (18–36 C.E.)			John the Baptist (late 20s C.E.)
				Jonathan son of Ananus (36–37 C.E.)	Galilean Cave Brigands (30s C.E.)		Jesus (ca. 30)
	Marcellus (36–37 C.E.)			Theophilus son of Ananus (37–? C.E.)	Eleazar ben Dinai (30s–50s C.E.)		The "Samaritan" (ca. 26–36 C.E.)
Gaius Caligula (37–41 C.E.)	Marullus (37–41 C.E.)	Herod Agrippa I (40 C.E.)					
Claudius (41–54 C.E.)	Herod Agrippa I (41–44 C.E.)			Simon Cantheras son of Boethus (41–? C.E.)	Tholomaus (early 40s C.E.)		
				Matthias son of Ananus (41–44 C.E.)			
	Fadus (44–46 C.E.)			Elionaeus son of Cantherus (44?–46? C.E.)			Theudas (ca. 45 C.E.)

Emperors	Governors/Procurators	High Priests	Rebel Leaders	Messianic/Rebel Figures	Prophetic Figures
Nero (54–68 C.E.)	Tiberius Alexander (46–48 C.E.)	Joseph son of Camei (46–48 C.E.)			The "Egyptian" (ca. 56 C.E.)
	Ventidius Cumanus (48–52 C.E.)	Ananias son of Nedebaeus (ca. 47–59 C.E.)			
	Felix (52–60 C.E.)	Ismael son of Phiabi (59–61 C.E.)	Jesus son of Sapphias (60s C.E.)		
	Porcius Festus (60–62 C.E.)	Joseph Cabi son of Simon (61–62 C.E.)			
	Albinus (62–64 C.E.)	Ananus son of Ananus (62 C.E.)			
		Jesus son of Damnaeus (62–63 C.E.)			
		Jesus son of Gamaliel (63–64 C.E.)			
	Gessius Florus (64–66 C.E.)	Matthias son of Theophilus (65–? C.E.)	John of Gischala (66–? C.E.)	Menahem son of Judas the Galilean (ca. 66 C.E.)	
Galba (68–69 C.E.)	Zealot Coalition (68–69 C.E.)	Phanni son of Samuel (68–70 C.E.)		Simon bar Giora (68–70 C.E.)	
Otho (69 C.E.)					
Vitellius (69 C.E.)	Simon bar Giora (69–70 C.E.)				
Vespasian (69–79 C.E.)					
Titus (79–81 C.E.)					
Domitian (81–96 C.E.)					
Nerva (96–98 C.E.)					
Trajan (98–117 C.E.)					
Hadrian (117–135 C.E.)				Bar Kokhba (132–135 C.E.)	

There are serious problems with this theory. In the *Antiquities,* written in the 90s, Josephus blames the fourth sect for all of the unrest of the first century. But in *J. W.* 2, written earlier, shortly after the end of the Jewish revolt, he does not claim that Judah's group was responsible. In fact, Judah's group is not mentioned anywhere in the *War* other than in the passage just cited, even though the *War's* purpose is to explain the causes of the revolt. It would be strange for Josephus to neglect describing in the *War* the actions of Judah's group after 6 C.E. if this group was really behind resistance to Roman rule. Further, nowhere in any of the passages does Josephus label Judah's group as Zealots. It is true that both Judah's group and the Zealots wanted freedom from Roman rule, but this is hardly enough to identify them as the same group. When Josephus summarizes in the *Antiquities* the things for which Judah's group is allegedly responsible, he includes almost every type of conflict and act of resistance of the first century. Even if Judah's group did exist in an organized form throughout the first century, which is unlikely, it could hardly have been responsible for all that Josephus attributes to it, nor would it be the only segment of the population responsible for the war.

When Josephus wrote the *Antiquities,* he wanted to blame everything on a single group that he categorized as a small minority of the population. He did not want the Jews to seem anti-Roman or troublesome to the empire. The philosophy of Judah's group was portrayed as alien to Judaism, an "innovation." But even here Josephus is inconsistent. In *Ant.* 18, he says that the fourth sect was like the Pharisees except for its emphasis on freedom. In *J. W.* 2, he says that the fourth sect was not like any of the others. The view in the *War* shows that even in the earlier period, Josephus wanted to portray the resisters as unrepresentative of the rest of the Jews, even though he does not carry this particular argument into the later work. A close look at Josephus's language shows that he does not really claim that Judah's group did all the things he lists. He only says that they were in some way responsible for them. What Josephus is saying is that their introduction of the idea of freedom into the Palestinian equation led to the troubles of the first century. This is quite different from claiming that the group continued in an organized way and that its members were engaged in revolutionary acts throughout the first century.

Judah is not portrayed as initiating full-scale rebellion. Rather, his actions have the contours of a tax revolt. Nowhere is it claimed that he took up arms. He merely refused to cooperate with the census and thus to pay taxes and urged his countrymen to do the same. Judah realized that the Romans would respond with repression, and he exhorted his followers to be ready to shed their own blood for the cause, confident that God would be on their side. God might even use their actions as an opportunity to restore Jewish independence.

Belief that God was Israel's only master was not new in Jewish thought. But Israel had lived for centuries under foreign rule. Jews had learned to reconcile devotion to God with submission to colonial powers. What was relatively new was Judah's insistence that one could not serve God and the Romans simultaneously. Jews had been paying taxes to the Romans for almost seven decades by the time Judah refused to do so. What was the new factor in 6 C.E. that made some see paying taxes as being enslaved? The most plausible answer is that the Romans began to rule Judea directly at that time. The shock of direct Roman rule generated resistance, and the census for the purposes of taxation made the Roman rule painfully obvious. In addition, conducting a census on God's people had traditionally been something that would be done only if God ordered it, since counting the people implied mastery of them in some way. In 2 Sam 24, David conducts an unauthorized census, and for this God punishes Israel with a plague that kills 70,000 people.

Josephus provides no evidence of widespread resistance under Judah. In the end, the high priest convinced the populace to cooperate with the Romans. Perhaps the memory of the repression of Varus ten years earlier dissuaded the people from defiance. Josephus says nothing about a Roman reaction, and he gives no details of what happened to Judah and his group. It can hardly have been a major rebellion, and it seems to have been nonviolent.

PONTIUS PILATE (26–36 C.E.)

Josephus mentions no major disturbance during the twenty years between 6 C.E. and the coming of Pontius Pilate as prefect of Judea. Far from fanning the flames of rebellion, Judah's tax resistance ushered in a peaceful period in Judea. Nor does Josephus castigate any of the prefects of those twenty years for trampling on Jewish sensitivities. But everything changed with the coming of Pontius Pilate. He stirred the Jews to protest several times. The first incident was at the beginning of Pilate's administration.

> Pilate, being sent by Tiberius as procurator to Judaea, introduced into Jerusalem by night and under cover the effigies of Caesar which are called standards. This proceeding, when day broke, aroused immense excitement among the Jews; those on the spot were in consternation, considering their laws to have been trampled under foot, as those laws permit no image to be erected in the city; while the indignation of the townspeople stirred the country-folk, who flocked together in crowds. Hastening after Pilate to Caesarea, the Jews implored him to remove the standards from Jerusalem and to uphold the laws of their ancestors. When Pilate refused, they fell prostrate around his house and for five whole days remained motionless in that position.

On the ensuing day Pilate took his seat on his tribunal in the great stadium and summoning the multitude, with the apparent intention of answering them, gave the arranged signal to his armed soldiers to surround the Jews. Finding themselves in a ring of troops, three deep, the Jews were struck dumb at this unexpected sight. Pilate, after threatening to cut them down, if they refused to admit Caesar's images, signaled to the soldiers to draw their swords. Thereupon the Jews, as by concerted action, flung themselves in a body on the ground, extended their necks, and exclaimed that they were ready rather to die than to transgress the law. Overcome with astonishment at such intense religious zeal, Pilate gave orders for the immediate removal of the standards from Jerusalem. (*J. W.* 2.169–174)

Thirty years after the incident of Herod's golden eagle, Pilate again tested Jewish concern for the divine command against images. The images were of the emperor and were on the standards carried by the Roman army. The violation may have been the more troublesome in that Roman soldiers worshiped their standards. Augustus and his successors allowed emperor worship in the East as a sign of loyalty to Rome, and emperor worship was enthusiastically embraced by Caligula (ruled 37–41 C.E.) and Nero (ruled 54–68 C.E.). Generally, Jews were not forced to worship the emperor, but they certainly would have found the presence of the emperor's images in Jerusalem offensive.

Pilate was aware of the Jewish prohibition against images, since he introduced the images of Caesar into Jerusalem at night. Daybreak brought discovery of the defilement, and the news spread quickly to the countryside. Since Pilate resided at Caesarea, a large crowd went there. This attests to the seriousness of the protest: a trip from Jerusalem to Caesarea involving a lengthy stay in the city and absence from one's work was a hardship. Pilate's first instinct was to intimidate the crowd. He did not want to start his term of office on the wrong foot. To show weakness early might mean trouble later. Using pretense to lure the protesters to the stadium, he showed his true colors when the soldiers drew their swords. The reaction of the crowd astonished Pilate. He must have expected that they would be terrified and give up. Instead they showed themselves willing to die rather than accept such a gross violation of Torah. Pilate capitulated.

This incident indicates something significant about the mood of the majority of Jews in 26 C.E. Far from being hotheaded, thirsty for revolt, and unruly, they turned to nonviolent protest to deal with Roman injustice. Their nonviolence was not from apathy, since they were willing to die for Torah. It is just that the overthrow of Roman rule was not their aim. Nonetheless, they would not allow Rome to defile Jerusalem. This time, events did not progress to the next step in the spiral of violence: repression. Even Pilate saw that such a step would be a mistake.

The Jewish philosopher Philo of Alexandria tells a similar story (*Embassy* 38.299–305). He says that Pilate installed in Herod's palace in Jerusalem some golden shields dedicated to the emperor Tiberius. When the residents of Jerusalem objected to the shields as violating their sacred customs, Pilate refused to remove the shields. The Jewish leaders appealed to the emperor Tiberius, who ordered the shields removed.

Later in his administration, Pilate again aroused the people:

On a later occasion he provoked a fresh uproar by expending upon the construction of an aqueduct the sacred treasure known as *Corbonas* [see Mark 7:11]; the water was brought from a distance of 400 furlongs. Indignant at this proceeding, the populace formed a ring round the tribunal of Pilate, then on a visit to Jerusalem, and besieged him with angry clamour. He, foreseeing the tumult, had interspersed among the crowd a troop of his soldiers, armed but disguised in civilian dress, with orders not to use their swords, but to beat any rioters with cudgels. He now from his tribunal gave the agreed signal. Large numbers of the Jews perished, some from the blows which they received, others trodden to death by their companions in the ensuing flight. Cowed by the fate of the victims, the multitude was reduced to silence. (*J. W.* 2.175–177; cf. *Ant.* 18.60–62)

Here Pilate uses temple funds for a public purpose. The construction of the aqueduct was for the public good, so, on one level, this is an example of Pilate acting as a responsible administrator. But he shows marked insensitivity to Jewish feeling in his disrespect for temple funds. The account in the *Antiquities* is kinder to Pilate. It says that his action was caused by abuse hurled at him by the crowd and that the soldiers got carried away and beat people harder than Pilate intended. Josephus may have softened his picture of the Roman prefect for his Roman audience in the 90s. The account in the *War* states that Pilate knew what was going to happen, and planned to beat the protesters as an example to those who would question his decisions. His strategy worked.

Josephus relates one more episode involving Pilate:

The Samaritan nation too was not exempt from disturbance. For a man who made light of mendacity and in all his designs catered to the mob, rallied them, bidding them go in a body with him to Mount Gerizim, which in their belief is the most sacred of mountains. He assured them that on their arrival he would show them the sacred vessels which were buried there, where Moses had deposited them. His hearers, viewing this tale as plausible, appeared in arms. They posted themselves in a certain village named Tirathana, and, as they planned to climb the mountain in a great multitude, they welcomed to their ranks the new arrivals who kept coming. But before they could ascend, Pilate blocked their projected route up the mountain with a detachment of cavalry and heavy-armed infantry, who in an encounter with the firstcomers in the village slew some in a pitched battle and put the others to flight. Many prisoners were taken, of whom Pilate put to death the principal leaders and those who were most influential among the fugitives.

When the uprising had been quelled, the council of the Samaritans went to Vitellius, a man of consular rank who was governor of Syria, and charged Pilate with the slaughter of the victims. For, they said, it was not as rebels against the Romans but as refugees from the persecution of Pilate that they had met in Tirathana. Vitellius thereupon dispatched Marcellus, one of his friends, to take charge of the administration of Judaea, and ordered Pilate to return to Rome to give the emperor his account of the matters with which he was charged by the Samaritans. (*Ant.* 18.85–89)

On the basis of Deut 18:15–19, the Samaritans believed that the eschatological figure would be a prophet like Moses (see also *Messianic Anthology* [4QTest]; Acts 3) who would restore the Samaritan nation. A man leading the Samaritans in this passage may well have thought he was this prophet. And the finding of the sacred vessels hidden by Moses would signal the beginning of the eschatological age. Because Pilate saw the people's eschatological fervor as a threat to public order, he reacted brutally. Vitellius's action implies that he found plausible the Samaritans' charges of injustice on the part of Pilate. Roman governor of Syria and Pilate's superior, he sent Pilate to Rome to answer to the emperor Tiberius. Thus Pilate's time in office ended in 36 C.E. because of his own ruthlessness. It should be noted, however, that Pilate's ten-year tenure was already quite long for a provincial prefect. The emperor Tiberius was criticized for neglecting to rotate such officials, a practice that could help limit abuse of power by provincial officials. A ten-year term of office offered too many possibilities for abuse.

Having dispatched Pilate, Vitellius visited Jerusalem. It was Passover, so the city was again filled with pilgrims, who received Vitellius warmly. In return, he remitted sales taxes on agricultural produce and awarded custody of the high-priestly vestments to the priests. Custody of the vestments was an important symbol. Herod had taken them away from the priests and allowed them to be used only at the festivals. The vestments had to be worn at specified times according to sacred law; by taking custody of them, Herod could control aspects of the high priest's activity and temple liturgy. And control of the vestments helped Herod to maintain some command of the situation during the festivals, which were volatile times. Until Vitellius, the prefects continued Herod's practice. Before leaving Jerusalem, Vitellius deposed Caiaphas, a friend of Pilate who had been high priest since 18 C.E.

Roman aqueduct near Caesarea Maritima. Herod the Great rebuilt Caesarea in Roman style and named it for the Roman emperor, thus demonstrating his loyalty to Rome.

Philo says that Pilate wanted to hide from the emperor "the briberies, the insults, the robberies, the outrages and wanton injuries, the executions without trial constantly repeated, the ceaseless and supremely grievous cruelty" that characterized his administration (*Embassy* 38.302). Given the descriptions by Philo and Josephus of Pilate's administration, it is remarkable that most Jewish protest against Pilate's abuses was nonviolent. There may have been some armed resistance under Pilate, however. The Gospels imply such resistance at the time of Jesus' ministry: "Now a man called Barabbas was in prison with the rebels who had committed murder during the insurrection" (Mark 15:7). Furthermore, Jesus is crucified between two "bandits" (Mark 15:27). The Greek word for "bandits" here is *lēstai,* precisely the same word used by Josephus to designate political resisters. Despite these hints, we have no other evidence for widespread violent resistance during Pilate's administration.

JOHN THE BAPTIST

Two figures of considerable importance for Christians—John the Baptist and Jesus Christ—carried on their public ministries during the time of Pilate. Christians extensively revised Josephus's account of Jesus, as we shall see. In contrast, Josephus's report on John the Baptist is free of Christian rewriting. He makes no connection between John and Jesus. Josephus tells of John in the context of a story about Herod Antipas, who had been married to the daughter of King Aretas of the Nabateans in a political marriage. The Nabateans were an Arabic people who lived east and southeast of the Dead Sea. But Herod then rejected Aretas's daughter in favor of Herodias, his half-brother's wife, causing bad feeling between Herod and Aretas. There were also boundary disputes between the two rulers. War broke out, and Herod suffered a defeat.

In the Gospels, John castigates Herod for his unlawful taking of his brother's wife, and Herod has him beheaded (Mark 6:17–29 and parallels). Josephus does not say that John accused Herod concerning his marriage:

> To some of the Jews the destruction of Herod's army seemed to be divine vengeance, and certainly a just vengeance, for his treatment of John, surnamed the Baptist. For Herod had put him to death, though he was a good man and had exhorted the Jews to lead righteous lives, to practise justice towards their fellows and piety towards God, and so doing to join in baptism. In his view this was a necessary preliminary if baptism was to be acceptable to God. They must not employ it to gain pardon for whatever sins they committed, but as a consecration of the body implying that the soul was already cleansed by right behaviour. When others too joined the crowds about him, because they were aroused to the highest degree by his sermons, Herod became alarmed. Eloquence that had so great an effect on mankind might lead to some form of sedition, for it looked as if they would be guided by John in everything that they did. Herod decided therefore that it would be much better to strike first and be rid of him before his work led to an uprising, than to wait for an upheaval, get involved in a difficult situation and see his mistake. (*Ant.* 18.116–118)

There are three possible reasons Herod saw John as a threat. First, John's reading of Torah did not coincide with Herod's. Josephus's characterization of John as one who taught people to practise justice toward others is consonant with the Gospels' portrayal of John as one who prophetically demands that Israel live as God demands in Torah and who is critical of King Herod as biblical prophets were critical of kings in their own times. Second, John drew a large following, and the crowds were enough to make Herod nervous. Finally, John's preaching concerned more than morality; it also had an eschatological content. Josephus does not make explicit the eschatological nature of John's message, but it is evident in the Gospels. John's baptism prepared a person for the intervention of God in history. At Qumran also, baptism had eschatological significance. In 1QS 3, it is made clear that baptism depends on one's inner disposition; this passage furnishes a further parallel to Josephus's description of John's baptism. Of course, there were differences between the baptisms as well. For example, John's seems to have been once-for-all, whereas Qumran seems to have in mind repeated ablutions. Efforts to see John as an Essene and related to the Qumran community have failed.

We cannot be sure that the Gospels preserve John's exact words, but it is likely that the following is true to the tone of John's message:

> You brood of vipers! Who warned you to flee from the wrath to come? Bear fruit worthy of repentance. Do not presume to say to yourselves, "We have Abraham as our ancestor"; for I tell you, God is able from these stones to raise up children to Abraham. Even now the ax is lying at the root of the trees; every tree therefore that does not bear good fruit is cut down and thrown into the fire.
>
> I baptize you with water for repentance, but one who is more powerful than I is coming after me; I am not worthy to carry his sandals. He will baptize you with the Holy Spirit and fire. His winnowing fork is in his hand, and he will clear his threshing floor and will gather his wheat into the granary; but the chaff he will burn with unquenchable fire. (Matt 3:7–12)

John urged people to accept baptism in the face of the wrath to come. "Wrath" is a technical term in apocalypticism referring to God's anger at sin, soon to be manifest in the destruction of evil. John was a "hell-fire and brimstone" apocalyptic preacher whose message attracted many and who paid the price when Herod realized the political potential of his movement. John did not plan armed rebellion, but he was convinced that God would soon come to change the world. His message challenged the establishment, and Herod knew it.

CALIGULA AND AGRIPPA I (37–44 C.E.)

Caligula (Gaius) was Roman emperor from 37 to 41 C.E. During his rule, a dispute developed between the Jews and Gentiles of Alexandria in Egypt, which had a sizable Jewish population. Among other things, the Alexandrian Jews may have wanted full citizenship in the city. The Gentiles charged the Jews with being unwilling to worship statues of Caligula and told the emperor that this demonstrated Jewish disloyalty. The situation became violent, resulting in a pogrom against the Jews in 38 C.E. Philo led an unsuccessful delegation to Rome to defuse this terrible situation and to seek justice for the Jews. In the *Embassy to Gaius,* he tells of Caligula's disrespectful attitude toward the Jewish embassy and toward Judaism in general.

Caligula later decided to confront his Jewish subjects by attacking them through their monotheism. He ordered the governor of Syria, Petronius, to march to Jerusalem and set up a statue of Caligula in the temple. Caligula took his pretensions to divinity seriously. Such a desecration of the temple had not taken place since Antiochus IV erected a statue of Zeus there. Following Caligula's orders, Petronius brought his army to Ptolemais, a city on the coast west of Galilee, to winter. Tens of thousands of Jews gathered and begged him not to carry out the ill-conceived plan. When he told them that he had no choice, they replied, "In order to preserve our ancestral code, we shall patiently endure what may be in store for us, with the assurance that for those who are determined to take the risk there is hope even of prevailing; for God will stand by us if we welcome danger for His glory" (*Ant.* 18.267). Petronius recognized that the Jews would not back down, so he withdrew to Tiberias by the Sea of Galilee. Another crowd gathered. Petronius asked whether they were willing to go to war over the issue.

> "On no account would we fight," they said, "but we will die sooner than violate our laws." And falling on their faces and baring their throats, they declared that they were ready to be slain. They continued to make these supplications for forty days. Furthermore, they neglected their fields, and that, too, though it was time to sow the seed. For they showed a stubborn determination and readiness to die rather than to see the image erected. (*Ant.* 18.271–272)

The protesters did not have arms, nor did they intend to fight. Since their absence from seed meant that the fields would not be sown, they must have been peasants, in large part. The abandonment of their fields amounted to a peasant strike, a strike that would have been costly to them, to the landowners, and to the Romans.

The native aristocracy intervened, begging Petronius to inform Caligula of the people's resolve. Part of their argument stressed the economic factor: "Let him point out that, since the land was unsown, there would be a harvest of banditry, because the requirement of tribute could not be met" (*Ant.* 18.274). This argument assumes that banditry results from peasants being caught between crop failure and the demands of taxation. In this case, the lack of crops would be due to the peasant strike. Petronius saw the force of the argument and appealed to Caligula. Agrippa I, grandson of Herod the Great, was in Rome, and had become the friend of Caligula. He persuaded Caligula to rescind his order. Nonetheless, when Caligula received Petronius's appeal on behalf of the Jews, he was angry and ordered Petronius to commit suicide. Fortunately, Caligula himself was assassinated before Petronius could carry out the order. Both Philo and Josephus present Petronius in a positive light.

This incident of Caligula's statue shows that Jews were willing to live in peace under Roman rule, but they refused to see temple and Torah violated. It also shows the importance of economic factors and the extent to which these are tied up with religion and politics. Finally, it is another example of the alliance between the Herodian family, in this case Agrippa I, and the Romans.

In 37 C.E., Caligula appointed Agrippa I king of the territory of Herod's son, Philip, who had died in 34 C.E. Agrippa's kingdom grew in size over the next few years. Josephus records no disturbances during Agrippa's rule, perhaps because he was sympathetic to the Jews. His Gentile subjects may not have enjoyed his rule, however: the cities of Caesarea and Sebaste celebrated the news of his death in 44 (*Ant.* 19.356–357). Agrippa died of natural causes, and Rome turned his kingdom over to a procurator. This was a return to a previous status for Judea, but it was the first time that Galilee came under direct Roman rule.

Between 4 B.C.E. and 44 C.E., there is no evidence for sustained, organized Jewish resistance to Roman rule. On the contrary, except for the tax revolt of Judah the Galilean, evidence indicates a willingness to accept Roman rule. The people would not be docile, however, at the price of gross violations of divine laws. Jewish reaction to such violations during this time was primarily peaceful protest (although there are intriguing hints of violence in the references to the brigands crucified with Jesus and to Barabbas the insurrectionist). The few prophets who expected God's imminent intervention, such as John the Baptist, did not encourage military preparation for the event. God would do it all. The picture in Josephus contrasts starkly with the common view that the Jews were "nationalistic" and were spoiling for a fight with the Romans. That view furnished a convenient foil for a peaceful Jesus who taught love of enemies, but it does not survive close scrutiny.

FADUS AND TIBERIUS JULIUS ALEXANDER (44–48 C.E.)

Fadus was procurator from 44 to 46 C.E. He tried to regain control of the priestly vestments but was overruled by the emperor, who awarded them and the power to appoint high priests to Herod of Chalcis, a member of the Herodian family who ruled the small territory of Chalcis north of Galilee. Fadus captured a bandit named Tholomaeus, who operated in Idumea and in Arab territory, but nothing specific is known of Tholomaeus or his motivations. There was one other noteworthy occurrence during Fadus's administration.

> During the period when Fadus was procurator of Judaea, a certain impostor named Theudas persuaded the majority of the masses to take up their possessions and to follow him to the Jordan River. He stated that he was a prophet and that at his command the river would be parted and would provide them an easy passage. With this talk he deceived many. Fadus, however, did not permit them to reap the fruit of their folly, but sent against them a squadron of cavalry.

> These fell upon them unexpectedly, slew many of them and took many prisoners. Theudas himself was captured, whereupon they cut off his head and brought it to Jerusalem. (*Ant.* 20.97–98)

The word translated "impostor" here is the Greek word *goēs.* It means "wizard," "sorcerer," "enchanter." It is a pejorative term, with the connotation of "con man" in colloquial American. Josephus applies it to those he thinks mislead the people with false promises of miracles, liberation, and God's intervention. Theudas undoubtedly thought of himself as a real prophet, as his actions prove. He did not advocate armed resistance but depended upon God's miraculous action. He showed remarkable trust in God. Theudas knew Israel's traditions and remembered that when the people were liberated from Egypt, God had split the Reed Sea. When Joshua led the people into the promised land across the Jordan, God had split the Jordan so that they could cross on foot. Theudas believed that as God had come to Israel's aid in Joshua's time and given them the land, so now God would do the same. Divine action in the past was the model for present and future divine action. Fadus understood the implications of Theudas's actions. He moved quickly and brutally.

The next procurator was Tiberius Julius Alexander (46–48). A Jew from Alexandria, he was the nephew of Philo of Alexandria. He had given up Judaism and was thoroughly hellenized.

> It was in the administration of Tiberius Alexander that the great famine occurred in Judaea, during which Queen Helena bought grain from Egypt for large sums and distributed it to the needy, as I have stated above. Besides this James and Simon, the sons of Judas the Galilaean, were brought up for trial and, at the order of Alexander, were crucified. This was the Judas who, as I have explained above, had aroused the people to revolt against the Romans while Quirinius was taking the census in Judaea. (*Ant.* 20.101–102)

Josephus narrates two significant events during the administration of Tiberius Julius Alexander. Queen Helena was a convert to Judaism from a kingdom called Adiabene. We are not accustomed to think of Judaism as a missionary religion, but there is some evidence for Jewish missionary activity at this time, although it is debated (see McKnight). Ancient Jewish authors such as Philo and Josephus claim that although many looked down on Judaism, others were attracted to it, perhaps because of its monotheism, high ethical ideals, and community values. The famine at this time means that there was increased economic pressure on Jewish society, especially peasants. This pressure may have had something to do with the crucifixion of James and Simon, the second important event Josephus mentions. Famine often led to banditry. It is possible that James and Simon were involved in anti-Roman or at least anti-ruling-class activity, since crucifixion was the punishment for such crimes. Anti-Roman activity seems to have run in the family of Judah the Galilean.

CUMANUS (48–52 C.E.)

> As procurator of the rest of the province (Tiberius) Alexander was succeeded by Cumanus; under his administration disturbances broke out, resulting in another large loss of Jewish lives. The usual crowd had assembled at Jerusalem for the feast of unleavened bread, and the Roman cohort had taken up its position on the roof of the portico of the temple; for a body of men in arms invariably mounts guard at the feasts, to prevent disorders arising from such a concourse of people. Thereupon one of the soldiers, raising his robe, stooped in an indecent attitude, so as to turn his backside to the Jews, and made a noise in keeping with his posture. Enraged at this insult, the whole multitude with loud cries called upon Cumanus to punish the soldier; some of the more hot-headed young men and seditious persons in the crowd started a fight, and, picking up stones, hurled them at the troops. Cumanus, fearing a general attack upon himself, sent for reinforcements. These troops pouring into the porticoes, the Jews were seized with irresistible panic and turned to fly from the temple and make their escape into the town. But such violence was used as they pressed round the exits that they were trodden under foot and crushed to death by one another; upwards of thirty thousand perished, and the feast was turned into mourning for the whole nation and for every household lamentation. (*J.W.* 2.223–227)

Feasts were dangerous times for the authorities, but Passover (celebrated with the feast of Unleavened Bread) was especially volatile. In the temple, the holiest place in Judaism, at one of the holiest times of the year, at a feast celebrating the liberation of Israel from foreign oppression, the pilgrims were subjected to a painful reminder of their subordinate position when a Gentile soldier showed contempt for everything they held most sacred. Cumanus reacts with force, and the result is disaster. Despite this, Josephus blames the crowd for its hostile response.

There were further problems during Cumanus's administration:

> This calamity was followed by other disorders, originating with brigands. On the public road leading up to Bethhoron some brigands attacked one Stephen, a slave of Caesar, and robbed him of his baggage. Cumanus, thereupon, sent troops round the neighboring villages, with orders to bring up the inhabitants to him in chains, reprimanding them for not having pursued and arrested the robbers. On this occasion a soldier, finding in one village a copy of the sacred law, tore the book in pieces and flung it into the fire. At that the Jews were

roused as though it were their whole country which had been consumed in the flames; and, their religion acting like some instrument to draw them together, all on the first announcement of the news hurried in a body to Cumanus at Caesarea, and implored him not to leave unpunished the author of such an outrage on God and on their law. The procurator, seeing that the multitude would not be pacified unless they obtained satisfaction, thought it fit to call out the soldier and ordered him to be led to execution through the ranks of his accusers. On this the Jews withdrew. (*J. W.* 2.228–231)

The attack on the caravan of Caesar's servant came from bandits. The extent of their political motivation is unknown. They may well have become bandits because of the earlier famine, or because of Roman repression, as in the temple incident under Cumanus. In any case, Cumanus suspected the villagers of being in league with the bandits. He may have been close to the truth, since bandits often survive with the support of the populace. The hostility of the procurator's soldiers is evident in the contemptuous desecration of a Torah scroll. Cumanus was pressured into executing the perpetrator. The Jews were satisfied with righting the wrong, and did not rebel.

The next incident under Cumanus involved the Samaritans (*J. W.* 2.232–246). A Galilean was murdered while passing through Samaria on the way to Jerusalem for a feast (see Luke 9:52–55). When Cumanus refused to take action, Jewish bandits, supported by a crowd of Jews, took justice into their own hands. This is an example of bandits effecting the justice that the government will not. Cumanus then had to intervene to prevent war between the Jews and the Samaritans, and he killed many of the bandits. Jewish aristocrats pleaded with the rest of the people to return home. Most did so, but the remaining Jewish bandits continued their fight. Samaritan and Jewish notables appealed to the Syrian governor, the Jews blaming Cumanus for his failure to attend to his duties. This was one case in which the Jewish aristocrats sided with the people. The governor went to Caesarea and crucified those Cumanus had taken prisoner, the appropriate punishment for political offenders. He then sent Jewish and Samaritan nobles, as well as Cumanus and another Roman official, to Rome for a hearing. The emperor heard the case in the presence of Agrippa II, son of Agrippa I. As noted above, Agrippa II had received the kingdom of Chalcis when Herod of Chalcis died in 48 C.E. He did not rule over Judea directly, but as a Jewish king, he had some influence over it. He also exerted some legal power because he had inherited authority over the priestly vestments and authority to appoint the high priest.

Claudius banished Cumanus and condemned the other Roman official, thus acknowledging Roman responsibility. He then found fault with the Samaritans and executed three of them. Claudius did not see Jewish actions as

unwarranted or seditious. The Jews had no revolutionary intent, as is corrob-
orated by the fact that when the governor of Syria went from Caesarea to Jerusalem, he found the people "peacefully celebrating the feast of unleavened
bread" (*J. W.* 2.244), and so he returned to Antioch.

FELIX (52–60 C.E.)

Felix was procurator of Judea, Samaria, Galilee, and Perea from 52 to 60
C.E. He was a freed slave, not even a member of the equestrian order. Such an
appointment was unusual. His corrupt administration aggravated the deteriorating situation.

Felix first took on the problem of banditry:

> Felix took prisoner Eleazar, the brigand chief, who for twenty years had rav-
> aged the country, with many of his associates, and sent them for trial to Rome.
> Of the brigands whom he crucified, and of the common people who were con-
> victed of complicity with them and punished by him, the number was incalcu-
> lable. (*J. W.* 2.253)

Again, peasants support banditry. Eleazar had operated with impunity for
twenty years.

The procuratorship of Felix saw the emergence of a new form of Jewish
resistance to oppressive rule:

> But while the country was thus cleared of these pests, a new species of
> banditti was springing up in Jerusalem, the so-called *sicarii,* who committed
> murders in broad daylight in the heart of the city. The festivals were their spe-
> cial seasons, when they would mingle with the crowd, carrying short daggers
> concealed under their clothing, with which they stabbed their enemies.
> Then, when they fell, the murderers joined in the cries of indignation and,
> through this plausible behaviour, were never discovered. The first to be assas-
> sinated by them was Jonathan the high-priest; after his death there were nu-
> merous daily murders. The panic created was more alarming than the
> calamity itself; every one, as on the battlefield, hourly expecting death. Men
> kept watch at a distance on their enemies and would not trust even their
> friends when they approached. Yet, even while their suspicions were aroused
> and they were on their guard, they fell; so swift were the conspirators and so
> crafty in eluding detection. (*J. W.* 2.254–257)

The Sicarii took their name from the weapon they used, the dagger (Latin:
sica). Although Josephus calls them a "new species" of bandit, they do not resemble other bandits he describes. Bandits operated in the countryside,
whereas the Sicarii operated in the city. Bandits lived by raiding. Frequently,

they did not kill unless forced to fight. The Sicarii's whole program was assassination and terrorism. While bandits were often well known to peasants and to authorities who tried to catch them, the identities of the Sicarii were secret.

Judging from their tactics, the Sicarii had a specific political program. Their targets were not Romans but the Jewish upper classes that collaborated with the Romans. The high priest was their first victim. The assassinations caused panic among the aristocrats, and members of the ruling class grew to distrust each other. The social structure in Jerusalem began to break down, and the aristocracy's hold on the people weakened. The political program of the Sicarii went beyond righting specific wrongs. It extended to the destabilization of the ruling structure of Jerusalem. They were more advanced than rural bandits in terms of political awareness, organization, and goals.

A later procurator, Albinus (62–64 C.E.), managed to capture some Sicarii. The group evolved a new tactic to deal with this development:

> Once more the sicarii at the festival, for it was now going on, entered the city by night and kidnapped the secretary of the captain Eleazar—he was the son of Ananias the high priest—and led him off in bonds. They then sent to Ananias saying that they would release the secretary to him if he would induce Albinus to release ten of their number who had been taken prisoner. Ananias under this constraint persuaded Albinus and obtained this request. This was the beginning of greater troubles; for the brigands contrived by one means or another to kidnap some of Ananias' staff and would hold them in continuous confinement and refuse to release them until they had received in exchange some of the sicarii. (*Ant.* 20.208–210)

The Sicarii were an organized group capable of devising a strategy and putting it into effect. The priestly aristocracy was caught between the Sicarii and the Romans.

During Felix's term troubles were rife: "In Judaea matters were constantly going from bad to worse. For the country was again infested with bands of brigands and impostors who deceived the mob. Not a day passed, however, but that Felix captured and put to death many of these impostors and brigands" (*Ant.* 20.160–161). Josephus goes on to describe the deeds of the Sicarii, calling them simply "brigands" in this passage. He accuses Felix of bribing them to kill the high priest Jonathan because Jonathan was a thorn in Felix's side, always trying to get him to rule more justly. This accusation points to a more nuanced role for high priests than is often imagined. They are usually seen simply as collaborators with Rome, party to Rome's less honorable practices, including exploitation and repression of the people. In this passage and elsewhere, however, Josephus also gives evidence of individual high priests doing their best to hold the Romans accountable and to procure better treatment for the people. That Josephus can even entertain the idea that a Roman government would plot the death of a high priest shows awareness that Roman officials and Jewish aristocrats were not always in agreement and that the aristocracy could at times act in the best interests of the people. It also shows that the Romans could use civil unrest to their own advantage.

Josephus asserts that bloodshed by the resisters within the holy city and even in the temple precincts was a desecration that turned God against them and their cause. This passage typifies Josephus's outlook in that it blames the increasing violence on a small portion of the population and claims that the people as a whole were deceived by those few.

As events escalated, Sicarii, prophets, and bandits were all active:

> With such pollution did the deeds of the brigands infect the city. Moreover, impostors and deceivers called upon the mob to follow them into the desert. For they said that they would show them unmistakable marvels and signs that would be wrought in harmony with God's design. Many were, in fact, persuaded and paid the penalty for their folly; for they were brought before Felix and he punished them. At this time there came to Jerusalem from Egypt a man who declared that he was a prophet and advised the masses of the common people to go out with him to the mountain called the Mount of Olives, which lies opposite the city at a distance of five furlongs. For he asserted·that he wished to demonstrate from there that at his command Jerusalem's walls would fall down, through which he promised to provide them an entrance into the city. When Felix heard of this he ordered his soldiers to take up their arms. Setting out from Jerusalem with a large force of cavalry and infantry, he fell upon the Egyptian and his followers, slaying four hundred of them and taking two hundred prisoners. The Egyptian himself escaped from the battle and disappeared. And now the brigands once more incited the populace to war with Rome, telling them not to obey them. They also fired and pillaged the villages of those who refused to comply. (*Ant.* 20.167–172)

The specific example of an "impostor" (the Egyptian, an eschatological prophet) shows that such prophets thought that God would intervene to save Israel as in the past. This confirms what we learned above of the prophet Theudas, who said that the Jordan River would divide as it did for Joshua. The Egyptian also looked to the time of Joshua, for his promise that the walls of Jerusalem would fall recalls the battle of Jericho in Josh 6. This prophet was apparently a Jew from Egypt. Josephus makes no claim that the masses who gathered to the Egyptian's side were armed or militarily organized. They came to witness the sign offered as proof of God's imminent liberation of the people. But again, the Roman government recognized the political implications of these religious claims.

This passage also indicates the difficult positions in which peasants found themselves when caught between occupiers and resisters. Bandits might inflict violence on Jewish peasants who did not join the resistance, but if they did join, they were in danger from the occupiers and their collaborators. This scenario has played itself out countless times in history.

The Egyptian's efforts were aimed at defeating the Roman garrison in Jerusalem: "From there [the Mount of Olives] he proposed to force an entrance into Jerusalem and, after overpowering the Roman garrison, to set himself up as tyrant of the people, employing those who poured in with him as his bodyguard" (*J. W.* 2.262). Felix did not wait to see if the Egyptian's prediction would come to pass. He reacted with harsh repression. But rather than quell the Jews' rebellious attitude, Felix's measures increased it:

> No sooner were these disorders reduced than the inflammation, as in a sick man's body, broke out again in another quarter. The impostors and brigands, banding together, incited numbers to revolt, exhorting them to assert their independence, and threatening to kill any who submitted to Roman domination and forcibly to suppress those who voluntarily accepted servitude. Distributing themselves in companies throughout the country, they looted the houses of the wealthy, murdered their owners, and set the villages on fire. The effects of their frenzy were thus felt throughout all Judaea, and every day saw this war being fanned into fiercer flame. (*J. W.* 2.264–265)

In the course of the 50s, resistance to Roman rule became more widespread and better organized. Violence was directed more at fellow Jews than at Romans. In colonial situations, native collaborators are handy targets. Attacking them could have a major affect on the empire, since the empire needed the native aristocracy. The wealthy in particular were singled out.

The priests among the wealthy aristocracy were not the only priests in Jewish society. Priesthood was hereditary in Judaism, but only the leading priestly families belonged to the ruling class. Toward the end of Felix's rule, there was a clash in Jerusalem that pitted priest against priest:

> At this time Agrippa [II] conferred the high priesthood upon Ishmael, the son of Phabi. There now was enkindled mutual enmity and class warfare between the high priests, on the one hand, and the priests and the leaders of the populace of Jerusalem, on the other. Each of the factions formed and collected for itself a band of the most reckless revolutionaries and acted as their leader. And when they clashed, they used abusive language and pelted each other with stones. And there was not even one person to rebuke them. No, it was as if there was no one in charge of the city, so that they acted as they did with full

licence. Such was the shamelessness and effrontery which possessed the high priests that they actually were so brazen as to send slaves to the threshing floors to receive the tithes that were due to the priests, with the result that the poorer priests starved to death. Thus did the violence of the contending factions suppress all justice. (*Ant.* 20.179–181)

Class conflict divided priest from priest. Poor priests had more in common with the workers of the city than with the ruling priests. The unrest and disorder in the city was not addressed by Felix, who did not live there.

In addition to conflicts between priests of different classes, there were also conflicts between priests of different factions. Factions compete for power and resources; often they do not disagree with each other on ideology, nor do they come from different ethnic groups or social classes. Rather, each faction wishes to be dominant (see Hanson and Oakman). Factionalism was rife among Palestinian Jews at this time.

Jewish Resistance (4 B.C.E.–66 C.E.)

Eagle incident	4 B.C.E.
Tax revolt	Judah the Galilean and Saddok the Pharisee (4 B.C.E.)
Revolts with messianic overtones	Judah ben Hezekiah (4 B.C.E.) Simon (4 B.C.E.) Athronges (4 B.C.E.) Menahem ben Judah the Galilean (ca. 66 C.E.; see ch. 10) Simon bar Giora (68–70 C.E.; see ch. 10) Bar Kokhba (132–135 C.E.; see ch. 10)
Eschatological prophets	John the Baptist (ca. 30 C.E.) Jesus of Nazareth (ca. 30 C.E.) The Samaritan prophet (30s C.E.) Theudas (ca. 45 C.E.) The "Egyptian" (ca. 56 C.E.) Jesus ben Hananiah (Ananias) (62–69 C.E.; see ch. 10)
Banditry	Hezekiah (ca. 47–38 B.C.E.) Eleazar (30s-50s C.E.; captured by Felix) Tholomaeus (early 40s C.E.; captured by Fadus)
Peasant strike	Protest by peasants against Caligula's plans to erect his statue in the temple (41 C.E.)

Felix lived in Caesarea, and this city was not immune from the disturbances shaking the country. The discord in Caesarea was different in kind from that in Jerusalem. In Jerusalem, it was Jew against Jew; in Caesarea, it was Jew against Gentile. Caesarea was a mixed city, and each group aspired to dominance in terms of civic rights and privileges. Clashes between the groups grew increasingly violent. Felix finally sent in the troops, who killed many Jews, captured others, and plundered their houses. He then sent representatives from the Jewish and Gentile segments of Caesarea to Rome to argue their cases before Nero. The Jews sent to Rome by Felix used this opportunity to accuse Felix of maladministration, but Nero gave the Jews no satisfaction.

FESTUS (60–62 C.E.) AND ALBINUS (62–64 C.E.)

In 60 C.E., Festus replaced Felix and held office until 62. He devoted his time to campaigning against the bandits in the countryside, and Josephus credits him with some success. When Festus died in office, Nero sent Albinus (62–64) to replace him. Meanwhile, Agrippa II appointed Ananus, son of the previous high priest Ananus, as high priest.

> The younger Ananus, who, as we have said, had been appointed to the high priesthood, was rash in his temper and unusually daring. He followed the school of the Sadducees, who are indeed more heartless than any of the other Jews, as I have already explained, when they sit in judgment. Possessed of such a character, Ananus thought that he had a favourable opportunity because Festus was dead and Albinus was still on the way. And so he convened the judges of the Sanhedrin and brought before them a man named James, the brother of Jesus who was called the Christ, and certain others. He accused them of having transgressed the law and delivered them up to be stoned. Those of the inhabitants of the city who were considered the most fair-minded and who were strict in observance of the law were offended at this. They therefore secretly sent to King Agrippa [II] urging him, for Ananus had not even been correct in his first step, to order him to desist from any further such actions. Certain of them even went to meet Albinus, who was on his way from Alexandria, and informed him that Ananus had no authority to convene the Sanhedrin without his consent. Convinced by these words, Albinus angrily wrote to Ananus threatening to take vengeance upon him. King Agrippa, because of Ananus' action, deposed him from the high priesthood which he had held for three months and replaced him with Jesus the son of Damnaeus. (*Ant.* 20.199–203)

Ananus's deed did not have the support of all members of the Jerusalem aristocracy. In fact, their indignation at his high-handedness and disregard for legal proceedings led them to protest to both Agrippa and Albinus. Ananus's prosecution of James and the others led to his downfall. (For New Testament references to James the brother of Jesus, see Mark 6:3; Matt 13:55; Gal 1:19; 2:9, 12; Acts 15.)

Under Albinus, conflicts between the upper and lower echelons of the priesthood continued (*Ant.* 20.206–207). Power struggles within the aristocracy even sank to the level of street fights (*Ant.* 20.213–214). Things were deteriorating in Jerusalem. Josephus's summary of Albinus's term of office is scathing:

> The administration of Albinus, who followed Festus, was of another order; there was no form of villainy which he omitted to practise. Not only did he, in his official capacity, steal and plunder private property and burden the whole nation with extraordinary taxes, but he accepted ransoms from their relatives on behalf of those who had been imprisoned for robbery [banditry] by the local councils or by former procurators; and the only persons left in gaol as malefactors were those who failed to pay the price. Now, too, the audacity of the revolutionary party in Jerusalem was stimulated; the influential men among their number secured from Albinus, by means of bribes, immunity from their seditious practices. (*J. W.* 2.272–274)

The result of Albinus's actions was that "the prison was cleared of inmates and the land was infested with brigands" (*Ant.* 20.215). If Josephus's accusations are accurate, they show how the personal ambition and greed of Roman officials could lead them to actions of which even their superiors would not approve. Albinus' corruption pushed the country further toward war.

FLORUS (64–66 C.E.)

Albinus was succeeded in 64 C.E. by Gessius Florus. It was his rule that finally pushed the Jews to revolt: "It was Florus who constrained us to take up war with the Romans, for we preferred to perish together rather than by degrees" (*Ant.* 20.257). Around the beginning of his term, the rebuilding of the temple begun by Herod the Great reached completion, throwing 18,000 workers (according to Josephus's count) out of work and making social unrest a danger. To employ the workers and to keep temple funds from being diverted into Roman hands, Agrippa II approved plans to pave Jerusalem with white stone. But before this could happen, the city was destroyed.

Josephus condemns Florus for being in league with the bandits. He says that they had a free hand during Florus's term as long as they paid him bribes. Josephus charges him with despoiling individuals, villages, and cities on a grand scale. The Jews appealed to the governor of Syria without success (*J. W.* 2.280–283). Josephus even accuses Florus of intentionally provoking the Jewish revolt in order to disguise his own crimes.

During Florus's term, Nero resolved the dispute between the Jews and the Gentiles of Caesarea in favor of the Gentiles. This exacerbated already tense relations between the two groups. Things escalated when some Gentiles performed sacrifices near the synagogue to provoke the Jews. When the Jews turned to Florus, he treated them with disdain. When Florus decided to take money from the temple treasury (as had Pilate earlier), perhaps to pay tribute to Rome, the Jews protested. In one demonstration, they took up a mock collection for "poor" Florus. Florus then went to Jerusalem with troops, and when some Jews came out of the city to greet him, he dispersed them with cavalry. His troops then plundered parts of the city, and scourged and crucified some citizens. The city crowd was ready to go to war with Florus, but their prominent citizens urged caution. The ruling priests in particular tried to check the emotions of the crowd. Florus made their job harder when he forced the Jews to go out to greet a new contingent of Roman soldiers coming from Caesarea and then had the troops attack them. The Jews began to fight back and prevented Florus and his men from reaching the temple or the fortress of Antonia adjoining it. Florus then left the city, leaving a company of troops behind under the command of the chief priests.

Agrippa II now went to Jerusalem to try to persuade the people to remain peaceful. He induced them to collect the taxes that were in arrears, but when he counseled them to submit to Florus until a new procurator could be sent out, they drove him out of the city. He withdrew to his own kingdom to the north. Insurgents now captured the fortress of Masada. Eleazar, the temple captain and son of the former high priest Ananias, convinced the priests to terminate the daily temple sacrifice for Rome and emperor. Cessation of sacrifices was tantamount to a declaration of independence.

CONCLUSION

Israel suffered much under the oppression of Herod the Great. When he died, revolts erupted in Judea, Perea, and Galilee. The revolts were popular uprisings and may have drawn ideological support from Israel's ancient traditions of popular kingship. Varus, governor of Syria, crushed the revolts, and Judean Jews endured ten years of Archelaus's cruelty. Eventually even the Romans admitted Archelaus's failure and began to rule Judea directly.

Transition to direct rule was marked by the tax revolt under Judah the Galilean. The next decades saw a sustained effort by most segments of the population to live in peace with the Roman occupiers. Crises were caused by the Romans—Pilate, Cumanus, and Caligula especially—and the Jews in each case reacted with nonviolent protest. That Pilate and Cumanus were sent to Rome to answer for their maladministration shows that the emperor was not unconcerned about the conduct of his representatives, but in general, the prefects and procurators were allowed fairly free reign.

To counter Roman abuses, the Jews resorted to direct appeal to the prefect or procurator, the governor of Syria, or the emperor. During the crisis over the statue of Caligula, they effectively conducted a peasant strike. Eschatological prophets such as John the Baptist, the Samaritan prophet, Theudas, the Egyptian Jew, and perhaps Jesus of Nazareth arose to criticize the aristocracy and to predict imminent divine relief. The famine of the mid-40s increased economic pressure on the peasants and their landlords and may have led to an increase in banditry. Organized, politically aware resistance emerged in the Sicarii movement, aimed at terrorizing the local aristocracy. Growing Roman corruption and incompetence under Felix, Festus, Albinus, and Florus brought things to the boiling point. With Florus's ruthless repression, the pot finally boiled over.

In the broad sweep of the events of the first century, we can discern the fourfold pattern of injustice, protest, repression, and revolt. As injustices multiplied, so did protests, at first nonviolent, then violent. As protests grew stronger, so did repression. When repression reached its peak under Florus, the population finally resorted to total renunciation of Roman rule and to violent revolt.

SELECT BIBLIOGRAPHY

Anderson, Robert T. "Samaritans." *ABD* 5:940–47.

Applebaum, S. "Judea as a Roman Province: The Countryside as a Political and Economic Factor." *ANRW* 2.8:355–96.

Attridge, Harold. "Jewish Historiography." *EJMI* 311–43.

Bowman, John. *The Samaritan Problem: Studies in the Relationships of Samaritanism, Judaism, and Early Christianity.* Pittsburgh: Pickwick, 1975.

Farmer, W. R. *Maccabees, Zealots, and Josephus: An Inquiry into Jewish Nationalism in the Greco-Roman Period.* New York: Columbia University Press, 1973.

Feldman, Louis H. "Josephus." *ABD* 3:981–98.

Feldman, Louis H., and Gohei Hata, eds. *Josephus, Judaism, and Christianity.* Detroit: Wayne State University Press, 1987.

Goodman, Martin. *The Roman world, 44 BC–AD 180.* New York: Routledge, 1997.

————. ed. *Jews in a Graeco-Roman World*. New York: Oxford University Press, 1998.

Grant, Michael. *The Jews in the Roman World*. New York: Scribner's, 1973.

Hanson, K.C., and Douglas Oakman. *Palestine in the Time of Jesus: Social Structures and Social Conflicts*. Minneapolis: Fortress, 1998.

Hengel, Martin. *The Zealots: Investigations into the Jewish Freedom Movement in the Period from Herod I until 70 A.D.* Edinburgh: T&T Clark, 1989.

Hjelm, Ingrid. *The Samaritans and Early Judaism: A Literary Analysis*. Sheffield: Sheffield Academic Press, 2000.

Hobsbawm, E. J. *Bandits*. Rev. ed. New York: Pantheon, 1981.

————. *Primitive Rebels*. New York: Norton, 1965.

————. "Social Banditry." Pages 142–57 in *Rural Protest: Peasant Movements and Social Change*. Edited by H. A. Landsberger. New York: Macmillan, 1974.

Horsley, Richard A. *Jesus and the Spiral of Violence: Popular Jewish Resistance in Roman Palestine*. San Francisco: Harper & Row, 1987.

Horsley, Richard A., and John S. Hanson. *Bandits, Prophets, and Messiahs: Popular Movements at the Time of Jesus*. Minneapolis: Winston, 1985.

Jeremias, Joachim. *Jerusalem in the Time of Jesus*. Philadelphia: Fortress, 1969.

Mason, Steve. *Josephus and the New Testament*. Peabody, Mass.: Hendrickson, 1992.

McKnight, Scot. *A Light among the Gentiles: Jewish Missionary Activity in the Second Temple Period*. Minneapolis: Fortress, 1991.

Millar, Fergus. *The Emperor in the Roman World, 31 BC–AD 337*. Ithaca, N.Y.: Cornell University Press, 1977.

Millar, Fergus, and Graham Burton. "Equites." Pages 550–52 in the *Oxford Classical Dictionary*. 3d ed. New York: Oxford, 1996.

Purvis, James D. "The Samaritans and Judaism." *EJMI* 81–98.

Rajak, Tessa. *Josephus: The Historian and His Society*. Philadelphia: Fortress, 1983.

Rhoads, David M. *Israel in Revolution: A Political History Based on the Writings of Josephus*. Philadelphia: Fortress, 1976.

Safrai, S., and M. Stern, eds. *The Jewish People in the First Century*. 2 vols. CRINT. Assen: Van Gorcum, 1974–1976.

Saldarini, Anthony J. "Reconstructions of Rabbinic Judaism." *EJMI* 437–77.

Schürer, Emil. *The History of the Jewish People in the Age of Jesus Christ (175 B.C.–A.D. 135)*. Revised and edited by Geza Vermes, Fergus Millar, and Matthew Black. 3 vols. Edinburgh: T&T Clark, 1973–1987.

Sherwin-White, A. N. *Roman Society and Roman Law in the New Testament*. Oxford: Clarendon Press, 1963.

Smallwood, E. Mary. "High Priests and Politics in Roman Palestine." *JTS* 13 (1962): 17–37.

———. *The Jews under Roman Rule from Pompey to Diocletian: A Study in Political Relations.* Leiden: Brill, 1981.

Smith, Morton. "Zealots and Sicarii, Their Origins and Relation." *HTR* 64 (1971): 1–19.

CHAPTER 9

JESUS THE JEW

PRIMARY READINGS: Matthew ◆ Mark ◆ Luke ◆ John

JESUS

Jesus was not a Christian. He was a Jew. Not only was he a Jew; he was a religious Jew, deeply dedicated to his people's sacred traditions. His conflicts with other Jews of his time must not be read as "Jesus against Judaism." Rather, they exemplify a Jew of Second Temple Judaism interacting, and at times disagreeing, with his Jewish contemporaries. Such conflicts do not make Jesus different from his compatriots; they make him similar to them. Second Temple Judaism was marked by variety in belief and practice. There was no single, overarching orthodoxy, nor was there a central authority that could have enforced such an orthodoxy. So Jesus was very much a man of his times. Everything that we have been studying—priestly religion, apocalypticism, scribes, Pharisees, Sadducees, Roman conquerors, and so on—was part and parcel of his world. If, to some degree, Jesus is a stranger to us, the reason is that his world was so much different from ours. To begin to bridge the gap, we must venture into his world and strive to appreciate it.

The question of the historical Jesus generates a tremendous amount of scholarly interest (see Powell). This chapter does not provide a full treatment of this topic; instead it focuses on the Jewishness of Jesus and suggests ways in which he fits into his own environment. Its interest is the *humanity* of Jesus. We shall not address theological questions per se, such as the question of Christian belief that Jesus is divine. This is an exercise in history rather than theology.

Christian presentations of the historical Jesus have traditionally underplayed his Jewishness. Instead his uniqueness has been emphasized. The result is that Jesus becomes a universal: a person without a homeland, native language, or traditional religion. The trend begins as early as the New Testament. For example, Jesus is portrayed in the Gospel of John as speaking with or arguing with "the Jews," who appear as his enemies. Jesus says something, and "the Jews" answer. This is a strange way of speaking. Suppose that an American professor is teaching a class in an American college, that there are no foreign students in the class, and that after the class he tells a colleague, "I mentioned this subject, and when I did, the Americans reacted strongly." The colleague might be puzzled and ask whether there were any non-Americans in the group. Otherwise, to specify Americans makes no sense.

Where John has Jesus interacting with "the Jews," no one is present but Jews. Jesus is Jewish, his disciples are Jewish, and his listeners are Jewish. Nonetheless, John's language sets Jesus off from the Jews: Jesus alone knows God. John uses this technique to convey a particular theological point, but he does so at the expense of distorting history. The other gospels do not set Jesus off from Jews in the same way. They let us get a more realistic picture of what Jesus would have looked like within Second Temple Judaism. But because of their own theological agendas, they too distort the historical picture. This book aims to provide a more adequate picture of Jesus within his own context.

THE HISTORICAL JESUS

We define the historical Jesus as that human being who walked and spoke in Galilee and Judea in the first century C.E. To oversimplify somewhat, what is historical is what actually happened, what could have been observed by an eyewitness. We recognize, of course, the difficulty in discovering what actually happened two thousand years ago, both because of the insufficiency of our sources and because of our distance from the events. And what actually happened is a problematic concept. It sounds simpler than it is. Observation itself entails interpretation and point of view. And how one reconstructs the past depends a good deal on how one views the world. Despite such problems, we can surely agree that there are more and less satisfactory historical reconstructions.

John Meier (*Marginal Jew*, 1.1–3) suggests a hypothetical situation. Suppose four historians familiar with first-century religious movements were to get together to study the historical Jesus. One is a Catholic, one a Protestant, one a Jew, and one an agnostic. They proceed as historians, evaluating the evidence. What could they agree on? It is clear that the Christians could not convince the Jew or the agnostic on the basis of faith alone. Hard evidence and persuasive reasoning, not faith, would have to be the basis for agreement. The picture becomes still more complex if we admit interpreters of widely differing philosophies into the discussion—postmodernists and structuralists, for example.

THE CHRIST OF FAITH AND THE REAL JESUS

The Christ of faith is the object of Christian worship. Many things are claimed for the Christ of faith that cannot be proved or disproved by historical method and are indeed a matter of faith and theology (e.g., that he is divine or that he took away human sin; the resurrection poses a special problem that we shall not address here). Our interest here is not the Christ of faith but the historical Jesus.

The "real" Jesus is an elusive concept. There is a certain commonsense quality to the desire to know the real Jesus, but if this means to comprehend the totality of his being, it is obviously an impossible task. How well can we know the "reality" even of our friends or ourselves, much less of someone who lived two millennia ago? What does it mean, after all, to speak of the "real me"? If we say that Jesus lives, that believers have a personal relationship with him, and that this is the real Jesus, then we are in the sphere of the Christ of faith. On the whole, therefore, it is best to avoid such terms as "the real Jesus."

THE QUEST FOR THE HISTORICAL JESUS

Study of the historical Jesus began with the dawn of the Enlightenment and the birth of modern historical method. The Enlightenment was a movement that began to flourish in the eighteenth century although its seeds were planted before that time. Basic to the Enlightenment is a high regard for the power of reason. Knowledge comes from the application of reason to experience and to evidence from careful observation. One should not arrive at one's views simply by accepting traditional answers offered by the church or any other authority. This philosophical approach was considered a threat by many in the church. Once scholars began to analyze the past with critical methods, it was inevitable that these methods would be applied to the objects of religious belief, including Jesus.

True to its roots in the Enlightenment, much research on the historical Jesus was driven by the conviction that one must separate the Jesus of history from the Christ of faith. Only by freeing oneself from church doctrine, which demanded specific answers to historical questions and therefore predetermined the outcome, could one do authentic historical research on Jesus. This caused conflict with church members for whom the New Testament was to be taken at face value, true not only theologically but historically and even scientifically. Over the subsequent centuries, most mainline Christian churches have come to accept critical historical inquiry as necessary and beneficial to Christianity, while more fundamentalist churches, which read the

Bible literalistically, still object to critical inquiry as inappropriate and even harmful, or use it to prove the truth of the Christian religion "scientifically."

The title of this section comes from the title of a book by Albert Schweitzer, published in 1906 in German and in 1910 in English, *The Quest of the Historical Jesus*. In it Schweitzer recounts nineteenth-century efforts to reconstruct the historical Jesus. He shows that such efforts were not so much objective history as portraits conforming to the agendas of the writers, be they theological, rationalistic, or other. Often the agenda was that of liberal Protestantism, an approach that downplayed aspects of Jesus foreign to the world of nineteenth-century Europe and focused on "universals"—what became known as "the fatherhood of God and the brotherhood of man." Jesus became an ethical preacher, stripped of "mythical" characteristics or those which made him too much a person of his time. His Jewishness was often thought to be too specific, not universal enough, so it was de-emphasized. For example, if it was accepted that he saw himself as the Messiah, his conception of what this meant was thought to be radically different from that of his contemporaries. While they were "nationalistic," he was "spiritual." While they thought in terms of this world, he thought in terms of eternity. Miracles were treated in a rationalistic way—that is, they were explained as natural happenings that the people in antiquity interpreted as supernatural because they lacked scientific knowledge.

In the period after Schweitzer, most scholars gave up on the quest for the historical Jesus, finding it methodologically impossible (the sources did not contain reliable historical information) or theologically unnecessary (religious faith cannot be based on historical research). Rudolph Bultmann, the most influential New Testament scholar of the twentieth century, held these views. He was supported by the great theologian Karl Barth. But in 1953, one of Bultmann's students, Ernst Käsemann, called for a new quest for the historical Jesus, declaring that it was both possible and necessary. This "new quest" used critical criteria for authenticity, as well as new methods of gospel analysis that helped distinguish between material originating with the evangelists, the church before them, and the historical Jesus.

The new quest recognizes the limitations of our materials and acknowledges that a full biographical treatment of Jesus is not possible. The chronological order within the gospel narratives is seen to be the work of the evangelists, for example. Nonetheless, the new quest believes that the historical study of Jesus is possible, and even theologically necessary, if Jesus is to be the center of the Christian religion.

The new quest continues to the present day, although some authors now speak of a third quest. Not all describe this third quest the same way. Indeed, it is characterized by variety in methods and conclusions. It applies new ways of thinking about Second Temple Judaism, which include challenging Christian stereotypes of Judaism, appreciating the diversity and richness of Second Temple Judaism, and employing all of the available evidence—treating each piece of evidence in its own right, without subordinating it to preconceived notions. The third quest also uses comparative methods, such as cultural anthropology and sociology. Ancient Judaism is seen as a specific instance of broader realities in religion in general; comparisons with other religions and cultures can therefore be fruitful.

The historian must disentangle the historical from the nonhistorical within the Gospels and then put the "facts" into a comprehensible historical framework. The job is difficult, some would say impossible. The problem with giving up entirely is that each of us has an implicit view of the historical Jesus that colors what we think about him. This is true of believers and non-believers alike. If we do not ask critical historical questions, chances are we will assume that whatever we think about Jesus is historically accurate. Indeed, we may even find ourselves heatedly defending our view against "false" views, and we will easily slip into the field of theology and doctrine, not making distinctions between theological and historical judgments. We will assume that our view is right not only historically but also doctrinally, so that defending it becomes a matter of defending the faith.

Even if no definitive, compelling answers to the historical questions asked in historical-Jesus research are forthcoming, the exercise of asking and trying to answer the questions makes explicit our implicit picture of the historical Jesus and allows us to examine its historical bases. Further, although the canonical gospels, as expressions of faith, will remain fundamental to the church, believers can gain insight into the message and meaning of Jesus by taking Jesus seriously as a historical figure. For many theologians, insights gleaned from study of the historical Jesus have transformed and energized their Christology.

THE SOURCES

The earliest New Testament documents are Paul's letters. Paul supplies us with some information about the historical Jesus, but he is far less interested in the details of Jesus' life than in Jesus' death and resurrection as eschatological events that begin a new creation and a new humanity rescued from Satan's power. Despite the paucity of historical information about Jesus in Paul's letters, they can confirm certain aspects of Jesus' ministry, such as that he had twelve apostles or that he forbade divorce.

The most fruitful sources for the historical Jesus are the canonical gospels of Matthew, Mark, Luke, and John. The first three are called the Synoptic

Gospels. Because of the large amount of material they have in common, they can be "seen together," the root meaning of the Greek *synopsis*. The Gospels are not unbiased. They are selective in what they report. Their aim is not to write "objective history" in a modern sense. They are expressions of faith meant to encourage and support belief. Further, each gospel author (called an evangelist, from the Greek word for "gospel," *euangelion*) has his own particular interpretation of the story of Jesus. There is good historical information in the Gospels, but they are not themselves histories. One might more accurately call them sermons in narrative form. A modern preacher might retell a biblical story to make a point. As he or she does so, gaps are filled in, details are changed, problems are resolved. The Gospels do something similar. They add, subtract, and rewrite material to present their own perspectives on Jesus.

Mark was the first gospel written (ca. 70 C.E.). It used oral and written sources, but they no longer exist. These materials had been shaped by the church's needs for about forty years. This means that there had already been a long process of selection, adaptation, and rewriting of traditions. Matthew and Luke wrote around the mid-80s. They both used Mark extensively, and they also had another written source, Q, consisting primarily of sayings of Jesus (see ch. 6, above). Q no longer exists, but reasonable reconstructions of it are possible based on comparisons of Matthew and Luke. It dates to a time before Matthew and Luke, since they used it. Matthew and Luke each have material peculiar to themselves that comes from various sources. Matthew's special sources are collectively referred to as M, and Luke's as L. These designations do not imply that the sources are connected, literary sources, like Mark and Q. When Matthew and Luke combined and rewrote their sources, they did so according to their own conceptions and concerns.

The Gospel of John is probably independent of the Synoptics, although this point is disputed. There are certainly intriguing parallels between John and the Synoptics, but nowhere can literary dependence be proven. John used sources no longer extant, but scholars do not agree on their precise nature and extent. John is so different from the Synoptics that it is untenable that Jesus was both like he is in the Synoptics and like he is in John. A few examples will suffice. In the Synoptics, Jesus says little directly about himself; rather, he preaches a message whose focal point is the kingdom of God. In John, Jesus speaks of little else besides himself, claiming for himself a whole range of titles, and he mentions the kingdom only twice, in a single story (John 3:3, 5). Jesus' exorcisms figure prominently in each of the Synoptics, while John has none. One of Jesus' most characteristic forms of teaching in the Synoptics is the parable, whereas there are no Synoptic-style parables in John. The teaching of Jesus in the Synoptics has been preserved, for the most part, in short sayings or collections of sayings, while in John Jesus delivers long, connected discourses. The list could go on. Most scholars think that Jesus more likely was as he appears in the Synoptics and that John's community then developed this picture theologically, rather than the reverse. This is not to deny that one can derive historical information from John; still, the Synoptics are the basis of most reconstructions, with John supplementing the Synoptics at times.

Besides the New Testament, there is little written evidence about Jesus close to his time. Most think that the early Christian noncanonical gospels are late and provide evidence primarily for what early Christians thought in the second century and later. As we shall see, Josephus contains a paragraph about Jesus that confirms some things learned from the Gospels. Roman sources refer briefly to Jesus but add nothing substantial to our knowledge. Some passages in rabbinic literature may refer to Jesus, but they are late and add nothing to our knowledge.

CRITERIA OF AUTHENTICITY

Scholars have devised criteria by which to judge the historicity of a given saying or deed of Jesus. Scholars differ in explaining and using them. What follows mainly combines the insights of Perrin and Meier.

DISSIMILARITY.   Something may be considered authentic (going back to Jesus himself) if it is contrary to the typical emphases of first-century Judaism and early Christianity—in other words, if it is not what we would expect from a first-century Jew or an early Christian. The problem with such a criterion is that it excludes material that would make Jesus a Jew of his time, as well as material that provides continuity between Jesus and the church. Another difficulty is that knowledge about first-century Judaism and the early church is fragmentary, so that we cannot be sure that something was not present in them. N. T. Wright suggests what he calls the "double criterion of similarity and dissimilarity." Something might be authentic if it makes sense within the Second Temple Jewish setting but at the same time can be seen as leading to something in later Christianity. In other words, it makes sense within first-century Judaism but is not necessarily typical of it, and it explains a development that appears in Christianity.

EMBARRASSMENT.   Some things in the Gospels are unlikely to have been invented by the church because it found them embarrassing. This is one of the most persuasive of the criteria.

MULTIPLE ATTESTATION.   Some things occur in more than one independent source. Sources that would count as independent are Mark, Q, M,

L, Paul, and John. Others are the *Gospel of Thomas,* and perhaps the *Gospel of Peter,* although there is debate over the degree of usefulness of these two sources. Meier adds that multiplicity of form can also be important—for example, miracles that can be attested not only in miracle stories but also in sayings. A combination of multiplicity of source and form is still stronger. Something found in parables, sayings, and other sorts of narratives, as well as in Mark, Q, and John, for example, would have a strong claim to authenticity.

COHERENCE. Once a core of material has been established by the preceding criteria, one might include other material that does not pass the stricter tests of authenticity but still fits with the core of material that does pass these tests.

LINGUISTIC AND ENVIRONMENTAL CONTEXT. This criterion is used to reject material that does not fit the environment of first-century Galilee and Judea.

REJECTION AND EXECUTION. Because Jesus was rejected by the Jerusalem establishment and executed by the Romans, any reconstruction of his life and work that portrays him as politically harmless would be inadequate.

RESULT. Some claim that historical-Jesus research must make sense of the fact that the Jesus movement turned into Christianity.

Criteria for Determining Authenticity

Dissimilarity: Does it differ from what we know of first-century Judaism and the early church?

Embarrassment: Is it something that we would not expect the church to preserve, since in some sense it is embarrassing to it?

Multiple Attestation: Is it found in more than one source? In more than one literary form?

Coherence: Does it cohere with what we have found using the more demanding criteria?

Linguistic and Environmental Context: Does it fit into the time and place of Jesus' ministry?

Rejection and Execution: Can it help to explain why Jesus was rejected by many of his contemporaries and why he was executed?

Result: Can it help to explain developments after Jesus' death, such as the foundation and growth of the church?

Even if we use these criteria, very different reconstructions of the historical Jesus are still possible. Approaches fall along a range between what might be called minimalist and maximalist. Minimalists think that the burden of proof falls on anyone who claims that something about Jesus is authentic. Maximalists assume that Jesus traditions are trustworthy unless an argument can be made for excluding them. It is better to say that whatever one's position, one must be prepared to argue it—that is, the burden of proof falls on whoever is making the argument. Another basic difference of approach concerns whether, on the one hand, one begins by judging individual bits of tradition and slowly builds up a store of material on which to build a hypothesis or, on the other hand, one begins with a general hypothesis and tests elements of tradition to see whether they fit.

Study of the titles of Jesus in the Gospels was once popular but is much less so now, for reasons that will be detailed below. Much research was also concentrated on Jesus' teaching, optimistically searching for the exact form of Jesus words by stripping sayings of their later accretions and then retranslating them back into Aramaic. Most now think that, at best, one can arrive at the "sort of thing" Jesus said.

THE "FACTS" ABOUT JESUS

In 1985, E. P. Sanders published *Jesus and Judaism,* which argues for seeing Jesus as a prophetic figure in the context of Jewish restoration eschatology. That is, Jesus is a prophet who expects God to intervene soon and decisively in history to restore Israel to its proper state in the world. When God reconstitutes things as they ought to be, Israel will occupy the position it should as God's chosen people, the temple will be rebuilt and become the center of worship of God for everyone, including Gentiles, and so on. This is the basic approach followed here. Sanders's work has been refined and augmented recently by Allison, who uses insights about millenarian movements to shed light on Jesus as a prophet and on his following as a community. His study is convincing and illuminating.

Recognizing the difficulty of reconstructing Jesus' teaching, Sanders takes as the starting point what he considers secure "facts" concerning Jesus. In *The Historical Figure of Jesus* (1993), Sanders offers a slightly different list of these facts. The table below combines his two lists, quoting from each. We will take a closer look at some of the items in the list.

Sanders's "Virtually Indisputable Facts"

Jesus was born ca. 4 B.C.E. near the time of the death of Herod the Great.

He spent his childhood and early adult years in Nazareth, a Galilean village.

He was baptized by John the Baptist.

He was a Galilean who preached and healed.

He called disciples and spoke of there being twelve.

He taught in the towns, villages, and countryside of Galilee (apparently not in the cities).

He confined his activity to Israel.

He preached "the kingdom of God."

About the year 30 he went to Jerusalem for Passover.

He engaged in a controversy about the temple and created a disturbance in the temple area.

He had a final meal with his disciples.

He was arrested and interrogated by Jewish authorities, specifically the high priest.

He was executed on the orders of the Roman prefect, Pontius Pilate, by being crucified outside Jerusalem by the Roman authorities.

His disciples at first fled.

They saw him (in what sense is uncertain) after his death.

As a consequence, they believed he would return to found the kingdom.

They formed a community to await his return and sought to win others to faith in him as God's Messiah.

At least some Jews persecuted at least parts of the new movement (Gal 1:13, 23; Phil 3:6), and it appears that this persecution endured at least to a time near the end of Paul's career (2 Cor 11:24; Gal 5:11; 6:12; cf. Matt 23:34; 10:17).

BAPTIZED BY JOHN THE BAPTIST

Chapter 8, above, spoke of John the Baptist in the context of first-century prophetic movements. Herod Antipas executed John because his message attracted the masses and because of John's eschatological, seditious tone. John's apocalyptic message is summarized in Matt 3:7–12. He preached that the eschaton was coming soon, when God's wrath would descend upon sinners. He urged repentance and baptized those who accepted his message. John believed that baptism would protect against God's wrath if it was accompanied by genuine repentance. John's message expressed dissatisfaction with the present world and so was a potential challenge to Israel's leaders and to the Romans. John presumed to speak for God, as prophets do, and this seldom wins the friendship of the religious establishment.

Jesus began his ministry by being baptized by John. This embarrassed early Christians both because it seemed to indicate a consciousness of sinfulness on Jesus' part and because it implied that John was superior to Jesus. A story unique to Matthew tries to deal with the latter problem:

> Then Jesus came from Galilee to John at the Jordan, to be baptized by him. John would have prevented him, saying, "I need to be baptized by you, and do you come to me?" But Jesus answered him, "Let it be so now; for it is proper for us in this way to fulfill all righteousness." Then he consented. (Matt 3:13–15)

Here John recognizes the implications of baptizing Jesus. The greater baptizes the lesser. Jesus responds that his subjection to John is temporary and in accord with God's plans. What is significant is that such an explanation is needed. Luke deals with the issue by avoiding a direct description of the baptism of Jesus by John. The Gospel of John evades the issue altogether by omitting the baptism.

In the Gospel of John, when members of the Jerusalem establishment came to ask John why he baptized, "He confessed and did not deny it, but confessed, 'I am not the Messiah' " (John 1:20). His emphatic denial suggests that some thought that John was the Messiah. Rivalry between John and Jesus is also suggested by the following passages:

> They came to John and said to him, "Rabbi, the one who was with you across the Jordan, to whom you testified, here he is baptizing, and all are going to him." John answered, "No one can receive anything except what has been given from heaven. You yourselves are my witnesses that I said, 'I am not the Messiah, but I have been sent ahead of him.' " (3:26–28)

> Now when Jesus learned that the Pharisees had heard, "Jesus is making and baptizing more disciples than John"—although it was not Jesus himself but his disciples who baptized. . . . (4:1–2)

These verses conflict with the synoptic contention that Jesus began his ministry only after John ended his. Here Jesus and John carry on simultaneous ministries. Since the Gospels claim that the Baptist was merely the forerunner of Jesus, it is more likely that the Synoptics came up with the neat succession of ministries, rather than that the Fourth Gospel made them simultaneous. In John's Gospel, the disciples of the Baptist are puzzled because Jesus carries on an independent ministry, and they are distressed that he is more successful than their master. The confusion over whether Jesus himself baptized may be due to the embarrassment of the relation between John and Jesus. Early Christians may have wanted to avoid any appearance that Jesus was merely copying the Baptist. Thus, although John 3:26 and 4:1 state that Jesus was baptizing, 4:2 denies it.

John the Baptist speaks of a human being to come after him who would be stronger than he. But did he think that Jesus was that greater person to come? Matthew and Luke (and so Q) claim that, well into Jesus' ministry, John sent his own disciples to Jesus asking, "Are you the one who is to come, or are we to wait for another?" (Matt 11:3; see Luke 7:19). If John had recognized Jesus as Messiah, it would be strange for this story to circulate among Christians. Indeed, it is striking that, even in the stories of the baptism, John never explicitly indicates Jesus as the one for whom he has been preparing. He does so in John 1:36, but since this happens in the Gospel of John but not the Synoptics, it is suspect. Surely the Synoptics would not have suppressed such a memory.

Given this evidence, it is likely that, at some point in his life, Jesus went out to hear John the Baptist's message, found it convincing, was baptized, and joined John's followers. This does not necessarily imply a consciousness of personal sinfulness on Jesus' part; it may be acceptance of belonging to a sinful people. This fits what we said in chapter 1, above, in that the emphasis falls more on the communal and less on the individual. Later Jesus went his own way, perhaps taking some of the Baptist's followers along with him (as in John 1). There is a saying of Jesus that provides a clue about why Jesus left John: "For John came neither eating nor drinking, and they say, 'He has a demon'; the Son of Man came eating and drinking, and they say, 'Look, a glutton and a drunkard, a friend of tax collectors and sinners!'" (Matt 11:18–19; see Luke 7:33–34). This saying is authentic, for the early church would not have made up such charges against Jesus. This slanderous charge may well be grounded in Jesus' own practice. Throughout the Gospels, he is often depicted at a meal. Indeed, Jesus' last act before his passion was a last meal with his disciples in which wine was consumed. And Jesus compares the kingdom of heaven to a banquet (Matt 22:1–14; Luke 14:15–24). The Baptist was an ascetic; Jesus was not.

The tone of Jesus' ministry was certainly different from that of John's. John's was grim, full of warning about the wrath to come, and his attitude to food and drink is harsh. In contrast, Jesus acted as if the kingdom was somehow present. Explaining why he and his disciples did not fast (Mark 2:18–20), Jesus says that feasting is appropriate when God's kingdom has come so near. Also, Jesus did miracles, while John did not. The miracles were another expression of the presence of God's kingdom. When John asks Jesus whether he is the one to come, Jesus responds by saying to John's messengers, "Go and tell John what you hear and see: the blind receive their sight, the lame walk, the lepers are cleansed, the deaf hear, the dead are raised, and the poor have good news brought to them. And blessed is anyone who takes no offense at me" (Matt 11:4–6). Jesus sees his miracles as signs that the kingdom is being made present through him, but he realizes that John may take offense at him.

Jesus retained a good deal of respect for John, even after he left him. For example, he says, "Truly I tell you, among those born of women no one has arisen greater than John the Baptist; yet the least in the kingdom of heaven is greater than he" (Matt 11:11). This saying expresses respect for John, but it also acknowledges that, to some degree, God's plan has passed him by.

Some scholars today deemphasize, reinterpret, or deny altogether an eschatological aspect to Jesus' message and actions (Crossan, Borg). But a substantial number of important scholars continue to defend the more established

View of Arbel, a modern town on to the west of the Sea of Galilee, near Tiberias. Many of the gospel stories about Jesus take place on or near this lake.

position that Jesus was an eschatological prophet (see Sanders above). Most recently, Allison has made a thorough and convincing case that Jesus was a millenarian prophet. That is, Jesus expected a definitive intervention in history by God in the near future that would decisively transform social relations and that would have cosmic consequences. Among other powerful arguments, Allison points out that if John the Baptist, who in some sense was Jesus' mentor, was an eschatological prophet and if the early church had an acute sense of the impending eschaton, then it seems likely that Jesus, the connecting link between John and the church, would also have an eschatological viewpoint. Allison also reviews the sayings tradition and finds much material that fits his general hypothesis.

A GALILEAN WHO PREACHED AND HEALED

Both Matthew and Luke say that Jesus was born at the end of the reign of Herod the Great (died 4 B.C.E.; Matt 2:1; Luke 1:5). Luke 2:1–2 adds that Jesus was born during the census under Quirinius (6 C.E.; see ch. 8, above). But Luke is confused, since the census occurred ten years after Herod's death. The earlier date, attested independently by Matthew and Luke, is more likely. Jesus was from the Galilean town of Nazareth, in the hills just north of the valley separating Galilee from Samaria. There would be no reason to invent this. Nazareth was an insignificant town. It is mentioned in neither the Hebrew Bible nor Josephus. Nazareth was about three miles southeast of the Hellenistic city of Sepphoris, which was an administrative center for Galilee under Herod Antipas (ruled 4 B.C.E.–39 C.E.). The Gospels never say that Jesus entered Sepphoris. Rather, he spent most of his time in the small villages of Galilee. If the tradition about Jesus being a carpenter is correct, he was a rural artisan and so a member of the lower classes. His native language was Aramaic, although some argue that he would have had at least a smattering of Greek (maybe more) and perhaps some Hebrew.

Herod Antipas ruled Galilee during Jesus' life, while Judea was under direct Roman jurisdiction. It is not clear how much influence the Jerusalem temple establishment had over Galilee, perhaps only as much as Herod allowed. The Synoptics imply that Jesus spent most of his ministry in Galilee and went to Jerusalem only at the end of his life. John has Jesus making at least three trips to Jerusalem. Most of Jesus' active ministry was in Galilee. Thus, the "scribes" with whom he interacts in Galilee would be Herodian officials or Galilean village scribes. There may have been some Pharisees there, but their presence was not strong. When Jesus went to Jerusalem, he came into direct conflict with the temple priests and scribes and with Jerusalem's elders (leading citizens).

Few question that Jesus was known to his contemporaries as a healer and an exorcist. Even Jesus' enemies admitted his powers. The issue was not whether Jesus could heal and exorcise but why he could do so. The following passage shows the debate:

> And the scribes who came down from Jerusalem said, "He has Beelzebul, and by the ruler of the demons he casts out demons." And he called them to him, and spoke to them in parables, "How can Satan cast out Satan? If a kingdom is divided against itself, that kingdom cannot stand. And if a house is divided against itself, that house will not be able to stand. And if Satan has risen up against himself and is divided, he cannot stand, but his end has come. But no one can enter a strong man's house and plunder his property without first tying up the strong man; then indeed the house can be plundered." (Mark 3:22–27)

Beelzebul is another name for the leader of the demons, otherwise known as Satan. Christians would not have invented a charge of collaboration with Satan, so this charge can be ruled authentic by the criterion of embarrassment. The accusers thus believed that Jesus did have special powers, but thought that he was in league with the devil. Jesus' answer discloses his own interpretation of his exorcisms, identifying them with tying Satan up and plundering his house. This is comprehensible within an apocalyptic worldview. The world is controlled by Satan, and God will soon intervene to defeat Satan and recapture the world. Jesus claims that God's intervention begins with his exorcisms.

According to Mark, the scribes from Jerusalem were not the only ones to interpret Jesus' activities negatively. Mark says of Jesus' family, "They went out to restrain him, for people were saying, 'He has gone out of his mind' " (Mark 3:21). According to this verse, which may well be judged authentic on the basis of the criterion of embarrassment, Jesus' family either agreed that Jesus had gone insane or were at least shamed by the accusations into taking action against him.

The eschatological element in Jesus' wonder-working sets him apart from other figures of the time with whom he has been compared. Vermes suggests comparison of Jesus with two Jewish holy men (*Jesus the Jew*, 69–80): Honi the Circle-Drawer lived in the first century B.C.E. His prayers ended a drought, according to Josephus and rabbinic sources. The rabbinic story compares his behavior toward God to that of a son toward his father. The other holy man was Hanina ben Dosa, from a Galilean village ten miles north of Nazareth. Like Jesus, Hanina cured people from a distance, controlled nature, and performed exorcisms. He showed little interest in ritual matters, instead focusing on moral issues. Parallels with Jesus are clear, especially in the case of Hanina ben Dosa. But neither man preaches an eschatological message.

TWELVE DISCIPLES

Jesus chose twelve disciples, as attested in the Gospels and in Paul (1 Cor 15:5, ca. 54 C.E.). It is the number twelve, rather than the individuals involved, that is important here, as we can see from the fact that lists of the twelve in the New Testament are not entirely consistent and from the fact that we know little to nothing about most of the apostles. Further, if the idea of twelve apostles had been invented by the early church, the church would not have included Judas, Jesus' betrayer, among their number, so the criterion of embarrassment comes into play.

The most obvious explanation for the number twelve is that there were twelve tribes of Israel. Jesus' words support such an interpretation: "Truly I tell you, at the renewal of all things, when the Son of Man is seated on the throne of his glory, you who have followed me will also sit on twelve thrones, judging the twelve tribes of Israel" (Matt 19:28). An argument for the authenticity of the second half of this verse is that it includes Judas among the twelve. The church would not have created a saying of Jesus promising a throne to Judas, so it meets the criterion of embarrassment.

There is some question about what "judging" means in this context. Eschatological judgment is suggested by the connection of the thrones of the twelve with the throne of the Son of Man. The Son of Man sits on a throne at the final judgment in Matt 25:31–46 and *1 En.* 62:5–8. Another possibility is that "judging" here means "ruling." There may be a reference to Israel's premonarchical judges (Horsley, 203–7). If so, Jesus may envision a restoration of Israel along the lines of a relatively egalitarian model of society. In any case, the fact that Jesus thinks in terms of twelve tribes suggests that he expects Israel's restoration.

HIS MINISTRY CONFINED TO ISRAEL

Jesus had little to do with Gentiles. Although the Gospels favor the church's Gentile mission, they also preserve material that opposes it. When Jesus sends the twelve on a mission in Matt 10:5–6, he says, "Go nowhere among the Gentiles, and enter no town of the Samaritans, but go rather to the lost sheep of the house of Israel" (see also 10:23). Although the authenticity of this saying has been questioned, it coheres with the general picture implied in the Gospels, that Jesus had little interest in approaching Gentiles.

The Gospels contain only two stories in which Jesus has any extended contact with Gentiles. In the first, Jesus helps the daughter of a Gentile woman.

Jesus left that place and went away to the district of Tyre and Sidon. Just then a Canaanite woman from that region came out and started shouting, "Have mercy on me, Lord, Son of David; my daughter is tormented by a demon." But he did not answer her at all. And his disciples came and urged him, saying, "Send her away, for she keeps shouting after us." He answered, "I was sent only to the lost sheep of the house of Israel." But she came and knelt before him, saying, "Lord, help me." He answered, "It is not fair to take the children's food and throw it to the dogs." She said, "Yes, Lord, yet even the dogs eat the crumbs that fall from their masters' table." Then Jesus answered her, "Woman, great is your faith! Let it be done for you as you wish." And her daughter was healed instantly. (Matt 15:21–28; see Mark 7:24–30)

Jesus' reluctance to have anything to do with the Gentile woman is striking. The explanation that he was testing her faith is pure speculation and not grounded in the text. The contrast of Jews and Gentiles as "children" and "dogs" is startling in its harshness. The healing itself is done from a distance.

There is one other story where Jesus heals a Gentile, this time a centurion's servant who is also healed from a distance (Matt 8:5–13; Luke 7:1–10; from Q). Jesus does not approach a Gentile; the Roman approaches him. In Luke, the Gentile approaches Jesus through the mediation of Jews, who appeal to Jesus by saying that the centurion loves the Jews and has built them a synagogue. In both versions of this story, Jesus is amazed to find such faith outside Israel.

If these two stories are authentic, they are evidence that Jesus saw his mission as being to Israel alone. If they are not, then we have no concrete stories about Jesus' interaction with Gentiles. It is remarkable that, given the interest in the Gentile mission and the numbers of Gentiles coming into the church fairly early, there are not more gospel stories supporting the Gentile mission.

Whether Jesus anticipated a mission to the Gentiles after his death is debatable, but there is little evidence for it. The Acts of the Apostles and the letters of Paul attest to a lively debate over allowing the Gentiles into the church. This implies that Jesus had not settled the question. He may have thought that the Gentiles would come to worship the God of the Jews at the eschatological restoration of Israel. Such an expectation would be fully consonant with Jewish belief, especially that which expected that Zion would be the place of worship for all nations (e.g., Isa 2, 60, 65; Zech 14; see also Rev 22). It would be the kind of universalism that preserves the centrality of Israel as God's chosen people and true worshipers. But Israel did not anticipate that when the Gentiles came to worship God, it would be the end of Torah. Rather, if Gentiles were to come into Israel, they would obey Torah just as Jews did. This is the position of Paul's opponents and of an important group

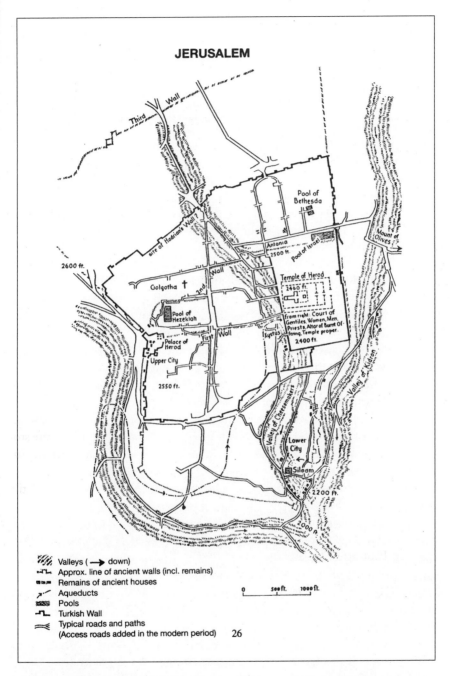

JERUSALEM

Third Wall

site of Hadrian's Wall ?

Pool of Bethesda

2600 ft.

Antonia 2500 ft.

Pool of Israel

Mount of Olives

Golgotha †

2nd Wall

Temple of Herod 2460 ft.

from right. Court of Gentiles, Women, Men, Priests, Altar of Burnt Offering, Temple proper.

2400 ft.

Pool of Hezekiah

First Wall

Xystus

Palace of Herod

Upper City

2550 ft.

Valley of Cheesemakers

Valley of Kidron

Lower City

Siloam

2200 ft.

2000 ft.

Valleys (➔ down)
Approx. line of ancient walls (incl. remains)
Remains of ancient houses
Aqueducts
Pools
Turkish Wall
Typical roads and paths
(Access roads added in the modern period)   26

0   500 ft.   1000 ft.

within the Jerusalem church in Acts. There were Gentile proselytes (converts) to Judaism even before the time of Jesus, and they were expected to live by Torah.

JESUS AND THE TEMPLE

Each Gospel recounts a scene in which Jesus disrupts the temple. The incident led to his death.

> Then they came to Jerusalem. And he entered the temple and began to drive out those who were selling and those who were buying in the temple, and he overturned the tables of the money changers and the seats of those who sold doves; and he would not allow anyone to carry anything through the temple. He was teaching and saying, "Is it not written, 'My house shall be called a house of prayer for all the nations'? But you have made it a den of robbers." And when the chief priests and the scribes heard it, they kept looking for a way to kill him; for they were afraid of him, because the whole crowd was spellbound by his teaching. (Mark 11:15–18)

The next day the chief priests, scribes, and elders confront Jesus and demand to know by what authority he acted (11:27–33). In his answer, Jesus associates his own ministry with that of John the Baptist (11:30).

The temple was a very large place, and on Passover it would have been filled with thousands of people. During the major feasts, it was well policed. In addition, the Roman prefect came to Jerusalem for the feast, accompanied by his soldiers. To disrupt temple activity substantially, Jesus would have needed a small army. And if he had seriously disrupted temple services, he would have been arrested immediately, as Roman responses to other disturbances at feasts amply demonstrate.

The Synoptic Gospels take Jesus' action as symbolic of cleansing the temple of commercial activity. But to bring all commercial activity in the temple to a halt would have undermined the temple itself by making it difficult to pay the temple tax, contribute to the temple, or make sacrifices. The money changers were there because Torah forbids images of animals or humans, so currency containing such images had to be changed to that which did not, for temple purposes. Further, pilgrims had to purchase ritually clean animals in Jerusalem, since it would be impractical for them to transport such animals all the way from their homes. It is thus doubtful that the synoptic interpretation of the temple scene is correct (but see Evans, Chilton). Nor is there evidence that Jesus opposed the sacrificial system as such. He was not against the temple on principle. He taught there, seems to have considered it central to Judaism, and called it his father's house.

The key to Jesus' action may lie in his overturning of the tables (Sanders, ch. 1). His was a symbolic action. Israel's prophets often performed public acts symbolizing their message. For example, in Jer 19 the prophet breaks a jug to symbolize the imminent destruction of Jerusalem. Sanders *(Jesus and*

Judaism) argues that the overturning of the tables symbolizes the coming destruction of the temple. The temple would be destroyed to make way for a new temple in a restored Israel. An alternative view is that Jesus opposed the social structure implied by the temple and its hierarchy. In that case, the temple would be destroyed and not rebuilt because it was an obstacle to the egalitarian society God wanted (Horsley). However Jesus' symbolic action is interpreted, it can hardly have seemed benign to the temple establishment. Since the Jerusalem leaders delivered Jesus to Pilate, they clearly saw him as a threat.

There is extensive evidence that Jesus predicted a destruction of the temple. In Mark 13:2, Jesus tells his disciples, "Do you see these great buildings? Not one stone will be left here upon another; all will be thrown down." In Jesus' trial, Mark accuses "false witnesses" of saying, "We heard him say, 'I will destroy this temple that is made with hands, and in three days I will build another, not made with hands' " (14:58). In Matthew, "false witnesses" say, "This fellow said, 'I am able to destroy the temple of God and to build it in three days' " (Matt 26:61). Luke omits the charge in the trial scene, but in the Acts of the Apostles, the second volume of Luke's work, Stephen proclaims, "This Jesus of Nazareth will destroy this place [the temple]" (Acts 6:14). The crowds at the cross claim that Jesus said he "would destroy the temple and build it in three days" (Mark 15:29; see Matt 27:40). In John, Jesus says, "Destroy this temple, and in three days I will raise it up" (John 2:19). The widespread nature of the temple sayings makes it likely, according to the principle of multiple attestation, that Jesus made some such statement against the temple. The principle of embarrassment is also relevant here, since the later church attributes the words against the temple to "false witnesses."

There is an important precedent for Jesus' prophetic challenge to the temple. Centuries before, Jeremiah had mounted a similar challenge. The gospel accounts of Jesus' action in the temple recall Jer 7 (see ch. 1, above). At God's command, Jeremiah goes to the temple to warn the Israelites that the temple cannot protect them if they fail to act righteously and pursue social justice. God asks through Jeremiah, "Has this house, which is called by my name, become a den of robbers in your sight?" (Jer 7:11). Jeremiah 26 retells the same episode, and there Jerusalem's priests and prophets say to the people and their other leaders, "This man deserves the sentence of death because he has prophesied against this city, as you have heard with your own ears" (26:11). Jeremiah escapes death, but a contemporary of Jeremiah, Uriah son of Shemaiah, was also preaching against Jerusalem and was executed.

It is impossible to say for sure whether Jesus saw himself in the tradition of Jeremiah and consciously drew on his example or whether it was the early church that saw the similarity and drew the parallel. Jesus certainly knew Scripture, and he thought of himself as a prophet. It would be surprising if he did not have Jeremiah in mind when he challenged the temple. Even if Jesus did not refer to Jeremiah openly, he must have been aware that his criticism of the temple echoed earlier prophets such as Jeremiah, Isaiah (see Isa 58), and Ezekiel (see Ezek 8–11).

Jesus was critical of the temple establishment, as was Jeremiah. Jeremiah berated those in the temple for breaking the basic commandments against stealing, murdering, committing adultery, bearing false witness, and worshiping idols, all covered in the Ten Commandments. He also criticized them for their lack of attention to social justice: "If you truly act justly one with another, if you do not oppress the alien, the orphan, and the widow . . . , then I will dwell with you in this place" (Jer 7:5–7). There is a parallel in the Gospels: the incident of the widow's mite, just before the apocalyptic discourse in Mark 13, where Jesus predicts the destruction of the temple. In this story, a widow gives a small amount of money that Jesus refers to as her "life," while rich people make much larger contributions. The story is often taken to illustrate true self-sacrifice as opposed to doing good for the sake of recognition. But the context shows that Jesus' intention may have been different. Just before the story of the widow, Jesus accuses the scribes as follows: "They devour widows' houses" (Mark 12:40). And the widow's story is followed by Jesus' prediction of the destruction of the temple. As Mark has arranged the material, there is a connection between the establishment scribes' willingness to take money from the poor and the temple's destruction. This coheres with the many other gospel passages where social justice is central.

CRUCIFIED OUTSIDE JERUSALEM DURING PASSOVER BY ROMAN AUTHORITIES

Jesus was crucified outside the walls of Jerusalem around Passover. Passover brought together the Romans, the Jewish governing class and their retainers, the population of Jerusalem, and Jewish pilgrims from Judea, Galilee, and the Diaspora. The combination of large crowds with the feast of liberation was volatile. Jesus had a sizeable following, and so he would have attracted the attention of the authorities, particularly during the feast.

Sometime around Passover, Jewish authorities arrested Jesus. Exactly what happened over the next twenty-four hours is disputed. There are several possibilities: (1) a night trial before the Sanhedrin with the high priest presiding, as in Matthew and Mark (although the night trial would seem to be a violation of Jewish law); (2) an early-morning meeting of the Sanhedrin, as in Luke; (3) an informal hearing, on the night of the arrest, before the high priest and several other notables, as in John and Luke. Whichever of these hypotheses is correct, or even if none is entirely accurate, members of the

Jerusalem establishment did see Jesus as a threat and decided to eliminate him. And what concerned the priestly establishment also concerned Rome, since Rome ruled Judea through the priests. The Romans reacted brutally to threats to public order.

The charge against Jesus is also a matter for discussion. The Gospels see Jesus' death as a result of his claim to be the Messiah, Son of God. When the church later attributed divinity to Jesus, the charges at the trial were taken as a recognition that Jesus was claiming to be divine, for which blasphemy they executed him. But it is debatable whether the Synoptics intend "Son of God" to be interpreted this way. As will become clear (see "The Titles of Jesus," below), this title did not imply divinity in Jewish traditions before this time.

In searching for the reasons for Jesus' death, two facts must be kept firmly in mind: (1) he was executed by the Romans by crucifixion; (2) the charge the Romans put on the cross read, "King of the Jews." Crucifixion was a Roman punishment reserved for political offenders, hardened criminals, and slaves. Jesus does not fit either of the last two categories. The charge on the cross makes his crime a political one. Many scholars think that the writing above the cross is authentic. We know that the Romans sometimes did post the charge against the condemned in this fashion, although they did not always do so. So the posting of the charge above Jesus is plausible. Further, since the title "king of the Jews" was not important in the early church, there would be little reason for the church to fabricate it. The title may reflect Pilate's understanding of messianic claims that were being made for Jesus. It is unclear whether Jesus explicitly claimed to be a messiah. But he did claim authority that came from God. Basing himself on that authority, he proclaimed judgment against the temple establishment. And Jesus' actions had political import. The best interpretation of this evidence is that Jesus, whether or not he claimed to be a messiah, looked enough like one to Jewish and Roman authorities to justify his execution. Jesus' attack on the temple could easily be seen as part of a messianic program, since it symbolized his attack on the priestly establishment and the Roman power that lay behind it.

FORMATION OF THE JESUS MOVEMENT

The fact that the Jesus movement continued to exist and to grow after his death says something about what it must have been during his life. Jesus probably intended to build a lasting movement. Some foundations must have been laid for the movement to have survived his death. This is not to say that Jesus intended to begin a religion different from Judaism. He seems to have wished to restore Israel to its proper state and relation with God. The Twelve would form the nucleus of the restored Israel.

In Sanders's list of 1993, he says of Jesus' disciples, "They saw him (in what sense is uncertain) after his death; as a consequence, they believed he would return to found the kingdom; they formed a community to await his return and sought to win others to faith in him as God's Messiah." It is notoriously difficult to deal with the resurrection in a historical presentation. Many historians do not think that consideration of the resurrection belongs to the study of the historical Jesus. After all, a person's life begins with his birth and ends with his death. In addition, even if the resurrection happened, it lies beyond history and certainly beyond historical research. But what the historian can say with assurance is that the earliest Christians experienced something that they interpreted as seeing the risen Jesus. Not only does all the evidence point in this direction; it is difficult to imagine that the Jesus movement would have survived the horrendous and humiliating execution of its leader and the flight of his disciples unless the disciples had some experience that turned things around for them.

JEWISH PERSECUTION OF THE MOVEMENT

It is misleading to picture Jews throwing Christians to the lions. Jews certainly did not have authority to mount a full-scale persecution of Christians. But Jewish communities, both in the Diaspora and in the homeland, did have a certain amount of authority to run their internal affairs. And there would have been reason for non-Christian Jews to react negatively to Christians in their midst. Christian presence could lead to conflict that might attract unwanted attention from local authorities. Paul says that before his conversion he himself persecuted Christianity, which probably means he tried to stamp it out within Jewish communities.

Conflict escalated after 70 C.E., when Judaism was being reconstituted according to Pharisaic and scribal principles and some Christians were beginning to see themselves as quite different from non-Christian Jews (see Dunn, *Partings*). Both claimed the same Scriptures and traditions. From the Jewish point of view, Christians were using Jewish Scriptures and tradition against Judaism. From the Christian point of view, Judaism had missed the boat by not recognizing Jesus as the Messiah.

THE TEACHING OF JESUS

THE KINGDOM OF GOD

This section depends largely on Perrin and Duling (412–25). The coming of the kingdom of God was central to Jesus' preaching. Although the precise phrase "kingdom of God" is not frequent in biblical and Jewish literature, the idea of God as King was widespread. In Israel, God was frequently called King (Hebrew: *melek*), or was said to reign *(malak)*. At times the kingdom of God was identified with the existing Israelite kingdom, as in 1 Chron 28:5. More often the notion of God's rule was not a geographical place but denoted God's powerful activity in ruling Israel and the world. The following passage illustrates this notion:

> They shall speak of the glory of your kingdom,
>   and tell of your power,
> to make known to all people your mighty deeds,
>   and the glorious splendor of your kingdom.
> Your kingdom is an everlasting kingdom,
>   and your dominion endures throughout all generations. (Ps 145:11–13)

During most of the Second Temple period, Israel lived under foreign domination. In such circumstances, it was difficult to believe that God ruled the world. Some circles hoped for a restoration of God's rule. The following sayings of Jesus should be read in the context of an expectation that God's rule was about to reassert itself:

> The kingdom of God is not coming with things that can be observed; nor will they say, "Look, here it is!" or "There it is!" For, in fact, the kingdom of God is among you. (Luke 17:20–21)

> From the days of John the Baptist until now the kingdom of heaven has suffered violence, and the violent take it by force. (Matt 11:12)

> But if it is by the finger of God that I cast out the demons, then the kingdom of God has come to you. (Luke 11:20)

The first of these sayings does not mean that Jesus thought the kingdom was an inner reality, a matter only of the heart (some translations read "within you" rather than "among you"—either is a possible translation of the Greek). Rather, it means that God's intervention will come too suddenly to be predicted. The saying also discourages efforts to date God's coming. Jesus' rejection of seeking signs is reflected in another saying: "Why does this generation ask for a sign? Truly I tell you, no sign will be given to this generation" (Mark 8:12). Early Christians were not content with Jesus' refusal of a sign; Matthew and Luke elaborate the text by considering Jesus himself as a sign like the prophet Jonah (Matt 12:38–42; 16:4; Luke 11:29–32), and Matthew goes on to say that Jesus' resurrection is a sign.

The second saying may refer to the violent fate of John the Baptist and the potentially similar fate of those who seek the kingdom of God. There is a war going on between God and Satan, and wars involve casualties.

The third saying occurs in a context in Luke that corresponds to Mark 3, where Jesus, because he does exorcisms, is accused of being possessed by Beelzebul. "Finger of God" alludes to Exod 8:19, where the Egyptians who have witnessed the plagues sent through Moses say, "This is the finger of God." Jesus' saying implies that God acts through Jesus, as he did through Moses. In Exodus, God's opponent was Pharoah; in Jesus' ministry, it is Satan. This would make sense in an apocalyptic context.

A famous question, still debated vigorously today, is whether Jesus thought that the kingdom was present (perhaps in his deeds and words), was future, or combined present and future elements. The most thorough recent review of the evidence is in Meier, *A Marginal Jew*. Perhaps the best solution is that Jesus expected soon the definitive intervention of God in history and saw his own work as the beginning of that intervention. This explanation has been called "inaugurated eschatology." In any case, the combination of present and future elements with respect to God's kingship is not foreign to Judaism (see Theissen, 251–52).

We have barely scratched the surface of what the kingdom might mean for Jesus. Much of what is said below helps to fill out Jesus' teaching about the kingdom. His symbol of the kingdom is so central that all other aspects of his ministry, including his attack on the temple, must be related to it.

THE PARABLES

In this section, *parable* means the kind of short story exemplified by the Good Samaritan (Luke 10:30–35), the Prodigal Son (Luke 15:11–32), and the Sower (Mark 4:3–8). Similar stories were used to teach lessons by the rabbis, and before them by Israel's wisdom tradition. Here again the double principle of similarity and dissimilarity comes into play. Jesus the teller of parables can look much like any other Jewish wisdom teacher. But he uses the form to proclaim the coming of God's kingdom and to shock people into hearing his message. Parables even help to bring the kingdom about by causing a shift of worldview among the hearers so that they begin to see things as God does. An example is the Good Samaritan:

> A man was going down from Jerusalem to Jericho, and fell into the hands of robbers, who stripped him, beat him, and went away, leaving him half dead. Now by chance a priest was going down that road; and when he saw him, he passed by on the other side. So likewise a Levite, when he came to the place and saw him, passed by on the other side. But a Samaritan while traveling came

near him; and when he saw him, he was moved with pity. He went to him and bandaged his wounds, having poured oil and wine on them. Then he put him on his own animal, brought him to an inn, and took care of him. The next day he took out two denarii, gave them to the innkeeper, and said, "Take care of him; and when I come back, I will repay you whatever more you spend." (Luke 10:30–35)

Jesus is a Jew telling a story to Jews. The parable has an anticlerical bent in that the "bad guys" are a priest and a Levite. This fits the critical attitude toward the temple establishment that we have already discovered in material about Jesus in the Gospels. In Jesus' parable, the priest and Levite may not have helped the wounded man because they thought that the man was dead and so saw no reason to defile themselves with the result that they could not take part in temple services. The prioritizing of human needs over other types of duties seems characteristic of Jesus.

If Jesus had simply made a pious Jewish layperson the one who finally helps the wounded man, the anticlerical strain would be clearer and might well win the sympathy of his audience. The shock of the story for the Jewish listeners comes when the Samaritan appears. Chapter 8, above, spoke of the antagonism between Jews and Samaritans. To portray a Samaritan as good would be distasteful, but to contrast the goodness of the Samaritan not only with a Jew but with the Jewish religious establishment would scandalize Jesus' audience. The basic message is that the human way of seeing is not God's way of seeing. To enter into the world of the parable and accept it implies giving up one's own presuppositions (see Crossan, *In Parables;* Scott).

In the parable of Workers in the Vineyard (Matt 20:1–15), the vineyard owner hires workers at various times during the day. At the end of the day he pays them each the same amount although some worked the entire day and others only an hour. Hearers of the story identify with the workers who complain about working the longest but getting paid only what the late workers were paid. This is hardly fair. But the point is that human fairness does not equal God's justice. Divine generosity cannot be limited by human boundaries. God will bypass religious systems if, instead of granting humans access to God, they serve the powerful in society and religion. This sort of teaching would not win Jesus friends among the rich and powerful.

Another example of a parable challenging preconceptions is that of the Rich Man and Lazarus (Luke 16:19–31). The rich man lives luxuriously during his life and goes to hell after his death. The poor man, Lazarus, lies suffering at the rich man's gate, and after his death he goes to heaven. This is a reversal of fates. The parable expresses God's judgment on a society in which there is a tremendous gap between rich and poor. The reversal theme is typical of apocalypticism, and the concern with social justice is characteristic of Israel's prophets and Jesus. The parable also attacks the idea that wealth indicates God's favor.

The theme of God's generosity evident in the parable of the Workers in the Vineyard also expresses itself as an emphasis on God's forgiveness. The parable of the Prodigal Son embodies this theme (Luke 15:11–32). A son takes his inheritance from his father while the father still lives. The son then goes to a foreign land, where he squanders the inheritance. Reduced to abject poverty, he returns home, asking only that he be treated as a servant. The father receives him joyously, sweeps aside the son's request to be treated as a servant, and holds a feast to celebrate his return. This is a graphic portrayal of forgiveness. But the parable does not end there. At the end of the parable, the prodigal son is inside at the banquet, while the other brother, who has stayed at home and done his duty all along, is outside. He condemns himself to be outside because he cannot accept his father's generosity to the other brother. Paradoxically, the dutiful brother misses out on the father's banquet, while the irresponsible one enjoys it. The attitude of the dutiful brother is the same as that of Matthew's laborers in the vineyard. He resents his father's generosity.

The two parables preceding the Prodigal Son in Luke 15 have a similar theme. The good shepherd seeks the lost sheep and rejoices when it is found, and the housewife searches for the lost coin and rejoices when she discovers it. The interpretation Luke's Jesus offers for the parable of the Lost Sheep is, "There will be more joy in heaven over one sinner who repents than over ninety-nine righteous persons who need no repentance" (15:7). Luke 15 begins, "The Pharisees and the scribes were grumbling and saying, 'This fellow welcomes sinners and eats with them' " (15:2). Thus the evangelist wants all three parables—the Lost Sheep, the Lost Coin, and the Prodigal Son—to be seen in the context of Jesus' relationship to sinners and of his conflict with the leaders of the religious establishment. The context is true to the ministry of Jesus. His association with those whom the religious elite considered sinners is well established in the tradition. Jesus' preaching of the kingdom of God emphasized the forgiveness of God, who approached people through him.

The theme of reversal appears also in the parable of the Wedding Guests (Luke 14:7–11), where the feast contains the unlikeliest of guests while those originally invited are not present. Those who are present at the messianic banquet will be a surprise. It will not be those whom conventional wisdom expects. Those who we thought would be there will not, and those who we were sure would be absent will be the very ones who are present.

SHORT SAYINGS: RADICAL DEMANDS, ESCHATOLOGICAL REVERSAL

Much material authentic to Jesus took the form of pithy, memorable sayings uttered by Jesus and passed down in the tradition. Some sayings were elaborated as they were passed down, and some were given narrative contexts.

"Another of his disciples said to him, 'Lord, first let me go and bury my father.' But Jesus said to him, 'Follow me, and let the dead bury their own dead' " (Matt 8:21–22). The saying "Let the dead bury their own dead" is probably authentic because it does not fit the ethics of Second Temple Judaism nor is it part of early Christian teaching. Jesus demands something that contradicts the commandment to honor one's father and mother, one of the Ten Commandments. Jesus insists that following him takes precedence over all other obligations, even the most sacred. Such a demand makes sense in the social context of Jesus' itinerant preaching.

Another saying also reveals that accepting Jesus means changing one's ways of thinking: "If anyone strikes you on the right cheek, turn the other also; and if anyone wants to sue you and take your coat, give your cloak as well; and if anyone forces you to go one mile, go also the second mile" (Matt 5:39–41). Did Jesus mean it literally? Was he speaking of how Jews should relate to occupying powers such as the Romans, who pressed people into forced service or confiscated their goods? Was he encouraging pacifism? Was he speaking of how peasants should relate to each other within villages? At the very least, Jesus is demanding a transformation of one's way of looking at the world, and so it means radical change in one's life and a radical change in society as a whole.

A well-attested theme in the teachings of Jesus is that of eschatological reversal, as found in the following sayings:

> For those who want to save their life will lose it, and those who lose their life for my sake, and for the sake of the gospel, will save it. (Mark 8:35)

> How hard it will be for those who have wealth to enter the kingdom of God! . . . It is easier for a camel to go through the eye of a needle than for someone who is rich to enter the kingdom of God. (Mark 10:23, 25)

> But many who are first will be last, and the last will be first. (Mark 10:31)

> For all who exalt themselves will be humbled, and those who humble themselves will be exalted. (Luke 14:11)

The first saying continues the theme of radical demands made by the kingdom and of opposition between values of the kingdom and those of this world. The second saying introduces an economic factor. Jesus thinks that the eschatological reversal will mean that few, if any, rich will be saved. The third saying is a general principle that things will be reversed at the eschaton. The final saying shows that striving for success according to the norms of this world results in being humbled.

The transformation of self and society that Jesus' proclamation commands is not easy, as demonstrated by this collection of sayings:

No one who puts a hand to the plow and looks back is fit for the kingdom of God. (Luke 9:62)

Enter through the narrow gate; for the gate is wide and the road is easy that leads to destruction, and there are many who take it. For the gate is narrow and the road is hard that leads to life, and there are few who find it. (Matt 7:13–14)

Truly I tell you, whoever does not receive the kingdom of God as a little child will never enter it. (Mark 10:15)

But I say to you, Love your enemies and pray for those who persecute you, so that you may be children of your Father in heaven; for he makes his sun rise on the evil and on the good, and sends rain on the righteous and on the unrighteous. For if you love those who love you, what reward do you have? Do not even the tax collectors do the same? And if you greet only your brothers and sisters, what more are you doing than others? Do not even the Gentiles do the same? Be perfect, therefore, as your heavenly Father is perfect. (Matt 5:44–48)

The precise meaning of each saying depends on the context in which it is read. As a group, they reinforce the conclusions already drawn about the profound change in attitude and the challenge to society that the kingdom represents. The saying about entering the kingdom like a child may refer to entering it without the fixed assumptions typical of adults. But how we read this saying depends, to some degree, on our cultural assumptions. Children in ancient society were low on the social scale, so in that context it may mean that only the lowliest are open to the kingdom. Absolute commitment to the new way of life symbolized by the kingdom means that one cannot look back, as Luke 9:62 makes clear. The difficulty of entering the kingdom is likened to going through a narrow gate (see 4 Ezra 7:3–9 for the same idea and image).

The importance of context for interpretation is illustrated by Matt 5:44–48. What did Jesus mean by the command to love one's enemies? This saying is similar to Matt 5:39–41, mentioned above. Were the "enemies" everyone with whom one had negative relations? Did Jesus mean political enemies, such as the Romans, or perhaps the Jerusalem hierarchy, or just personal enemies? Was he speaking to peasants about the squabbles among themselves? Does "love" imply pacifism, or can one love someone whom one finds it necessary to kill, such as an enemy in war?

THE LORD'S PRAYER

The Lord's Prayer is both Jewish and eschatological. It appears in a short form in Luke and a long form in Matthew; Luke's is closer to the original. The prayer resembles one still said by Jews, called the Kaddish. Perrin supplies an English version of its ancient form:

> Magnified and sanctified be his great name in the world that he has created according to his will. May he establish his kingdom in your lifetime and in your days and in the lifetime of all the house of Israel, even speedily and at a near time. (*Jesus and the Language*, 28)

Jesus' prayer may be his adaptation of the Kaddish.

> Father, hallowed be your name. Your kingdom come. Give us each day our daily bread. And forgive us our sins, for we ourselves forgive everyone indebted to us. And do not bring us to the time of trial. (Luke 11:2–4)

Christians are perhaps more familiar with the longer form of this prayer found in Matt 6:9–13. The shorter form is more likely to be authentic. "Hallow" and "sanctify" mean "make holy." Central to both the Kaddish and the Lord's Prayer is the hope that God's name will be treated as holy in the world. Ezekiel 36 and 39 indicates that making God's name holy means causing God to be recognized as God, for holiness is intrinsic to divinity. When God comes in power and kingship and is recognized by the peoples, God's name will truly be considered holy among them. In both the Kaddish and the Lord's Prayer, the coming of God's kingdom is the object of prayer, and both express this in terms of holiness.

Jesus asks for daily sustenance, a petition that would have been meaningful to peasants struggling to survive. The next petition is for forgiveness but makes it contingent on one's treatment of other people. The same point is made in the parable of the Unforgiving Servant in Matt 18:23–35. In particular, forgiveness is dependent upon the forgiving of debts, an economic term that, if taken literally, would mean that Jesus was in favor of releasing people from debts (see Hollenbach, "Liberating"). The final petition speaks of "temptation," a term found in eschatological contexts to denote the troubles of the end time and the potential for apostasy that they represent. The Lord's Prayer is deeply rooted in a Jewish milieu concerned with daily existence but with an eschatological outlook and an interest in the way people treat one another economically.

THE BEATITUDES

The word "beatitude" comes from the Latin *beatus,* meaning "blessed" or "happy." Beatitudes are common in the wisdom tradition. The gospel Beatitudes exist in two versions, Matt 5:3–12 and Luke 6:20–23. Matthew has nine Beatitudes, while Luke has four Beatitudes followed by four woes. The theme of eschatological reversal is embodied in the Beatitudes (as well as in Luke's woes). Matthew's version of the Beatitudes softens the eschatological harshness of Luke's version, so Luke's are closer to the original form:

> Blessed are you who are poor,
>   for yours is the kingdom of God.
> Blessed are you who are hungry now,
>   for you will be filled.
> Blessed are you who weep now, for you will laugh.
> Blessed are you when people hate you, and when they exclude you, revile you, and defame you on account of the Son of Man. Rejoice in that day and leap for joy, for surely your reward is great in heaven; for that is what their ancestors did to the prophets. (Luke 6:20–23)

Luke then adds woes that continue the theme of reversal, this time addressing the well-to-do of society:

> Woe to you who are rich,
>   for you have received your consolation.
> Woe to you who are full now,
>   for you will be hungry.
> Woe to you who are laughing now,
>   for you will mourn and weep.
> Woe to you when all speak well of you, for that is what their ancestors did to the false prophets. (Luke 6:24–26)

The eschatological reversal demanded by God's justice is concrete, and it concerns wealth, food and drink, and human relations. The future to which Jesus refers is when the kingdom of God comes in its fullness. There will be a reversal within society, and the first will be last and the last first.

JESUS AND TORAH

The vast majority of Jews shared a respect for the importance of Torah, but groups disagreed on how to interpret and apply it. Christians often assume that since the church came to see itself as separate from Judaism and not bound by rules of Torah such as circumcision and kosher laws, Jesus must have abrogated or overruled Torah. A closer inspection of the evidence reveals this to be untrue.

Some early Christians thought that obedience to Torah was necessary for all Christians, Jew or Gentile, and others thought the opposite. Such diametrically opposed positions on this key issue would be impossible to explain if Jesus had already decided it. Since the Gospels portray Jesus as concerned about Israel and Torah, it is hardly likely that he saw himself as abrogating Torah. If Jesus thought that he was nullifying Torah, he certainly would have seen fit to mention it.

Traditions in Matthew attribute to Jesus the command to obey Torah:

> Do not think that I have come to abolish the law or the prophets; I have come not to abolish but to fulfill. For truly I tell you, until heaven and earth pass away, not one letter, not one stroke of a letter, will pass from the law until all is accomplished. Therefore, whoever breaks one of the least of these commandments, and teaches others to do the same, will be called least in the kingdom of heaven; but whoever does them and teaches them will be called great in the kingdom of heaven. For I tell you, unless your righteousness exceeds that of the scribes and Pharisees, you will never enter the kingdom of heaven. (Matt 5:17–20)

Here Jesus insists on rigorous obedience to Torah. He does not draw a distinction between ethical and ritual prescriptions, nor does he say that all that matters is the spirit of the Law. Indeed, he insists that those in the kingdom of God must obey all of the laws, including the least.

Matthew 23 begins by having Jesus tell his disciples to obey the scribes and Pharisees because they have the authority of Moses and so can interpret Torah. Jesus says (Matt 23:23) that the Pharisees' rules about tithing spices, often seen as examples of Pharisaic legalism, are proper and should be obeyed as long as the more important aspects of the Law are not neglected.

SABBATH OBSERVANCE

Mark recounts the following story:

> One Sabbath he was going through the grainfields; and as they made their way his disciples began to pluck heads of grain. The Pharisees said to him, "Look, why are they doing what is not lawful on the Sabbath?" And he said to them, "Have you never read what David did when he and his companions were hungry and in need of food? He entered the house of God, when Abiathar was high priest, and ate the bread of the Presence, which it is not lawful for any but the priests to eat, and he gave some to his companions." Then he said to them, "The Sabbath was made for humankind, and not humankind for the Sabbath; so the Son of Man is lord even of the Sabbath." (Mark 2:23–28)

This is a *pronouncement story*, a story in which the narrative was invented to frame a saying or pronouncement of Jesus. Therefore, the narrative surrounding Jesus' sayings has no independent historical value. Indeed, it is hardly likely that Pharisees passed their Sabbaths in Galilean grainfields waiting to catch Sabbath violators. It is not Jesus who is accused of breaking Sabbath but his disciples. This hints that whoever made up the narrative framework thought that Sabbath work was an issue more for the early church than for Jesus.

The sayings in this narrative represent several different solutions to the problem of the disciples' action. In the first, Jesus defends his disciples on the basis of Scripture. He argues that there is no Sabbath violation because there is legal precedent in Scripture for breaking regulations in the face of human need (hunger). The next sayings are introduced with a new narrative beginning, "And he said to them," indicating originally independent material. The saying about the Sabbath being made for humans has potentially radical consequences for religious institutions but would not necessarily imply an abrogation of Torah. In rabbinic literature, love of God and neighbor was seen as the essence of Torah, and humanitarian concerns could override Sabbath regulations. The final saying, "The Son of man is lord even of the Sabbath," implies that Jesus has the authority to override Sabbath rules, but it does not state that any violation of Torah has occurred. In any case, the saying may be a faith statement characteristic of early Christianity. A more radical interpretation is that "Son of Man" here should have its basic meaning of "human being"; Jesus would then be saying that human beings are more important than the Sabbath or even that humans have authority to define Sabbath rules. The upshot is that, according to Mark, Jesus was not guilty of violating Sabbath. Matthew goes even further than Mark to insist that Jesus did not violate Torah in this incident. He makes clearer the element of hunger, and he adds further legal argument.

Mark 3:1–6 relates another story about Jesus' Sabbath activity. The story gives the impression that he was breaking a law by healing a man's hand, but in fact Jesus does no work in the healing, and so no violation takes place. Speaking healing words on the Sabbath is forbidden nowhere in Torah. Jesus asks, "Is it lawful to do good or to do harm on the Sabbath, to save life or to kill?" (3:4). Jesus' position, that it is legal to save a life on the Sabbath, is attributed in rabbinic literature to one of the Pharisaic schools. In general, there is no substantial evidence that Jesus broke the Sabbath.

FOOD LAWS

Food laws, laws about what foods can be eaten and under what circumstances, are important in Torah. Mark introduces the issue of food laws into a controversy narrated in Mark 7, a chapter that has been extensively reworked in the tradition. It begins,

> Now when the Pharisees and some of the scribes who had come from Jerusalem gathered around him, they noticed that some of his disciples were eating with defiled hands, that is, without washing them. (For the Pharisees, and all the Jews, do not eat unless they thoroughly wash their hands, thus observing the tradition of the elders; and they do not eat anything from the market unless they wash it; and there are also many other traditions that they observe, the washing of cups, pots, and bronze kettles.) So the Pharisees and the scribes asked him, "Why do your disciples not live according to the tradition of the elders, but eat with defiled hands?" (Mark 7:1–5)

The opponents are scribes and Pharisees. Once again the story has an air of artificiality about it. Mark explains Jewish customs to his audience, so it is likely that they were Gentiles. The assertion that all Jews follow the strict purity rules of the Pharisees is dubious. The question posed by the Pharisees and scribes concerns washing of hands, a matter covered not by Torah but by Pharisaic rules. Jesus responds to the accusers by quoting Isa 29:13 and asserting that his opponents worry about human rules and ignore God's will. He argues that their traditions nullify Torah, citing the case where they allow contributions to the temple, so that parents are deprived of support. Jesus continues with the claim that nothing going into a person can defile. Only what comes out of a person (evil thoughts, wickedness, and so on) can defile. Mark concludes, "Thus he declared all foods clean" (7:19). These last words are not presented as Jesus' but are editorial.

Matthew 15 tells the same story, but it keeps the focus firmly on unwashed hands. It omits Mark 7:19 and so does not apply Jesus' statements to dietary laws. After listing the inner things that defile, Matthew summarizes, "These are what defile a person; but to eat with unwashed hands does not defile" (Matt 15:20). Matthew firmly brings the discussion back to unwashed hands. He does not agree with Mark that Jesus abrogated Jewish food laws. He sees the issue as much more limited.

Matthew, retelling the controversy about picking grain on the Sabbath, has Jesus quote Hosea: "I desire mercy and not sacrifice" (12:7). Hosea's words do not mean that God has changed his mind about the sacrifices he demands in Torah. Rather, this is prophetic hyperbole meaning that God wants both mercy and sacrifice—what might be called *inclusive antithesis*. Jesus may be using the same prophetic form in Matt 15. In other words, Jesus is insisting that what comes from within may defile, but he does not deny that food laws are to be kept as well.

DIVORCE

Paul and the Gospels state that Jesus forbade divorce (Matt 5:31–32; 19:3–9; Mark 10:2–12; Luke 16:18; 1 Cor 7:10–11). By the principle of multiple attestation, we can conclude that Jesus probably did forbid it. It is more difficult to decide whether he made an exception in the case of unchastity, that is, sexual misconduct on the part of one's spouse, as in Matt 5:32 and 19:9. Jesus' prohibition of divorce is based on a scriptural argument, according to Mark 10 and Matt 19. When some Pharisees ask him why Moses permitted divorce, he says,

> Because of your hardness of heart he wrote this commandment for you. But from the beginning of creation, "God made them male and female." "For this reason a man shall leave his father and mother and be joined to his wife, and the two shall become one flesh." So they are no longer two, but one flesh. Therefore what God has joined together, let no one separate. (Mark 10:5–9)

Here Jesus does not rule on divorce on the basis of his own authority but makes a legal argument based on Torah (but see Matt 5:31–32; Luke 16:18, where Jesus' authority is enhanced by the omission of the scriptural argument). Moses did allow divorce, but Jesus does not negate Torah by his prohibition of divorce. It does not negate Torah to be stricter than Torah itself. The prophet Malachi also argues against divorce (fifth century B.C.E.), although he may do so only for priests.

In the fourth column of the *Damascus Document,* there is a parallel to Jesus' argument concerning divorce. There the followers of the "Spouter" of lies "shall be caught in fornication twice by taking a second wife while the first is alive, whereas the principle of creation is, *Male and female he created them* (Gen. i, 27)." Like Jesus, this document uses Gen 1:27 to argue for restrictions on divorce. Both Jesus and Qumran use one section of Scripture to interpret another.

Jesus' position on divorce may be part of his program of restoration. That is, things at the end should be as they were at the beginning, as in Genesis. This fits an apocalyptic viewpoint. It is also typical of millenarian movements, as shown by Allison.

BURYING THE DEAD

Some suggest that Jesus' saying about leaving the dead to bury the dead (Matt 8:21–22) is the clearest example of his opposing Torah. But here Jesus is stressing how urgent it is to follow him. Jewish tradition attests to the notion that one religious obligation can override another. For example, in

1 Macc 2:39–41, the Maccabees suspend Sabbath obligations so as to defend Torah against Antiochus IV. It is also possible that Jesus uses prophetic hyperbole here or that he intends another inclusive antithesis—that is, he wishes for his followers to fulfill both family duties and those of discipleship.

ASSOCIATION WITH SINNERS

The Gospels portray Jesus associating with sinners. Several of Jesus' parables—for example, the Prodigal Son, the Lost Sheep, the Lost Coin, and perhaps the Workers in the Vineyard—address this aspect of his ministry. Jesus is shown eating with sinners, an act said to shock the pious. A number of traditions indicate that Jesus saw his table fellowship as an anticipation of the messianic banquet to be celebrated in the kingdom of God, a joyful feast symbolizing restoration of Israel's relationship with God (Matt 8:11; Mark 14:25 and parallels; Matt 22:1–14; Luke 14:16–24; etc.). When Jesus is criticized in Mark 2 for eating with sinners, he responds, "Those who are well have no need of a physician, but those who are sick; I have come to call not the righteous but sinners" (Mark 2:17).

A distinction must be drawn between sin and impurity (see Sanders). First-century Judaism is often mistakenly seen as identical with Pharisaism, itself stereotyped as empty ritualism. Jesus is then seen as combating senseless ritual-purity rules that smothered genuine religion. His opponents are seen as identifying sin with impurity in a superficial and legalistic way. But this view distorts and denigrates ancient Judaism. It also shows a basic misunderstanding of what ancient religion was all about. Several misconceptions need to be addressed. First, as noted in chapter 1, above, all religions include both ritual and rules for behavior, including what we call ethics. Careful attention to ritual purity need not preclude a lively moral sensibility, as Lev 19 proves. Second, impurity is not equivalent to sin. Touching a dead body, for example, was not sinful, but doing so would make one ritually impure, unable to participate in the cult. Third, it is not clear that the Pharisees looked upon the Jews who did not follow their purity rules (probably the vast majority) as "sinners" for that reason. Finally, the Pharisees were a distinctive group with practices that set them apart from others. One cannot equate Pharisaic practice with Judaism itself. It is but one among many forms of Judaism.

Another misconception is that Jesus was willing to forgive whereas mainstream Judaism had no place for forgiveness. Jesus draws his attitudes on forgiveness directly from his Judaism. God's forgiveness was every bit as important to Judaism as it was to Christianity later. Second Temple Judaism, like Christianity after it, had specified ways of obtaining God's forgiveness. In some cases, there were reparations to be made and rituals to undergo.

What may have offended many of Jesus' contemporaries is his preaching that God's forgiveness could be obtained outside normal channels. Jesus was willing to offer forgiveness directly even to those recognized by society as sinners, on his own authority as God's agent, without insisting on the usual restitution and rituals.

The following words attributed to Jesus make it clearer who some of the "sinners" were, contrasting them with "religious" people: "Truly I tell you, the tax collectors and the prostitutes are going into the kingdom of God ahead of you. For John came to you in the way of righteousness and you did not believe him, but the tax collectors and the prostitutes believed him" (Matt 21:31–32). Tax collectors, who collected tolls at border crossings, were not popular characters. An argument for the authenticity of this saying can be made from the principle of dissimilarity: its viewpoint is not that of first-century Judaism, and the early church did not invent the shocking saying about harlots entering the kingdom.

We might ask whether Jesus was attacking Torah in bypassing cultic institutions, since Torah required these institutions. The question should not be answered in isolation from Second Temple Judaism. As central as the cultic establishment was, it was not above criticism. For example, the people of Qumran withdrew from Jerusalem altogether and devised an alternative mode for atonement—obedience to Torah and prayer. The Qumran community did not think of itself as violating Torah, just the opposite. Criticizing the temple establishment was not uncommon. There are Jewish texts envisioning the replacement of the second temple by a more glorious temple (*1 En.* 90:28–29; Tob 14:4–7). Both the *Testament of Moses* and the *Psalms of Solomon* were harshly critical of the temple establishment. Jesus was not against the temple in principle, any more than prophets who protested cultic activity in the midst of social injustice were. Rather, like many of his contemporaries, Jesus looked forward to a restoration of Israel that would overcome injustice and evil.

That Jesus freely offered sinners forgiveness and inclusion in the kingdom challenged the religious establishment, but there is little reason to believe that Jesus thought of this as founding a new religion or as undermining Judaism.

THE TITLES OF JESUS

Gospel traditions confer many titles on Jesus—Christ (Messiah), Son of God, Son of Man, Son of David, Prophet, Rabbi, Teacher, King of Israel, and so on. It was once believed that such titles held the key to Jesus' identity, but years of research have proven this assumption unjustified. All of the titles applied to Jesus are ambiguous. Some had a wide range of meaning in Second Temple Judaism, and others are not well enough attested for scholars to be able to supply any definitive meaning.

Another problem with Jesus' titles is that they cannot be confidently traced back to him. There are no sayings in the Synoptic Gospels in which Jesus states, "I am the Messiah," or, "I am the Son of God." The Gospel of John is replete with such sayings but is suspect for precisely this reason. The synoptic Jesus who proclaimed God's kingdom becomes the one proclaimed in John; this is a development within early Christianity.

CHRIST (MESSIAH)

The term "messiah" (Hebrew: *mashiah*, "anointed") was fluid in Israelite and Jewish society up to the time of the destruction of the second temple. To anoint meant to pour or smear oil on someone. It was a sign of being chosen by God for a specific task. The Hebrew Bible contains examples of kings, priests, prophets, and even a foreign emperor (Cyrus) being anointed. Postbiblical Jewish literature presents an equally varied set of possibilities for defining "messiah." Qumran expected two messiahs, one priestly and one royal, in addition to an eschatological prophet. The scrolls call major interpreters of Torah messiahs. The *Similitudes of Enoch* portray a heavenly messiah who will judge the powerful and the wealthy. *Testament of Levi* 18 expects a priestly messiah with royal and priestly functions. The *Testament of Judah* expects two messiahs, one priestly and one royal. Some Jews (e.g., the Sadducees) did not expect divine intervention. Others expected God to intervene in history soon, but directly, not through an intermediary. Hoped-for mediators of God's action were sometimes, but not always, called messiahs, and they assumed a multitude of forms, few of them supernatural. There is simply no consistent pattern.

Christians sometimes wonder how the Jews missed the fact that the Messiah had arrived in the person of Jesus if Jesus so clearly fulfilled their messianic expectations, as demonstrated by the fulfillment of specific prophecies. Such Christians confidently state that first-century Jews were waiting for *the* Messiah. But the portrait of the Messiah Christians have in mind simply did not exist before Christians composed it on the basis of their experience of the risen Jesus. The full picture of messiahship as found in Christianity does not conform to any Jewish expectation. In fact, Christian ideas of messiahship contradicted some Jewish expectations, such as the restoration of the Davidic monarchy in Jerusalem or the rebuilding of the temple and the return of the Diaspora. The variety of messianic expectations found among Jews reflects the variety of ways of being Jewish in the Second Temple period. Ideas of messiahship, or, as Neusner puts it, the messiah myth, give insight into Jewish thought on what history is all about, into Jewish hopes for Israel, and so on (see Neusner). A recent collection of studies of the subject is aptly named *Judaisms and Their Messiahs* (Neusner, Green, and Frerichs).

The accusation placed by the Romans on Jesus' cross, that he was "king of the Jews," has a strong claim to authenticity, as noted above. This raises the question whether Jesus claimed to be a messianic king. Many scholars doubt that Jesus explicitly applied the term "messiah" to himself, and it is still not certain why this particular title became so important in early Christianity. Whether or not Jesus ever used the word of himself, others may have done so even during his lifetime. The Gospel of Mark explicitly deals with the discrepancy between what Jesus thought and what his disciples thought about messiahship. Some may even have expected overt political action by Jesus because of his eschatological preaching. There is certainly no indication that Jesus intended to begin a revolution or to take power violently; he was not a messiah in this sense. But it is not the only way in which one could use the term. There surely must have been aspects of his ministry that led people to call him a messiah, aspects already laid out above in some detail: the eschatological tone of his message and ministry, his claim to speak for God, his message about the kingdom of God, his supernatural powers to heal and exorcise, the political import of his activity, and so on.

PROPHET

In the Synoptics, the closest Jesus comes to speaking of himself as the Messiah is in the Gospel of Luke (Luke 4:16–21). Here Jesus quotes Isa 61:1–2, a passage that identifies messiahship with a prophetic role and with the prophetic task to "bring good news to the poor," "release to the captives and recovery of sight to the blind, to let the oppressed go free, to proclaim the year of the Lord's favor."

There are other passages where Jesus refers to himself as a prophet (Mark 6:4 and parallels; Luke 4:24; 13:33–35 and parallels; John 4:44). He certainly acted like a prophet in his willingness to speak for God and to criticize Israel and its institutions. Many of the things he said resemble prophetic teaching. We have already discussed Jesus' similarity to Jeremiah in his actions toward the temple. The early church did not make much of the title of prophet for Jesus, probably because it did not think the title was lofty enough for him. This is an additional reason to think that if such traditions concerning Jesus as prophet have survived, they may well be true.

SON OF DAVID

Mark seems reticent about the title "Son of David." He may be uncomfortable with the more military or glorious aspects of messiahship, since he emphasizes the suffering and death of Jesus. In this gospel, the title appears only in Mark 10 and 12. In Mark 10, the blind beggar whom Jesus cures shouts it out. Mark 12 is puzzling because it can be read as challenging the very idea that the Messiah will be of the Davidic line:

> While Jesus was teaching in the temple, he said, "How can the scribes say that the Messiah is the son of David? David himself, by the Holy Spirit, declared, 'The Lord said to my Lord, "Sit at my right hand, until I put your enemies under your feet' " [Ps 110:1]. David himself calls him Lord; so how can he be his son?" (Mark 12:35–37)

It is unclear whether this passage denies that the Messiah is the son of David, or simply says that, although his son, the Messiah is greater than David. Matthew and Luke are much less reticent about calling Jesus Son of David.

That Jesus is of the lineage of David is attested in Paul (Rom 1:3). This is striking, for Paul himself makes little of this information. If it is accurate that Jesus was of the lineage of David, this would make more understandable the application of the title "Messiah" to him.

SON OF GOD

Christians usually assume that the title "Son of God" refers to Jesus' divinity. In a Greek context, the phrase could well indicate divinity. But Gentiles had a more fluid idea of divinity than did Jews. For Greeks and others in the Hellenistic world, there were humans, gods, and beings in-between. There were offspring of divine fathers and human mothers (e.g., Dionysus and Hercules). Humans could become divine, as in the case of Roman emperors voted into the Roman pantheon at their deaths by the senate. But Jews were strict monotheists. God was one, and no human being could claim divinity. Jews looked with disdain upon pretensions to divinity among Hellenistic and Roman rulers. When the title "Son of God" moved from a Jewish to a Greek setting as Christianity spread beyond its Jewish origins, it took on overtones of divinity. It is not likely, however, that a Jew would have understood it this way.

The "son" saying with the strongest claim to authenticity may be Mark 13:32. Speaking of the coming of the eschaton, Jesus says, "But about that day or hour no one knows, neither the angels in heaven, nor the Son, but only the Father." The saying's claim to authenticity lies in the suggestion that the early church would not have made up a saying admitting ignorance on the part of Jesus. Jesus does not explicitly use the title "Son of God" here, but the absolute use of "Son" seems to imply that.

Much has been made of the fact that in Mark 14:36 Jesus calls God Abba, an Aramaic word that means "the father." Later literature shows that it could be used as a vocative, that is, as a direct address. Early Christian usage of the term in prayer is attested in Gal 4:6 and Rom 8:15. As an address to God, it is not attested in Jewish literature before Galatians and Romans. Mark 14:36 supplies the only occurrence of the term in the Gospels, and Jesus is alone when he uses it in prayer while the apostles are asleep. The claim to authenticity of Mark 14:36 is weak, since no one would have heard him say it. But it is striking that the word appears in two letters of Paul, which means that it was used in early Christianity as an address to God; but then the early church dropped it. The specific incident in Mark 14:36 may not be authentic, but it may preserve the accurate memory that usage of the term "Abba" goes back to Jesus himself. This coheres with the extensive evidence in the Gospels that Jesus and then the church spoke of God as Father—evidence that spans various sources and literary forms and so is multiply attested. The Lord's Prayer, for example, attests to it, as it begins "Father" (Luke) or "Our Father" (Matthew). So it is likely that Jesus did use the term "Abba" to address God. It is often claimed that "Abba" is an intimate form of address and means something like "Daddy." This has been interpreted to mean that Jesus felt himself to have a unique relationship with God. As attractive as this thesis may be, it is not based on solid evidence.

The term "son of God" appears in many Jewish contexts. In 2 Sam 7:14, God tells David that Solomon will be God's son. "Son of God" may have remained an epithet for Jewish kings. The setting of Psalm 2 is the enthronement of the king-messiah, in which God adopts the king as son on his coronation day: "You are my son, today I have begotten you" (2:7). The application of "son of God" to an Israelite king is consonant with what we know of other kings in the ancient world, who were often thought to be divine or the offspring of gods. In Israel, such terminology was used, but it never denotes actual divinity. Matthew 2:15 quotes from Hos 11:1, "Out of Egypt I [God] have called my son," applying it to Jesus, but the prophecy in Hosea originally applied to the people of Israel as a whole. In Isa 1:2, the Israelites are called God's sons. In Wis 2:13, the righteous one calls himself a child of God and incurs the enmity of his fellows, who then plot his death. All of this is evidence that use of the term "son of God" in Judaism was devoid of later Christian connotations of divinity. The Apostle Paul conforms to Jewish usage when he uses the term for anyone in a proper relationship with God (e.g., Gal 4:1–7; Rom 8:14–17, 29). This is similar to what we saw in the *Psalms of Solomon* (see ch. 7, above); there, in psalm 17, one role of the Messiah was to bring Israel into conformity with the Torah, to make them all sons of God. If Jesus thought of himself as Son of God, it might well have been in one of the Jewish senses.

The connection between the titles "Son of God" and "Messiah," already suggested in traditions such as the one behind Psalm 2, is made explicit in Mark 14:61. Here the high priest asks Jesus, "Are you the Messiah, the Son of the Blessed One [God]?" Matthew's version of the confession of Peter reads, "You are the Messiah, the Son of the living God" (Matt 16:16; see Mark 1:1). The connection of the two titles suggests that, in this case, New Testament usage remains within Jewish limits.

SON OF MAN

Jesus uses the phrase "Son of Man," but it is not clear that he is speaks of himself each time. In the gospel tradition, Son of Man sayings fall into three categories. The apocalyptic Son of Man sayings refer to one who is to come at the end of time to rescue the righteous and to judge the wicked (Mark 8:38; 14:62). He will judge people according to how they have related to Jesus. The earthly Son of Man sayings deal with the authority of the earthly Jesus to forgive sins and to rule on Sabbath observance (Mark 2:10, 28), as one who comes "eating and drinking," in contrast to John the Baptist (Luke 7:34), as one with no home (Luke 9:58), and as the one who seeks and saves the lost (Luke 19:10). The suffering Son of Man sayings speak of the suffering that Jesus must endure and of his resurrection (Mark 8:31; 9:31; 10:33–34).

Scholars debate the issues raised by this title. Some recent interpretation questions whether Jesus ever used the term as a title for himself or anyone else, arguing that he may have used it only in a generic sense of "human being," as in Ezekiel (e.g., Ezek 2:1, 3, 6, 8) or more specifically as a circumlocution for "I" (see Vermes). The early church could then have picked up on the term and interpreted it in terms of the one like a son of man in Dan 7. Use of "son of man" to mean "I," however, is not attested in the Aramaic of Jesus' day, nor would this explain why the church adopted it as a major title of Jesus.

The church probably did not initiate the use of the title. And since it does not seem to have been a messianic title in Jesus' day, it is difficult to explain why the early church would have applied it to Jesus. Further, in the Gospels the term is found only on the lips of Jesus. Nor was it a popular title for Jesus beyond New Testament times. It does not occur in the church's creeds, liturgical formulas, or teaching summaries. Still, the title is well entrenched in the tradition. It enjoys the attestation of multiple sources and literary forms. Therefore, Jesus himself probably initiated use of the term.

If Jesus did originate its use, his reference was most likely to the apocalyptic son of man. Both the suffering and the earthly Son of Man sayings then evolved under the influence of early Christian reflection on Jesus in the light of his death and resurrection. If Jesus was an eschatological preacher, he expected an eschaton and a judgment. He may have settled on his vision of the Son of Man through reflection on Dan 7, as did the *Parables of Enoch*. Since he speaks of the Son of Man in the third person, he may have expected an eschatological figure other than himself to vindicate his ministry (see Mark 8:38). But others find it hard to believe that Jesus would deprive himself of a role in the judgment he predicted, and so they see Jesus as referring to himself in his prediction of the Son of Man.

A PASSAGE ABOUT JESUS IN JOSEPHUS

Josephus contains an important passage dealing with Jesus. The section is jarring in that it makes claims for Jesus that only a Christian would make, and Josephus was definitely not a Christian. Therefore, scholars conclude that the original was altered by Christians, and some feel that it deserves no consideration as historical evidence. Meier argues convincingly, however, that when one deletes obvious Christian additions, there remains a core that could easily go back to Josephus and that provides a valuable clue to how non-Christians would have perceived Jesus (*A Marginal Jew*, 1.56–69). The passage from Josephus reads as follows (Meier's translation, 1.60; *Ant.* 18.63–64):

> At this time there appeared Jesus, a wise man, if indeed one should call him a man. For he was a doer of startling deeds, a teacher of people who receive the truth with pleasure. And he gained a following both among many Jews and among many of Greek origin. He was the Messiah. And when Pilate, because of an accusation made by the leading men among us, condemned him to the cross, those who loved him previously did not cease to do so. For he appeared to them on the third day, living again, just as the divine prophets had spoken of these and countless other wondrous things about him. And up until this very day the tribe of Christians, named after him, has not died out.

By excising parts of the passage that are obviously Christian, Meier arrives at a plausible version of what Josephus wrote. These parts are as follows: "if indeed one should call him a man"; "He was the Messiah"; "For he appeared to them on the third day, living again, just as the divine prophets had spoken of these and countless other wondrous things about him." The resulting text reads,

> At this time there appeared Jesus, a wise man. For he was a doer of startling deeds, a teacher of people who receive the truth with pleasure. And he gained a following both among many Jews and among many of Greek origin. And when Pilate, because of an accusation made by the leading men among us, condemned him to the cross, those who loved him previously did not cease to do so. And up until this very day the tribe of Christians (named after him) has not died out. (Meier, *A Marginal Jew*, 1.61)

Meier notes that miracles ("startling deeds") and teaching would have been two activities of a "wise man" in Josephus's world, and Christian tradition attributes both to Jesus. The collusion of Pilate and Jewish leaders in Jesus' death corresponds to what the Gospels report and what is historically likely. There is no reason to doubt that Josephus knew that the Jesus movement survived his death and was eventually called after the title "Christ" that was applied to him.

Although Josephus's testimony adds nothing specific to what we already know from the Gospels, it affords an intriguing glimpse at how Jesus was viewed by a non-Christian, Jewish contemporary. It also supplies independent witness for Jesus' miracles, his teaching, and the account that both Pilate and some Jewish leaders were involved in his death.

CONCLUSION

This chapter sketches a plausible picture of the historical Jesus. It is incomplete, and many of the issues raised here are insoluble given the present state of knowledge. Still, the underlying assumption that Jesus was a Jew living in Galilee and Judea at the end of the Second Temple period is crucial. Although no one denies that Jesus was a Jew, the fact of his Jewishness is often rendered almost irrelevant because Christians often contrast him with his fellow Jews, to the denigration of Judaism and Jewish society. Any historical reconstruction that does not see Jesus within first-century Jewish society is highly problematic. And any treatment that uses the Jewish context simply to prove that Judaism is inferior to Christianity, or to put all Jews of Jesus' time into a negative category, is neither good history nor good theology. Further, a theology that does not see Jesus' humanity in terms of his Jewishness deprives that humanity of any but the most abstract qualities.

SELECT BIBLIOGRAPHY

Allison, D. C., Jr. *Jesus of Nazareth: Millenarian Prophet.* Minneapolis: Fortress, 1998.

Ashton, John. "Abba." *ABD* 1:7–8.

Borg, Marcus J. *Conflict, Holiness, and Politics in the Teachings of Jesus.* Lewiston, N.Y.: Edwin Mellen, 1984.

———. *Jesus: A New Vision.* San Francisco: Harper & Row, 1988.

Bornkamm, Günther. *Jesus of Nazareth.* London: Hodder & Stoughton, 1960.

Bultmann, Rudolf. *The History of the Synoptic Tradition.* New York: Harper & Row, 1963.

Charlesworth, James H. *Jesus' Jewishness: Exploring the Place of Jesus within Early Judaism.* Philadelphia: Crossroad, 1991.

———. *Jesus within Judaism: New Light from Exciting Archeological Discoveries.* New York: Doubleday, 1988.

———, ed. *The Messiah: Developments in Earliest Judaism and Christianity.* Minneapolis: Fortress, 1992.

Chilton, Bruce D. *The Temple of Jesus: His Sacrificial Program within a Cultural History of Sacrifice.* University Park: Pennsylvania State University Press, 1992.

Collins, Adela Yarbro. "The Origins of the Designation of Jesus as 'Son of Man.' " *HTR* 80 (1987): 391–407.

Crossan, J. Dominic. *The Historical Jesus: The Life of a Mediterranean Jewish Peasant.* San Francisco: HarperCollins, 1991.

———. *In Parables: The Challenge of the Historical Jesus.* New York: Harper & Row, 1973.

———. *Jesus: A Revolutionary Biography.* San Francisco: HarperSanFrancisco, 1994.

Crossan, John Dominic, and Jonathan L. Reed. *Excavating Jesus: Beneath the Stones, Behind the Texts.* San Francisco: HarperSanFrancisco, 2001.

Dunn, J. D. G. *The Evidence for Jesus.* Philadelphia: Westminster, 1985.

———. *The Partings of the Ways: Between Christianity and Judaism and Their Significance for the Character of Christianity.* Philadelphia: Trinity Press International, 1991.

Evans, Craig. *Jesus and His Contemporaries: Comparative Studies.* Leiden: Brill, 1995.

———. *Life of Jesus Research: An Annotated Bibliography.* Leiden: Brill, 1989.

Evans, Craig, and Bruce Chilton, eds. *Studying the Historical Jesus: Evaluations of the State of Current Research.* Leiden: Brill, 1994.

Fredriksen, Paula. *Jesus of Nazareth, King of the Jews: A Jewish Life and the Emergence of Christianity.* New York: Knopf, 2000.

Freyne, Sean. *Galilee from Alexander the Great to Hadrian, 325 B.C.E. to 135 C.E.* Wilmington, Del.: Michael Glazier, 1980.

———. *Galilee, Jesus, and the Gospels: Literary Approaches and Historical Investigations.* Philadelphia: Fortress, 1988.

Funk, Robert W. *Honest to Jesus: Jesus for a New Millenium.* San Francisco: HarperSanFrancisco, 1996.

Funk, Robert W., Roy W. Hoover, and the Jesus Seminar. *The Five Gospels: The Search for the Authentic Words of Jesus.* New York: Macmillan, 1993.

Funk, Robert W., and the Jesus Seminar. *The Acts of Jesus: The Search for the Authentic Deeds of Jesus.* San Francisco: HarperSanFrancisco, 1998.

Gnilka, Joachim. *Jesus of Nazareth: Message and History.* Peabody, Mass. Hendrickson, 1997.

Gowan, Donald E. "The Messiah." Pages 387–95 in *Bridge Between the Testaments: A Reappraisal of Judaism from the Exile to the Birth of Christianity.* Edited by Donald E. Gowan. 3d ed., rev. Allison Park, Pa.: Pickwick, 1986.

Hare, Douglas R. A. *The Son of Man Tradition.* Philadelphia: Fortress, 1990.

Harrington, Daniel J. "The Jewishness of Jesus: Facing Some Problems." *CBQ* 49 (1987): 1–13.

Harvey, A. E. *Jesus and the Constraints of History.* Philadelphia: Westminster, 1982.

Hollenbach, Paul W. "The Conversion of Jesus: From Jesus the Baptizer to Jesus the Healer." *ANRW* 2.25.1:196–219.

———. "Liberating Jesus for Social Involvement." *BTB* 15 (1985): 151–57.

Horsley, Richard A. *Jesus and the Spiral of Violence: Popular Jewish Resistance in Roman Palestine.* San Francisco: Harper & Row, 1987.

Hurtado, Larry W. *One God, One Lord: Early Christian Devotion and Ancient Jewish Monotheism.* Philadelphia: Fortress, 1988.

Jeremias, Joachim. *New Testament Theology: The Proclamation of Jesus.* New York: Scribner, 1971.

———. *The Parables of Jesus.* Rev. ed. New York: Scribner, 1963.

Johnson, Luke Timothy. *The Real Jesus.* San Francisco: HarperSanFrancisco, 1995.

Lindars, Barnabas. *Jesus Son of Man: A Fresh Examination of the Son of Man Sayings in the Gospels.* Grand Rapids: Eerdmans, 1983.

Loader, William. *Jesus' Attitude towards the Law: A Study of the Gospels.* Tübingen: Mohr Siebeck, 1997.

Mack, Burton. *A Myth of Innocence: Mark and Christian Origins.* Philadelphia: Fortress, 1988.

Meier, John P. "Jesus." *NJBC* 1316–28.

———. *A Marginal Jew: Rethinking the Historical Jesus.* 3 vols. New York: Doubleday, 1991–2001.

Meyer, Ben. *The Aims of Jesus*. London: SCM, 1979.

Neusner, Jacob. *Messiah in Context: Israel's History and Destiny in Formative Judaism*. Philadelphia: Fortress, 1984.

Neusner, Jacob, William S. Green, and Ernest Frerichs, eds. *Judaisms and Their Messiahs at the Turn of the Christian Era*. Cambridge: Cambridge University Press, 1987.

Oakman, Douglas E. *Jesus and the Economic Questions of His Day*. Lewiston, N.Y.: Edwin Mellen, 1986.

Perrin, Norman. *Jesus and the Language of the Kingdom: Symbol and Metaphor in New Testament Interpretation*. Philadelphia: Fortress, 1976.

———. *Rediscovering the Teaching of Jesus*. San Francisco: Harper & Row, 1976.

Perrin, Norman, and Dennis Duling. "The Presupposition of the New Testament: Jesus." Chapter 13 in *The New Testament: An Introduction*. New York: Harcourt Brace Jovanovich, 1982.

Powell, Mark Allan. *Jesus as a Figure in History: How Modern Historians View the Man from Galilee*. Louisville: Westminster John Knox, 1998.

Reumann, John. "Jesus and Christology." Pages 501–64 in *The New Testament and Its Modern Interpreters*. Edited by Eldon Jay Epp and George W. MacRae. Philadelphia: Fortress, 1989.

Riches, John. *Jesus and the Transformation of Judaism*. New York: Seabury, 1982.

Rousseau, John J., and Rami Arav. *Jesus and His World*. Minneapolis: Fortress, 1995.

Sanders, E. P. *The Historical Figure of Jesus*. London: Penguin, 1993.

———. *Jesus and Judaism*. Philadelphia: Fortress, 1985.

Schweitzer, Albert. *The Quest of the Historical Jesus: A Critical Study of Its Progress from Reimarus to Wrede*. New York: Macmillan, 1968.

Scott, Bernard Brandon. *Hear Then the Parable: A Commentary on the Parables of Jesus*. Philadelphia: Fortress, 1989.

Stegemann, Ekkehard W., and Wolfgang Stegemann. *The Jesus Movement: A Social History of Its First Century*. Minneapolis: Fortress, 1999.

Tatum, W. Barnes. *In Quest of Jesus: A Guidebook*. Nashville: Abingdon, 1999.

Theissen, Gerd, and Annette Mertz. *The Historical Jesus: A Comprehensive Guide*. Minneapolis: Fortress, 1998.

Tödt, Heinz Eduard. *The Son of Man in the Synoptic Tradition*. London: SCM, 1965.

Vermes, Geza. *Jesus and the World of Judaism*. Philadelphia: Fortress, 1984.

———. *Jesus the Jew: A Historian's Reading of the Gospels*. Philadelphia: Fortress, 1973.

————. *The Religion of Jesus the Jew.* Minneapolis: Fortress, 1993.

Westerholm, S. *Jesus and Scribal Authority.* Lund: Gleerup, 1978.

Wilcox, M. "Jesus in the Light of His Jewish Environment." *ANRW* 2.25.1:129–95.

Wright, N. T. *Jesus and the Victory of God.* Minneapolis: Fortress, 1996.

————. "Jesus Christ." *ABD* 3:773–96.

————. "Jesus, Quest for the Historical." *ABD* 3:796–802.

CHAPTER 10

ISRAEL IN REVOLT

PRIMARY READINGS: *4 Ezra* ♦ *2 Baruch*

Roman rule over Israel was never easy. Since the days of Pompey's take-over of the area, the Romans had tried a shifting patchwork of jurisdictions and methods of administration, none of which was fully successful. Perhaps there were simply too many competing interests. The Romans, like all colonial powers, had their own best interests at heart. And their internal power struggles complicated their relations with the provinces during the late Second Temple period. The instability of Roman politics did not foster stability and security on the Palestinian front. Further, like all colonized powers, Palestinian Jews fragmented into rival groups that sometimes cooperated and sometimes worked against each other.

Chapter 8, above, recounted the unhappy story of first-century Palestinian Judaism. In 66 C.E., Rome and the Jews of Judea and Galilee descended into the abyss of a long and costly war. We can debate whether such a war was inevitable and what the history of Judaism and Christianity would have been if had it not been for the war. But it is not difficult to see why war engulfed Judea and Galilee. The case can be made that war was in the making from the time that Pompey first set foot in Jewish territory. When the Romans took Jerusalem in 70 C.E., they destroyed the temple that had stood there for six hundred years. Thus the Second Temple period came to a tragic end.

CAUSES OF THE WAR

Wars are not simple events. They usually result from a complex interplay of nations, personalities, institutions, events, economic factors, and religious elements. The causes of wars are often difficult to unravel and to present systematically. And we cannot always point to one main factor as *the* cause of a war. When we examine the war between the Jews and the Romans in 66–70 C.E., our job is made more difficult by the distance in time between us and the events and by a lack of evidence. What evidence we have comes from Josephus, who is biased, and he leaves much unsaid. Despite these obstacles, we can understand the main causes of the war.

ROMAN MALADMINISTRATION

Josephus details the misdeeds of the Roman administrators. The fact that Josephus is pro-Roman and even had the Flavian emperors as patrons makes his accusations the more credible. Crises in Pilate's and Cumanus's administrations resulted in their recall, a sign that even Rome recognized their inadequacy.

ROMAN OPPRESSION

Rome's rule began with Pompey's desecration of the temple and was marked by repression, high taxes, various forms of humiliation, enslavement and crucifixion of resisters, and even the effort of Gaius Caligula to force emperor worship on the Jews.

JUDAISM AS A RELIGION

For centuries the Jews reconciled scriptural promises of independence and an anointed Jewish king with the reality of colonialism. Jewish religion thus did not automatically produce rebellion. On the contrary, Second Temple Judaism had its origins in the reconstitution of Jewish society under Persian auspices. But when foreign oppression grew strong, sacred traditions promised relief and supplied hope. That is clear in such documents as the *Psalms of Solomon* and the *Testament of Moses* and in some of the popular movements of the first century C.E. The tax revolt of Judas the Galilean, for example, championed the idea that the Jews should accept no ruler but God, and Horsley and Hanson speculate that the rebellions after Herod the Great's death arose from ideas of popular kingship exemplified in stories about David and Saul.

The Romans allowed the Jews to live by their own customs to some degree, but tensions inevitably arose. The presence and influence of foreign culture aroused resentment. Such was the case with the military standards brought into Jerusalem by Pilate, Herod's golden eagle, Caligula's statue, foreign marriage practices, confiscation of temple funds, and so on.

CLASS TENSIONS

In the *Jewish War*, Josephus lists the horrors of warfare. He speaks of "those in power oppressing the masses, and the masses eager to destroy the powerful. These were bent on tyranny, those on violence and plundering the property of the wealthy" (*J. W.* 7.260–261). The colonial situation positioned the local aristocracy between the Romans and the lower classes. Some aristocrats used this position to oppress peasants and workers, and at times the lower classes resisted.

CONFLICTS WITH GENTILES

Many non-Jewish inhabitants of the area preferred Roman to Jewish rule. Gentiles living in Greek cities did not support the revolt of 66–70. Josephus reports violence between Jews and Gentiles during the time leading up to the war and during the war, and he says that the Gentiles furnished the Romans with auxiliary troops. This must be balanced with the observation that Jews and Gentiles had been living peacefully together over many centuries. Increasing movement toward Jewish independence may have aroused Gentile opposition and embittered Jews against them.

THE RULING CLASS

The upper classes displayed factionalism and a range of attitudes toward the war. We have seen similar divisions within Israel throughout the Second Temple period. Herodian rule introduced new and disruptive factors into the Jewish aristocracy, and not all segments of this aristocracy benefited equally from Roman and Herodian rule. Disaffected aristocrats may have made common cause with elements of resistance in the lower classes.

THE WAR AGAINST THE ROMANS

THE BEGINNING OF THE WAR

In 66 C.E., the temple captain Eleazar and the lower priests refused to accept any sacrifices from foreigners.

> This action laid the foundation of the war with the Romans; for the sacrifices offered on behalf of that nation and the emperor were in consequence rejected. The chief priests and the notables earnestly besought them not to abandon the customary offering for their rulers, but the priests remained obdurate. (*J. W.* 2.409–410)

The rebels barricaded themselves in the temple and blocked the chief priests from entering. The chief priests and prominent Pharisees appealed to the people, hoping to avoid a hopeless struggle with the Romans. They produced Torah experts who argued that it was unlawful to refuse the sacrifices of foreigners. Finally, they sent messengers to Florus and Agrippa II, asking for troops to crush the revolt. With this military aid, the antiwar factions controlled the upper city, while the rebels occupied the lower city and the temple. This was civil war, and aristocratic elements were enlisted on both sides.

After some days, the Sicarii joined Eleazar and the rebel priests. With their augmented numbers, the rebels ousted the loyalists from the upper city and captured most of Jerusalem, except for the fortress of Antonia and Herod's palace, which were still occupied by Roman troops. They then proceeded to besiege the palace.

> At this period a certain Menahem, son of Judas surnamed the Galilaean—that redoubtable doctor who in old days, under Quirinius, had upbraided the Jews for recognizing the Romans as masters when they already had God—took his intimate friends off with him to Masada, where he broke into king Herod's armory and provided arms both for his fellow-townsmen and for other brigands; then, with these men for his bodyguard, he returned like a veritable king to Jerusalem, became the leader of the revolution, and directed the siege of the palace. (*J. W.* 2.433–434)

The procurator Tiberius Alexander had already crucified two sons of Judah the Galilean in the mid-40s. Resistance seems to have run in Judah's family. Josephus accuses Menahem ben Judah the Galilean of royal (messianic) pretensions. Eleazar's followers resented Menahem. "So they laid their plans to attack him in the temple, whither he had gone up in state to pay his devotions, arrayed in royal robes and attended by his suite of armed fanatics" (*J. W.* 2.443–444). Menahem was killed, and his surviving supporters fled to Masada. Among them were Sicarii who spent the rest of the war at Masada, leaving it only to raid the surrounding area (*J. W.* 4.398–409). Shortly afterward the Romans in Herod's palace were lured out of their refuge with promises of safe passage but then slaughtered.

Syria's Roman governor, Cestius Gallus, then advanced on Jerusalem. Deprived of quick victory, he withdrew to Antioch, sustaining considerable casualties along the way. The rebel victory caused the antiwar factions to flee from Jerusalem to the Romans. A provisional government composed of the remaining aristocrats was formed, and it appointed generals for the Jewish forces. Josephus assumed charge of Galilee, which attests to his status among Jerusalem's ruling elite. He set about fortifying Galilee and training its citizens for war.

JOSEPHUS IN GALILEE

Josephus gives two accounts of his activity in Galilee, one in the *War* and the other in his autobiography, *The Life*. Both reports are brimming over with scathing indictments of those who opposed him. His main rival was John of Gischala in Galilee. John, suspecting that Josephus was pro-Roman, did not trust him (*J. W.* 2.594). Much of what Josephus says gives substance to John's suspicions. Josephus admits that he was a reluctant revolutionary who did all he could to leave the door open for reconciliation with the Romans, an attitude probably in accord with other Jerusalem leaders. One of the main tasks given him by those leaders was disarming the bandits in Galilee, probably because the bandits could not be controlled by the ruling elite.

John was unable to oust Josephus, though not for lack of trying. John complained about Josephus to the provisional government in Jerusalem (*Life* 189–194). He had a friend in Jerusalem in the person of Simon son of Gamaliel, a prominent citizen and a Pharisee. Simon had no authority to remove Josephus, but he tried to exert his influence with the Sanhedrin to accomplish this. The high priest Ananus, however, blocked the move. The incident is significant from a number of perspectives. First, John himself may have been a member of the ruling class, since he was prominent in his town of Gischala and he had an eminent friend in Jerusalem. Second, Simon was a prominent Pharisee, but Ananus the high priest had the final word. Third, Ananus had to decide between two aristocrats, Josephus and John; this indicates that not all aristocrats were in accord. Fourth, if John was more intent on revolution than Josephus, then the high priest's decision favored moderation, since Josephus retained his office. The moderate position advocated preparing for war with Rome but hoped not so much for victory as for a strong negotiating position.

Vespasian's Advance

Nero appointed Vespasian to conduct the war. Vespasian assembled a large army and in the spring of 67 C.E. was poised to retake Galilee. The city of Sepphoris requested a Roman garrison, which Vespasian supplied, thus bloodlessly regaining one of Galilee's major cities. As the Romans advanced, Josephus's army fled before them. Many ended up in the fortress of Jotapata, north of Sepphoris. After a siege the fortress was taken, most of its inhabitants killed or enslaved, and Josephus captured. From then on he viewed the war from the Roman side, first as a prisoner, and later as aide to Titus, Vespasian's son. His change from prisoner to aide occurred when a prediction he made to Vespasian that Vespasian would become emperor came true in 69 C.E. (*J. W.* 3.399–408). Titus assumed command of the war, and Josephus became his interpreter and guide.

When Vespasian retook the rest of Galilee and environs, John of Gischala and his men escaped to Jerusalem. There he gained admittance to the inner group of aristocrats running the city under Ananus the high priest. The rest of the war centered mostly on Jerusalem. As the Romans advanced in the winter of 67–68, civil strife flared up in Jerusalem between prowar and antiwar factions. Jews from countryside and villages withdrew before the Roman advance, and many ended up in Jerusalem, where they aggravated the situation.

THE ZEALOTS

Josephus first uses the name "Zealots" as an organized party when he describes the effects of the entrance of "bandits" into Jerusalem in the winter of 67–68 (*J. W.* 4.135–161). He says that bandits active in Judea joined together and entered Jerusalem as a group, and it is these who were the Zealots. Lack of strong leadership in Jerusalem made resistance to their entrance impossible. It is likely that the Zealots were joined by other Jews fleeing before the Roman advance. We have no evidence of the Zealots' existence before this time.

> The brigands [Zealots], however, were not satisfied with having put their captives in irons, and considered it unsafe thus to keep for long in custody influential persons, with numerous families quite capable of avenging them; they feared, moreover, that the people might be moved by their outrageous action to rise against them. They accordingly decided to kill their victims. . . . For such a monstrous crime they invented as monstrous an excuse, declaring that their victims had conferred with the Romans concerning the surrender of Jerusalem and had been slain as traitors to the liberty of the state. In short, they boasted of their audacious acts as though they had been the benefactors and saviours of the city. (*J. W.* 4.143–146)

Josephus reports the Zealots' rationale for their behavior, a rationale that is plausible. They suspected—perhaps rightly—the rulers of wanting to reach accomodation with the Romans. They thought it advisable to do away with the "traitors" rather than take the chance that they would be rescued by their supporters or influence the people, thus undermining the revolt.

The Zealots then took action with respect to the priesthood:

> They actually took upon themselves the election to the high priesthood. Abrogating the claims of those families from which in turn the high priests had always been drawn, they appointed to that office ignoble and low-born individuals, in order to gain accomplices in their impious crimes; for persons who had undeservedly attained to the highest dignity were bound to obey those who had conferred it. Moreover, by various devices and libelous statements, they brought the official authorities into collision with each other, finding their own opportunity in the bickerings of those who should have kept them in check; until, glutted

with the wrongs which they had done to men, they transferred their insolence to the Deity and with polluted feet invaded the sanctuary.

An insurrection of the populace was at length pending, instigated by Ananus, the senior of the chief priests, a man of profound sanity, who might possibly have saved the city, had he escaped the conspirators' hands. At this threat these wretches converted the temple of God into their fortress and refuge from any outbreak of popular violence, and made the Holy Place the headquarters of their tyranny. To these horrors was added a spice of mockery more galling than their actions. For, to test the abject submission of the populace and make trial of their own strength, they essayed to appoint the high priests by lot, although, as we have stated, the succession was hereditary. As pretext for this scheme they adduced ancient custom, asserting that in old days the high priesthood had been determined by lot; but in reality their action was the abrogation of established practice and a trick to make themselves supreme by getting these appointments into their own hands.

They accordingly summoned one of the high priestly clans, called Eniachin, and cast lots for a high priest. By chance the lot fell to one who proved a signal illustration of their depravity; he was an individual named Phanni, son of Samuel, of the village of Aphthia, a man who not only was not descended from high priests, but was such a clown that he scarcely knew what the high priesthood meant. At any rate they dragged their reluctant victim out of the country and, dressing him up for his assumed part, as on the stage, put the sacred vestments upon him and instructed him to act in keeping with the occasion. To them this monstrous impiety was a subject for jesting and sport, but the other priests, beholding from a distance this mockery of their law, could not restrain their tears and bemoaned the degradation of the sacred honours. (*J. W.* 4.147–157)

Josephus rails against the Zealots' decision to use lots to choose a high priest, but the use of lots to determine God's will is well attested in the Bible. Had the Zealots wanted simply to appoint someone whom they could control, they probably could have found a better system and a better candidate. They used lots for the same reason that lots are used in the Bible, to ensure that the priest was chosen by God. The Zealots were careful to put forth candidates from one of the recognized high-priestly clans, although not from the approved aristocratic families. Josephus professes shock that the Zealots appointed a high priest from a family not of the Jerusalem elite. But the families that controlled the high priesthood in the first century C.E. themselves were interlopers, comparatively speaking, for Herod had brought in priestly families from the Diaspora to replace the Hasmoneans. And the Hasmoneans themselves were not originally of high priestly stock, for that matter. The Zealots' actions can be read as a genuine attempt to restore the priesthood by replacing unworthy priests with priests, properly credentialed, of God's own choosing. So, as we have seen before, reform is seen as restoration. The Zealots made the temple their headquarters. It was both a fortress and the center of religious and political authority. It was natural that their new high priest should rule from there.

The high priest Ananus led the protest against the Zealots, but they eliminated him. Other members of the priestly elite bemoaned the new order, as we might expect. The leading citizens and chief priests "vehemently upbraided the people for their apathy and incited them against the Zealots; for so these miscreants called themselves, as though they were zealous in the cause of virtue and not for vice in its basest and most extravagant form" (*J.W.* 4.160–161). The name "Zealots" was adopted by the group itself. In Jewish texts, "zeal" usually means devotion to Torah. The word "zeal" was also used to characterize the Maccabees two centuries earlier. The name embodied the Zealots' ideology. They came to Jerusalem from the countryside, so there may have been a city-country antipathy. Perhaps because of this same tension, the chief priests were able to arouse the city residents against these Zealots from the countryside, and they were trapped in the temple. A contingent of Zealots occupied part of the temple until war's end. Josephus expresses priestly indignation that each time the Zealots came out to fight and were wounded, they went back to the inner sanctuary and defiled it with their blood. He also alleges that Ananus would not attack the inner sanctuary because his men were not properly purified to enter it, but he admits that the Zealots' weapons may have figured in Ananus's calculations.

JOHN OF GISCHALA, THE ZEALOTS, AND THE IDUMEANS

At this point, John of Gischala reenters the story. He pretended to work for the priests, but Josephus says that he was in fact on the Zealots' side (*J.W.* 4.209). The priests chose him as their liaison with the Zealots, but John used his position to keep the Zealots informed of the priests' plans. John told the Zealots that Ananus was about to hand Jerusalem over to the Romans, and he advised them to seek help from the Idumeans, inhabitants from the area that had been brought into the Judean ambit by John Hyrcanus I.

The Idumeans marched to Jerusalem, but the gates were closed and barred by Ananus and the city populace. The Zealots, however, admitted the Idumeans into the city, and the Idumeans killed many there.

> Thinking their energies wasted on the common people, they went in search of the chief priests; it was for them that the main rush was made, and they were soon captured and slain. . . . I should not be wrong in saying that the capture of the city began with the death of Ananus; and that the overthrow of the walls

and downfall of the Jewish state dated from the day on which the Jews beheld their high priest, the captain of their salvation, butchered in the heart of Jerusalem. (*J. W.* 4.315–318)

For Josephus, the real end of Jerusalem comes when the leader of the priestly aristocracy is killed. He suggests that God allowed the temple to be burned to cleanse it of the Zealots' pollutions.

The Zealots and Idumeans initiated a bloody campaign against Jerusalem's ruling class. Josephus says that eventually even many of the Idumeans were alienated by Zealot excesses. Most Idumeans left the city, but not before liberating many prisoners taken by the Zealots. At this point, John of Gischala made a bid for more power among the Zealots. This produced a split of the Zealots into two factions, although there were no open battles between them. The Idumeans remaining in the city sided with John. Josephus says that those who did not join John's group were suspicious of monarchical authority and dedicated to an egalitarian power structure (*J. W.* 4.393–394). The Zealots continued to control the city until the spring of 69. Meanwhile the Romans bided their time, having received intelligence that civil strife divided the Jews.

SIMON BAR GIORA

Simon bar Giora led one of the bandit groups operating in Judea and Idumea, preying upon the wealthy of northeast Judea. Ananus had tried to disarm him, without success. "He withdrew to the hills, where, by proclaiming liberty for slaves and rewards for the free, he gathered around him the villains from every quarter" (*J. W.* 4.508). It is not clear whether Simon espoused a program of social reform or whether his social policies were purely pragmatic. He resembled the ancient King David, who began his rise to power by gathering a gang of bandits in the countryside composed of the disaffected of society (1 Sam 22:1–2). Like David, Simon knew how to hold people together, and he gained a reputation for being an effective leader. Simon attracted increasing numbers of people to his band as his reputation spread. They obeyed him "as a king" (*J. W.* 4.510). This suggests that Simon was the sort of popular king described in chapter 8, above.

As the Romans reconquered Idumea and parts of Judea, Simon began to harass Jerusalem. The Idumeans still under John of Gischala's command turned against John, forcing him and his supporters into the temple's outer precincts. Together with the remnants of the priestly aristocracy, the Idumeans then invited Simon into the city. In the spring of 69, Simon attained mastery of Jerusalem, and his only Jewish rivals were confined to the temple. Simon's rule was marked by frequent battles with the Zealots that destroyed much of Jerusalem's supplies, and by iron discipline featuring the death penalty for all who opposed him.

THE FALL OF JERUSALEM

Around Passover in 70, Titus began to besiege Jerusalem. Inside the city, when Eleazar opened the gates to the inner temple for the festival, John smuggled his armed men into that area. They then attacked and defeated Eleazar, leaving John and Simon sole leaders. The two came to terms with one another in the face of the Roman enemy. But in 70, Jerusalem fell to superior Roman strength, and John and Simon were captured and taken to Rome. Simon was treated as the main leader by the Romans. He was paraded through Rome in a triumphal march and then executed. John was sentenced to life imprisonment. Titus consigned Jerusalem and its temple to the flames. The Roman soldiers planted their idolatrous standards in the ruined courts of the temple and sacrificed to them.

	Main Dates of the War (All Dates Are C.E.)
66	Eleazar, the temple captain, ceases offering sacrifices for Rome
	Menahem ben Judah the Galilean claims the kingship; he is supported by the Sicarii
	Menahem is killed, and the Sicarii take over Masada
	Roman governor of Syria, Cestius Gallus, invades Judea but then conducts a costly retreat
	Josephus appointed as commander in Galilee
67	Josephus surrenders
	John of Gischala goes to Jerusalem
Winter 67–68	Zealots enter Jerusalem and take control
Spring 68	All of Judea except Jerusalem controlled by the Romans
	Qumran attacked and the community destroyed
Spring 69	Zealots confined to the inner temple
	Simon bar Giora invited into Jerusalem and John is confined to the outer temple area
	Temple and city are divided among revolutionary groups
Summer 69	Vespasian becomes emperor
	Titus becomes commander of the forces in Judea
Summer 70	Jerusalem falls; city and temple are destroyed
73	Masada falls to the Romans

DIVINE SIGNS

After narrating Jerusalem's fall, Josephus says that there had been numerous supernatural signs predicting the city's doom, but that those who should have been able to read the signs misled the people, giving them false hope.

> At the feast which is called Pentecost, the priests on entering the inner court of the temple by night, as their custom was in the discharge of their ministrations, reported that they were conscious, first of a commotion and a din, and after that of a voice as of a host, "We are departing hence." (*J. W.* 6.299–300)

The words "We are departing hence" recall God's departure from the temple in Ezekiel, before the Babylonians destroyed Jerusalem and its temple (Ezek 9–11). Josephus blames God's abandonment of the second temple not on the Jews as a whole but on the insurgents, especially the Zealots, who defiled the holy city.

There was another means by which Josephus claims that God told the Jews that they did not have divine support for their revolt:

> Four years before the war, when the city was enjoying profound peace and prosperity, there came to the feast at which it is the custom of all Jews to erect tabernacles to God, one Jesus, son of Ananias, a rude peasant, who, standing in the temple, suddenly began to cry out, "A voice from the east, a voice from the west, a voice from the four winds; a voice against Jerusalem and the sanctuary, a voice against the bridegroom and the bride, a voice against all the people." Day and night he went about all the alleys with this cry on his lips. Some of the leading citizens, incensed at these ill-omened words, arrested the fellow and severely chastised him. But he, without a word on his own behalf or for the private ear of those who smote him, only continued as before. Thereupon, the magistrates, supposing, as was indeed the case, that the man was under some supernatural impulse, brought him before the Roman governor; there, although flayed to the bone with scourges, he neither sued for mercy nor shed a tear, but, merely introducing the most mournful of variations into his ejaculation, responded to each stroke with "Woe to Jerusalem!" When Albinus, the governor, asked him who and whence he was and why he uttered these cries, he answered him never a word, but unceasingly reiterated his dirge over the city, until Albinus pronounced him a maniac and let him go. During the whole period up to the outbreak of war he neither approached nor was seen talking to any of the citizens, but daily, like a prayer that he had conned, repeated his lament, "Woe to Jerusalem!" He neither cursed any of those who beat him from day to day, nor blessed those who offered him food: to all men that melancholy presage was his one reply. His cries were the loudest at the festivals. So for seven years and five months he continued his wail, his voice never flagging nor his

strength exhausted, until in the siege, having seen his presage verified, he found his rest. For, while going his round and shouting in piercing tones from the wall, "Woe once more to the city and to the people and to the temple," as he added his last word, "and woe to me also," a stone hurled from the *ballista* struck and killed him on the spot. So with those ominous words still upon his lips he passed away. (*J. W.* 6.300–309)

There are numerous parallels between this account and traditions about Jesus Christ: the name Jesus; the message about the destruction of Jerusalem; the supernatural origins of the message; the movement from the countryside to the city to deliver the message; the charge of insanity by some; the investigation before Jewish authorities followed by the appearance before the Roman governor; the scourging; the silence before their accusers; the importance of the context of a Jewish feast; the imagery of bride and bridegroom. Of course, there are major differences as well. The parallels are noted only to bring home the fact that Jesus of Nazareth was a person of his own times and was similar, in many ways, to his contemporaries.

THE FORTRESS OF MASADA

Masada was not taken by the Romans until 73. During most of the war, it was occupied by the Sicarii under the command of Eleazar son of Jair,

Relief from the Arch of Titus in the Roman Forum depicting the triumphal march celebrating Titus's victory over the Jewish rebels in Jerusalem in 70 C.E. Clearly visible is the seven-branched menorah from the temple.

another descendant of Judah the Galilean. The fortress held out for so long because it was built on a high hill with very steep sides and was well supplied. Before it fell, its last defenders committed suicide, a fate considered more honorable than submission to the Romans.

BETWEEN THE REVOLTS, 73–135

The fall of Jerusalem and its temple in 70 marks the end of the Second Temple period. A brief sketch of the next sixty-five years indicates the direction Judaism took after the destruction. The sources that date from this period are scarce and give little historical information.

After the war, the area received a governor of senatorial status, and so it was no longer subject to the province of Syria. The Romans recognized that the area needed more direct attention and that rule through members of the equestrian order had not worked. The Sanhedrin no longer existed. The city of Jerusalem had been heavily damaged, and it became a Roman military encampment.

After some decades, Jews in parts of the Diaspora revolted against Rome (115–117). Just as the Diaspora Jews did not take part in the uprising of 66–70, so the Jews in the homeland did not participate in that of the Diaspora.

In 132, about fifteen years into Hadrian's reign (ruled 117–138), the Jews revolted again. We do not know for sure what started the war, and the precise order of events is unclear. Some scholars, depending on a late Jewish legend, have claimed that Hadrian gave permission to rebuild the temple and then revoked it, but this theory is now recognized as unhistorical. Two other potential causes have been put forward. First, Hadrian issued a decree against circumcision that was not aimed at the Jews in particular but was an attempt to stamp out what many in the empire considered to be a barbarous practice. (Hadrian's successor, Antoninus Pius, revoked the decree.) Second, Hadrian's plans to turn Jerusalem into a Greek-Roman city, complete with a temple to Jupiter (the chief Roman god), may have provoked the Jews.

The revolt lasted until 135. Its leader was Simon bar Kosiba. A pun on his name turned it into Bar Kokhba, Aramaic for "Son of a Star." This is probably an allusion to his messianic claims. Numbers 24:17 mentions a star that will arise from Jacob; this star was interpreted messianically during the period discussed here (see the *Messianic Anthology* [4QTest] from Qumran). Tradition has it that Rabbi Akiba, a prominent teacher of the period, acknowledged Bar Kokhba as the Messiah. One of Bar Kokhba's coins features a star over the temple, suggesting that a rebuilt temple was one of his goals. Documents from the Judean desert indicate that restoration of traditional religion was a priority of Bar Kokhba.

The close of the war in 135 brought retribution on the Jews, but its details are unclear. Circumcision was forbidden. This stricture was so odious to the Jews that it caused yet another uprising under the next emperor, Antoninus Pius, who rescinded the order. Hadrian built a new city on the site of Jerusalem. It was named Aelia Capitolina—Aelia after Hadrian's family and Capitolina after Jupiter Capitolinus. Jews were forbidden under pain of death to enter the city except on the Day of Atonement to mourn the loss of the temple.

THE BEGINNINGS OF RABBINIC JUDAISM

The war against the Romans completely changed the face of Jewish society in the land of Israel. The priestly elite lost its power base when Jerusalem and the temple were destroyed. The Qumran community was attacked and destroyed by the Romans around 68. With the decrease of the power, land, and wealth of the Judean aristocracy, the Sadducees faded from view. The Jerusalem Sanhedrin no longer existed. Some of the Sicarii fled to the Diaspora, where they fomented further disturbances, but they were soon eliminated (*J.W.* 7.409–419; 7.437–440). Other groups, such as the Zealots, were neutralized.

During the war, a prominent Pharisee named Yohanan ben Zakkai, a member of the antiwar faction, escaped from Jerusalem and obtained Roman permission to go to the coastal city of Yavneh (also called Jamnia) to found a school. Yohanan and his school survived the war, and when peace came, he gathered to himself many of the surviving Pharisees, scribes, and priests. The Pharisees dominated at Yavneh, and they were poised to take the reins of leadership after the war. They had always been a political interest group, and prominent Pharisees were engaged in the governing of Israel at various points in its history. Their claim to true interpretation of Torah amounted to a claim for the right to implement Torah as the constitution and law of Israel.

The Pharisaic worldview offered hope after the war. Yohanan taught that atonement could be attained through prayer, fasting, and good works and so was possible without the temple. Rules for sanctification of the temple and of those who participated in its liturgies were widened to include everyday Jewish life, especially food, its production, and its consumption. This afforded the Jews a powerful symbolic system and set of practices to embody the belief that they were God's chosen people and therefore holy. It also enabled the maintenance of Jewish identity in the face of loss of territorial nationhood. Distinctive practices would mark the Jews as a special people, and since these practices were based on Torah, they were divinely ordained.

After the war, the experts in Torah who became the authorities in Judaism became known as rabbis; "rabbi" literally means "my great one" but can be roughly translated as "teacher." The parts of Torah dealing with the temple and cult received special attention from the rabbis even though the cult was not in operation and the temple no longer existed. There was still hope for the restoration of the temple, of course, but even beyond this motive was the strong belief that all of Torah came directly from God and deserved detailed explanation. Increased concentration on Torah led to standardization of the list of books that were considered authoritative, or canonical. There was also a move to standardize the text of the Hebrew Bible.

Pharisaic oral traditions afforded Judaism a vehicle through which new ideas and new interpretations of Torah could enter. Over time, the interpretations themselves assumed the authority of Torah. This authority was expressed in the later rabbinic notion of Oral Torah. The idea was that God gave Moses both a written Torah and an Oral Torah on Sinai. The written Torah was contained in the Hebrew Bible, while the Oral Torah was passed down from generation to generation and finally written down in the rabbinic documents called the Mishnah (ca. 200 C.E.), the Tosefta (written shortly after the Mishnah), the Jerusalem Talmud (ca. 400 C.E.), and the Babylonian Talmud (ca. 600 C.E.).

Belief in resurrection was not exclusively Pharisaic, but its acceptance by Pharisaism made the Pharisaic worldview helpful for a defeated people needing hope. It is possible that many Pharisees still hoped for a messiah. If so, then Pharisaic belief also gave the people a this-worldly hope that may have contributed to the second revolt against Rome. After the second devastating defeat, however, messianic hopes were treated cautiously. Most apocalyptic texts of Second Temple Judaism were preserved not by Jews but by Christians, for whom the apocalyptic worldview furnished a context for belief about Christ. But apocalyptic images and ideas did contribute substantially to later Jewish mysticism.

All of this being said, it must be emphasized that it took some time for the rabbinic movement to develop, and it took longer still for it to come to dominate Judaism. That story is best told by experts in the rabbinic texts. Especially important is the work of Jacob Neusner and his students.

4 EZRA

Fourth Ezra is a Jewish apocalypse written as a response to the destruction of Jerusalem by the Romans. It expresses an eloquent and anguished struggle with the issues raised by the catastrophe. *Fourth Ezra* consists of chapters 3–14 of 2 Esdras, which is part of the Apocrypha. Chapters 1–2 and 15–16 of 2 Esdras are later Christian additions to the Jewish apocalypse.

Fourth Ezra attempts to reconcile the disaster with divine justice. Such defenses of divine justice are called theodicies. It was probably written in the homeland sometime around 100. The aftermath of the Jewish revolt is the historical context for the writing of the apocalypse, but the fictional setting of the book is the destruction and exile under the Babylonians in the sixth century B.C.E. The first destruction became paradigmatic for the second. In typically apocalyptic fashion, the destruction of the second temple is put into perspective by seeing it as the playing out of a pattern that goes beyond the particular event. The perspective supplied by this analogy allows the readers (Jews distressed over the events of 70) to see their own time in the context of the broad sweep of history and of God's plans for the cosmos. The book demonstrates how apocalypticism supplied a solution for the problems raised by Jerusalem's fall.

Fourth Ezra has seven sections. The first three are dialogues between Ezra (the priestly scribe who brought the Torah from Persia to Judah) and the angel Uriel. In these dialogues, Ezra complains bitterly against God. Sections 4–6 are a series of visions. In section 4, the central section of the book, Ezra undergoes a conversion in which he comes to accept God's ways. Ezra's movement from desolation to consolation is a key element in the apocalypse and is intended to cause the same transformation in *4 Ezra's* readers (see Breech). The remaining visions interpret Israel's present and reveal the future. Section 7 is an epilogue in which God speaks directly to Ezra.

The Structure of *4 Ezra*

Section 1	3:1–5:19	Ezra's dialogue with Uriel
Section 2	5:20–6:34	Ezra's second dialogue with Uriel
Section 3	6:35–9:25	Ezra's third dialogue with Uriel
Section 4	9:26–10:59	Vision of the woman who becomes Zion
Section 5	10:60–12:51	The eagle (Rome) and the lion (Messiah)
Section 6	13:1–58	Battles involving the one like a son of man
Section 7	14:1–48	Rewriting of the public and secret books

SECTION 1 (3:1–5:19)

Fourth Ezra begins,

In the thirtieth year after the destruction of the city, I was in Babylon—I, Salathiel, who am also called Ezra. I was troubled as I lay on my bed, and my thoughts welled up in my heart, because I saw the desolation of Zion and the wealth of those who lived in Babylon. (3:1–2)

Ezra has his first vision while lying on his bed at night, just as Daniel does (Dan 7:1). The problem Ezra ponders as he lies on his bed is the desolation of Zion (the temple built on Mount Zion and Jerusalem) and the distress of the Jewish people. The desolation contrasts with Rome's prosperity.

Because he is distraught over Zion's misfortune, Ezra prays. His prayer reviews history, starting with creation and leading up to the "present," the destruction of Jerusalem by the Babylonians. The review is pessimistic, stressing the failure of almost everyone to obey God's will. The cause of the failure is the evil inclination in human hearts:

> Yet you did not take away their evil heart from them, so that your law might produce fruit in them. For the first Adam, burdened with an evil heart, transgressed and was overcome, as were also all who were descended from him. Thus the disease became permanent; the law was in the hearts of the people along with the evil root; but what was good departed, and the evil remained. (3:20–22)

God could have made humans differently, but God left the evil inclination in place. God thus left humanity powerless to obey Torah, and so, ultimately, God is responsible for sin.

Israel's sinfulness makes its punishment understandable, but Ezra's experience of Babylon (Rome) throws God's justice into question: "Then I said in my heart, Are the deeds of those who inhabit Babylon any better? Is that why she has gained dominion over Zion?" (3:28). The obvious answer is, No. Ezra challenges God to find any nation on earth that is righteous, and says, "You may indeed find individuals who have kept your commandments, but nations you will not find" (3:36).

At the conclusion of Ezra's prayer, Uriel confronts him and says that he will answer Ezra's questions if Ezra solves three problems: "Go, weigh for me the weight of fire, or measure for me a blast of wind, or call back for me the day that is past" (4:5). Of course, Ezra is at a loss. Uriel responds, "You cannot understand the things with which you have grown up; how then can your mind comprehend the way of the Most High?" (4:10–11). Ezra is not deterred and says bitterly, "It would have been better for us not to be here than to come here and live in ungodliness, and to suffer and not understand why" (4:12). Using the analogy that trees cannot conquer the sea nor the sea conquer the forest, Uriel says, "Those who inhabit the earth can understand only what is on the earth, and he who is above the heavens can understand what is above the height of the heavens" (4:21). (This discussion is similar to that in

John 3 between Jesus and Nicodemus; see esp. John 3:8–13.) The events into which Ezra inquires cannot be comprehended without knowledge of what happens above the heavens, where God is. This is typically apocalyptic. Uriel's emphasis on the inadequacy of human knowledge and reason to penetrate God's mysteries is a way of expressing Jewish despair at making sense of the tragedy and of establishing that special revelation is the only way to understand it.

Ezra is unwilling to admit that the answers to his questions require esoteric knowledge:

> I implore you, my lord, why have I been endowed with the power of understanding? For I did not wish to inquire about the ways above, but about those things that we daily experience: why Israel has been given over to the Gentiles in disgrace; why the people whom you loved has been given over to godless tribes, and the law of our ancestors has been brought to destruction and the written covenants no longer exist. We pass from the world like locusts, and our life is like a mist, and we are not worthy to obtain mercy. But what will he do for his name that is invoked over us? It is about these things that I have asked. (4:22–25)

In the apocalyptic outlook, direct revelation of God's plans is the only way to comprehend what happens on earth. At this point, Ezra does not grasp that.

The rest of the vision consists of revelations of the future. At the end of time, the good will receive their reward, and the evil their punishment. Chapter 5 enumerates the traditional apocalyptic signs of the end, among them cosmic disturbances: "The sun shall suddenly begin to shine at night, and the moon during the day. Blood shall drip from wood, and the stone shall utter its voice; the peoples shall be troubled, and the stars shall fall" (5:4–5). (Similar cosmic images are ascribed to Jesus in Mark 13; see also *T. Mos.* 10.)

SECTION 2 (5:20–6:34)

The second section begins with a prayer of Ezra reminding God that Israel is the chosen people yet it has been brought lower than any other nation. In the ensuing dialogue, the angel reminds Ezra that he cannot understand God's ways. The rest of the section stresses that God has a plan older than creation and that God's imminent intervention will affect the whole universe. In 6:20, we again encounter the idea of heavenly books that will serve as the basis of judgment. The judgment will be preceded by the usual apocalyptic signs.

SECTION 3 (6:35–9:25)

The third section begins with a prayer of Ezra recalling the six days of creation and reminding God that all was created for Israel's sake. The angel agrees that God made the world for Israel, but says that Israel must pass through dangers in order to inherit the world. He uses the analogies of a river that must go through narrow passages to reach the wide sea, and of a city that can be reached only through a narrow and difficult entrance (cf. Jesus' words in Matt 7:13–14). Ezra pities sinners, who are the vast majority of humanity. Uriel reproaches Ezra for questioning God's judgment and says, "Let many perish who are now living, rather than that the law of God that is set before them be disregarded!" (7:20).

Next comes an eschatological timetable:

> For my son the Messiah shall be revealed with those who are with him, and those who remain shall rejoice four hundred years. After these years my son the Messiah shall die, and all who draw human breath. Then the world shall be turned back to primeval silence for seven days, as it was at the first beginnings, so that no one shall be left. After seven days the world that is not yet awake shall be roused, and that which is corruptible shall perish. (7:28–31)

After this comes resurrection, judgment, rewards, and punishments. The Messiah is human, since he is mortal. He is called God's son, as is the Davidic king in 2 Sam 7 and Psalm 2. This passage in *4 Ezra* represents the combination of the hope for the establishment of an earthly messiah with the expectation that this world will pass away and a new one take its place. There will be a messianic kingdom of four hundred years, followed by the reduction of all to the silence that reigned before creation. Then there will be a new beginning and a new world.

This does not comfort Ezra. News of a future world comforts only those who will enjoy it. They are such a tiny minority that Ezra is left with his grief. Uriel is unmoved: "For this reason the Most High has made not one world but two" (7:50). Ezra should look to the future world and not fasten on this one. Uriel has no pity for sinners who get what they deserve. Ezra despairs because he is convinced that almost all humanity is sinful. He even goes further and claims that *everyone* is unrighteous: "For all who have been born are entangled in iniquities, and are full of sins and burdened with transgressions" (7:68). In response to an appeal to God's mercy, the angel says,

> The Most High made this world for the sake of many, but the world to come for the sake of only a few. But I tell you a parable, Ezra. Just as, when you ask the earth, it will tell you that it provides a large amount of clay from which

earthenware is made, but only a little dust from which gold comes, so is the course of the present world. Many have been created, but only a few shall be saved. (8:1–3)

This passage recalls the words of Jesus: "Many are called, but few are chosen" (Matt 22:14). Uriel discloses that Ezra is among the righteous.

SECTION 4 (9:26–10:59)

This section is the turning point because here Ezra turns from despair to acceptance of the angel's message. Ezra prays about Israel's situation, then he spies a woman in deep mourning over the death of her son. Ezra reproaches her:

You most foolish of women, do you not see our mourning, and what has happened to us? For Zion, the mother of us all, is in deep grief and great distress. . . . For if you acknowledge the decree of God to be just, you will receive your son back in due time, and will be praised among women. (10:6–7, 16)

The woman refuses to be diverted from her grief. Ezra continues,

Let yourself be persuaded—for how many are the adversities of Zion?—and be consoled because of the sorrow of Jerusalem. For you see how our sanctuary has been laid waste, our altar thrown down, our temple destroyed; our harp has been laid low, our song has been silenced, and our rejoicing has been ended; the light of our lampstand has been put out, the ark of our covenant has been plundered, our holy things have been polluted, and the name by which we are called has been almost profaned; our children have suffered abuse, our priests have been burned to death, our Levites have gone into exile, our virgins have been defiled, and our wives have been ravished; our righteous men have been carried off, our little ones have been cast out, our young men have been enslaved and our strong men made powerless. And, worst of all, the seal of Zion has been deprived of its glory, and given over into the hands of those that hate us. (10:20–23)

Ezra utters a litany of Israel's losses. It is a moving expression of the desolation the Jews suffered because of the revolt. Central to Ezra's concern is the loss of the cult.

Suddenly the woman becomes a large city with "huge foundations." Uriel appears and supplies an allegorical explanation of the vision of the woman and the city, the key element of which is the identification of the woman as Zion, mourning over the destruction of Jerusalem. The woman's transformation into a city symbolizes Jerusalem's restoration.

After this vision and interpretation, Ezra no longer challenges God's judgments. Somehow his experience has reconciled him to God's ways. Precisely how this takes place is disputed. Perhaps in the act of consoling the woman who turns out to be Zion, Ezra sees his own sorrow in a new light. Perhaps Ezra finds comfort in seeing the future-restored city. The end result is that he takes the very advice he offers the woman, acknowledging the decree of God to be just. Now Ezra can do what the angel has encouraged him to do all along, that is, turn his attention to the future. He now becomes the recipient and the conveyor of revelation.

SECTION 5 (10:60–12:51)

This section is a vision and interpretation. It contains the kind of strange imagery seen in the book of Daniel. The central figure is an eagle, the symbol of Rome. Then a lion appears. The lion makes a speech to the eagle that begins,

> Listen and I will speak to you. The Most High says to you, "Are you not the one that remains of the four beasts that I had made to reign in my world, so that the end of my times might come through them? You, the fourth that has come, have conquered all the beasts that have gone before; and you have held sway over the world with great terror, and over all the earth with grievous oppression; and for so long you have dwelt on the earth with deceit. You have judged the earth, but not with truth, for you have oppressed the meek and injured the peaceable; you have hated those who tell the truth, and have loved liars; you have destroyed the homes of those who brought forth fruit, and have laid low the walls of those who did you no harm." (11:38–42)

Rome's hegemony is portrayed harshly. *Fourth Ezra* details here for the first time Rome's social injustice. God's sovereignty is asserted by the lion's claim that Rome is but one of the powers to which God gave power. Rome's power serves God's purposes, as it brings the end of times, planned by God. Its rule is interpreted within a pattern of four kingdoms, a pattern known from Dan 2, 7, and other Hellenistic documents. The four-kingdom scheme puts the present kingdom into historical perspective. After the succession of kingdoms comes liberation through God. By appealing to this pattern with its deep roots in Israel and the ancient Near East, the message of hope resonates in the people's consciousness. The lion announces to the eagle that the Most High has noted its injustices and will soon destroy its kingdom. In the interpretation of the vision (12:10–35), the eagle's heads and wings represent kings. Then the lion is interpreted as the messiah, son of David. The Davidic messiah plays the role of judge of Israel's oppressor.

SECTION 6 (13:1–58)

The section begins with a night dream of Ezra:

> And lo, a wind arose from the sea and stirred up all its waves. As I kept looking the wind made something like the figure of a man come up out of the heart of the sea. And I saw that this man flew with the clouds of heaven; and wherever he turned his face to look, everything under his gaze trembled, and whenever his voice issued from his mouth, all who heard his voice melted as wax melts when it feels the fire.

> After this I looked and saw that an innumerable multitude of people were gathered together from the four winds of heaven to make war against the man who came up out of the sea. And I looked and saw that he carved out for himself a great mountain, and flew up on to it. (13:2–7)

The passage depends upon Dan 7. It draws on Daniel's images of the one like a son of man accompanied by clouds, and of the mystery and power of the sea. A crowd of humans from all over the earth gathers to fight the one like a man. In the next verses, the man causes a stream of fire to destroy his enemies, so that only ashes are left. Then the man descends from the mountain and gathers to himself a peaceable crowd.

Uriel interprets the man from the sea as the Messiah, God's son, whom God has hidden until the last days. At the eschaton, the messiah ascends Mount Zion, judges the wicked, and liberates Israel. The wicked are the assembled nations, and the peaceable crowd is the lost tribes of Israel, exiled in 721 B.C.E. (13:35–40). The idea that God's enemies wage a final, huge battle against God's forces is common in apocalypses, and it appears also in Ezek 38–39. The site of the battle is Mount Zion. When asked why the man arose from the sea, Uriel explains, "Just as no one can explore or know what is in the depths of the sea, so no one on earth can see my Son or those who are with him, except in the time of his day" (13:52). Only Ezra is given the secret because he has been loyal to Torah and loves wisdom (13:53–56).

SECTION 7 (14:1–48)

Now God speaks to Ezra. "On the third day, while I was sitting under an oak, suddenly a voice came out of a bush opposite me and said, 'Ezra, Ezra!' And I answered, 'Here I am, Lord,' and I rose to my feet. Then he said to me, 'I revealed myself in a bush and spoke to Moses when my people were in bondage in Egypt' " (14:1–3). The parallel between Ezra and Moses is obvious. The apocalypse reaches back into Israel's sacred traditions to find paradigms for God's action. God says concerning Moses, "I told him many wondrous things, and showed him the secrets of the times and declared to him the end of the times. Then I commanded him, saying, 'These words you shall publish openly, and these you shall keep secret' " (14:5–8). So Moses allegedly received precisely the kind of eschatological knowledge granted to Ezra. Moses is told that he must publish some of the revelation, presumably the Torah, and that he must keep the esoteric knowledge hidden, corresponding to the "secret" knowledge in apocalypses.

Ezra reminds God that the Torah and the secret revelations to Moses no longer exist. They perished in the destruction of Jerusalem. He says, "Send the holy spirit into me, and I will write everything that has happened in the world from the beginning, the things that were written in your law" (14:22). The Torah contains the whole history of the world. God agrees with Ezra's proposal. He tells Ezra to instruct the people not to seek him for forty days (the length of time Moses spent on Sinai receiving the Torah), to gather five skilled scribes, and to bring them to God. God will dictate things to be published (Torah), and things to be kept secret (esoteric knowledge).

> A voice called me, saying, "Ezra, open your mouth and drink what I give you to drink." So I opened my mouth, and a full cup was offered to me; it was full of something like water, but its color was like fire. I took it and drank; and when I had drunk it, my heart poured forth understanding, and wisdom increased in my breast, for my spirit retained its memory, and my mouth was opened and was no longer closed. Moreover, the Most High gave understanding to the five men, and by turns they wrote what was dictated, using characters that they did not know. They sat forty days; they wrote during the daytime, and ate their bread at night. But as for me, I spoke in the daytime and was not silent at night. So during the forty days, ninety-four books were written. And when the forty days were ended, the Most High spoke to me, saying, "Make public the twenty-four books that you wrote first, and let the worthy and the unworthy read them; but keep the seventy that were written last, in order to give them to the wise among your people. For in them is the spring of understanding, the fountain of wisdom, and the river of knowledge." And I did so. (14:38–48)

So ends *4 Ezra.* Ezra, under the power of the Holy Spirit, dictates the complete body of divine revelation conveyed to Moses but lost in the destruction of Jerusalem. The twenty-four published books are the Hebrew Bible. The seventy unpublished books are even more important than the public Torah. For *4 Ezra,* they contain the true spring of understanding. Torah is the word of God, but the esoteric knowledge obtained by the seer is also direct revelation, and it surpasses Torah because it is the secret wisdom necessary for grasping God's plans. This claim for secret revelation is striking.

This book offers an apocalyptic solution to the problem of the destruction of Jerusalem. Ezra voices the concerns and complaints that many Jews of the postwar era felt. Uriel repeatedly tells Ezra to stop concentrating on present woes and look to the brilliant but hidden future. Ezra is finally convinced to accept God's will when he tours the future city of God. From then on, he becomes a willing recipient of apocalyptic knowledge. As with other apocalyptic works, *4 Ezra* consoles and exhorts by putting things into historical and cosmological perspective. To restrict oneself to looking at worldly events leads to despair. Knowledge of heavenly secrets produces hope and understanding.

2 BARUCH

Second Baruch is another apocalyptic response to the destruction of Jerusalem, written around the same time as *4 Ezra*. Baruch was the secretary of the prophet Jeremiah, who lived before and during the destruction of Jerusalem in the sixth century B.C.E. The earlier destruction is the paradigm for interpreting the second, as in *4 Ezra*. There are many points of contact between *4 Ezra* and *2 Baruch* that make some sort of relationship between them likely, but the nature of the relationship is disputed.

This section will not analyze *2 Baruch* in detail, as was done with *4 Ezra*. Rather, it will examine several key passages that deal directly with the fall of Jerusalem and Israel's situation after the fall.

Second Baruch's basic solution to the loss of Jerusalem is apocalyptic, as is *4 Ezra*'s. Another world is coming that rewards the good and punishes the evil. The destruction of Jerusalem is punishment for Israel's sins, but it also helps to hasten the eschaton. The movement from distress to comfort that the book seeks to effect in its readers is embodied in Baruch himself. In the first sections, he is at the point of despair over the destruction of Zion, but as the book progresses, he accepts God's will and encourages his fellow Jews. As in *4 Ezra,* the seer voices thoughts that are answered and often corrected by an angel or by God.

The book opens with God telling Baruch that Jerusalem is about to fall because of the people's sins. Baruch's response embodies Zion theology:

O Lord, my Lord, have I come into the world for this purpose that I might see the evils of my mother? Not so, my Lord. If I have found grace in your sight, first take my spirit, that I may go to my fathers and not behold the destruction of my mother. For two things vehemently constrain me: for I cannot resist you, and my soul, moreover, cannot behold the evils of my mother. But one thing I will say in your presence, O Lord. What, therefore, will there be after these things? For if you destroy your city, and deliver up your land to those that hate us, how shall the name of Israel be remembered? Or how shall one speak of your praises? Or to whom shall that which is in your law be explained? Or shall the world return to its former nature, and the age revert to primeval silence? And shall the multitude of souls be taken away, and the nature of man not again be named? And where is all that which you said to Moses concerning us? (3:1–9)

For Baruch, the loss of Jerusalem has dire implications. It means the destruction of Israel and the cessation of God's worship. There will be no one to listen to Torah, the world may cease to exist, humanity will perish, and the promises to Moses will be nullified. Such an extreme reaction is a reminder of the central role of Jerusalem and the temple in Israel's history as a people and in priestly religion as a worldview. The temple was the site of both God's presence with his people and the Creator's presence to his creation. In the ancient world, temples and the mountains on which they were situated were often thought to have cosmic significance (see Clifford).

God says that Jerusalem's destruction is temporary, as is the coming exile, and that the world will not pass out of existence. God goes on to say,

Do you think that this is that city of which I said: "On the palms of my hands I have graven you"? This building now built in your midst is not that which is revealed with me, that which was prepared beforehand here from the time when I took counsel to make Paradise, and showed it to Adam before he sinned, but when he transgressed the commandment it was removed from him, as also Paradise. And after these things I showed it to My servant Abraham by night among the portions of the victims. And again also I showed it to Moses on Mount Sinai when I showed to him the likeness of the tabernacle and all its vessels. And now, behold, it is preserved with me, as also Paradise. (4:2–6)

God quotes from Isa 49:16, where God's complete devotion to Jerusalem is expressed vividly. Yet Baruch hears that God is about to destroy Zion. God's words reconcile Zion theology with Jerusalem's ruin: The divine oracle in Isaiah never applied to the earthly Zion in the first place. There is a heavenly sanctuary to which God's promises applied. This draws on the ancient Near Eastern idea that earthly temples have heavenly counterparts. In 2 Baruch, it is the heavenly temple that matters. Second Baruch never says that the heavenly temple will descend to earth. The importance of the earthly temple is downplayed throughout in favor of the heavenly world. Although an earthly messianic kingdom is anticipated (chs. 72–74), it is but a prelude to the next world. In chapter 51, the faithful go to heaven and live with the stars.

Baruch objects that if the Gentiles conquer Jerusalem and pollute the sanctuary, it will reflect badly on God's name. Although this may seem a strange argument to modern ears—that God's reputation might be harmed by Israel's fate—it appears several places in the Hebrew Bible (e.g., Exod 32:9–14; Num 14:10b–25; 16:19b–24; Ezek 36:20–38; see Murphy, *Structure*, 72–77). God replies that the divine name, which is eternal, is unaffected by such events. God adds that divine judgment will descend on the destroyers in due time. In the meanwhile, Baruch is assured that it is not the Gentiles who will destroy Zion. Rather, angels will destroy Jerusalem lest the enemy boast. Then "a voice was heard from the interior of the temple, after the wall had fallen, saying: 'Enter, you enemies, and come, you adversaries; for he who kept the house has forsaken it' " (8:1–2). As Ezekiel says about its fall in 587 B.C.E. (Ezek 9–11) and as Josephus says about the destruction of 70 C.E. (*J. W.* 6.299–300), *2 Baruch* asserts that God left the temple before it fell. If God leaves, the temple falls.

Second Baruch blames the people and especially the priests (10:18) for Jerusalem's destruction, which is God's punishment. But as in the Hebrew Bible, the agents of God's wrath, in this case the Romans, do not escape unscathed. They themselves will be punished for their deeds against Israel (*2 Bar.* 12–14). God, however, counsels attention to proper obedience to Torah instead of preoccupation with the defeat of Israel's enemies (see Murphy, "Romans").

In chapter 44, Baruch addresses the people. Baruch first says that he is about to die. He exhorts the people to obey the Law, using Zion's destruction as an example of the consequences of disobedience. The rest of the speech contrasts the present world, corruptible, passing, full of sorrows, with the future world, eternal and full of hope: "Because whatever is now is nothing, but that which shall be is very great" (44:8). The people react fearfully to the news of Baruch's impending death: "For where again shall we seek the law, or who will distinguish for us between death and life?" (46:3) As Moses says in Deut 30:15–20, the choice of whether to obey Torah is a choice between life and death.

> There shall not be wanting to Israel a wise man nor a son of the law to the race of Jacob. But only prepare your hearts, that you may obey the law, and be subject to those who in fear are wise and understanding; and prepare your souls that you may not depart from them. For if you do these things, good tidings shall come to you. (46:4–6)

The major trait of the wise man is that he knows Torah. The presence of the wise in Israel is crucial because it makes obedience to the Law possible.

In chapter 77, Baruch addresses the people, urging them to obey Torah. They promise to do so, but utter another lament over their loss:

> For the shepherds of Israel have perished,
> And the lamps that gave light are extinguished,
>   and the fountains have withheld their stream where we used to drink.
> And we are left in the darkness,
> And amid the trees of the forest,
> And the thirst of the wilderness. (77:13–14)

Baruch answers them,

> Shepherds and lamps and fountains come from the law:
> And though we depart, yet the law abides.
> If therefore you have respect to the law,
> And are intent upon wisdom,
> A lamp will not be wanting,
> And a shepherd will not fail,
> And a fountain will not dry up. (77:15–16)

Chapters 78–86 are a letter of Baruch to the exiled northern tribes. He recalls that formerly Israel had righteous men and prophets. "But now the righteous have been gathered, and the prophets have fallen asleep, and we also have gone forth from the land, and Zion has been taken from us, and we have nothing now save the Mighty One and His law" (85:3). This verse aptly describes Israel after 70 C.E. The rest of the letter exhorts the people to prepare their souls by submission to God and thereby to escape this corruptible world and inherit the future glorious world.

Second Baruch expects rewards and punishments after death. Thus, its ultimate solution to the problem that in this life the good suffer while the evil prosper is apocalyptic, as in *4 Ezra*. But also as in *4 Ezra*, *2 Baruch* expects a messiah. In *2 Baruch* this messiah will slay Israel's oppressors (29:2; 40; 72).

CONCLUSION

The destruction of Jerusalem and its temple by the Romans in 70 C.E. was a watershed in Jewish history, comparable only to the earlier destruction by the Babylonians in the sixth century B.C.E. Before 70, the Jews had a land of their own and a physical temple staffed by priests and Levites in which a sacrificial cult was performed. They lost all this. But they were not caught unprepared. Even before 70, Jewish groups were developing ways of living as Jews that could survive the loss of land, temple, and sacrifices. The Torahcenteredness of Judaism made possible the reconstitution of Judaism around written Torah and its interpretation. The Pharisees were especially well equipped to remold Judaism according to their own worldview, and the post-war teachers, now called rabbis, were particularly influenced by Pharisaic teaching and practices.

Apocalypticism afforded comfort to some Jews after Jerusalem's fall. Apocalyptic solutions to Israel's situation are found in *4 Ezra, 2 Baruch*, and also another work: the *Apocalypse of Abraham,* which we have not analyzed. Hopes for a restoration of Israel in this world were kept alive between 70 and 132 and may have played a role in the second Jewish uprising of 132–135. After that time, apocalyptic expectations were discouraged by the rabbis, for the most part. Judaism was now to concentrate on the sanctification of every-day life and on the maintenance of a Jewish identity in the midst of a foreign and often hostile world.

SELECT BIBLIOGRAPHY

Aberbach, M. *The Roman-Jewish War (66–70 A.D.): Its Origins and Conse-quences.* London: R. Golub, 1966.

Breech, E. "These Fragments I Have Shored against My Ruins: The Form and Function of *4 Ezra.*" *JBL* 92 (1973): 267–74.

Clifford, Richard. *The Cosmic Mountain in Canaan and the Old Testament.* Cambridge: Harvard University Press, 1972.

Cohen, Shaye J. D. *Josephus in Galilee and Rome.* Leiden: Brill: 1979.

———. "The Significance of Yavneh: Pharisees, Rabbis, and the End of Jew-ish Sectarianism." *HUCA* 55 (1984): 36–41.

Collins, John J. *The Scepter and the Star: The Messiahs of the Dead Sea Scrolls and Other Ancient Literature.* New York: Doubleday, 1995.

Goodman, Martin. *The Ruling Class of Judaea: The Origins of the Jewish Re-volt against Rome, A.D. 66–70.* Cambridge: Cambridge University Press, 1987.

Farmer, W. R. *Maccabees, Zealots, and Josephus: An Inquiry into Jewish Na-tionalism in the Greco-Roman Period.* Westport, Conn.: Greenwood Press, 1973.

Gruenwald, Ithamar. *Apocalyptic and Merkavah Mysticism.* Leiden: Brill, 1980.

Horsley, Richard A., and John S. Hanson. *Bandits, Prophets, and Messiahs: Popular Movements at the Time of Jesus.* Minneapolis: Winston, 1985.

Levine, L. I. "Jewish War (66–73 C.E.)." *ABD* 3:839–45.

Murphy, Frederick J. "*2 Baruch* and the Romans." *JBL* 104 (1985): 663–69.

———. *The Structure and Meaning of Second Baruch.* SBLDS 78. Atlanta: Scholars Press, 1985.

Neusner, Jacob. *First Century Judaism in Crisis: Yohanan ben Zakkai and the Renaissance of Torah.* New York: Ktav, 1982.

———. "The Formation of Rabbinic Judaism: Yavneh (Jamnia) from A.D. 70 to 100." *ANRW* 2.19.2:3–42.

Rhoads, David M. *Israel in Revolution: A Political History Based on the Writings of Josephus.* Philadelphia: Fortress, 1976.

Saldarini, Anthony J. "Reconstructions of Rabbinic Judaism." *EJMI* 437–77.

Sayler, Gwendolyn. *Have the Promises Failed? A Literary Analysis of 2 Baruch.* SBLDS 72. Chico, Calif.: Scholars Press, 1984.

Schürer, Emil. *The History of the Jewish People in the Age of Jesus Christ (175 B.C.–A.D. 135).* Revised and edited by Geza Vermes, Fergus Millar, and Matthew Black. 3 vols. Edinburgh: T&T Clark. 1973–1987.

Stone, Michael E. "The Concept of the Messiah in IV Ezra." Pages 295–312 in *Religions in Antiquity: Essays in Memory of E. R. Goodenough.* Edited by Jacob Neusner. Leiden: Brill, 1968.

———. Fourth Ezra: *A Commentary on the Book of* Fourth Ezra. Minneapolis: Fortress, 1990.

———. "Reactions to Destructions of the Second Temple: Theology, Perception, and Conversion." *JSJ* 12 (1981): 195–204.

Thompson, A. L. *Responsibility for Evil in the Theodicy of* IV Ezra. SBLDS 29. Missoula, Mont.: Scholars Press, 1977.

Yadin, Yigael. *Bar Kochba.* New York: Random House, 1971.

CHAPTER 11

JEWISH FOUNDATIONS OF NEW TESTAMENT VIEWS OF CHRIST

PRIMARY READINGS: Matthew ◆ Luke 1–2 ◆ Acts of the Apostles
◆ Hebrews ◆ Revelation

Every page of the New Testament attests to Christianity's deep roots in Second Temple Judaism. Our increased knowledge of Judaism in the time of Jesus makes the New Testament come alive. So many things we have learned about Jewish history, groups, concepts, symbols, institutions, traditions, and so on apply directly to the texts of Christian Scripture. This chapter chooses several texts to illustrate this point, but it is by no means complete or exhaustive. The reader is encouraged to go beyond the texts examined here to see how what we have learned about Second Temple Judaism enhances reading the New Testament.

THE GOSPEL OF MATTHEW: JESUS AS TEACHER OF TORAH

Matthew, written around 85 C.E., presents Jesus as a Torah teacher of supreme authority whose mission is only to Israel. Jesus teaches his apostles the true interpretation of Torah, and after his death and resurrection they bring this interpretation to all nations. The author was probably a Jewish Christian who did not conceive of Christianity as a new religion. Rather, Christianity for him was the true Israel, following the correct interpretation of Torah as taught by God's own representative, Jesus.

THE INFANCY NARRATIVE

Matthew 1–2 tells of the birth and infancy of Jesus. It opens thus: "An account of the genealogy of Jesus the Messiah, the Son of David, the son of Abraham" (1:1). Here Matthew presents two of Jesus' main credentials: Jesus is a true Jew, descended from Abraham, and he can be the Davidic Messiah because he is of David's line. The title "Son of David" receives more attention in this gospel than in any of the other gospels. The word translated "genealogy" here is the Greek word *genesis,* meaning "beginning" or "origin." Matthew may be alluding to the first book of the Torah, Genesis. There follows a genealogy of Jesus illustrating that he is truly son of Abraham and Son of David. A genealogy is a chronological list of one's ancestors. Genealogies were especially important in postexilic Judaism, where it was crucial to define the community (see Hanson and Oakman, 26–31). We have seen the crucial role genealogies play in Ezra and Nehemiah (see also Gen 5, 10, 11).

The rest of the Infancy Narrative is structured around formula quotations, a frequent form in Matthew. A *formula quotation* is a citation of the Hebrew Bible, accompanied by a formulaic statement that Jesus fulfills the passage cited. According to Matthew, the following items fulfill predictions in the Hebrew Bible: Jesus was born of a virgin (1:22–23), in Bethlehem (2:5–6), and went to Egypt (2:15); the innocent children were slaughtered by Herod (2:17–18); and Jesus grew up in Nazareth (2:23). The point is that God predicted Jesus' ministry in detail and that Jesus' ministry is indeed God's work. Jesus is the goal of Israel's history. Such use of Israel's Scripture recalls Qumran's mode of interpretation in the pesharim, for Qumran also treated Scripture as predictive of its own history.

Matthew 1–2 contradicts Luke's Infancy Narrative in several ways (see Meier, *A Marginal Jew,* 1.205–30). (Mark and John do not have an Infancy Narrative.) In Matthew, Jesus' family flees to Egypt for fear that Herod the Great will murder the infant, but in Luke, they appear publicly and confidently in the temple shortly after Jesus' birth, attracting much attention there, and do not go to Egypt. In Luke, Jesus' family lives in Nazareth, goes to Bethlehem because of the census in the time of Quirinius (6 C.E.), and then returns to Nazareth. In Matthew, Jesus' family lives in Bethlehem and is forced to flee to Egypt by Herod. When Herod's son Archelaus comes to power in Judea in 4 B.C.E., the family goes to Nazareth of Galilee, ruled by Herod Antipas, to escape the rule of Archelaus (Matt 2:22). Both gospels have Jesus born in Bethlehem and growing up in Nazareth, but they do so in very different ways.

The discrepancies between Matthew and Luke are due in part to their differing theological emphases. Matthew's narrative is structured around formula quotations; he was less interested in writing history in the sense of what actually happened, and more interested in what he saw as the meaning behind the events. (The same is true of Luke. See "Luke's Infancy Narrative" below.) Matthew wanted to show how Jesus fulfilled the words of the prophets. A brief examination of the first formula quotation in Matthew will help to show how the author uses Scripture.

Matthew quotes Isa 7:14: "All this took place to fulfill what had been spoken by the Lord through the prophet: 'Look, the virgin shall conceive and bear a son, and they shall name him Emmanuel,' which means, 'God is with us' " (Matt 1:22–23). Isaiah spoke his prophecy in Jerusalem in the eighth century B.C.E., when Ahaz was king of Judah. At that time, Assyria was threatening the kingdoms of Syria, Israel, and Judah. Syria and Israel were pressuring Ahaz to join them in an anti-Assyrian alliance. Through Isaiah, God tells Ahaz not to worry about Syria and Israel because they are both about to fall. Then Isaiah gives a sign:

> Look, the young woman is with child and shall bear a son, and shall name him Immanuel. He shall eat curds and honey by the time he knows how to refuse the evil and choose the good. For before the child knows how to refuse the evil and choose the good, the land before whose two kings you are in dread will be deserted. (Isa 7:14–16)

Christian interpretation of this passage is so deeply engrained in Christian consciousness that it seems obvious that Isaiah was referring to Jesus, who came almost eight centuries after Isaiah uttered these words. But a closer reading of the text shows that Isaiah could not have had in mind someone to be born in the far distant future. Isaiah was speaking of a child soon to be born, while the crisis of his own time was still happening. He says that Syria and Israel would fall before the child spoken of in the prophecy reached the age of reason: "Before the child knows how to refuse the evil and choose the good, the land before whose two kings you are in dread will be deserted" (7:16). Indeed, the two kingdoms did fall shortly after the prophecy.

The NRSV translation, quoted above, has Isaiah speak of a "young woman," the basic meaning of the Hebrew word here, *almah.* A different Hebrew word, *betulah,* is the technical term for "virgin." There is no indication in the Hebrew that Isaiah refers to a virgin. When the Hebrew Bible was translated into Greek, *almah* was translated by the Greek term *parthenos,* meaning "maiden" or "virgin." Some early Christians, reading the Greek text, took *parthenos* to mean "virgin" and saw it as predicting a miraculous birth of Jesus.

Isaiah says that the child to be born will be called Immanuel, the Hebrew for "God with us," as Matthew correctly translates. For Isaiah, the name does not define the nature of the child; he does not mean that the child will be divine. It is a symbolic name, indicating that God is with Judah and will act soon. Such symbolic names are common in Israelite and Jewish history. Isaiah gives his own child a symbolic name in 8:1–4.

Isaiah thus spoke of one to be born in his own time, the eighth century B.C.E., not in the distant future; he did not speak of a child to come as a divine being among humans; and he did not speak of a miraculous birth. But we have reached these conclusions as historical critics, concerned with what the historical Isaiah actually meant and how his original audience would have understood it. Matthew was not interested in historical criticism, any more than his contemporaries were. For them, Scripture was inspired word for word, which implied that verses could be lifted from their context and interpreted completely apart from it.

Some conservative Christians still look at Scripture this way, but many of the larger, mainstream churches do not. For the latter, Scripture is divinely inspired, but they avoid literalism in interpretation (see, e.g., Pontifical Biblical Commission, esp. 72–75). As historians, we must admit that Isaiah was not consciously referring to Jesus. But this does not mean that, as believers, we may not hold that God used Isaiah's prophecy for that purpose. In other words, God may have used Isaiah's prophecy both to speak the divine word to Isaiah's contemporaries, a meaning of which Isaiah was aware, and to use that same word to speak of other things to later Christians, as discovered by Matthew. Similarly, the *Commentary on Habakkuk* from Qumran admits that Habakkuk did not fully understand his own prophecies; for the Qumran sectaries, the only meaning seems to be for their own time.

One further point is important, given the fact that Isaiah is Scripture both to Jews and to Christians. Too often Christians have had the attitude that, for their own interpretation of Scripture to be correct, Jewish interpretation must be wrong. In other words, if Jews do not recognize the prediction of Jesus in Isa 7, they are wrong. But this limitation of how God may act is unworthy of Christian theology. Surely God can use the same text to say different things to different faith communities.

Like the members of the Qumran sect, the early Christians did not only comment on history by means of Scripture; they read history through the lens of Scripture. Their view of what happened was colored by their reading of what Scripture said must have happened. Matthew's interpretation could not be expected to convince the rabbis of Yavneh who were his contemporaries (much less the Jews of today), any more than similar interpretations by the Qumran community convinced the Jerusalem establishment.

In Matt 1–2, Jesus looks like Moses, and there are also parallels between Jesus and Israel. As is the case with Moses in the book of Exodus, the birth of Matthew's Jesus is connected with the slaughter of innocent male babies. Both Moses and Jesus escape the slaughter. Like Israel, Jesus goes down into Egypt and is later called from Egypt by God. The quote from Hosea that Matthew says is fulfilled in Jesus, "Out of Egypt I called my son" (Hos 11:1), originally referred to Israel, spoken of as God's son. As Moses entered and then left Egypt, Jesus did the same.

TEACHER OF TORAH

Matthew collects the sayings of Jesus in five sermons. The first is the Sermon on the Mount (Matt 5–7). In Matthew, this sermon is Jesus' chief statement of his message. As Moses received the Torah on Mount Sinai, Jesus goes up onto a mountain to deliver the definitive interpretation of Mosaic Torah. Toward the beginning of the sermon, Jesus states emphatically that his ministry should not be interpreted as abrogation of Torah but as confirmation of it (5:17). Torah lasts until the end of the world (5:18). Torah is to be obeyed, right down to its "least commandments" (5:19). Scribes and Pharisees do not go far enough in observing their own stringent interpretations (5:20; 23:2–3).

Jesus as Fulfiller of Torah

Do not think that I have come to abolish the law or the prophets; I have come not to abolish but to fulfill. For truly I tell you, until heaven and earth pass away, not one letter, not one stroke of a letter, will pass from the law until all is accomplished. Therefore, whoever breaks one of the least of these commandments, and teaches others to do the same, will be called least in the kingdom of heaven; but whoever does them and teaches them will be called great in the kingdom of heaven. For I tell you, unless your righteousness exceeds that of the scribes and Pharisees, you will never enter the kingdom of heaven. (Matt 5:17–20)

The Sermon on the Mount continues with a series of six antitheses in which Jesus quotes Torah, saying, "You have heard that it was said . . ." In each case, Jesus interprets Torah. In several of these antitheses, Jesus "builds a fence" around Torah, just as the sectarians of Qumran and the Pharisees did. That is, he makes rules that are stricter than those found in Torah, thus insuring that Torah's rules will not be broken (see ch. 5, above). Thus, for example, whereas Torah says not to kill, Jesus says not even to get angry (5:21–22). Whereas Torah says not to commit adultery, Jesus says not even to have lustful thoughts (5:27–28). Jesus does not abrogate Torah; he supports it. Still, we must admit that the particular form here—"You have heard it said [Torah] . . . , but I [Jesus] say to you . . ."—does seem to claim more authority for Jesus in interpreting Torah than other Jews could accept (see Neusner).

Matthew 6 treats three pillars of Jewish piety—prayer, almsgiving, and fasting. Jesus teaches his disciples a prayer, the Lord's Prayer, that is close in form and content to an ancient Jewish prayer called the Kaddish (see ch. 9, above). Toward the end of the Sermon on the Mount, Jesus makes the following general statement: "In everything do to others as you would have them do to you; for this is the law and the prophets" (7:12). The verse is also found in Luke 6:31, but without the words about the Law and the Prophets. The verse makes the point again that Matthew's Jesus thinks of his teaching as identical with Torah.

Matthew's view of Jesus as Torah teacher influences the Gospel in many of its details. For example, in all three Synoptic Gospels, Jesus is asked what is the greatest commandment (Mark 12:28–31; Matt 22:34–40; Luke 10:25–28). Each of the gospels has him answer by quoting Deut 6:5, concerning love of God, and Lev 19:18, which enjoins love of neighbor. These biblical verses would have been dear to most, if not all, Jews. Only Matthew ends the story with the words "On these two commandments hang all the law and the prophets" (Matt 22:40).

Chapter 9, above, looked at the conflict between Jesus and the Pharisees and scribes (Mark 7; Matt 15). Mark's version makes the issue one of kosher foods—Jesus "declared all foods clean" (Mark 7:19). Matthew drops this line and insists that the issue is the washing of hands, a purity rule peculiar to the Pharisees (Matt 15:20). For Matthew, Jesus did not annul the dietary rules.

Matthew probably wrote his Gospel partially in reaction to what was happening at Yavneh after the destruction of Jerusalem (see ch. 10, above). This may account for his long, harsh attack on the scribes and Pharisees in Matt 23. Pharisees and scribes were central players in the reconstitution of Judaism at Yavneh. Although Matthew attacks the Pharisees, he shares many of their presuppositions. In 23:2–3, Jesus even recognizes their authority: "The scribes and the Pharisees sit on Moses' seat; therefore, do whatever they teach you and follow it; but do not do as they do, for they do not practice what they teach."

In the final scene of the Gospel, the eleven apostles (minus Judas Iscariot, the betrayer) meet Jesus on a mountain in Galilee. Jesus says to them,

> All authority in heaven and on earth has been given to me. Go therefore and make disciples of all nations, baptizing them in the name of the Father and of the Son and of the Holy Spirit, and teaching them to obey everything that I have commanded you. And remember, I am with you always, to the end of the age. (28:18–20)

Torah language permeates these verses. The Greek for "disciples" comes from the word meaning "to teach" and denotes students. The apostles are to make learners of all nations, teaching them to observe Jesus' commandments. This echoes Jewish tradition, where teaching people to observe God's commandments is central. For example, Moses says, "Now this is the commandment—the statutes and the ordinances—that the LORD your God charged me to teach you to observe" (Deut 6:1). Matthew's idea of what Jesus has done and what the church does is modeled on Judaism.

Matthew adds an eschatological touch characteristic of his Gospel when Jesus reminds the disciples of the end of the age (Matt 28:20). The Gospel contains frequent reminders that the eschaton is coming, in which people will be judged according to their reaction to the message of Jesus and his disciples. Matthew 25 is the only place in the New Testament giving a detailed description of the Last Judgment. It begins, "When the Son of Man comes in his glory, and all the angels with him, then he will sit on the throne of his glory. All the nations will be gathered before him, and he will separate people from one another as a shepherd separates the sheep from the goats" (25:31–32). The scene recalls the judgment scene in Dan 7, although in that account, God is the Judge, not the one like a son of man. The *Similitudes of Enoch* likewise transformed the one like a son of man in Daniel into a judge who sits on a throne and judges all nations (e.g., *1 En.* 62). And Ezekiel 34 has a scene in which God judges sheep and goats. Again, Matthew finds his inspiration in Jewish traditions.

JESUS AND THE GENTILES

In Matt 28:18, Jesus instructs the disciples to go to all nations. But the mission of Jesus, and of the disciples during his life, was limited to Israel. In 10:5, when Jesus sends the disciples out on a mission, he warns them, "Go nowhere among the Gentiles, and enter no town of the Samaritans, but go rather to the lost sheep of the house of Israel." In 15:21–28, Jesus is unwilling to heal the daughter of a Gentile woman. He says, "I was sent only to the lost sheep of the house of Israel" (15:24). Matthew reconciles the church's later Gentile mission by saying that, during the life of Jesus, he and his disciples ministered only to Israel whereas, after the resurrection, the mission expanded to include all nations.

LUKE'S INFANCY NARRATIVE

Luke considered it a substantial theological problem that Jesus had not been accepted as the Messiah by the Jewish people as a whole. Like Mark and Matthew, Luke presents Jesus as the fulfillment of Jewish hopes. Luke emphasizes this in his Infancy Narrative, and he writes a second volume, the Acts of the Apostles, in which he explains that, during the period of the early church, God continued to send missionaries to the Jews to make them realize their mistake in rejecting Jesus.

Luke is well versed in Jewish Scripture. This is nowhere more evident than in his Infancy Narrative, where his language echoes that of the Greek translation of the Hebrew Bible. After a brief introduction customary for Hellenistic historical works, Luke recounts the annunciations of the births of John the Baptist and Jesus, the births themselves, and the journey of Jesus' parents with their new baby to Jerusalem to bring him to the temple.

Luke opens with a revelation given to John the Baptist's father, Zechariah, a priest, in the Jerusalem temple. The angel Gabriel (known to us through various Jewish apocalypses) appears to Zechariah and tells him that his son will have the "spirit and power of Elijah," the ancient Israelite prophet who did not die but was taken up into heaven in a fiery chariot. The end of the book of Malachi expects Elijah to return to warn Israel before God comes in judgment. Early Christians saw John the Baptist as Elijah returned to announce the coming of Jesus (see esp. Matt 11:14; 17:13).

Gabriel then announces to Mary the birth of Jesus, emphasizing that Jesus is the Davidic Messiah. God had said that David's line would rule forever. Speaking to David about Solomon, God says, "I will establish the throne of his kingdom forever. I will be a father to him, and he shall be a son to me" (2 Sam 7:13–14). There had not been a king on the throne in Jerusalem since the beginning of the Babylonian exile in 587 B.C.E., in apparent contradiction to God's words. Luke references this stream of tradition as the angel says to Mary, "He will be great, and will be called the Son of the Most High, and the Lord God will give to him the throne of his ancestor David. He will reign over the house of Jacob forever, and of his kingdom there will be no end" (Luke 1:32–33).

The main characters in this narrative are faithful, Torah-abiding Jews who represent an Israel prepared for its messiah. For example, John's parents are introduced as follows:

> In the days of King Herod of Judea, there was a priest named Zechariah, who belonged to the priestly order of Abijah. His wife was a descendant of Aaron, and her name was Elizabeth. Both of them were righteous before God, living blamelessly according to all the commandments and regulations of the Lord. (1:5–6)

Jesus' parents are portrayed similarly. They circumcise their son at the appropriate time, eight days after his birth. Later they bring the infant to the temple:

> When the time came for their purification according to the law of Moses, they brought him up to Jerusalem to present him to the Lord (as it is written in the law of the Lord, "Every firstborn male shall be designated as holy to the Lord"),

and they offered a sacrifice according to what is stated in the law of the Lord, "a pair of turtledoves or two young pigeons." (2:22–24)

This passage is thoroughly Jewish, with its emphasis on obedience to the Torah of Moses, on purification, sacrifice, holiness, the temple, and Jerusalem.

In Jerusalem, Simeon testifies to the significance of Jesus' birth: "Now there was a man in Jerusalem whose name was Simeon; this man was righteous and devout, looking forward to the consolation of Israel, and the Holy Spirit rested on him. It had been revealed to him by the Holy Spirit that he would not see death before he had seen the Lord's Messiah" (2:25–26). The scene is set. Simeon has the spirit of God and therefore sees things from God's perspective and can speak for God. He waits in the temple, center of Judaism, for the Messiah whom God has promised. Jesus' parents bring him to the temple "to do for him what was customary under the law" (2:27). Simeon takes Jesus into his arms, praises God, and makes the solemn pronouncement that the coming of Jesus is "a light for revelation to the Gentiles and for glory to your people Israel" (2:32). In speaking of Jesus' significance for Gentiles, Simeon relies on Isa 49:6.

The temple scene ends with the confirmation of Simeon's words by the prophetess Anna: "At that moment she came, and began to praise God and to speak about the child to all who were looking for the redemption of Jerusalem" (2:38). The Infancy Narrative ends with the scene of the boy Jesus in the temple, amazing its teachers with his understanding, and saying to his worried parents, "Did you not know that I must be in my Father's house?" (2:49).

In Luke 2, both Mary and Zechariah utter canticles. Remarkable in both is the extent to which they portray Jesus as the fulfillment of God's promises to Israel. These promises concern not only spiritual realities but this-worldly ones as well, not only forgiveness of sin but also deliverance from enemies. Mary's canticle speaks of the pulling down of the mighty from their thrones and the raising up of the lowly. This is the sort of reversal we know from Jewish apocalypses and from the teaching of Jesus. She ends her canticle as follows:

> He [God] has helped his servant Israel,
> > in remembrance of his mercy,
> according to the promise he made to our ancestors,
> > to Abraham and to his descendants forever. (1:54–55)

The descendants of Abraham are Israel, and God now intervenes in history on Israel's behalf.

Similarly, Zechariah's canticle interprets Jesus' coming as Israel's salvation:

> Blessed be the Lord God of Israel,
>> for he has looked favorably upon his people and redeemed them.
> He has raised up a mighty savior for us
>> in the house of his servant David,
> as he spoke through the mouth of his holy prophets from of old,
>> that we would be saved from our enemies and from the hand of all who hate us.
> Thus he has shown the mercy promised to our ancestors,
>> and has remembered his holy covenant,
> the oath that he swore to our ancestor Abraham,
>> to grant us that we, being rescued from the hands of our enemies,
> might serve him without fear, in holiness and righteousness
>> before him all our days. (1:68–75)

Zechariah goes on to predict that John the Baptist will be a prophet who announces this great salvation to Israel. Zechariah's picture is of an Israel delivered from its enemies, living in peace under a Davidic ruler, free to worship its God.

Luke uses his first two chapters to express clearly and graphically the idea that Jesus comes to Israel in fulfillment of God's promises to Israel, that he comes into the midst of Torah-abiding Jews, and that his coming means the salvation of Jerusalem and Israel.

THE ACTS OF THE APOSTLES: CHRISTIAN JUDAISM BECOMES CHRISTIANITY

Jewish Unbelief

The Acts of the Apostles—written by the author of the Gospel of Luke—is in the form of a history of the early church, covering the period from just after the death of Jesus (ca. 30 C.E.) to Paul's arrival in Rome as a prisoner (ca. 60 C.E.). As with each of the Jewish and Christian documents we have examined, it would be unwise to read Acts as straight history in the modern sense. It is embued with its author's theology. This does not mean, however, that it has no historical value. Indeed, historians of the earliest church make extensive use of Acts, for it is one of our few sources for the period and is the only one written in the form of a history.

Central to Acts is a theological problem: the vast majority of Jews did not become followers of Jesus. This problem was exacerbated by the fact that

Luke lived in the great Hellenistic world, which he wished to convert to Jesus. To grasp Luke's problem, it is helpful to consider the following scenario. Suppose one were an early Christian preaching belief in Jesus to non-Jewish members of a Roman Hellenistic city. One would be preaching that Jesus the Jew was the Jewish Messiah, sent to the Jews by the God of Israel in fulfillment of promises to the Jews, in fulfillment of the Jewish Scriptures. Indeed, this is precisely the way that Luke portrays Jesus in the first two chapters of his Gospel. Then suppose that one's hearers were to say, "That sounds interesting. Let's go to the local synagogue to hear more about this." One would have to answer, somewhat sheepishly, that in fact the Jews in the local synagogue had already rejected the claims of Christian missionaries. One would then have a lot of explaining to do. Indeed, much of the New Testament is dedicated to precisely that sort of explaining.

The Acts of the Apostles is especially concerned with this problem. Part of Luke's answer is that many Jews did believe. Acts says that when Peter preached his first missionary sermon, a Jew preaching to Jews in Jerusalem, three thousand believed and were baptized (2:41). In Acts 6:7, Luke says that "the number of the disciples increased greatly in Jerusalem" (at this point in the story, these had to be Jews) and that "a great many of the priests became obedient to the faith." Acts 9 assumes a Jewish-Christian community in Damascus shortly after Jesus' death. Acts 9:31 says that the church grew in Judea, Galilee, and Samaria. Acts 14:1 says that many Jews in the city of Iconium in Asia Minor believed. And Acts 15 says that there was an influential Pharisaic contingent in the Jerusalem church. However one evaluates these claims, part of Luke's strategy is to assert that a very large number of Jews did in fact become Christians. Even when Luke does not claim that Jews converted, he often says that many in a given Jewish community were sympathetic to Christian preaching. Despite these claims, Luke is very aware that the great majority of Jews do not believe.

Luke is concerned to show that although Jesus had been rejected by most Jews, God had not given up on the Jews. As Acts opens, there are no Gentile disciples. Just before Jesus ascends to heaven, the disciples ask him, "Lord, is this the time when you will restore the kingdom to Israel?" (1:6). Christian readers may expect Jesus to correct the disciples' expectations, pointing out that their desire for an earthly Jewish kingdom misinterprets God's plans. This does not happen. Rather, Jesus answers, "It is not for you to know the times or periods that the Father has set by his own authority" (1:7). This implies that the disciples were not wrong to expect the coming of a Jewish kingdom, only in their desire to know precisely when it would happen.

In Acts 2, Peter preaches to Jews gathered in Jerusalem for the feast of Weeks, Pentecost, fifty days after Passover. Peter addresses his audience as

"Israelites" (2:22) and uses scriptural arguments that Jesus' resurrection was foretold by David and that Jesus is the Messiah awaited by the Jews. Sometime later, Peter makes another speech to Jews in Jerusalem (Acts 3). There he attributes to ignorance the Jewish participation in the death of Jesus, and assures his hearers that Jesus stands ready in heaven to come back as Israel's messiah.

Peter's Speech—Jesus as Prophet like Moses and Messiah To Come

> And now, friends, I know that you acted in ignorance, as did also your rulers. In this way God fulfilled what he had foretold through all the prophets, that his Messiah would suffer. Repent therefore, and turn to God so that your sins may be wiped out, so that times of refreshing may come from the presence of the Lord, and that he may send the Messiah appointed for you, that is, Jesus, who must remain in heaven until the time of universal restoration that God announced long ago through his holy prophets. Moses said, "The Lord your God will raise up for you from your own people a prophet like me. You must listen to whatever he tells you. And it will be that everyone who does not listen to that prophet will be utterly rooted out of the people." And all the prophets, as many as have spoken, from Samuel and those after him, also predicted these days. You are the descendants of the prophets and of the covenant that God gave to your ancestors, saying to Abraham, "And in your descendants all the families of the earth shall be blessed." When God raised up his servant, he sent him first to you, to bless you by turning each of you from your wicked ways. (Acts 3:17–26)

Here Jesus is the prophet about whom Moses spoke in Deut 18:15 (see the *Messianic Anthology* [4QTest]). As is common in the rest of Luke–Acts, Peter sees Jesus as the fulfillment of all of the prophets. It was necessary that Jesus, as the fulfillment of all the promises to Israel, be sent first to Israel. Although Israel rejected him, God is determined to give Israel another chance. Even now Jesus waits in heaven for Jews to believe. When they do, God will send the Messiah appointed for them, Jesus.

Despite these claims about Jewish belief, Luke must reckon with the fact that the vast majority of Jews did not become Christian. At the end of a speech to Jews in Pisidian Antioch in Asia Minor, Paul concludes, "It was necessary that the word of God should be spoken first to you. Since you reject it and judge yourselves to be worthy of eternal life, we are now turning to the Gentiles" (13:46). At the very end of the book, Paul addresses the Jews of Rome. Some are convinced by him, but others are not. Paul, angered at their lack of belief, quotes Isa 6:9–10, a verse favored by the early Christians to explain Jewish unbelief. It begins, "You will indeed listen, but never understand, and you will indeed look, but never perceive" (Acts 28:26). Paul finishes by saying, "Let it be known to you then that this salvation of God has been sent to the Gentiles; they will listen" (28:28). Thus Luke explains Jewish unbelief and the development of a Gentile church by relating the two to each other and saying the prophets had predicted it.

GENTILE BELIEVERS

Luke acknowledges that admitting Gentiles into the emerging Christian group did not come without a struggle. Indeed, one gets the impression from the first nine chapters of Acts that it did not even occur to the earliest Christians to pursue a Gentile mission. Even the mission to Samaria, depicted in Acts 8, does not count as counterevidence to this, since the Samaritans were monotheistic Yahweh worshipers who followed the law of Moses. It appears that the earliest Christians saw Christianity as a group within Judaism, even as the true Judaism. Perhaps they thought that at the eschaton the Gentiles would come to worship Israel's God, but initially there was no Gentile mission, according to Luke.

Acts 10 explains the Gentile mission as God's decision. The Gentile Cornelius, an admirer of Judaism, has a vision in which he is told to summon Peter to his house. Meanwhile, Peter also has a vision, in which he is told to eat animals that are ritually impure. He does not understand the vision and refuses to eat, protesting that he has never eaten impure food. Chapter 9, above, used the fact that the earliest Christians kept Jewish dietary rules to argue that Jesus did not disobey the Jewish food laws nor did he abrogate them for his disciples. When the emissaries from Cornelius arrive, Peter is told in a vision to go with them, and he does. He says, "Your yourselves know that it is unlawful for a Jew to associate with or to visit a Gentile; but God has shown me that I should not call anyone profane or unclean" (10:28). Thus he interprets his dream in terms not of food but of people.

Peter then preaches to Cornelius and his household about Jesus. He says that he now understands that God's message of forgiveness is not limited just to the Jews. He finishes with these words: "All the prophets testify about him that everyone who believes in him receives forgiveness of sins through his name" (10:43). What comes next is a turning point for Christianity, according to Luke:

> While Peter was still speaking, the Holy Spirit fell upon all who heard the word. The circumcised believers who had come with Peter were astounded that the gift of the Holy Spirit had been poured out even on the Gentiles, for they heard them speaking in tongues and extolling God. Then Peter said, "Can anyone withhold the water for baptizing these people who have received the Holy Spirit just as we have?" So he ordered them to be baptized in the name of Jesus Christ. (10:44–48)

In other words, it was not Peter or any other human being who decided that Gentiles should be admitted to the church. It was God.

8EARLY JUDAISM: THE EXILE TO THE TIME OF JESUS

Not all Christians are delighted to hear of what had happened with Cornelius and his household:

Now the apostles and the believers who were in Judea heard that the Gentiles had also accepted the word of God. So when Peter went up to Jerusalem, the circumcised believers criticized him, saying, "Why did you go to uncircumcised men and eat with them?" (11:1–3).

Of course, the phrase "circumcised believers" is redundant at this point in the narrative, since *all* believers were circumcised, ie., were Jews. Peter tells those assembled in Cornelias's house the whole story, beginning with his initial vision. Speaking of his experience at Cornelius's house, he says,

"And as I began to speak, the Holy Spirit fell upon them just as it had upon us at the beginning. And I remembered the word of the Lord, how he had said, 'John baptized with water, but you will be baptized with the Holy Spirit.' If then God gave them the same gift that he gave us when we believed in the Lord Jesus Christ, who was I that I could hinder God?" When they heard this, they were silenced. And they praised God, saying, "Then God has given even to the Gentiles the repentance that leads to life." (11:15–18)

But the battle over the admission of the Gentiles is not yet over. As the Gentile mission grows larger, particularly through the work of Paul and his coworker Barnabas, some in Jerusalem continue to have misgivings. In particular, some in Jerusalem are disturbed that new Gentile converts are not required to keep Torah. After all, what sense does it make for a movement whose original members were all Jews and that has remained heavily Jewish, a movement that followed the Jewish Messiah and exists in fulfillment of promises to Israel recorded in the Jewish Scriptures, to then abandon the most sacred laws and customs that these very Scriptures clearly demand? This was one of the most important issues the early church faced. Paul struggles with it in three letters—Romans, Galatians, and Philippians.

Acts 15 tells what happened when members of the Jerusalem church hear that Paul, Barnabas, and other Christians in Antioch of Syria do not require Gentile Christians to observe Torah:

Then certain individuals came down from Judea and were teaching the brothers, "Unless you are circumcised according to the custom of Moses, you cannot be saved." And after Paul and Barnabas had no small dissension and debate with them, Paul and Barnabas and some of the others were appointed to go up to Jerusalem to discuss this question with the apostles and the elders. (15:1–2)

Paul describes the same meeting in Gal 2. When those from Antioch arrive, "Some believers who belonged to the sect of the Pharisees stood up and said, 'It is necessary for them to be circumcised and ordered to keep the law of Moses' " (Acts 15:5). After discussion, James, leader of the Jerusalem church, declares that the entrance of the Gentiles into the church has been predicted by the prophet Amos (Amos 9:11–12) and that the only rules the Gentile Christians must follow are that they not eat meat sacrificed to idols, that they abstain from sexual immorality, and that they not eat blood.

HELLENISTS AND HEBREWS

In Acts 6, "Hellenists" and "Hebrews" begin to squabble with each other. Both groups must be Jewish Christian, since the conflict reported is an inner-church affair and the mission to the Gentiles has not yet started. One opinion is that the Hellenists are Jewish Christians from the Diaspora, perhaps more hellenized than Palestinian Jews, while the Hebrews are Aramaic-speaking Jews from the homeland (authors in Greek and Latin usually do not distinguish between Hebrew and Aramaic).

The conflict between the Hellenists and Hebrews within the church is over distribution of food to widows. The Hellenists complain against the Hebrews that their widows are being neglected in the distribution. Acts mentions no theological content to the dispute. The solution reached is that Hellenists will be in charge of the distribution of food to their own widows. The seven men appointed to this task all have Greek names. Prominent among them is Stephen. But then Jews of the so-called synagogue of the Freedmen (freed slaves, who constituted a special class within the Roman Empire) begin to complain against Stephen. They say, "We have heard him speak blasphemous words against Moses and God," and they bring "false witnesses" who say, "This man never stops saying things against this holy place and the law; for we have heard him say that this Jesus of Nazareth will destroy this place and will change the customs that Moses handed on to us" (6:11, 14). In Acts 7, Stephen makes a speech condemning Israel for rejecting Moses and then Jesus, both of whom were sent to liberate Israel. Toward the end of the speech, Stephen denies that God could live in a temple built by human hands. He is stoned by the crowd and so becomes the first Christian martyr.

Luke seems to be papering over a serious disagreement within the early church. The charges by "false witnesses" that Stephen speaks of the destruction of the temple sound much like the charges brought against Jesus in the Gospels. Significantly, Luke does not contain these charges in Jesus' trial. Rather, they are transferred to Stephen's trial. Luke wishes to deny that either Jesus or Stephen spoke against the temple in this way, but he admits that some said that they did. Stephen faces added allegations. They claim he speaks against Moses, the Law, and Jewish customs. Precisely these sorts of accusations were leveled against Paul and others who thought like him. Although the circumstances are not entirely clear, the basic issues are the Jewish nature of earliest Christianity and the problems the earliest church had in deciding on the status of Torah within the community. These problems were exacerbated when substantial numbers of Gentiles began entering the church. At least some Hellenistic Jews, certainly Paul and perhaps Stephen, thought that Gentile converts need not obey Torah.

Later it is reported, "A severe persecution began against the church in Jerusalem, and all except the apostles were scattered throughout the countryside of Judea and Samaria" (8:1). It seems strange that a persecution would exclude the leaders of the new movement. But this may be explained if the apostles belonged to the Hebrew section of the Jewish-Christian movement, the section that remained observant of Torah. In fact, although Paul claims the support of the Jerusalem Christian leaders for his Torah-free mission to the Gentiles, he also locates there the more conservative Jewish Christians who insist on circumcision and complete observance of Torah by Gentile Christians (Gal 2). If indeed there was a persecution by non-Christian Jews in Jerusalem against the Jewish Christians there, they may well have directed it only at those who were a threat to Torah.

THE LETTER TO THE HEBREWS: JESUS AS HIGH PRIEST

JESUS AS HIGH PRIEST AND MEDIATOR

The Letter to the Hebrews is an anonymous New Testament work. Every step of the argument in Hebrews depends upon interpretation of the Hebrew Bible. Hebrews uses priestly concepts and images to explain Jesus and his function. Its major categories are high priest and sacrifice. The author notes that high priests are mediators between God and the people. Their function is to remove any obstacles, particularly sin and impurity, between God and the congregation, and they accomplish this through sacrifice. For Hebrews, Jesus is the perfect mediator, being both human and Son of God. Further, Jesus' work is effective because he is both priest and victim, sacrificer and sacrificed.

Hebrews 1–3 establishes that Jesus is greater than the prophets, the angels, and Moses. The book begins,

> Long ago God spoke to our ancestors in many and various ways by the prophets, but in these last days he has spoken to us by a Son, whom he appointed heir of all things, through whom he also created the worlds. He is the reflection of God's glory and the exact imprint of God's very being, and he sustains all things by his powerful word. When he had made purification for sins, he sat down at the right

hand of the Majesty on high, having become as much superior to angels as the name he has inherited is more excellent than theirs. (1:1–4)

This passage speaks of Jesus in terms that recall the personification of wisdom seen in Prov 8–9, Sir 24, *1 En.* 42, Wis 7, and elsewhere. In the Jewish wisdom tradition of the Hellenistic period, Jewish speculation stopped just short of considering Wisdom a goddess. She was present at the creation, and God created the world through her. In Wis 7, she is the perfect representation of God, and she is the one who holds the universe together. Hebrews uses such ideas to interpret Jesus. Jesus becomes more than human. He becomes the one through whom the universe was created, the perfect reflection of God.

Hebrews 1:4 conceives of Jesus' work as purification, the task proper for priests. At the end of chapter 4, Jesus' high priesthood begins to receive detailed treatment. The author sees Jesus as one who is fully human but also as one who is more than human. Therefore, Jesus is the perfect mediator, the ideal priest, since he has a foot in both worlds. Jesus suffered as do all humans, and so he represents humans before God. At the same time, he represents God to humans because he reflects the glory of God and bears "the exact imprint of God's very being." Two passages from Scripture are taken to refer to God's choice of Jesus as high priest. The first is from a messianic context: "You are my Son, today I have begotten you" (Heb 5:5, quoting Ps 2:7). The second demonstrates the possibility of being a priest outside the tribe of Levi: "You are a priest forever, according to the order of Melchizedek" (Heb 5:6, quoting Ps 110:4). This gets around the problem of seeing Jesus as a priest even though he is of the tribe of Judah.

JESUS AND MELCHIZEDEK

Chapter 7 takes up the idea of Melchizedek's priesthood again to solve a basic problem: how can Jesus be a priest if he is not of the tribe of Levi? The author has searched the Scriptures and found another important priest, Melchizedek, whose priesthood even Abraham recognized, and he concludes that Jesus is a priest like Melchizedek. Melchizedek is an obscure figure who appears in Gen 14:17–20. He is mentioned elsewhere in the Hebrew Bible only in Ps 110:4, quoted above.

For the author of Hebrews, Melchizedek is a *type* of Jesus; that is, Melchizedek foreshadows Jesus. King of Salem (probably Jerusalem), he brings out bread and wine to Abraham, who is returning from war (Gen 14:18). Melchizedek is also "priest of God Most High." Abraham gives him tithes from the spoils of his battles, as later Israel will give tithes to its priests in Jerusalem. Since Genesis mentions neither Melchizedek's parents nor his death, Hebrews concludes that he has no parents and that he did not die: "Without father, without mother, without genealogy, having neither beginning

of days nor end of life, but resembling the Son of God, he remains a priest forever" (Heb 7:3). Because Abraham gives tithes to him, Hebrews concludes
that Melchizedek is superior to Abraham, and since Levi is in the loins of
Abraham when he pays tithes, Melchizedek is also superior to Levi and to the
priestly tribe descended from him. Such interpretation may not be persuasive
to many today, but it accords with the allegorical interpretation known in
Jewish and Gentile circles in the Hellenistic and Roman periods.

Hebrews then introduces Jesus into the argument:

> Now if perfection had been attainable through the levitical priesthood—for
> the people received the law under this priesthood—what further need would
> there have been to speak of another priest arising according to the order of
> Melchizedek, rather than one according to the order of Aaron? For when there
> is a change in the priesthood, there is necessarily a change in the law as well.
> Now the one of whom these things are spoken belonged to another tribe, from
> which no one has ever served at the altar. For it is evident that our Lord [Jesus]
> was descended from Judah, and in connection with that tribe Moses said noth-
> ing about priests. (7:11–14)

That a priest (Jesus) arises who is outside the Levitical priesthood proves that
the Levitical priesthood was inadequate, for God does not do unnecessary
things. The text goes further and claims that since the priesthood and the
Law are so closely associated, the change in the priesthood implied by Jesus'
appointment must entail a change in the Law. In the view of the Letter to the
Hebrews, Christianity leaves the Torah behind. This clearly puts the author
beyond the pale of Judaism. As the author says, "There is, on the one hand,
the abrogation of an earlier commandment because it was weak and ineffec-
tual (for the law made nothing perfect); there is, on the other hand, the introduction of a better hope, through which we approach God" (7:18–19).

The permanence of Jesus, who has no beginning or end, demonstrates
the superiority of his priesthood.

> Consequently he is able for all time to save those who approach God through him,
> since he always lives to make intercession for them. For it was fitting that we
> should have such a high priest, holy, blameless, undefiled, separated from sinners,
> and exalted above the heavens. Unlike the other high priests, he has no need to
> offer sacrifices day after day, first for his own sins, and then for those of the people;
> this he did once for all when he offered himself. For the law appoints as high
> priests those who are subject to weakness, but the word of the oath, which came
> later than the law, appoints a Son who has been made perfect forever. (7:25–28)

Hebrews characteristically combines Hellenistic philosophical notions with
biblical concepts and images (see MacRae). The Greek word for "perfect" is

common in Hellenistic religions and philosophies. It can mean initiates in Hellenistic mystery religions who have a special relationship with the patron gods of the mysteries. Hebrews 9 says that the earthly sanctuary stands for the present age and that the sanctuary through which Jesus has passed is a "greater and more perfect tent (not made with hands, that is, not of this creation)" (9:11). In other words, "perfect" describes the heavenly sanctuary, and it is used in opposition to terms that can describe the present, earthly sanctuary. To enter the heavenly sanctuary, one must become perfect. This means that in Hebrews the term "perfect" is used in a way analogous to the term "pure" or "holy" in cultic contexts. Indeed, Jesus is described in chapter 7 with a string of phrases that combines both types of language. Jesus is "high priest, holy, blameless, undefiled, separated from sinners, and exalted above the heavens . . . perfect forever" (7:26, 28).

JESUS' SACRIFICE

Hebrews 8 maintains this contrast between the heavenly and the earthly, or, to use terms familiar in a Hellenistic philosophical and religious setting, between shadow and reality, real and apparent. The author sums up his argument by saying, "Now the main point of what we are saying is this: we have such a high priest, one who is seated at the right hand of the throne of the Majesty in the heavens, a minister in the sanctuary and the true tent that the Lord, and not any mortal, has set up" (8:1–2). He then characterizes the earthly sanctuary as "a sketch and shadow of the heavenly one" (8:5). The term "shadow" recalls Plato's parable of the cave from the *Republic*. The idea is that most humans are as if chained in a cave, facing away from the entrance. The images they see moving on the wall of the cave are but shadows of the realities that exist outside the cave. For Plato, the sensory world presents us with shadows of the real world, and the real can be perceived only with the mind. By using this sort of conception, the author of Hebrews uses the Hebrew Bible as a pointer to Jesus, but at the same time he denies the efficacy of Israel's cult. Jewish cult is the shadow; Jesus is the reality.

Chapter 7 notes that a change in priesthood and cult means a change in the Law, and chapter 8 goes on to say that such a change in turn means that the old covenant is abrogated. The new covenant had been predicted by the prophet Jeremiah in Jer 31, which Heb 8:8–12 quotes. The people of Qumran, too, thought that they were the fulfillment of the "new covenant" passage of Jer 31, but they remained within the Mosaic Torah. They did not see a "new covenant" as implying the end of Torah or the beginning of a new religion.

Hebrews 9 describes the earthly temple in Jerusalem. The climax of the description comes in 9:6–7: "The priests go continually into the first tent to carry out their ritual duties; but only the high priest goes into the second, and he but once a year, and not without taking the blood that he offers for himself and for the sins committed unintentionally by the people." There follows an allegorical interpretation of the temple, making the outer tent symbolic for the present age, which must be passed through in order to reach the sanctuary, where God is (9:8–10). But 9:11–28 supplies an alternative allegorical interpretation, in which the sanctuary is heaven, the abode of God, and the outer tent stands for this world. In this second interpretation, Jesus as high priest enters the sanctuary, heaven, once and for all. Such allegorical interpretation, in which the literal meaning of a text gives way to a figurative one, was common in the Hellenistic world.

Once a year, on the Day of Atonement, the high priest goes into the sanctuary. He brings the blood of animals to cleanse the sanctuary, thereby atoning for the sins of priests and people (Lev 16). Jesus' activity is analogous to that of the high priest. When Jesus enters the heavenly sanctuary, of which the earthly is but a shadow, he, too, must bring blood. The general priestly principle is stated in Heb 9:22: "Under the law almost everything is purified with blood, and without the shedding of blood there is no forgiveness of sins." The text continues,

> Thus it was necessary for the sketches of the heavenly things to be purified with these rites, but the heavenly things themselves need better sacrifices than these. For Christ did not enter a sanctuary made by human hands, a mere copy of the true one, but he entered into heaven itself, now to appear in the presence of God on our behalf. Nor was it to offer himself again and again, as the high priest enters the Holy Place year after year with blood that is not his own; for then he would have had to suffer again and again since the foundation of the world. But as it is, he has appeared once for all at the end of the age to remove sin by the sacrifice of himself. (9:23–26)

The "Holy Place" here denotes the innermost room of the temple, as is clear from the fact that the high priest enters it only once a year. Jesus has attained access to God in the true holy of holies, heaven, and he has done this by sacrificing himself. Jesus is both priest and sacrificial victim. Just as the Levitical high priest does not enter the holy of holies for himself alone, neither does Jesus enter heaven only for his own benefit. His death purifies not only himself but all Christians, who then gain access to God:

> Therefore, my friends, since we have confidence to enter the sanctuary by the blood of Jesus, by the new and living way that he opened for us through the curtain (that is, through his flesh), and since we have a great priest over the house of God, let us approach with a true heart in full assurance of faith, with our hearts sprinkled clean from an evil conscience and our bodies washed with pure water. (10:19–22)

FLESHLY AND HEAVENLY

Throughout Hebrews, there is a contrast between the Jewish and the Christian cults. The Jewish cult is fleshly, and the Christian is heavenly. This contrast is informed by a Platonic view of the universe as divided between the physical world, accessible to the senses, and the world accessible only to the mind. Hebrews 12 contrasts the literal Mount Sinai and Mount Zion, taken as a symbol of the heavenly Jerusalem.

> You have not come to something that can be touched, a blazing fire, and darkness, and gloom, and a tempest, and the sound of a trumpet, and a voice whose words made the hearers beg that not another word be spoken to them. (For they could not endure the order that was given, "If even an animal touches the mountain, it shall be stoned to death." Indeed, so terrifying was the sight that Moses said, "I tremble with fear.") But you have come to Mount Zion and to the city of the living God, the heavenly Jerusalem, and to innumerable angels in festal gathering, and to the assembly of the firstborn who are enrolled in heaven, and to God the judge of all, and to the spirits of the righteous made perfect, and to Jesus, the mediator of a new covenant, and to the sprinkled blood that speaks a better word than the blood of Abel. (12:18–24)

Fire, darkness, and tempest refer to the theophany (divine appearance) at Sinai, where God gave Israel the Torah. As terrifying as that theophany was, its holiness was but a shadow of the true access to heaven, figuratively called Mount Zion, that Christians now enjoy through Christ. Similarly, the earthly Jerusalem is but a shadow of the heavenly Jerusalem.

Hebrews 13 draws the conclusion to which the letter has been leading: since Judaism possesses only the shadows of the reality Christians have attained in Christ, Christians should break with Judaism. In 13:13, Christians are exhorted to "go to him [Jesus] outside the camp." "Camp" is a biblical term for Israel. It is taken from a military context: Israel is encamped and ready for holy war.

THE BOOK OF REVELATION: JESUS AS WITNESS AND ESCHATOLOGICAL WARRIOR

HISTORICAL CONTEXT

The New Testament is full of apocalyptic imagery, symbols, and concepts, but Revelation is its only apocalypse. Like all apocalypses, Revelation tells the story of a revelation given to a seer (John) concerning the

*Albrecht Dürer's woodcut depicting the Son of Man from the
first chapter of the book of Revelation.*

heavenly world and the eschaton. The book was written during the rule of
the Roman emperor Domitian, around 96 C.E. Earlier scholarship
thought that, unlike most of his predecessors, Domitian insisted on emperor worship and that persecution was threatened against those who refused, especially Christians. More recent scholarship has challenged this

picture (see Thompson). In fact, there was little persecution of Christians in the first century C.E. There was a persecution under Nero, but Christians were not killed for the mere fact of being Christians but because Nero blamed them for a devastating fire in Rome in 64 C.E., possibly to divert suspicion from himself. Revelation itself offers little evidence of widespread persecution, but its author does think that a general persecution is impending (e.g., Rev 3:10). The book sees the coming persecution as a showdown between God and Satan.

Chapters 2–3 consist of seven messages from the glorified Christ to seven churches in western Asia Minor. Christ is distressed at developments within the churches. They were, for the most part, located in important cities in the Roman province of Asia, and their culture was Roman Hellenism. The author feels that some Christians are too much at home in the local culture, and he writes to convince them that Christianity is incompatible with it. God's sovereignty is irreconcilable with that of Caesar. The author praises those who share his views, and he threatens with judgment those who do not.

The author of Revelation, like the author of Matthew, does not see Christianity as a new religion, separate from Judaism. He thinks of Christianity as the true Judaism. Twice he attacks non-Christian Jewish communities in Asia Minor. Josephus tells us that these communities were prosperous and respected in their cities. Our author may be upset at them both because they do not accept Jesus as the Messiah and because they advocate peaceful coexistence with the Roman Empire. In Rev 2:9, the author refers to them as "those who say that they are Jews and are not, but are a synagogue of Satan," and in 3:9, he asserts that they "say that they are Jews and are not, but are lying." Signs of the author's Jewishness are his heavy use of allusions to the Hebrew Bible and his use of Jewish concepts and symbols. The author's language is a very strange sort of Greek, apparently deeply influenced by Hebrew. Some think that the author was a Jewish Christian who had migrated from the homeland to Asia Minor after the war between the Jews and the Romans in 66–73 C.E. He thought of himself as a prophet, and he had been active in the seven churches. His was a conservative, apocalyptic Jewish Christianity that had little room for accomodation to the open, Hellenistic urban culture he found in western Asia Minor. He found emperor worship, used by eastern cities as a means of expressing loyalty and gaining prestige for themselves, particularly repugnant. His radical views led him to be exiled to the rocky island of Patmos, from which he wrote. His alienation from the surrounding culture led him to compose a work that has proven of great use down through the ages to those alienated from their own environments.

SATAN AND THE ROMAN EMPIRE

To understand the author's antipathy to the Roman Empire, it is necessary to recall that religion and politics were closely intertwined in the ancient world. Rome was no exception. Roman imperial propaganda and ceremony were expressed in terms that can only be called religious. Israelite and Jewish tradition conceived of God in royal and even imperial terms. So it was not surprising that Rome's claims were seen to clash with God's kingship. When the author faced what he saw as Jewish and Christian accomodation to Rome's idolatrous claims and when he encountered emperor worship as a popular way of claiming one's place in the empire, he reacted as did the ancient prophets of Israel when they faced Israel's adaptation to its polytheistic environment.

Many inhabitants of the Roman Empire were convinced that there was a superhuman power behind the empire. Such tremendous might must have a supernatural source. The Romans themselves sometimes attributed their hegemony over the world to their piety toward their own gods and even toward the gods of others. Josephus thought that the Romans were granted lordship over Israel by Israel's God, although he did not think this lordship permanent. Paul thought that God was the power behind the empire (Rom 13).

For Revelation's author, the supernatural force behind the empire had to be evil, since for him Rome was hostile to Christianity and since Roman religious pretensions were incompatible with the exclusive worship of God and Christ. Revelation 12–13 offers the author's explanation of the supernatural evil force that gave the empire its power and authority. Chapter 12 opens with the vision of a woman in heaven, probably representing Israel. She is pregnant, and although the author does not say so explicitly, her son is the Messiah. The idea is that the Messiah comes from Israel. Since the woman is the Messiah's mother, it would be natural to see her as Mary, mother of Jesus, but things are said about her later in the chapter that do not fit Mary.

Now another figure appears: "a great red dragon, with seven heads and ten horns, and seven diadems on his heads. His tail swept down a third of the stars of heaven and threw them to the earth" (12:3–4). As is revealed further on, the dragon is Satan. His portrayal as a red dragon with horns and a long tail is the source of modern depictions of the devil. The dragon causes havoc among the stars of heaven. The stars are heavenly beings (angels), and the dragon wages war directly on them. He also wishes to devour the Messiah.

The heavenly war is described more explicitly in the next verses:

And war broke out in heaven; Michael and his angels fought against the dragon. The dragon and his angels fought back, but they were defeated, and there was no longer any place for them in heaven. The great dragon was thrown down, that ancient serpent, who is called the Devil and Satan, the deceiver of the whole world—he was thrown down to the earth, and his angels were thrown down with him. (12:7–9)

The description of Satan derives from his identification with the "ancient serpent" that deceived Adam and Eve and, through them, the whole world (Gen 3). Satan was originally an angel in heaven. As mentioned earlier, in Job 2 and Zech 3, he is the heavenly prosecuting attorney. Later he was identified with the prince of demons. Eventually Satan was associated, in Jewish and Christian tradition, with the serpent that tempted Eve in the Garden of Eden (Gen 3).

The *Book of the Watchers* develops a mythic fragment from Gen 6:1–4 in which angels descend from heaven and have intercourse with human women (see ch. 4, above). Revelation 12 draws on a different tradition concerning the departure of rebellious angels from heaven, a tradition that attributes their departure to a war with God's loyal angels. The rest of Rev 12 hails Satan's defeat as a victory for God and for those faithful to God. Thrown down to earth from heaven, the dragon tries to pursue the woman, who is now also on earth. He sends after her a torrent of water, but the earth opens up and swallows it, saving the woman. There are echoes of the exodus here, given the elements of the desert, a threat from water, and being saved from water. The book of Revelation contains many allusions to the exodus.

"Then the dragon was angry with the woman, and went off to make war on the rest of her children, those who keep the commandments of God and hold the testimony of Jesus. Then the dragon took his stand on the sand of the seashore" (12:17–18). The rest of the woman's children are those whom Revelation considers faithful Christians. Satan's anger at Christians explains their impending suffering. The sea symbolizes supernatural forces against God, as it does in Dan 7.

Chapter 13 opens with a strange and terrifying beast rising out of the sea. This scene, too, recalls Dan 7, in which four beasts from the sea represent kingdoms. The beast in Revelation has ten horns and seven heads. In Dan 7, there are a total of seven heads and ten horns on the beasts. Revelation's beast has characteristics of a leopard, a bear, and a lion, precisely the animals to which Daniel compares his beasts. The beast mirrors the heavenly dragon in that the latter, too, has seven heads and ten horns. This draws a close connection between the dragon (Satan) and the beast (Rome). In Rev 13 the beast symbolizes the Roman Empire: "And the dragon gave it his power and his throne and great authority. . . . They worshiped the dragon, for he had given his authority to the beast, and they worshiped the beast, saying, 'Who is like the beast, and who can fight against it?' " (13:2, 4). The might of the Roman

Empire is thus explained: Satan gave it his authority and power. And emperor worship is explained: people recognize the cosmic power at work in the Roman Empire, and so they worship Rome and the emperor, but in so doing, they really pledge loyalty to Satan.

GOD'S SOVEREIGNTY

Defense of God's sovereignty is common in apocalypses. Many apocalypses are written to demonstrate that the world is alienated from God and that God will soon take it back. These texts, and those texts from the Hebrew Bible that they draw from, often depict God's ultimate authority through throne scenes (e.g., Isa 6, Ezek 1, Dan 7, *1 En.* 14) where the seer beholds God in heaven. Revelation follows this pattern. The eschatological visions open with a throne scene in chapters 4–5, and the rest of the book makes frequent reference to God's throne. "Throne" is one of the most common words in the book, occurring forty-seven times, mostly in reference to God's throne. The throne represents God's sovereignty over the whole universe. Revelation shows that the events that effect Rome's downfall, the defeat of Satan, and the establishment of God's new Jerusalem on earth all originate at God's throne—that is, they are the work of God.

THE APOCALYPTIC JESUS

Satan's defeat in heaven is a prelude to his final defeat at the end of time at the hands of Jesus the eschatological warrior. But Jesus has already defeated Satan because, when Jesus walked the earth, he resisted Satan, even to death (1:5; 3:21; 5:9–10; 12:10–12). He was the "faithful witness" to God's sovereignty who resisted Rome's idolatrous claims. Christian martyrs are assured that, by their witness and death, they too overcome Satan and gain entry into the heavenly sanctuary. Martyrdom thus becomes conquest.

As noted above, Rev 4–5 is a heavenly throne scene that serves as the basis for the rest of the eschatological revelations in the book. In chapter 4, God sits on the throne, surrounded by worshiping angels. At the beginning of chapter 5, the seer notices a scroll in God's hand, sealed with seven seals. When he learns that no one in the universe is worthy to open the scroll, he weeps because he realizes that the scroll contains the end time events, which cannot happen if the scroll is not opened. We have encountered the idea of heavenly books in the apocalypses we studied. Heavenly books can be of various types. That in Rev 5 contains future events. (Close parallels are found in Dan 10:21; Ps 139:16; and *1 En.* 81:1–3; 93:1–3; 103:2; 106:19; 107:1; 108:7). An angel reveals to the seer that there is, after all, one who is worthy, "the Lion of the tribe of Judah, the Root of David" (Rev 5:5; see Gen 49:9–10; Isa

11:10; *4 Ezra* 11:36–12:25). These are Davidic messianic terms. The seer then sees "a Lamb standing as if it had been slaughtered, having seven horns and seven eyes" (5:6). The Lamb is an apocalyptic representation of Christ. The image of a slaughtered lamb may derive from the Passover lamb, or perhaps it is an allusion to the Suffering Servant song of Isa 53 (see ch. 3, above), a passage often applied to Christ in Christian tradition.

When the Lamb takes the book from God's hand, God's heavenly attendants (angels) sing,

> You are worthy to take the scroll
>   and to open its seals,
> for you were slaughtered and by your blood you ransomed for God
>   saints from every tribe and language and people and nation;
> you have made them to be a kingdom and priests serving our God,
>   and they will reign on earth. (Rev 5:9–10)

Jesus' death begins the execution of God's end time plans. When the Lamb, Jesus, takes the scroll and opens the seals one by one, the divine plan is set in motion, and the battle between the forces of God and those of Satan begins. His death also results in the formation of a community loyal to God. It is priestly and kingly, a description taken from God's words on Sinai about Israel in Exod 19:6. Christians participate in the cosmic battle as they resist Satan's onslaughts on earth by means of the Roman Empire.

Jesus is first introduced in Revelation with the following words: "Jesus Christ, the faithful witness, the firstborn of the dead, and the ruler of the kings of the earth" (1:5). Jesus' "witness" is his testimony to God in the midst of persecution. "Firstborn of the dead" refers to Jesus' resurrection. His resurrection vindicates him, and the term "firstborn" indicates that it is but the first of many resurrections. All who are faithful to God will rise in the end. We have seen that resurrection is a common expectation in the Jewish apocalypses. What is new in Christianity is the claim that one person has already been raised, Jesus, proof that the rest of the righteous will also be raised. In Jesus, the consummation of history has begun.

Jesus' power is expressed in 1:5: he is "the ruler of the kings of the earth." Christians have nothing to fear from the Roman emperor, who is but a king of the earth. The idea that God rules the kings of the earth is common in Jewish apocalypses. What is new is that Jesus rules these kings on God's behalf.

The seer, John, receives a vision of Christ in all his glory and strength. He sees

> one like the Son of Man, clothed with a long robe and with a golden sash across his chest. His head and his hair were white as white wool, white as snow; his

eyes were like a flame of fire, his feet were like burnished bronze, refined as in a furnace, and his voice was like the sound of many waters. In his right hand he held seven stars, and from his mouth came a sharp, two-edged sword, and his face was like the sun shining with full force. (1:13–16)

Jesus' portrait here is based on two passages from the book of Daniel, along with some touches from elsewhere in the Hebrew Bible. The first is Daniel's throne scene, which opens,

> Thrones were set in place,
>   and an Ancient One took his throne,
> his clothing was white as snow,
>   and the hair of his head like pure wool;
> his throne was fiery flames,
>   and its wheels were burning fire. (Dan 7:9)

The second passage from Daniel concerns the revealing angel of Dan 10:

> I looked up and was a man clothed with linen, with a belt of gold from Uphaz around his waist. His body was like beryl, his face like lightning, his eyes like flaming torches, his arms and legs like the gleam of burnished bronze, and the sound of his words like the roar of a multitude. (10:5–6)

Jesus portrayed in these terms would be a comfort to Christians who thought that they faced Satan himself. A Christ of such supernatural and terrifying magnitude could be a match for the prince of demons.

Warlike imagery is employed in Rev 19 to depict Jesus' going out to the final battle with Satan. It is this eschatological warrior who conquers Satan.

> Then I saw heaven opened, and there was a white horse! Its rider is called Faithful and True, and in righteousness he judges and makes war. His eyes are like a flame of fire, and on his head are many diadems; and he has a name inscribed that no one knows but himself. He is clothed in a robe dipped in blood, and his name is called The Word of God. And the armies of heaven, wearing fine linen, white and pure, were following him on white horses. From his mouth comes a sharp sword with which to strike down the nations, and he will rule them with a rod of iron; he will tread the wine press of the fury of the wrath of God the Almighty. On his robe and on his thigh he has a name inscribed, "King of kings and Lord of lords." (Rev 19:11–16)

Revelation is roughly contemporary with *4 Ezra* and *2 Baruch*. The latter two works envision an earthly messianic kingdom that has an end, followed by a more complete fulfillment of eschatological hopes. Revelation follows this same pattern. In 20:1–6, Satan is bound in the abyss, and the martyrs rise to rule the earth with Christ for a thousand years. Then Satan is released, a final battle is fought in which he is defeated, and all the forces of evil are thrown into a lake of fire to be tormented forever. The binding of Satan pending his final punishment recalls similar scenarios in the *Book of the Watchers* (*1 En.* 10:4–6) and the *Similitudes of Enoch* (*1 En.* 53–54). A similar scene is supposed by a section of what is often called the "Isaiah Apocalypse" (Isa 24–27), so called because it stands out from the rest of First Isaiah (Isa 1–39) because of its apocalyptic outlook. The lake of fire in Revelation corresponds to the fiery abyss in *1 Enoch.*

THE NEW JERUSALEM

Revelation 21 describes the descent onto earth of a new Jerusalem. In the new Jerusalem, the faithful live without suffering or sorrow. God's blessings are showered on it:

> I saw no temple in the city, for its temple is the Lord God the Almighty and the Lamb. And the city has no need of sun or moon to shine on it, for the glory of God is its light, and its lamp is the Lamb. The nations will walk by its light, and the kings of the earth will bring their glory into it. Its gates will never be shut by day—and there will be no night there. People will bring into it the glory and the honor of the nations. But nothing unclean will enter it, nor anyone who practices abomination or falsehood, but only those who are written in the Lamb's book of life. (21:22–27)

The new Jerusalem is the goal of history. Zion theology supplies the images for the description of God's eschatological city, including the idea that God is present there (see Ezek 43:1–5; 48:35) and that the nations stream to it to worship Israel's God (see Hag 2:7; Zech 14:14; Tob 13:11; 14:5–6). Priestly terminology is used to speak of the holiness of the city. But entry into the new Jerusalem is determined by whether one's name is written in the "Lamb's book of life." Again we encounter the idea of heavenly books, this time books that contain judgments on humans and angels. Here it is the followers of the Lamb who are saved.

The absence of a temple in the new Jerusalem is remarkable when one considers the significance of the temple for Jerusalem over the better part of a thousand years of Israel's history. On the other hand, many Jews in the Second Temple period disapproved of the Jerusalem priesthood and thought that it had defiled the temple. Jesus himself attacked the temple and predicted its destruction. The lack of a temple means that inhabitants of the world now have direct, unmediated access to God.

CONCLUSION

Jesus and his first followers were Jews. To understand the historical Jesus, we must see him in the context of first-century Galilee and Judea. The same is true of the earliest Christian movement, which initially was composed of Jews. An appreciation of late Second Temple Judaism is essential to understanding interpretations of Jesus that emerged after his death. If according to the early Christians Jesus was the Jewish Messiah foretold by the Hebrew Bible, then it is in Jewish terms that the early Christians had to understand him.

It is often thought that Christianity split from Judaism when Christians claimed that Jesus was divine, a belief incompatible with Jewish monotheism. But things were not so simple. J. D. G. Dunn shows that the split did not happen all at once nor was only one issue involved. Acts sees the initial tensions as resulting from attitudes to Torah and temple, not from conflicts over the divinity of Christ. Over time, Christianity did become a separate religion from Judaism. But this can blind us to the fact that it began as a group within Second Temple Judaism. It is important to remember Christianity's Jewish roots; otherwise we misunderstand both Christianity and Judaism. As Segal expresses it, Judaism and Christianity were born "as twins in the lst years of Judean statehood" (p. 181).

SELECT BIBLIOGRAPHY

Attridge, Harold W. *Hebrews.* Philadelphia: Fortress, 1989.
Bourke, Myles M. "The Epistle to the Hebrews." *NJBC* 920–41.
Caird, G. B. *A Commentary on the Revelation of St. John the Divine.* London: Adam & Charles Black, 1966).
Charles, R. H. *A Critical and Exegetical Commentary on the Revelation of St. John.* 2 vols. New York: Scribner's, 1920.
Collins, Adela Yarbro. "The Apocalypse (Revelation)." *NJBC* 996–1016.
———. *The Combat Myth in the Book of Revelation.*, Missoula, Mont.: Scholars Press, 1976.
———. *Crisis and Catharsis: The Power of the Apocalypse.* Philadelphia: Westminster, 1984.
Davies, W. D. *The Sermon on the Mount.* Cambridge: Cambridge University Press, 1966.
deJonge, Marinus. *Christology in Context: The Earliest Christian Response to Jesus.* Philadelphia: Westminster, 1988.
Dunn, J. D. G. *The Partings of the Ways between Christianity and Judaism and Their Significance for the Character of Christianity.* Philadelphia: Trinity Press International, 1991.

—. *Christology in the Making: A New Testament Inquiry into the Origins of the Doctrine of the Incarnation.* Philadelphia: Westminster, 1980.

Fredriksen, Paula. *From Jesus to Christ: The Origins of the New Testament Images of Jesus.* New Haven: Yale, 1988.

Hanson, K. C., and Douglas E. Oakman. *Palestine in the Time of Jesus: Social Structures and Social Conflicts.* Minneapolis: Fortress: 1998.

Hurtado, Larry W. *One God, One Lord: Early Christian Devotion and Ancient Jewish Monotheism.* Philadelphia: Fortress, 1988.

Jeremias, Joachim. *New Testament Theology.* New York: Scribners, 1971.

Kingsbury, Jack Dean. *Matthew: Structure, Christology, Kingdom.* Philadelphia: Fortress, 1975.

Levine, Amy-Jill. *The Social and Ethical Dimensions of Matthean Salvation History.* Lewiston: Edwin Mellen, 1988.

MacRae, George. "Heavenly Temple and Eschatology in the Letter to the Hebrews." *Semeia* 12 (1978): 179–99.

Meier, John. *A Marginal Jew: Rethinking the Historical Jesus.* 2 vols. New York: Doubleday, 1991–1994.

—. *The Vision of Matthew.* New York: Paulist, 1979.

Murphy, Frederick J. *Fallen Is Babylon: The Revelation to John.* Harrisburg, Pa.: Trinity Press International, 1998.

Neusner, Jacob. *A Rabbi Talks with Jesus: An Intermillennial, Interfaith Exchange.* New York: Doubleday, 1993.

Overman, J. Andrew. *Church and Community in Crisis.* Harrisburg, Pa.: Trinity Press International, 1996.

—. *Matthew's Gospel and Formative Judaism: The Social World of the Matthean Community.* Minneapolis: Fortress, 1990.

Pontifical Biblical Commission. *The Interpretation of the Bible in the Church.* Boston: St. Paul, 1993.

Saldarini, Anthony. *Matthew's Christian-Jewish Community.* Chicago: University of Chicago Press, 1994.

Segal, Alan E. *Rebecca's Children: Judaism and Christianity in the Roman World.* Cambridge: Harvard University Press, 1986.

Thompson, Leonard L. *The Book of Revelation: Apocalypse and Empire.* New York: Oxford University Press, 1990.

Wilson, Stephen G. *Related Strangers: Jews and Christians, 70–170 C.E.* Minneapolis: Fortress, 1995.

GLOSSARY OF TERMS

Anatolia. See Asia Minor.

Aniconic. Without images. An icon is an image.

Anointed. Smeared with oil as a sign of designation for a special task. "Messiah" is from the Hebrew and "Christ" is from the Greek for "anointed."

Apocalypse. "A genre of revelatory literature with a narrative framework, in which a revelation is mediated by an otherworldly being to a human recipient, disclosing a transcendent reality which is both temporal, insofar as it envisages eschatological salvation, and spatial insofar as it involves another, supernatural world" (*AI* 5).

Apocalyptic. Relating to, or indicative of apocalypses.

Apocalyptic multivalence. Ability of apocalypses to be applied to many different situations due to their ambivalent symbolism and lack of specific references.

Apocalypticism. Worldview typical of apocalypses.

Apocrypha. Books and parts of books contained in the Septuagint but not in the Hebrew Bible. Most are accepted by Catholics as canonical (and so are called deuterocanonical), but not by Protestants or Jews.

Apostasy. Abandonment of one's religious faith or loyalty to God. One who does this is called an "apostate."

Ark of the covenant. Box that served as a traveling shrine for the Israelites and that contained tablets of the covenant. It was deposited in the holy of holies in Solomon's temple but apparently did not survive the destruction of the temple by the Babylonians.

Asia Minor. Ancient name for what is now Asian Turkey. Also called Anatolia.

Astral immortality. An afterlife state consisting of eternal existence among the stars, themselves thought of as heavenly beings.

B.C.E. Before the Common Era. The same time period is also often designated B.C.

Babylonian exile. The deportation of the leading citizens of the kingdom of Judah to Babylonia in 587 B.C.E. Cyrus allowed them to return in 538 B.C.E.

Bandits. Members of groups (bands) who lived on the fringes of society by raiding.

Berith. Hebrew word for "covenant."

C.E. Common Era. The same time period is also often designated A.D.

Canon. Sacred books considered normative. Books considered to be part of the Bible.

Canonical. Belonging to the canon.

Centurion. Commander of a hundred men in the Roman army.

Chaldeans. Another name for the Babylonians.

Christ. "Anointed"; from the Greek *christos.*

Circumcision. Cutting off of the foreskin of Jewish males as a sign of the covenant.

Clean. Pure; undefiled; capable of coming into God's sacred temple precincts.

Cosmology. A system of knowledge dealing with the nature of the universe.

Cosmopolis. The entire known world conceived as a single city *(polis);* a Stoic ideal.

Cosmos. From the Greek *kosmos,* meaning "world" or "ordered universe."

Covenant. An agreement or pact between two parties. Hittite suzerainty covenants (treaties) were the model for Israel's relation with God.

Cult. Practices centering on the temple, its sacrifices, and its liturgy.

Day of Atonement. Major feast day in the fall when atonement was made for the people and priests and the temple was cleansed.

Dead Sea Scrolls. Scrolls discovered in 1947 and in following years, thought to be connected to the nearby ancient settlement of Qumran.

Decalogue. The Ten Commandments. From the Greek *deka,* "ten," and *logos,* "word"; in the Bible, the Ten Commandments are called the "ten words."

Determinism. The belief that everything is preordained, including human history.

Deuterocanonical. *See* canon. A second group of books considered canonical by Catholics but not by Protestants or Jews.

Deuteronomistic. Characteristic of the biblical books Deuteronomy through 2 Kings (the Deuteronomistic History).

Diadochoi. Successors of Alexander the Great.

Diaspora. A general name for the Jewish communities outside the Jewish homeland.

Dirt. Matter out of place.

Dispersion. The Diaspora. English meaning of the Greek *diaspora.*

Divine Warrior. God depicted as a man of war.

Dualism. Looking at the world in terms of polar opposites. Social dualism entails seeing all humanity as divided into good and bad, for example. Cosmic dualism sees two opposed forces in the universe, such as God against Satan.

Economics. Arrangements determining the production, distribution, and consumption of goods and services.

Eden. Garden where Adam and Eve first lived.

Elder. A group within the ruling classes of ancient Israel. Elders were prominent citizens, probably the leading members of the leading families.

Endogamy. Marriage within the group.

Eschatology. Teaching concerning the end of things. Apocalyptic eschatology refers to the end of the world and society as presently constituted.

Eschaton. A Greek word meaning "end." In apocalypticism it refers to the end of the world as presently constituted.

Essenes. A Jewish sect believed by many to be responsible for the Qumran library.

Ethnarch. Ruler of a people (Greek: *ethnos*).

Ex eventu prophecy. Prophecy after the event, typical of apocalypses.

Exegesis. Interpretation of Scripture.

Exile. See Babylonian exile.

Exodus. Israel's escape from Egypt through the power of God and under the leadership of Moses.

Exogamy. Marriage outside the group.

Factions. Rival groups within a society that compete for limited power and resources but do not differ in ideology, class, or ethnicity.

Genealogy. A list of one's ancestors.

Gentiles. Non-Jews.

Gerizim. The sacred mountain of the Samaritans, located near ancient Shechem.

Gnosis. Literally, knowledge. It often designates a particular kind of religion in which the possession of knowledge, usually esoteric, is the key to salvation.

Halakah. Jewish law.

Hanukkah. A feast celebrating the Maccabean victory over the Seleucids and the cleansing and re-dedication of the sanctuary.

Hasidim. A group or groups devoted to Torah that supported the Maccabees in the early stages of the revolution.

Hasmoneans. Name used for the Jewish dynasty established by the priest Mattathias and his five sons, who revolted against the Seleucids.

Hellenism. Multifaceted culture created through the interaction of Greek culture and local cultures, beginning with the conquests of Alexander the Great.

Hellenistic reform. An attempt, begun in 175 B.C.E. by some members of the upper classes of Jerusalem, to make the city and its institutions Hellenistic.

Herem. Spoils of war belonging to God and meant to be offered to God in holocaust.

Hesed. God's loving-kindness for Israel, expressed in God's deeds on behalf of Israel.

Holiness. An attribute belonging to God and that which is close to God.

Holy of holies. Innermost and most sacred room of the temple.

Holy place. The nave of the temple. The temple's second holiest room, where most of the activity within the building took place.

Holy war. War in which God fights on behalf of Israel.

Horeb. See Sinai.

Idumeans. Natives of the territory south of Judah. They were forcibly circumcised by John Hyrcanus. Herod the Great was an Idumean.

Israel. Name of God's people in the Hebrew Bible. Also name of the northern kingdom after the split with the Davidic dynasty.

Jamnia. See Yavneh.

Jews. All those descended from the natives of the ancient kingdom of Judah. The name was applied to Yahweh worshipers after the exile.

Judah. One of the twelve patriarchs (children of Jacob). Also, the tribe from which David came, and the area around Jerusalem.

Judea. Name given by the Romans to the area controlled by the city of Jerusalem.

Kingdom of God. God's rule, expressed through mighty deeds. Precisely how the kingdom works itself out in history (or at the eschaton) varies with different authors and contexts.

Kinship. Family relationship; descent.

Levi. The priestly tribe.

Levites. Israel's lower clergy, of the tribe of Levi.

Liturgy. Public worship.

LORD. See Yahweh.

Lots. Objects cast or drawn to make decisions in accord with God's will. This is analogous to throwing dice or drawing straws today.

Maccabee. Name meaning "hammer," applied to Judah, son of Mattathias, probably for his military feats against the Seleucids. Applied by extension to his brothers.

Masada. Herodian fortress, west of the Dead Sea, where the Sicarii held the Romans off until 73 C.E.

Messiah. From the Hebrew word for "anointed." One who is set aside and anointed to perform a special task for God.

Mikra. Literally, "reading." This Hebrew word denotes Jewish Scripture.

Mishnah. Written collection of rabbinic legal rulings, written ca. 200 C.E.

Monolatry. Worship of (service to) one God.

Monotheism. Belief in one God.

Mystery. A technical term in apocalypticism, denoting God's plans kept secret from the beginning of the world and now revealed to a human intermediary. The term can also refer to a particular kind of religious express in which one is initiated into the good graces of a particular god or goddess through mystical rites.

Nabateans. Arab people from east of the Jordan.

Oral Torah. Rabbinic term, applied to the oral traditions of the Pharisees and then the rabbis. The traditions were collected and written down in rabbinic literature and were thought to have been given to Moses on Sinai with the written Torah and then passed down through the generations orally.

Parable. In its broad meaning, any sort of figurative speech, from similes and analogies to prophetic oracles to extended narrative metaphors. In a more restricted sense, short stories told by Jesus.

Paradise. From a Persian loanword that in the Septuagint indicates the Garden of Eden.

Parthians. Rulers of the empire east of the Roman Empire until the third century C.E.

Passover. Feast, celebrated in the spring, that commemorates God's liberation of Israel from Egypt.

Patriarchy. Rule by the father. Also, dominance of men over women.

Patron-client relationship. Vertical organization of social status and interaction in which members of the upper class bestow tangible benefits on members of the lower class in return for loyalty, honor, and so on.

Peasants. Members of the lower classes who made their living by cultivating the land.

Pentateuch. The first five books of the Hebrew Bible.

Pericope. A short unit of text.

Persia. Empire that ruled most of the eastern Mediterranean from the middle of the sixth century B.C.E. until the conquests of Alexander the Great.

Pharaoh. The name for the ancient Egyptian kings.

Pharisees. Political interest and religious group that existed from the second century B.C.E. through the first century C.E.

Politics. The set of mechanisms and interactions, formal and informal, by which power is distributed and exercised.

Polytheism. Belief in many gods.

Priest. One of a hereditary class that had traditional rights to serve God in the sanctuary.

Prophet. One who speaks for God.

Proselytes. Converts.

Pseudepigrapha. Books written in the name of others, usually figures from the distant past. The name is applied to a large body of literature falling outside the limits of the canon.

Pseudonymity. False or fictional attribution of a literary work.

Ptolemies. Hellenistic dynasty that ruled Egypt after the conquest by Alexander.

Purify. To put things back in their proper category. To remove that which defiles so that persons or things are restored to their proper state.

Purity rules. Rules safeguarding the distinction between sacred and profane.

Qumran. A settlement, now in ruins, among the cliffs at the northwest shore of the Dead Sea. The settlement is associated with the library, called the Dead Sea Scrolls, found in neighboring caves.

Rabbinic literature. Literature produced by the rabbis. The parts mentioned in this book are the Mishnah (ca. 200 C.E.), the Tosefta (ca. 250 C.E.), the Palestinian Talmud (ca. 400–450 C.E.), and the Babylonian Talmud (ca. 500–600 C.E.).

Rabbi. Term meaning "my great one" in Hebrew. It was applied to teachers of Torah after the destruction of the temple in 70 C.E.

Recapitulation. Technique in apocalypses in which the same event or sequence of events or symbol is repeated in differing ways, thereby reinforcing a basic pattern.

Religion. A set of beliefs, symbols, practices, and social structures thought to be of divine origin and enabling humans to interact with the world of the sacred.

Replication. The repetition of basic patterns in various realms, such as cult, society, and architecture, thus reinforcing a culture's symbolic system.

Restoration. The period of rebuilding Jerusalem, the temple, and Jewish society after the Babylonian exile (from 520 B.C.E. onward).

Retainer. One whose occupation was to serve the ruling class, such as a scribe or a soldier.

Ritual purity. A state of purity enabling one to participate in the cult.

Sabbath. The seventh day, sacred to the Lord, on which no work was to be done.

Sacrifice. Something offered to God. In the case of an animal, it involves ritually slaughtering it, burning some (or all) of it on the altar, and dividing the rest between the priests and the offerers or, in some cases, giving it entirely to the priests.

Sadducees. A political interest group, probably composed of some of the leading priests and landowners, which existed at least from the latter half of the second century B.C.E. to the destruction of Jerusalem in 70 C.E.

Salvation. Rescue; liberation. In most of the Hebrew Bible, the term refers to rescue from enemies, oppression, natural disasters, and so on. Later the term could refer to being brought to heaven to live.

Samaritans. Inhabitants of Samaria, the land between Judea and Galilee. Most Judean traditions portray the Samaritans negatively. The Samaritans revere Moses and have a version of the Torah.

Sanctification. Making something or someone holy, pure, able to approach God.

Sanctuary. From the Latin *sanctus,* meaning "holy." A sanctuary is a holy place. "The sanctuary" often means the temple or the holy of holies.

Sanhedrin. Governing council in Jerusalem, composed of leading priests, elders, and scribes. Sadducees and some Pharisees were members.

Sapiential. Concerning wisdom.

Scribe. One whose occupation was that of reading and writing.

Scroll. Roll of papyrus or treated leather used for writing.

Sect. Minority group that sees itself as separate from, and opposed to, the dominant society and is very conscious of its social boundaries.

Seer. One who sees visions or receives special revelations in apocalypses.

Seleucids. Dynasty that ruled Syria and other lands after the breakup of Alexander's empire.

Septuagint. Greek translation of the Hebrew Bible and some other books begun in the third century B.C.E. It was the main version used by the early Christians. Books in the Septuagint but not in the Hebrew Bible are called the Apocrypha.

Shema. One of the most sacred prayers in Judaism, recited daily. It begins with the words of Deut 6:4.

Sheol. Name for the shadowy underworld inhabited by the dead.

Sicarii. A Jewish group, emerging in the 50s C.E. that used terrorist tactics against the ruling class of Judea.

Sinai. The mountain on which God gave Moses the Torah. (Also called Horeb.)

Society. A broad term encompassing the religious, cultural, political, economic, and kinship institutions and practices of a group of people.

Son of God. Term applied in Jewish tradition to a Davidic king, Israel as a whole, a righteous Jew, an angel, and so on.

Son of Man. Often means simply "human being." The term can be applied to an angel, in which case it is usually said that the angel is *like* a son of man. It is applied to the angelic representative of Israel, Michael, in Dan 7, and by the early Christians to Jesus as eschatological judge, a use that parallels that found in the *Similitudes of Enoch.*

Stoics. An influential Hellenistic philosophical school to which Josephus compares the Pharisees.

Synagogue. Jewish institution whose origins are obscure. It is the place where Jews meet weekly for prayer and for Torah reading and exposition.

Syncretism. Interaction of elements from diverse cultures to form a new cultural entity.

Synoptic Gospels. Matthew, Mark, and Luke, so called because are very similar and so can be placed side by side and compared ("seen together") in detail.

Tabernacle. The tent in the Israelite desert camp, symbolizing the presence of God. It is described in terms that fit the Jerusalem temple.

Tabernacles. Autumnal festival, timed to coincide with the harvest of fruits.

Talmud. Two bodies of rabbinic commentary on Mishnah, one from Babylon and the other from the land of Israel.

Tanak. Jewish name for the Hebrew Bible. It is an acronym for the three parts of Scripture, Torah *(torah),* Prophets *(nebi'im),* and Writings *(ketubim).*

Testament. A literary genre composed of a narrative of the last hours of an important figure and his/her last words. In "New Testament" and "Old Testament," the term means "covenant."

Tetrarch. A ruler who was less than a king and an ethnarch. The term originally literally meant perhaps the ruler of a fourth of a territory or one of four rulers.

Theodicy. A defense of God's righteousness, particularly in the face of experiences that seem to contradict that righteousness. See especially *4 Ezra.*

Theophany. A divine appearance.

Throne scene. Scene in an ancient text featuring God's throne; such scenes were often used to validate the message of a prophet or an apocalyptic seer.

Tithes. An offering to God, given to the priests, consisting of a tenth of agricultural produce.

Torah. The term's earliest use meant "instruction," applied to priestly rulings or instructions. It came to be applied to the first five books of the Hebrew Bible. Later it was also used for all of Scripture, and later still for the entire Jewish way of life.

Unclean. Impure, defiled, unable to be brought into God's presence.

Watcher. An angelic figure who watches, or guards.

Weeks. Feast celebrating the wheat harvest, fifty days after Passover.

Wisdom. Knowledge of how the universe, including human life, works. Folk wisdom is often passed on through proverbs. In the wisdom tradition, it is available to those with the time to study wisdom handed on orally and in writing, to observe human life, and to reflect on their observations. Apocalyptic wisdom is esoteric wisdom given to an elite.

Yahweh. The proper name of the God of the Israelites. Today the name is considered too sacred even to pronounce, except once a year, on the Day of Atonement. When Jews are reading Scripture aloud and come to this name, they substitute the Hebrew word *Adonai,* meaning "my Lord." In respect for this usage, some biblical translations such as the NRSV, do not print the name "Yahweh," substituting instead the word "LORD," with small capital letters.

Yavneh. Town on the Mediterranean coast to which Johanan ben Zakkai was allowed to go by Vespasian during the siege of Jerusalem. It became the center for the reformulation of Judaism after the war.

Zadokites. Priests descended from Solomon's high priest Zadok.

Zealots. Group of Jews from the countryside who fled to Jerusalem before the Roman advance in 67–68 C.E. "Zealots" was a self-designation alluding to their zeal for the Torah.

Zion. Name of the mountain on which the temple was built. The word could be used more broadly to speak of all of Jerusalem.

Zion ideology; Zion theology. General term for a set of beliefs about Zion—for example, that it is God's dwelling place, that God will protect it, that it will become the center of worship for all nations at the end of time.

GLOSSARY OF PERSONS

Abraham. The ancestor of Israel (through Isaac) and of the Arabs (through Ishmael).

Agrippa I. Grandson of Herod the Great. During the first century C.E. he ruled over an area equal to Herod's old kingdom (37–44 C.E.).

Agrippa II. Son of Agrippa I. He ruled the small northern kingdom of Chalcis beginning in 48 C.E.

Alexander Jannaeus. Hasmonean king who ruled 103–76 B.C.E.

Alexander the Great. Macedonian leader who united the Greek cities, conquered the Persian Empire, and initiated the Hellenistic era.

Alexandra Salome. Hasmonean queen who ruled 76–67 B.C.E. Wife of Alexander Jannaeus. Josephus says that the Pharisees were her advisors.

Antiochus IV Epiphanes. Seleucid king (ruled 175–164 B.C.E.) who persecuted Judaism.

Antipater. An Idumean, the principal military commander of the Hasmonean Hyrcanus II. He was made procurator of Judea in 47 B.C.E. He was the father of Herod the Great.

Archelaus. Son of Herod the Great; ruled Judea from 4 B.C.E. to 6 C.E. The Romans removed him from office and instituted direct Roman rule in Judea.

Aristobulus I. Hasmonean king, ruled 104–103 B.C.E. Son of John Hyrcanus I.

Aristobulus II. Hasmonean king, ruled 67–63 B.C.E. Son of Alexandra Salome. He fought his brother, Hyrcanus II, over the rule.

Athronges. Rebel in 4 B.C.E., perhaps with messianic pretensions.

Augustus. The first Roman emperor (or the second, if one counts Julius Caesar). He was effectively sole emperor from the battle of Actium (31 B.C.E.) until his death in 14 C.E.

Azazel. One of the leaders of the bad angels in the *Book of the Watchers*.

Bar Kokhba. A messianic figure who led a revolt against Rome 132–135 C.E.

Baruch. Secretary of the prophet Jeremiah. An apocalypse was written in Baruch's name in response to the destruction of the second temple *(2 Baruch).*

Belial. Name for the angelic or demonic leader of the supernatural forces against God. The name is especially common in the Dead Sea Scrolls.

Caiaphas. Jewish high priest during Jesus' ministry.

Caligula. Nickname for Gaius; means "little boots." He was Roman emperor 37–41 C.E.

Cyrus. Persian emperor who conquered the Babylonian Empire and allowed the Jews to return to Judah and rebuild. Second Isaiah calls him a messiah.

Daniel. Fictional author of the book of Daniel.

David. King of Israel, successor of Saul. David united the northern and southern tribes, and chose Jerusalem as the capital of the united kingdom. Later generations looked back to his rule as a golden period, and messianic hopes were patterned on him. He ruled in the tenth century B.C.E.

Deborah. Female judge of Israel.

Domitian. One of the three Flavian emperors. Son of Vespasian. Ruled as emperor 81–96 C.E.

Elijah. A prophet who decried foreign religious influences in the northern kingdom under King Ahab and his wife, Jezebel. Elijah is said to have been taken to heaven in a fiery chariot at the end of his career, and Mal 4:5–6 expects him to return before God's day of judgment to warn Israel.

Elisha. Prophetic follower of Elijah; carried on Elijah's career after Elijah's ascension.

The Egyptian prophet. Jewish eschatological prophet who was active during the administration of the procurator Felix in the 50s C.E.

Enoch. Enigmatic figure in Gen 5 who represents the seventh generation from Adam and becomes an apocalyptic seer in a series of Jewish apocalypses.

Ezekiel. Priest and prophet who prophesied in Babylonia before and during the exile.

Ezra. Priest, scribe, and agent of the Persian crown; came to Judah with the written Torah some time during the fifth century or the early fourth century B.C.E.

Gaius. Roman emperor 37–41 C.E. His nickname was Caligula.

Hadrian. Roman emperor 117–138 C.E.

Haggai. Prophet who in 520 B.C.E. urged the restored community to begin rebuilding the temple.

Herod Antipas. Son of Herod the Great and tetrarch of Galilee and Perea 4 B.C.E.–39 C.E.

Herod the Great. King of Judea 40–4 B.C.E. He was known for his loyalty to Rome, repression of dissent, execution of those he suspected of conspiracy against him, and widespread building programs. He rebuilt Jerusalem's temple on a grand scale.

Hezekiah. Reforming king of Judah. Ruled 715–687 B.C.E.

Hyrcanus II. Hasmonean high priest and ruler, son of Alexandra Salome. High priest 76–67 and 63–40 B.C.E.

Isaac. Son of Abraham and Sarah, through whom the promises were passed down.

Isaiah. Eighth-century B.C.E. prophet. The book in his name dates from at least three different periods—the eighth century, the period just before Cyrus allowed the Jews to return from the exile to rebuild Jerusalem and its temple, and the early restoration period; thus we speak of First Isaiah (Isa 1–39), Second Isaiah (Isa 40–55), and Third Isaiah (Isa 56–66).

Jacob. Son of Isaac and Rebekah. He had twelve sons, whose descendants became the twelve tribes of Israel. He was renamed Israel by God.

Jason. Jewish high priest who ousted his brother Onias III from that position in 175 B.C.E. and began the Hellenistic reform.

Jeremiah. Prophet who prophesied at the end of the kingdom of Judah and at the beginning of the exilic period.

Jesus. An eschatological prophet who began as a follower of John the Baptist. He started a movement whose goal was probably the restoration of Israel in some sense. He was crucified by the Romans under the prefect Pontius Pilate.

Johanan ben Zakkai. See Yohanan ben Zakkai.

John Hyrcanus I. Hasmonean high priest and ruler 134–104 B.C.E.

John of Gischala. Rival of Josephus in Galilee during the early part of the war against the Romans. He then went to Jerusalem and played a prominent role there until the war's end.

John the Baptist. Eschatological prophet who was put to death by Herod Antipas ca. 30 C.E. Christians considered him to be Jesus' forerunner.

Josephus. A priest from Jerusalem, born in 37 C.E. After the war against Rome, he went to Rome and under the patronage of the Flavian emperors wrote four works that are our main historical sources for first-century Israel.

Joshua. Moses' successor who led the people across the Jordan into the promised land.

Joshua the high priest. High priest of the early restoration.

Josiah. Reforming king of Judah. Ruled 640–609 B.C.E. During his reign, a book of the Torah was found in the temple.

Judah ben Hezekiah. Led a revolt in Galilee at the time of Herod the Great's death and claimed kingship for himself.

Judah Maccabee. Took over the revolt against Judah's Seleucid overlords in 167 B.C.E. He recaptured the temple after its defilement by Antiochus IV, and he rededicated it in 164 B.C.E. The Feast of Hanukkah commemorates this rededication. He died in 161 B.C.E.

Judah the Galilean. Led an unsuccessful tax revolt in 6 C.E. and was executed.

Luke. Name given to the writer of the Gospel of Luke; was also the writer of the Acts of the Apostles.

Marc Antony. Member of the second triumvirate, whom Augustus defeated in 31 B.C.E. to become sole ruler of the Roman Empire.

Mark. Name given to the writer of the second gospel in the New Testament, which is probably the first of the four to be written.

Manasseh. King of Judah. Son of King Hezekiah, he undid Hezekiah's reforms.

Matthew. Name given to the author of the first gospel in the New Testament.

Menahem ben Judah the Galilean. Leader early in the war against the Romans. Had messianic pretensions and was killed.

Moses. Ancient Israelite leader who led the people out of Egypt and received the Torah for them on Sinai.

Nebuchadnezzar. Babylonian emperor who ordered the deportations of Judahites to Babylonia in the first part of the sixth century B.C.E.

Nehemiah. Jewish cupbearer to the Persian emperor. He went to Judah as its governor in 445 B.C.E. and instituted a series of reforms.

Nero. Roman emperor 54–68 C.E. During his rule, the war between Rome and the Palestinian Jews broke out. He blamed the Christians for burning Rome and persecuted them.

Onias III. See Jason.

Petronius. Roman governor of Syria, ordered by Caligula to set up a statue of the emperor in Jerusalem.

Philo of Alexandria. A Jewish philosopher from a wealthy family in Alexandria. Lived ca. 20 B.C.E.–ca. 50 C.E.

Pompey. Roman general who brought Judea under Roman control.

Pontius Pilate. Roman prefect of Judea 26–36 C.E. He condemned Jesus to die.

Samuel. Ancient Israelite prophet who anointed Saul and David as kings.

Sarah. Abraham's wife.

Satan. From the Hebrew for "accuser." He was originally an angelic figure who served as God's prosecuting attorney. Over time his figure developed into leader of the demons and God's enemy.

Saul. The first king of Israel; ruled ca. 1020–1000 B.C.E.

Semyaza. One of the leaders of the bad angels in the *Book of the Watchers.*

Simon. One of three rebels with messianic pretensions in 4 B.C.E.

Simon bar Giora. One of the Jewish leaders during the war against the Romans 66–70 C.E. The Romans captured him and brought him to Rome to display in the parade celebrating the Roman triumph.

Simon the Hasmonean. Hasmonean ruler 142–134 B.C.E.

Solomon. David's son. He built the temple in Jerusalem and engaged in many other building projects, including palaces and fortifications. Later generations credited him with great wisdom.

Taxo. Old man who, with his seven sons, is ready for martyrdom in *T. Mos.* 9.

Theudas. Jewish eschatological prophet in Judea during the Roman procuratorship of Fadus (44–46 C.E.).

Tiberius. Roman emperor 14–37 C.E.

Tiberius Julius Alexander. Philo's nephew and son of Alexandria's alabarch (collector of customs). He was governor of Judea (46–48 C.E.), governor of Egypt (66–70), and chief of staff for Titus when he captured Jerusalem in 70.

Titus. Son of Vespasian. Roman general for the final part of the war against the Palestinian Jews. He captured Jerusalem in 70 C.E. and destroyed the temple. He was emperor 79–81 C.E.

Tobiah. Yahweh worshiper from east of the Jordan; an opponent of Nehemiah.

Vespasian. Roman general who conducted the war against the Jews from 66 until 69 C.E., when he became emperor.

Yohanan ben Zakkai. A Pharisee who fled Jerusalem during the siege by the Romans in the war of 66–70 C.E. He founded a school in Yavneh that became the first center of formative Judaism, leading to rabbinic Judaism.

Zadok. One of David's two chief priests, with Abiathar. Zadok was sole chief priest under Solomon.

Zechariah. Prophesied in the early postexilic period, insisting on the rebuilding of the temple.

Zerubbabel. Jewish governor of Judah under the Persians in the early restoration. He is credited with rebuilding the temple.

INDEX OF NAMES AND SUBJECTS

INDEX OF ANCIENT SOURCES

25:10 24
37 204
37:11 139, 267
41:9 210
48 42–43
50:12–13 48
66:8 151
69:28 151
72 29
105 114
110:4 421
139:16 151, 430
145 132
145:11–13 351
146:7–8 207

Proverbs
1:5 32
2:9–11 32
8 34
8–9 269, 421
8:22–31 32
11 32
14 32

Isaiah
1–5 150
1–39 433
1:2 257, 368
2 344
4:2 68
4:3 151
6 134, 143, 430
6:3 267
6:9–10 416
7 408
7:14–16 407
7:17 184
8:1–4 407
11:1 68
11:10 430–31
24:17 182
24–27 433
26:19 163
28:14 179
28:22 179
29:13 361
29:20 179
30:10 179
40–55 21, 70
43:18–19 72
44:24–45:7 21
49:6 413
49:16 400

53 431
55:13–53:12 111–12
56–66 70
56:6–7 72
57:14–21 70
58:2–7 73–74
58:12 74
60 344
60:11 70
60:14–16 71
61:1 207
61:1–2 366
61:1–4 71
61:6 72
62:1 72
62:6–7 72
62:11–12 72
63:1 70
63:16 73
63:18 73
65 178, 344
65:13–15 73
65:17–18 73
65:17–25 70
66:10–14 70

Jeremiah
7 20, 74
7:5–7 348
7:11 347
23:5 68
24:5–7 21
25:11–12 160
26 74
26:11 347
26:20–24 21
28 32
29 21, 64
29:10 160
31 423
31:31 174
31:31–34 21
33:15 68

Ezekiel
1 143, 430
1–3 21
1:4–14 268
2:1 157, 369
2:3 157, 369
2:6 157, 369
2:8 157, 369
9–11 21, 348, 386, 401
14:14 152

14:20 152
34 411
36 357
36:20–38 401
37 163
38–39 397
39 357
40–48 21
43:1–5 433
48:35 433

Daniel
1:18–20 153
1–6 152–53
2 148, 396
2:19 154
2:27–28 154
2:31–45 154
2:46–47 155
3:28–29 155
3–6 154
4:13 137
4:17 137, 159
4:19–37 253
4:23 137
4:34–35 155
4:37 155
6:26–27 155
7 143, 148, 156, 197,
264, 266, 271, 272, 275,
369, 370, 396, 397, 411,
429, 430
7–8 253
7–12 153, 154
7:1 392
7:2–3 155
7:7 155
7:9 158, 270, 432
7:9–10 156–57
7:10 139, 151
7:11 157
7:13 158, 199
7:13–14 157, 158
7:14 159
7:17 155
7:17–18 159
7:21 159
7:22 159
7:23 155
7:25 159
7:27 159, 199
8 271
8:13 159
8:15 158